California
Atlas & Gazetteer™

W9-BDN-280

Grid numbers refer to detailed map pages

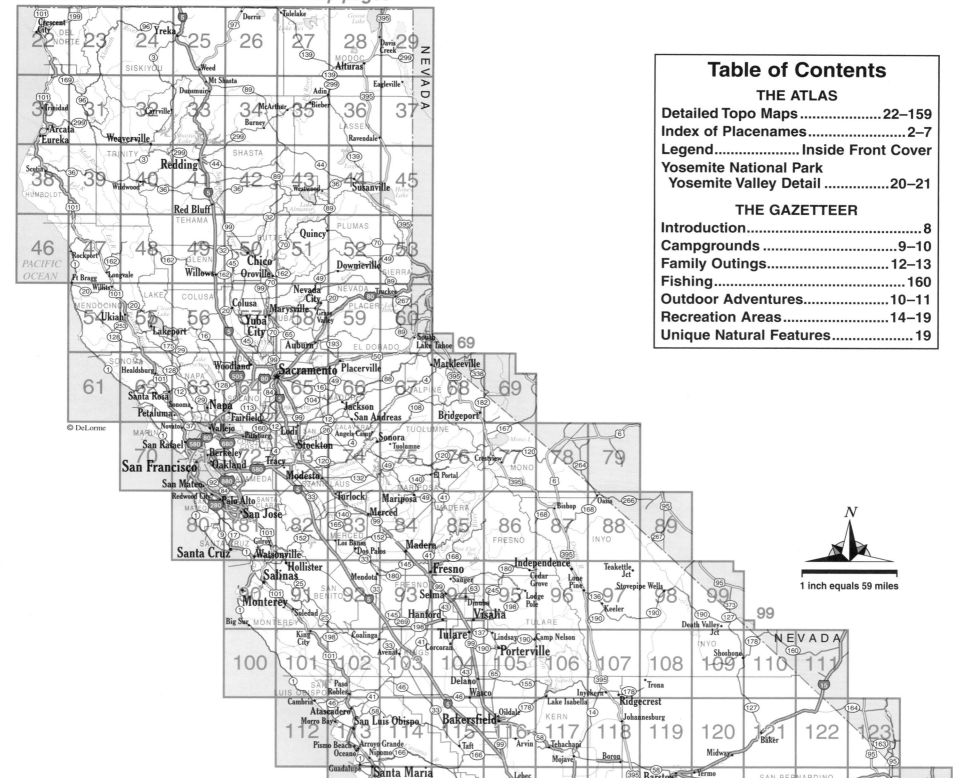

Table of Contents

THE ATLAS

Detailed Topo Maps 22–159
Index of Placenames 2–7
Legend .... Inside Front Cover
Yosemite National Park
  Yosemite Valley Detail 20–21

THE GAZETTEER

Introduction 8
Campgrounds 9–10
Family Outings 12–13
Fishing 160
Outdoor Adventures 10–11
Recreation Areas 14–19
Unique Natural Features 19

N

1 inch equals 59 miles

SECOND EDITION.
Copyright © 2010 DeLorme. All rights reserved.
P.O. Box 298, Yarmouth, Maine 04096
(207) 846-7000   www.delorme.com
Printed in Canada.
1 2 3 TR 12 11 10

© DeLorme

Index of Placenames

A

Abbott 57 E10
Aberdeen 87 F9
Academy 85 G7
Acampo 65 G8
Acolita 152 G5
Actis 117 G9
Acton 128 F4
Adams 55 G10
Adela 74 E1
Adelaida 102 G1
Adelanto 130 E1
Adin 35 B10
Adobe Corners 130 E1
Advance 95 D8
Aerial Acres 118 F2
Aetna Springs 63 B7
Afton 120 G5
Afton 57 A7
Ager 25 B7
Agnew 81 B7
Agoura Hills 139 B9
Agra 148 D5
Agua Caliente 63 F7
Agua Dulce 128 E3
Agua Fria 84 A3
Aguanga 149 C10
Ahwahnee 85 B6
Ainshea Butte 27 D7
Ainsworth Corner 26 A5
Airbase 124 A5
Akers 73 B7
Al Tahoe 60 F4
Alameda 116 D2
Alameda 71 E9
Alamitos 81 C7
Alamo 72 D1
Alamo Oaks 72 D1
Alamorio 157 A7
Alba 73 D10
Albany 71 C9
Alberhill 142 G1
Albion 54 C1
Albrae 81 A6
Alder Creek 65 B8
Alder Springs 85 E9
Aldercroft Heights 81 D7
Alderglen Springs 55 G7
Alderpoint 39 F8
Alemandra 57 D9
Alessandro 142 E2
Algerine 74 C5
Algoma 34 B2
Algoso 116 C3
Alhambra 140 C5
Alicia 57 D10
Aliso Viejo 148 A3
Alleghany 52 G1
Allen 67 B8
Allendale 64 D2
Allensworth 104 E4
Alliance 30 F3
Alliance Redwood 62 D3
Almanor 43 F8
Almanor 43 G9
Almonte 71 C7
Alpaugh 104 D3
Alpine 155 C6
Alpine 54 A3
Alpine Heights 155 C6
Alpine Station 67 D8
Alpine Village 150 A4
Alpine Village 67 A10
Alray 129 G10
Alta 59 C7
Alta Hill 58 C4
Alta Loma 141 C9
Alta Mesa 80 B5
Alta Sierra 106 F1
Alta Sierra 58 D4
Alta Vista 87 B6
Altadena 140 B5
Altamont 72 E4
Altaville 74 A4
Alto 71 C7
Alton 38 B3
Alturas 28 F4
Alum Rock 81 B8
Alvarado 72 G1
Alviso 81 A7
Amador City 66 E1
Ambler 94 G5
Amboy 132 E5
Ambrose 27 F10
Ambrose Station 27 F10
American Camp Station 75 A6
American Canyon 63 G9
American Flat 59 C7
American House 51 E10
Amesti 81 G8
Amos 152 F4
Ampere 73 A8
Amsterdam 83 A9
Anaheim 141 F6
Anchor Bay 54 G3

Anderson 41 D9
Andersonia 47 B6
Andesite 25 F10
Andover 60 B1
Andrade 158 D4
Andrade Corner 128 D2
Angeles Crest Station 140 A4
Angels Camp 74 A4
Angelus Oaks 142 B4
Angiola 104 C3
Angwin 63 C8
Anita 50 C2
Annapolis 61 A10
Annette 103 G7
Ansel 128 A4
Antelope 65 B7
Antelope Acres 128 C3
Antelope Center 129 E6
Antelope Station 128 B1
Antes 95 G6
Antioch 72 B3
Antlers 33 F8
Antonio 124 B4
Anza 150 B2
Anza 157 C7
Apex 66 A1
Apple Valley 130 E3
Applegate 58 E5
Aptos 81 F7
Arastraville 75 B7
Araz Junction 158 D4
Arbee 57 C6
Arbios 92 B5
Arboga 57 E10
Arbolada 126 F5
Arbuckle 57 E6
Arcade 64 D5
Arcadia 140 B5
Arcilla 141 F10
Arcata 30 F4
Arch Rock Entrance Station 76 F1; 20 G1
Archer 133 F8
Arden Town 65 C7
Arena 83 B7
Argos 132 C1
Arguello 124 E3
Argus 108 F1
Arlanza 141 D10
Arlight 124 E3
Arlington 141 E10
Arlington Station 141 E10
Arlynda Corners 38 B2
Armistead 118 A1
Armstrong 73 A8
Arnold 47 G9
Arnold 66 F5
Arnold Heights 142 E2
Aromas 81 G9
Arrowbear Lake 142 B3
Arrowhead Highlands 142 A2
Arrowhead Junction 134 A3
Arrowhead Springs 142 B2
Arrowhead Springs Station 142 B2
Arroyo Grande 113 F8
Arroz 64 B2
Artesia 140 E5
Artois 49 F10
Arvin 116 E4
Asco 72 F2
Ash Hill 132 C2
Ashford Junction 109 D7
Ashford Mill (Ruins) 109 D7
Ashland 71 F10
Aspen Valley 75 D10
Aspendell 87 D6
Asti 62 A3
Asuncion 113 A8
Asylum 55 D6
Atascadero 113 B8
Athens 140 E3
Atherton 80 A5
Athlone 83 D10
Atlanta 73 D9
Atlas 63 E9
Atolia 118 D4
Atwater 83 B8
Atwood 141 E7
Auberry 85 E8
Auburn 58 F4
Auckland 95 D6
August 73 B8
Avalon 139 F8
Avalon Village 140 F3
Avena 73 D9
Avenal 103 C7
Avery 66 G5
Avila Beach 113 E7
Avinsino Corner 66 B3
Avocado 94 A4
Avon 72 B1
Azalea 33 A9
Azusa 141 B6

B

Badger 95 C7
Badwater 109 A6
Bagby 75 C7
Bagdad 132 E4
Bahia 71 A10
Bailhache 62 C4
Baker 121 D7
Bakersfield 116 C2
Balboa 148 A1
Balboa Island 148 A2
Balch 121 F8
Balderson Station 59 F7
Baldwin Park 141 C6
Ballarat (Ghost Town) 108 C2
Ballard 125 D8
Ballico 83 A7
Ballou 141 C9
Bancroft 72 C1
Bangor 58 A1
Bankhead Springs 156 E1
Banner 150 G3
Banning 142 E5
Bannock 134 A3
Banta 73 E7
Barber 50 E3
Bard 158 C5
Bardi 73 E9
Bardsdale 127 G8
Barkerville 56 D2
Barlett Springs 55 C10
Barlow 62 E4
Barnwell 122 D4
Baroda 124 C3
Barona 154 A5
Barrett 155 E7
Barro 63 C7
Barstow 130 A4
Barstow 93 A9
Barsug 113 G9
Barths Retreat 71 C6
Bartle 34 B3
Bartlett 96 E5
Barton 66 D4
Bass Lake 85 C9
Bassett 141 C6
Bassetts 52 F3
Batavia 64 E3
Battles 124 A5
Baumberg 71 F10
Baxter 59 D7
Bay Park 154 C2
Bayley 36 A4
Bayliss 50 F1
Bayo Vista 71 B9
Bayshore 71 E8
Bayside 30 F4
Bayview 30 G3
Bayview District 71 E8
Bayview-Montalvin 71 B9
Baywood Park 113 C6
Beale AFB 58 D2
Bealville 116 D5
Bear Creek 73 A8
Bear Creek 83 C10
Bear Creek Station 55 B9
Bear River Pines 58 C5
Bear Valley 67 D8
Bear Valley 75 G7
Bear Valley Springs 116 E5
Beatrice 38 A2
Beatrice 64 B5
Beatty Junction 98 D5
Beaumont 142 E4
Beckwourth 52 C5
Bee Rock 101 E10
Beegum 40 E4
Bel Air 140 C2
Belden 51 A8
Belfast 44 D5
Belfort 68 E5
Bell 140 D4
Bell Gardens 140 D4
Bell Mountain 130 D2
Bell Springs 47 B9
Bella Vista 106 C3
Bella Vista 41 A9
Belle Monte 71 G9
Belleview 38 C3
Belleview 75 B6
Bellevue 62 E5
Bellflower 140 E5
Bellota 73 B10
Belltown 142 D1
Bellview (Site) 85 F6
Belmont 71 G9
Belmont Shore 140 G4
Belvedere 71 D7
Belvedere Heights 142 D2
Ben Hur 84 B4
Ben Lomond 81 E6

Bena 116 C4
Benbow 47 A6
Bend 41 F10
Benicia 71 B10
Benito 92 A5
Benton 78 D2
Benton Hot Springs 78 D1
Berenda 84 F2
Berg 57 C10
Berkeley 71 D9
Bermuda Dunes 143 G10
Berros 113 F9
Berry Creek 51 E6
Berry Glenn 30 A4
Berryessa 81 B8
Bertram 151 D10
Bertsch-Oceanview 22 C3
Berwick 25 A9
Bethel Island 72 A2
Betteravia 124 A4
Beulah Park 81 F6
Beverly Hills 140 C2
Bicknell 124 B5
Bieber 35 C9
Big Bar 32 G1
Big Bar 66 F2
Big Basin 80 D4
Big Bear City 143 A6
Big Bear Lake 142 A5
Big Bend 34 G2
Big Bend 51 E6
Big Bend 63 G7
Big Bunch 94 B2
Big Creek 85 D10
Big Lagoon 30 C3
Big Meadow 67 E8
Big Oak Flat 75 D6
Big Pine 87 D8
Big Pines 129 G8
Big River 147 B7
Big Rock Springs 129 F7
Big Springs 25 E8
Big Stump Entrance Station 95 B7
Big Sur 90 G3
Big Trees 67 F6
Big Tujunga Station 140 A4
Bigelow 87 B8
Biggs 57 A9
Bijou 60 F4
Bijou Park 60 F4
Binghamton 64 E3
Binney Junction 57 D10
Biola 93 A8
Biola Junction 93 A10
Birchville 58 B4
Birds Landing 72 A2
Bishop 87 B7
Bismarck 119 G10
Bissell 118 G1
Bitney Corner 58 C4
Bitterwater 91 F10
Bivalve 70 A4
Bixby Knolls 140 F4
Bixler 72 C5
Black Bear 32 B1
Black Butte 25 G8
Black Lands 73 B8
Black Oak Villa (Site) 63 A7
Black Oaks 55 G9
Black Point 71 A7
Blackwells Corner 103 G10
Blairsden 52 D3
Blanchard 75 E6
Blanco 104 C3
Blanco 90 C4
Blavo 50 F4
Blocksburg 39 E7
Bloomfield 62 F4
Bloomington 142 C1
Blossom 41 F8
Blue Canyon 59 C7
Blue Hills 81 C6
Blue Jay 142 A2
Blue Lake 30 F4
Blunt 41 F9
Blythe 153 A10
Boards Crossing 67 F6
Boca 60 A3
Bodega 62 E3
Bodega Bay 62 F2
Bodfish 117 A6
Bodie 69 G7
Bogue 57 D10
Boiling Point 128 E3
Bolam 25 F9
Boles 27 F9
Bolinas 70 C5
Bolsa Knolls 90 B4
Bombay Beach 151 D10
Bonadelle Ranchos-Madera Ranchos 84 G4
Bonanza Springs 55 G10
Bonds Corner 157 D8

Bonetti 66 B5
Bonita 154 E4
Bonita 84 G2
Bonnefoy 66 E2
Bonnie Bell 143 D7
Bonnie View 55 A10
Bonny Doon 80 F5
Bonny Nook 59 C7
Bonsall 149 E7
Boonville 54 E5
Bootjack 84 A4
Borden 84 G3
Boron 118 G4
Boronda 90 B4
Borosolvay 108 F1
Borrego 150 E5
Borrego Springs 150 E5
Boston Ravine 58 C4
Bostonia 154 C5
Bouquet Guard Station 128 E2
Bowerbank 115 C9
Bowles 94 C1
Bowman 58 F5
Box Springs 142 D2
Box Springs 142 E2
Boyes Hot Springs 63 F7
Boys Republic 141 D8
Brackney 81 E6
Bradbury 141 B6
Bradley 102 E2
Bragur 124 A4
Brainard 30 G3
Brandon Corner 65 C10
Brandy City 51 F10
Branscomb 47 E7
Brant 122 D3
Brawley 157 A7
Bray 26 D2
Brazos 63 G9
Brea 141 E6
Brea Chem 141 E7
Brela 65 C10
Brents Junction 139 B10
Brentwood 140 C2
Brentwood 72 C4
Brentwood Park 75 B6
Briceburg 75 G9
Briceland 38 G5
Bridge Haven 62 D2
Bridge House 65 D9
Bridgehead 72 B3
Bridgeport 75 G9
Bridgeport 84 F5
Bridgeport 84 A3
Bridgeville 39 C6
Brighton 65 C6
Brisbane 71 F8
Brito 83 F7
Broadmoor 71 F7
Broadwell (Site) 132 A1
Brock 58 F2
Brockman 36 E4
Brockmans Corner 87 B7
Brockway 60 C3
Broderick 64 C5
Bromela 113 G8
Brookdale 80 E5
Brooks 63 A10
Brooks Mill 37 A6
Brown (Site) 107 F7
Browning 141 G7
Browns Corner 64 B3
Browns Flat 74 B5
Browns Valley 58 C1
Brownsville 51 G8
Bruceville 65 F6
Brush Creek 51 E7
Bryants 66 A4
Bryman 130 D1
Bryn Mawr 142 C2
Bryson 101 E9
Bryte 64 C5
Buchanan 75 C7
Buchli 63 G9
Buck Meadows 75 D8
Buckeye 41 A8
Buckeye 51 D7
Buckeye 59 F7
Buckhorn Station 40 A5
Buckingham Park 55 E10
Bucktail 40 A4
Bucktown 64 E1
Buellton 125 D7
Buena 149 F7
Buena Park 141 E6
Buena Vista 50 A2
Buena Vista 63 F8
Buena Vista 66 F1
Buena Vista 75 E10
Buffalo Hill 59 F6
Buhach 83 B9

Bull Creek 38 E4
Bullard 65 C10
Bully Hill (Site) 33 G10
Bumblebee 67 G9
Bummerville 66 E4
Bunker 64 E3
Bunker Hill 66 E1
Buntingville 44 E4
Burbank 140 B3
Burbank 81 C7
Burbeck 54 A4
Burdell 71 A7
Burlingame 71 G8
Burlington 38 E5
Burness 94 B3
Burney 34 F4
Burnham 73 C9
Burnt Ranch 31 G9
Burr 95 G6
Burrel 93 E9
Burson 66 G1
Bush 144 B5
Butano Park 80 D4
Butera 104 E5
Butler 141 B6
Butte City 50 G1
Butte Meadows 50 A5
Butte Valley 50 E5
Buttonwillow 115 C8
Byron 72 D4
Byron Hot Springs 72 D4

C

Cabazon 143 E6
Cabin Cove 95 E10
Cable 117 G9
Cachuma Village 125 D9
Cactus 158 B2
Cactus City 144 G3
Cadenasso 63 A10
Cadiz 133 E7
Cadwell 62 E5
Cahuilla 150 B1
Cahuilla Hills 143 G9
Cain Rock 39 G8
Cairns 95 E6
Cairns Corner 105 A6
Cajon 141 A10
Cajon Junction 129 G10
Calabasas 139 B10
Calabasas Highlands 139 B10
Calada 122 A3
Calaveritas 74 A3
Calavo Gardens 154 C5
Calders Corner 115 C10
Caldor 66 C5
Caldwell Pines 55 G9
Calexico 157 D7
Calflax 93 F8
Calgro 94 E5
Caliente 116 D5
California City 118 F1
California Heights 140 F4
California Hot Springs 105 D10
California Valley 114 C3
Calimesa 142 D4
Calipatria 152 F2
Calistoga 63 C6
Calla 73 E8
Callahan 32 A4
Callender 113 F8
Calneva 45 G8
Calpack 83 C10
Calpella 55 C6
Calpine 52 E5
Calville 30 E3
Calwa 94 B1
Calzona 147 B6
Camarillo 139 B7
Cambria 112 A4
Cambrian Park 81 C7
Camden 93 E10
Cameo 94 B1
Cameron 117 F8
Cameron 54 B3
Cameron Corners 155 E9
Cameron Creek Colony 94 G5
Camino 66 A3
Camp Meeker 62 E3
Camp Nelson 105 A10
Camp Richardson 60 F3
Campana 59 G9
Campbell 81 C7
Campbell Hot Springs 53 F6
Campbellville 50 A4
Camphora 91 E7
Campo 155 D10
Campo Seco 66 G1

Camptonville 51 G10
Camulos 127 F9
Canby 28 G1
Canebrake 106 F4
Cannon 64 F2
Canoga Park 140 B1
Cantil 118 D1
Cantrall Mill 37 A6
Cantua Creek 93 E6
Canyon 71 D10
Canyon Acres 148 B3
Canyon City 155 E8
Canyon Crest Heights 142 D1
Canyon Lake 141 G2
Canyondam 43 G9
Capay 50 D1
Capay 64 B1
Cape Horn 59 D6
Capetown 38 C1
Capistrano Beach 148 C3
Capital Hill 102 G3
Capitan 125 F8
Capitola 81 F7
Caratan 104 E5
Carbona 73 F6
Carbondale 65 E10
Cardiff-by-the-Sea 154 A2
Caribou 51 A9
Caric 104 E5
Carlotta 38 C1
Carlsbad 149 F6
Carlton 141 E7
Carlton Hills 154 B4
Carmel Highlands 90 E2
Carmel Valley 90 E4
Carmel-by-the-Sea 90 D2
Carmen City 74 B3
Carmet 62 E2
Carmichael 65 B7
Carnadero 81 F10
Carnelian Bay 60 C3
Carpenter 72 F1
Carpinteria 126 G3
Carquinez Heights 71 A9
Carr 124 A4
Carr Scale 124 A4
Carrick 25 G8
Carrizo Gorge 156 D1
Carrolton 73 D9
Carrville 32 D5
Carson 140 F3
Carson Hill 74 B4
Cartago 96 G5
Caruthers 93 D10
Casa Blanca 142 E1
Casa de Oro 154 D4
Casa Diablo Hot Springs 77 F8
Casa Loma 59 C7
Cascade 51 E8
Cascade Creek 67 F9
Casey Corner 58 C3
Casitas Springs 126 G4
Casmalia 124 B4
Caspar 54 A1
Cassel 34 E5
Castaic 127 F10
Castaic Junction 127 F10
Castella 33 C9
Castle Crag 33 C9
Castle Gardens 83 B9
Castle Park 154 E4
Castle Rock Springs 62 A5
Castro Valley 72 F1
Castroville 90 B3
Caswell (Site) 127 C9
Cat Town 75 F8
Cathedral City 143 F9
Catheys Valley 84 A3
Catlett 57 G10
Cavin 127 G8
Cawelo 116 B1
Cayley 72 E5
Cayucos 113 B6
Cazadero 62 C2
Cecile 94 B1
Cecilville 32 C2
Cedar Glen 142 A3
Cedar Grove 95 A10
Cedar Ridge 58 C5
Cedar Ridge 75 B6
Cedar Slope 106 A1
Cedar Springs 129 G5
Cedar Valley 85 G7
Cedarbrook 95 B7
Cedarpines Park 142 A1
Cedarville 29 F7
The Cedars 24 G2
The Cedars 32 C4
The Cedars 59 C10
Cella 94 C3
Ceneda 118 C2
Centerville 41 C7
Centerville 50 D4
Centerville 72 G1
Centerville 94 B3
Central 64 E5

2

Central Valley 41 A8
Centralia 65 F8
Century City 140 C2
Ceres 73 G10
Cerritos 140 E5
Cerro 71 B7
Cerro Villa Heights 141 F7
Chabot Terrace 71 A9
Chadbourne 64 G1
Chaffee 117 F9
Chalfant 78 G3
Challenge 51 G8
Chambers Lodge 60 E2
Chambless 133 E7
Champagne 141 C9
Champagne Fountain 81 C6
Chantry Flat Station 140 B5
Chapmantown 50 D3
Chappo 149 E6
Charlton Station 141 A6
Charter Oak 141 C7
Chase 122 E2
Chatsworth 139 A10
Chatsworth Lake Manor 139 A10
Cheeseville 24 F4
Chemeketa Park 81 D7
Chemurgic 83 A6
Cherokee 50 E5
Cherokee 58 A5
Cherokee 65 G8
Cherokee 75 B6
Cherokee Strip 115 B10
Cherry Creek Acres 58 D4
Cherry Valley 142 D4
Chester 43 E8
Chianti 62 A3
Chicago Park 58 D5
Chico 50 D3
Chilao Station 128 G5
Chilcoot 53 D7
Chili Bar 66 A1
China Lake 107 G9
Chinatown 71 D8
Chinese Camp 74 D5
Chino 141 D8
Chino Hills 141 D8
Chinowths Corner 94 F4
Chipps 72 B2
Chips Flat 52 G1
Chiquita 62 B4
Chiriaco Summit 151 A10
Chittenden 81 G10
Chloride City 98 B5
Cholame 103 F6
Chorro 113 C8
Chowchilla 84 E1
Chrisman 138 A5
Christie 71 B10
Chrome 49 D7
Chualar 90 D5
Chubbuck 133 G9
Chula Vista 154 E3
Cima 122 D2
Cimarron 93 G10
Cinco 117 D10
Cincotta 94 B1
Cisco 59 B9
Cisco Grove 59 B9
Citro 95 F7
Citrona 64 B2
Citrus 141 C7
Citrus 65 C8
Citrus Heights 65 B8
City Creek Station 142 B3
City Terrace 140 C4
Clairemont 154 C3
Clam Beach 30 E3
Claraville 117 B8
Claremont 141 C8
Claribel 74 E1
Clarksburg 64 E5
Clarksville 65 B9
Clarsona 65 E10
Claus 74 F1
Claussenius 59 G8
Clay 65 F9
Clayton 58 F2
Clayton 72 C2
Clear Creek 23 D9
Clear Creek 43 E10
Clear Creek Junction 43 E9
Clear Creek Station 140 A4
Clearing House 75 F10
Clearlake 56 F1
Clearlake Oaks 56 E1
Clearlake Park 56 F1
Clements 65 G9
Cleone 47 G6
Cliff 116 D5
Clifton 140 F2
Clint 93 E10
Clinton 66 E3
Clio 52 D4
Clipper Gap 58 F5
Clipper Mills 51 G9
Clotho 94 B2
Clover Flat 155 D9
Cloverdale 41 C7
Cloverdale 55 G8
Clovis 94 A1
Clyde 158 B2
Clyde 72 B1
Coachella 144 G1
Coalinga 102 B5
Coalinga Mineral Springs 102 A4
Coarsegold 85 C6
Cobb 55 G10
Coburn 91 G9
Cochrane 73 E7
Codora 50 G1
Codora Four Corners 50 G1
Cohasset 50 B4
Cold Fork 41 G6
Cold Spring 125 E10
Cold Springs 66 A1
Cold Springs 67 G8
Cole 25 A6
Coles Station 66 B3
Coleville 68 C3
Colfax 58 D5
Colfax Spring 75 D8
Colima 141 D6
College City 57 E6
College Heights 141 C8
College Park 81 B7
Collegeville 73 C9
Collierville 65 G8
Collins 63 G9
Collinsville 72 A3
Colma 71 F7
Coloma 66 A1
Colton 142 C2
Columbia 74 B5
Colusa 57 C6
Colusa Junction 57 D9
Cometa 73 D10
Commerce 140 D4
Como 141 G7
Comptche 54 B3
Compton 140 E4
Conant 33 C9
Conaway 64 B4
Concepcion 124 F5
Concord 72 B1
Conejo 94 D1
Confederate Corners 90 C4
Confidence 75 B7
Confidence Mill (Site) 109 E8
Conner 116 E1
Constantia 53 B8
Cooks Station 66 C5
Cooks Valley 47 A6
Cool 58 G5
Coolidge Springs 151 C7
Cooper 90 B4
Cooperstown 74 E4
Copic 27 B7
Copper City (Site) 119 C8
Copper City 48 D4
Copperopolis 74 B3
Coram 41 A8
Corcoran 104 B2
Cordelia 63 G10
Cordelia Junction 63 G10
Cordero Junction 64 F2
Cordova 65 D6
Cornell 139 C9
Cornell 27 C7
Corning 49 B10
Corona 141 E9
Corona del Mar 148 A2
Coronado 154 D3
Corporal 81 G10
Corralitos 81 F8
Corte Madera 71 C7
Cortena 56 C5
Cortez 83 A7
Cory 49 D10
Coso 107 A9
Coso 107 C6
Coso Junction 107 C6
Costa Mesa 148 A1
Cosumne 65 D8
Cosy Dell 141 A10
Cotati 62 F5
Cotners Corner 130 F3
Cottage Corners 91 A6
Cottage Springs 67 E7
Cotton Center 105 B6
Cottonwood 41 D9
Coulterville 75 E7
Counsman 65 A6
County Industrial Road Camp 126 A4
Courtland 64 F5
Covelo 48 D1
Covina 141 C7
Covington Mill 32 E5
Cow Creek 67 G9
Cowan Heights 141 F8
Cowell 72 C1
Cox 146 F3
Coyote 81 D9
Coyote Wells 156 D3
Coyoteville 66 C3
Cozzens Corner 62 B3
Crabtree 95 A6
Crafton 142 C3
Craig 57 B10
Cranmore 57 E8
Crannell 30 D3
Crater 88 D3
Creed 64 G3
Creegan 83 C10
Crescent City 22 C2
Crescent Mills 44 G1
Cressey 83 B8
Crest 154 C5
Crest 44 A5
Crest Park 142 A3
Cresta 51 C6
Crestline 142 A2
Crestmore 142 C1
Creston 113 A9
Creston 63 G10
Crestview 77 E7
Crimea House 74 D4
Crockett 71 B10
Croft 66 C5
Cromberg 52 C3
Crome 115 B10
Cromir 92 A5
Cronise Valley 120 F5
Cross 94 E3
Cross Roads 147 B8
Crowley 54 A4
Crown 63 F6
Crown Jewel 142 C2
Crows Landing 82 B4
Crucero 121 F6
Crystal Cove 148 A2
Crystal Lake 59 B9
Cudahy 140 D4
Cuesta 113 C8
Cuesta-by-the-Sea 113 C6
Culver City 140 D2
Cummings 47 C7
Cunard 57 G9
Cunningham 62 E5
Cupertino 81 C6
Curlew 157 A8
Curry Village 76 E2; 21 E6
Curtis 34 B3
Curtner 81 A7
Cushenbury 130 G5
Cushing 113 B8
Cutler 94 D5
Cutten 30 G3
Cuyama 126 A2
Cygnus 72 A1
Cypress 140 F5
Cypress Grove 62 G4

D

Daggett 130 A5
Dairyland 84 F1
Dairyville 41 G10
Dales 42 E1
Dalton 27 A6
Dalton Station 141 B7
Daly City 71 E7
Dana 34 C5
Dana Point 148 C3
Danby 133 D8
Danielson 63 G10
Dantoni 58 D1
Danville 72 D1
Daphnedale Park 28 F4
Dardanelle 67 F10
Darlington 66 A5
Darrah 75 G10
Darwin 97 G9
Date City 157 C9
Daulton 84 E4
Davenport 80 F5
Davis 64 C4
Davis Creek 28 D5
Day 35 B7
Day Canyon Station 141 B10
Day Valley 81 F8
Dayton 50 E2
De Luz 149 C6
Deadmans Corners 93 E8
Deadwood 24 D4
Deadwood 40 A5
Deadwood 50 D5
Dearborn Park 80 C4
Death Valley Junction 99 G9
Declezville 141 C10
Dedrick 32 F2
Deep Springs 88 B1
Deer Creek 43 F7
Deer Creek Colony 105 C7
Deer Creek Station 43 E6
Deer Lick Station 142 B3
Deer Park 63 C7
Deer View 59 G8
Deetz 33 A8
DeHaven 47 E6
Del Dios 149 G8
Del Mar 154 A2
Del Monte Heights 90 C3
Del Paso 65 B6
Del Rey 94 C2
Del Rey Oaks 90 D3
Del Rio Woods 62 B4
Del Rosa 142 B2
Del Sur 128 C3
Del Valle 127 F10
Delano 104 F5
Delevan 56 A5
Delevan 56 A5
Delft Colony 94 D3
Delhi 83 A7
Delleker 52 C4
DelLoma 31 G10
Delphos 56 C5
Delta 33 E8
DeLuz 149 D7
Democrat Hot Springs 116 A5
Demuth 35 A8
Denair 74 G2
Denis 128 D5
Denny 31 E9
Denverton 64 G2
Derby Acres 115 D7
Des Moines 141 E6
DeSabla 50 C5
Descanso 155 B8
Descanso Junction 155 C8
Desert 122 A4
Desert Beach 151 B8
Desert Center 145 G8
Desert Heights 144 B2
Desert Hot Springs 143 D8
Desert Lake 118 G3
Desert Shores 151 C7
Desert View Highlands 128 D4
Devil Canyon Station 142 B1
Devils Den 103 F9
Devon 124 B4
Devore 142 B1
Devore Heights 142 A1
Dew Drop 58 D4
Di Giorgio 116 D3
Diablo 72 D2
Diamond Bar 141 D7
Diamond Springs 66 B2
Dillard 65 E8
Dillon Beach 62 F3
Dinsmore 39 C8
Dinuba 94 D4
Dirigo 33 C9
Division 155 E8
Dixie 35 E8
Dixieland 156 C5
Dixon 64 D3
Dobbins 58 A3
Doble 143 A6
Dogtown 48 F5
Dogtown 65 G9
Dogtown 74 A4
Dogtown 75 E7
Dolomite 97 D6
Dorrington 67 F6
Dorris 26 A2
Dos Cabezas 156 D2
Dos Palmas Corners 143 E8
Dos Palos 83 F8
Dos Palos Y 83 F8
Dos Rios 47 D10
Dougherty 65 G8
Dougherty 72 E2
Douglas City 40 A3
Douglas Flat 74 A5
Douglas Park 22 C4
Downey 140 E5
Downieville 52 F1
Doyle 53 A8
Doyles Corner 34 F5
Dozier 64 F3
Drake 125 F6
Drakesbad 43 D6
Drawbridge 81 A7
Dresser 72 G2
Drytown 66 D1
Duarte 141 B6
Dublin 72 E2
Ducor 105 D7
Dufour 64 A3
Dugan 65 C10
Dulah 126 G4
Dulzura 155 E6
Dumont (Site) 110 F1
Duncan Springs 55 F7
Duncans Mills 62 D2
Dunderberg Mill 76 A5
Dunes 158 C3
Dunlap 95 B6
Dunlap Acres 142 D3
Dunmovin 107 B6
Dunn 120 F4
Dunneville 82 G1
Dunnigan 57 G7
Dunsmuir 33 B9
Durham 50 E3
Durmid 151 C9
Dustin Acres 115 E9
Dutch Flat 59 C6
Dutch Flat Station 59 C6
Dutton 72 A2

E

Eagle Mountain 145 E7
Eagle Rock 140 B4
Eagles Nest 150 E3
Eagleville 37 A8
Eagleville 51 F9
Earlimart 104 D5
Earp 147 B7
East Arboga 57 E10
East Biggs 57 A9
East Blythe 153 A10
East Farmersville 94 G5
East Fork Station 141 A8
East Garrison 90 C4
East Gridley 57 A9
East Highlands 142 C3
East Irvine 141 G8
East La Mirada 141 E6
East Los Angeles 140 D4
East Nicolaus 57 F10
East Oakdale 74 D2
East Orosi 94 D5
East Palo Alto 80 A5
East Pleasanton 72 F3
East Porterville 105 B7
East Quincy 52 B1
East Richmond 71 C9
East San Diego 154 D3
East Side 73 A8
Easton 93 C10
Eastport 71 D10
Eberly 72 G1
Echo Lake 60 G3
Eckley 71 B10
Eden Gardens 154 A2
Eden Hot Springs 142 E4
Edenvale 81 C8
Eder 60 B1
Edgar 156 C5
Edgemar 71 F7
Edgewood 25 G8
Edison 116 C3
Edmiston 94 B2
Edmundson Acres 116 D4
Edna 113 E8
Edom 143 F9
Edwards 129 A6
Edwards Siding 118 G2
Edwin 65 E10
Eel Rock 39 E7
Egan 142 G4
El Bonita 62 D3
El Cajon 154 C5
El Camino 49 A10
El Campo 71 C7
El Casco 142 D3
El Centro 157 C7
El Cerrito 141 F10
El Cerrito 71 C9
El Dorado 66 B1
El Dorado Hills 65 B9
El Granada 80 A2
El Macero 64 C4
El Mirador 105 A7
El Mirage 129 D9
El Modena 141 F7
El Monte 140 C5
El Nido 139 C9
El Nido 83 E9
El Portal 75 F10
El Rancho Del Obispo 62 C4
El Rio 139 A6
El Rio Villa 64 C2
El Roble 55 D6
El Segundo 140 E2
El Segundo Station 140 E2
El Sobrante 71 B9
El Sueno 125 F10
El Toro 148 A3
El Verano 63 F7
Elders Corner 58 F4
Elderwood 95 E6
Elderwood Station 95 E6
Eldridge 63 E7
Electra 66 F3
Elk 54 D2
Elk 94 B3
Elk Creek 49 F7
Elk Creek Maintenance Station 39 E6
Elk Grove 65 E7
Elk Mountain Station 55 B8
Elk River 30 G3
Elk River Corners 30 G3
Elk Valley 23 A7
Elkhorn 90 A4
Ellicott 81 G8
Elliott Corner 84 A5
Ellis 142 F2
Ellis Place 95 D7
Ellwood 125 F9
Elm View 93 D10
Elmco 105 C7
Elmira 64 E2
Elmo 104 G4
Elora 122 E2
Elsa 91 G9
Elsey 50 F5
Elston Spur 64 B3
Elvas 65 C6
Elverta 65 A6
Emerald Bay 148 B2
Emerald Bay 60 F3
Emeryville 71 D9
Emigrant Gap 59 B8
Emmaton 72 A4
Empire 74 F1
Encanto 154 D4
Encinal 57 C5
Encinitas 149 G7
Encino 140 B1
Engineer Springs 155 E6
Englewood 38 D5
English Town (Site) 81 D8
Ensley 57 G9
Enson 94 D4
Enterprise 41 B8
Enterprise 55 A8
Enterprise 66 C1
Epworth 127 G8
Erickson 25 D10
Escalon 73 D10
Escondido 149 F8
Escondido Junction 149 F6
Esex 133 C9
Esparto 64 B1
Esperanza 141 E8
Esquon 50 F3
Essex 133 C9
Essex 30 F4
Estelle 152 F2
Estrella 102 F3
Etheda Springs 95 B7
Etiwanda 141 B10
Etna 24 G4
Ettawa Springs 55 G10
Ettersburg 38 G4
Eucalyptus Hills 154 B5
Eugene 74 C1
Eureka 30 G3
Evelyn (Site) 109 A10
Everglade 57 F8
Evergreen 81 C8
Ewing 58 F2
Exeter 95 G6

F

Fagan 57 B9
Fair Oaks 65 B8
Fair Oaks 73 C8
Fair Play 66 C3
Fairbanks 59 G8
Fairfax 71 B6
Fairfield 64 G1
Fairhaven 30 G2
Fairmead 84 E2
Fairmont 128 C2
Fairview 106 D1
Fairview 127 G8
Fairview 72 F1
Fairview 94 B2
Fairville 63 G8
Fales Hot Springs 68 E4
Fall River Mills 35 D6
Fallbrook 149 D7
Fallbrook Junction 149 E6
Fallen Leaf 60 G3
Falling Springs 141 A7
Fallon 141 D7
Fallon 62 F4
The Falls 85 C7
Famoso 104 G5
Fane 95 F6
Farley 47 F10
Farmersville 94 G5
Farmington 73 C10
Farr 149 F6
Farwell 72 G2
Favinger Place 50 A2
Fawnskin 142 A5
Fayette 105 A7
Feather Falls 51 F8
Feather River 43 E7
Feather River Park 52 D3
Felix 74 B2
Fellows 115 E7
Felton 81 F6
Femmons 75 C8
Fenner 133 B10
Fergus 83 C9
Fern 42 A2
Fern Ann Falls 139 A10
Fern Valley 143 F7
Fernbridge 38 B2
Fernbrook 154 A5
Ferndale 38 B2
Fernwood 139 C10
Fernwood 30 F5
Ferrum 151 C9
Fetters Hot Springs 63 F7
Fiddlers Green 48 D5
Fiddletown 66 D2
Field 120 G3
Fieldbrook 30 E4
Fields Landing 38 A2
Fig Garden 93 A10
Figueroa Station 125 C8
Fillmore 127 G8
Finley 55 E9
Fire Mountain 43 E6
Firebaugh 92 A5
Firebrick 66 F1
Fish Camp 85 A7
Fish Rock 54 G3
Fish Springs 87 E8
Fishel 133 G9
Fisher 30 E3
Fisher 33 D8
Fisher Place 66 G5
Five Brooks 70 B5
Five Corners 51 C6
Five Corners 66 C5
Five Corners 73 D9
Five Mile Terrace 66 A2
Five Points 117 F6
Five Points 154 D3
Five Points 52 C4
Five Points 93 E8
Fivemile House 58 B5
Flamingo Heights 143 A9
Fleta 117 G9
Flinn Springs 154 B5
Flonellis 65 C10
Florence 140 D4
Florin 65 D6
Floriston 60 A3
Flosden Acres 71 A9
Flournoy 49 B8
Flowing Wells 152 E2
Fluhr 83 B9
Flumeville 54 F2
Flynn 121 G10
Folsom 65 B8
Folsom Junction 65 B8
Fondo 152 G1
Fontana 141 C10
Foothill Farms 65 B7
Foppiano 73 B8
Forbestown 51 G8
Ford City 115 E8
Forebay 59 C7
Forest 52 G1
Forest Falls 142 C5
Forest Glen 39 D10
Forest Home 38 C3
Forest House 24 D5
Forest Knolls 70 B5
Forest Lake 55 G10
Forest Meadows 66 G5
Forest Park 128 F2
Forest Park 80 E5
Forest Ranch 50 C4
Forest Springs 80 E5
Foresta 76 F1; 20 G1
Foresthill 59 E6
Forestville 62 D4
Forks of Butte 50 B5
Forks of Salmon 31 B10
Fornis 59 F6
Fort Bidwell 29 B7
Fort Bragg 47 G6
Fort Dick 22 B3
Fort Goff 24 B1
Fort Jones 24 E4
Fort McDowell 71 D8
Fort Piute 123 F6
Fort Romie 91 F7
Fort Ross 62 D1
Fort Scott 71 D7
Fort Seward 39 F7
The Forks 55 C6
The Forks 85 C7
Fortuna 38 B3
Foster 154 B5
Foster 32 B3
Foster City 71 G9
Fountain Springs 105 D8
Fountain Valley 141 G6
Four Corners 25 E8
Four Corners 144 B2
The Four Corners 57 D6
Four Points 128 E5
Four Trees 51 C7
Fourth Crossing 74 A3
Fouts Springs 56 A1
Fowler 94 C1
Frances 141 G8
Franklin 65 E6
Frazier Park 127 B8
Freda 146 C2
Fredalba 142 B3
Frederickburg 60 G5
Freedom 81 G8
Freeman Junction 107 G6
Freeport 65 D6
Freestone 62 E4
Freight Station 140 D5
Fremont (Site) 118 E4
Fremont 64 B4
Fremont 72 G1
Fremont Ford 83 C6
French Bar 51 A8
French Camp 73 C8
French Corral 58 B4
French Gulch 41 A6
Frenchtown 58 A3
Frenchtown 66 B1
Fresh Pond 66 A4
Freshwater 30 G4
Freshwater Corners 30 G3
Fresno 93 B10
Fresno Crossing 84 D5
Friant 85 F6
Friendly Hills 141 D6
Frink 152 D1

Frost 130 E2
Fruitland 39 E6
Fruitridge Manor 65 D6
Fruitvale 116 C1
Fruitvale Station 71 E9
Fruto 49 F7
Frying Pan 40 G3
Fuller 157 B8
Fuller Acres 116 D3
Fullerton 141 E6
Fulton 62 D5
Furnace (Site) 109 A7
Furnace Creek 98 E5

G

Gabilan Acres 90 B5
Gale 131 B6
Gales Orchard 51 G10
Galivan 148 B3
Gallinas 71 B7
Galt 65 F7
Ganns 67 E7
Garberville 39 G6
Garden City Station 118 B4
Garden Farms 113 B8
Garden Grove 141 F6
Garden Valley 59 G6
Gardena 140 E3
Gardenland 65 C6
Garey 125 A6
Garlock 118 C2
Garnet 143 E8
Gas Point 41 D7
Gasoline Alley 58 F4
Gasquet 22 B4
Gaston (Site) 59 A7
Gateley 71 B9
Gates 124 A5
Gateway 60 B2
Gato 124 F5
Gaviota 125 F7
Gazelle 25 F7
Genesee 52 A2
Genevra 57 E6
Georgetown 59 F6
Gepford 93 F10
Gerber 49 A10
Geyserville 62 B4
Ghirardelli Square 71 D8
Giant 71 B8
Gibson 33 D8
Gibsonville 52 D1
Gilberts 66 B4
Gillete 105 A7
Gillis 26 A1
Gillis 73 C7
Gilman Hot Springs 142 F4
Gilroy 81 F10
Gilroy Hot Springs 82 E1
Girvan 41 C8
Glamis 158 A1
Glasgow 121 G9
Glen Arbor 81 E6
Glen Avon 141 D10
Glen Ellen 63 E7
Glen Frazer 71 B10
Glen Ivy Hot Springs 141 G10
Glen Oaks 155 C6
Glen Valley 142 E1
Glenblair 47 G7
Glenburn 35 D6
Glencoe 66 E3
Glencove 71 A10
Glendale 140 B3
Glendale 30 F4
Glendora 141 B7
Glenhaven 55 E10
Glenn 50 G1
Glennville 105 F10
Glenview 154 C5
Glenview 55 F10
Glenwood 81 E6
Globe 105 B9
Glorietta 71 D10
Glorietta 94 A1
Goat Rock 62 C2
Goffs 134 A1
Gold Flat 58 C5
Gold Hill 58 F3
Gold Hill 66 A1
Gold Run 59 C6
Goldleaf 94 B1
Goldstone 119 D10
Goler Heights 118 B3
Goleta 125 F10
Gonzales 91 E6
Goodale 95 F7
Goodmans Corner 65 G10
Goodyears Bar 52 F1
Gorda 101 D6
Gordola 80 F5
Gordon 85 G6
Gordons Well 158 D2
Gorman 127 B8
Gosford 116 D1
Goshen 94 F3
Gottville 24 B5
Government Flat 48 C3
Government Holes 122 E3
Grabtown 80 B3
Graeagle 52 D3
Graino 57 E7
Granada Hills 140 A1
Grand Island 57 E7
Grand Terrace 142 C2
Grandview 130 A3
Grangeville 94 F1
Granite Bay 65 A8
Granite Springs 75 E6
Graniteville 59 A7
Grant 62 C4
Grant Grove Village 95 B7
Grantville 154 C3
Grape 141 C10
Grapeland 141 B9
Grapevine 127 A8
Grapit 49 E10
Grass Flat 51 E10
Grass Lake 25 E10
Grass Valley 58 C4
Graton 62 D4
Gravelly Ford 76 G3
Gravenstein 62 E4
Graves 90 B4
Gravesboro 94 B4
Grays Flat 51 A9
Grayson 73 G8
Greeley Hill 75 E7
Green Trees 54 E5
Green Valley 128 D2
Green Valley 63 F10
Green Valley Lake 142 A4
Greenacres 116 C1
Greenbrae 71 C7
Greendale 64 E5
Greenfield 116 D2
Greenfield 91 G8
Greens Mill 111 F6
Greenview 24 E4
Greenville 141 G6
Greenville 43 G10
Greenville 58 A3
Greenwater (Site) 109 A8
Greenwich Village 139 B8
Greenwood 49 E10
Greenwood 59 F6
Gregg 84 G4
Grenada 25 D7
Gridley 57 A9
Grimes 57 E7
Griminger 66 A5
Grizzly Bear House 58 F5
Grizzly Flat 66 B4
Grossmont 154 C4
The Grove 83 B8
Grove 54 A2
Groveland 75 D7
Grover Beach 113 F8
Guadalcanal Village 71 A9
Guadalupe 113 G9
Gualala 61 A8
Guasti 141 C9
Guatay 155 B8
Guerneville 62 D3
Guernewood 62 D3
Guernewood Park 62 D3
Guernsey 104 A2
Guernsey Mill 105 E10
Guild 73 A8
Guinda 56 G5
Gulf 116 E1
Gum 124 A4
Gustine 82 C5
Gypsite 118 C1

H

Hacienda 62 D3
Hacienda Heights 141 D6
Hackamore 27 E9
Hacketsville 38 C3
Hagginwood 65 B6
Haight 73 A8
Haines 127 G6
Haiwee 107 A6
Halcyon 113 F8
Hales Grove 47 C6
Half Moon Bay 80 A3
Halfway House 116 A2
Hall 90 A4
Hall Station 72 G1
Hallelujah Junction 53 D8
Halloran Springs 121 C9
Halls Corner 93 F10
Halls Flat 35 G8
Hamblin 94 F2
Hambone 34 A4
Hamburg 24 C2
Hamilton Branch 43 E9
Hamilton City 50 D1
Hamlet 62 G3
Hammil 78 F2
Hammond 93 B10
Hammond 95 E8
Hammonton 58 C1
Hanford 94 F2
Hanks Exchange 66 B2
Hansen 141 F6
Happy Camp 23 C10
Happy Valley 66 B4
Harbin Springs 63 A6
Harbison Canyon 155 C6
Harbor City 140 F3
Harbor Side 154 E4
Harden Flat 75 D9
Hardwick 94 F1
Hardy 47 E6
Hardy Station 68 E3
Harlem 91 F8
Harmony 112 A5
Harmony Grove 149 G8
Harold 128 E5
Harp 73 G10
Harpertown 116 D3
Harrington 57 F6
Harris 39 G7
Harrisburg 98 F3
Harrison Park 155 A8
Harry Floyd Terrace 71 A9
Hart (Site) 122 D5
Hartland 95 C7
Hartley 64 E2
Harvard 120 G2
Haskell Creek 52 E4
Hat Creek 35 G6
Hatch 82 A5
Hatfield 26 A5
Hathaway Pines 66 G5
Havasu Lake 135 F6
Havasu Palms 135 G8
Havilah 117 A6
Hawaiian Gardens 140 F5
Hawkins Bar 31 F8
Hawkinsville 25 C6
Hawley 52 C5
Hawthorne 140 E3
Hayden 122 F1
Hayden Hill 36 E1
Hayfield 145 G6
Hayfork 40 B1
Haystack 63 G6
Hayward 72 F1
Hayward 74 F5
Hayward Park 71 G9
Hazelton 115 F9
Healdsburg 62 C4
Hearst 48 G1
Heber 157 D7
Hector 131 B9
Hector Station 77 A6
Helena 32 G2
Helendale 130 C1
Hell 145 G9
Hells Gate 98 B4
Helltown 50 C4
Helm 93 D8
Helm Corner 104 B2
Hemet 142 G4
Henderson 80 A5
Henderson Village 73 A7
Henley 25 B7
Henleyville 49 B9
Henry 113 B8
Herald 65 F8
Hercules 71 B9
Herlong 45 G7
Herlong Junction 45 G6
Hermosa Beach 140 E2
Herndon 93 A9
Herpoco 71 B9
Hershey 57 F6
The Hermitage 47 C7
Hesperia 130 F2
Hess Mill 75 A6
Hessel 62 E5
Hetch Hetchy Junction 74 D4
Hi Vista 129 C8
Hickman 74 F2
Hidden Hills 139 B10
Hidden Meadows 149 E8
Hidden River 143 B10
Hidden Springs 128 G5
Hidden Valley 65 A9
Higby 94 G5
Higgins Corner 58 E4
Highgrove 142 D1
Highland 142 B2
Highland Court 142 C2
Highland Park 140 C4
Highland Springs 142 D5
Highland Springs 55 F9
Highlands-Baywood Park 71 G8
Hights Corner 115 B10
Highway City 93 A9
Hilarita 71 C7
Hildreth 85 E7
Hill Crest 58 C3
Hillcrest 154 D3
Hillcrest 34 F2
Hillgrove 141 D6
Hillmaid 95 F6
Hills Flat 58 C4
Hillsborough 71 G8
Hillsborough Park 71 G8
Hillsdale 154 C5
Hillsdale 71 G9
Hilmar 83 B6
Hilt 25 A6
Hinda 142 D4
Hinkley 130 A3
Hinsdale 57 E8
Hinton 60 A3
Hiouchi 22 C4
Hirschdale 60 A3
Hobart Mills 60 A2
Hobergs 55 G10
Hoboken 31 F9
Hodge 130 B3
Holcomb Village 150 D1
Hollenbeck 27 F8
Hollis 104 G5
Hollister 91 A6
Hollydale 140 E4
Hollydale 62 D3
Hollywood 140 C3
Hollywood Beach 138 B5
Hollywood by the Sea 138 B5
Hollywood Riviera 140 F2
Holmes 38 D5
Holt 73 C6
Holtville 157 C8
Holy City 81 D7
Home Gardens 141 E10
Homeland 142 G3
Homelands 154 D4
Homer 134 A2
Homestead 27 B6
Homewood 60 D2
Honby 128 F1
Honcut 57 B10
Honda 124 D3
Honeydew 38 F3
Hood 64 E5
Hooker 41 E9
Hookston 72 C1
Hookton 38 A2
Hoopa 31 D7
Hooperville 24 D4
Hope Ranch 126 F1
Hopeton 83 A9
Hopland 55 F7
Hoppaw 22 F4
Hornbrook 25 B7
Hornitos 84 A1
Horrs Four Corners 34 C5
Horse Creek 24 C3
Horstville 58 E2
Hotlum 25 F9
Hough Springs 56 D1
House Mountain 56 D3
Hovley 157 A7
Howard 33 A9
Howard Mill Station 55 B8
Howard Springs 56 G1
Howland Flat 52 E1
Huasna 113 F10
Hub 93 F10
Hubbard Station 39 F6
Hudner 82 G1
Hughson 74 G1
Hulburd Grove 155 B7
Hume 95 A8
Humphreys 128 F2
Humphreys Station 85 G8
Hunter-Liggett 101 C8
Huntington Beach 140 G5
Huntington Lake 85 D10
Huntington Park 140 D4
Huntley 73 E10
Hurleton 51 G7
Huron 103 A8
Hyampom 39 B9
Hydesville 38 B3
Hydril 103 C8

I

Ibis 134 A3
Ice House 59 G10
Iceland 60 A3
Idlewild 105 E10
Idlewild 23 B6
Idlewild 60 D2
Idria 92 E3
Idyllwild 143 G7
Ignacio 71 A7
Igo 41 C7
Ilmon 116 D5
Imperial 157 B6
Imperial Beach 154 E3
Imperial Gables 153 F7
Inca 146 F3
Incline 75 F10
Independence 66 E4
Independence 96 A4
Indian Falls 51 A10
Indian Springs 128 G3
Indian Springs 154 D5
Indian Springs 47 D10
Indian Springs 58 C3
Indian Springs 85 F6
Indian Village 98 E5
Indian Well 36 G1
Indian Wells 107 G7
Indian Wells 143 G10
Indianola 30 G4
Indianola 38 A2
Indio 144 G1
Industry 141 D6
Ingle 93 B6
Inglenook 47 G6
Ingleside 71 E7
Inglewood 140 D3
Ingomar 82 D5
Ingot 34 G1
Inskip 50 B5
Inspiration Point 76 E1; 20 F3
Interlaken 81 G9
Inverness 70 A4
Inverness Park 70 B4
Inwood 42 C2
Inyokern 107 G7
Ione 66 E1
Iowa City 58 B1
Iowa Hill 59 D6
Iris 152 F3
Irmulco 54 A3
Iron Mountain 41 A7
Irrigosa 84 G4
Irvine 141 G7
Irvine Siding 141 G7
Irvington 72 G2
Irwin 83 B6
Irwindale 141 C6
Irwindale Siding 141 C6
Isla Vista 125 F10
Island Crossing 77 G6
Island Mountain 47 A9
Isleton 64 G5
Ivanhoe 94 F5
Ivanpah 122 C4
Ivesta 94 B2
Ivory 94 D3
Ivory Mill Station 48 F5

J

Jacinto 50 F1
Jackass Hill 74 B4
Jackson 66 E2
Jackson Gate 66 E2
Jacobs Corner 64 B2
Jacumba 156 E1
Jalama 124 E4
Jamacha 154 D5
James 50 E5
Jamesan 93 B7
Jamesburg 90 F5
Jamestown 74 C5
Jamul 154 D5
Janes Place 31 G7
Janesville 44 E4
Jasmin 105 F6
Jastro 116 C1
Java 134 A4
Jellico 35 F7
Jenner 62 D2
Jenny Lind 74 A1
Jerome 26 D1
Jerseydale 75 G10
Jesmond Dene 149 F8
Jesus Maria 66 F3
Jet 82 A4
Jewell 70 B5
Jimgrey 118 G5
Jimtown 62 B4
Jofegan 149 D6
Johannesburg 118 C4
John Rains House 141 C9
Johnsondale 106 C1
Johnsons 30 A5
Johnston Corner 81 G9
Johnstons Corner 130 B3
Johnstonville 44 D3
Johnstown 154 C5
Johnsville 52 D3
Jolon 101 C8
Jones Corner 105 B6
Jonesville 43 G6
Josephine 57 D8
Joshua 122 D3
Joshua Tree 143 B10
Jovista 105 E6
Julian 150 G3
Junction City 32 G2
June Lake 77 E6
June Lake Junction 77 D7
Juniper 28 F4
Juniper Hills 129 F6
Juniper Springs 142 F3
Jupiter 75 A6

K

Kadota 83 C10
Kaiser 141 C10
Kaktus Korner 94 B4
Kalina 27 A6
Kanawyers 96 A1
Kandra 27 B7
Kane Spring 151 G9
Karlo 45 B6
Karnak 64 A4
Kathryn 141 G8
Kaweah 95 E8
Kayandee 116 C2
Kearsarge 96 A5
Kecks Corner 103 G8
Keddie 51 A10
Keeler 97 E7
Keenbrook 141 A10
Keene 117 E6
Kegg 26 D1
Keith 127 G7
Kekawaka 39 G8
Kellogg 63 B6
Kelsey 66 A1
Kelseyville 55 F9
Kelshaw Corners 85 D6
Kelso 122 G1
Kenny (Site) 46 B5
Kensington 71 C9
Kentfield 71 C7
Kenton Mill 131 D10
Kentucky House 66 G3
Kentwood-In-The-Pines 150 G3
Kenwood 63 E7
Keough Hot Springs 87 C7
Kephart 27 E7
Kerens 121 G9
Kerman 93 B8
Kern City 116 C1
Kern Lake 116 E1
Kernell 104 F4
Kernville 106 F2
Keswick 41 B7
Kett 41 B7
Kettenpom 39 G9
Kettleman 73 A8
Kettleman City 103 C9
Kevet 127 G7
Keyes 74 G1
Keyesville 106 G1
Keystone 74 D4
Kibesillah 47 F6
Kiesel 64 B5
Kilaga Springs 58 F3
Kilkare Woods 72 F2
Kilowatt 115 C8
Kincaid 141 B6
King City 101 A9
King Salmon 30 G2
Kingdon 73 A7
Kings Beach 60 C3
Kingsburg 94 D2
Kingsville 66 B1
Kingvale 59 B10
Kinyon 34 B2
Kirker Pass 72 C2
Kirkville 57 F8
Kirkwood 67 B8
Kiska 49 A10
Kismet 84 F3
Klamath 22 F4
Klamath Glen 22 F4
Klamath River 24 B4
Klamathon 25 B7
Klau 102 G1
Klinefelter 134 A3
Klondike 132 D3
Kneeland 30 G4
Knights Ferry 74 D3
Knights Landing 64 A4
Knightsen 72 C4
Knob 40 D3
Knowles 84 D5
Knowles Corner 62 E4
Knowles Junction 84 D4
Knoxville 56 G3
Komandorski Village 72 E2
Korbel 30 F5
Korbel 62 D3
Korblex 30 F4
Kramer Junction 118 G5
Kramm 50 F5
Krug 63 D7
Kyburz 67 A6

L

La Barr Meadows 58 C5
La Canada Flintridge 140 B4
La Crescenta 140 A4
La Cresta 154 C5
La Delta 130 D1
La Grange 74 F5
La Habra 141 E6
La Habra Heights 141 D6
La Honda 80 C4
La Honda Park 74 A4
La Jolla 141 E7
La Jolla 154 C2
La Jolla Amago 149 E10
La Mesa 154 C4
La Mirada 141 E6
La Palma 140 F5
La Paloma 141 F7
La Panza 114 C2
La Porte 51 E10
La Presa 154 D4
La Puente 141 D6
La Quinta 150 A5
La Riviera 65 C7
La Salle 124 D4
La Selva Beach 81 G8
La Sierra 141 E10
La Sierra Heights 141 D10
La Verne 141 C8
La Vida Mineral Springs 141 E7
La Vina 84 G3
Lachusa Fire Patrol Station 139 C8
Lacjac 94 C3
Ladera 80 B5
Lafayette 71 C10
LaFinca Orchards 57 C10
Lagol 139 A7
Laguna 65 E6
Laguna Beach 148 B3
Laguna Hills 148 A3
Laguna Junction 155 C8
Laguna Niguel 148 B3
Laguna Woods 148 A3
Lagunitas 70 B5
Lairds Corner 104 B5
Lake Alpine 67 D8
Lake Arrowhead 142 A3
Lake City 29 D7
Lake City 58 A5
Lake Elsinore 142 G1
Lake Forest 148 A3
Lake Forest 60 C3
Lake Hughes 128 C2
Lake Isabella 106 G1
Lake Los Angeles 129 D7
Lake of the Woods 127 B7
Lake of the Woods 44 B2
Lake San Marcos 149 F7
Lakehead 33 F8
Lakeland Village 149 A6
Lakeport 55 E9
Lakeshore 33 F8
Lakeshore 86 C1
Lakeside 154 B5
Lakeside Park 139 A10
Lakeview 116 F1
Lakeview 142 F3
Lakeview 154 C5
Lakeview Hot Springs 142 F3
Lakeview Junction 28 F4
Lakeville 63 G7
Lakewood 140 E4
Lamoine 33 E8
Lamont 116 D3
Lanare 93 E9
Lancaster 128 C5
Landco 116 C2
Landers 143 A9
Lane 73 B8
Lanes 66 F1
Lanfair 122 F5
Lang 128 F2
Larabee 38 D5
Largo 55 E7
Largo Vista 129 F8
Larkmead 63 C7
Larkspur 71 C7
Las Cruces 125 E7
Las Flores 139 C10
Las Flores 148 E5
Las Flores 49 A10
Las Gallinas 71 B7
Las Juntas 72 C1
Las Lomas 62 B2
Las Lomas 90 A4
Las Palmas 94 B1
Lasco 43 D10
Last Chance (Site) 59 D8
Lathrop 73 D8
Laton 94 E1
Latrobe 65 C10
Laughlin 55 B6
Laurel 71 G9
Laurel 81 E7
Lavic 131 C10
Lawndale 140 E3
Lawndale 63 E6
Lawrence 81 B6
Laws 87 B8
Laytonville 47 E9
Le Grand 84 D1
Leadfield 98 A4
Leaf 26 D1
Lebec 127 B8
Lee Vining 77 C6
Leesdale 139 B6
Leesville 56 C3
Leggett 47 C7
Leisure Town 64 E2
Lemon 138 A5
Lemon Grove 154 D4
Lemon Heights 141 F8
Lemona 142 D1
Lemoncove 95 F7
Lemoore 93 G10
Lennox 140 E3
Lento 125 F7
Lenwood 130 A3
Leon 130 E2
Leona Valley 128 D3
Leonardi 59 G9
Lerdo 116 B1
Lerona 85 E8
Letter Box 51 C8
Leucadia 149 G7
Levee Spur 115 E10
Levis 92 C5
Lewiston 40 A4
Liberty 62 F5
Libfarm 64 E4
Lick 81 C8
Lido Isle 148 A1
Likely 36 B4

Lilac 149 E8
Lily Cup 142 D1
Limon 127 G6
Limoneira 127 G6
Lincoln 58 G2
Lincoln Acres 154 D4
Lincoln Crest 128 D3
Linda 57 D10
Linda Vista 140 B4
Linda Vista 154 C3
Lindcove 95 F7
Linden 73 B9
Lindsay 105 A6
Lingard 83 D10
Linnie 107 E7
Lira 57 D7
Liskey 27 B6
Lisko 105 B7
List 95 G6
Litchfield 44 D5
Little Grass Valley 51 E10
Little Hayen 51 A8
Little Lake 107 D6
Little Morongo Heights 143 C8
Little River 54 B1
Little Rock Station 128 E5
Little Shasta 25 D8
Little Tujunga Station 140 A3
Little Valley 35 F8
Littlerock 129 E6
Live Oak 57 B9
Live Oak 81 F7
Live Oak Acres 126 F4
Live Oak Springs 155 D10
Livermore 72 F3
Livingston 83 B7
Llanada 92 C1
Llano 129 E7
Lobitos 80 B3
Locans 94 B1
Loch Lomond 55 G10
Locke 65 F6
Lockeford 65 G9
Lockhart 119 G6
Lockwood 101 D9
Lodgepole 43 B9
Lodgepole 95 C9
Lodi 73 A8
Lodi Junction 73 A8
Lodoga 56 B2
Log Spring Station 48 C5
Logan 81 G10
Logandale 56 A5
Loganville 52 F3
Lois 105 C7
Lokern 115 C7
Lokoya 63 E8
Loleta 38 A2
Loma 94 G5
Loma Linda 142 C2
Loma Mar 80 C4
Loma Portal 154 D2
Loma Rica 58 B1
Lombard 63 G9
Lomita 140 F3
Lomita Park 71 F8
Lomo 50 A5
Lomo 57 C9
Lompico 81 E6
Lompoc 124 D5
London 94 E3
Lone Hill 141 C7
Lone Pine 96 C5
Lone Pine Station 96 C5
Lone Star 48 E4
Lone Star 94 B1
Lone Star Junction 38 B5
Lone Wolf Colony 130 F3
Long Barn 75 A7
Long Beach 140 F4
Long Bell Station 27 F6
Longvale 47 F9
Longville 43 G8
Lonoak 91 G10
Lonoke 81 F10
Lonsmith 116 C3
Lookout 35 B9
Lookout Junction 35 B8
Loomis 58 G3
Loomis Corners 41 B9
Loope 68 B1
Loraine 117 D7
Lorenzo Station 71 F10
Lort 95 F6
Los Alamitos 140 F5
Los Alamitos Junction 141 F6
Los Alamos 125 C6
Los Altos 140 F5
Los Altos 81 B6
Los Altos Hills 80 B5
Los Angeles 140 C3
Los Banos 83 F6
Los Gatos 81 D7
Los Medanos 72 B3
Los Molinos 49 A10
Los Nietos 140 D5
Los Olivos 125 D8
Los Osos 113 D6
Los Serranos 141 D8
Los Terrentos 155 C7
Los Trancos Woods 80 B5
Los Tules 150 E2
Lost City 74 A2
Lost Creek Maintenance Station 43 F7
Lost Hills 104 G1
Lotus 59 G6
Lovdal 64 C5
Lovelock 50 C5
Low Gap Station 48 D3
Lowell 63 G9
Lower Forni 60 G2
Lower Lake 56 F1
Lower San Antonio Station 141 B8
Lowes Corner 104 B5
Lowrey 49 A7
Loyalton 53 E6
Loyola Corners 81 B6
Lucca 95 G6
Lucerne 55 D10
Lucerne 94 F1
Lucerne Valley 130 F4
Lucia 100 C5
Ludlow 132 C1
Lugo 130 G1
Lumer 105 C7
Lumpkin 51 F8
Lundy 76 B5
Luzon 71 B9
Lynwood 140 E4
Lynwood Gardens 140 E4
Lynwood Station 140 E4
Lyons Crossing 157 D6
Lyonsville 42 E4
Lyoth 73 E7
Lytle Creek 141 A10
Lytton 62 B4

M

Mabie 52 D4
Macdoel 26 B1
Mad River 39 C8
Madeline 36 D4
Madera 84 G3
Madison 64 B2
Madrone 81 D9
Magalia 50 C5
Magnolia 105 C7
Magra 59 D6
Magunden 116 C3
Maine Prairie 64 F3
Majors 80 F5
Malaga 94 C1
Malby Crossing 65 C9
Malibu 139 C10
Malibu Bowl 139 C9
Malibu Hills 139 C9
Malibu Junction 139 B9
Malibu Riviera 139 D9
Malibu Vista 139 C9
Maltby 72 B1
Maltha 116 B2
Mammoth 27 D7
Mammoth Lakes 77 F7
Manchester 54 F2
Manhattan Beach 140 E2
Manila 30 F3
Manix 120 G3
Mankas Corner 63 F10
Manlove 65 C7
Manor 71 B6
Manteca 73 D8
Manteca Junction 73 D8
Manton 42 D2
Manzana 62 D4
Manzanita 155 D10
Manzanita 71 D7
Manzanita Lake 42 C5
Maple Creek 30 G5
Maple Grove 39 C6
Mar Vista 140 D2
Marcel 117 E6
March Field 142 E2
Marchant 57 G9
Marconi 70 A4
Maricopa 115 F9
Marigold 142 C2
Marin City 71 D7
Marina 90 C3
Marina Del Rey 140 D2
Marina District 71 D8
Marinwood 71 B7
Mariposa 84 A4
Mark West 62 D5
Mark West Springs 62 C5
Markleeville 67 B10
Marne 141 D6
Marsh Creek Springs 72 C3
Marshall 62 G4
Marshall Station 85 F7
Martell 66 E2
Martinez 151 B7
Martinez 71 B10
Martinez Place 114 D2
Martins 127 E10
Martins Beach 80 B3
Martins Ferry (Site) 31 B6
Martinus Corner 101 D9
Marysville 57 D10
Mason Station 43 D10
Masonic (Site) 69 E6
Massack 52 B1
Matchin 95 F6
Mather 75 D10
Matheson 41 A7
Mattei 94 B1
Maxwell 56 B5
May 141 E10
Mayaro 51 C6
Mayfair 116 C3
Mayhew 65 C7
Mayo Spur 127 F10
Maywood 140 D4
McArthur 35 D7
McArthur 36 A4
McCann 39 E6
McCloud 33 B10
McColl 33 G9
McConnel 65 E7
McCulloh 59 F9
McFarland 104 G5
McGill 63 G8
McHenry 73 E10
McKay 102 E2
McKay 67 G6
McKinleyville 30 E3
McKittrick 115 D7
McManus 66 A4
McNear 63 G6
McNears Beach 71 B7
McPherson 141 F7
Meadow Brook 59 G6
Meadow Lakes 85 E8
Meadow Valley 51 B9
Meadow Vista 58 E5
Meadowbrook Woods 142 A2
Meadowsweet 71 C7
Meares 27 E8
Mecca 151 B7
Meeks Bay 60 E2
Meiners Oaks 126 F5
Meinert 72 C1
Meiss 67 B6
Melbourne 54 B2
Melita 63 D6
Mello 57 C10
Meloland 157 C8
Melones 74 B4
Melsons Corner 66 C2
Melvin 94 A1
Mendocino 54 B1
Mendocino Woodlands 54 B2
Mendota 92 B5
Menifee 142 G3
Menlo Park 80 A5
Mentone 142 C3
Merced 83 C9
Merced Falls 75 G6
Mercey Hot Springs 92 B1
Mercuryville 62 A4
Meridian 116 F3
Meridian 57 D7
Meridian 81 C7
Merlin 51 C7
Merrimac (Site) 51 D7
Merritt 64 C3
Merryman 95 F6
Mesa Grande 150 F1
Mesa Vista 67 A10
Mesaville 146 G4
Mesquite 157 A10
Mesquite Oasis 156 B1
Metropolitan 38 C3
Mettler 116 F2
Metz 91 F8
Mexican Colony 115 B10
Meyers 60 G3
Meyers 73 E10
Michigan Bluff 59 E7
Midas 59 C7
Middle River 72 C5
Middleton 63 G9
Middletown 63 A6
Midland 146 E3
Midoil 115 E8
Midpines 75 G9
Midvalley 94 G4
Midway 120 G4
Midway 42 C2
Midway 72 E5
Midway City 141 G6
Midway Well 158 D1
Mile High 129 F8
Miles 113 E7
Miley 94 C2
Milford 44 G5
Mill City 77 F7
Mill Creek 42 E5
Mill Spur 64 B3
Mill Valley 71 C7
Millbrae 71 G8
Millbrae Meadows 71 G8
Millersville 117 D7
Millerton 70 A4
Milligan 145 A10
Mills 65 C7
Mills Orchard 50 D1
Mills Orchards 56 B4
Millspaugh 107 C10
Millux 115 E10
Millville 41 B10
Milo 105 A9
Milpitas 81 A7
Milton 74 B1
Mina 47 B10
Mineral 42 E5
Mineral King 96 E1
Minkler 94 B3
Minneola 131 B6
Minnesota 41 A7
Mint Canyon 128 F2
Minter Village 116 A1
Minturn 84 E1
Mira Loma 141 D10
Mira Mesa 154 B3
Mira Monte 126 F5
Mirabel Heights 62 D4
Miracle Hot Springs 117 A6
Mirador 105 A7
Miraleste 140 G3
Miramar 154 B3
Miramar 80 A2
Miramonte 95 B7
Miranda 39 F6
Mission Beach 154 C2
Mission District 71 E8
Mission Highlands 63 F7
Mission Hills 124 C5
Mission Hills 140 A2
Mission San Jose 72 G2
Mission Springs 81 E6
Mission Viejo 148 A3
Missouri Flat 66 A1
Missouri Triangle 115 B6
Mitchell Corner 94 F5
Mitchells Corner 116 E3
Mi-Wuk Village 75 B7
Moccasin 51 A10
Mococo 71 B10
Modesto 73 F10
Modjeska 141 G9
Mohawk 52 D3
Mojave 117 F9
Mojave Heights 130 E1
Mokelumne City 65 F6
Mokelumne Hill 66 F2
Molena 72 A2
Molino 62 E4
Molus 91 E7
Monmouth 94 D1
Mono Hot Springs 86 C2
Mono Mills (Site) 77 C7
Mono Village 76 A4
Mono Vista 75 B6
Monola 87 E9
Monolith 117 F7
Monroe 62 D5
Monrovia 141 B6
Mons 143 E6
Monsanto 72 B1
Monson 94 E4
Monta Vista 81 C6
Montague 25 D7
Montalvo 138 A5
Montara 71 G7
Montclair 141 C8
Monte Nido 139 C10
Monte Rio 62 D3
Monte Sereno 81 D6
Monte Toyon 81 F7
Monte Vista 59 C6
Montebello 140 D5
Montecito 126 F2
Monterey 90 C2
Monterey Park 140 C5
Montesano 62 D3
Montezuma 64 G2
Montezuma 72 A2
Montezuma 74 C5
Montgomery 54 C4
Montgomery City 78 D2
Montgomery Creek 34 F2
Montgomery Village 62 D5
Montpelier 74 G2
Montrose 140 B4
Mooney Flat 58 C3
Moonridge 142 A5
Moonstone 30 D3
Moore 122 C4
Moores Flat 59 A6
Moorpark 139 A8
Moorpark Home Acres 139 A8
Morada 73 B8
Moraga 71 D10
Moran 36 F4
Morena Village 155 D8
Moreno 154 B5
Moreno Valley 142 D2
Morettis Junction 150 F2
Morgan Hill 81 E9
Morgan Springs 43 D6
Mormon 73 C8
Mormon Bar 84 A4
Morningside Park 140 D3
Morongo Valley 143 C8
Morrison 67 A6
Morristown 52 E1
Morro Bay 113 C6
Morse 91 A6
Mortmar 151 B8
Moss 157 A8
Moss Beach 71 G7
Moss Landing 90 A3
Mossdale 73 E7
Motion 41 A7
Motor City 66 A2
Mott 33 B9
Mount Aukum 66 C2
Mount Baldy 141 A9
Mount Bullion 68 B1
Mount Bullion 84 A3
Mount Eden Station 71 F10
Mount Hebron 26 C1
Mount Hermon 81 F6
Mount Hope 59 E7
Mount Jackson 62 D4
Mount Laguna 155 B9
Mount Ophir 84 A3
Mount Shasta 33 A9
Mount Shasta Woods 26 E1
Mount Signal 157 D6
Mount Wilson 140 A5
Mountain Center 143 G7
Mountain Gate 41 A9
Mountain Home 43 A7
Mountain Home Village 142 C4
Mountain House 25 G6
Mountain House 51 E7
Mountain House 72 E5
Mountain Mesa 106 G2
Mountain Pass 122 B2
Mountain Ranch 66 G4
Mountain Top Junction 129 G9
Mountain View 71 B10
Mountain View 81 B6
Mountain View Acres 130 E1
Mountclef Village 139 A8
Mt Eden 72 F1
Mugginsville 24 E3
Muir 52 A5
Muir Beach 71 D6
Mulford Gardens 71 E10
Mundo 152 E1
Murphy Crossing 81 G9
Murphys 74 A5
Murray 103 B8
Murray Park 71 C7
Murrieta 149 B7
Murrieta Hot Springs 149 B8
Muscatel 93 A10
Muscoy 142 B1
Myers Flat 38 F5
Myoma 143 G10
Myricks Corner 115 A10
Myrtletown 30 G3
Mystic 60 A3

N

Nacimiento 102 E2
Nanceville 105 B6
Napa 63 F9
Napa Junction 63 G9
Napa Soda Springs 63 E9
Naples 125 F9
Naples 140 G5
Naranjo 95 F7
Narlon 124 B3
Nashmead 47 C9
Nashua 90 B3
Nashville 66 C1
National City 154 D3
Natividad 90 B5
Natoma 65 B8
Navarro 54 D3
Navelencia 94 C4
Neal 80 B5
Nealeys Corner 141 B10
Nebelhorn 60 G3
Nebo 130 A5
Needles 134 B5
Negro Hill 74 G5
Neighbors 153 B9
Nelson 50 F3
Neponset 90 B3
Nervo 62 B4
Nestor 154 E3
Neufeld 104 G4
Nevada 142 C2
Nevada City 58 B5
Nevada Dock 71 B10
New Almaden 81 D8
New Auberry 85 E8
New Chicago 66 D1
New Cuyama 126 A1
New England Mills 58 E5
New Monterey 90 C2
Newark 72 G1
Newberry Springs 131 B7
Newburg 38 B3
Newbury Park 139 B8
Newcastle 58 G4
Newell 27 B7
Newhall 128 G1
Newlove 72 B3
Newman 82 C5
Newman Springs 55 C10
Newport 47 F6
Newport Beach 148 A1
Newport Heights 148 A1
Newtown 41 A8
Newtown 58 C4
Newtown 66 B3
Newville 49 D7
Nicasio 70 B5
Nice 55 D9
Nicholls Warm Springs 153 A9
Nicklin 142 D4
Nicks Cove 62 G3
Nicolaus 57 F10
Niland 152 E2
Niles 72 G2
Niles Junction 72 G2
Nimbus 65 B8
Nimshew 50 C5
Nipinnawassee 85 B6
Nipomo 113 F9
Nipton 122 B4
Nitro 71 B8
Noel Heights 62 D3
Nolton 23 B10
Norco 141 E9
Nord 50 D2
Norden 59 B10
Norman 56 A5
North Beach 71 D8
North Bloomfield 59 A6
North Clairemont 154 C2
North Columbia 58 A5
North Dinuba 94 D4
North Edwards 118 G2
North Elsinore 142 G1
North Fair Oaks 80 A5
North Fillmore 127 F8
North Fork 85 D8
North Highlands 65 B7
North Hollywood 140 B2
North Jamul 154 D5
North Palm Springs 143 E8
North Park 154 D3
North Pomona 141 C8
North Richmond 71 C8
North San Juan 58 A4
North Santa Maria 113 G10
North Shafter 115 A10
North Shore 142 A3
North Star 51 F9
North Wawona 76 G2
Northridge 140 A1
Northspur 54 A3
Northwood 62 D3
Norton 64 C2
Norton 73 A8
Nortonville 72 C2
Norwalk 140 E5
Notarb 84 F2
Novato 71 A6
Noyo 54 A1
Nubieber 35 C8
Nuestro 57 C9
Nuevo 142 F3
Nyland 139 A6

O

O'Brien 33 G9
O'Neals 85 E6
Oak Bottom F S Station 23 G9
Oak Glen 142 C5
Oak Glen 39 E6
Oak Grove 150 D1
Oak Grove 74 A1
Oak Grove 95 E9
Oak Knoll 63 E8
Oak Park 102 G3
Oak Park 139 B9
Oak Run 42 A1
Oak Valley 51 G10
Oak View 126 G4
Oak Village 127 G7
Oakdale 74 E1
Oakhurst 85 C7
Oakland 71 D9
Oakley 72 B4
Oakmont 63 D6
Oaks 113 F8
The Oaks 58 C4
Oakville 63 D8
Oasis 151 C7
Oasis 88 A1
Oban 128 B4
Obie 34 C4
Obregon 158 B3
Occidental 62 E3
Ocean Beach 154 D2
Ocean Park 140 D1
Ocean Roar 62 G3
Ocean View 141 G6
Ocean View 62 E2
Oceano 113 F8
Oceanside 149 F6
Ockenden 85 E9
Ocotillo 156 D3
Ocotillo Wells 151 F7
Octol 104 B4
Ogilby 158 C3
Ogo Station 40 D5
Ohm 73 F7
Oil City 116 B2
Oil Junction 116 B2
Oildale 116 B2
Oilfields 93 G6
Ojai 126 F5
Ojala 126 F5
Olancha 97 G6
Olcott 64 F3
Old Adobe 102 F3
Old Carrizo Stage Station 156 B2
Old Dale 144 C5
Old Forbestown 51 G8
Old Fort Jim 66 A2
Old Gilroy 81 F10
Old Hilltown 90 C4
Old Hopland 55 F7
Old Hulbert Place 27 G9
Old Pino 59 G8
Old Point Comfort 129 F7
Old River 116 D1
Old Station 43 A6
Old Station 43 A6
Old Town 117 E6
Old Town 126 F3
Oleander 94 C1
Olema 70 B5
Oleum 71 B9
Olinda 41 D8
Olive 141 F7
Olive Hill 58 B1
Olive View 128 G2
Olivehurst 57 D10
Olivenhain 149 G7
Olympia 81 E6
Olympic Valley 60 C2
Omega 59 B7
Omira 53 B8
Omo Ranch 66 C4
Omus 62 A3
100 Palms 151 B6
101 Ranch 85 E6
Ono 41 C6
Ontario 141 C9
Onyx 106 F4
Opal Cliffs 81 G7
Ophir 58 G4
Ora 103 A6
Orange 141 F7
Orange Avenue Junction 141 C6
Orange Cove 94 C4
Orange Park Acres 141 F8
Orangevale 65 B8
Orcutt 124 A5
Ordbend 50 E1
Ordway 142 D3
Oregon City 50 F5
Oregon House 58 A3
Orford 73 B8
Orick 30 A4
Orinda 71 D10
Orinda Village 71 C10
Orita 157 A8
Orland 49 D10
Orleans 31 A8
Orleans Flat 59 A6
Ormand 142 D1
Oro Fino 24 E3
Oro Grande 130 D1
Oro Loma 83 G8
Oroleve 51 G8
Orosi 94 D5
Oroville 50 G5
Oroville East 51 G6
Oroville Junc 50 G4
Orris 105 E7
Orrs Springs 54 C5
Ortega 73 C8
Ortonville 126 G5
Orwood 72 C5
Ostrom 58 E1
Oswald 57 E10
Otay 154 E4
Oteys Sierra Village 87 B7
Otterbein 141 D7
Outingdale 66 C2
Outlet 47 G10
Owenyo 96 C5
Owl 143 E6
Oxalis 83 G9
Oxford 64 F5
Oxnard 139 A6
Oxnard Beach 138 B5
Ozol 71 B10

P

Pabrico 72 G1
Pachappa 142 D1
Pacheco 72 B1
Pacific 66 A4
Pacific Beach 154 C2
Pacific Grove 90 C2
Pacific Manor 71 F7
Pacific Palisades 140 C1
Pacifica 71 F7
Pacoima 140 A2
Pagliarulo 104 E5
Paicines 91 B8
Paige 104 A3
Paintersville 64 F5
Pajaro 81 G9
Pala 149 D9

Pala Mesa 149 D8
Palermo 57 A10
Palm Beach 90 A3
Palm City 154 E3
Palm Desert 143 G9
Palm Springs 143 F8
Palm Springs Station 143 E7
Palmdale 128 E5
Palmetto 51 C7
Palmo 115 A9
Palo Alto 80 A5
Palo Cedro 41 B9
Palo Verde 153 C9
Paloma 66 F2
Palomar Mountain 149 D10
Palos Verdes Estates 140 F2
Panama 116 D2
Panamint (Ghost Town) 108 B3
Panamint Springs 97 F10
Panoche 92 D1
Panoche Junction 92 D4
Panorama City 140 A2
Panorama Heights 105 E10
Panorama Heights 141 F7
Paradise 50 D5
Paradise Camp 86 A5
Paradise Cay 71 C7
Paradise Park 81 F6
Paradise Springs 129 G7
Paraiso Springs 91 F7
Paramount 140 E4
Paris 128 F4
Park Village 98 D5
Parker Dam 147 A9
Parkfield 102 D5
Parkfield Junction 102 B4
Parkhill 51 D6
Parkway 65 D6
Parlier 94 C3
Parramore Springs 55 B9
Parsnip Springs 37 C6
Pasadena 140 B4
Pasatiempo 81 F6
Paskenta 49 C7
Paso Robles 102 G3
Patch 116 D3
Patrick Creek 23 B6
Patricks Point 30 C3
Patterson 82 A4
Patton 142 B2
Paulsell 74 E3
Pauma Valley 149 D9
Paxton 51 A10
Payne 40 F2
Paynes Creek 42 E2
Paynesville 60 G5
Peaceful Pines 67 E10
Peachton 57 A9
Peanut 40 C1
Pearblossom 129 E6
Peardale 58 C5
Pearland 128 E5
Pearson 57 E10
Pearson 73 A8
Pearsonville 107 E7
Peavine 53 E8
Pebble Beach 90 D2
Pebbly Beach 139 G8
Pecwan 30 A5
Pedley 141 D10
Peltier 65 G8
Pena House (Site) 64 F1
Pendola Gardens 75 G8
Peninsula Village 43 E9
Penney 40 F2
Penngrove 63 F6
Pennington 57 B8
Penoyar 26 D1
Penryn 58 G3
Pentland 115 F9
Pentz 50 E5
Penvir 91 D6
Pepper Corner 141 E9
Pepperwood 38 D4
Pepperwood Grove 55 E10
Peral 94 E5
Peralta Hills 141 F7
Perez 27 D8
Perkins 65 C7
Perks Corner 66 A1
Perris 142 F2
Perry 81 D9
Perrys Corner 157 B8
Pescadero 80 C3
Petaluma 63 G6
Peters 73 B10
Peterson Mill 87 C7
Petrolia 38 E2
Phelan 129 F9
Phelps Corner 155 D6
Phillips 60 G3
Phillipsville 39 F6
Philo 54 E4
Picacho 158 A5
Pico 127 G10
Pico Rivera 140 D5
Piedmont 71 D9
Piedra 94 A4
Pierce 33 B10
Pierce 71 A10
Piercy 47 B6
Pierpont Bay 138 A5
Pike 58 A5
Pilliken 66 B5
Pilot Hill 58 G5
Pine City (Site) 144 C2
Pine Cove 143 F6
Pine Flat 105 D10
Pine Grove 155 A7
Pine Grove 41 A8
Pine Grove 54 B1
Pine Grove 55 G10
Pine Grove 66 E3
Pine Hill 30 G3
Pine Hills 150 G2
Pine Log 74 A5
Pine Ridge 85 E9
Pine Town 43 E10
Pine Valley 155 C8
Pine Wood 143 F6
Pinecrest 67 G9
Pinecroft 58 D5
Pinedale 93 A10
Pinehurst 95 B7
Pinezanita 142 B5
Pinnacles 91 D9
Pinnio 36 D4
Pino Grande 59 G8
Pinole 71 B9
Pinon Hills 129 F9
The Pines 50 D5
The Pines 85 C7
Pinto Wye 144 D3
Pinyon Crest 150 A4
Pinyon Pines 150 A4
Pioneer 33 A9
Pioneer 66 E4
Pioneer Point 108 E1
Pioneertown 143 B9
Pippin Corner 113 D10
Piru 127 F9
Pisgah 131 C10
Pismo Beach 113 E8
Pit River 35 D9
Pitco 94 F1
Pittsburg 72 B2
Pittville 35 D7
Pixley 104 C5
Pizona (Site) 78 C1
Placentia 141 E7
Placerville 66 A2
Plainfield 64 C3
Plainsburg 84 D1
Plainview 105 A6
Planada 84 C1
Plano 105 C7
Plantation 61 C10
Plaskett 101 D6
Plasse 67 B7
Plaster City 156 C4
Platina 40 D4
Playa del Rey 140 D2
Plaza 94 F4
Pleasant Grove 58 G1
Pleasant Hill 72 C1
Pleasant Valley 66 B3
Pleasant View 51 G10
Pleasanton 72 F2
Plumas Eureka 52 D3
Plumbago 52 G1
Plymouth 66 D1
Poe 51 D6
Point Arena 54 F2
Point Loma 154 D2
Point Pleasant 65 F6
Point Reyes Station 70 A4
Poker Flat 52 E1
Polaris 60 B2
Polk 65 C6
Polk Springs 42 G4
Pollard Flat 33 E8
Pollock 33 E8
Pollock Pines 66 A3
Pomo (Site) 55 B7
Pomona 141 C8
Ponca 105 C7
Pond 104 F4
Pondosa 34 B4
Ponto 149 G7
Pope 151 D10
Pope 73 A8
Pope Valley 63 C8
Poplar 105 B6
Porphyry 141 E10
Port Costa 71 B10
Port Hueneme 138 B5
Port Kenyon 38 B2
Port Orford (Site) 125 F7
Port San Luis 113 E7
Port Wine 51 E10
Porterville 105 B7
Portola 52 C4
Portola Valley 80 B5
Ports O'Call Village 140 G3
Portuguese Bend 140 G2
Posey 105 E10
Poso Park 105 E10
Post 124 D4
Posts 100 A3
Potrero 155 E8
Potrero District 71 E8
Potter Valley 55 B7
Potwisha 95 D9
Poverty Hill 51 F10
Poway 154 A4
Powellton 50 B5
Pozo 113 D10
Prairie City (Site) 65 B9
Prather 85 F8
Pratton 93 B9
Prattville 43 F9
Prenda 142 E1
Presswood 55 C6
Preston 55 G8
Priest 75 D6
Princeton 57 A6
Princeton 80 A2
Princeton Siding 57 A6
Pritchard Hill 63 D8
Proberta 49 A10
Progress 57 E8
Project City 41 A8
Prospero 116 B1
Prunedale 90 B4
Puente Junction 141 D6
Puerta La Cruz 150 D2
Pulga 51 D6
Pumpkin Center 116 D2
Pumpkin Center 35 C9
Punta 126 G3
Purdys Gardens 55 D7

Q

Quail 104 C4
Quail Valley 142 G2
Quaker Meadow 106 B1
Quality 105 E6
Quartz 74 C5
Quartz Hill 128 D4
Queen City 51 E10
Queen Dicks 78 E2
Quincy 51 B10
Quincy Junction 52 B1
Quintette 59 F8

R

Rackerby 58 A2
Raco 93 A9
Radec 149 C10
Radnor 104 E5
Radum 72 F3
Rafael Village 71 A7
Raffetto 59 G10
Rag Dump 51 C6
Ragtown 132 D1
Rail Road Flat 66 F4
Rainbow 149 C8
Rainbow 59 B9
Rainbow Wells 122 E1
Raisin City 93 C9
Ralph 75 C6
Ramada 50 F4
Ramal 63 G8
Ramirez 57 B10
Ramona 149 G10
Rampart 60 D2
Ramsey 47 B9
Rana 142 C1
Ranch 54 A2
Ranch House 149 D6
Rancheria 66 D2
Ranchita 150 E3
Rancho Bernardo 154 A4
Rancho Calaveras 74 A1
Rancho Cordova 65 C7
Rancho Cucamonga 141 C9
Rancho Mirage 143 G9
Rancho Murieta 65 D9
Rancho Palos Verdes 140 G2
Rancho Santa Clarita 128 F1
Rancho Santa Fe 154 A2
Rancho Santa Margarita 148 A4
Rancho Seco 118 D1
Rand 118 B3
Randolph 52 F5
Randsburg 118 C4
Ravendale 36 G5
Ravenna 128 F4
Rawson 41 G10
Raymer 140 B2
Raymond 84 D4
Rayo 94 E5
Readings Bar (Site) 40 A3
Reclamation 71 A7
Rector 94 G5
Red Ant 52 F1
Red Apple 66 G5
Red Bank 41 G8
Red Bluff 41 F9
Red Bluff Omni Radio Range Station 41 G9
Red Box Station 140 A5
Red Hill 141 G7
Red Mountain 118 C4
Red Rock 53 B8
Red Top 83 E9
Redbanks 95 E6
Redcrest 38 D5
Redding 41 B8
Redlands 142 C3
Redman 129 C6
Redondo Beach 140 F2
Redway 39 G6
Redwood City 80 A4
Redwood Estates 81 D6
Redwood Grove 80 D5
Redwood House 38 C5
Redwood Retreat 81 F9
Redwood Terrace 80 C4
Redwood Valley 55 B6
Redwoods 42 B2
Reed 71 C7
Reedley 94 D3
Regina Heights 55 D6
Reilly Heights 54 D3
Relief 59 A6
Remnoy 94 F2
Reno Junction 53 D8
Renoville (Site) 121 A6
Requa 22 F4
Rescue 65 A10
Reseda 140 B1
Reward 115 C6
Reward 96 B5
Rex 124 A5
Reynolds 70 A4
Rheem 71 D10
Rheem Valley 71 D10
Rialto 142 C1
Ribier 116 D3
Ricardo (Site) 118 C1
Riccas Corner 62 E5
Rice 146 C3
Riceton 50 G4
Rich 118 G3
Rich Bar 51 A8
Rich Gulch 66 F3
Richardson Springs 50 C3
Richfield 49 B10
Richgrove 105 E6
Richmond 71 C8
Richmond District 71 E7
Richvale 50 G4
Rico 157 C8
Ridge 54 B5
Ridgecrest 107 G8
Ridgeville 32 F4
Ridgewoods Heights 30 G3
Riego 65 A6
Rimforest 142 A2
Rimlon 143 F9
Rimrock 143 B8
Rincon 149 E10
Rincon 81 F6
Rio Bravo 115 C10
Rio Del Mar 81 F7
Rio Dell 38 C3
Rio Dell 62 D4
Rio Linda 65 B6
Rio Nido 62 D3
Rio Oso 57 F10
Rio Vista 72 A4
Rio Vista Junction 64 G2
Ripley 153 B9
Ripon 73 E9
Ripperdan 93 A8
River Oaks 81 G10
River Pines 66 C2
Riverbank 73 E10
Riverbend 94 B3
Riverdale 47 C6
Riverdale 93 E10
Riverdale Park 73 F10
Riverside 142 D1
Riverside Grove 80 D5
Riverside Park 38 C4
Riverside Station 75 B7
Riverton 66 A5
Riverview 33 E8
Riverview 64 D5
Riverview Farms 154 B5
Riz Siding 49 G10
Roads End 106 D1
Rob Roy Junction 81 F7
Robbers Creek 43 D10
Robbins 57 G9
Robertsville 81 C7
Robinson Mills 51 G7
Robinsons Corner 57 A10
Robla 65 B6
Roblar 62 F5
Robles Del Rio 90 E4
Rochester 141 C10
Rock Creek 51 B7
Rock Haven 85 E9
Rockaway Beach 71 F7
Rocklin 65 A8
Rockport 47 D6
Rocktram 63 F9
Rockville 63 G10
Rockwood 152 G2
Rocky Hill 95 G6
Rodeo 71 B9
Rogerville 51 F8
Rohnert Park 62 F5
Rohnerville 38 B3
Rolands 62 D3
Rolinda 93 B9
Rolling Hills 140 G3
Rolling Hills Estates 140 F3
Rollingwood 71 C9
Romoland 142 G3
Roosevelt 129 C6
Rosamond 128 A4
Rose Place 55 D9
Rosedale 116 C1
Roseland 62 E5
Rosemary 124 A5
Rosemead 140 C5
Rosemont 154 A5
Rosemont 65 C7
Roseville 65 A7
Rosewood 30 G3
Rosewood 41 E7
Ross 62 D4
Ross 71 C7
Ross Corner 158 C5
Rossi 93 G10
Rossmoor 140 F5
Rotavele 50 E1
Rough and Ready 58 C4
Round Mountain 34 G2
Round Valley 43 F6
Rovana 86 B5
Rowen 117 D6
Rowland 141 D6
Rowland Heights 141 D6
Rubidoux 142 D1
Rucker 81 F10
Rumsey 56 G4
Running Springs 142 B3
Rupert Siding 57 D10
Rush Creek 75 D9
Russ 128 F3
Russell 64 G1
Russell City 71 F10
Ruth 39 E10
Rutherford 63 D8
Ruthven 158 A1
Ryan 99 G7
Ryde 64 G5

S

Sablon 146 B1
Sacate 125 F6
Saco 116 B1
Sacramento 65 C6
Saddle Junction 143 F7
Sage 149 A10
Sage Hen 36 C4
Sageland 117 B9
Saint Bernard 43 F7
Saint Helena 63 D7
Saint Johns 95 F6
Saint Louis 52 E1
Salida 73 E9
Salinas 90 C4
Salmon Creek 62 E2
Saltdale 118 C2
Saltmarsh 146 A1
Salton 151 C9
Salton City 151 E8
Salton Sea Beach 151 D8
Saltus 132 E5
Salvador 63 F9
Salvia 143 E8
Salyer 31 F8
Samoa 30 F3
Samuel Springs 63 C9
San Andreas 66 G3
San Anselmo 71 C7
San Antonio Heights 141 B9
San Ardo 102 C1
San Augustine 124 F5
San Benito 91 D9
San Bernardino 142 C2
San Bruno 71 F8
San Carlos 80 A4
San Clemente 148 C4
San Diego 154 D3
San Diego Country Estates 155 A6
San Dimas 141 C7
San Dimas Station 141 B8
San Felipe 150 F3
San Felipe 82 F1
San Fernando 140 A2
San Francisco 71 E8
San Gabriel 140 C5
San Geronimo 71 B6
San Gregorio 80 C3
San Ignacio 150 D3
San Jacinto 142 F5
San Joaquin 93 C7
San Jose 81 C7
San Juan Bautista 90 A5
San Juan Capistrano 148 B4
San Juan Hot Springs 148 A5
San Juan Station 148 A5
San Lawrence Terrace 102 F3
San Leandro 71 E10
San Lorenzo 71 F10
San Lorenzo Park 80 D5
San Lucas 101 B10
San Luis Obispo 113 D8
San Luis Rey 149 E6
San Luis Rey Heights 149 D7
San Marcos 149 F8
San Marino 140 C5
San Martin 81 E10
San Mateo 71 G9
San Mateo Park 71 G8
San Miguel 102 F3
San Onofre 148 D4
San Pablo 71 C8
San Pasqual 149 G10
San Pedro 140 G3
San Pedro Valley 71 G7
San Quentin 71 C7
San Rafael 71 C7
San Ramon 72 E2
San Ramon Village 72 E2
San Simeon 101 G8
San Tomas 81 C7
San Ysidro 150 E3
San Ysidro 154 F4
Sanborn 117 G10
Sanchez Adobe 71 G7
Sand City 90 C3
Sand Hill 72 C4
Sandberg 127 C10
Sanders 57 C9
Sandia 157 B8
Sands 121 G8
Sandy Gulch 66 E4
Sandy Korner 151 A6
Sandyland 126 F2
Sandyland Cove 126 G3
Sanger 94 B2
Sankey 65 A6
Santa Ana 141 G7
Santa Ana Heights 148 A2
Santa Barbara 126 F1
Santa Clara 81 B7
Santa Clarita 128 F1
Santa Cruz 81 F6
Santa Fe Springs 140 D5
Santa Margarita 113 C8
Santa Maria 113 G10
Santa Monica 140 D1
Santa Nella Village 82 E5
Santa Paula 127 G7
Santa Rita 90 B4
Santa Rita Park 83 F8
Santa Rosa 62 D5
Santa Susana 139 A10
Santa Susana Knolls 139 A10
Santa Venetia 71 B7
Santa Ynez 125 D8
Santa Ysabel 150 G2
Santee 154 C4
Saratoga 81 C6
Saratoga Springs 55 C8
Sargent 81 G10
Saticoy 139 A6
Sattley 52 F5
Saugus 128 F1
Sausalito 71 D7
Sawmill Flat 74 B5
Sawyers Bar 32 A2
Saxon 64 D4
Scales 51 F10
Scarface 27 G7
Scheelite 86 B5
Schelville 63 G8
Schilling 93 F9
Scissors Crossing 150 G4
Scotia 38 C3
Scotland 141 A10
Scott Bar 24 C3
Scotts 53 C8
Scotts Corner 72 G2
Scotts Valley 81 F6
Scottsville 56 F2
Scottys Castle 89 F6
Scranton 99 E8
Sea Cliff 126 G3
Seal Cove 71 G7
Searles 118 B4
Searles Valley 108 F1
Sears Point 71 A8
Seaside 90 C3
Sebastopol 58 A4
Sebastopol 62 E4
Second Crossing 77 G7
Second Garrotte 75 D7
Secret Town 59 D6
Sedco Hills 149 A7
Seeley 156 C5
Seguro 116 B2
Seiad Valley 24 B1
Seigler Springs 55 G10
Selby 71 B9
Selma 94 D2
Seminole Hot Springs 139 C9
Semitropic 104 G3
Seneca 43 G9
Sequoia 95 E6
Serena 126 F2
Serena Park 126 F2
Serra 148 C3
Serra Mesa 154 C3
Sespe 127 G7
Sespe Village 127 G7
Seven Oaks 142 B5
Seven Pines 96 A3
Seville 94 E5
Shady Glen 58 D5
Shafter 115 A10
Shafter 70 B5
Shake City 54 A4
Shake House 42 E3
Shandon 102 G5
Sharon 84 E2
Sharon Valley 51 G8
Shasta 41 B7
Shasta Retreat 33 B9
Shasta Springs 33 B9
Shaver Lake 85 E9
Shaver Lake Point 85 E9
Shaw Mine Mill 66 B1
Shaws Flat 74 B5
Sheep Ranch 66 G5
Sheepshead 36 F1
Sheldon 65 E7
Shell 94 F2
Shell Beach 113 E8
Shelter Cove 71 G7
Sheridan 62 D2
Sherman Acres 67 D8
Sherman Oaks 140 B2
Shiloh 62 D5
Shingle Springs 66 B1
Shingletown 42 C2
Shinn 72 G2
Shippee 50 F4
Shipyard Acres 63 F9
Shirley 94 F1
Shirley Meadows 106 F1
Shively 38 D4
Shore Acres 72 B2
Shoshone 109 C10
Shuman 124 A4
Shumway 44 A4
Siberia 132 D3
Sicard Flat 58 C2
Sidds Landing 50 F1
Sierra 52 B1
Sierra Glen 95 C7
Sierra Heights 105 A7
Sierra Madre 140 B5
Sierra Sky Park 93 A10
Sierraville 52 F5
Signal Hill 140 F4
Silt 118 G3
Silver City 95 E10
Silver Lake 121 C7
Silver Strand 138 B5
Silverado 141 G9
Silverado Station 141 G9
Silverthorn 41 A8
Simi 62 B4
Simi Station 139 A9
Simi Valley 139 A9
Simmler 114 C4
Simms 73 D9
Sims 33 D8
Singing Springs 128 G5
Sisquoc 125 A6
Sites 56 B3
Sixmile Station 57 C10
Ski Hi 48 F5
Skidoo 98 E3
Skinners 65 B10
Sky Londa 80 B4
Sky Valley 143 E10
Skyforest 142 A3
Skyhigh 67 E8
Skyland 142 A2
Skytop 107 F10
Slagger 34 A4
Slater 115 A10
Sleepy Hollow 141 D8
Sleepy Valley 128 E3
Sloat 52 C2
Sloughhouse 65 D8
Small 33 B9
Smartville 58 C2
Smeltzer 141 G6
Smiley Park 142 B3
Smith Corner 115 B10
Smith River 22 A3
Smithflat 66 A2
Snelling 74 G5
Snoboy 81 A7
Snow Creek 143 E7
Snowden 32 A2
Snowdon 25 C7
Soapweed 59 G8
Soboba Hot Springs 142 F5
Sobrante 71 B8
Soda Bay 55 E9
Soda Creek Station 55 A8
Soda Springs (Site) 61 B10
Soda Springs 105 C9
Soda Springs 42 G5
Soda Springs 59 B10
Solana Beach 154 A2
Soledad 91 E7
Solemint 128 F2
Solromar 139 C7
Solvang 125 D7
Solyo 73 F8
Somerset 66 B3
Somersville (Site) 72 C3
Somes Bar 23 G9
Somis 139 A7
Sonoma 63 F7
Sonora 74 B5
Sonora Junction 68 E3
Soquel 81 F7
Sorensens 67 A9
Sorrento 154 B2
Sorroca 64 E5

Soulsbyville 75 B6
Sousas Corner 62 D4
South Coyote 81 D9
South Dos Palos 83 G8
South El Monte 140 C5
South Entrance Station 85 A7
South Fontana 141 C10
South Fork 38 E5
South Fork 54 A2
South Fork 75 F9
South Fork 85 D8
South Gate 140 D4
South Laguna 148 B3
South Lake 106 G2
South Lake Tahoe 60 F4
South Leggett 47 C7
South Oceanside 149 F6
South Oroville 50 G5
South Pasadena 140 C4
South San Diego 154 E3
South San Francisco 71 F8
South San Gabriel 140 C5
South San Jose Hills 141 D6
South Santa Ana 141 G7
South Taft 115 E8
South Trona 108 F1
South Wawona 76 G2
South Whittier 140 D5
South Yuba 57 D10
Southern Pacific Station 125 F10
Southern Pacific Station 71 E8
Spadra 141 C7
Spalding Corner 34 C5
Spangler 118 A5
Spanish Creek 52 B1
Spanish Dry Diggings 59 F6
Spanish Flat 59 G7
Spanish Flat 63 C9
Sparkle 72 C1
Spaulding 44 A2
Spear Creek Summer Home Tract 106 E1
Spellacy 115 F8
Spence 90 C5
Sperry (Site) 110 F1
Spicer City 115 A7
Spinks Corner 104 A5
Spoonbill 72 B2
Sportshaven 39 D9
Spreckels 90 C4
Spreckels Junction 90 C5
Spring Gap 67 G8
Spring Garden 52 C2
Spring Hill 58 C5
Spring Valley 154 D4
Springfield 74 B5
Springville 105 B9
Springville 139 A6
Spruce Point 30 G3
Spyrock 47 C9
Squab 63 G9
Squabbletown 74 B5
Squaw Hill 50 B1
Squaw Valley 94 B5
Squirrel Mountain Valley 106 G2
Stacy 45 F8
Stafford 38 C4
Stage Station 108 B2
Stallion Springs 116 F5
Stallman Corners 65 A9
Standard 75 C6
Standish 44 D5
Stanfield Hill 58 B2
Stanford 80 B5
Stanislaus 74 A5
Stanley 63 G9
Stanton 141 F6
Stauffer 127 C6
Stedman 132 D1
Steelhead 24 C2
Steelhead 39 G7
Steeplehollow Crossing 59 C6
Stege 71 C9
Stegeman 57 A6
Stent 74 C5
Stevens 115 D10
Stevinson 83 C6
Stewart Springs 25 G7
Stewarts Point 61 B9
Stinson Beach 71 C6
Stirling City 50 B5
Stirling Junction 50 E3
Stockton 73 C7
Stoil 104 D3
Stomar 82 B5
Stone House 58 B2
Stonehouse (Site) 32 E3
Stonehouse 84 B3
Stonestown 71 E7
Stony Creek 50 E1
Stony Point 62 F5
Stonyford 56 A2
Storey 84 F3
Storrie 51 B7
Stout 105 A6
Stovepipe Wells 98 D3
Stratford 103 A10
Strathearn 139 A9
Strathmore 105 A7
Strawberry 67 G8
Strawberry Point 71 C7
Strawberry Valley 51 F9
Stronghold 27 B6
Stuart 149 E6
Studio City 140 B2
Styx 146 E3
Subaco 57 F9
Subeet 64 G1
Sucker Flat 58 C2
Sucro 64 G3
Sudden 124 E4
Sugar Pine 85 A7
Sugarfield 64 A3
Sugarloaf 143 A6
Sugarloaf 33 F8
Sugarpine 75 B7
Suisun City 64 G1
Sullivan 57 C9
Sulphur Bank 56 E1
Sulphur Springs 127 F10
Sulphur Springs 127 F6
Sulphur Springs 91 G10
Sultana 94 D4
Summer Home 73 D8
Summerhome 62 D3
Summerland 126 F2
Summertown 42 B5
Summerville 32 C2
Summit 117 F7
Summit 128 E4
Summit 130 G1
Summit 152 A2
Summit 54 A4
Summit 55 C7
Summit City (Site) 59 A9
Summit City 41 A8
Summit House 84 C5
Sun City 142 G3
Sun Valley 140 A2
Suncrest 154 C5
Sunfair 144 B1
Sunfair Heights 144 A1
Sunkist 142 C3
Sunland 105 C7
Sunland 140 A3
Sunny Brae 30 F4
Sunny Hills 141 E6
Sunnybrook 66 E1
Sunnyside 154 D4
Sunnyside 48 C4
Sunnyside 60 D2
Sunnyside 94 B1
Sunnyslope 141 D10
Sunnyslope 58 A1
Sunnyvale 81 B6
Sunol 72 G2
Sunrise 128 D5
Sunrise Vista 55 G10
Sunset 57 C9
Sunset Beach 140 G5
Sunset Cliffs 154 D2
Sunset District 71 E7
Sunset Ridge Station 140 B4
Sunset View 58 C4
Sunsweet 141 C8
Surf 124 C3
Surfside 140 G5
Susanville 44 D3
Sutter 57 D9
Sutter Creek 66 E2
Sutter Hill 66 E2
Suval 64 G1
Sveadal 81 E8
Swall 94 G5
Swansea 97 D6
Swanston 65 C6
Swanton 80 E4
Sweeneys Crossing 66 B3
Sweetbriar 33 C9
Sweetland 58 B4
Swingle 64 C4
Switzer Station 140 A4
Swobe 34 A2
Sycamore 57 D7
Sycamore Flat 91 G7
Sycamore Springs 113 E7
Sycamore Station 142 B1
Sykes 107 C6
Sylmar 140 A2
Sylvan Corners 65 B7

T

Taft 115 E8
Taft Heights 115 E8
Taft Point 76 E2; 20 F5
Tagus 94 G4
Tahoe City 60 C2
Tahoe Pines 60 D2
Tahoe Valley 60 F3
Tahoe Vista 60 C3
Tahoma 60 E2
Tajiguas 125 F8
Talich 149 F6
Tallac Village 60 F3
Talmage 55 D6
Tamalpais Valley 71 D7
Tamarack 67 D8
Tambo 57 C10
Tan Oak Park 47 C8
Tancred 63 A10
Tangair 124 C3
Tara Hills 71 B9
Tarke 57 D8
Tarpey 94 A1
Tarpey Village 94 A1
Tarzana 140 B1
Tassajara 72 D3
Tassajara Hot Springs 90 G5
Tatu 47 E10
Taurusa 94 E5
Taylor 150 A4
Taylorsville 52 A1
Teakettle Junction 97 B10
Tecate 155 E7
Tecnor 26 C3
Tecopa 110 E1
Tecopa Hot Springs 110 D1
Tehachapi 117 F7
Tehama 49 A10
Telegraph City 74 C2
Temecula 149 B8
Temecula Hot Springs 149 B8
Temescal Station 141 F10
Temple City 140 C5
Templeton 113 A7
Tennant 26 E2
Terminous 73 A6
Terminus (Site) 95 F7
Termo 36 F5
Terra Bella 105 C7
Terra Cotta 142 G1
Terra Linda 71 B7
Tesla (Site) 72 F5
Tharps Log 95 D9
Thermal 151 A7
Thermalito 50 G5
Thoman 63 D7
Thomas Lane 115 B10
Thomasson 63 G10
Thompson 63 G9
Thorn 130 F2
Thorn 130 G5
Thorn Junction 46 A5
Thornton 65 G6
Thousand Oaks 139 B8
Thousand Palms 143 F9
Thousand Palms Oasis 143 F10
Three Arch Bay 148 B3
Three Cabins 38 A5
Three Corners 102 A5
Three Crossing 55 B8
Three Forks 40 G1
Three Points 129 G6
Three Rivers 95 E8
Three Rocks 92 E5
Thyle 113 C8
Tiber 113 E8
Tiburon 71 D7
Tie Summit Station 128 G5
Tierra Buena 57 D9
Tiger Lily 66 B2
Timba 82 B5
Timbuctoo 58 C2
Tionesta 27 D7
Tipton 104 B4
Tisdale 57 E8
Titus 156 E1
Toadtown 50 C5
Tobin 51 B7
Tocaloma 70 B5
Todd Place 114 D2
Todd Valley 59 E6
Tokay 94 D4
Tolenas 64 F1
Tollhouse 85 F9
Tomales 62 G4
Toms Place 77 G10
Tomspur 73 B8
Tonyville 95 G6
Toolville 95 G6
Toomey 131 A6
Top of the World 148 B3
Topanga 139 C10
Topanga Beach 140 C1
Topanga Park 139 C10
Topaz 68 C3
Tormey 71 B9
Toro Canyon 126 F2
Torrance 140 F3
Tortuga 152 F3
Tower House 41 A6
Towle 59 C7
Town Talk 58 C5
Toyon 41 A8
Toyon 66 G2
Trabucco Gardens 75 G8
Trabuco Canyon 148 A4
Tracy 73 E6
Trancas 139 D8
Tranquillity 93 C6
Transfer 42 G5
Traver 94 E3
Travis Field 64 F2
Treadwell 116 B2
Tremont 64 D4
Trent 83 E6
Trenton 62 D4
Tres Pinos 91 A7
Trevarno 72 F4
Trigo 84 G4
Trimmer 85 G10
Trinidad 30 D3
Trinity Alps 32 F4
Trinity Center 32 D5
Trinity Village 31 F8
Triunfo Corner 139 B9
Trocha 105 E6
Trona 108 F1
Trowbridge 57 F10
Troy 59 B10
Truckee 60 B2
Truckhaven 151 E8
Trull 73 C6
Tryon Corner 22 B3
Tuber 27 A6
Tudor 57 E10
Tujunga 140 A3
Tulare 104 A4
Tulelake 27 A6
Tunnel 128 G1
Tunnel 15 Spur 156 D1
Tuolumne 75 C6
Tupman 115 D9
Turk 103 A7
Turlock 83 A6
Turner 62 F5
Turner 73 D8
Tustin 141 G7
Tustin Foothills 141 F7
Tuttle 83 C10
Tuttletown 74 B5
Twain 51 A10
Twain Harte 75 B7
Twentynine Palms 144 B2
Twin Bridges 35 C9
Twin Bridges 60 G2
Twin Buttes 94 E5
Twin Cities 65 F7
Twin Creeks 81 D8
Twin Lakes 81 F6
Twin Oaks 117 D7
Twin Oaks 149 F8
Twin Peaks 142 A2
Twin Pines 58 E5
Two Bunch Palms 143 D9
Two Harbors 139 E7
Two Rivers 52 C3
Two Rock 62 F5
Tyee City 30 E3
Tylers Corner 66 C3
Tyrone 62 D3

U

Ukiah 55 D6
Ulmar 72 E4
Ultra 105 C7
Una 116 B1
Underwood Park 47 C7
Union 63 F9
Union City 72 G1
Union Hill 51 F10
Union Landing 47 E6
Union Point 73 C6
Union Point 76 E2; 20 E5
Universal City 140 B3
University City 154 B2
University Heights 154 C3
University Of California Experiment Station 142 D1
University of California Marine Laboratory 62 F2
Upland 141 C9
Upper Crossing 25 B10
Upper Forni 60 G2
Upper Lake 55 D9
Upton 33 A8
Urgon 73 A8
Usal 47 C6
Uva 94 C3

V

Vacation Beach 62 D3
Vacaville 64 E1
Val Verde 127 F10
Val Verde 142 F2
Valdez 64 F5
Vale 64 F3
Valencia 128 F1
Valerie 151 B6
Valinda 141 C6
Valjean (Site) 121 A7
Valle Vista 142 G5
Valle Vista 71 D10
Vallecito 74 A4
Vallejo 71 A9
Vallemar 71 F7
Valleton 102 D2
Valley Acres 115 E9
Valley Center 149 E9
Valley Crossing 61 B9
Valley Ford 62 F3
Valley Home 74 D1
Valley of Enchantment 142 A2
Valley of the Moon 142 A2
Valley Springs 66 G1
Valley View 76 E1
Valley View Park 142 A2
Valley Wells 108 E1
Valley Wells 121 B10
Valona 71 B9
Valyermo 129 F7
Van Allen 73 D9
Van Nuys 140 B2
Vance 105 A6
Vandenberg 124 C4
Vandenberg Village 124 C4
Vanguard 93 G9
Venado 62 C3
Venice 140 D2
Venida 95 F6
Venola 116 D2
Ventucopa 126 B3
Ventura 138 A5
Verdant 152 F2
Verde 113 E9
Verdemont 142 B1
Verdugo City 140 B4
Vernalis 73 F7
Vernon 140 D4
Verona 64 A5
Vestal 105 E6
Vichy Springs 55 C6
Victor 73 A8
Victorville 130 E2
Victory Palms 144 G5
Vidal 147 C6
Vidal Junction 146 B5
View Park 140 D3
Viewland 45 D6
Villa Park 141 F7
Villinger 73 A7
Vina 50 B1
Vincent 128 E5
Vine Hill 72 B1
Vineburg 63 F8
Vineyard 65 D7
Vinland 104 F5
Vinton 53 D7
Viola 42 C4
Virgilia 51 A9
Virginia Colony 139 A8
Virginiatown 58 F3
Visalia 94 F5
Vista 149 F7
Vista Robles 57 A10
Volcan 116 B2
Volcano 66 D3
Volcanoville 59 F7
Vollmers 33 E8
Volta 83 E6
Vorden 64 F5
Voss 66 B5

W

Waddington 38 B2
Wadstrom 126 G5
Wagner 67 E10
Wagner 73 D9
Wahtoke 94 C3
Waits Station 66 D1
Waldo 71 D7
Waldo Junction 58 D2
Waldorf 124 A4
Waldrue Heights 63 E7
Walerga 65 B7
Walker 68 D3
Wallace 65 G10
Wallace Center 115 E8
Walltown 65 C9
Walmort 65 E8
Walnut 141 D7
Walnut Creek 72 C1
Walnut Grove 65 G6
Walnut Park 140 D4
Walnut Siding 141 D7
Walong 117 E6
Walsh Station 65 C7
Walter Springs 63 B8
Walteria 140 F3
Walthal 73 B9
Warm Springs 81 A7
Warner 142 C3
Warner Springs 150 E2
Warnerville 74 E3
Wasco 104 G4
Waseck 31 B6
Washington 59 A7
Waterford 74 F2
Waterloo 73 B8
Waterman Canyon Station 142 A2
Watermans Corner 157 C8
Watsonville 81 G8
Watsonville Junction 81 G9
Watts 140 E4
Waukena 104 B3
Wave 126 G3
Wawona 76 G1
Wayne 81 B7
Weaverville 32 G3
Webster 64 C4
Weed 25 G8
Weed Patch 116 D3
Weeds Point 51 G10
Weimar 58 E5
Weisel 141 F10
Weitchpec 31 B7
Welby 101 A9
Weldon 106 G3
Wellsona 102 F3
Wendel 45 E6
Wengler 34 E2
Weott 38 E5
Werner 72 C5
West Anaheim 141 F6
West Antelope Station 128 A2
West Butte 57 C7
West Colton 142 C1
West Covina 141 C6
West Highlands 142 B2
West Hollywood 140 C3
West Los Angeles 140 C2
West Manteca 73 D8
West March 142 E2
West Menlo Park 80 A5
West Modesto 73 F10
West Park 93 B10
West Pittsburg 72 B2
West Point 66 E4
West Sacramento 64 C5
West Saticoy 139 A6
West Venida 95 F6
West Whittier 140 D5
Westchester 140 D2
Westend 108 F1
Western Addition 71 E8
Westhaven 103 A9
Westhaven 30 D3
Westlake 71 F7
Westlake Village 139 B9
Westley 73 G8
Westminster 141 F6
Westminster Woods 62 D3
Westmorland 152 G1
Westport 47 E6
Westside 93 F7
Westville 59 C8
Westwood 140 C2
Westwood 43 E10
Westwood Junction 43 D10
Westwood Village 140 C2
Whalan Station 33 C7
Wheatland 58 E1
Wheaton Springs 122 B2
Wheeler (Site) 46 C5
Wheeler Guard Station 68 E3
Wheeler Ridge 116 G3
Wheeler Springs 126 E5
Whiskey Springs 54 A2
Whiskeytown 41 A7
Whisky Falls 85 C8
Whispering Pines 150 G3
White 67 B6
White Hall 66 A5
White Heather 128 E3
White Pines 67 F6
White River 105 E8
White Rock 65 B9
White Wolf 76 D2
Whitehorse 35 A6
Whitethorn 46 A5
Whitley Gardens 102 G4
Whitlow 39 E6
Whitmore 42 B2
Whitmore Hot Springs 77 F9
Whitney 58 G2
Whitney Portal 96 D4
Whittier 140 D5
Wible Orchard 116 C2
Wicks Corner 50 F5
Wiest 152 G3
Wilbur Springs 56 E3
Wild Crossing 130 B2
Wildflower 94 E1
Wildomar 149 A7
Wildwood 40 D2
Wildwood 80 E5
Wilfred 62 E5
Williams 56 D5
Willits 54 A5
Willota 63 G10
Willow Brook 140 E4
Willow Creek 31 E7
Willow Creek 43 D7
Willow Glen 81 C7
Willow Ranch 28 B5
Willow Springs 128 A3
Willow Springs 35 F8
Willow Springs 68 G5
Willows 49 G10
Wilmington 140 F3
Wilseyville 66 E4
Wilsie 157 C6
Wilson 57 F10
Wilson Corner 113 B10
Wilson Grove 62 D4
Wilsona Gardens 129 D7
Wilsonia 95 B7
The Willows 155 C7
Wilton 65 E8
Wimp 94 E5
Winchester 142 G3
Windsor 62 C4
Windsor Hills 140 D3
Wineland 94 D2
Wingo 63 G8
Winnetka 140 B1
Winter Gardens 154 C5
Winterhaven 158 D4
Winters 64 D2
Wintersburg 141 G6
Winterwarm 149 D7
Winton 83 B8
Winton Corners 22 A3
Wise Station 39 A8
Wister 152 D1
Witch Creek 150 G2
Wofford Heights 106 F2
Wolf 58 E4
Wolf 94 B2
Woodacre 71 B6
Woodbridge 73 A7
Woodcrest 142 E1
Woodford 117 E6
Woodfords 67 A10
Woodlake 73 A8
Woodlake 95 F6
Woodland 64 B3
Woodland Hills 139 B10
Woodlands 143 A6
Woodlands Station 54 B1
Woodleaf 51 G8
Woodman 47 D9
Woods Ridge 75 C9
Woodside 80 A4
Woodside Glens 80 A4
Woodville 104 B5
Woodville 70 C5
Woody 105 F8
Woolsey Flat 59 A6
Worswick 38 B3
Worth 105 B8
Wrightwood 129 G9
Wunpost 102 D1
Wyandotte 51 G6
Wye 62 D5
Wyeth 94 D5
Wynola 150 G2
Wyntoon 34 B1
Wyo 49 D10

YZ

Yager Junction 39 B6
Yankee Hill 50 E5
Yankee Hill 74 B5
Yankee Jims 59 E6
Yellowjacket 42 F4
Yermo 131 A6
Yettem 94 E5
Yokohl 95 F6
Yolano 64 E4
Yolo 64 A3
Yontocket (Site) 22 B3
Yorba 141 E7
Yorba Linda 141 E7
Yorba Slaughter Adobe 141 E9
Yorkville 55 F6
Yosemite Forks 85 B7
Yosemite Junction 74 C4
Yosemite Village 76 E2; 20 E5
Youngstown 65 G8
Yountville 63 E8
Yreka 25 C6
The Y 107 G10
Yuba City 57 D10
Yuba City South 57 D9
Yuba Gap 59 B8
Yuba Pass 59 B8
Yucaipa 142 C4
Yucca Valley 143 C9
Zamora 64 A2
Zante 105 B7
Zayante 81 E6
Zediker 94 B3
Zenia 39 F9
Zentner 105 F6
Zinfandel 63 D8
Zurich 87 D8
Zuver 59 F8
Zzyzx 121 E7

California is aptly known as the Golden State. With its lush variety of climates, resplendent resources and unique opportunities, California provides unlimited possibilities for travel and outdoor recreation.

California's history is filled with explorers and settlers. The first known inhabitants were Native Americans. Explorers reached California coming west from England, and east from Russia before the Spanish built missions along the coast. The Golden State was booming by the onset of the Gold Rush in 1848. California was soon connected to the eastern seaboard by the trans-continental railroad and it never stopped growing. It ranks today as our most populous state.

Modern California has not seen a lack of innovation. Hollywood and Los Angeles have been synonymous with the entertainment business for a century. Visitors can explore its history on the Walk of Fame or ride the movies at Universal Studios. In recent decades yet another California gold mine, the tech sector, was discovered in what was dubbed Silicon Valley.

The geography of California is as varied as its inhabitants. Visitors can tour Death Valley, the lowest point in North America, then travel just seventy-six miles to Mount Whitney, the highest point in the lower 48 states. The central valley boasts some of the most productive farmland in the world. The coastal ranges create a

rugged scenic coastline. Inland, the snow-covered volcanic peaks of the Sierra Nevada mountain range provide a worthy sight. The Mojave Desert sprawls over the state's southwest corner. The northern third of the state is thickly forested and as wet as the south is dry. In the east Yosemite National Park is a destination for the outdoor enthusiast.

The Golden State glories in its three record-setting trees. Its famed Coast Redwoods are the tallest on Earth. Redwood groves are scattered throughout the northern coastal area. The Giant Sequoia is the world's largest tree. Its seven meter diameter ensures that it's easily spotted in Sequoia National Park. The mountains of southeastern California are home to the Bristlecone Pine. Their elder statesman is Methuselah of the White Mountains in the Inyo National Forest. This golden oldie is over 4,800 years old and is the oldest living organism in the world.

Whether your interest is in exploring the greatest of outdoors locations, experiencing a diverse history, or partaking in modern forms of entertainment, California has something for you. It is truly the Golden State.

As a starting point, the Gazetteer features a selection of activities for all ages and activity levels. For a more comprehensive list of destinations and activities contact the following state and federal agencies.

RECREATION

The California Travel and Tourism Commission provides information on a wide range of activities including performing arts, spectator sports, outdoor recreation and excursions. The Tourism Commission also includes information on cultural attractions such as museums, galleries, history and ancient Indian ruins. California offers countless trails for hikers, bikers and horseback riders as well as miles of rivers and streams for canoeing and kayaking. Scenic beaches offer chances for swimming, boating and surfing. In addition to information on events and activities, the California Travel and Tourism Commission also supplies maps, brochures, and information about accommodations.

California Travel and Tourism Commission www.visitcalifornia.com
(916) 444-4429

California State Parks manages more than 270 parks, wilderness areas and historic sites. These parks preserve wildlife habitats, natural resources, and locations of cultural interest. At the same time these parks provide nearly unlimited opportunities for outdoor recreation. With more than 3,000 miles of trails, outdoor enthusiasts can hike, bike, horseback ride, rock climb, cross-country ski or snowshoe. The state lands include thousands of miles of waterfront for swimming, surfing, waterskiing and fishing. For information about park programs, reservations and fees contact California State Parks.

California State Parks
www.parks.ca.gov
(916) 653-6995

California offers a multitude of diverse recreational opportunities on a variety of federal lands. Memorable experiences are abundant in eight national parks and dozens of national monuments, historic sites and recreational areas. Visitors can rock climb in Yosemite National Park, relive history along the California National Historic Trail or marvel at the surf along Point Reyes National Seashore. In addition 18 national forests provide more than 20 million acres so visitors can hike, bike, swim, surf, fish or camp. Wildlife refuges preserve valuable ecosystems and allow opportunities for wildlife viewing, photography and educational programs. Dozens of other scenic sites and recreational areas offer visitors activities surrounding features of natural, historic and cultural interest. For additional information on recreation activities on federal lands contact the following agencies.

National Park Service
www.nps.gov/state/ca

USDA Forest Service
www.r5.fs.fed.us
(707) 562-8737

Bureau of Land Management
www.blm.gov/ca
(916) 978-4400

National Wildlife Refuges
www.fws.gov/refuges/
(800) 344-WILD

US Army Corps of Engineers
www.corpslakes.us
(877) 444-6777

TRAVEL

The California Department of Transportation (CalTrans) provides comprehensive information for all forms of travel. CalTrans maintains roadside rest areas for visitor safety and provides visitor information about mass transit and Amtrak travel. CalTrans has information on bicycle routes as well as network maps for busses trucks and motor homes. In addition, CalTrans provides up-to-date information on road conditions, travel restrictions and weather delays.

California Department of Transportation
www.dot.ca.gov
(916) 654-5266

Road and travel conditions
511 or (800) 427-ROAD

If you plan to travel outside the US, you can receive information and assistance from US Customs and Border Protection. This agency will provide information about travel requirements, documents, travel alerts and wait times at border crossings. For information about passports, contact the US Department of State.

US Customs and Border Protection
www.cbp.gov
(202) 354-1000

Passport information
www.travel.state.gov
(877) 4USA-PPT

STATE FACTS

Admitted to the Union:
September 9, 1850; 31st state
Capital: Sacramento
Size: 163,707 square miles
Population: 36,961,664 (2009 estimate)
Nickname: The Golden State
Motto: Eureka (I have found it)
Bird: California Valley Quail
Flower: Golden Poppy
Tree: Redwood
Mineral: Gold
Animal: Grizzly Bear
Fish: Golden Trout
Reptile: Desert Tortoise
Fossil: Sabre-toothed Tiger
Song: "I Love You, California"
Major Industries: Agriculture, Oil, Mining, Electronics, Movie Making/Entertainment, and Tourism

Major cities (with population):
Los Angeles 3,849,378
San Diego 1,256,951
San Jose 929,936
San Francisco 744,041
Highest Mountains:
Mount Whitney.................. 14,491 feet
Mount Williamson .... 14,370 feet
White Mountain .... 14,246 feet
Lowest Point: Death Valley, 282 feet below sea level
Major Lakes:
Salton Sea.................. 376 square miles
Lake Tahoe .... 191 square miles
Shasta Lake .... 47 square miles
Major Rivers:
Sacramento River...................447 miles
San Joaquin............................330 miles
Pit River...................................315 miles

FISHING AND HUNTING

California has an abundance of wilderness lands and waterways that entice people to the outdoors. Hunting and fishing opportunities abound throughout the state. The Gazetteer features a selection of fishing locations on state and federal lands. It is important to be familiar with local rules, regulations and restrictions

before hunting or fishing in any area. California Department of Fish and Game provides information on hunting and fishing regulations and licensing requirements in the state of California.
California Department of Fish and Game
www.dfg.ca.gov
(916) 928-5805

CAMPGROUNDS

Campgrounds with a variety of different facilities are located on state, federal and private lands. The public campground symbol, as shown in the Legend (see inside front cover), identifies campgrounds located within national forests and parks. For information on fees, services and reservations at public campgrounds, con-

tact one of the state or federal agencies listed above. The Gazetteer also includes a selected list of private campgrounds that are members of the California Travel Parks Association (CTPA). To locate private campgrounds in this Atlas, look on the appropriate map for the campground symbol and corresponding four-digit number.

Campgrounds

NUMBER, NAME, LOCATION	PAGE & GRID	RV SITES	TENTING
4000 49er RV Ranch, Columbia	74 B5	45	●
4003 A Country RV Park, Algoso	116 C3	120	●
4006 Alameda County Fairgrounds, Pleasanton	72 F2	100	●
4009 All Seasons RV Park, Hidden Meadows	149 E8	150	●
4015 Almond Tree RV Park, Chico	50 D2	42	
4018 Anaheim Harbor RV Park, Anaheim	141 F6	75	●
4021 Anaheim Resort RV Park, South Anaheim	141 F6	150	●
4024 Angels Camp RV & Camping Resort, Melones	74 B4	64	●
4027 Annett, Mono Village	76 A4	350	●
4030 Antlers RV Park & Campground, Antlers	33 F8	110	●
4033 Anza RV Resort, Anza	150 B2	89	●
4036 Auburn Gold Country RV Park, Elders Corner	58 F4	66	●
4039 Audiss RV Park, El Cerrito	71 C9	28	
4045 Bakersfield KOA, Shafter	115 B10	31	●
4048 Bakersfield Palms RV Resort, Magunden	116 C3	116	
4051 Bakersfield River Run RV, Bakersfield	116 C2	123	
4054 Bakersfield Travel Park, Algoso	116 C3	100	
4057 Barstow KOA, Daggett	130 A5	78	●
4060 Bashford, Frink	152 C1	143	●
4063 Bay Pines Travel Trailer Park, Morro Bay	113 C6	112	
4069 Beaver Creek RV Park & Campground, Glenbrook	55 G10	107	●
4072 Benbow Valley RV Resort & Golf Course, Benbow	47 A6	112	
4075 Bernardo Shores RV Resort, Imperial Beach	154 E3	124	
4078 Betabel RV Resort, San Juan Bautista	81 G10	170	
4081 Big River RV Park, Big River	147 B7	182	●
4084 Big Sur Campground & Cabins, Big Sur	90 G2	81	●
4087 Bigfoot Campground & RV Park, Junction City	40 A2	45	●
4090 Black Meadow Landing, Parker Dam	135 G8	350	●
4093 Blue Herron RV Park, Ager	25 A7	27	
4096 Bodega Bay RV Park, Bodega Bay	62 F2	72	
4099 Boulder Creek RV Resort, Lone Pine	96 D5	80	●
4102 Bowman RV Park, Bowman	58 F4	39	
4105 Bridgeport Reservoir Recreation Area, Bridgeport	68 F5	42	●
4108 Butterfield Ranch Resort, Julian	155 A9	106	●
4111 C C Camperland, Anaheim	141 F6	65	●
4114 Cabana Holiday Resort, Prunedale	90 A4	78	●
4117 Cal Expo RV Park, Swanston	65 C6	144	
4120 Californian RV Resort, Vincent	128 F4	128	
4123 Calizona RV Park, Parker Junction	134 B5	64	
4126 Camanche Recreation Area, Goodmans Corner	65 G10	150	●
4129 Camp Edison, Dora Belle	85 E9	252	●
4132 Camp Lotus, Lotus	59 G6	43	●
4135 Camp Williams Resort and Campground, Falling Springs	141 A7	51	●
4138 Camper Corral, Hoppaw	22 F4	120	●
4141 Campland On The Bay, Pacific Beach	154 C2	600	●
4144 Candlestick RV Park, Bayview District	71 E8	118	●
4147 Canyon RV Park, Esperanza	141 E8	120	●
4150 Capitol West RV & MH Park, Mikon	64 C5	87	
4153 Carmel By The River RV Park, Del Rey Oaks	90 D3	35	
4156 Casa de Fruta Orchard Resort, San Felipe	82 F2	300	●
4159 Casini Ranch Family Campground, Sheridan	62 D2	225	●
4162 Caspar Beach RV Park and Campground, Caspar	54 A1	110	●
4165 Castaic Lake RV Park, Castaic	127 F10	103	
4168 Champagne Lakes RV Resort, Hidden Meadows	149 E8	94	●
4171 Chateau Shasta, Mount Shasta	33 A9	29	
4174 Childs Meadow Resort, Morgan Springs	43 E6	24	●
4177 Chula Vista RV Resort and Marina, Boal	154 E3	237	
4180 Circle RV Resort, Granite Hills	154 C5	179	
4183 Cisco Grove Campground & RV Park, Cisco Grove	59 B9	406	●
4186 Clio's Rivers Edge RV Park, Clio	52 D4	220	
4189 Cloverdale KOA, Asti	62 A3	100	●
4192 Coachland RV Park, Polaris	60 A2	131	
4195 Collins Lake Recreation Area, Stanfield Hill	58 B2	150	●
4198 Coloma Resort at Sutters Mill, Coloma	59 G6	100	●
4201 Costanoa Coastal Lodge & Resort, Butano Park	80 D3	50	●
4204 Cotillion Gardens RV Park, Mount Hermon	81 F6	80	●
4207 Crane Lakeside Park & Resort, Lakeland Village	149 A6	116	●
4210 Creekside Cabins and RV Resort, Outlet	47 G10	50	●
4213 Crescent City KOA, Bertsch-Oceanview	22 C3	94	●
4216 Cypress Morro Bay, Morro Bay	113 C6	36	
4219 De Anza Springs Resort, Titus	156 E1	311	●
4222 Dean Creek Resort, Redway	38 G5	60	●
4225 Deer Creek RV Park, Ponca	105 C7	78	●
4228 Del Loma RV Park & Campground, DelLoma	31 G10	41	●
4231 Del Yermo RV Park, Calipatria	152 F2	45	●
4234 Delta Bay RV Resort & Marina, Isleton	72 A5	122	●
4237 Delta Marina RV Resort, Rio Vista	72 A4	25	
4240 Desert View RV Resort, Java	134 A4	65	
4243 Destiny's Mc Intyre RV Park, Blythe	153 B10	183	●
4246 Diamond Jack, Phelps Corner	155 D6	35	●
4249 Dinkey Creek Campground, Ross Crossing	86 F1	128	●
4252 Dockweiler Beach RV Park, El Segundo	140 E2	117	
4255 Dolphin Isle Marina & RV, Fort Bragg	54 A1	86	
4258 Doney Creek Lakeshore Village, Lakehead	33 F8	92	●
4261 Duncans Mills Camping Club, Duncans Mills	62 D2	125	
4264 Dutcher Creek RV Park and Campground, Asti	62 A3	38	●
4267 Eagle Lake RV Park, Spaulding Tract	44 A2	60	●
4270 East Shore RV Park, San Dimas	141 C7	518	
4273 Eddo's Harbor and RV Park, Emmaton	72 B4	40	●
4276 Edgewater Resort & RV Park, Buckingham Park	55 E10	61	●
4279 El Solana MH & RV Park, Brown	107 F7	44	
4282 Elk Creek Campground & RV Park, Happy Camp	23 C9	35	●
4285 Emerald Cove Resort, Cross Roads	147 A8	800	●
4288 Escondido RV Resort, Escondido	149 F8	122	
4291 Evergreen RV Park, Oxnard	139 A6	81	
4294 Far Horizons 49er Village RV Resort, Plymouth	66 D1	329	
4297 Far West Resorts, Sulphur Springs	127 F6	74	●
4300 Fawndale Lodge & RV Resort, McColl	33 G9	23	●
4303 Fawndale Oaks RV Park, McColl	33 G9	43	●
4306 Feather River RV Park, Mabie	52 D4	68	●
4309 Flag City RV Resort, Villinger	73 A7	180	
4312 Flying Flags RV Resort & Campground, Buellton	125 D7	300	●
4315 Forest Park RV Spaces, Prattville	43 F8	55	●
4318 Fort Bragg Leisure Time RV Park, Noyo	54 A1	70	●
4321 Fort Independence Reservation RV Park, Independence	96 A4	48	●
4324 Fountain Of Youth Spa, Frink	152 D1	1000	
4327 Frandy Park, Kernville	106 F2	88	●
4330 French Camp RV Park & Golf Course, Turner	73 D8	196	
4333 Fridays RV Retreat, McCloud	33 C10	30	
4336 Funtime RV Park & Watersports, Clearlake	56 F1	60	●
4339 Giant Redwoods RV & Camp, Myers Flat	39 F6	82	●
4342 Glen Eden Sun Club, Alberhill	141 G10	295	●
4345 Glen Ivy RV Park, Glen Lvy Hot Springs	141 F10	350	●
4348 Gold Strike Village, San Andreas	66 G3	45	●
4351 Golden Coach RV Park, Cromberg	52 C3	50	
4354 Golden Gate Trailer Park, Greenbrae	71 C7	39	
4357 Golden Pines RV Resort & Campground, Big Trees	67 F6	62	●
4360 Golden Shore RV Resort, Thenard	140 F4	80	
4363 Golden Village Palms RV Resort, Hemet	142 G4	1019	
4366 Green Acres RV Park, Girvan	41 B8	33	
4369 Gualala River Redwood Park, Gualala	61 A8	114	●
4372 Happy Traveler RV Park, Palm Springs	143 F8	130	
4375 Hat Creek Resort & RV Park, Hat Creek	35 G6	57	●
4378 Heritage RV Park, Corning	49 B10	92	●
4381 High Sierra RV & Mobile Park, Oakhurst	85 C6	53	●
4384 High Sierra RV & Mobile Park, Yosemite Forks	85 B7	102	●
4387 Hilton Park Family Campground, Forestville	62 D3	49	●
4390 Hiouchi RV Resort, Stout Grove	22 C4	120	●
4393 Holiday Harbor RV Pk & Marina, Nice	55 D9	34	
4396 Holloway's Marina & RV Park, Boulder Bay	142 A5	112	
4399 Hope Valley Resort, Sorensens	67 A9	24	●
4402 Huntington By The Sea RV Park, Newport Beach	148 A1	92	
4405 Indian Flat RV Park, Incline	75 F10	28	●
4408 Indian Hill Ranch RV Park, Five Points	117 F6	74	
4411 Indian Oaks Trailer Ranch, Sage	149 A9	75	●
4414 Islander Mobile/RV Park, Mossdale	73 E7	40	
4417 JGW RV Park, Anderson	41 C9	82	
4420 Johnny, Cutten	30 G3	53	
4423 Kamp Klamath RV Park and Campground, Requa	22 F4	54	●
4426 Kaweah Park Resort, Three Rivers	95 E8	83	●
4429 Keough's Hot Springs, Keough Hot Springs	87 C7	18	●
4432 Kit Fox RV Park, Patterson	82 A3	91	
4435 Klamath River RV Park, Requa	22 F4	52	●
4438 La Pacifica RV Resort, San Ysidro	154 F4	179	
4441 Laguna Del Sol, Sloughhouse	65 D8	150	●
4444 Laguna Seca Recreation Area, Confederate Corners	90 C4	102	●
4447 Lake Berryessa Marina Resort, Sugarloaf Park	63 C9	53	●
4450 Lake Casitas Recreation Area, Ventura	126 F4	170	●
4453 Lake Cove Resort & Marina, East Shore	43 F9	55	●
4456 Lake Elsinore Marina & RV Resort, Terra Cotta	142 G1	197	
4459 Lake Henshaw Resort Inc, Morettis Junction	150 F2	110	●
4462 Lake Morena RV Park, Morena Village	155 D8	41	
4465 Lake of The Woods Mobile Village, Lebec	127 B8	44	
4468 Lake Pillsbury Resort, Booth Crossing	48 G3	41	●
4474 Lake San Antonio, Bee Rock	101 E10	563	●
4477 Lake Siskiyou Camp Resort, Pioneer	33 B8	360	●
4480 Lakeridge Camping & Boating Resort, Piedra	94 A4	107	
4483 Lakeshore Inn & RV, Antlers	33 F8	35	●
4486 Lakeside Trailer Park, Worth	105 B8	45	●
4489 Lakeview Terrace Resort, Lewiston	32 G5	40	
4492 Lassen Pines RV Park, Pittville	35 D8	45	●
4498 Le Sage Riviera, Grover Beach	113 F8	50	
4501 Leapin' Lizard RV Ranch, Ocotillo Wells	151 F7	60	
4504 Lemon Cove Sequoia Campground, Lemoncove	95 F7	55	●
4507 Lighthouse Trailer Resort & Marina, Fawnskin	142 A5	88	
4510 Likely Place RV Resort & Golf, Likely	36 B4	50	●
4513 Lilac Oaks Campground, Lilac	149 E9	60	●
4516 Little Bear RV Park, Mohawk	52 D3	92	
4519 Long Ravine Campground, Cape Horn	58 D5	58	●
4522 Loomis RV Park and Campground, Loomis	58 G3	74	●
4525 Lundborg Landing, Bethel Island	72 B5	70	●
4528 Mad River Rapids RV Park, Alliance	30 F3	92	
4531 Malibu Beach RV Park, Solromar	139 C7	150	●
4534 Mammoth Mountain RV Park, Mammoth Lakes	77 F7	115	●
4537 Manchester Beach KOA, Manchester	54 F2	124	●
4540 Manor Oaks Overniter, Asylum	55 D6	52	
4543 Maple Leaf RV Park, San Martin	81 E10	270	
4546 Marble Quarry RV Park, Columbia	74 B5	85	●
4549 Marin Park, Greenbrae	71 C7	89	●
4552 Marina Dunes RV Park, Marina	90 B3	62	●
4555 Marina RV Park, Redding	41 B8	86	
4558 Mariner, Spaulding Tract	44 A2	70	●
4561 McCloud Dance Country RV Park, McCloud	33 B10	130	●
4564 McGee Creek RV Park, Whitmore Hot Springs	77 G9	30	●
4567 Merced River RV Park, Delhi	83 B7	160	●
4570 Midway RV Park, Vacaville	64 E2	51	
4573 Midway RV Park, Trinidad	30 D3	60	
4576 Mission Bay RV Park, Bay Park	154 C2	260	
4579 Mission Farm RV Park, San Juan Bautista	90 A5	140	
4582 Monterey Vacation RV Park, Aromas	90 A4	88	●
4585 Moonshine Campground, Freemans Crossing	58 A4	25	●
4588 Morro Dunes Travel Trailer Park & Resort Campground, Morro Bay	113 C6	178	●
4591 Moss Landing RV Park, Moss Landing	90 A3	46	
4594 Mountain Gate RV Park, Project City	41 A8	120	
4597 Mountain Gate RV Park, Redding	41 A8	300	
4600 Mountain Valley RV Resort, Hemet	142 G4	171	
4603 Mountain View RV Park, Haines	127 G6	77	
4606 Mountain View RV Park, Susanville	44 D3	28	●
4609 Mountain Village RV Park, Etna	24 F4	44	●
4612 Movin' West RV Park, Johnsville	52 D3	50	●
4615 Mystic Forest RV Park, Requa	22 E4	30	●
4618 Narrows Lodge Resort, Saratoga Springs	55 C8	30	●
4621 Needles Marina Park, Needles	134 B5	158	●
4624 Nevada County Fairgrounds, Boston Ravine	58 C4	115	
4627 New Horizons Mobile RV Park, Muscatel	93 B10	64	
4630 Newberry Mountain RV & Motel Park, Newberry Springs	131 B8	18	
4633 Newport Dunes Waterfront RV Resort, Balboa Island	148 A2	406	●
4636 North Shore Campground, Chester	43 E8	100	●
4639 Northport Trailer Resort, North Lakeport	55 D9	20	
4642 Novato RV Park, Novato	71 A7	69	
4645 Oak Creek RV Resort, Flinn Springs	155 B6	120	
4648 Oak Dell Park, Redwood Retreat	81 F9	57	
4651 Oak Haven RV Park, Sacramento	65 B6	90	
4654 Oak Knoll Campground, Palomar Mountain	149 D10	38	●
4657 Ocean Canyon Resort, Miles	113 E7	30	
4663 Ocean Mesa at El Capitan Canyon, Capitan	125 F9	100	●
4666 Oceanside RV Park, Escondido Junction	149 F6	141	●
4669 Old Lewiston Bridge RV Resort, Lewiston	40 A4	64	●
4672 Olema Ranch Campground, Point Reyes Station	70 B4	203	●
4675 Orangeland RV Park, Marlboro	141 F7	203	
4678 Orchard Springs Resort, Chicago Park	58 D5	102	●
4681 Ortega Oaks RV Park & Campground, Lakeland Village	149 A6	70	●
4684 Outdoor World Retreat, Live Oak Springs	155 E10	151	●
4687 Palm View RV Park, Quail Valley	142 G2	45	●
4690 Paradise By The Sea, Escondido Junction	149 F6	102	
4693 Paradise Shores RV Park, Bridgeport	68 F5	38	●
4696 Parkway Lakes RV Park, Perry	81 D9	104	
4699 Pechanga RV Resort, Temecula	149 C8	168	
4702 Pelican Point RV Park, Half Moon Bay	80 A3	75	
4705 Peninsula Camping & Boating, Grass Valley	58 D5	70	●
4708 Pine Acres Blue Lake Resort, Summit	55 C8	31	●
4711 Pine Acres Resort RV Park & Campground, Pine Grove	66 E3	80	●

Continued on page 10

Campgrounds, *continued*

NUMBER, NAME, LOCATION	PAGE & GRID	RV SITES	TENTING
4714 Pine Ranch RV Park, Banning	142 E5	100	
4717 Pine Tree RV Park, Fawnskin	142 A5	22	
4720 Pinezanita Campground & RV Park, Harrison Park	150 G3	82	●
4723 Pinnacles Campground, Pinnacles	91 E9	36	●
4726 Pioneer RV Park, Cedar Mill	52 B1	62	●
4729 Pismo Coast Village RV Resort, Pismo Beach	113 F8	400	●
4732 Pismo Sands RV Park, Oceano	113 F8	134	
4735 Plasse's Resort, Plasse	67 B7	56	●
4738 Playland Park, Lakeland Village	149 A6	40	
4741 Pomo RV Park & Campground, Fort Bragg	54 A1	100	●
4744 Premier RV Resorts - Redding, Redding	41 B8	82	●
4747 Pyramid Lake RV Resort, Gorman	127 C9	117	
4750 Quail Trails Village, Paradise	50 D5	20	●
4753 Quail Valley RV Park, California Hot Springs	105 D10	67	●
4756 Rancheria RV Park, Hat Creek	35 G6	75	●
4759 Rancho Colina, Morro Bay	113 C6	57	
4762 Rancho Los Coches RV Park, Johnstown	154 C5	142	●
4765 Rancho Marina Resort, Terminous	72 A5	29	●
4768 Rancho Seco Recreational Area, Clay	65 E9	38	●
4771 Redcrest Resort, Englewood	38 D5	23	●
4774 Redding RV Park, Redding	41 B8	110	
4777 Redwood Empire Fair RV Park, Presswood	55 D6	42	
4780 Redwood River Resort & Campground, Riverdale	47 C7	50	●
4783 Reflection Lake RV Park, San Jacinto	142 F4	121	●
4789 Rio Viento Resort Campground, Emmaton	72 A3	70	
4792 River Bend Resort, Hilton	62 D3	100	●
4795 River Grove Resort, Mount Hermon	81 F6	90	●
4798 River Lodge Resort, Parker Strip	147 A8	300	●
4801 River Oaks Resort, Lewiston	40 A4	35	●
4804 River Ranch RV Park, Quincy	51 B10	32	
4807 Riverland RV Resort, Cienega Springs	147 B8	60	
4810 Rivernook Campground, Kernville	106 F2	286	●
4813 Riverpoint Landing Marina–Resort, Country Club	73 B7	32	
4816 River's Edge RV Park, Rio Dell	38 C3	49	●
4819 Riverside Campground and Cabins, Big Sur	90 G3	45	●
4822 Riverview Trailer Park, Kernville	106 F2	81	●
4825 Riverwalk RV Park & Campground, Rohnerville	38 B3	89	●
4828 Riviera RV Resort & Marina, Ehrenberg	153 A10	300	●
4831 Rollerville Junction, Flumeville	54 F2	19	●
4834 Rosedale Village RV Park, Rosedale	116 C1	156	
4837 Sacramento KOA, Lovdal	64 C5	100	●
4840 Sacramento River RV Park, Anderson	41 C9	140	●
4843 Salmon Harbor Resort, Winton Corners	22 A3	93	●
4846 San Andreas RV Park, Isleton	72 A5	26	
4849 San Bernardino RV Park, San Bernardino	142 C2	112	
4852 San Diego KOA, Chula Vista	154 E4	200	●
4855 San Francisco North KOA, Crown	63 F6	300	●
4858 San Francisco RV Resort, Pacific Manor	71 F7	182	
4861 San Lorenzo County Park, King City	101 A9	83	●
4864 San Luis RV Resort, Santa Nella	82 F5	101	●
4867 Sandev Mobile Park, San Lorenzo	71 F10	29	
4870 Sands RV & Golf Resort, Desert Hot Springs	143 E9	507	
4873 Sans End RV Park, Winterhaven	158 D4	104	●
4876 Santa Barbara Sunrise RV Park, Santa Barbara	126 F1	33	
4879 Santa Cruz KOA, Ellicott	81 G8	230	●
4882 Santa Cruz Ranch RV Park, Scotts Valley	81 F6	110	●
4885 Santa Fe Travel Park, Elvira	154 C2	129	
4888 Santa Margarita KOA, Pippin Corner	113 C9	36	●
4891 Santee Lakes Recreation Preserve, Carlton Hills	154 B4	300	●
4894 Saratoga Springs, Saratoga	81 C6	42	●
4897 Scotts Flat Lake Recreation Area, Fivemile House	58 B5	150	●
4900 Sea Breeze RV Resort, Seal Beach	140 G5	86	
4903 Sea View RV Park, Crescent City	22 C3	22	
4906 Seacliff Center Trailer Park, Aptos	81 F7	32	
4909 Shadow Hills RV Resort, Bermuda Dunes	143 G10	120	●
4912 Shasta Lake RV Resort and Campground, Antlers	33 F8	70	●
4915 Sierra Lakes Campground, Badger	95 C7	25	●
4918 Sierra Skies RV Park, Sierra City	52 F3	29	
4924 Sierra Trails RV Park, Mojave	117 F9	25	●
4927 Sierra Valley RV Park, Beckwourth	52 C5	43	●
4930 Silver Valley Sun Club, Newberry Springs	131 A8	20	●
4933 Sky Valley Resorts, Coachella	144 G1	285	
4936 Skyline Ranch RV Park & Campground, Phelps Corner	155 D6	35	
4939 Smithwoods RV Park, Felton	81 F6	84	
4942 Smoke Tree RV Park, Wible Orchard	116 D2	61	
4945 Snug Harbor Resort, Ryde	64 G5	64	
4948 Sonoma Grove, Rohnert Park	62 F5	152	●
4951 Sounds of the Sea, Trinidad	30 C3	70	
4954 Southland RV Park & Mini Storage, Greenfield	116 D2	91	
4957 Spaceport RV Park, Mojave	117 F9	48	●
4960 Spanish Flat Resort, Spanish Flat	63 C9	104	●
4963 Stafford RV Park, Stafford	38 C4	75	●
4966 Stockton Delta KOA, Terminous	73 A6	275	
4969 Stockton Lodi RV Park, Tomspur	73 B7	98	●
4972 Stone Lagoon RV Park, Orick	30 B3	100	●
4975 Stone Villa RV Park, Costa Mesa	148 A1	34	
4978 Sugar Barge RV Park & Marina, Bethel Island	72 B5	114	●
4981 Sugar Pine RV Park, Mi-Wuk Village	75 B7	52	●
4984 Sun & Fun RV Park, Paige	104 A3	89	
4987 Sunbeam Lake RV Resort, Seeley	157 C6	340	
4990 Suncrest Village RV Park, Rosedale	116 C1	40	
4993 Sunshine Resort, Parker Dam	147 A9	28	●
4996 Sycamore Ranch RV Park, Browns Valley	58 C1	68	●
4999 Sylvan Harbor RV Park, Trinidad	30 D3	73	
5002 Tahoe Valley Campground, Tahoe Valley	60 F4	413	●
5005 Tecopa Hot Springs Campground & Pools, Tecopa Hot Springs	110 D1	200	●
5008 Terrace Village RV Park, Grand Terrace	142 C1	53	
5011 The Emerald Forest Of Trinidad, Trinidad	30 D3	50	●
5014 The Florence Village, Cudahy	140 D4	60	
5017 The Garlic Farm RV Park, Old Gilroy	82 F1	158	
5020 The Parkway RV Resort, Orland	49 D10	40	●
5023 The Redwoods RV Resort, Crescent City	22 B3	102	●
5026 The Springs at Borrego, Borrego Springs	150 E5	90	
5029 Three Rivers Hideaway, Hammond	95 E8	42	●
5032 Town & Country Trailer Park, Del Paso Heights	65 B7	65	
5035 Tradewinds RV Park, Carquinez Heights	71 A9	78	
5038 Trail in RV Park, Antlers	33 F8	39	●
5044 Trailer Lane RV Park, Weed	25 G8	20	●
5047 Trailer Rancho, Leucadia	149 G7	60	
5050 Trailer Villa RV Park, North Fair Oaks	80 A5	100	
5053 Travelers' RV Park, Kettleman City	103 C9	46	●
5056 Travelhome Park, Yuba City	57 D10	48	
5059 Trinity Lake KOA, Trinity Center	32 D5	139	●
5062 Trinity Lake Resorts at Pinewood Cove, Trinity Alps	32 F4	75	●
5065 Twentynine Palms Resort, Twentynine Palms	144 B2	175	●
5068 Twin Lakes RV Park, Harvard	131 A7	104	●
5074 Uvas Pines RV Park, Redwood Retreat	81 E9	40	
5077 U-Wanna Camp, Lakeport	55 E8	30	●
5080 Vacationer RV Resort, Granite Hills	154 C5	160	
5083 Vail Lake Village & Resort, Radec	149 C9	350	●
5086 Valencia Travel Village, Del Valle	127 F10	400	
5089 Ventura Oaks, Oak View	126 F4	60	
5092 Victorville KOA, Victorville	130 E2	136	●
5095 View Crest Lodge & RV Park, Trinidad	30 C3	20	●
5098 Viking RV Park, Wineland	94 D2	48	●
5101 Vineyard RV Park, Hartley	64 E2	113	
5104 Walnut RV Park, Northridge	140 A1	114	
5107 Westport Beach RV & Camping, Hardy	47 E6	126	●
5110 Wheel-Er In Family Resort, Earp	147 B7	55	●
5113 White Rock Resort, Winton Corners	22 A2	25	
5116 Widow White Creek RV Park, Fisher	30 E3	40	●
5119 Willits KOA, Summit	54 A4	50	●
5122 Willow Creek RV Campground, Weeds Point	51 G10	35	●
5125 Willow Springs Motel & RV, Willow Springs	68 G5	27	
5128 Windsorland RV Park, Windsor	62 C4	56	●
5131 Wine Country RV Resort, Capital Hill	102 G3	166	
5134 Wishon Village, Ross Crossing	86 E1	120	●
5137 Wooden Shoe RV Park, Goshen	94 F3	57	
5143 Woods Valley Kampground, Valley Center	149 F9	89	●
5146 Woodson Bridge RV Park, Vina	50 B1	60	●
5149 Yosemite KOA, Midpines	75 G9	50	●
5152 Yosemite Pines RV Resort & Family Lodging, Second Garrotte	75 D7	200	●
5155 Yosemite South–Coarsegold Ranch, Coarsegold	85 D6	60	●
5158 Yreka RV Park, Yreka	25 C6	100	
5161 Yucca Valley RV Park, Yucca Valley	143 C9	18	

Outdoor Adventures

BIKING

BALD MOUNTAIN BICYCLE TRIP – Sequoia National Forest – 106 C3 Begins just east of Sherman Pass, trip goes 13 miles northeast along paved FR 22S05. Views of granite bluffs, meadows, creeks and mountains. Continue 0.1 mile onto dirt access road to locked gate. Easy 0.4-mile hiking trail to lookout on Bald Mountain.

COLUMBIA/SONORA LOOP – Columbia – 74 B5 Start at Columbia. Travel loop counterclockwise. Parrots Ferry Road to Springfield Road. Springfield and Shaws Flat are old mining towns. From Springfield, ride south on Shaws Flat Road, which leads into Sonora. Route travels through oak woodlands and past small farms. Many old buildings in Sonora. Return to Columbia via Columbia Way and SR 49 for short stretch. Gently rolling terrain. Moderate to heavy traffic.

GEORGETOWN LOOP – Georgetown – 66 A1 Starts uphill from Coloma to Pilot Hill on SR 49. Good view of Sierra Nevada. From Cool, take SR 193 uphill to Greenwood. From Greenwood continue on SR 193 to Georgetown. At either Georgetown or Garden Valley, return to Coloma on Marshall Road. Traffic moderate to light. Some steep climbs and descents.

JEDEDIAH SMITH NATIONAL RECREATION TRAIL – Sacramento – 65 C6 Rolling hills with steep grade near Rainbow Bridge. Paved bikeway starts at west end of Discovery Park in Sacramento, follows American River Parkway and continues into Folsom Lake State Recreation Area. Bicycle-in campsites are available at Beals Point.

LAKE PERRIS BIKE TRAIL – Lake Perris SRA – 142 E3 Paved hiking and bicycling trail circles Lake Perris.

OJAI VALLEY TRAIL – Ojai – 126 F5 Paved multiuse trail extends south from Fox Street to Foster Park. Follows historic route of Southern Pacific Railroad.

PACIFIC COAST BICYCLE ROUTE – Oregon Border–Mexico Border – 22 A2 509-mile route from Oregon Border to Mexico. Follows US 101 and SR 1 with exception of occasional city and county roads and bike paths. Flat to rolling terrain through redwoods, with steep descent to SR 1 along ocean. Climbs and descents occur both north and south of San Francisco on SR 1. Very hilly terrain between Monterey and San Simeon, then becomes flat. Climb occurs near Lompoc and then route remains rolling to flat past San Diego. Heavy traffic near and through all cities.

POINT MUGU STATE PARK BIKE TRAILS – Point Mugu State Park – 139 C7 Big Sycamore Canyon, Wood Canyon and Ranch Center Trails connect to form 13-mile route suitable for mountain bikes.

SAN LORENZO RIVERWAY – Santa Cruz – 81 G6 Paved bike paths atop levees along both sides of San Lorenzo River from river mouth near Santa Cruz Beach Boardwalk to SR 1. Passes through San Lorenzo Park on east side of river.

SOUTH BAY BICYCLE TRAIL – Los Angeles County – 140 C1 Uninterrupted bike paths from Will Rogers State Beach, in Pacific Palisades, to Torrance Beach, north of Palos Verdes. Through Santa Monica, Venice and Marina Del Rey and by Manhattan, Hermosa and Redondo Beaches.

SOUTHERN TIER BICYCLE ROUTE – San Diego–Blythe – 154 C2 California's portion of 3,180-mile coast-to-coast route that ends in St. Augustine, Florida. Winds through San Diego metropolitan area via bike paths and city streets. Uses portions of I-8 and frontage roads to In-Ko-Pah Pass and then descends into Yuha Desert. Heads northeast on SR 86 and SR 78 through flat and slightly rolling terrain to Chocolate Mountains. Continues on to Blythe before crossing Colorado River into Arizona.

VOLCANO LOOP – Volcano – 66 D3 Starts in old mining town with some original buildings still standing. From Volcano, head south on Volcano–Pioneer Road to SR 88 past limestone caves, then north again on Aqueduct Road to Pine Grove–Volcano Road. Some heavy traffic on SR 88. Fairly steep terrain with steep descent before return to Volcano.

SKIING

ALPINE MEADOWS – Tahoe City – 60 D1 MOUNTAIN: 11 chairlifts. 100+ trails, Beginner 25%, intermediate 40%, advanced 35%, uphill capacity 16,000/hr. VERTICAL DROP: 1,802 feet. FACILITIES: Ski shop, rentals, ski school, 2 restaurants, snowboarding, 4 terrain parks, bowl skiing.

BEAR MOUNTAIN – Big Bear Lake – 142 A5 MOUNTAIN: 8 chairlifts including 2 high-speed quads. 748 permit acres, Beginner 30%, intermediate 40%, advanced 30%, uphill capacity 16,590/hr. VERTICAL DROP: 1,665 feet. FACILITIES: Rentals, ski school.

BEAR VALLEY – Bear Valley – 67 D8 MOUNTAIN: 9 chairlifts. 67 trails, Beginner 30%, intermediate 40%, advanced 30%, uphill capacity 12,000/hr. VERTICAL DROP: 1,900 feet. CROSS-COUNTRY TRAILS: 75 km, groomed and set. FACILITIES: Ski shop, rentals, ski school, cafeteria, snowboarding, terrain park.

BOREAL – Truckee – 60 B1 MOUNTAIN: 9 chairlifts. 41 trails, Beginner 30%, intermediate 55%, advanced 15%, uphill capacity 13,200/hr. VERTICAL DROP: 600 feet. FACILITIES: Ski shop, rentals, ski school cafeteria, snack bar, lounge, snowboarding, terrain parks, night-skiing.

DODGE RIDGE – Pinecrest – 67 G9 MOUNTAIN: 8 chairlifts. 59 trails, Beginner 20%, intermediate 40%, advanced 40%, uphill capacity 13,200/hr. VERTICAL DROP: 1,600 feet. FACILITIES: Ski shop, rentals, ski school, 2 cafeterias, restaurant, snowboarding, terrain park.

DONNER SKI RANCH – Norden – 60 B1 MOUNTAIN: 6 chairlifts. 52 trails, Beginner 25%, intermediate 50%, advanced 25%, uphill capacity 7,800/hr. VERTICAL DROP: 750 feet. FACILITIES: Ski shop, rentals, ski school, restaurant.

EAGLE MOUNTAIN CROSS COUNTRY SKI AREA & MOUNTAIN BIKE RESORT – Emigrant Gap – 59 B8 CROSS-COUNTRY TRAILS: 65 km, groomed and tracked, beginner–advanced, meadows to steep winding hills. FACILITIES: Ski shop with rentals, instruction, guided ski tours, cafe, 2 warming huts and skating and telemark clinics.

GRANLIBAKKEN – Tahoe City – 60 D2 MOUNTAIN: 2 surface lifts. 1 trail, Beginner 50% and intermediate 50%. VERTICAL DROP: 300 feet. CROSS-COUNTRY TRAILS: 4 km, groomed and tracked through Page Meadows, intermediate. FACILITIES: Rentals, ski school, snack bar, snowboarding, snowshoeing.

HEAVENLY – South Lake Tahoe – 60 F4 MOUNTAIN: 30 lifts including gondola, aerial tram and 9 high speed chairs. 95 trails, Beginner 35%, intermediate 45%, advanced 20%, uphill capacity 52,000/hr. VERTICAL DROP: 3,500 feet. FACILITIES: Ski shop, rentals, ski school, restaurants, snowboarding, 4 terrain parks.

HOMEWOOD – Homewood – 60 D2 MOUNTAIN: 7 total lifts. 60 trails, Beginner 15%, intermediate 50%, advanced 35%, uphill capacity 8,500/hr. VERTICAL DROP: 1,650 feet. FACILITIES: Rentals, ski school, cafeteria, snowboarding, terrain park.

JUNE MOUNTAIN – June Lake – 77 E6 MOUNTAIN: 6 chairlifts. 35 trails, Beginner 20%, intermediate 45%, advanced 35%, uphill capacity10,000/hr. VERTICAL DROP: 2,590 feet. FACILITIES: Rentals, ski school, dining, snowboarding.

KIRKWOOD – Kirkwood – 67 B8 MOUNTAIN: 10 chairlifts. Beginner 15%, intermediate 50%, advanced 35%, uphill capacity 17,905/hr. VERTICAL DROP: 2,000 feet. CROSS-COUNTRY TRAILS: 75 km, groomed and tracked.FACILITIES: Ski shop, rentals, ski school, restaurants, snowboarding, terrain parks, snowtubing, snowshoeing.

LASSEN PARK NORDIC SKI AREA – Lassen Volcanic National Park – 42 D5 TRAILS: 20 km, groomed and tracked, marked ungroomed trails through Lassen Volcanic National Park, beginner–advanced, flat to mountainous terrain, overnight trips possible. FACILITIES: Rentals, instruction, cafeteria and guided tours available.

MAMMOTH MOUNTAIN – Mammoth Lakes – 77 F7 MOUNTAIN: 2 gondolas and 22 chairlifts. 107 trails, Beginner 25%, intermediate 40%, advanced 35%, uphill capacity 50,000/hr. VERTICAL DROP: 4,000 feet. FACILITIES: Rentals, ski school, restaurants, snowboarding, terrain park, nordic skiing, snowshoeing, bowl skiing.

MOUNTAIN HIGH – Angeles National Forest – 129 G8 MOUNTAIN: 11 chairlifts including 2 high-speed quads. 60 trails, beginner 22%, intermediate 41%, advanced 37%. VERTICAL DROP: 1,600 feet. FACILITIES: Rentals, ski school, restaurant, lounge.

MT BALDY – Mt Baldy – 141 A9 MOUNTAIN: 4 double chairlifts. 28 trails, beginner 20%, intermediate 50%, advanced 30%, uphill capacity 2,500/hr. VERTICAL DROP: 2,100 feet. FACILITIES: Ski school, rentals, restaurant.

MT SHASTA BOARD & SKI PARK – Mt Shasta – 33 A10 MOUNTAIN: 3 triple chairlifts. 32 trails, beginner 20%, intermediate 55%, advanced 25%, uphill capacity 4,500/hr. VERTICAL DROP: 1,390 feet. CROSS-COUNTRY TRAILS: 75 km, groomed. FACILITIES: Rentals, ski school, cafeteria, snowboarding, superpipe, 2 terrain parks, night-skiing.

NORTHSTAR-AT-TAHOE – Truckee – 60 B2 MOUNTAIN: 17 lifts including gondola and 6 express quads. 83 trails, beginner 13%, intermediate 62%, advanced 25%, uphill capacity 21,800/hr. VERTICAL DROP: 2,280 feet. CROSS-COUNTRY TRAILS: 42 km, groomed and tracked. FACILITIES: Ski shop, rentals, ski school, day care, 2 restaurants, snowboarding, superpipe, terrain parks.

ROCK CREEK WINTER LODGE – Southeast of Toms Place – 86 A4 TRAILS: 25 km, groomed and tracked, skating lanes, 50 km marked trail through John Muir Wilderness, beginner–advanced, valley meadow to steep terrain. FACILITIES: Backcountry ski facility, 2 miles to lodge. Full range of lessons, rentals with demo skis, 3 huts for warming or overnight, rustic cabins, central dining facilities with family-style meals, guided tours and seminars available.

ROYAL GORGE CROSS-COUNTRY SKI RESORT – Soda Springs – 59 B10 TRAILS: 330 km, groomed and tracked, skating lanes, beginner–advanced, flat to hilly. FACILITIES: Rentals, ski shop, instruction, children's ski school, 10 warming huts, 4 cafes, lounge and lodging with meals.

SEQUOIA SKI TOURING – King's Canyon National Park – 95 D9 TRAILS: 50 km, groomed for classic and skate skiers, beginner–advanced. FACILITIES: Lessons, lodge, 3 warming huts.

SIERRA SUMMIT – Lakeshore – 86 D1 MOUNTAIN: 7 chairlifts, 45+ trails, beginner 39%, intermediate 33%, advanced 28%, uphill capacity 9,200/hr. VERTICAL DROP: 1,679 feet. CROSS-COUNTRY TRAILS: Flat course at base, marked trails through Sierra National Forest. FACILITIES: Ski shop, rentals, ski school, restaurant, snowboarding, 3 terrain parks.

SIERRA-AT-TAHOE RESORT – Twin Bridges – 60 G3 MOUNTAIN: 12 lifts including 3 express quads. 46 trails, beginner 25%, intermediate 50%, advanced 25%, uphill capacity 14,000/hr. VERTICAL DROP: 2,212 feet. FACILITIES: Ski shop, rentals, ski school, 3 cafeterias, snowboarding, superpipe, 6 terrain parks.

SNOW SUMMIT – Big Bear Lake – 142 A5 MOUNTAIN: 9 chairlifts including 2 high-speed quads. 31 trails, beginner 35%, intermediate 40%, advanced 25%, uphill capacity 18,550/hr. VERTICAL DROP:1,200 feet. FACILITIES: Rentals, ski school, restaurant, lounge, lodging.

SNOW VALLEY – Running Springs – 142 A4 MOUNTAIN: 5 triple, 6 double chairlifts, 1 moving carpet. 35 trails, beginner 30%, intermediate 35%, advanced 35%, uphill capacity 16,590/hr. VERTICAL DROP: 1,041 feet. FACILITIES: Rentals, ski school, restaurant, lounge.

SQUAW VALLEY NORDIC CENTER – Olympic Valley – 60 C2 TRAILS: 25 km, groomed and tracked, additional 20 km of marked trails, beginner–advanced, varied terrain. FACILITIES: Rentals, ski shop, instruction and all facilities shared with downhill area.

SQUAW VALLEY USA – Olympic Valley – 60 C1 MOUNTAIN: 33 lifts including 4 express six-passenger chairs. 100+ trails, beginner 25%, intermediate 45%, advanced 30%, uphill capacity 49,000/hr. VERTICAL DROP: 2,850 feet. CROSS-COUNTRY TRAILS: 18 km, groomed and tracked. FACILITIES: Ski, shop, restaurants, ski school, rentals, snowboarding, superpipe, terrain parks, snowtubing, bowl skiing, night-skiing.

SUGAR BOWL – Norden – 60 B1 MOUNTAIN: Gondola and 10 chairlifts. 84 trails, beginner 17%, intermediate 45%, advanced 38%, uphill capacity 21,740/hr. VERTICAL DROP: 1,500 feet. FACILITIES: Ski shop, restaurant, ski school, rentals, snowboarding, superpipe, terrain parks.

TAHOE DONNER – Truckee – 60 B1 MOUNTAIN: 4 lifts. 14 trails, Beginner 40%, intermediate 60%, uphill capacity 2,500/hr. VERTICAL DROP: 600 feet. CROSS-COUNTRY TRAILS: 50 km, groomed and tracked. FACILITIES: Ski shop, rentals, ski school, cafeteria, snowboarding.

TAHOE NORDIC SKI CENTER – Tahoe City – 60 C3 TRAILS: 55 km, groomed and tracked, additional marked trails in Tahoe National Forest, beginner–advanced, smooth, rolling terrain to steep hills. FACILITIES: Rentals including telemark and racing skis, instruction, children's ski school, snack bar and guided tours including moonlight and gourmet tours.

TAMARACK CROSS-COUNTRY SKI CENTER – Mammoth Lakes – 77 F7 TRAILS: 50 km, groomed and tracked, beginner–advanced, flat to hilly terrain in Mammoth Lake Basin, high elevation. FACILITIES: Rentals, racing ski rentals available, instruction, restaurant, lunches on weekends and tours by reservation.

YOSEMITE'S BADGER PASS SKI AREA – Yosemite National Park – 76 F1 MOUNTAIN: 4 chairlifts. 10 trails, Beginner 35%, intermediate 50%, advanced 15%. VERTICAL DROP: 800 feet. CROSS-COUNTRY TRAILS: 32 km groomed. FACILITIES: Rentals, ski school, snowboarding.

HIKING

AGUA TIBIA WILDERNESS LOOP – Agua Tibia Wilderness – 149 C9 Begins along FT 1W03 to panoramic view at peak and follows unimproved road to FR 8S06. Returns to Dripping Springs Station by SR 79.

ALTA/SEVEN MILE HILL/HIGH SIERRA TRIP – Sequoia National Park – 95 D9 Moderate to strenuous trail with some steep areas. Passes through sequoia groves, mixed conifers, meadows and wildflowers. Begins at General Sherman Tree on Congress Trail and continues onto Alta Trail. Follows 7 Mile Hill Trail and High Sierra Trail to Crescent Meadows. Trail of Sequoias leads to Congress Trail which returns to General Sherman Tree. Camping at Merhten Meadows.

BAYSIDE TRAIL – Cabrillo National Monument – 154 D2 Marked trail, begins at Old Point Loma Lighthouse and follows old military road through coastal chaparral zone. View of harbor at Ballast Point.

BOUCHER LOOKOUT LOOP – Palomar Mountain State Park – 149 D10 From park headquarters, take short northeast connector to Scott's Cabin and continue on to Cedar Grove Campground, where Adams Trail heads off to left. Beyond Harrison Road, trail continues as Boucher Trail to Boucher Lookout. Returns to headquarters on paved road south of Boucher Mill.

COASTAL TRAIL – California – 22 D3 Flat trail will traverse entire length of state, along coast. Completed sections include trips through Golden Gate Recreation Area and Redwood National Park.

CRAGS TRAIL/INDIAN SPRINGS TRAIL – Castle Crags State Park – 33 C9 From Vista Point parking take Crags Trail to Castle Dome with rise of 2,250 feet over 2.7 miles. Or take turnoff onto Indian Springs Trail, to Indian Springs where water bubbles up from underground stream.

CRYSTAL LAKE HIKE – Sequoia National Park – 96 E1 From Sawtooth Parking Area, just over 0.5 mile to fork in trail. Right at fork, trail climbs with switchbacks for nearly 3 miles, crossing Monarch Creek. Leaving trail to Monarch Lakes and heading southeast, trail continues uphill to ruins of Chihuahua Mine. More switchbacks to Crystal Lake at 10,800 feet elevation and panoramic view of surrounding area. Strenuous hike.

CULP VALLEY TRAIL – Anza–Borrego Desert State Park – 150 E4 Culp Valley turnoff from SR S22. Trail begins in parking area of campground. Marked trail through transitional flora. Views along ridge of Hellhole and Dry Canyons. Trail ends on SR S22, 1 mile south of park headquarters and visitor center.

EAST BAY SKYLINE NATIONAL RECREATION TRAIL – Richmond – 71 C9 Wildcat near El Cerrito to southern end of Anthony Chabot Park, Castro. Rolling hills, creeks, views, redwoods. Camping at Anthony Chabot Park.

FEATHER FALLS NATIONAL RECREATIONAL TRAIL – Plumas National Forest—Feather Falls Scenic Area – 51 F8 3.5 miles to Feather Falls. Last mile on return is uphill.

GABRIELINO NATIONAL RECREATION TRAIL – Angeles National Forest – 140 B5 Hilly terrain. Trailheads at both Chantry Flat Station and Nino Gould Mesa. Moderately difficult from Chantry Flat Station; moderate from Nino Gould Mesa. Canyon bottoms and forested ridges.

IDES COVE LOOP TRAIL – Mendocino National Forest—Yolla Bolly–Middle Eel Wilderness – 48 A4 Moderately steep trail through streams, wooded areas and dry meadows. Loop passes Square Lake and Long Lake. Browns Camp Trail leads back to trailhead.

JOHN MUIR TRAIL – Lone Pine – 96 D3 Trail passes through John Muir Wilderness from Mt Whitney to Happy Isles in Yosemite National Park. Peaks, meadows, streams, lakes, canyons. Waterfalls. Wildflowers. Steep climbs and descents.

KING CREST TRAIL – King Range National Conversation Area – 38 F3 Passes along main coastal ridge north of Shelter Cove, leading to top of King Peak.

MIST FALLS HIKE – Kings Canyon National Park – 96 A1 Trail begins at road end of SR 180. 3.5 miles to fork and bridge crossing Kings River. Trail continues straight without crossing bridge. 4.5 miles along river to Mist Falls. Many small cascades and waterfalls on creeks in canyon.

MOUNT WHITNEY TRAIL – Inyo National Forest – 96 D4 Strenuous trail at high altitude with frequent switchbacks. From Whitney Portal, trail passes Lone Pine Lake, Outpost Camp, Mirror Lake, Trail Camp, Trail Crest Pass, John Muir Junction and reaches 14,495 feet in elevation at summit of Mt Whitney.

NOBLE CANYON NATIONAL RECREATION TRAIL – Cleveland National Forest – 155 B8 Hike begins at Pine Creek Road, 3 miles north of Pine Valley. Trail goes through chaparral, riparian woodlands and forested areas. Trail ends few hundred feet from Pacific Crest Trail in Laguna Mountain Recreation Area.

PACIFIC CREST TRAIL – Kings Canyon National Park – 87 F7 1,615 miles of this national scenic trail pass through California. Trail traverses variety of terrain with features including high peaks, meadows, vistas, chaparral, desert and woodlands. Six national forests, two national parks, one national monument, three state parks, one state recreation area and several wilderness areas.

PFEIFFER BIG SUR TRAIL – Pfeiffer Big Sur State Park – 90 G3 Follows Valley View Trail from Pfeiffer Falls to Oak Grove Trail. Gradual incline proceeds through redwood groves and evergreen forests. Trail passes Homestead Cabin and joins Big Sur River Gorge Trail, which features waterfalls and swimming holes. Fishing, swimming and picnicking.

PINE CREEK – Modoc National Forest—South Warner Wilderness – 37 A6 Easy to moderate trail through meadows and forests. Starts at Pine Creek parking area and continues uphill to and along Pine Creek before reaching Patterson Lake, 9,700 feet. Fishing in lake and ponds. Connects with Summit Trail.

REDWOOD CREEK TRAIL – Redwood National Park – 30 A4 Flat trail along Redwood Creek through old-growth redwoods. Connects to Tall Trees Trail and old logging road.

RUBICON TRAIL – D L Bliss State Park – 60 E3 From Calawee Cove to Eagle Falls. Passes by Vikingsholm, Norse fortress reproduction.

SAN BERNARDINO PEAK LOOP – San Gorgonio Wilderness – 142 B4 Loop begins at Forsee Ridge Trailhead, one mile on dirt road from Jenks Lake Road. Continues along FT 1E16 past Johns Meadow wilderness camp for 4.5 miles, turns left on FT 1W07 to San Bernardino Peak. Trail passes Limber Pine Bench camp and has frequent switchbacks to peak at 10,649 feet elevation. 2.5 miles from peak to Trail Fork Springs camp, where trail goes left on FT 1E06, 6 miles, returning to Forsee Ridge Trailhead.

SAN GABRIEL RIVER AND SKYLINE TRAILS – Los Angeles County – 140 F5 Rolling hills, urban areas and views of San Gabriel Valley and Mountain Ranges. Trail begins at San Diego Freeway and follows along flood control channel of San Gabriel River for 19 miles, through River Park. Turns right on Skyline Trail, passing through Whittier Narrows County Recreation Area, Puente Hills Landfill, Otterbein County Park and Walnut Creek County Park.

SCOUT TRAIL – Joshua Tree National Park – 144 C1 Strenuous hike with some scrambling and climbing along westernmost edge of Wonderland of Rocks. 13 miles round trip from Indian Cove to Hidden Valley.

SKYLINE-TO-THE SEA TRAIL – Big Basin Redwoods State Park – Castle Rock State Park – 81 D6 Moderately strenuous trail through Big Basin Redwoods and Castle Rock State Parks. Reaches Pacific Ocean at Rancho del Oso. Santa Cruz Mountains, waterfall, vistas, woodlands, redwoods. Connects with other trails. Trail camps.

SOUTH YUBA TRAIL – Lake City – 58 B5 Difficult trail along rugged river canyon. Connects with Malakoff Diggins State Historic Park. Reaches to Tahoe National Forest.

SUMMIT NATIONAL RECREATION TRAIL – Seqoia National Forest – 67 B10 Gradual climb through mixed conifer forest from Quaking Aspen to Maggie Lakes on FR 31E14 and continues on to Twin Lakes through Golden Trout Wilderness. Fishing. Access to other trails. Moderate.

SUMMIT TRAIL – Modoc National Forest—South Warner Wilderness – 37 B7 Marked trail from Pepperdine to Patterson along west ridge of Warner Mountains. Wooded areas, alpine meadows. Views of Mt Shasta and Mt Lassen. Moderate with some uphill climbs. Forms loop with Owl Creek Trail.

VALENCIA PEAK TRAIL – Montana de Oro State Park – 113 D6 Begins at park headquarters on Pecho Rd, proceeding inland, switchbacks as trail rises. Views of 90 miles of coastline on clear day from summit of Valencia Peak (1,346 ft.). Moderately strenuous.

WESTERN STATES PIONEER EXPRESS TRAIL – Folsom Lake SRA – 65 B8 Rolling terrain in foothills of Sierra Nevada from Nimbus Overlook at Lake Natoma, along Folsom Lake to Auburn Fairgrounds.

WESTERN STATES TRAIL – Foresthill – 59 E7 Strenuous route through Tahoe National Forest and Granite Chief Wilderness. Intersects Pacific Crest Trail.

PADDLING

CACHE CREEK – Rumsey Run – Rumsey – 56 F4 8.5-mile run for novices with easy vehicle access from SR 16. Mandatory portage around low water bridge.

COLORADO RIVER – Havasu NWR Run – 153 A10 70-mile run. Flat, but moving water. Several put-in and take-out points.

COLORADO RIVER – Lower Colorado River – 135 C6 27 miles through Havasu National Wildlife Refuge. Several portages. Open waters may become rough in high winds.

EAST FORK OF CARSON RIVER – Cave Rock to Diversion Dam – South of Loope – 68 C1 27-mile run through scenic wilderness. Upper 7 miles continuous Class III rapids. Infrequent commercial raft trips.

KINGS RIVER – Kings River – Sierra National Forest – 95 A7 Run begins at Mill Flat Campground and goes to Kirch Flat. 3.5-mile trip. Primarily used for commercial rafting. Experience necessary.

KLAMATH RIVER – Sarah Totten Campground to Weitchpee – Yreka – 24 C2 Remote scenic 100-mile run with many rapids and portages. Convenient access points from road.

LOWER KERN RIVER – Lower Kern Run – South of Isabella Lake – 106 G1 18-mile run for experienced kayakers and rafters. Convenient access from road. Portages. Commercial rafting trips.

LOWER STANISLAUS RIVER – Goodwin Dam to Knights Ferry – Oakdale – 74 D3 Three-mile run through scenic canyon. Experts only. Portages.

LOWER TRINITY RIVER – Hawkins Bar to Weitchpec – East of Willow Creek – 31 F8 39-mile run. Slow releases from large reservoir. Easy rapids. Wilderness sections.

MERCED RIVER – Red Bug to Bagby – El Portal – 75 F10 28-mile run with several major rapids and portage around 25-feet. North Fork Falls.

MOKELUMNE RIVER – Electra Run – Jackson – 66 F3 Three-mile beginners' run through scenic canyon.

RUSSIAN RIVER – Squaw Rock Run – North of Cloverdale – 55 F7 Eight-mile beginner's run from Pieta Creek with easy road access. Below Cloverdale 50 miles of Class I rapids

SOUTH FORK OF AMERICAN RIVER – Chili Bar and Gorge Runs – Placerville – 66 A1 Popular 20-mile run through canyon, valley and gorge.

SOUTH YUBA RIVER – Washington to Edwards Crossing – 59 A7 14-mile run through gorge. Mandatory portage around waterfall several miles upstream from take-out.

TUOLUMNE RIVER – Cherry Creek to Wards Ferry – North Harden Flat – 75 D9 27-mile run for experts only with over 20 rapids rated Class IV–V and at least one portage.

UPPER KERN RIVER – Upper Kern Run – North of Fairview – 106 C1 15-mile run. Accessible from road. Commercial rafting trips.

ALCATRAZ ISLAND – Golden Gate National Recreation Area – 71 D8 Prison building remains, along with old military fortifications. Exhibits, audio tour and guided tours.

ALCAZAR GARDEN – San Diego – 154 D3 Floral display in Balboa Park, modeled and named after gardens of Spanish castle. Flowers bloom year round.

ANGEL STADIUM – Anaheim – 141 F7 Angel Stadium of Anaheim has been the home of the Los Angeles Angels of Anaheim since 1966.

AQUARIUM OF THE PACIFIC – Long Beach – 140 F4 World class aquarium dedicated to study of the Pacific Ocean, with a focus on local waters as well as features on the North Pacific and tropical sections. Over 500 aquatic species.

THE ARBORETUM – Arcadia – 140 B5 127-acre sanctuary of plants from Australia, South Africa, South America, Asia and North America. Lasca Lagoon. Guided tram tours. Demonstrations. Lectures.

ARCO ARENA – Sacramento – 64 B5 Home stadium of the Sacramento Kings of the NBA. Built in 1988, it is known for the high volume of its crowds.

ARTISTS DRIVE – Death Valley National Park – 9 miles – 99 F6 Loops through brightly colored canyon and badlands in foothills of Black Mountains. Begins south of Furnace Creek.

ASIAN ART MUSEUM OF SAN FRANCISCO – San Francisco – 71 E8 Vast collection of Asian art, items from Neolithic times to present. Includes personal collection of Chicago millionaire Avery Brundage.

AT&T PARK – San Francisco – 71 E8 The home stadium of baseball's San Francisco Giants is a modern stadium overlooking the waters of McCovey Cove.

AVENUE OF THE GIANTS (SR 254) – North of Garberville – 33 miles – 38 D4 Scenic bypass of US 101 splits off between Garberville and Phillipsville. Follows Eel River, past redwood groves including Rockefeller Forest and Children's Forest. Avenue of the Giants rejoins US 101 in several places including Greenlaw Vista Point where SR 254 ends.

BALE GRIST MILL STATE HISTORIC PARK – 3 miles northwest of St. Helena – 63 C7 Mill built in 1846 by Edward Turner Bale. Using waterpower from Mill Creek, mill ground flour and meal until early 1900s when Napa Valley began producing grapes in place of grains.

BATTERY POINT LIGHTHOUSE – Crescent City – 22 C2 Lighthouse built in 1865 on island 20 yards from shore. Can only be reached at low tide. Lighthouse museum exhibits original light, photographs of shipwrecks and Indian artifacts.

BAY MODEL VISITOR CENTER – Sausalito – 71 D7 Hydraulic model of San Francisco Bay–Delta area. Reproduces action of bay and various conditions. Used to study effects of different projects.

BERKELEY ART MUSEUM AND PACIFIC FILM ARCHIVE – Berkeley – 71 D9 20th-century paintings, sculptures, drawings and prints. Hans Hofman paintings and archives. Film collection. Oriental paintings.

BIDWELL MANSION STATE HISTORIC PARK – Chico – 50 D3 Italian Villa–style mansion built in 1868 by John Bidwell, pioneer, farmer, statesman, politician, soldier and philanthropist. Tours and exhibits.

BILLY JONES WILDCAT RAILROAD – Los Gatos – 81 D7 Miniature steam locomotive in Oak Meadow Park. Originally created by miniature railroad pioneer Billy Jones.

BODIE STATE HISTORIC PARK – Bridgeport – 69 G7 Genuine ghost town abandoned since 1940s. During its heyday, Bodie had reputation as toughest, most lawless mining town in West with 10,000 residents and about $100 million in ore.

BOTANICAL BUILDING AND LILY POND – San Diego – 154 D3 Balboa Park's immense greenhouse. Exotic species include flowering orchids and philodendron. More than 500 species of tropical and subtropical plants.

THE BOWERS MUSEUM OF CULTURAL ART – Santa Ana – 141 F7 World cultures explored through their visual arts. History and culture of California explorers, settlers and Native Americans. Pre-Columbian art and artifacts from Mexico, Central and South America. Changing exhibits. Adjacent Kidseum offers interactive exhibits for children.

CABLE CARS – San Francisco – 71 D8 Moving National Historic Landmark. Only cable car system of its kind left. Covers 69 blocks with three routes: Powell and Market to Fisherman's Wharf; Powell and Market to Victoria Park at Beach and Hyde; and California from Market to Van Ness. Cable Car Museum houses three vintage cable cars, scale models of 57 cars that once operated in city and complex winding gear system. 40 cable cars are housed in barn.

CABOT'S PUEBLO MUSEUM – Desert Hot Springs – 143 D9 35-room Hopi pueblo hand-made by Cabot Yerxa. Pioneer museum, art gallery and trading post. Tours.

CABRILLO MARINE AQUARIUM – San Pedro – 140 G3 Seaside aquarium with local marine plants, animals and ecology. Over 30 exhibits, including small sharks. Large seashell collection. Nautical equipment. Museum extends to beach and ocean. Hands-on exhibits. Tide pool tours. Whale watching.

CABRILLO NATIONAL MONUMENT – San Diego – 154 D2 Lighthouse, furnished in period. Visitor center. Maritime collection. Museum tours.

CALICO EARLY MAN ARCHAEOLOGICAL SITE – Barstow – 131 A6 Pleistocene archaeology and geology. Artifacts of earliest-known Americans. Stone tools. Guided tours. Museum. Self-guided trail.

CALIFORNIA ACADEMY OF SCIENCES – San Francisco – 71 E7 Houses Steinhart Aquarium, Natural History Museum and Morrison Planetarium. Hands-on exhibits and guided tours. Foucault pendulum.

CALIFORNIA AFRICAN AMERICAN MUSEUM – Los Angeles – 140 D3 Artifacts documenting history of African-American experience. Workshops. Lectures. Tours.

CALIFORNIA HERITAGE MUSEUM – Santa Monica – 140 D1 Re-creation of 1875–1915 Los Angeles. Residences, church and railroad station.

CALIFORNIA MUSEUM OF PHOTOGRAPHY – Riverside – 142 D1 19th- and 20th-century photographs. Regional and national photographs. Bingham Camera Collection. Permanent and changing exhibits.

CALIFORNIA OIL MUSEUM – Santa Paula – 127 G7 Restored 1890s oil company offices and 1930s apartment. Exact scale model of cable tool drilling rig. Changing exhibits focus on art, history and science. Guided tours.

CALIFORNIA PALACE OF THE LEGION OF HONOR – San Francisco – 71 E7 Reproduction of French palace by same name. Fine art museum hosts French paintings, tapestries and furniture. Rodin sculpture collection.

CALIFORNIA SCIENCE CENTER – Los Angeles – 140 D3 Hands-on exhibits explore life sciences, physical sciences and technology. Air and Space Gallery. IMAX Theater.

CALIFORNIA STATE CAPITOL MUSEUM – Sacramento – 65 C6 California State Capitol, finished in 1869 and restored from 1976–1982. Tours are available, including Restored Capitol Tour, Legislative Process Tour and Capitol Park Tour. Museum features exhibits on restoration.

CALIFORNIA STATE INDIAN MUSEUM – Sacramento – 65 C6 Large collection of basketry, clothing, jewelry and art. Displays of Indian ceremonial life.

CALIFORNIA STATE MINING AND MINERAL MUSEUM – Mariposa – 84 A4 Site of first gold mine in California. Museum explores importance of minerals to California's history. Gems, paleontology, rocks and minerals, geologic mapping, mine models and gold stamp mill.

CALIFORNIA WESTERN RAILROAD SKUNK TRAIN – Fort Bragg/Willits – 47 G6 Trips on old 1885 logging locomotives with open observation cars. Route winds through redwoods and along Noyo River. Leave from either Fort Bragg or Willits.

CANDLESTICK PARK – San Francisco – 71 E8 Home for the San Francisco Forty-Niners of the NFL. Built originally for baseball's Giants, it sits on the westside of the San Francisco Bay, where swirling wind has long been a hallmark of the field.

CARTOON ART MUSEUM – San Francisco – 71 E8 Permanent and changing exhibits of cartoon and animation arts in wide variety of forms.

THE CHILDREN'S MUSEUM AT LA HABRA – La Habra – 141 E6 Scientific, cultural and historic exhibits. Train and aviation models, local history and mounted animals. Bee observatory.

COLONEL ALLENSWORTH STATE HISTORIC PARK – Allensworth – 104 E4 Reconstructed home of black pioneer, Colonel Allensworth. Restored school. Picnic area.

COLUMBIA STATE HISTORIC PARK – Columbia – 74 B5 Once prosperous gold mining town, never completely abandoned. Park preserves days of gold rush. Costumed performers.

CRAFT AND FOLK ART MUSEUM – Los Angeles – 140 C3 Focuses on contemporary crafts in traditional styles. Japanese folk art, East Indian quilts. Changing exhibits of crafts, folk paintings, artifacts and utensils.

CROCKER ART MUSEUM – Sacramento – 65 C6 15th- to 20th-century paintings and drawings. Contemporary art, crafts, costumes and Asian art.

DESCANSO GARDENS – La Canada Flintridge – 140 B4 Garden features camellias, roses and native plants of California. Japanese Tea House and Hospitality House. Education and Exhibition Center for lectures and demonstrations. 165 acres. Picnic facilities. Tram tours.

DISCOVERY MUSEUM – Sacramento – 65 B7 History, Science, Space and Technology. Exhibits illustrate government, commercial and domestic history of Sacramento region. Lure of Gold exhibit. Other programs explore natural history, geology and space. Planetarium. Nature trail. Challenger Learning Center.

DISNEYLAND RESORT – Anaheim – 141 F6 Walt Disney's original theme park brings to life his timeless characters and stories. Guests enter through Mainstreet USA, throwback to days gone by and reflection of Walt's Missouri hometown. From there, eight meticulously themed lands present guests with thrilling rides, live shows and chances to get involved in magic. Disney's California Adventure features history and resources of California. Hollywood Pictures Backlot recreates golden days of studios. Paradise Pier recollects traditional pier amusement park. The Golden State area explores natural spaces of state, while *Soarin'* allows guests to fly high above them. Outside parks, Downtown Disney provides extensive shopping, dining and entertainment.

DODGER STADIUM – Los Angeles – 140 C4 Baseball park built for the Los Angeles Dodgers in 1962 following their relocation from Brooklyn, NY.

EL PRESIDIO DE SANTA BARBARA STATE HISTORIC PARK – Santa Barbara – 126 F1 Spanish presidio founded in 1782. Museum. El Cuartel. Royal Presidio Chapel. Caneda Adobe.

EL PUEBLO DE LOS ANGELES STATE HISTORIC MONUMENT – Los Angeles – 140 C4 Original settlement of Los Angeles. Restored marketplace. Avila Adobe, Mission Plaza Church and old Pico House. Old Plaza Firehouse. Guided tours.

EMPIRE MINE STATE HISTORIC PARK – Grass Valley – 58 C4 Oldest and richest hard-rock mine in California. Yielded 5,800,000 ounces of gold before closing in 1956. Park includes mine shaft, historic mine yard, formal gardens of mine owner, scale model of mine and mining film.

EXPLORATORIUM – San Francisco – 71 D8 Participatory exhibits on science, technology, mathematics, animal behavior and perception.

FILOLI CENTER – Woodside – 80 A4 Plants from Middle Ages. 16 acres of enclosed gardens. Willis Polk designed 43-room house built in 1916.

FORT ROSS STATE HISTORIC PARK – Jenner – 62 D1 Partially restored fort, settled in 1812 by Russians and native Alaskans. Southern limit of Russian expanse. Original house, several restored buildings.

FORT TEJON STATE HISTORIC PARK – Lebec – 127 A8 Living history museum. Restored barracks building, officers' and orderlies' quarters. Picnic area.

FORTY NINE MILE SCENIC DRIVE – San Francisco – 49 miles – 71 D8 Scenic tour of San Francisco. Marked by blue/white seagull signs. Views of city include waterfront area, Chinatown, Japan Center, Mission Dolores, Golden Gate Park, parts of Golden Gate National Recreation Area and Presidio. Begin loop at Lombard and Lyon Streets.

FRANKLIN D MURPHY SCULPTURE GARDEN – Los Angeles – 140 C2 Over 70 works by 20th-century artists situated on over five acres at University of California, Los Angeles campus.

FRESNO ARTS MUSEUM – Fresno – 93 B10 Pre-Columbian and modern Mexican art. Contemporary works by local and international artists. American sculpture and graphics. Traveling and temporary exhibits.

FRESNO METROPOLITAN MUSEUM – Fresno – 93 B10 Museum of art and science. 3,000 artifacts. Jigsaw puzzles. Ansel Adams photos. Salzer collection of European and American still life paintings. Reeves ASK Science Center.

FULLERTON ARBORETUM – Fullerton – 141 E7 A wide variety of plant habitats including desert, forest and Mediterranean. Groomed orchards. Carnivorous plants. Guided and self-guided tours.

THE GETTY CENTER – Los Angeles – 140 C2 Modern museum dedicated to the visual arts. Established due to the philanthropy of famous industrialist J Paul Getty. Sculpture, European paintings, manuscripts, photographs.

THE GETTY VILLA – Malibu – 140 C1 Re-creation of Roman villa. Museum exploring ancient Greek and Roman culture. Over 40,000 Greek and Roman antiquities.

GONDOLA AT HEAVENLY – South Lake Tahoe – 60 F4 Views of Lake Tahoe and Sierra Nevada. Deck, restaurant and lounge at top, 8,300 feet up.

GOVERNOR'S MANSION STATE HISTORIC PARK – Sacramento – 65 C6 15-room Victorian mansion built in 1878. Home of 13 governors, 1903–1967. Tours.

GRAUMAN'S CHINESE THEATRE – Hollywood – 140 C3 World famous movie theatre, constructed in 1927. Footprints of movie stars line concrete sidewalk in front of theatre.

GREAT AMERICA – Santa Clara – 81 B7 Amusement park with over 100 rides, shows and attractions. Children's area, shops and restaurants.

GUINNESS WORLD OF RECORDS MUSEUM – Hollywood – 140 C3 Hands-on displays, videos and life-size replicas illustrate archives found in *Guinness World Records* book.

THE HAGGIN MUSEUM – Stockton – 73 C7 Art and history museum. 19th-century French and American paintings, decorative arts and folk arts. Displays on history of Stockton area, including gold rush.

HAKONE GARDENS – Saratoga – 81 C6 Mid-17th-century Japanese Zen–style garden. 16 acres of Japanese gardens and structures.

HALL OF CHAMPIONS – San Diego – 154 D3 Sports museum in Balboa Park. Displays, photographs, films of nationally acclaimed San Diego athletes.

HEARST–San Simeon State Historical Monument – San Simeon – 101 F8 Castle, guesthouses and 127 acre estate of publisher William Randolph Hearst. Art collection and antiques displayed. Landscaped gardens.

HONDA CENTER – Anaheim – 141 F7 The home stadium of the Anaheim Ducks is often referred to as The Pond.

HP PAVILION – San Jose – 81 C7 Known as the Shark Tank, it is the home of the San Jose Sharks, an NHL team.

THE HUNTINGTON LIBRARY, ART GALLERY AND BOTANICAL GARDENS – San Marino – 140 B5 Research center founded by railroad developer Henry Huntington, set on 120 acres of gardens with 15,000 plants. Library houses rare books and manuscripts. Art gallery features 18th-century British and European paintings. Tapestries and porcelains. 17th- to early-19th-century American paintings.

INDIAN GRINDING ROCKS STATE HISTORIC PARK – Pine Grove – 66 E3 Northern Miwok Indian grinding rock with rock carvings and mortar cups. Indian dwelling, round house and football field. Museum, cultural center.

JACK LONDON STATE HISTORIC PARK – Glen Ellen – 63 E7 Memorial park to one of America's most popular writers. Includes London's grave, ruins of Wolf House and Charmian London's House of Happy Walls.

JOHN MUIR NATIONAL HISTORIC SITE – Martinez – 71 B10 Residence of early preservationist John Muir. Adobe residence of Muir's daughter. Self-guided tour and film on Muir's life. Nine acres of orchards. Bird walks in oak woodlands.

KINGDOM OF THE DOLLS – Desert Hot Springs – 143 D9 Display of dolls depicting The History of Man. From prehistoric times to 1900.

KNOTT'S BERRY FARM – Buena Park – 141 F6 Amusement park loosely themed on Old West and early California. Camp Snoopy features rides and attractions for young children. Restaurants and shops.

KRUSE RHODODENDRON STATE RESERVE – Plantation – 61 C10 317 acres with rhododendrons, redwoods and fern canyons. Adjacent to Salt Point State Park. Rhododendrons bloom in late May and early July.

LA PURISIMA MISSION STATE HISTORIC PARK – Lompoc – 124 D5 Nine restored buildings on more than 900 acres preserve eleventh Spanish mission, established in 1787. Museum. Self-guided tour.

LAGUNA ART MUSEUM – Laguna Beach – 148 B2 California art of all periods. Photography and contemporary art collections.

LINDSAY WILDLIFE MUSEUM – Walnut Creek – 72 C1 Natural history exhibitions on flora and fauna, geology, marine life and astronomy. Working animal hospital. Wildlife encounters.

THE LIVING DESERT – Palm Desert – 143 G10 Gardens re-create different deserts of world. Numerous plant and animal species native to deserts. African savanna. American southwest. Various gardens. Self-guided trails. Picnic area.

LONG BEACH MUSEUM OF ART – Long Beach – 140 F4 Southern California art from 1890 to present. 20th-century American art. Video art archives. Contemporary sculpture. Works from Laguna Canyon School of 1920's. WPA pieces.

LOS ANGELES COUNTY MUSEUM OF ART – Los Angeles – 140 C3 Far Eastern, Pre-Columbian, Indian, Islamic, American and European paintings. Glass, photography, sculpture and decorative art collections.

LOS ANGELES MARITIME MUSEUM – Los Angeles – 140 G3 Remodeled ferry building. Exhibits nautical history, history of harbor. Scale models of ships.

LOS ANGELES TIMES – Los Angeles – 140 C4 Modern building built in 1934. Tour of newspaper production process and history of Los Angeles Times.

LOS ANGELES ZOO – Los Angeles – 140 B3 1,200 animals from around world, grouped by area of origin. Naturalistic enclosures. Aquatics, Aviary and Reptile House. Children's Zoo with Baby Animals' Nursery and barnyard area. Tram rides. Picnic areas and snack bars.

MALAKOFF DIGGINS STATE HISTORIC PARK – North Bloomfield – 59 A6 Once California's largest hydraulic mining operation. Cliffs stand where monitors directed streams over hillside gravel. Museum with interpretive exhibits and several restored buildings.

MANZANAR NATIONAL HISTORIC SITE – Independence – 96 B4 Site of World War II internment camp for Japanese-American citizens and resident Japanese aliens. Guided walking tours. Self-guided auto tour.

MARITIME MUSEUM – San Diego – 154 D3 *Star of India* (1863), full-rigged merchant ship. *Berkeley* (1898), ferry. *Medea* (1904), steam yacht. Nautical and oceanographic exhibits.

MARSHALL GOLD DISCOVERY STATE HISTORIC PARK – Coloma – 66 A1 Location where James Marshall discovered gold in 1848. Reconstruction of Sutter's Mill. Museum with exhibits on Gold Rush, films on mining and discovery of gold and tools of mining trade.

MCAFEE COLISEUM AND ORACLE ARENA – Oakland – 71 E10 The Oakland Coliseum complex is famed for the Black Hole a section of rowdy and costumed fans of the Oakland Raiders. The NFL team shares the coliseum with the Oakland A's of the American League. The NBA's Golden State Warriors are the tenants of the Arena.

Family Outings

MENDOCINO COAST BOTANICAL GARDENS – Fort Bragg – 54 A1 Gardens of flowering plants including rhododendron and fuchsia. Wooded areas, fern canyon and lily pond. Paths and ocean access.

MISSION SAN ANTONIO DE PALA – Pala – 149 D9 Only California mission still serving Indians. Museum and mineral room.

MISSION SAN CARLOS BORROMEO DEL RIO CARMELO – Carmel – 90 D2 Second California mission, founded in Monterey in 1770. Moved in 1771. Museum includes replica of mission kitchen.

MISSION SAN DIEGO DE ALCALA – San Diego – 154 C3 First of California's missions, founded in 1769. Self-guided taped tours. Visitor center.

MISSION SAN FERNANDO REY DE ESPANA – Mission Hills – 140 A2 Alta California Franciscan Mission, founded in 1797. Self-guided tour of church, workshops, residences, wine vats and gardens.

MISSION SAN JUAN CAPISTRANO – San Juan Capistrano – 148 B4 Seventh California mission, site dedicated in 1776. Tour of tanning vat ruins, kitchens, sleeping quarters and jail.

MISSION SAN LUIS OBISPO DE TOLOSA – San Luis Obispo – 113 D8 Spanish mission established in 1772. Museum displays include Indian relics and early settlers' artifacts. Gardens.

MISSION SANTA INES – Solvang – 125 D7 Nineteenth California mission, founded in 1804. Museum displays Indian artifacts.

MONTEREY BAY AQUARIUM – Monterey – 90 C2 Open-air shorebird aviary. Touch Tide Pool. Bat Ray Petting Pool. California sea otters. Marine Mammals Gallery. Monterey Bay and Kelp Forest exhibits. Restaurant. Gift shop and bookstore.

MONTEREY MUSEUM OF ART – Monterey – 90 D2 Works by California and early Monterey artists. Oriental, contemporary and folk art. Sculpture, graphics and international photography.

MONTEREY STATE HISTORIC PARK – Monterey – 90 C2 Custom House museum. Casa Del Oro houses trade items exhibit. California's first theatre. Pacific House museum of California history and Indian artifacts. Stevenson and Larkin Houses are period homes.

MULHOLLAND SCENIC CORRIDOR – Santa Monica National Recreation Area – 50 miles – 140 C3 Winds along Santa Monica Mountains, westward from Hollywood Freeway to Leo Carrillo State Beach.

MUSEUM OF CONTEMPORARY ART – Los Angeles – 140 C3 International collections include sculpture, paintings and environmental works. Full range of media and performing arts.

MUSEUM OF CONTEMPORARY ART SAN DIEGO – La Jolla – 154 B2 20th-century avant-garde design, Pop and other post-1950 American art, California art, architectural and industrial design. Latin American art, installation art. Changing exhibits.

NORTON SIMON MUSEUM – Pasadena – 140 B4 Old Master paintings. Goya etchings. Tapestries. 20th-century European and American art. South Asian art.

THE OAKLAND MUSEUM OF CALIFORNIA – Oakland – 71 D9 Exhibitions in areas of art, history and natural sciences pertaining to California. Includes botany, entomology, geology, zoology, ornithology, oceanography, mineralogy and mammalogy. California art. Paintings, sculpture, graphics, decorative arts, textiles and costumes.

OAKLAND ZOO – Oakland – 71 E10 African Veld environment with over 200 animals. Baby Zoo and children's petting zoo. Aerial tram.

OLD SACRAMENTO STATE HISTORIC PARK – Sacramento – 65 B6 Historic district of over 50 restored 19th–century buildings on 28 riverside acres in downtown Sacramento. Western Terminus of Pony Express and Transcontinental Railroad. California Railroad Museum features 21 restored railroad cars and locomotives dating 1862–1944. Train rides from old Central Pacific station. California Military Museum and Wells Fargo Museum.

OLD TOWN SAN DIEGO STATE HISTORIC PARK – San Diego – 154 C3 La Casa de Estudillo contains period furnishings and relics. San Diego Union Museum. Collection of horse-drawn vehicles at Seeley Stables.

ORANGE EMPIRE RAILWAY MUSEUM – Perris – 142 F2 Display of railway equipment and trolleys. Streetcar and train rides. Picnic area.

ORCUTT RANCH HORTICULTURE CENTER – Canoga Park – 139 A10 The 200 acre estate of oil executive William Warren Orcutt. 16 acres of citrus trees. Oak trees, gardens.

PACIFIC ASIA MUSEUM – Pasadena – 140 B4 Pacific and Asian art. Chinese courtyard garden.

PAGE MUSEUM LA BREA TAR PITS – Los Angeles – 140 C3 Collection of fossils from ice age, recovered from Rancho La Brea Tar Pits by industrialist George C Page. Remains of saber-toothed cats, mammoths, wolves and other mammals and plants. Life size models of extinct animals.

PALM SPRINGS AERIAL TRAMWAY – Palm Springs – 143 F8 2.5 miles up Mount San Jacinto, to Mountain Station (elevation 8,516 feet), in 18 minutes. Passes through five different climate zones. Top of mountain is 6-mile hike from tram station. Restaurant. Gift shops. Seasonal cross-country skiing. Picnic area. Self-guided nature trail. Hiking trails.

PALOS VERDES SCENIC DRIVE – Palos Verdes Peninsula – 15 miles – 140 F3 Cliff top section of roads following Palos Verdes Drive. Begins at Palos Verdes Estates and goes to Point Fermin Park in San Pedro. Affords many views.

PANORAMA GONDOLA AT MAMMOTH MOUNTAIN – Mammoth Lakes – 77 F7 Gondola ride to over 11,000 feet. Views of Mammoth Lakes Basin, Minaret Range, Mono Lake, Ritter and Banner peaks.

PEBBLE BEACH SCENIC DRIVE – Monterey Peninsula – 17 miles – 90 C2 17-Mile Drive loops Monterey Peninsula through Pescadero Canyon, along coast and by Forest Lake.

PETALUMA ADOBE STATE HISTORIC PARK – Petaluma – 63 F6 Rancho Petaluma, 66,000-acre agricultural estate of General Mariano Guadalupe Vallejo. Built 1836–1846. Authentic furniture. Interpretive displays depict early rancho life.

PETCO PARK – San Diego – 154 D3 New downtown stadium built in 2004 for The San Diego Padres of baseball's National League.

PIGEON POINT LIGHT STATION STATE HISTORIC PARK – Pescadero – 80 D3 Classically designed lighthouse. Guided history walks around lighthouse grounds including 1902 fog signal building.

POINT PINOS LIGHTHOUSE – Monterey – 90 C2 Cape Cod-style Pacific Grove structure. Working third-order lens.

POINT SUR STATE HISTORIC PARK – Point Sur – 90 G2 Light station, 361 feet above water, on towering volcanic rock. Still in operation. Tours.

PRESIDIO OF SAN FRANCISCO – Golden Gate National Recreation Area – 71 D7 Military garrison under flags of Spain (1776–1822), Mexico (1822–48) and United States (1848–1994). Over 500 historic buildings, coastal defense fortifications, national cemetery and historic airfield.

PYGMY FOREST – Mendocino – 54 B1 Stunted, 1–3 foot cypress and pine trees, caused by chemicals in soil and poor drainage, in Van Damme State Park.

QUAIL BOTANICAL GARDENS – Encinitas – 149 G7 31 acres specializing in cacti, succulents, semitropicals and native plants. Self-guided trails.

QUALCOMM STADIUM – San Diego – 154 C3 Home of San Diego Chargers of the NFL. Originally built to attract the Padres and Chargers to the city, in part due to the efforts of sportswriter Jack Murphy.

QUEEN MARY – Long Beach – 140 G4 One of largest, fastest ocean liners. Historic tours. Paranormal tours. Moored permanently at Pier J Tours.

RAGING WATERS – San Dimas – 141 C7 50-acre water park. Numerous water slides, speed slides, family raft ride. Lazy river, wave pool, sandy beach, children's pool.

RAILTOWN 1897 STATE HISTORIC PARK – Jamestown – 74 C5 Roundhouse, railroad cars, locomotives, repair shops, tools and equipment. Audio-visual presentation. Steam-powered train takes 40-minute, 6-mile round-trip excursion through California's gold-mining country. Railroad and surroundings have been used in over 100 films.

RANCHO LOS ALAMITOS – Long Beach – 140 F5 Furnished ranch house, built in 1806. Blacksmith shop and barns. Guided tour.

RANCHO LOS CERRITOS – Long Beach – 140 F4 Furnished 1844 period house. Research library.

REUBEN H FLEET SPACE THEATER AND SCIENCE CENTER – San Diego – 154 D3 IMAX Theater and planetarium. Space shows. Science center features variety of participatory displays.

RIM OF THE WORLD DRIVE SCENIC BYWAY – San Bernardino – 101 miles – 142 A2 Follows SR 18 from SR 30 to Big Bear Lake through San Bernardino National Forest. Winding road at 5,000–7,200 feet affords many panoramic views.

ROARING CAMP RAILROADS – Felton – 81 F6 Roaring Camp & Big Trees Narrow Gauge Railroad provides 1-hour round-trip excursion through redwood forest to Bear Mountain summit. Santa Cruz, Big Trees & Pacific Railway offers 3-hour round-trip train ride through redwood forest and along San Lorenzo River gorge to Santa Cruz.

ROSICRUCIAN EGYPTIAN MUSEUM – San Jose – 81 B7 One of largest Egyptian artifact collections in western United States. Mummies, canopic jars, funerary boats and models, jewelry, pre-dynastic pottery, bronze tools, sculpture and Coptic textiles. Egyptian rock-cut tomb replica.

SAN DIEGO MUSEUM OF ART – San Diego – 154 D3 Italian Renaissance, Dutch and Spanish Baroque Old Masters. Oriental art. Contemporary American works. Sculpture Garden Cafe. Changing exhibitions.

SAN DIEGO MUSEUM OF MAN – San Diego – 154 D3 Anthropology museum in historic Balboa park. Focus on people of Western Americas. Ceramics, basketry and photographs. Ecology. Egyptian artifacts.

SAN DIEGO NATURAL HISTORY MUSEUM – San Diego – 154 D3 Hall of Shore Ecology. Eels, insects, birds, shells, minerals and gems, fossils. Foucault pendulum.

SAN DIEGO RAILROAD MUSEUM – Campo – 155 E9 Over 80 major pieces of railroad equipment, including steam and diesel locomotives, passenger cars, freight cars and cabooses. Train ride from Campo to Miller Creek. 1.5-hour round trip. Guided walking tour of museum's restoration area.

SAN DIEGO SCENIC DRIVE – San Diego – 52 miles – 154 D2 Scenic tour of San Diego marked with blue/white seagull signs. Sites include Sunset Cliffs, Mission Bay Park, Balboa Park, Shelter Island and Cabrillo National Monument.

SAN DIEGO WILD ANIMAL PARK – Escondido – 149 G9 2,200 animals on 1,800 acres resembling native habitats. Wgasa Bush monorail. Outdoor aviary. Petting kraal. Kilimanjaro Hiking Trail. Animal shows and rides.

SAN DIEGO ZOO – San Diego – 154 D3 World famous zoo contains over 4,000 animals on 100 acres of natural habitat enclosures with moats or low walls. Walk-through aviaries. Rare and endangered species. Children's zoo with animals to pet, newborns, primate nursery. Animal shows. Skyfari aerial tram. Bus tours.

SAN FRANCISCO BOTANICAL GARDENS AT STRYBING ARBORETUM – San Francisco – 71 E7 55 acres with over 7,000 species of plants. Garden of Fragrance with Braille labels. Native California plants. Exotic plants including natives of South America, New Zealand and southeast Asia. Moon-viewing Garden. Succulent Garden. Tours and picnicking.

SAN FRANCISCO MARITIME NATIONAL HISTORICAL PARK – San Francisco – 71 D8 National Maritime Museum. Maritime Museum Library. Fleet of six turn-of-the-20th-century vessels. Submarine museum. Interpretive programs.

SAN FRANCISCO MUSEUM OF MODERN ART – San Francisco – 71 E8 European and American paintings, sculpture, graphics, ceramics and photography.

SAN FRANCISCO ZOOLOGICAL GARDENS – San Francisco – 71 E7 1,000 animals in enclosures landscaped like natural habitats. Gorilla World. Primate Discovery Center. 130 endangered species. Children's zoo.

SAN JUAN BAUTISTA STATE HISTORIC PARK – San Juan Bautista – 90 A5 Original Mission, San Juan Bautista, founded in 1812 and still in operation. Other 19th–century buildings include, Castro House and 1858 Plaza Hotel. Stable with carriages and harness on display. Blacksmith shop.

SAN PASQUAL BATTLEFIELD STATE HISTORIC PARK – 2.5 miles west of San Pasqual – 149 G9 Monument commemorates December 6, 1846, battle between General Stephen Kearny and Andres Pico during Mexican-American War.

SANTA BARBARA MUSEUM OF ART – Santa Barbara – 126 F1 Oriental, American and European art. Egyptian, Greek and Roman antiquities. Photography. Paintings and watercolors. Drawings. Sculpture. Doll collection.

SANTA CRUZ BEACH BOARDWALK – Santa Cruz – 81 G6 Oceanfront amusement park maintains original turn-of-20th-century style, with over 30 rides. Includes 1924 Giant Dipper roller coaster and 1911 Looff Carousel. Also features variety of children's rides, games of skill, arcades, laser tag and two-story indoor miniature golf course. Shops and snack bars.

SCRIPPS AQUARIUM – La Jolla – 154 B2 22 marine tanks. Sharks, eels. Fish from San Diego area and Mexico. Oceanographic museum with wave channel display, tide pool, underwater telecast. Part of University of California.

SEAWORLD SAN DIEGO – San Diego – 154 C2 Marine park with animal attractions, including Shamu, the killer whale aquarium exhibits, thrill rides and live entertainment. Highlights include Shark Encounter with acrylic tunnel passing through tank full of sea predators; Rocky Point Preserve, interactive dolphin attraction; and Wild Arctic, simulated helicopter expedition to North Pole.

SHASTA STATE HISTORIC PARK – Shasta – 41 B7 Ruins and restorations of northern mining town. Museum houses Boggs collection of historic artifacts, books, California oil paintings and watercolors.

SIX FLAGS DISCOVERY KINGDOM – Vallejo – 71 A9 Combination theme park, oceanarium and land animal park. Thrill rides, animal attractions and live shows. Looney Tunes Seaport for smaller children.

SIX FLAGS MAGIC MOUNTAIN – Valencia – 128 F1 Rides, shows and entertainment on 260 acres. Includes 16 roller coasters, many among world's largest and fastest. 6-acre Bugs Bunny World for smaller children.

SONOMA DRIVE – San Francisco – 165 miles – 71 D7 From San Francisco go north on US 101 across Golden Gate Bridge. North of Ingnacio, head east on SR 37 to Sears Point. North on SR 121 than west on SR 12 through Santa Rosa to Sebastopol. North on SR 116 to Guerneville. Head southwest on SR 116 along Russian River to SR 1 and south along coast to US 101 in San Francisco.

SONOMA STATE HISTORIC PARK – Sonoma – 63 F7 Buildings of northern most mission. General Mariano Guadalupe Vallejo's home. Interpretive exhibits.

SONOMA TRAIN TOWN RAILROAD – Sonoma – 63 F7 Miniature steam and diesel locomotives travel through forests and two tunnels, cross five bridges and trestles and stop at miniature mining town.

SOUTH COAST BOTANIC GARDENS – Palo Verdes Peninsula – 140 F3 Plants from Australia, Mediterranean, South Africa and other areas. Reference library. Tram tours. Picnic area.

SQUAW VALLEY CABLE CAR – Olympic Valley – 60 C1 From base area (6,200 feet) to High Camp (8,200 feet). Views of Sierra Nevada and Lake Tahoe. Accesses downhill skiing, hiking, swimming, tennis and 3-season ice skating. Restaurants.

SR 1 – Dana Point – 440 miles – 148 C3 Southern section of Pacific Coast Highway follows shoreline of Pacific Ocean and its beaches and rugged cliffs. Through Orange County's beach towns, metropolitan Los Angeles, Santa Monica Mountains, dunes of San Luis Obispo County, scenic Big Sur and city of Santa Cruz. Northern section of Pacific Coast Highway follows rugged shoreline of Pacific with accessible beaches. Traverses Metro San Francisco. Coastal hills and cliffs of northern Sonoma and Mendocino Counties.

STAPLES CENTER – Los Angeles – 140 C3 Sports arena built in 1999. Home to the Lakers and Clippers of the NBA, and the Kings of the NHL.

STEINHART AQUARIUM – San Francisco – 71 E7 Dolphin and seal tank. Penguin Environment. Fish Roundabout with sharks and other fish. Ecological exhibits. Dolphin, seal and penguin feedings daily.

SUTTER'S FORT STATE HISTORIC PARK – Sacramento – 65 C6 Restored to 1848 condition. Exhibits. Self-guided audio tour. Demonstrations of skills and crafts.

TORREY PINES STATE RESERVE – La Jolla – 154 B2 2,000 acres of bluffs, woods and wildflowers. Rare Torrey pines.

TRAVEL TOWN – Los Angeles – 140 B3 Open-air transportation museum. Antique locomotives, planes, automobiles, railroad and street cars. Miniature train provides 1-mile ride through park and around Travel Town.

TURTLE BAY EXPLORATION PARK – Redding – 41 B8 300-acre park complex focuses on Sacramento River and surrounding region's natural history, culture and human history. Turtle Bay Museum, Paul Bunyan's Forest Camp, summer butterfly house, live animals, arboretum and trails.

UNIVERSAL STUDIOS HOLLYWOOD – Universal City – 140 B3 Combination working production studio and theme park features rides with film and television show themes, live entertainment and 45-minute narrated tram tours of studio. Universal CityWalk entertainment, dining and shopping complex adjoins.

UNIVERSITY OF CALIFORNIA BOTANICAL GARDEN – Berkeley – 71 D9 Over 10,000 species of plants arranged by region of origin. Collection of succulents and cacti. Visitors center.

UNIVERSITY OF CALIFORNIA MUSEUM OF PALEONTOLOGY – Berkeley – 71 D9 Vertebrate, invertebrate and plant fossils.

WARNER BROS. STUDIOS – Burbank – 140 B3 Tours (by reservation only) show inner workings of television show and feature film production. Warner Museum.

WATTS TOWERS OF SIMON RODIA STATE HISTORIC PARK – Watts – 140 E4 Sculptural Towers built 1921–1954 single-handedly by Simon Rodia. Made of assorted articles, such as tiles, glass, pebbles and dishes.

WAX MUSEUM AT FISHERMAN'S WHARF – San Francisco – 71 D8 Over 270 life-size wax figures from fiction, history and present. Chamber of Horrors. Hall of Religions.

WEAVERVILLE JOSS HOUSE STATE HISTORIC PARK – Weaverville – 32 G3 Oldest continuously used Chinese temple in California. Built in 1874. Exhibits on Chinese art, tools and weapons.

WESTERN RAILWAY MUSEUM – Fairfield – 64 G2 Various streetcars, trains, trams and miscellaneous equipment. Seasonal.

WILL ROGERS STATE HISTORIC PARK – Pacific Palisades – 140 C1 Home of actor Will Rogers and his family 1924–1935. Memorabilia. Self-guided audio tour of grounds. Hiking and picnicking. Polo matches in season.

WINCHESTER MYSTERY HOUSE – San Jose – 81 C7 Sarah Winchester's Victorian mansion. Sprawling garden and home built over 38 years by Winchester Rifle heiress. Numerous oddities include stairs that lead to ceilings and doors that open onto walls. 110 rooms open to tour.

WORLD'S BIGGEST DINOSAURS – Cabazon – 143 E6 Huge concrete models of dinosaurs on side of I-10. *Apatosaurus* with museum inside and *Tyrannosaurus Rex*.

YOSEMITE MOUNTAIN–Sugar Pine Railroad – 2 miles south of Fish Camp – 85 A7 Steam-powered narrow gauge railroad with cars carved from logs. 4-mile ride with stops along way. Some gas-powered railcars ride along same route.

Recreation Areas

NAME, LOCATION	PAGE & GRID	ADMINISTRATION	ACREAGE	BIKING	INTERPRETIVE OPPORTUNITIES	FISHING	HIKING	HORSEBACK RIDING	OFF-HIGHWAY VEHICLE AREA	SWIMMING	WILDLIFE VIEWING	PICNICKING	CAMPING	VISITOR CENTER	BOATING	DESCRIPTION
Admiral William Standley State Recreation Area, Branscomb	47 E7	CSP	45			●	●					●				Coastal redwoods in small park along South Fork of Eel River.
Agua Tibia Wilderness, Cleveland National Forests	149 C10	USFS	15,934				●									Northwest tip of Palomar Mountain Range, 1,400 to 5,400 feet. Canyons, chaparral. Views from the ridges.
Ahjumawi Lava Springs State Park, McArthur	35 C6	CSP	6,000			●	●					●			●	6,000-acre island of old lava flow in Big Lake. Views of Mount Shasta. Access by boat only.
Andrew Molera State Park, Big Sur	90 G3	CSP	4,800	●	●	●	●	●		●	●	●				Big Sur River. Sandy beach, meadows, mountains.
Angel Island State Park, Tiburon	71 D8	CSP	740	●	●	●	●					●		●	●	Several small sandy beaches. Reached by private boat or commercial ferry service from Tiburon, San Francisco, or Berkeley. Views of Bay area.
Angeles National Forest, Arcadia	140 A4	USFS	655,000	●	●	●	●	●	●	●		●	●	●	●	Mountainous park showcased by Mt San Antonio (Old Baldy), 10,064 feet and Mt Badden–Powell, 9,399 feet. Ancient limber pine trees, wildflowers and birds. Plentiful lakes and streams.
Annadel State Park, Santa Rosa	63 D6	CSP	5,000	●		●	●	●				●				Over 130 species of birds inhabit this picturesque park. Best birding at Ledson Marsh.
Ano Nuevo State Reserve, Pescadero	80 E3	CSP	4,000		●	●	●				●	●		●		Harbor seals and California and Steller sea lions. Northern elephant seal breeding ground (December–March) when visits are by guided tour only (reservations required).
Ansel Adams Wilderness, Sierra National Forest, Inyo National Forests	77 E6	USFS	230,258				●	●								San Joaquin River. Minarets Range. Granite outcroppings. Elevations range 7,600–13,157 feet. Pacific Crest Trail. Good mountain climbing.
Antelope Valley California Poppy State Reserve, Fairmont	128 C2	CSP	1,700		●		●					●		●		Natural area in California's best poppy growing country provides excellent opportunities for viewing poppies and other wildflowers.
Anza–Borrego Desert State Park, Borrego Springs	150 E4	CSP	600,000		●		●	●			●	●	●	●		Colorado Desert features canyons, badlands, vistas, dry lakes and sandstone formations. Over 200 species of birds. Specialized mammals and reptiles.
Anza–Borrego Desert State Wilderness, Borrego Springs	150 F4	CSP	460,000				●									Rugged, mountainous terrain. 360 to 6,193 feet. Valleys, canyons, mesas, springs. Tierra Blanca, Vallecito, Pinyon, San Ysidro, Santa Rosa, and Jacumba Mountains. Hot springs. Fan palms. Chaparral. Numerous wildlife species. Two self-guided nature trails near Elephant Trees Ranger Station.
Armstrong Redwoods State Reserve, Guerneville	62 C3	CSP	805		●		●	●				●		●		Coastal redwoods. Adjacent to Austin Creek State Recreation Area.
Arthur B Ripley Desert Woodland State Park, Fairmont	128 C1	CSP	566		●		●					●				A stand of Joshua and Juniper trees to be viewed and preserved.
Asilomar State Beach, Pacific Grove	90 C2	CSP	107		●	●	●							●		Beach with rocky shore and dunes. Tide pooling. Rip tides make swimming unsafe.
Auburn State Recreation Area, Auburn	58 F5	CSP	42,000	●		●	●	●		●		●			●	On Lake Clementine and Middle Fork of American River.
Austin Creek State Recreation Area, Guerneville	62 C3	CSP	6,000	●			●	●				●				Access through Armstrong Redwoods State Reserve. A variety of birds and wildlife.
Bean Hollow State Beach, Pescadero	80 D3	CSP	44		●	●	●					●				Rocky surf, rip tides, path to beach, sandy beach, and rocky shore. Paved parking area and restrooms.
Benbow Lake State Recreation Area, Garberville	47 A6	CSP	1,200	●	●	●	●			●		●	●		●	Eel River is dammed each summer to create Benbow Lake.
Benicia State Recreation Area, Benicia	71 A10	CSP	720			●	●				●	●				Along Upper San Pablo Bay. Marshland area by Dillon Point.
Bethany Reservoir State Recreation Area, Byron	72 E5	CSP	608	●		●						●			●	608-acre reservoir in gently rolling hills. California Aqueduct Bikeway.
Bidwell–Sacramento River State Park, Stony Creek	50 D2	CSP	180		●	●	●			●		●				Along the Sacramento River. Lush vegetation, oxbow sloughs, and wildlife, such as turtles, river otters, birds, and beavers. Nature trail.
Big Basin Redwoods State Park, Big Basin	80 D5	CSP	18,000	●	●		●	●		●		●	●	●		Redwood groves give way to scenic views of ocean.
Bighorn Mountains Wilderness, Rimrock	143 A7	BLM/ USFS	38,500				●									San Bernardino Mountains, 3,000 to 7,500 feet. Arid. Craggy peaks, valleys, canyons. Rattlesnake Canyon. Springs. Yucca, cactus, creosote. Pinyon–juniper. Chaparral. Ponderosa pine forests. Joshua trees. Wildflowers.
Bolsa Chica State Beach, Huntington Beach	140 G5	CSP	169	●		●	●			●		●	●			6 miles of beach. Bluffs at south end. Wayside camping. Paved bike path to the Santa Ana River Trail.
Border Field State Park, Imperial Beach	154 F3	CSP	418	●	●	●	●	●		●	●	●		●		Monument marks Mexican–American border. Tijuana River Estuary saltmarsh. Over 1 mile of beach. Wildflowers. Over 170 species of birds.
Bothe–Napa Valley State Park, Calistoga	63 C7	CSP	1,917	●	●		●	●		●	●	●	●	●		Stands of coast redwoods in Napa Valley wine country.
Brannan Island State Recreation Area, Rio Vista	72 A4	CSP	336		●	●	●			●	●	●	●	●	●	Junction of Sacramento and San Joaquin Rivers (gateway to Delta Region).
Bucks Lake Wilderness, Plumas National Forest	51 B8	USFS	21,000				●	●								Rolling terrain and granite outcroppings. Red fir trees. Pacific Crest Trail.
Burton Creek State Park, Tahoe City	60 C2	CSP	2,000	●			●									Forested park. Roadways for skiing in winter,
Butano State Park, Butano Park	80 D3	CSP	2,200		●		●					●	●	●		Santa Cruz Mountains. Coast redwoods. 114 species of birds sighted.
Calaveras Big Trees State Park, Arnold	67 F6	CSP	6,500		●	●	●			●		●	●	●		Two groves of giant sequoias. Lava outcroppings and scenic canyon on North Fork of Stanislaus River.
Candlestick Point State Recreation Area, San Francisco	71 E8	CSP	170	●	●	●	●					●				Rural park in urban setting. Beautiful view of San Francisco. Experienced windsurfers.
Cardiff State Beach, Cardiff-by-the-Sea	154 A2	CSP	14			●				●						Day use area. Broad sand beach. Tide pools. Surfing.
Caribou Wilderness, Lassen National Forest	43 C8	USFS	20,546				●	●								Forested plateau with many lakes. Red and white fir trees. Caribou Peaks, Black Cinder Rock, and Red Cinder Cone. Black-tailed deer.
Carlsbad State Beach, Carlsbad	149 F6	CSP	14			●				●		●				Sand beach with rocky areas. Bluff diving.
Carmel River State Beach, Carmel	90 D2	CSP	106		●	●	●				●					Sandy beach from Point Lobos to Carmel Point on Carmel Bay. Low bluffs. Carmel River Lagoon Wetlands Preserve to the east has good birding. Diving at Monastery Beach in the south. Wind surfing.
Carnegie State Vehicular Recreation Area, Tracy	72 F5	CSP	1,500						●			●		●		1,500 acres of hilly terrain for motorcycles and all-terrain-vehicles. Limited access for 4-wheel drives
Carpinteria State Beach, Carpinteria	126 G3	CSP	62		●	●	●			●	●	●	●	●		Beach with dunes and bluff. Shorebirds. Migrating grey whales. Tide pools. Surfing area.
Carson–Iceberg Wilderness, Stanislaus National Forest, Humboldt–Toiyabe National Forest	67 D10	USFS	160,000				●	●								Twelve prominent peaks with elevations over 12,000 feet. Steep ridges and narrow valleys. Red and white fir trees.
Caspar Headlands State Beach, Caspar	54 A1	CSP	75			●										Small sandy beach with stream corridor.
Castaic Lake State Recreation Area, Castaic	127 E10	CSP	8,800	●		●	●			●		●			●	Castaic lake and Afterbay Lagoon. 8,700 acres and 29 miles of shoreline.
Castle Crags State Park, Castella	33 C9	CSP	4,350		●	●	●	●		●		●	●	●		Views of Mount Shasta. Crags and geologic formations. Mineral springs. Pacific Crest Trail.
Castle Crags Wilderness, Shasta–Trinity National Forest	33 B8	USFS	10,500				●									Granite cliffs and spires. Elevations range 2,300–7,200 feet. Small lakes and numerous streams. Pacific Crest Trail.
Castle Rock State Park, Los Gatos	80 D5	CSP	3,600		●		●	●								Linked to Big Basin Redwoods State Park by Skyline-to-Sea Trail. Steep, mountainous terrain. Waterfalls. Rock climbing.
Caswell Memorial State Park, Ripon	73 E8	CSP	258		●	●	●			●	●	●	●			Wildlife includes blue heron rookery and wood ducks.
Cayucos State Beach, Cayucos	113 B6	CSP	16			●				●		●				White sand beach on Estero Bay. Fishing pier. Stream and surf fishing. Surfing.
Chanchelulla Wilderness, Shasta–Trinity National Forest	40 C3	USFWS	8,200				●									Highest point Chanchelulla Mountain, 6,600 feet. Views of Sacramento Valley. Brush field and mixed conifer. Trails for day hikes.
Channel Islands National Marine Sanctuary, Channel Islands	138 D3	NPS	249,354			●					●			●		Extends six nautical miles from Channel Islands National Park. Dolphins, porpoises, whales. Seals and sea lions. Migratory waterfowl, seabirds, and shorebirds.
Channel Islands National Park, Channel Islands	138 D4	NPS	108,800		●	●	●			●	●	●	●	●	●	Five of the eight Channel Islands. Cliffs, sea stacks, caves. Channel Islands National Marine Sanctuary. Marine mammals. Birding.
China Camp State Park, San Rafael	71 B7	CSP	1,640	●	●	●	●	●		●	●	●		●	●	Abandoned fishing village on San Francisco Bay. Salt marsh. Sandy beach.
Chino Hills State Park, Los Serranos	141 E8	CSP	12,452	●	●		●	●				●	●			Rolling hills, grasslands, oak woodlands, and riparian areas. Undeveloped. Aliso and Telegraph Canyons. Birds. Riding on old dirt roads and cowpaths.
Chuckwalla Mountains Wilderness, Hell	152 A4	BLM	84,614			●	●	●								Hills, peaks, washes, ridges, bajadas, canyons, valleys. Rocky spires. Springs. Chuckwalla Bench. Corn Springs area with fan palms. Bighorn sheep, desert tortoise, raptors.
Cibola National Wildlife Refuge, Palo Verde	153 D9	USFWS	2,785		●	●					●	●		●	●	In California and Arizona. Riverbottom, wetlands, lake. Waterfowl and migratory birds. Best viewing in winter. Auto tours.
Clay Pit State Vehicular Recreation Area, Oroville	50 G5	CSP	220						●							Area for dune-buggies, all-terrain vehicles and motorcycles. Good for beginning riders.
Clear Lake National Wildlife Refuge, Perez	27 C9	USFWS	46,460								●					Less accessible part of Klamath Basin National Wildlife Refuge Complex. Lake with dry grasslands. Pronghorn, sage grouse, some migratory waterfowl, pelicans, and cormorants.
Clear Lake State Park, Kelseyville	55 E9	CSP	290		●	●	●			●	●	●	●	●	●	Largest natural lake in California. Sulphur springs nearby.

Recreation Areas

NAME, LOCATION	PAGE & GRID	ADMINISTRATION	ACREAGE	BIKING	INTERPRETIVE OPPORTUNITIES	FISHING	HIKING	HORSEBACK RIDING	OFF-HIGHWAY VEHICLE AREA	SWIMMING	WILDLIFE VIEWING	PICNICKING	CAMPING	VISITOR CENTER	BOATING	DESCRIPTION
Cleveland National Forest, Alpine	155 C6	USFS	460,000	●		●	●	●	●			●	●	●		Hilly chaparral to high mountains with coniferous forests and plateaus. Palomar Mountain Observatory. Agua Tibia Wilderness. Pacific Crest Trail.
Colusa–Sacramento River State Recreation Area, Colusa	57 C6	CSP	67		●	●	●					●	●		●	Cottonwood- and willow-lined banks of Sacramento River. Major bird migration route of Pacific Flyway.
Corona Del Mar State Beach, Corona del Mar	148 A2	CSP	30			●				●		●				Broad sand beach with palm trees. East of jetty at Newport Harbor entry. Surfing.
Crystal Cove State Park, Corona del Mar	148 A2	CSP	2,791	●	●	●	●	●		●	●	●		●		3 miles of beach. Primarily undeveloped woodland. Designated underwater area for diving. Daylight hours only.
Cucamonga Wilderness, Angeles National Forest	141 A9	USFS	12,781				●	●								Rugged terrain with sharp peaks of 5,000 to 9,000 feet. Chaparral, canyons, fir, pine trees. Thunder, Telegraph, Timber, and Cucamonga Peaks are all over 8,000 feet. Middle and North Forks of the Lytle Creek. Bighorn sheep.
Cuyamaca Mountains State Wilderness, Hulburd Grove	155 A8	CSP	13,210				●									Gentle to rugged terrain. Mesas, grasslands, mixed conifer woodlands, meadows, springs, canyons. Cuyamaca Mountains. Juaquapin and Harper Creeks. Raptors.
Cuyamaca Rancho State Park, Descanso	155 B8	CSP	24,677	●	●	●	●	●			●	●	●	●		Mountainous, forested terrain with meadows and small streams. Almost 300 species of birds. 3.5-mile trail to top of Cuyamaca Peak, 6,512 feet
D L Bliss State Park, Tahoma	60 E3	CSP	1,830		●	●	●			●	●	●	●			Adjacent to Emerald Bay State Park, on shore of Lake Tahoe.
Death Valley National Park, Death Valley	98 E5	NPS	3,348,928	●	●		●	●					●	●		In the Mojave Desert. 120 miles long. 282 feet below sea level to 11,049 feet high. Telescope Peak. Sand dunes. Salt flats. Volcanic craters. Ghost town ruins. Mining. Self-guided auto tours.
Del Norte Coast Redwoods State Park, Crescent City	22 D3	CSP	6,400	●	●		●						●			Thick coastal redwood forests. Ocean beaches.
Desolation Wilderness, Eldorado National Forest	60 F2	USFS	63,960				●	●								Alpine timber and vegetation. Many small streams and lakes. Adjacent to Sierra Nevadas. Elevations range 6,500–10,000 feet. Granite outcroppings.
Devils Postpile National Monument, Mammoth Lakes	77 F6	NPS	798		●	●	●	●				●	●	●		Devils Postpile, 60-feet. columnar basalt formation. 101-feet. Rainbow Falls. Access by shuttle bus. Closed in winter.
Dick Smith Wilderness, Los Padres National Forest	126 D3	USFS	67,800			●		●								In the coast range. 3,750 to 6,541 feet at Madulce Peak. 12 by 18 miles. Canyons and creeks. Chaparral slopes. Pines at higher elevations. Scenic vistas from the slopes.
Dinkey Lakes Wilderness, Sierra National Forest	86 D2	USFS	30,000				●	●								Rolling, timbered terrain and large meadows. Grazing cattle. Highest point Three Sisters Peak, 10,619 feet. Separated from John Muir Wilderness by Ershim/Dusey Off-highway Vehicle Route.
Dockweiler State Beach, Playa del Rey	140 E2	CSP	91	●		●				●		●	●			3 miles of broad, sandy beach. South Bay Bike Path.
Doheny State Beach, Dana Point	148 C3	CSP	62	●	●	●	●			●		●	●	●		1.2-mile sandy beach. Surfing. Underwater park/marine life sanctuary for divers. San Juan Creek Bike Path.
Dome Land Wilderness, Sequoia National Forest	106 E4	BLM/ USFS	130,081			●	●	●								In the Sierra Nevadas. 3,000 to 9,730 feet. Basin, rolling terrain with sagebrush, wet meadows, conifer forests. Creeks and springs. South Fork of the Kern River. Granite domes, rock formations.
Don Edwards San Francisco Bay National Wildlife Refuge, Newark	72 G1	USFWS	30,000		●	●	●				●			●		Selected areas open. Salt marsh, mudflats, open water, and upland. Stop on Pacific Flyway. Over 200 species of birds including shorebirds and waterfowl. Interpretive center. Hiking.
Donner Memorial State Park, Truckee	60 B2	CSP	3,000		●		●			●		●	●	●		Commemorates early pioneers at the site of the infamous Donner Party. Museum.
Ed Z'berg–Sugar Pine Point State Park, Tahoma	60 E2	CSP	2,011	●		●	●			●		●	●	●		Forested western shore of Lake Tahoe. Sandy beach and pier.
El Capitan State Beach, Capitan	125 F8	CSP	133	●	●	●	●			●		●	●			Sand beach with occasional outcroppings. Surfing at El Capitan Point. 3 miles of ocean frontage.
Eldorado National Forest, Camino	66 A4	USFS	680,946	●		●	●	●	●	●		●	●	●	●	Sugar pine, white fir, Ponderosa pine, red fir, and Jeffrey pine trees. Along the western slope of the Sierra Nevada, south and southwest of Lake Tahoe.
Elkhorn Slough National Estuarine Research Reserve, Watsonville	90 A4	CDFG/ NOAA	1,400				●							●		Undisturbed coastal wetland. Channels, tidal creeks. Migratory flyway. Shorebirds, waterfowl. Sea otters. Viewing blind. Trails. Educational programs.
Emerald Bay State Park, South Lake Tahoe	60 F3	CSP	593		●		●			●	●	●	●	●	●	Adjacent to DL Bliss State Park, on Emerald Bay in Lake Tahoe. Eagle Falls. Fannette Island. Vickingsholm, reproduction of Ninth Century Norse fortress built as summer home in 1929.
Emigrant Wilderness, Stansislaus National Forest	67 G10	USFS	112,277				●	●								Abuts Yosemite National Park. Elevations range 6,000–12,000 ft. Granite-walled canyons. Lava-caped peaks.
Emma Wood State Beach, Ventura	138 A4	CSP	109	●	●	●	●			●		●	●			Sandy and rocky beach. Bike path runs to San Buenaventura State Beach. Surfing. Freshwater marsh.
Farallon National Wildlife Refuge, Inverness Park	70 E2	USFWS	211								●					Important breeding area for seabirds on group of islands west of San Francisco. Species include various gulls, three types of cormorants, guillemots, storm-petrels, and puffins. Marine mammals. Visitors not allowed on islands.
Folsom Lake State Recreation Area, Folsom	65 A8	CSP	18,000	●	●	●	●	●		●	●	●	●	●	●	Larger Folsom Lake and smaller, colder Lake Natoma. Sierra Nevada foothills and rolling oak woodlands.
Franks Tract State Recreation Area, Bethel Island	72 B4	CSP	3,515			●				●					●	Accessible only by water. Six-slip dock on Little Franks Tract. Most of area underwater.
Fremont Peak State Park, Morse	91 B6	CSP	37		●		●					●	●			Gabilan Mountains. Rolling hills. Trail to summit of Fremont Peak where there is a view of Monterey Bay and a plaque commemorating Captain John Fremont's raising of the American flag in 1846.
Garrapata State Park, Big Sur	90 E2	CSP	2,879			●	●									Ocean access to rocky shore with small coves. Trails on east side of Hwy 1. Diving.
Gaviota State Park, Fort Orford	125 F7	CSP	2,790			●	●	●		●		●				On both sides of US 101. Beach, pier and boat launch.
George J Hatfield State Recreation Area, Newman	82 B5	CSP	47			●				●			●			On the Merced River. Birds. Sandy beaches.
Golden Gate National Recreation Area, San Francisco	71 E7	NPS	75,398	●	●		●				●			●		World's largest urban park; series of sub-parks and sub-units covering over 72,000 acres in three counties. Varied terrain and many recreational opportunities. Hang gliding at Fort Funston. Several beaches. Fields for kite flying and games. Bird-watching. Tide pools. Views of San Francisco.
Golden Trout Wilderness, Inyo National Forest/Sequoia National Forest	96 F2	USFS	303,287				●	●								South end of Inyo National Forest and north end of Sequoia National Forest. Borders Sequoia National Park and John Muir Wilderness. 4,800 to 12,432 feet at Mt Florence and 12,900 feet at Cirque Peak. Kern Plateau. Little Kern Basin. Kern River and South Fork of the Kern River. Hot spring. Birds. Hunting.
Granite Chief Wilderness, Tahoe National Forest	60 D1	USFS	25,680				●	●								Remote alpine area with steep ridges, barren crags, and glacial valleys. Headwaters of American River.
Greenwood State Beach, Elk	54 D2	CSP	47			●	●					●		●		State beach and museum centered around the former existence of a lumber town.
Grizzly Creek Redwoods State Park, Carlotta	38 C5	CSP	399		●	●	●			●		●	●	●		Furthest inland of the redwood parks. Along Van Duzen River.
Grover Hot Spring State Park, Markleeville	67 B10	CSP	744			●	●			●		●	●			Alpine area surrounded by Humboldt–Toiyabe National Forest. Hot springs, pools.
Half Moon Bay State Beach, Half Moon Bay	80 A3	CSP	181	●	●	●	●	●			●	●	●	●		Long sandy beach with several access points.
Harry A Merlo State Recreation Area, Big Lagoon	30 B3	CSP	830			●										Landward side of Big Lagoon.
Hauser Wilderness, Cleveland National Forest	155 D8	USFS	7,547				●									Mountainous. Steep slopes. 1,800 to 3,900 feet. Canyons. Chaparral, coastal sage. Barrett Reservoir. Granite boulders. Rock outcroppings. Pacific Crest Trail.
Havasu National Wildlife Refuge, Needles	135 C6	USFWS	44,371	●		●	●		●	●	●	●	●		●	Majority in Arizona. Part of Topock Gorge in California. Along the Colorado River. Over 275 species of birds. Canada and snow geese.
Heber Dunes State Vehicular Recreation Area, El Centro	157 D8	CSP	343						●			●	●			Area used primarily for off-road vehicles.
Hendy Woods State Park, Philo	54 D4	CSP	850	●	●		●	●		●		●	●	●		Two groves of virgin coast redwoods.
Henry Cowell Redwoods State Park, Felton	81 F6	CSP	4,140	●	●		●	●		●		●	●	●		Second growth coast redwoods with one virgin stand. Along San Lorenzo River.
Henry W Coe State Park, Gilroy Hot Springs	81 D10	CSP	87,000	●	●	●	●	●			●	●	●	●		Largest state park in northern California. Rugged, beautiful terrain. Ridges and canyons.
Hollister Hills State Vehicular Recreation Area, Hollister	91 B6	CSP	3,200	●	●		●		●			●	●	●		Motorcycle and four-wheel-drive special events. Four-wheel-drive obstacle course. Call ahead for events and conditions.
Hoover Wilderness, Inyo National Forest, Humboldt–Toiyabe National Forest	76 B4	USFS	48,601				●	●								Glacial canyons, mountains, and meadows. Excelsior Mountain, 12,446 feet. Variety of wildlife.
Humboldt Bay National Wildlife Refuge, Bracut	30 F3	USFWS	2,200		●	●	●				●			●		Mudflats, marshes, and islands. Migratory black brant, snowy egret, great blue herons, waterfowl (winter), shorebirds, and seabirds. Harbor seal, porpoise, and sea lions. Migrating gray whale.
Humboldt Lagoons State Park, Orick	30 B3	CSP	1,036		●	●	●					●		●	●	Extensive beach area. Several lagoons. Headlands. Migratory waterfowl and shorebirds.
Humboldt Redwoods State Park, Weott	38 D5	CSP	53,000	●	●	●	●	●		●		●	●	●	●	Largest of state redwood parks lies on Eel River.
Humboldt–Toiyabe National Forest, Markleeville	67 A9	USFS	649,080	●		●	●	●	●		●	●	●			Abuts Yosemite National Park. Reaches from Nevada into eastern California and lies along rugged mountain ranges.

Continued on page 16

NAME, LOCATION	PAGE & GRID	ADMINISTRATION	ACREAGE	BIKING	INTERPRETIVE OPPORTUNITIES	FISHING	HIKING	HORSEBACK RIDING	OFF-HIGHWAY VEHICLE AREA	SWIMMING	WILDLIFE VIEWING	PICNICKING	CAMPING	VISITOR CENTER	BOATING	DESCRIPTION
Hungry Valley State Vehicular Recreation Area, Los Padres National Forest	127 C9	CSP	19,000		●				●			●		●		Motorcycles, dune buggies, four-wheel-drive, and all-terrain vehicles. Competitive events. Hills, valleys, canyons, and washes.
Huntington State Beach, Huntington Beach	148 A1	CSP	121	●		●	●			●	●	●				3 miles of sandy beach. Snack bar. 2-mile promenade. Surfing.
Imperial National Wildlife Refuge, Picacho	159 A6	USFWS	25,000		●		●				●	●		●	●	The majority is in Arizona. Colorado River. Lower Sonoran Desert. Marsh, open water, desert, woodland. Great blue herons, great and snowy egrets, Yuma clapper rails. Roadrunners, desert tortoise. Trails.
Inyo National Forest, Independence	96 F5	USFS	1,839,887			●	●						●			Rugged terrain with mountains and woodlands. Mt Whitney, 14,495 feet. 1,150 miles of trails. Pacific Crest Trail.
Ishi Wilderness, Lassen National Forest	42 G3	BLM/ USFS	41,339			●	●	●								Named after last ancestral member of Yahi Yana Indian Tribe. Rugged canyons and plateaus with chaparral and digger pine trees. Golden eagles and black-tailed deer.
Jackson Demonstration State Forest, Fort Bragg	54 A3	CDFFP	50,195	●	●		●	●		●		●				Coast redwood, Bishop pine, Douglas fir trees. Pygmy Forest Reserve. South Fork of Noyo River and North Fork of Big River. Rugged terrain.
Jacumba Outstanding Natural Area, Ocotillo	156 D3	BLM	31,194			●	●	●								Jacumba Mountains. Yuha Basin. Low desert. Valleys, canyons. Pinnacles, spires. Rock formations. Smuggler's Cave. Five springs. California fan palms. Crucifixion thorns. Peninsular bighorn sheep.
Jedediah Smith Redwoods State Park, Crescent City	22 C3	CSP	10,000	●	●	●	●	●		●		●	●	●		Old growth redwoods mixed with woodland trees and wildflowers. Smith River.
Jennie Lakes Wilderness, Sequoia National Forest	95 B9	USFS	10,500				●	●								In the Sierra Nevadas. 7,000 to 10,365 feet at Mitchell Peak. High peaks, meadows, mixed conifer forests, lakes, and streams. Rock outcroppings.
John Muir Wilderness, Inyo National Forest/Sierra National Forest	96 D3	USFS	580,323			●	●	●								In the Sierra Nevadas. 4,000 to 14,495 feet at summit of Mt Whitney. High peaks, woodlands, canyons, meadows, lakes, and streams. San Joaquin and Kings Rivers. John Muir and Pacific Crest Trails.
Joshua Tree National Park, Twentynine Palms	144 C2	NPS	770,595	●	●		●	●				●	●	●		High desert area on the south boundary of the Mojave. 1,000 to 6,000 feet. Little San Bernardino and Pinto Mountains. Groves of Joshua trees, giant yuccas. Spring wildflowers. California palm oases. Birds. Desert bighorn sheep.
Joshua Tree Wilderness, Joshua Tree National Park	144 F5	CSP	557,000				●									The backcountry of Joshua Tree National Park. Roadless high desert area. Transition zone between the Mojave and Colorado Deserts. Little San Bernardino and Pinto Mountains, 1,000 to 6,000 feet.
Julia Pfeiffer Burns State Park, Big Sur	100 A4	CSP	3,762				●					●				On the Big Sur coast. Rugged ridges and bluff above the ocean. Chaparral slopes. Redwood grove. At McWay Cove, a small waterfall feeds into the ocean. Some harbor seals and sea lions. Sea otters. Migrating gray whales. Shore and seabirds.
Kaiser Wilderness, Sierra National Forest	85 C10	USFS	22,700				●	●								Divided by Kaiser Ridge. Elevations range 7,000–10,000 feet. Red fir and Jeffrey pine trees. Small lakes.
Kenneth Hahm State Recreation Area, Los Angeles	140 D2	CSP	370			●	●					●				Rugged terrain amidst Los Angeles, coverd in walking trails. Scenic overlooks.
Kern National Wildlife Refuge, Alpaugh	104 F2	USFWS	10,618		●						●					Wetland habitat with flooded marsh, grasslands, scrub, and riparian habitats. 200 species of birds, shorebirds, waterfowl, wading birds. Pacific Flyway wintering area for ducks and geese. San Joaquin Desert Research Natural Area.
Kings Beach State Recreation Area, Kings Beach	60 C3	CSP	28							●						Beach next to Tahoe State Recreation Area.
Kings Canyon National Park, Three Rivers	95 B10	NPS	462,901		●	●	●	●				●	●	●		Giant sequoia groves in the high sierras. Deep canyons along Kings River. San Joaquin River.
Klamath National Forest, Yreka	23 E9	USFS	1,711,440			●	●	●	●	●			●			Mountainous. Dense wilderness forest with fast-flowing rivers cutting deep canyons.
Lake Del Valle State Recreation Area, Fourteenmile House	72 G4	CSP	3,997			●		●		●		●			●	Water recreation site on the South Bay Acqueduct. Ideal recreation site close to urban areas.
Lake Oroville State Recreation Area, Oroville	51 F6	CSP	16,100		●	●	●	●		●		●	●	●	●	Large lake in the Sierra Nevada foothills. Fish hatchery.
Lake Perris State Recreation Area, Perris	142 E3	CSP	8,800	●	●	●	●	●		●		●	●		●	Alessandro Island day use area, reached by boat only, has a picnic area and trails.
Lake Tahoe Basin Management Area, South Lake Tahoe	60 F4	USFS	150,000	●	●		●	●	●	●		●	●	●		Created to protect and preserve Lake Tahoe and surrounding areas.
Lake Valley State Recreation Area, South Lake Tahoe	60 G3	CSP	150													Golf course. Snowmobile rentals. Cross-country skiing.
Lassen National Forest, Susanville	42 E5	USFS	1,200,000	●		●	●	●	●			●	●		●	Gentle mountain terrain with pine and fir forests and meadows.
Lassen Volcanic National Park, Mineral	42 D5	NPS	106,000		●	●	●	●		●	●		●	●	●	Surrounded by Lassen National Forest. 50 lakes. Mountains. 10,457-foot plug dome volcano (Lassen Peak). Crags, volcanic hot springs, fumaroles, and sulphur vents. Wilderness area.
Lassen Volcanic Wilderness, Lassen Volcanic National Park	43 C7	CSP	78,982				●									Fantastic Lava Beds. Cinder Cone. Extensive lava fields. Lava tubes for cavers. High, rugged mountains and glaciated plateaus. Black-tailed deer, black bear, and martens.
LaTour Demonstration State Forest, Beal Place	42 A4	CDFFP	9,033	●		●	●	●								Pine, fir and cedar trees alongside wildlife in Cascade Range.
Lava Beds National Monument, Tulelake	27 D6	NPS	46,560		●		●				●	●	●	●		Rugged landscape features cinder cones, lava flows, spatter cones, lava tube caves, and pit craters. Modoc War (1872–1873) sites. Petroglyphs. Caving, bird-watching.
Lava Beds Wilderness, Lava Beds National Monument	27 C6	NPS	28,460				●	●								Lava flows, buttes, and craters. Numerous lava tubes. Cinder and spatter cones. Rattlesnakes and rodents. Trails and old roads. Caving.
Leo Carrillo State Park, Solromar	139 C8	CSP	2,513		●	●	●			●	●	●	●	●		Secluded beach. Caves. Tide pools.
Leucadia State Beach, Leucadia	149 G7	CSP	11			●				●		●				1.4 miles of sandy beach. Surfing.
Lighthouse Field State Beach, Santa Cruz	81 G6	CSP	38	●			●				●	●				The northern point of Monterey Bay. Sea Lions. Monarch Butterflies. Surfing.
Limekiln State Park, Lucia	100 C5	CSP	716			●	●					●	●			Beach area and redwood grove. Waterfall and old lime quarry.
Little River State Beach, Trinidad	30 D3	CSP	112			●										Adjacent to Clam Beach County Park. Path to sandy beach with dunes and access to Little River Delta.
Los Padres National Forest, Wheeler Springs	126 E5	USFS	1,761,950	●		●	●	●	●			●	●			Santa Ynez, Santa Lucia, La Panza, San Rafael, Sierra Madre Mountains. Santa Lucia (bristlecone) fir trees at Cone Peak. Five wilderness areas. Gowan Cypress at Cuesta Ridge Botanical Area. Beaches. Hot springs. Five rivers.
Lower Klamath National Wildlife Refuge, Hosley	26 A4	USFWS	50,092								●			●		Pacific Flyway stopover. In Klamath Basin National Wildlife Refuge Complex. Pelicans, cormorants, egrets, herons, three species of geese, and many types of ducks.
Machesna Mountain Wilderness, Los Padres National Forest	114 D1	BLM/ USFS	19,880			●	●	●								La Panza Mountain Range. 1,600 to 4,063 feet at the summit of Machesna Mountain. American Canyon. Limited access.
MacKerricher State Park, Fort Bragg	47 G6	CSP	1,598	●	●	●	●	●		●	●	●	●	●		Beach, forest, and wetland habitats. Tide pools.
Mailliard Redwoods State Reserve, Ornbaun Springs	54 F5	CSP	242									●				242 acres of preserved redwoods.
Malibu Creek State Park, Calabasas	139 C9	CSP	8,000	●	●	●	●	●		●	●	●	●	●		Undeveloped tract in the Santa Monica Mountains. Malibu Creek. Birds. Wildflowers.
Malibu Lagoon State Beach, Serra Relrea	139 C10	CSP	167		●	●	●			●	●	●				Estuary formed by Malibu Creek. Excellent bird-watching opportunities.
Manchester State Park, Manchester	54 F2	CSP	760			●	●				●	●	●			Sandy beach known for its driftwood. Dunes and grassland.
Mandalay State Beach, Hollywood Beach	138 B5	CSP	92							●						Sandy beach. Dunes and wetlands.
Manresa State Beach, La Selva Beach	81 G8	CSP	138		●	●				●						Sandy beach suitable for water recreation. Surfing.
Marble Mountain Wilderness, Klamath National Forest	24 F1	USFS	242,500			●	●	●		●						Forested area with many meadows. Numerous stocked lakes and fishing streams. Wildlife includes deer and bear.
Marina State Beach, Marina	90 B3	CSP	171		●	●	●					●				171 acres of sandy beach and dunes with spring wildflowers. Cliffs. Hang gliding.
McArthur–Burney Falls Memorial State Park, Four Corners	34 D4	CSP	910		●	●	●	●		●	●	●	●	●	●	Evergreen forests. Burney Falls. Water sports in Lake Britton.
McConnell State Recreation Area, Livingston	83 B7	CSP	74			●				●		●	●			Merced River. San Joaquin Valley. Streamside habitat with lawns and trees.
McGrath State Beach, Oxnard	138 A5	CSP	312		●	●	●				●		●	●		2 miles of beach frontage. Dunes. Lifeguards during summer and on spring and fall weekends. Nature trail.
Mendocino Headlands State Park, Mendocino	54 B1	CSP	347		●	●	●				●	●		●		Sandy beach and dunes with bluffs. Trails.
Mendocino National Forest, Willows	48 G3	USFS	913,000	●	●	●	●	●	●			●	●		●	Located in the North Coast Mountain Range. Ski touring and snowmobiling.
Millerton Lake State Recreation Area, Friant	85 F6	CSP	14,107	●	●	●	●	●		●	●	●	●		●	Lake formed from the San Joaquin River by Friant Dam. 43 miles of shoreline. Surrounded by hills and woodlands.
Modoc National Forest, Alturas	28 F3	USFS	1,663,401	●		●	●	●	●		●	●	●		●	High peaks, canyons, alpine meadows, and pine forest. Elevations range 5,000–9,892 feet at the summit of Eagle Peak. Obsidian cliffs, lava caves, craters, lakes, and streams.
Modoc National Wildlife Refuge, Alturas	28 G4	USFWS	7,000	●		●	●	●		●	●				●	Diverse habitat near Warner Mountains. Good summer birding. Migratory waterfowl in spring and fall.
Mojave National Preserve, Barstow	121 D7	NPS	1,462,154				●	●	●				●			Includes seven wilderness study areas and one state recreation area. Sand dunes, cinder cones, granite dome, spires, canyons, and washes. Petroglyphs. Wildflowers. Joshua trees. Kelso Dunes. Devil's Playground. Historic Mojave Trail.

Recreation Areas

NAME, LOCATION	PAGE & GRID	ADMINISTRATION	ACREAGE	BIKING	INTERPRETIVE OPPORTUNITIES	FISHING	HIKING	HORSEBACK RIDING	OFF-HIGHWAY VEHICLE AREA	SWIMMING	WILDLIFE VIEWING	PICNICKING	CAMPING	VISITOR CENTER	BOATING	DESCRIPTION
Mokelumne Wilderness, Eldorado National Forest, Stanislaus National Forest, Humboldt–Toiyabe National Forest	67 B8	USFS	99,161				●	●								Bisected by Mokelumne River. Scattered timber stands. Shallow valleys and small lakes. Highest point Mokelumne Peak, 9,332 feet. Deadwood and Fourth-of-July Canyons.
Monarch Wilderness, Sequoia National Forest/Sierra National Forest	95 A9	USFS	44,896				●	●								2,400 to 10,000 feet. Views from Spanish Mountain. Brush at lower elevations with pines at higher. Rock outcroppings. Rugged area with limited access. No trails in Sierra National Forest portion.
Mono Lake Tufa State Preserve, Lee Vining	58 A3	CSP	112		●		●			●		●		●	●	Lakeside recreation dedicated to peserving its tufas, natural rock formations. High salt content makes the lake denser than seawater.
Montana de Oro State Park, Los Osos	113 D6	CSP	8,000		●	●	●	●			●	●	●	●		Coastal plains, cliffs, sandy beaches, streams, canyons, chaparral hills. Rock formations. Tide pools. Valencia Peak, 1,342 feet. Spring wildflowers.
Montara State Beach, Montara	71 G7	CSP	773	●		●	●	●								Sandy beach with hazardous surf. Stairs and steep paths to beach. Bluff.
Monterey State Beach, Monterey	90 C2	CSP	90			●	●					●				Small, narrow sand beach. Dunes. Tide pools. Surfing.
Montgomery Woods State Reserve, Montgomery	54 C5	CSP	1,142		●		●					●				Old growth redwoods mixed with Woodwardia ferns on 1,142 acres. Nature trail.
Moonlight State Beach, Leucadia	149 G7	CSP	13			●				●		●				3 miles of sandy beach. Surfing.
Morro Bay State Park, Morro Bay	113 C6	CSP	2,700		●	●	●				●	●	●	●	●	Developed. Bay, lagoon, dunes, and marsh. Beach. Birds, including a protected great blue heron rookery. Spring wildflowers. Morro Rock. Golf course.
Morro Strand State Beach, Cayucos	113 B6	CSP	160			●				●		●	●			Sandy beach with bluff. Gentle surf. Day use only.
Moss Landing State Beach, Moss Landing	90 A3	CSP	60			●	●	●			●					Also called Jetty Beach. One of the Monterey Bay State Beaches. Views of the harbor. Surfing.
Mountain Home State Forest, Porterville	95 G10	CDFFP	4,807			●	●	●								Giant sequoias. Connects with Golden Trout Wilderness trails. Ski touring and snowmobiling.
Mt Diablo State Park, Diablo	72 D2	CSP	20,000	●	●		●	●			●	●	●	●		View of 35 California counties (weather permitting). Sandstone formations and fossils. Rock climbing.
Mt San Jacinto State Park, Pine Cove	143 F6	CSP	13,522		●		●	●			●	●	●	●		Adjacent to Mount San Jacinto State Wilderness. Nature trails. Many trails lead to wilderness area.
Mt San Jacinto State Wilderness, Idyllwild	143 F7	CSP	32,000				●									Granite peaks. Sub-alpine forests, meadows. San Jacinto Peak, 10,804 feet. Pacific Crest Trail. Palm Springs Aerial Tramway.
Mt Shasta Wilderness, Shasta–Trinity National Forest	25 G9	USFS	38,200				●	●								Rugged terrain surrounding Mount Shasta with steep slopes, glaciers and waterfalls. Elevations range 4,300–14,000 feet. Shasta red fir and whitebark pine trees. Spectacular views. No established mountain trails.
Mt Tamalpais State Park, Mill Valley	71 C6	CSP	6,218	●	●	●	●	●			●	●		●		In Golden Gate National Recreation Area. 30 miles of hiking and riding trails. Access to beaches. Views from summit.
Muir Woods National Monument, Mill Valley	71 C6	NPS	523		●		●									In Golden Gate National Recreation Area. Virgin stands of coast redwood trees. Albino baby redwood trees. Trails.
Natural Bridges State Beach, Santa Cruz	81 G6	CSP	65		●	●	●			●	●	●		●		Sandy beach on Monterey Bay. Tide pools. Sandstone outcroppings with arches. Annual monarch butterfly migration. Eucalyptus trees.
Navarro River Redwoods State Park, Elk	54 C2	CSP	727			●				●		●	●			Eleven mile stretch of redwood trees along the banks of the Navarro River. A road travels down the middle of what can be seen as a redwood tunnel.
New Brighton State Beach, Capitola	81 F7	CSP	93			●				●		●	●			Popular beach amidst a forest of pine and live oak trees.
North Fork Wilderness, Six Rivers National Forest	39 G1	USFS	7,999			●	●									Located on watershed of North Fork of Eel River. Steep, rugged terrain. Grass slopes with manzanita and scrub oak trees. Douglas fir and ponderosa pine trees. Winter range for black-tailed deer.
Oceano Dunes State Vehicular Recreation Area, Pismo Beach	113 F8	CSP	1,500		●	●	●	●	●	●		●	●	●		1,500 acres of coastal dunes. Motorcycles, dune buggies, four-wheel-drive and all-terrain vehicles.
Ocotillo Wells State Vehicular Recreation Area, Ocotillo Wells	151 F6	CSP	80,000						●			●				Dune buggy and motorcycle competitions. Four-wheel-drive and all-terrain vehicles. Sand dunes, hills, and washes.
Pacifica State Beach, San Pedro Valley	71 G7	CSP	21	●			●			●						Crescent shaped beach, very popular for surfing.
Palomar Mountain State Park, Palomar Mountain	149 D10	CSP	1,897		●	●	●				●	●	●	●		Forested area with pine, cedar, fir trees. West side of Palomar Mountain. Views of ocean and desert.
Patrick's Point State Park, Trinidad	30 C3	CSP	640		●	●	●				●	●	●	●		Headlands with meadows, forests, and cliffs. Beach, sea stacks, seals, sea lions, and migrating whales. Rock climbing.
Pelican State Beach, Winton Corners	22 A2	CSP	5			●						●				Path to sandy beach with dunes.
Pescadero State Beach, Pescadero	80 C3	CSP	665		●	●	●				●	●				Stairs and path to sandy beach with dunes and rocky shoreline. Stream corridor and bluff.
Pfeiffer Big Sur State Park, Big Sur	90 G3	CSP	821		●		●			●		●	●			Big Sur River. Canyons. Big Sur River Gorge. Coast redwoods. Pfeiffer Falls. Wildlife, birds, and spring wildflowers.
Picacho State Recreation Area, Picacho	158 A5	CSP	7,000		●	●	●			●	●	●	●		●	55 miles of open river. Picacho Peak, a plug-dome volcanic outcropping. Waterfowl (on Pacific Flyway). Wild burros. Bighorn sheep. Desert wildflowers. Desert and mountainous terrain with desert washes.
Pine Creek Wilderness, Cleveland National Forest	155 C8	USFS	13,480				●									2,000 to 4,000 feet. Gentle slopes. Pine Creek and other intermittent streams. Chaparral. Oak woodlands.
Pinnacles National Monument, Pinnacles	91 E8	NPS	26,470		●		●						●			Volcanic spires, canyons, crags, caves, rock formations. North Chalone Peak, 3,304 feet. Coast Range chaparral. Birds. Wildflowers. Rock climbing.
Pismo State Beach, Pismo Beach	113 E8	CSP	1,052		●	●	●	●		●	●	●	●	●		6 miles of beach. Extensive dune system. Pier. Surfing.
Placerita Canyon State Park, Newhall	128 G2	CSP	350				●					●				350-acre natural area. Oak trees. Stream.
Plumas National Forest, Quincy	51 B10	USFS	1,176,005	●		●	●	●	●	●		●	●		●	Grassy valleys, deep canyons, and mountainous terrain. Feather Falls Scenic Area. Lakes Basin with scenic lakes, interesting terrain, and historic areas. Skiing, and snowmobiling.
Plumas–Eureka State Park, Graeagle	52 D2	CSP	6,749	●	●	●	●					●	●	●		Mountainous terrain in the Sierra Nevada. Trails connect with Plumas National Forest. Winter snow play and cross-country skiing.
Point Dume State Beach, Malibu	139 D9	CSP	63		●					●	●					More than 0.5 mile of ocean frontage. Sandstone cliffs. Tide pooling. Surfing and diving.
Point Mugu State Park, Solromar	139 C7	CSP	15,000	●	●	●	●	●		●	●	●	●			Rocky bluffs, sandy beaches, sand dunes, hills, canyons and valleys among the Santa Monica Mountains. 5 miles of ocean shoreline. Birds and wildlife.
Point Reyes National Seashore, Point Reyes	70 B5	NPS	70,000	●	●		●	●			●	●		●		Peninsula in western Marin county. Highest point Mount Wittenberg, 1,407 feet. San Andreas fault. Variety of habitats. Over 300 species of birds. Marine mammals. Wildflowers. Point Reyes Lighthouse.
Pomponio State Beach, Pescadero	80 C3	CSP	421		●	●	●					●				Path to sandy beach with dunes and stream corridor. Bluff.
Portola State Park, La Honda	80 C5	CSP	2,800		●		●				●	●	●	●		Rugged canyon. Groves of redwoods. 14 miles of trails.
Prairie City State Vehicular Recreation Area, Alder Creek	65 C8	CSP	836						●			●				Varied off road terrain for motorcycles, all-terrain-vehicles and motorcycles includes open grasslands and rolling hills.
Prairie Creek Redwoods State Park, Orick	30 A4	CSP	14,500	●	●	●	●				●	●	●	●		Coast redwoods. Fern canyon. Herd of Roosevelt elk.
Providence Mountains State Recreation Area, Kelso	122 G2	CSP	5,900		●		●				●	●	●	●		Eastern Mojave Desert. Mitchell Caverns Nature Preserve. Rhyolite crags and cinder cones. Dunes. Wildflowers.
Red Buttes Wilderness, Klamath National Forest, Siskiyou National Forest, Rogue River National Forest	23 A10	USFS	20,230				●	●								Straddles California–Oregon border in Siskiyou Mountains. Steep and unstable slopes. Diverse and spectacular scenery. Abundant wildlife, including deer, bear, and bobcat.
Red Rock Canyon State Park, Cantil	118 C1	CSP	27,000		●		●		●			●	●	●		Colorful clay cliffs. Canyons. Buttes. Rock formations. Wildflowers.
Redwood National Park, Crescent City	22 D3	NPS	77,762	●	●	●	●	●			●	●	●	●		Redwood groves. Sandy beaches. Woodlands and streams. Birds, seals, sea lions, and Roosevelt elk.
Refugio State Beach, Capitan	125 F8	CSP	155	●	●	●	●			●		●	●			One of the Santa Barbara County State Beaches. 155 acres. 2.5-mile walk from El Capitan State Beach. Surfing.
Richardson Grove State Park, Garberville	47 A6	CSP	2,000		●	●	●			●		●	●	●		Coast redwoods on South Fork of Eel River.
Robert H Meyer Memorial State Beach, Malibu	139 C8	CSP	37							●		●		●		Sandy beach. Rocky cliffs.
Robert Louis Stevenson State Park, Calistoga	63 B6	CSP	5,000		●		●					●				Undeveloped parkland. Hike to summit of Mount St Helena. Old silver mines. Robert Louis Stevenson spent honeymoon here in 1880.
Robert W Crown Memorial State Beach, Alameda	71 E9	CSP	132	●						●		●		●		2.5-mile beach on east side of San Francisco Bay. Day use only. Sunbathing and windsurfing. Nature center and lawn areas. Paved trail.
Rogue River–Sisklyou National Forest, Dividend Bar	24 A3	USFS	53,800	●		●	●	●	●			●	●		●	Windy Peak and Scraggy Mountain of Siskiyou Mountains. Applegate River. Pacific Crest Trail on southern border.
Russian Gulch State Park, Mendocino	54 B1	CSP	1,162	●	●	●	●	●		●	●	●	●			Redwood groves. Sandy beaches with rocky shore. Bluff. Trails to Jackson Demonstration State Forest.
Russian Wilderness, Klamath National Forest	32 A3	USFS	12,000			●	●	●								Steep slopes, rock pinnacles, and glacial valleys. Alpine lakes. Abundant wildlife, including deer and bear.
Sacramento National Wildlife Refuge Complex, Logandale	56 A5	USFWS	35,000		●	●	●				●			●		Intensely managed area. Major stopover on Pacific Flyway. Geese, ducks, wading birds, raptors, quail, and pheasants.

Continued on page 18

Recreation Areas, *continued*

NAME, LOCATION	PAGE & GRID	ADMINISTRATION	ACREAGE	BIKING	INTERPRETIVE OPPORTUNITIES	FISHING	HIKING	HORSEBACK RIDING	OFF-HIGHWAY VEHICLE AREA	SWIMMING	WILDLIFE VIEWING	PICNICKING	CAMPING	VISITOR CENTER	BOATING	DESCRIPTION
Saddleback Butte State Park, Lancaster	129 C7	CSP	3,000		●		●	●				●	●	●		Antelope Valley. Saddleback Butte, 3,651 feet. Joshua trees. Birds. Wildlife includes the desert tortoise.
Salinas River State Beach, Moss Landing	90 A3	CSP	182			●	●	●			●	●				Wide sandy beach with extensive, undisturbed dune system. 3.5 miles of ocean frontage on Monterey Bay. Birds.
Salt Point State Park, Plantation	61 C10	CSP	5,970	●	●	●	●	●			●	●	●	●		Sandstone rocks; sandy coves; bluffs; and headlands with grassy areas, prairie, and pygmy forest. Gray whales sighted. Underwater park for divers.
Salton Sea State Recreation Area, Mecca	151 B9	CSP	336,000		●	●	●			●	●	●	●	●	●	Large 35-by-15-mile salt lake in the Colorado Desert. Birds include shore and wading birds and migratory waterfowl. Boat ramp. Nature trail.
Samuel P Taylor State Park, Jewell	70 B5	CSP	2,700	●	●		●	●				●	●			Fern-filled groves of redwoods contrast with dry grasslands.
San Bernardino National Forest, San Bernardino	142 A1	USFS	800,000	●		●	●	●	●		●	●	●			Meadows, rolling hills, peaks, cliffs, chaparral slopes, evergreen and oak forests. Lakes and streams. San Jacinto, Cucamonga, and San Gorgonio Wilderness Areas. Joshua trees. 227 species of birds.
San Bruno Mountain State Park, San Bruno	71 F8	CSP	2,326				●					●				Mountainous area. Trails.
San Buenaventura State Beach, Ventura	138 A5	CSP	109	●		●				●		●				Broad sandy beach. 2 miles of coastline.
San Clemente State Beach, San Clemente	148 C4	CSP	20		●	●	●			●		●	●			1 mile of long, narrow beach. Steep bluffs. Surfing.
San Elijo State Beach, Cardiff-by-the-Sea	154 A2	CSP	43		●					●			●			Sandy beach. 1.7 miles of ocean frontage. Bluff. Surfing.
San Gabriel Wilderness, Angeles National Forest	129 G6	USFS	36,118			●	●									San Gabriel Mountains, 1,600 to 8,200 feet. Rugged terrain. Grassy flats, streams, canyons. Chaparral. Mixed stands of spruce and oak.
San Gorgonio Wilderness, San Bernardino National Forest	143 C6	BLM/ USFS	94,702			●	●	●								Rugged San Gorgonio Mountains, 7,000 to 11,499 feet. High peaks. Vistas. Two small lakes. Meadows.
San Gregorio State Beach, San Gregorio	80 C3	CSP	172			●					●	●				Wetland. Path and stairs to sandy beach with rocky shore and stream corridor. Highly eroded bluffs.
San Jacinto Wilderness, San Bernardino National Forest	143 F7	USFS	32,248				●	●								On either side of Mount San Jacinto State Wilderness. Rugged and mountainous. San Jacinto Mountains. Desert to alpine.
San Luis Reservoir State Recreation Area, Santa Nella Village	82 E4	CSP	12,250		●	●	●	●		●		●	●		●	San Luis Reservoir, O'Neil Forebay, Los Banos Reservoir. Lakes are part of the California Aqueduct system.
San Onofre State Beach, San Onofre	148 D4	CSP	3,036			●	●						●			Actually two separate beaches: 3.5-mile San Onofre Beach North, and 1-mile Surf Beach, south of the power plant. Surfing. Whale-watching spot.
San Pablo National Wildlife Refuge, Sears Point	63 G8 71 A8	USFWS	20,000		●	●					●					North shore of San Pablo Bay. Mudflats, salt marsh, and open water. Pacific Flyway stop. Canvasbacks, loons, grebes, shorebirds, and wading birds.
San Rafael Wilderness, Los Padres National Forest	125 B10	USFS	197,380				●	●								San Rafael and Sierra Madre Mountains, 1,166 to 6,800 feet. Conifer forests. Chaparral slopes. Sisquoc and Manzana Rivers, Santa Cruz Creek. Hurricane Deck area rock formations.
San Simeon State Park, San Simeon	112 A4	CSP	541		●	●	●					●	●		●	Two miles of coastline. Sand beach. Stream through middle. Near Hearst–San Simeon State Historical Monument.
Santa Lucia Wilderness, Los Padres National Forest	113 D8	BLM/ USFS	21,678			●	●	●								Lopez Canyon, 800 to 3,000 feet. Riparian vegetation. Chaparral slopes.
Santa Monica Mountains National Recreation Area, Santa Monica	139 C10	NPS	154,000				●	●				●	●	●		Sandy beaches, lagoons. Hills, canyons, oak groves, meadows, waterfalls, valleys. Paramount Ranch. Whale watching. Surfing. Scuba diving.
Santa Monica State Beach, Santa Monica	140 D1	CSP	27							●		●				2 miles of wide sand beach. Pier cuts the beach into two sections. Bluff. Promenade. Volleyball. Basketball. Playground.
Santa Rosa Mountains State Wilderness, Anza–Borrego Desert State Park	150 C5	BLM/ USFS	70,132			●	●	●								Mountainous. Canyons, ridges, mesas, palm groves, and mountain mahogany. Wildlife includes bighorn sheep, mountain lions, bobcat, coyote, gray fox, and golden eagles.
Schooner Gulch State Beach, Point Arena	54 G2	CSP	54			●	●					●				Paths and stairs to sandy beach. Rugged headlands.
Seacliff State Beach, Aptos	81 F7	CSP	87		●	●	●			●		●	●	●		Sandy beach with pier and sunken concrete freighter.
Sequoia National Forest, Springville	117 A6	USFS	1,192,000	●		●	●	●	●	●		●	●		●	Canyons, lakes, streams, waterfalls, mountain meadows. High Sierra Primitive Area, Domeland Wilderness, Golden Trout Wilderness. Giant sequoias. Dome rock.
Sequoia National Park, Three Rivers	95 C9	NPS	403,879		●	●	●	●					●	●		Giant sequoias. Serrated ridges, peaks, cirques, canyons, peaks, moraines, valleys, glacial lakes. Mt Whitney, 14,495 feet. Kaweah River. Moro Rock. Giant Forest. Crystal Cave. Mineral King area.
Sheep Mountain Wilderness, Angeles National Forest	129 G9	USFS	44,000			●	●	●								Rugged. Mt Baldy, 10,064 feet. Chaparral. Conifer forest. Ancient limber pine trees. Nelson bighorn sheep.
Sierra National Forest, North Fork	85 D8	USFS	1,311,913			●	●	●	●			●	●		●	Grass, woodlands, river canyons, and mountainous areas. 13,986-foot Mount Humphreys. Adjoins Inyo National Forest and Kings Canyon National Park.
Silver Strand State Beach, Coronado	154 E3	CSP	3,709			●				●		●				On both sides of the sand spit connecting North Island to Imperial Beach. Over 1 mile of undeveloped beach on the south end.
Silverwood Lake State Recreation Area, Crestline	142 A1	CSP	2,400	●	●	●	●			●	●	●	●	●	●	Lake formed by the Cedar Springs Dam across the West Fork of the Mojave River. Migratory waterfowl. Chaparral.
Sinkyone Wilderness State Park, Four Corners	46 B5	CSP	7,367		●	●	●					●		●		Undeveloped wilderness. Rugged coast with small sandy beaches. Steep mountains. Redwoods. Seal, sea lion, and whale migrations. Roosevelt elk.
Siskiyou Wilderness, Klamath National Forest, Six Rivers National Forest, Siskiyou National Forest	23 B8	USFS	152,680				●	●								Open valleys and rock faces. Steep terrain and narrow ridgelines. Wet meadows and forests of Douglas fir and ponderosa pine trees.
Six Rivers National Forest, Eureka	22 C4	USFS	994,154			●	●	●				●	●		●	Named for six rivers (Smith, Klamath, Trinity, Mad, Van Duzen, Eel) that cut through area.
Smithe Redwoods State Reserve, Leggett	47 B6	CSP	665			●				●						Park with stands of redwoods along South Fork of Eel River.
Snow Mountain Wilderness, Mendocino National Forest	55 A10	USFS	37,679				●	●								Southernmost peak of North Coast Range. Varied terrain with rocky bluffs and flat, eroded areas. Chapparel brush, Douglas and red firs, and ponderosa pine trees. Wildlife includes black-tailed deer, black bear, and eagles.
Sonny Bono Salton Sea National Wildlife Refuge, Fondo	152 F1	USFWS	37,484		●						●			●		Desert scrub, freshwater marshes, farmlands, mudflats, treed coverstrips, open water and shore areas. Over 400 species of wildlife. Southernmost part of Pacific Flyway. Wintering waterfowl. Shorebirds. Yuma clapper rail.
Sonoma Coast State Beach, Bridge Haven	62 E2	CSP	9,044		●	●	●	●			●	●	●		●	13-mile stretch includes 17 beaches. Some steep paths, hazardous surf and strong currents. Underwater park for divers along full length.
Soquel Demonstration State Forest, Twin Creeks	81 E7	CDFFP	2,681	●			●	●				●				On the East Branch of Soquel River. Geologically active. Rugged terrain.
South Carlsbad State Beach, Carlsbad	149 G6	CSP	118		●	●				●		●	●			3.6 miles of sandy beach. Surfing.
South Sierra Wilderness, Inyo National Forest/Sequoia National Forest	106 A4	USFS	62,700				●	●								Sierra Nevada Crest. Steep terrain. 6,100 to 12,123 feet. South Fork of the Kern River. Pinyon–juniper, mixed pine trees, meadows, forested ridges, rolling hills, high peaks. Pacific Crest Trail.
South Warner Wilderness, Modoc National Forest	37 A7	USFS	70,614			●	●	●								Alpine meadows, lakes, and peaks of the Cascade Range. 90 miles of trails. Snowshoeing and cross-country skiing.
South Yuba River state Park, Edwards Crossing	58 B5	CSP	10,560		●	●	●			●		●				Mostly forested acres bisected by South Yuba River.
Standish–Hickey State Recreation Area, Leggett	47 C7	CSP	1,070		●		●			●		●	●			South Fork of Eel River offers up many scenic vistas in Gold Rush territory.
Stanislaus National Forest, Sonora	67 G8	USFS	898,121	●		●	●	●	●	●		●	●		●	Western slope of the Sierra Nevada. Several rivers cut deep canyons.
Sugarloaf Ridge State Park, Kenwood	63 D7	CSP	2,700		●		●	●				●	●	●		Coastal mountains with chaparral-covered ridges, wooded groves, and meadows. Wildflowers.
Sunset State Beach, Palm Beach	81 G8	CSP	300		●	●	●			●		●	●			Popular beach with soaring dunes, surrounded by agricultural fields.
Tahoe National Forest, Nevada City	60 B2	USFS	870,392	●		●	●	●	●	●		●	●		●	Steep canyons. At lower elevations forest composed of oak, brush, and grasslands giving way to pine, cedar, and fir trees. Excellent views from crest above tree line.
Tahoe State Recreation Area, Tahoe City	60 C2	CSP	57			●				●		●	●			Lakeshore park with boating facilities. Water sports.
The Forest of Nisene Marks State Park, Santa Cruz	81 F7	CSP	10,000	●			●	●				●				Rugged terrain. Trails and fire roads.
Thousand Lake Wilderness, Lassen National Forest	34 G5	USFS	16,355				●	●								Pine forests and open meadows. Elevations range 5,000–9,000 feet. Lava and granite formations. Thousand Lakes Valley. Magee and Crater Peaks.
Tolowa Dunes State Park, Crescent City	22 C2	CSP	5,000	●	●	●	●	●			●	●			●	Wetlands, forests, meadows, lakes, and ocean beaches provides a variety of ecological communities. Wildflowers, birds, deer, coyote, sea lions, harbor seals, and gray whales present.
Tomales Bay State Park, Marconi	70 A4	CSP	2,000		●	●	●			●		●				Point Reyes Peninsula. Shallow, surf-free beaches. Canyons and rocky headlands. Bishop pine trees. Wildflowers. Land and sea birds.

Recreation Areas

NAME, LOCATION	PAGE & GRID	ADMINISTRATION	ACREAGE	BIKING	INTERPRETIVE OPPORTUNITIES	FISHING	HIKING	HORSEBACK RIDING	OFF-HIGHWAY VEHICLE AREA	SWIMMING	WILDLIFE VIEWING	PICNICKING	CAMPING	VISITOR CENTER	BOATING	DESCRIPTION
Topanga State Park, Topanga	139 C10	CSP	12,655	●	●		●	●			●	●				Wilderness area within the city of Los Angeles, replete with trails transversing forested and grass areas. Chaparral, oak woodlands, grasslands, streams, canyons. Ocean view.
Torrey Pines State Beach, San Diego	154 A2	CSP	61		●	●	●			●		●				Sandy, wide 4.5-mile beach. Bluff. Formerly part of Torrey Pines State Reserve. Surfing.
Torrey Pines State Reserve, Sorrento	154 B2	CSP	1,446		●		●							●		The rare torrey pine tree is preserved in this piece of wilderness within the San Diego area. Mostly chapparal and marsh. Hiking on trails only.
Trinidad State Beach, Trinidad	30 D3	CSP	159			●	●	●				●				Sandy beach with rocky shore. Creek. Bluff.
Trinity Alps Wilderness, Six Rivers National Forest, Klamath, Shasta–Trinity National Forest	32 C4	BLM/ USFS	525,627			●	●	●								Rugged mountain ridges and deep canyons. Scattered timber stands, rock cliffs, and large meadows. Elevations range 2,000–9,000 feet.
Tule Elk State Reserve, Tupman	115 C9	CSP	953		●						●	●		●		Tule elk viewing area.
Tule Lake National Wildlife Refuge, Tulelake	26 A5	USFWS	39,116		●						●			●		Major Pacific Flyway migration stopover in Klamath Basin National Wildlife Refuge Complex. Raptors seen in cliffs. Marked canoe trail to viewing areas.
Turlock Lake State Recreation Area, Warnerville	74 F4	CSP	409		●	●	●			●	●	●	●		●	Aquatic recreation area bounded by Tuolumne River on north and Turlock Lake on South.
Twin Lakes State Beach, Twin Lakes	81 G6	CSP	94			●	●			●	●					1 mile of sandy shoreline is excellent for birdwatching.
Van Damme State Park, Mendocino	54 B1	CSP	1,831	●	●	●	●			●		●	●	●		Beach and upland area with pygmy forest, fern canyon, and bog.
Ventana Wilderness, Los Padres National Forest	100 A5	BLM/ USFS	240,024			●	●	●								Ridges, valleys, chaparral slopes, woodlands, pine, streams, canyons, waterfalls. Santa Lucia Mountains, 600 to 5,862 feet. Rock formations. Bristlecone pine trees (Santa Lucia fir).
Westport–Union Landing State Beach, Westport	47 E6	CSP	57			●	●					●				Sandy beach. Rocky shore. Creek.
Whiskeytown–Shasta–Trinity National Recreation Area, Whiskeytown	41 B6	NPS	203,587	●		●	●	●		●		●	●	●	●	Large area, including three lakes in separate units. Surrounding shorelines, islands, and uplands.
Will Rogers State Beach, Pacific Palisades	140 C1	CSP	82	●		●				●						Wide beach, several miles long with even surf. Surfing. Diving.
William R Hearst Memorial State Beach, San Simeon	101 G8	CSP	8		●	●				●		●			●	Sandy beach. Adjacent to Hearst Castle. San Simeon Point. Pier.
Woodson Bridge State Recreation Area, Corning	50 B1	CSP	325		●	●	●					●	●			Small park of oak woods along Sacramento River.
Yolla Bolly–Middle Eel Wilderness, Mendocino National Forest, Shasta–Trinity National Forest	40 G4	BLM/ USFS	180,877			●	●	●								Rugged terrain with dense stands of pine and firs. Yolla Bolly Mountains. Headwaters of Middle Fork of Eel River. Wildlife includes bear and deer.
Yosemite National Park, Yosemite	75 D10	NPS	759,539	●	●	●	●	●		●		●	●	●	●	Yosemite features waterfalls, domes, pinnacles, canyons, lakes, two rivers, and three groves of giant sequoia.
Zmudowski State Beach, Moss Landing	90 A3	CSP	156			●	●	●			●					Sandy beach. Undeveloped. Dune system. Surfing.

Unique Natural Features

AMBOY CRATER – 2 miles west of Amboy – 132 E5 Basalt cinder cone rises 246 feet above desert floor. Surrounded by lava flows. Moderately difficult hike on poorly maintained trail.

ARCH ROCK – Anacapa Island – 138 D4 40-foot natural bridge formed by sea erosion. Hiking and picnicking.

BADWATER – Death Valley National Park – 109 A6 Salt pools and formations, 282 feet below sea level.

BOYDEN CAVERN – Sequoia National Forest – 95 A9 Stalagmites, stalactites, columns and other formations. Guided tours.

BRANDY CREEK FALLS – Whiskeytown–Shasta–Trinity National Recreation Area – 41 B6 Falls form as series of underground springs come above ground. Located 5 miles down old logging trails, accessible by horse or foot.

BRIDALVEIL FALLS – Yosemite National Park – 76 E2; 20 E4 Powerful falls drop 620 feet to valley floor. Located across from face of El Capitan. Short walk from parking area to base of falls.

BRISTLECONE PINE FOREST – Big Pine – 87 B9 28,000 acres of gnarled pines up to 4,000 years old.

BUMPASS HELL – Lassen Volcanic National Park – 43 C6 Geothermal area featuring hot springs, steaming fumaroles, mudpots and boiling pools. Accessible only by 1.5-mile trail.

BURNEY FALLS – McArthur–Burney State Park – 34 D4 129-foot double waterfall cascades over basalt cliffs in lush forest setting.

CALIFORNIA CAVERNS AT CAVE CITY – Mountain Ranch – 66 G4 Large horizontal limestone cave with many chambers. Stalagmites and stalactites. Jungle Room with vinelike formations.

CASTLE CRAGS – Castle Crags State Park – 33 C9 Steep rugged rock formations rise 4,000 feet. Glacier-polished and weathered granite spires.

CHAGOOPA FALLS – Kings Canyon National Park – 96 E2 Falls of small stream drop 500 feet in Kern Canyon. Reached via hiking trails.

CHAOS CRAGS – Lassen Volcanic National Park – 42 C5 Young plug dome volcano formed by mass of molten lava. Last steaming in 1850.

CIMA DOME AND CIMA VOLCANIC FIELD – 55 miles northwest of Cima – 122 D1 Rounded granite pediment with lava formations and volcanic cones. Teutonia Peak is 5,755 feet high. Hiking trails.

CINDER CONE – Lassen Volcanic National Park – 43 B7 Extinct basaltic volcano formed from cinders and lava flows around vent.

CINDER CONES – 15 miles west of Cima – 121 E10 More than thirty cones including ash, cinder, parasitic and breached cones.

COLUMNS OF THE GIANTS – Stanislaus National Forest – 67 F10 Columns formed from two separate flows that cooled at different rates. Eroded basalt. 0.25-mile trail.

CONFUSION HILL – Piercy – 47 B6 Gravity appears to be defied through contradictory optical and physical sensations.

CRYSTAL CAVE – Sequoia National Park – 95 D9 Limestone formations. Guided tours.

CRYSTAL CREEK FALLS – Whiskeytown – 41 A6 Series of cascades in area of virgin timber, on East Fork of Crystal Creek. Falls drop about 200 feet. Accessible by 2-mile walk on old logging roads.

DARDANELLES CONES – Stanislaus National Forest – 67 E10 Part of lava flow from volcanoes near Bridgeport. Flowed down river bed. On ridge top, cones are large protrusions formed of basalt, turned brownish from weathering.

DARWIN FALLS – 5 miles northeast of Darwin – 97 G10 Falls formed by water from underground springs. Water disappears underground short distance from falls. Microhabitat in surrounding desert. Access via 0.75-mile hiking trail.

DEEP CREEK HOT SPRING – San Bernardino National Forest – 130 G3 Mineral water averages 108 degrees Fahrenheit. Accessible by 6-mile trail along Deep Creek.

DEVIL'S PLAYGROUND – 18 miles southeast of Baker – 121 F9 Westerly winds drive sand to area where winds from north, south and east converge.

DEVILS POSTPILE – Devils Postpile National Monument – 77 F6 60-foot columnar basalt formation created by volcanic flow.

FALLS OF THE MCCLOUD RIVER – McCloud – 34 B1 Three waterfalls tumble through sheer-walled gorge.

FEATHER FALLS – Plumas National Forest – 51 E8 640-foot waterfall. 3.5-mile access trail.

GLASS MOUNTAIN – Modoc National Forest – 27 E6 Volcanic flow of glossy obsidian, covering 4,210 acres.

GRIZZLY FALLS – Sequoia National Forest – 95 A9 100-foot falls on Grizzly Creek. Easily accessible from road.

GROVER HOT SPRINGS – South Lake Tahoe – 67 B10 Non-sulphurous springs fill two pools at 80 and 102 degrees Fahrenheit.

HOT CREEK GEYSER – north of Toms Place – 77 F8 Small hot geysers.

ILLILOUETTE FALLS – Yosemite National Park – 76 E2; 21 F6 Drop of 370 feet over granite walls.

KELSO SAND DUNES – 24 miles north of Amboy – 132 A5 Sand slides cause deep, rumbling sound. Tallest dune is about 560 feet.

KERN HOT SPRING – Sequoia National Park – 96 E2 Spring next to Upper Kern River averages 115 degrees Fahrenheit. Three days' hike from nearest road.

LA JOLLA CAVES – La Jolla – 154 B2 Caves in sandstone cliffs formed by wave action. Accessible via staircase. Gift shop.

LAKE SHASTA CAVERNS – O'Brien – 33 G9 Limestone caverns with stalactite and stalagmite formations.

LAS CRUCES HOT SPRING – 2 miles north of Gaviota State Park – 125 E7 Natural mineral water averages 90–96 degrees Fahrenheit. 1,100 yards by trail to spring.

LAVA BEDS NATIONAL MONUMENT CAVES – Tulelake – 27 D6 21 lava tube caves. Access by Cave Loop Road.

MASONIC CAVES – Volcano – 66 D3 Limestone caverns just south of town. Used by Masons for meetings in 1850.

MCWAY COVE WATERFALL – Julia Pfeiffer Burns State Park – 100 A4 Falls drop 70 feet from McWay Creek to ocean. Hiking. Picnicking.

MERCER CAVERNS – Murphys – 74 A4 Crystalline formations. Guided tours.

MIST FALLS – Kings Canyon National Park – 96 A1 Rolling falls on Kings River which drop 100 feet.

MITCHELL CAVERNS AND WINDING STAIR CAVERNS – Providence Mountains State Recreation Area – 133 A7 Dripstone, flowstone, curtains, pillars, stalactites and stalagmites. Lighting, stairs, and railings. Guided tours.

MOANING CAVERN – Vallecito – 74 A4 Vertical cave with large main chamber. First explored during Gold Rush Days. Stairs. Formations and Indian remains. Guided tours.

MONO LAKE TUFA – Lee Vining – 77 C7 Tufa formations formed from interaction of spring water with alkaline lake water. Self-guided nature trail.

MORRO ROCK – Morro Bay – 113 C6 Plug dome volcanic outcropping at entrance to Morro Bay. 576 feet above sea level. Peregrine falcon nesting site. Fishing, swimming and picnicking.

MT SAN ANTONIO (OLD BALDY) – Angeles National Forest – 141 A9 Highest peak in San Gabriel Mountains at 10,064 feet. Northeast of Los Angeles. Hiking trails.

MT SHASTA – Shasta–Trinity National Forest – 25 G10 14,162 foot peak. Timberline at 8,000 feet Glaciers, hot spring, crater and lake. Hiking trail to summit.

MT WHITNEY – Lone Pine, Sequoia National Park – 96 D3 At 14,495 feet, summit is highest point in contiguous United States. Hiking trails.

NATURAL BRIDGE – Weaverville – 40 C2 Limestone arch crosses 200-foot ravine.

NEEDLES – Sequoia National Forest – 106 B1 Pinnacle-shaped volcanic plugs. Highest peak is 2,200 feet.

NEVADA FALLS – Yosemite National Park – 76 E2; 21 E7 Falls drop 594 feet.

NOJOQUI FALLS – Los Padres National Forest – 125 E7 Year-round cascading falls drop 164 feet. Hiking. Picnicking.

OLD FAITHFUL GEYSER – Calistoga – 63 C6 Fed by underground river, water heats up and erupts every 40 minutes.

PETRIFIED FOREST – Calistoga – 63 C6 Redwood trees turned to stone through volcanic activity.

PINNACLES – Pinnacles National Monument – 91 E8 Ancient volcano carved by elements into precipitous bluffs, spires and crags. Formations 500–1,200 feet. high. Hiking. Picnicking.

THE RACETRACK – Death Valley National Park – 97 C9 Dry lake bed where large rocks are moved by high velocity winds. Trails of the rocks can be seen in mud.

RAINBOW BASIN – 12 miles north of Barstow Way Station – 119 G9 Fossilized bones in sedimentary rock include those of North American mastodon, pronghorn, large and small camel, three-toed horse, rhinoceros and oreodont. Hiking, riding and picnicking.

RAINBOW FALLS – Devils Postpile National Monument – 77 G6 101-foot falls on middle Fork of San Joaquin River.

RED ROCK CANYON STATE PARK – Cantil – 118 C1 Exposed rock consisting of lake sediment and volcanic materials. Scenic cliff faces. Hiking trails.

RIBBON FALLS – Yosemite National Park – 76 E2; 20 E4 Second tallest falls in Yosemite Valley with a drop of 1,612 feet.

ROARING RIVER FALLS – Kings Canyon National Park – 95 B10 Fast-moving, powerful falls drop 40 feet. Just off US 180. Short walk from parking area to base of falls.

SENTINEL FALLS – Yosemite National Park – 76 E2; 20 E5 Sentinel Falls stand along side towering Sentinel Rock.

SESPE HOT SPRING – Los Padres National Forest, Ojai RD – 127 D7 Natural mineral water spring averages 185 degrees Fahrenheit. Accessible by motorcycle or hiking trail. Camping.

SUBWAY CAVE – Lassen National Forest – 43 A6 Lava tube, 0.25 mile long. Several chambers. Trail from parking lot.

SULPHUR WORKS – Lassen Volcanic National Park – 42 D5 Thermal area. Steam vents, boilers and bubbling mud pots.

TOKOPAH FALLS – Sequoia National Park – 95 C10 Large falls cascade 1,200 feet. Accessible by 1.7-mile hiking trail from Lodgepole Ranger Station.

TRONA PINNACLES – 10 miles south of Trona – 108 G1 More than 500 pinnacles composed of deposits of calcium carbonate up to 100 feet tall. Hiking trails.

VASQUEZ ROCKS – Agua Dulce – 128 F3 Moon-like landscape consisting of massive slabs of smoothed and uplifted sandstone, some forming caves. Hiking. Picnic area.

VERNAL FALLS – Yosemite National Park – 76 E2; 21 E7 Vernal Falls, drop 317 feet. Especially impressive during spring melting.

WHIPPLE MOUNTAINS – 20 miles west of Parker Dam – 147 A6 Pinnacles, natural bridges, sedimentary rock and eroded spires.

YOSEMITE FALLS – Yosemite National Park – 76 E2; 20 D5 Yosemite Falls drops 2,425 feet over three steps.

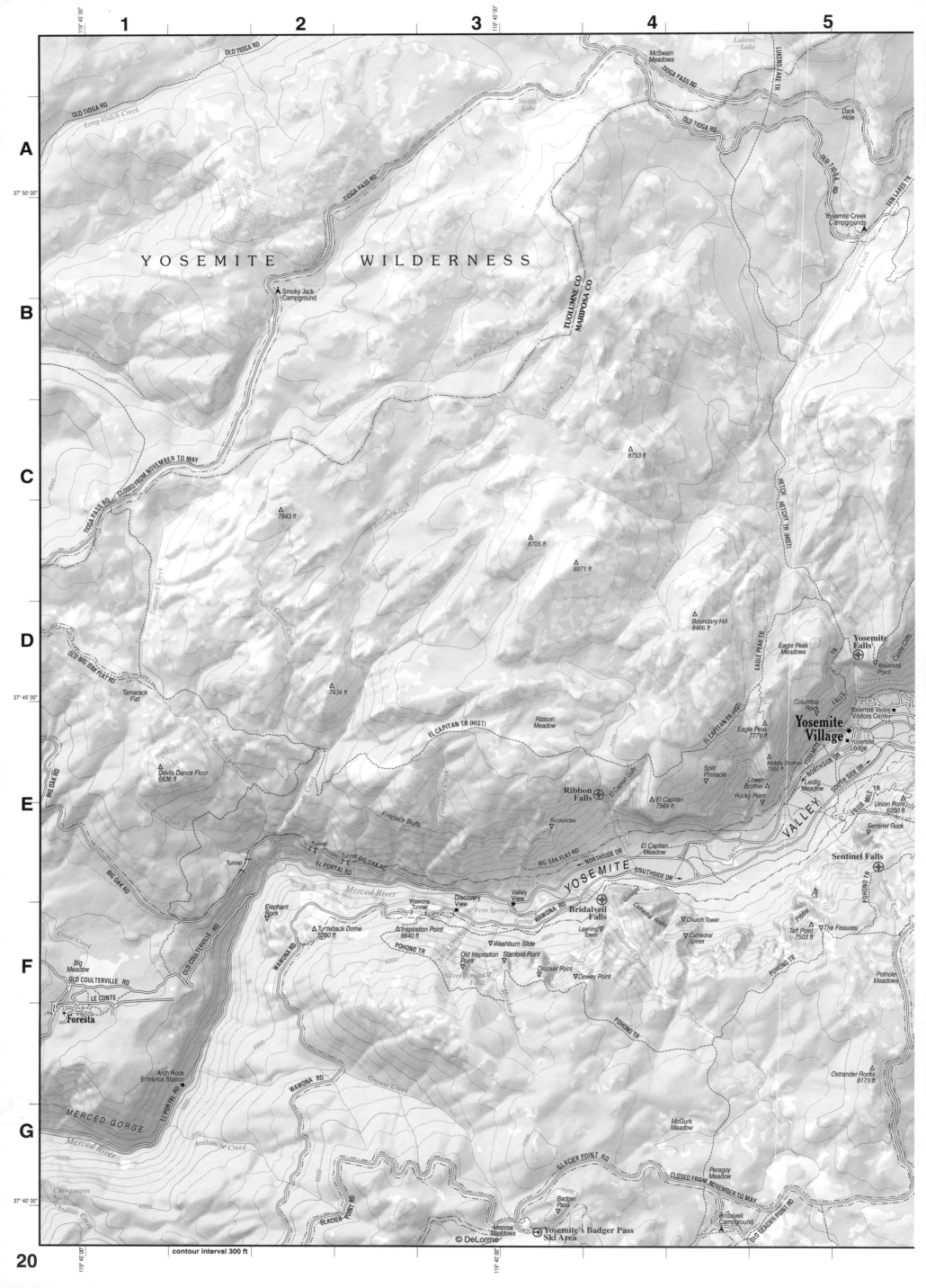

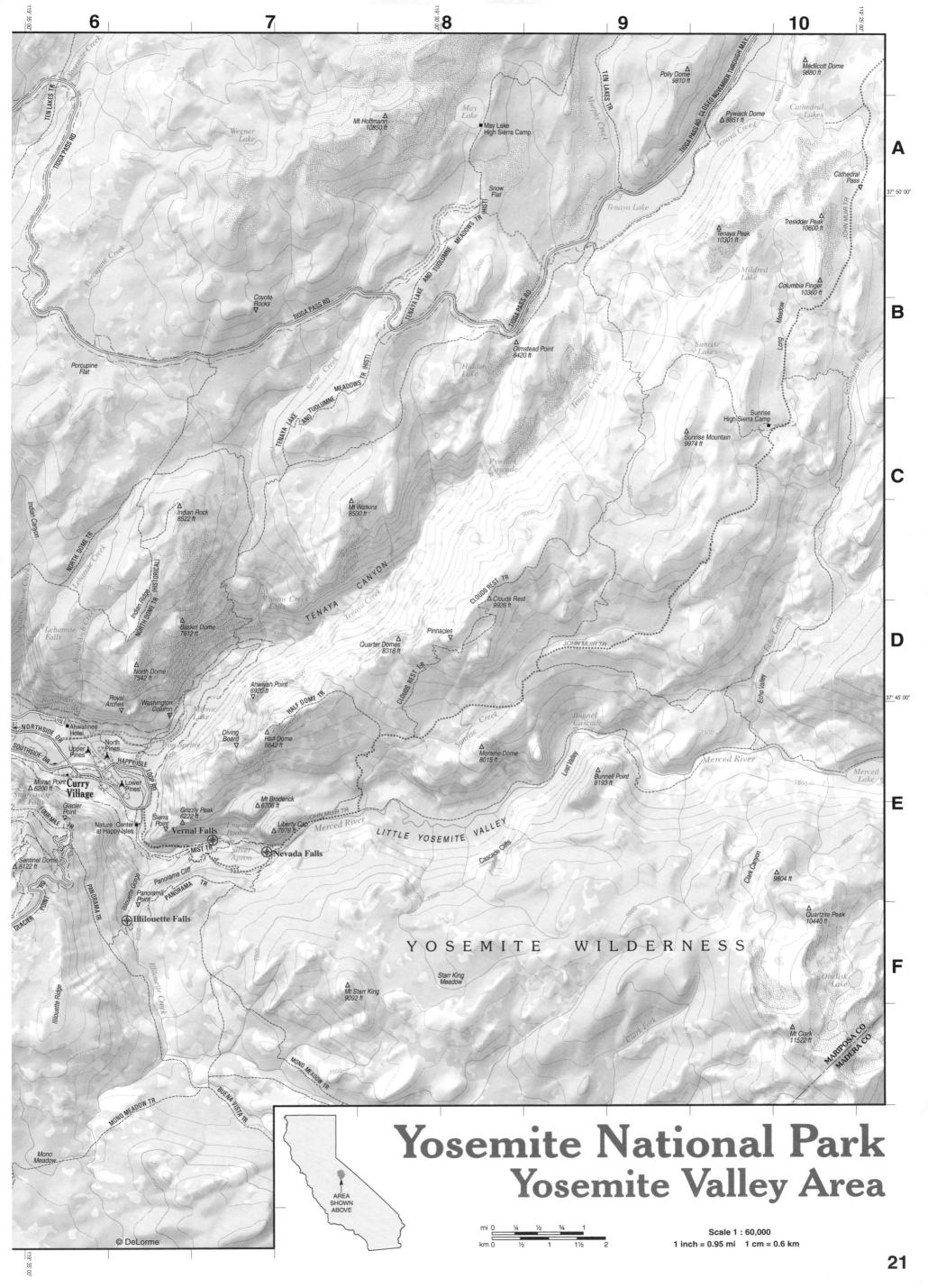

Yosemite National Park
Yosemite Valley Area

Scale 1 : 60,000
1 inch = 0.95 mi   1 cm = 0.6 km

mi 0   ¼   ½   ¾   1
km 0   ½   1   1½   2

AREA SHOWN ABOVE

© DeLorme

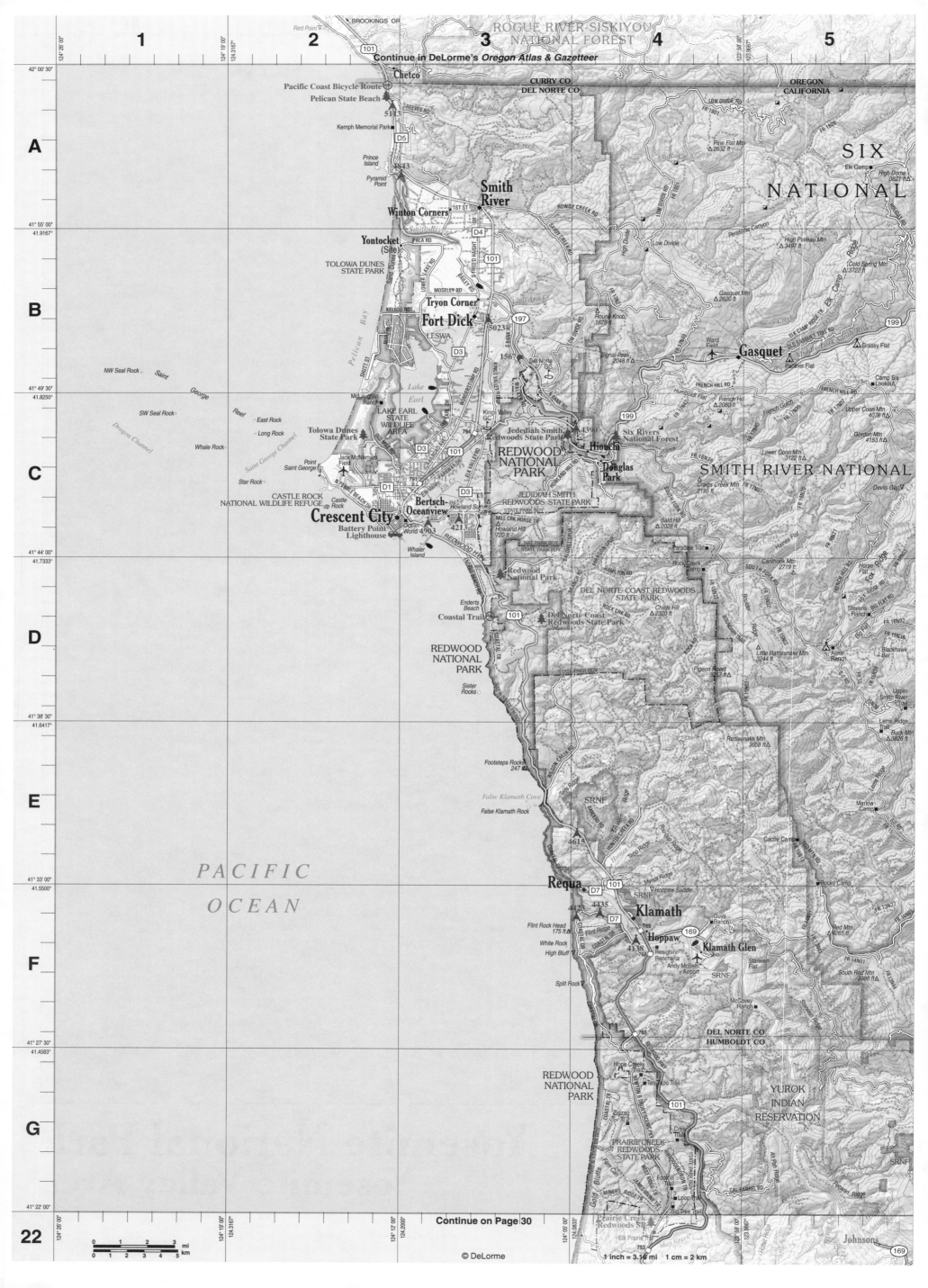

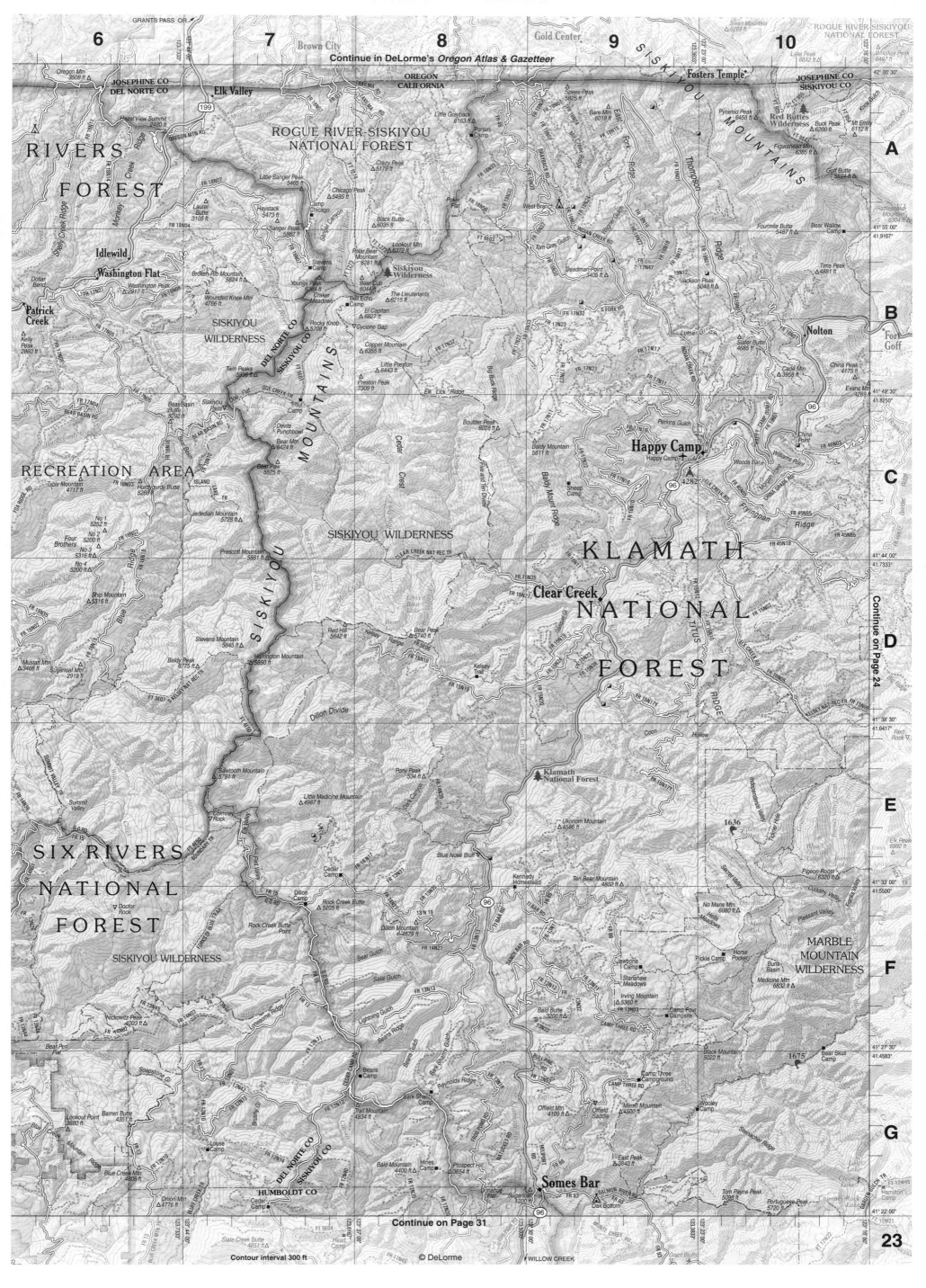

GRANTS PASS OR

ROGUE RIVER-SIKIYOU
NATIONAL FOREST

JOSEPHINE CO
DEL NORTE CO

JOSEPHINE CO
SISKIYOU CO

Fosters Temple

Red Buttes
Wilderness

Elk Valley

RIVERS

FOREST

ROGUE RIVER-SISKIYOU
NATIONAL FOREST

SISKIYOU MOUNTAINS

Idlewild

Washington Flat

Patrick
Creek

SISKIYOU
WILDERNESS

Nolton

Fort
Goff

SISKIYOU MOUNTAINS

RECREATION AREA

Happy Camp

KLAMATH

Clear Creek

NATIONAL

SISKIYOU WILDERNESS

FOREST

Klamath
National Forest

SIX RIVERS

NATIONAL

FOREST

SISKIYOU WILDERNESS

MARBLE
MOUNTAIN
WILDERNESS

DEL NORTE CO
SISKIYOU CO

HUMBOLDT CO

Somes Bar

A

B

C

D

E

F

G

23

Continue on Page 24

Continue on Page 31

Contour interval 300 ft

© DeLorme

WILLOW CREEK

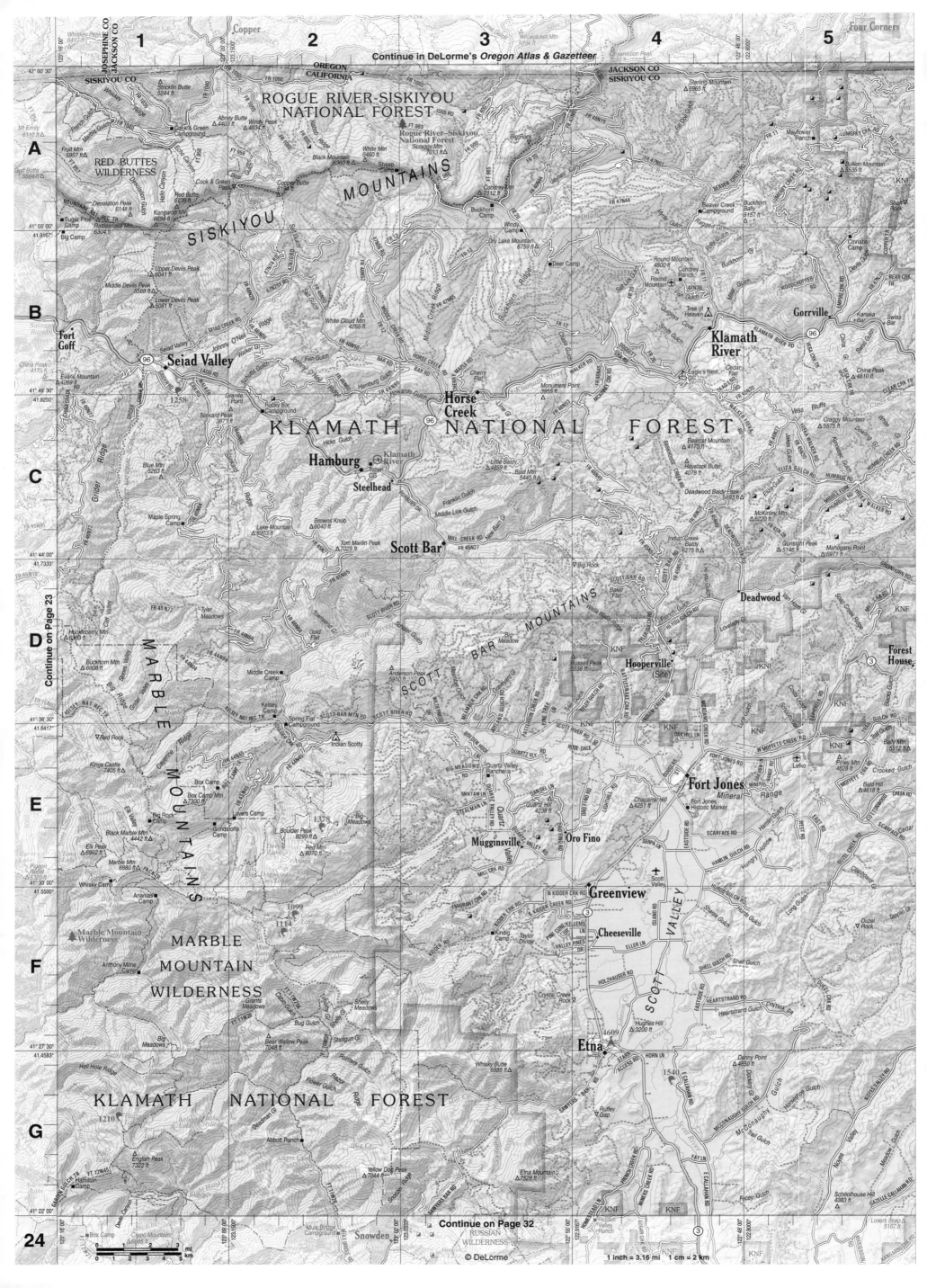

Continue in DeLorme's *Oregon Atlas & Gazetteer*

ROGUE RIVER-SISKIYOU
NATIONAL FOREST

SISKIYOU   MOUNTAINS

RED BUTTES
WILDERNESS

KLAMATH   NATIONAL   FOREST

Seiad Valley

Fort Goff

Horse Creek

Hamburg

Steelhead

Scott Bar

Klamath River

Gorrville

Deadwood

Forest House

Hooperville (Site)

SCOTT   BAR   MOUNTAINS

Continue on Page 23

MARBLE   MOUNTAINS

Fort Jones

Mugginsville

Oro Fino

Greenview

Cheeseville

MARBLE
MOUNTAIN
WILDERNESS

KLAMATH   NATIONAL   FOREST

Etna

Continue on Page 32

RUSSIAN
WILDERNESS

Snowden

24

1 inch = 3.16 mi   1 cm = 2 km

© DeLorme

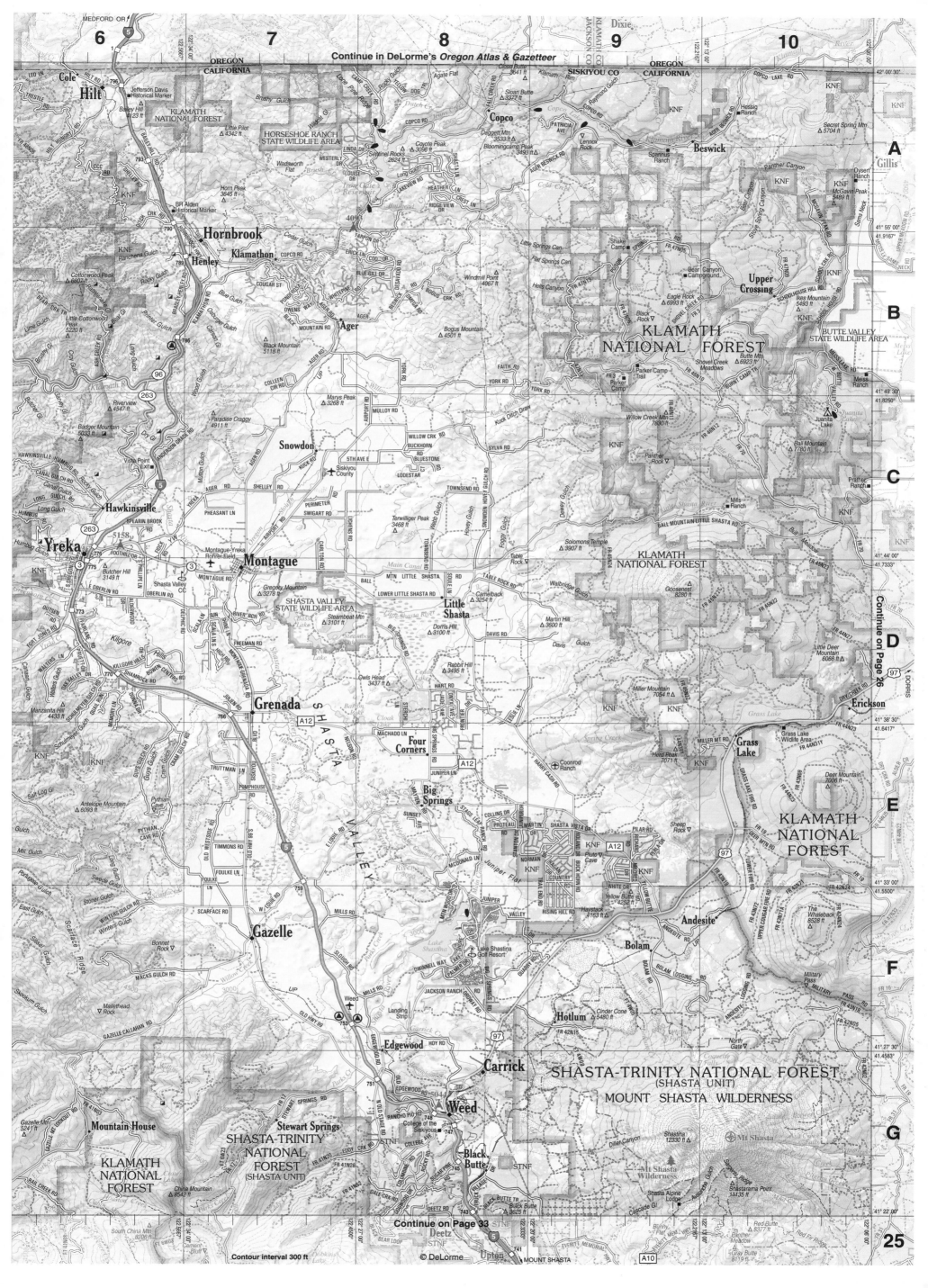

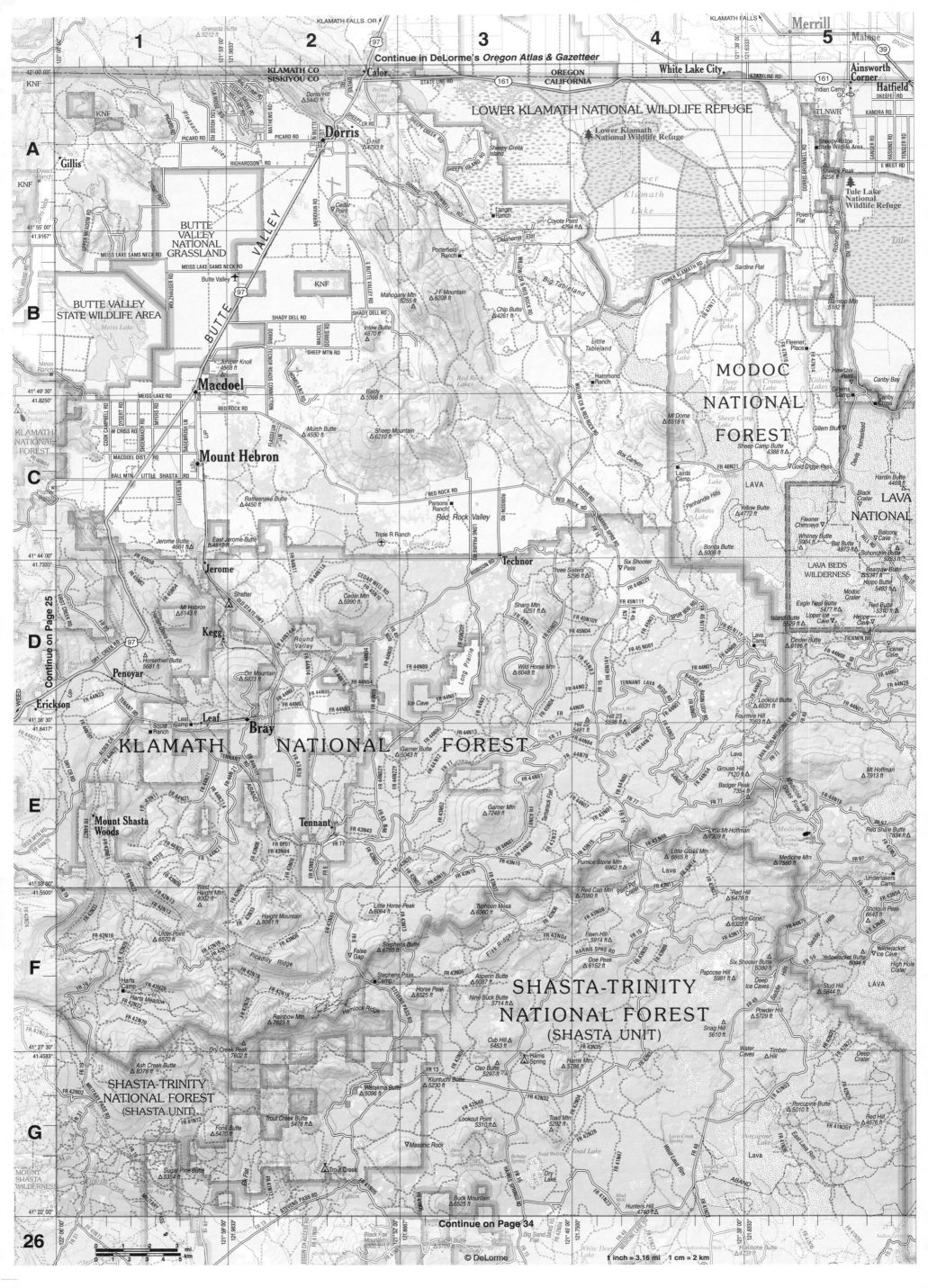

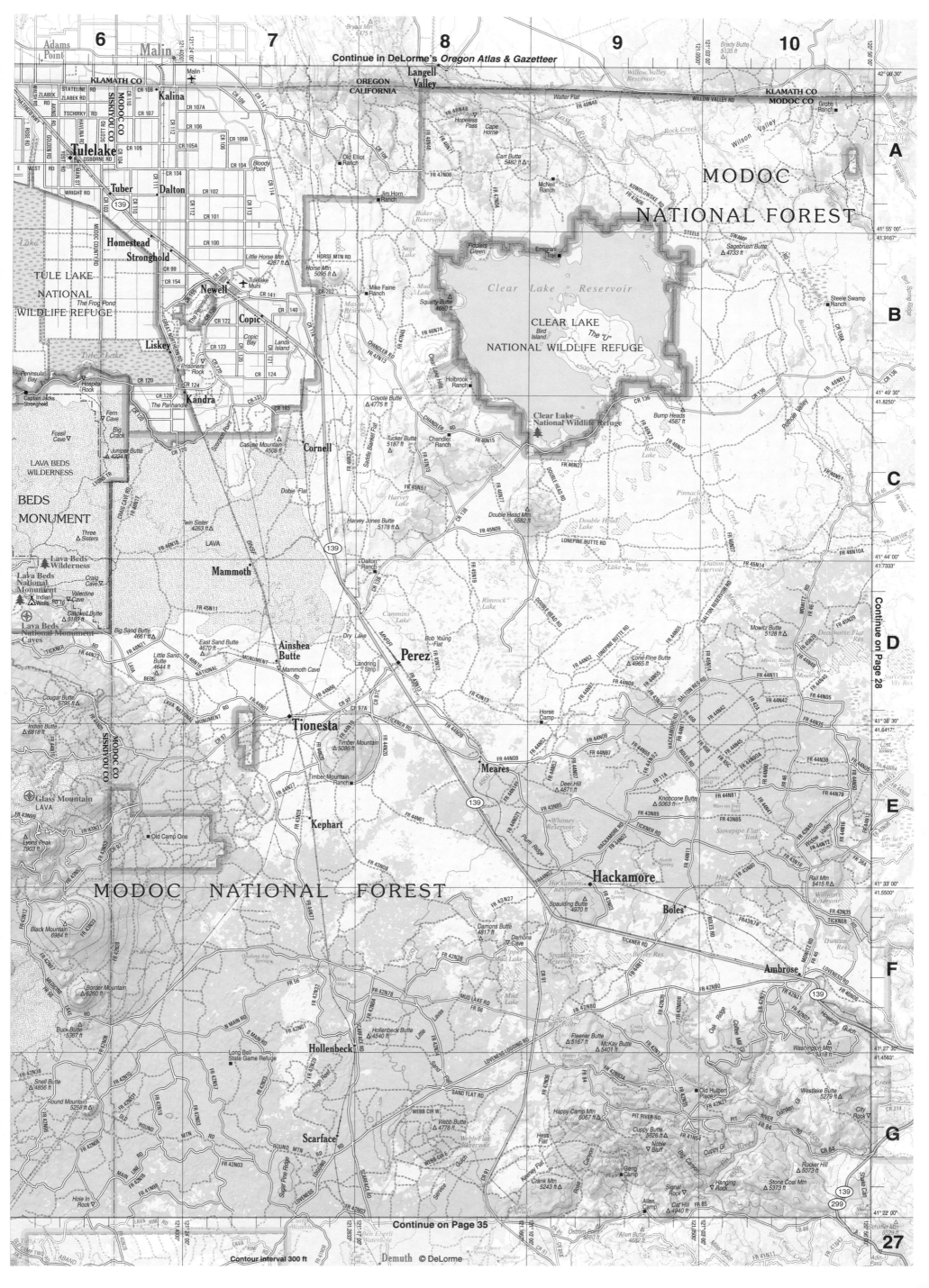

Continue in DeLorme's *Oregon Atlas & Gazetteer*

MODOC

NATIONAL FOREST

CLEAR LAKE
NATIONAL WILDLIFE REFUGE

Clear Lake Reservoir

The "U"

TULE LAKE
NATIONAL
WILDLIFE REFUGE

LAVA BEDS
WILDERNESS

BEDS
MONUMENT

Lava Beds
Wilderness

Lava Beds
National Monument

Lava Beds
National Monument
Caves

Tulelake

Malin

Newell

Copic

Liskey

Kandra

Cornell

Mammoth

Ainshea
Butte

Perez

Tionesta

Meares

Kephart

Glass Mountain
LAVA

MODOC   **NATIONAL**   **FOREST**

Hackamore

Boles

Ambrose

Hollenbeck

Scarface

Continue on Page 28

Contour interval 300 ft

Demuth © DeLorme

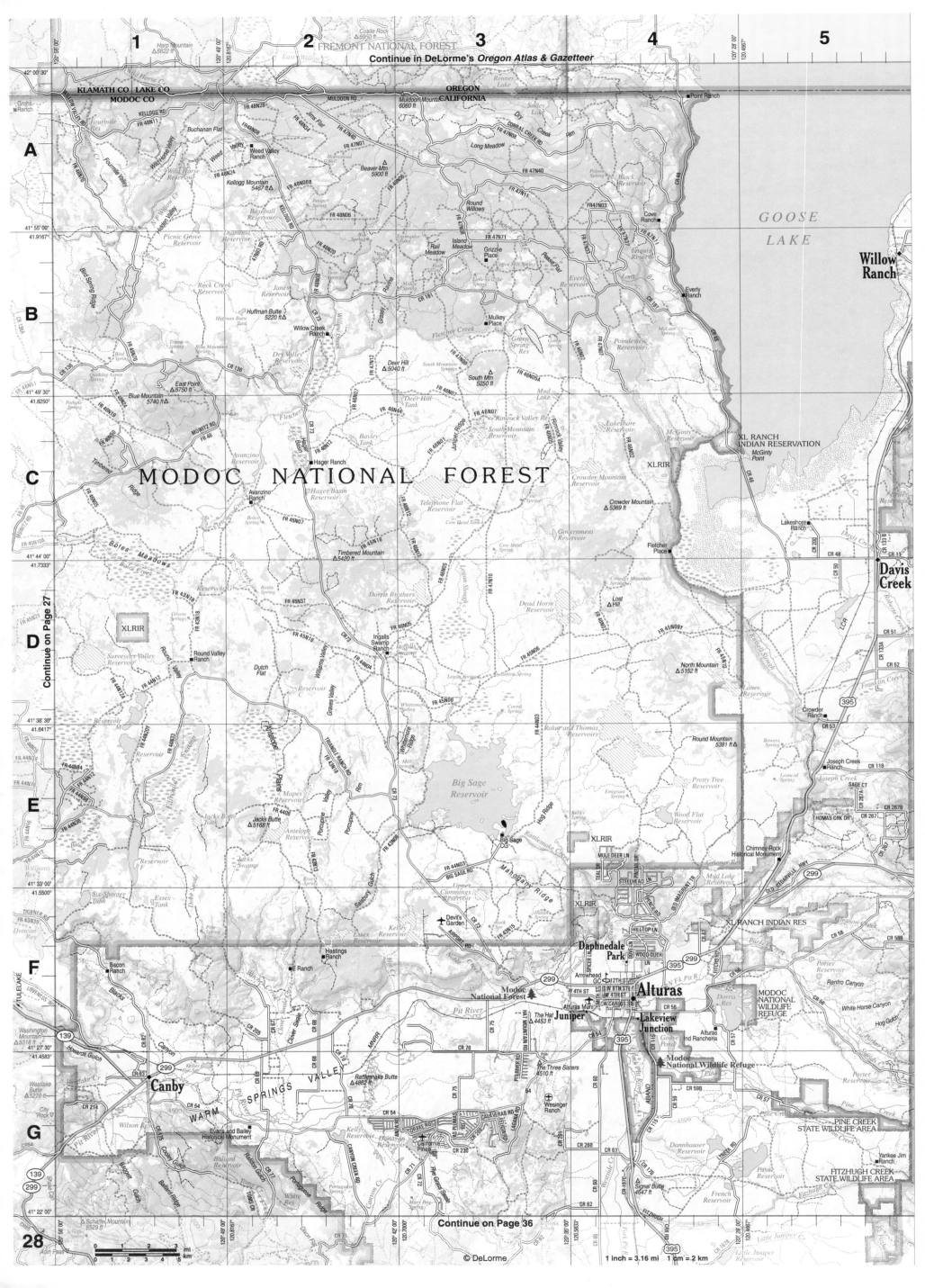

MODOC NATIONAL FOREST

Continue on Page 27

Continue on Page 36

1 inch = 3.16 mi   1 cm = 2 km

© DeLorme

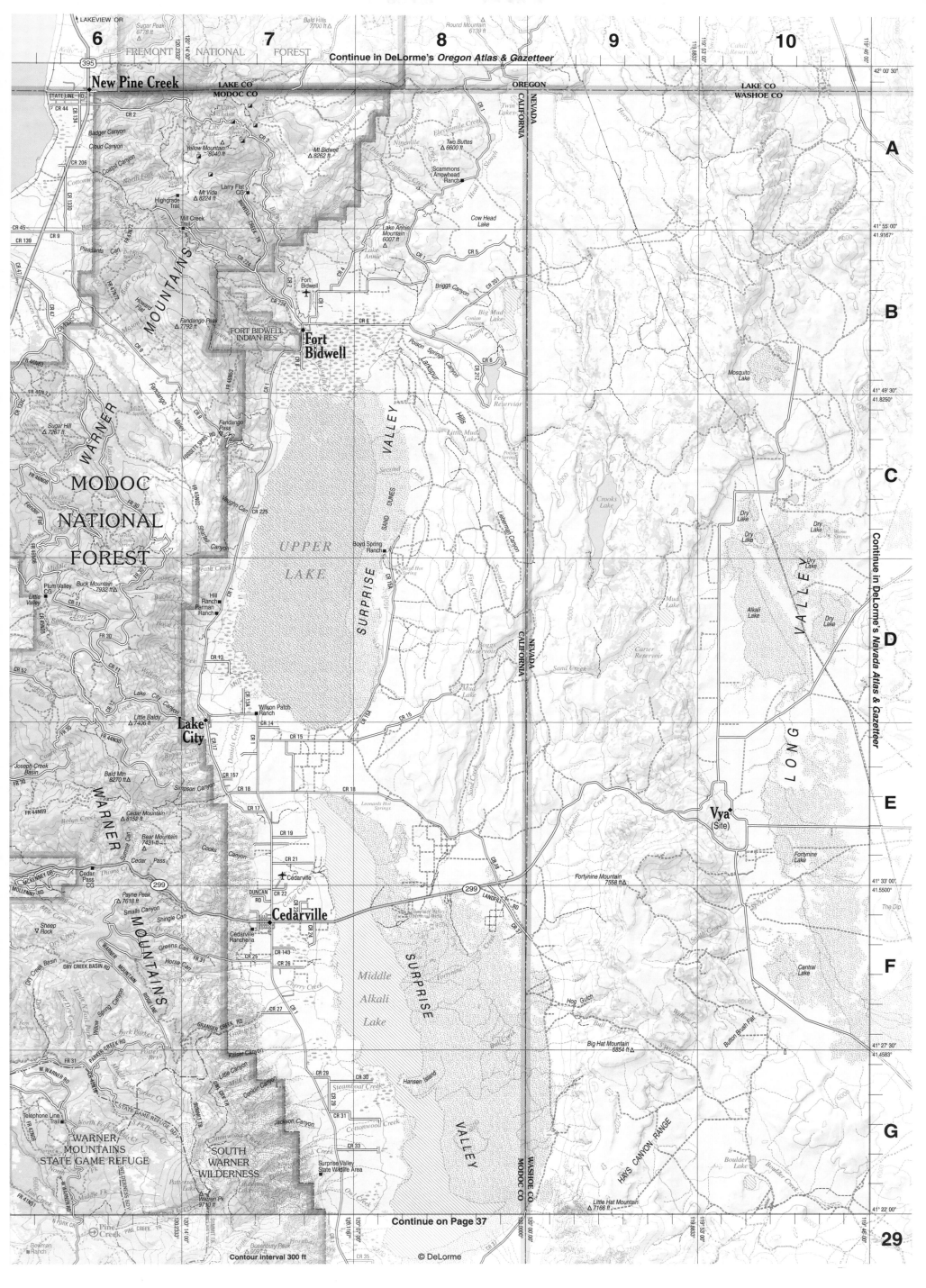

Continue in DeLorme's *Oregon Atlas & Gazetteer*

LAKEVIEW OR
FREMONT NATIONAL FOREST

New Pine Creek

LAKE CO
MODOC CO

OREGON

LAKE CO
WASHOE CO

CALIFORNIA
NEVADA

A

Sugar Peak 6778 ft
Bald Hills 7700 ft
Round Mountain 6139 ft
Cahill Reservoir

Badger Canyon
Cloud Canyon
Yellow Mountain 8040 ft
Mt Bidwell 8262 ft
Twin Lakes
Horse Creek
Cow Head Creek

B

Mt Vida 8224 ft
Highgrade Trail
Larry Flat CG
Mill Creek Trail
Scammons Arrowhead Ranch
Cow Head Lake

Lake Annie Mountain 6007 ft
Lake Annie

WARNER
MOUNTAINS

Pleasants Can
Fandango Peak 7792 ft
FORT BIDWELL INDIAN RES
Fort Bidwell
Fort Bidwell

Briggs Canyon
Big Mud Lake
Conlan Springs
Mosquito Lake

C

MODOC
NATIONAL
FOREST

Sugar Hill 7267 ft
Fandango Pass
FOSSETT SPRG RD

UPPER LAKE

SURPRISE VALLEY

Poison Springs Canyon
Fee Reservoir

Little Mud Lake

Crooks Lake

Dry Lake
Dry Lake
Dry Lake
Warm Springs

D

Plum Valley CG
Buck Mountain 7932 ft
Little Valley

Boyd Spring Ranch

SAND DUNES

Mud Lake

LONG VALLEY

Alkali Lake
Carter Reservoir
Dry Lake
Dry Lake

Continue in DeLorme's *Nevada Atlas & Gazetteer*

E

Little Baldy 7406 ft
Wilson Patch Ranch
Hill Ranch
Parman Ranch

Lake City

Bald Mtn 6270 ft
Simpson Canyon
Cedar Mountain 8158 ft
Bear Mountain 7431 ft
Cooks Canyon
Cedar Pass

Leonards Hot Springs

Vya (Site)

Fortynine Lake

F

WARNER
MOUNTAINS

Cedar Pass CG
Payne Peak 7618 ft
Smalls Canyon
Shingle Can
Sheep Rock

Cedarville
DUNCAN RD
Cedarville
Cedarville Rancheria
Greens Can
Horse Can

Fortynine Mountain 7558 ft
LANDFILL RD

The Dip

Central Lake

Middle Alkali Lake

SURPRISE VALLEY

Hog Gulch

Big Hat Mountain 6854 ft

G

WARNER MOUNTAINS STATE GAME REFUGE

SOUTH WARNER WILDERNESS

Cherry Creek
Granger Creek Rd
Steamboat Creek
Hansen Island
Cottonwood Creek
Jackson Canyon
Surprise Valley State Wildlife Area

HAYS CANYON RANGE

Little Hat Mountain 7166 ft

Boulder Lake

Pine Creek
Warren Pk 9710 ft
Dusenbury Peak 9097 ft

MODOC CO
WASHOE CO

Continue on Page 37

Contour interval 300 ft

© DeLorme

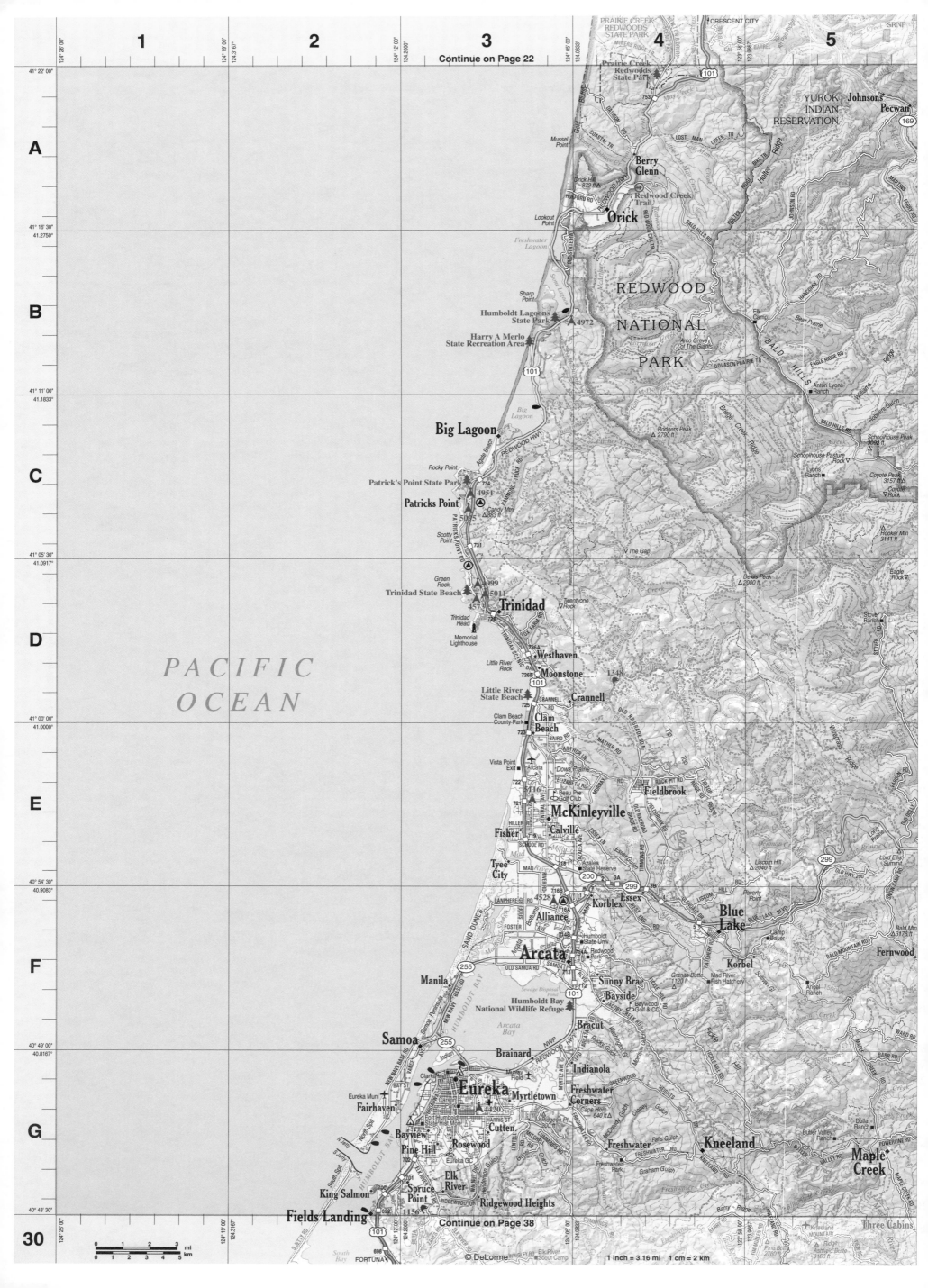

PACIFIC
OCEAN

REDWOOD
NATIONAL
PARK

YUROK
INDIAN
RESERVATION

Johnsons'
Pecwan

Berry
Glenn

Orick

Big Lagoon

Humboldt Lagoons
State Park

Harry A Merlo
State Recreation Area

Patrick's Point State Park
Patricks Point

Trinidad State Beach
Trinidad

Westhaven
Moonstone
Crannell

Little River
State Beach

Clam Beach
County Park
Clam
Beach

Vista Point
Exit

Fieldbrook

McKinleyville

Fisher
Calville

Tyee
City

Essex

Korblex

Blue
Lake

Alliance

Fernwood

Arcata

Korbel

Manila

Sunny Brae
Bayside

Humboldt Bay
National Wildlife Refuge

Bracut

Samoa

Brainard

Indianola

Freshwater
Corners

Eureka

Myrtletown

Kneeland

Fairhaven

Cutten

Bayview
Pine Hill

Rosewood

Freshwater

Maple
Creek

King Salmon
Elk
River

Spruce
Point

Ridgewood Heights

Fields Landing

Continue on Page 38

© DeLorme

1 inch = 3.16 mi   1 cm = 2 km

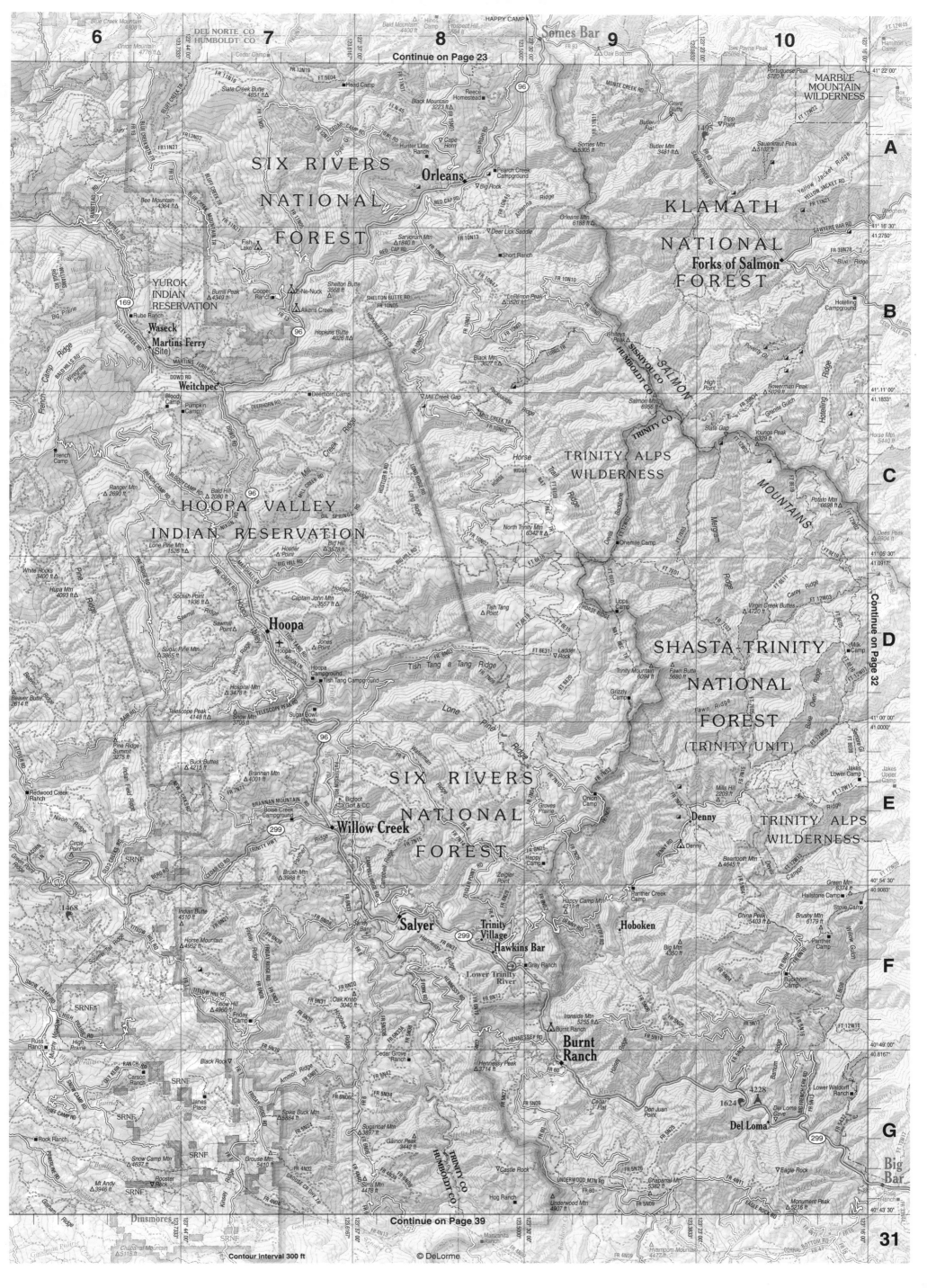

Continue on Page 23

DEL NORTE CO
HUMBOLDT CO

HAPPY CAMP

MARBLE
MOUNTAIN
WILDERNESS

SIX RIVERS

NATIONAL

FOREST

Orleans

KLAMATH

NATIONAL

FOREST

Forks of Salmon

YUROK
INDIAN
RESERVATION

Waseck

Martins Ferry
(Site)

Weitchpec

TRINITY ALPS
WILDERNESS

HOOPA VALLEY

INDIAN RESERVATION

MOUNTAINS

Hoopa

SHASTA·TRINITY

NATIONAL

FOREST

(TRINITY UNIT)

SIX RIVERS

NATIONAL

FOREST

Willow Creek

Denny

TRINITY ALPS
WILDERNESS

Salyer

Trinity
Village

Hawkins Bar

Hoboken

Lower Trinity
River

Burnt
Ranch

Del Loma

Big
Bar

Continue on Page 39

Contour interval 300 ft

© DeLorme

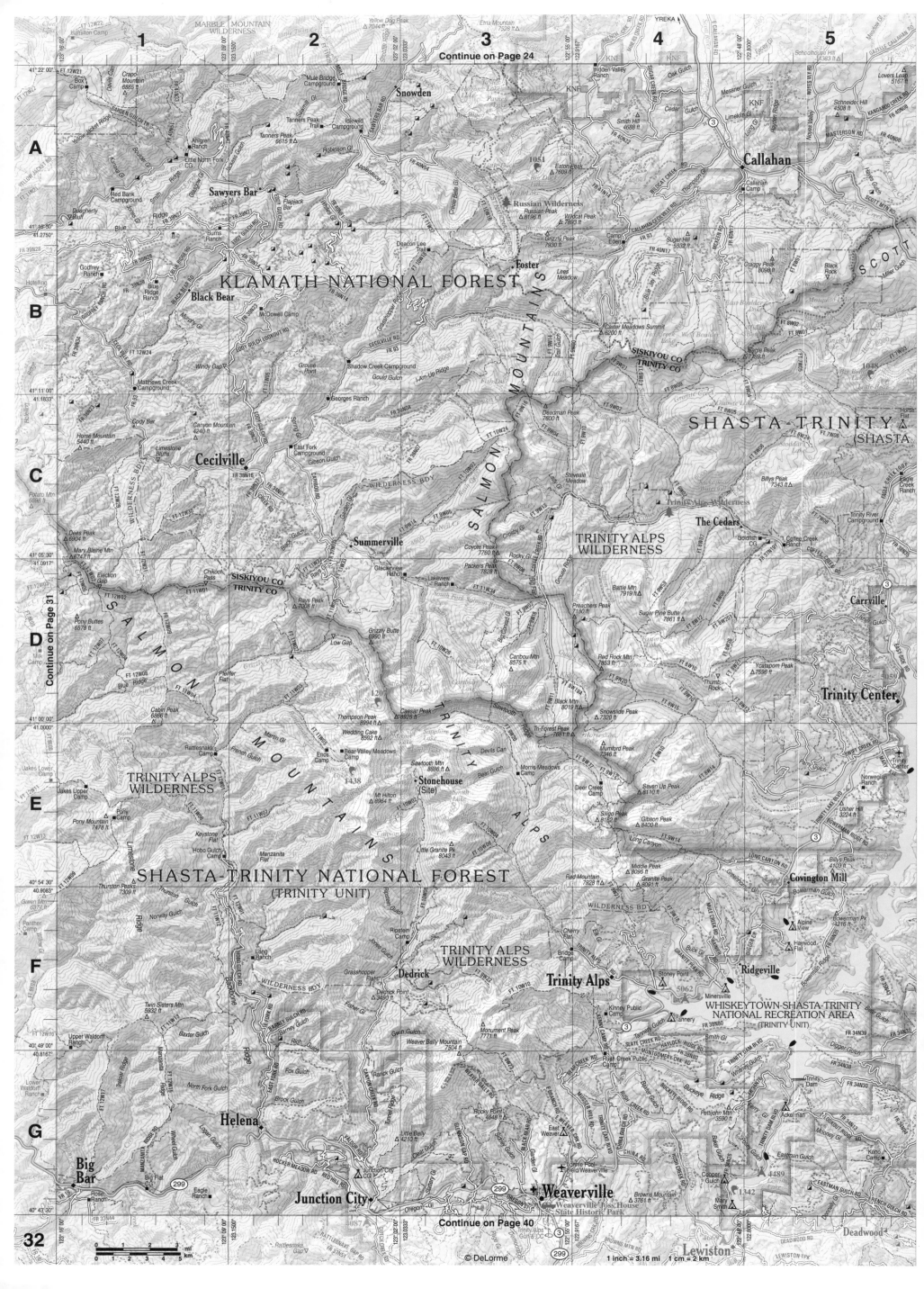

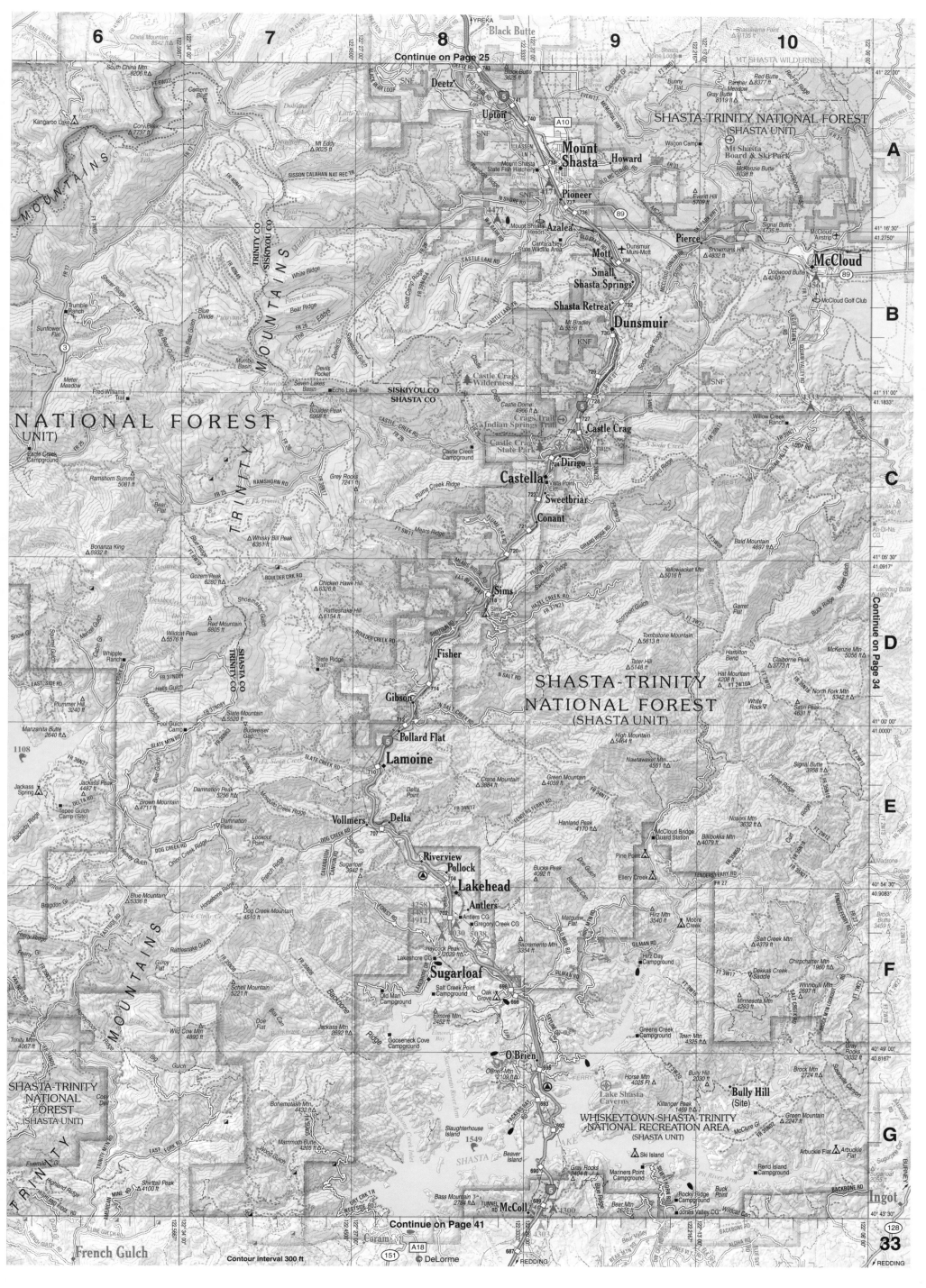

Continue on Page 25

YREKA
Black Butte

SHASTA-TRINITY NATIONAL FOREST
(SHASTA UNIT)

MT SHASTA WILDERNESS

Deetz

Upton

Mount
Shasta

Howard

Mt Shasta
Board & Ski Park

Pioneer

Pierce

McCloud

Azalea

Mott

Small

Shasta Springs

Shasta Retreat

Dunsmuir

McCloud Golf Club

SISKIYOU CO
SHASTA CO

Castle Crags
Wilderness

Castle Crag

NATIONAL FOREST
(UNIT)

T R I N I T Y   M O U N T A I N S

Dirigo

Castella

Sweetbriar

Conant

Sims

SHASTA-TRINITY
NATIONAL FOREST
(SHASTA UNIT)

Fisher

Gibson

Pollard Flat

Lamoine

Vollmers   Delta

Riverview
Pollock

Lakehead

Antlers

Sugarloaf

O'Brien

Bully Hill
(Site)

WHISKEYTOWN-SHASTA-TRINITY
NATIONAL RECREATION AREA
(SHASTA UNIT)

SHASTA-TRINITY
NATIONAL
FOREST
(SHASTA UNIT)

M O U N T A I N S

T R I N I T Y

McColl

Ingot

Continue on Page 41

French Gulch

Contour interval 300 ft

© DeLorme

REDDING

A

B

C

D

E

F

G

Continue on Page 34

33

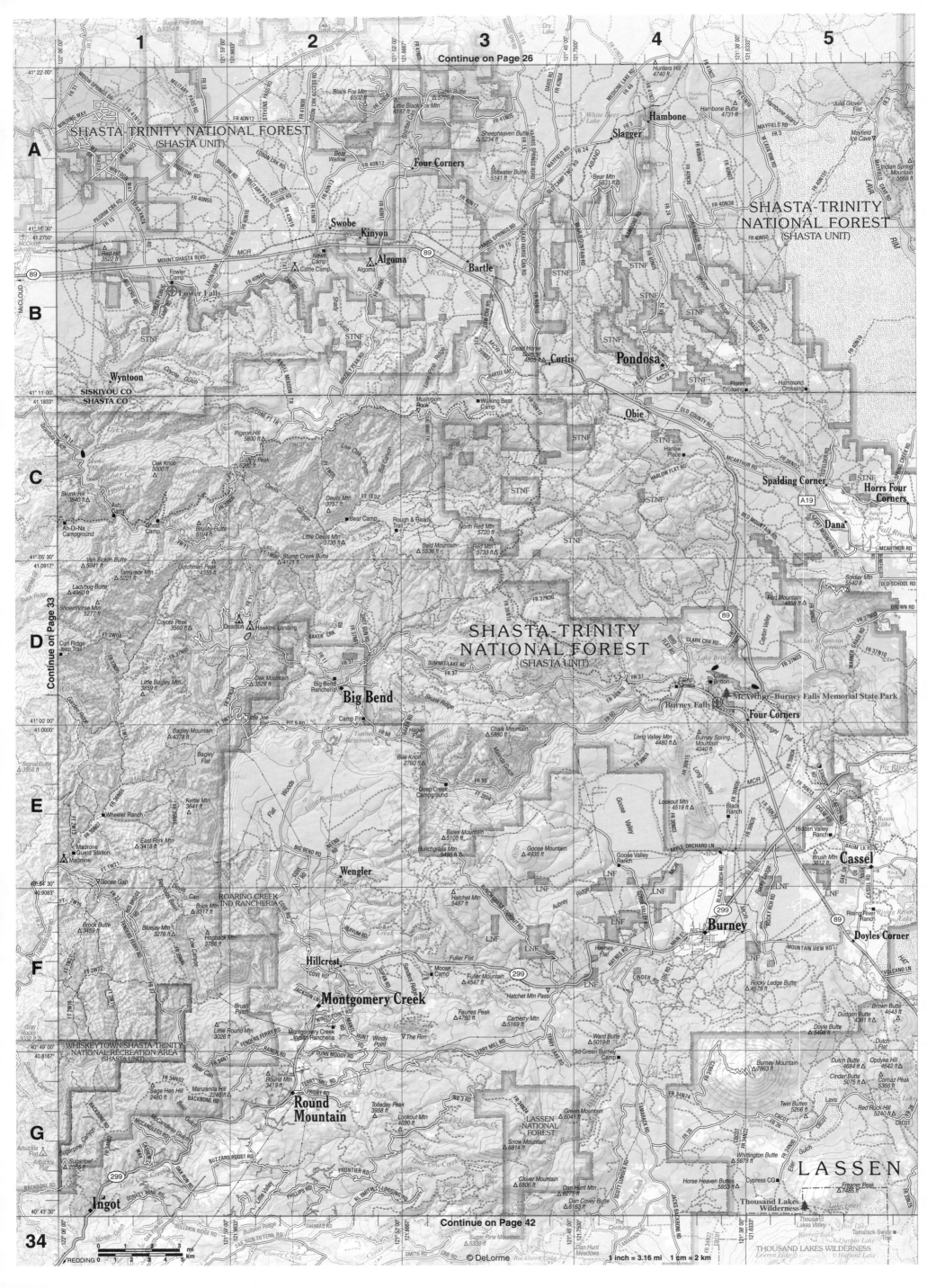

Continue on Page 26

Continue on Page 33

Continue on Page 42

SHASTA-TRINITY NATIONAL FOREST
(SHASTA UNIT)

SHASTA-TRINITY
NATIONAL FOREST
(SHASTA UNIT)

SHASTA-TRINITY
NATIONAL FOREST
(SHASTA UNIT)

WHISKEYTOWN SHASTA TRINITY
NATIONAL RECREATION AREA
(SHASTA UNIT)

LASSEN
NATIONAL FOREST

LASSEN

THOUSAND LAKES WILDERNESS

Four Corners

Swobe

Kinyon

Algoma

Bartle

Curtis

Pondosa

Obie

Hambone

Slagger

Spalding Corner

Horrs Four Corners

Dana

Wyntoon

Big Bend

Burney Falls

Four Corners

Wengler

Hillcrest

Montgomery Creek

Round Mountain

Ingot

Burney

Cassel

Doyles Corner

Lower Falls

SISKIYOU CO
SHASTA CO

MCCLOUD

REDDING

© DeLorme

1 inch = 3.16 mi   1 cm = 2 km

34

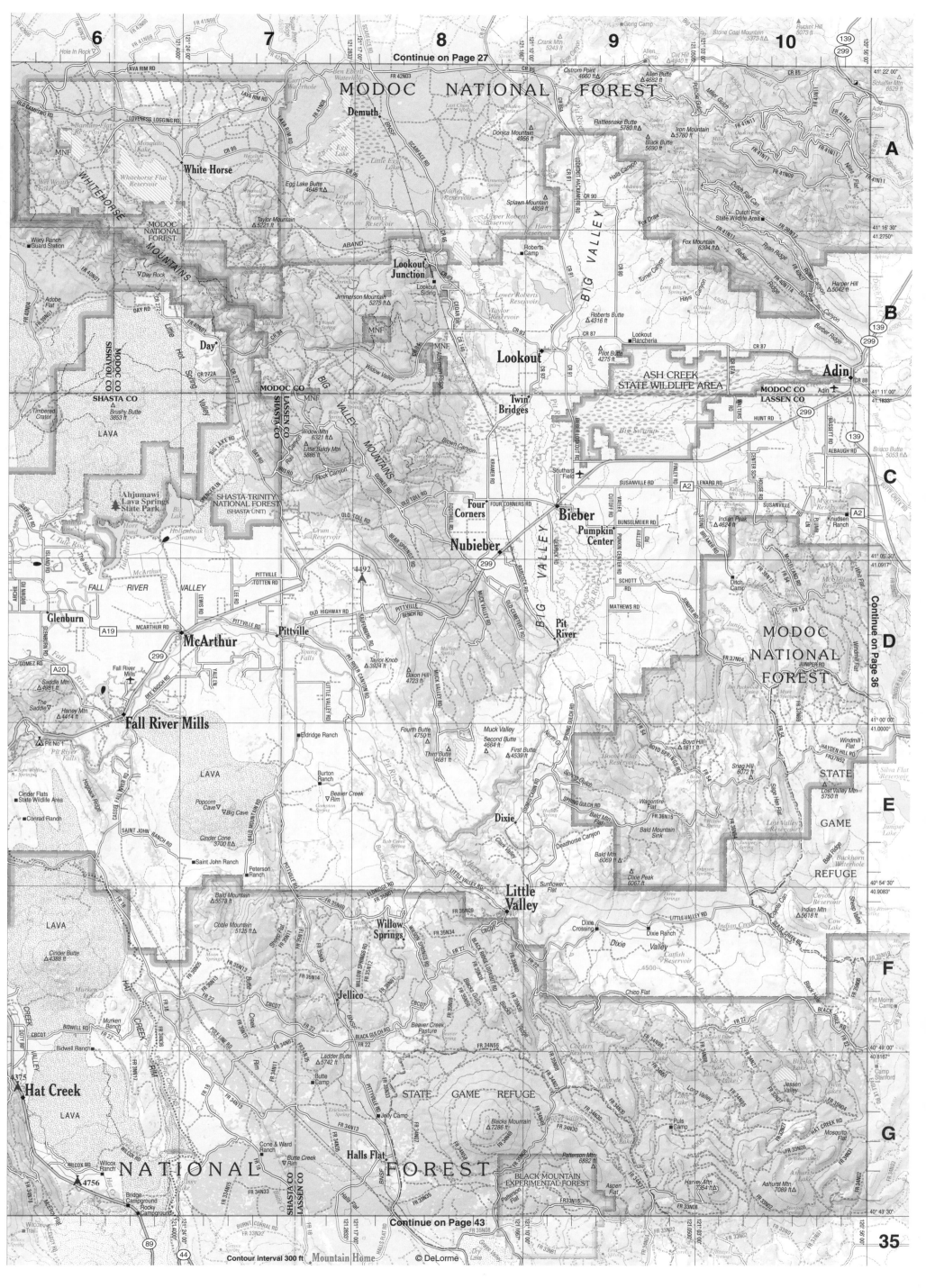

Continue on Page 27

MODOC NATIONAL FOREST

WHITEHORSE MOUNTAINS

Demuth

White Horse

MODOC NATIONAL FOREST GUARD STATION

Day

MODOC CO SISKIYOU CO

SHASTA CO

LAVA

Lookout Junction

MNF

MNF

BIG VALLEY MOUNTAINS

MODOC CO SHASTA CO

LASSEN CO SHASTA CO

Ahjumawi Lava Springs State Park

SHASTA-TRINITY NATIONAL FOREST (SHASTA UNIT)

FALL RIVER VALLEY

Glenburn

McArthur Pittville

Fall River Mills

LAVA

Lookout

Twin Bridges

Four Corners

Nubieber

ASH CREEK STATE WILDLIFE AREA

MODOC CO LASSEN CO

Adin

Bieber

Pumpkin Center

Pit River

BIG VALLEY

MODOC NATIONAL FOREST

STATE

GAME

REFUGE

Dixie

Little Valley

Willow Springs

Jellico

Hat Creek

LAVA

NATIONAL

Halls Flat

FOREST

BLACK MOUNTAIN EXPERIMENTAL FOREST

STATE GAME REFUGE

Continue on Page 43

Contour interval 300 ft Mountain Home ©DeLorme

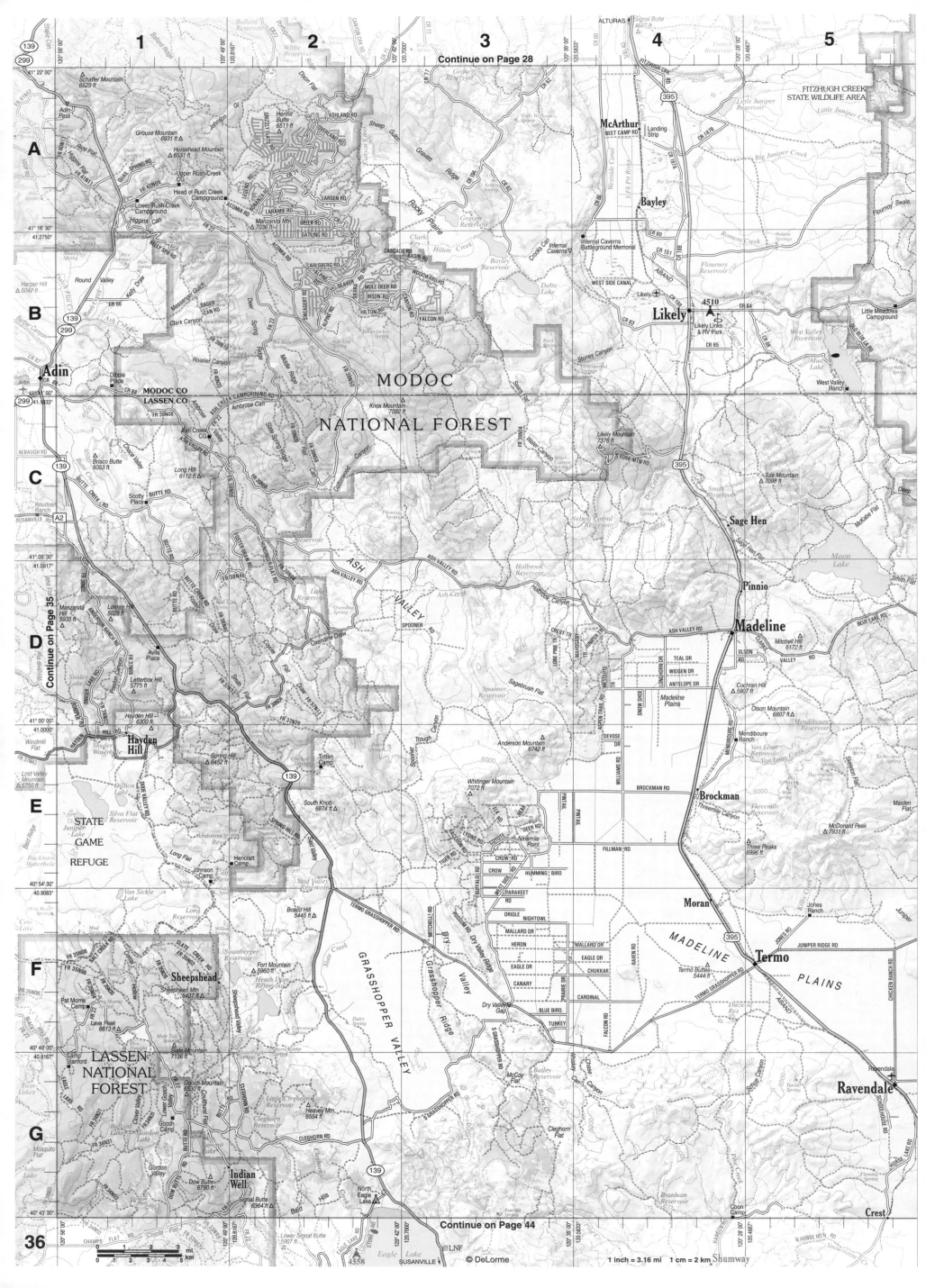

Continue on Page 28

Continue on Page 35

Continue on Page 44

MODOC

NATIONAL FOREST

LASSEN
NATIONAL
FOREST

STATE
GAME
REFUGE

1 inch = 3.16 mi   1 cm = 2 km

© DeLorme

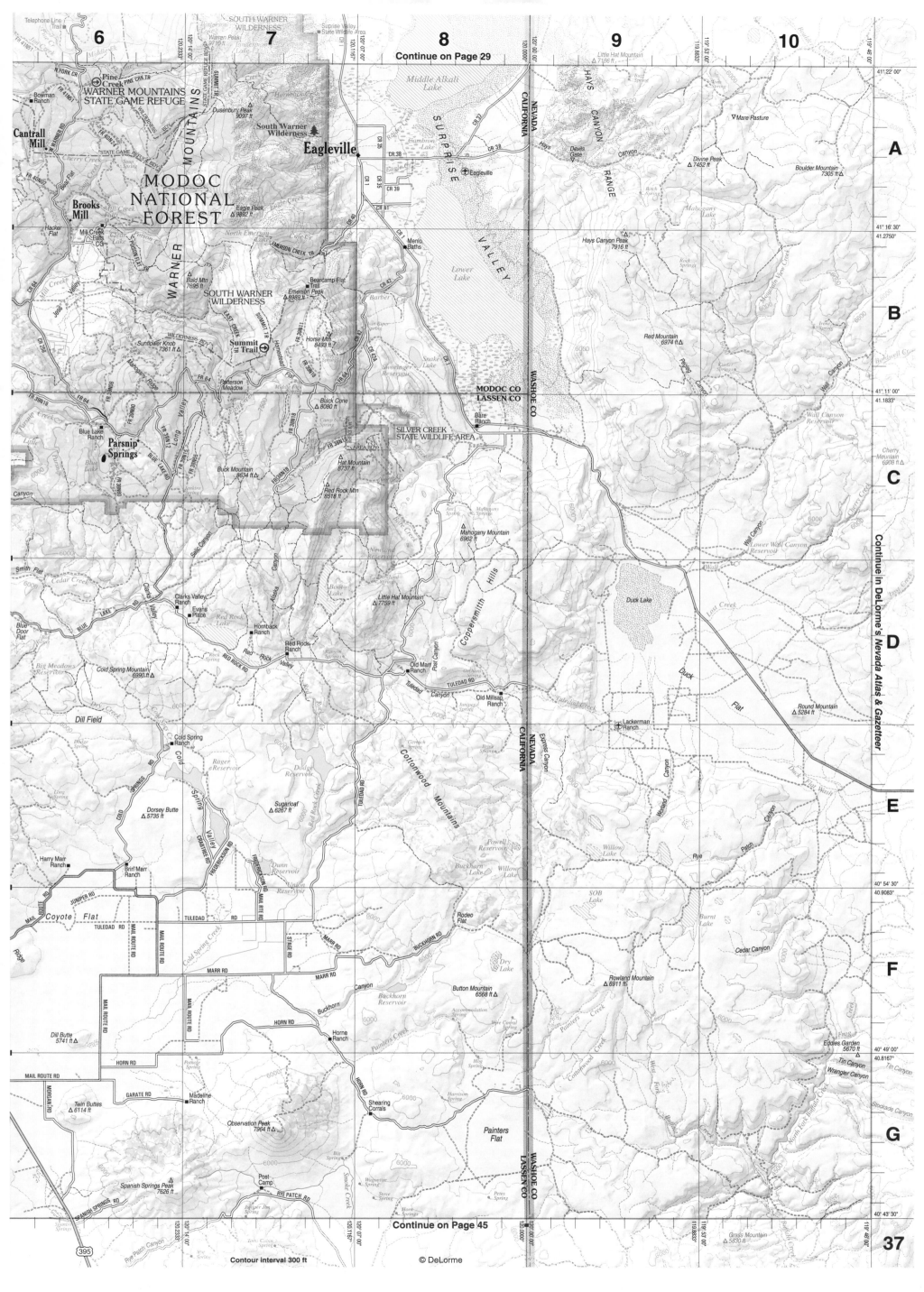

Continue on Page 29

WARNER MOUNTAINS
STATE GAME REFUGE

South Warner
Wilderness

Eagleville

MODOC
NATIONAL
FOREST

SOUTH WARNER
WILDERNESS

Summit Trail

MODOC CO
LASSEN CO

SILVER CREEK
STATE WILDLIFE AREA

Parsnip
Springs

Coppersmith
Hills

Cottonwood
Mountains

Coyote Flat

Painters
Flat

Continue on Page 45

Contour interval 300 ft

© DeLorme

Continue in DeLorme's Nevada Atlas & Gazetteer

A B C D E F G

37

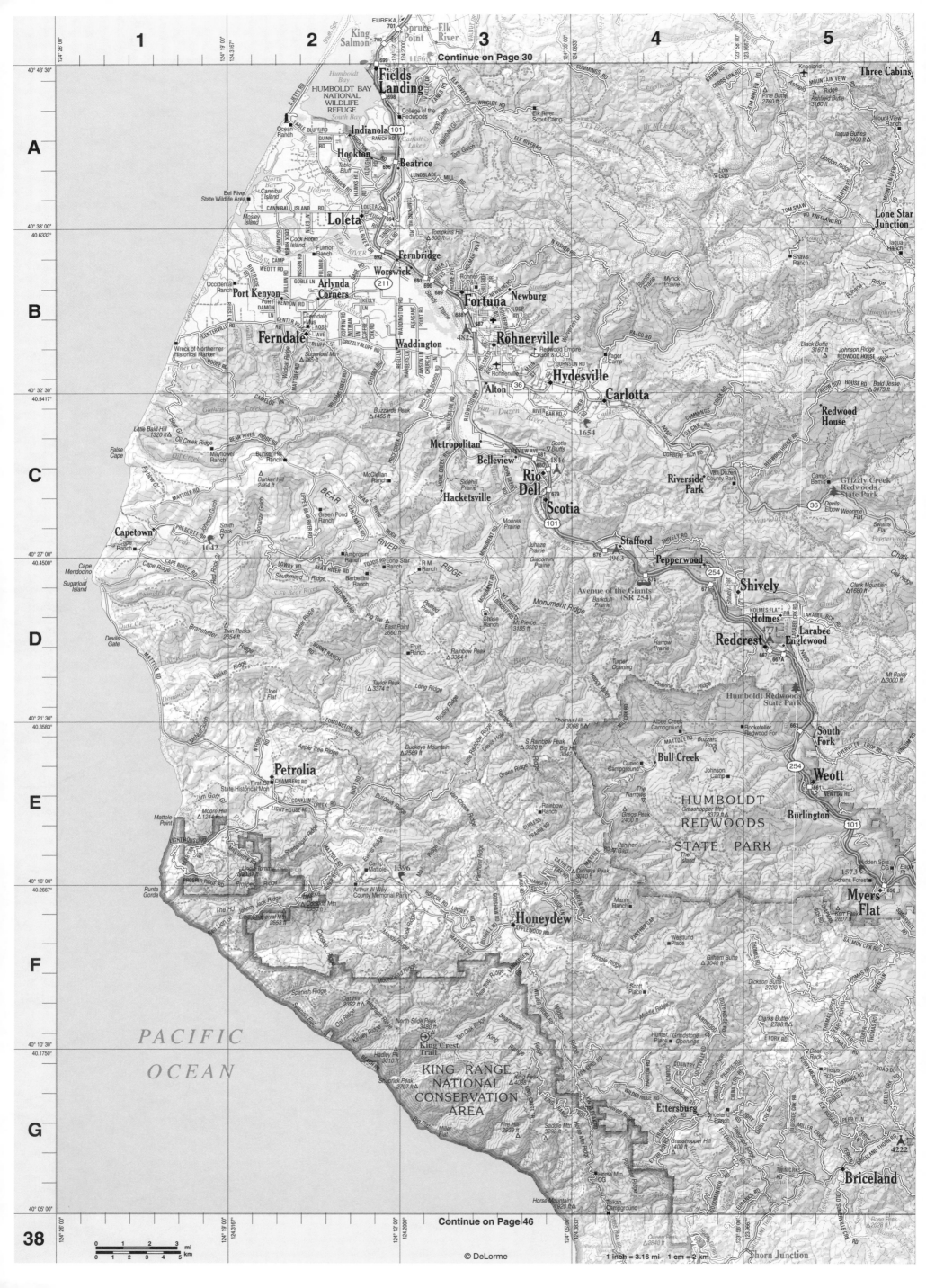

PACIFIC

OCEAN

HUMBOLDT
REDWOODS

STATE PARK

KING RANGE
NATIONAL
CONSERVATION
AREA

© DeLorme

1 inch = 3.16 mi   1 cm = 2 km

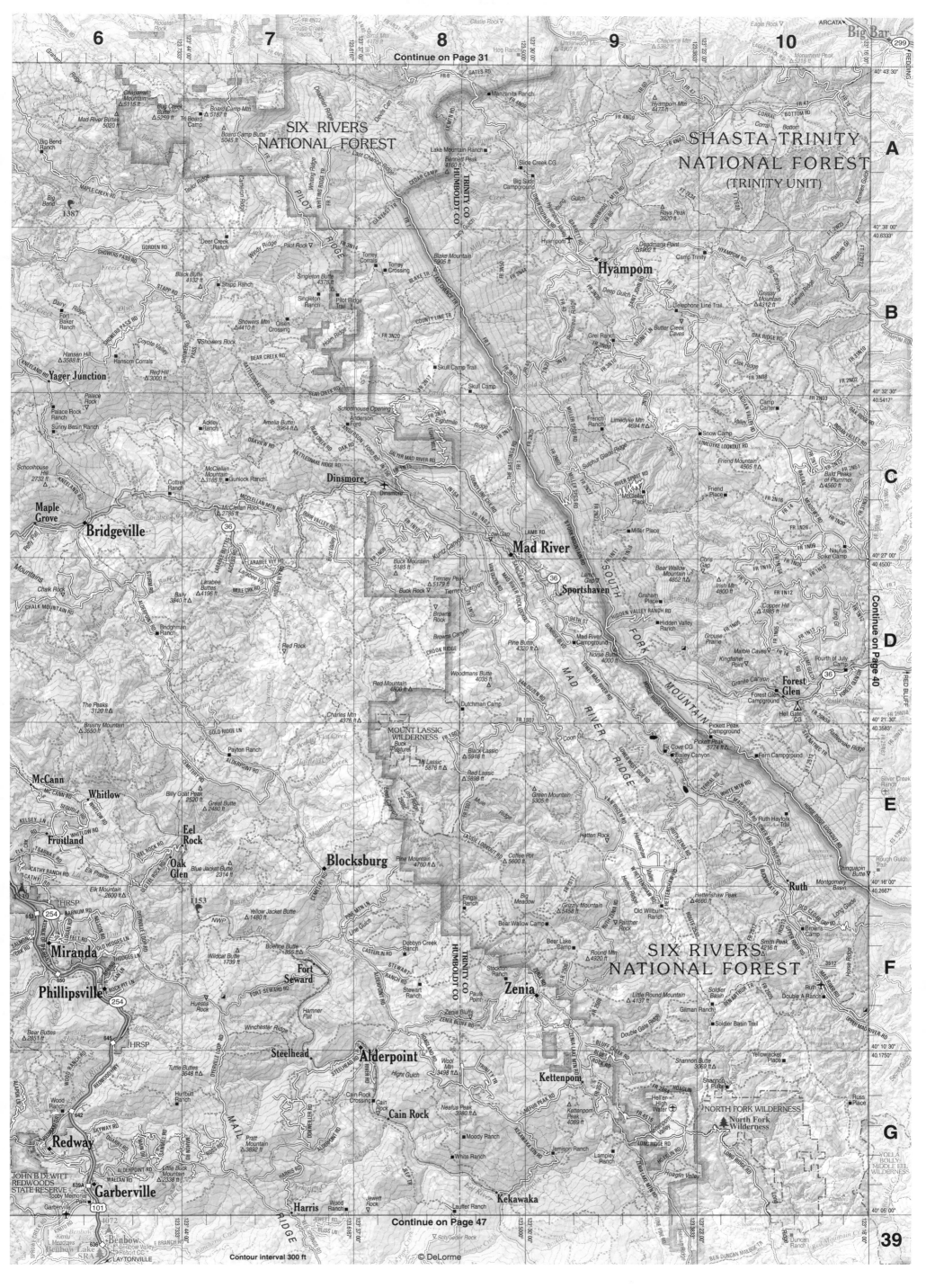

SIX RIVERS
NATIONAL FOREST

SHASTA-TRINITY
NATIONAL FOREST
(TRINITY UNIT)

Hyampom

Dinsmore

Mad River

Sportshaven

MOUNT LASSIC
WILDERNESS

Blocksburg

**Forest
Glen**

SIX RIVERS
NATIONAL FOREST

**Maple
Grove**

Bridgeville

Yager Junction

McCann

Whitlow

Fruitland

**Eel
Rock**

**Oak
Glen**

Miranda

Phillipsville

Redway

Zenia

Ruth

Steelhead

Alderpoint

Kettenpom

Cain Rock

NORTH FORK WILDERNESS
North Fork
Wilderness

Garberville

Harris

Kekawaka

YOLLA
BOLLY
MIDDLE EEL
WILDERNESS

Continue on Page 40

Contour interval 300 ft

© DeLorme

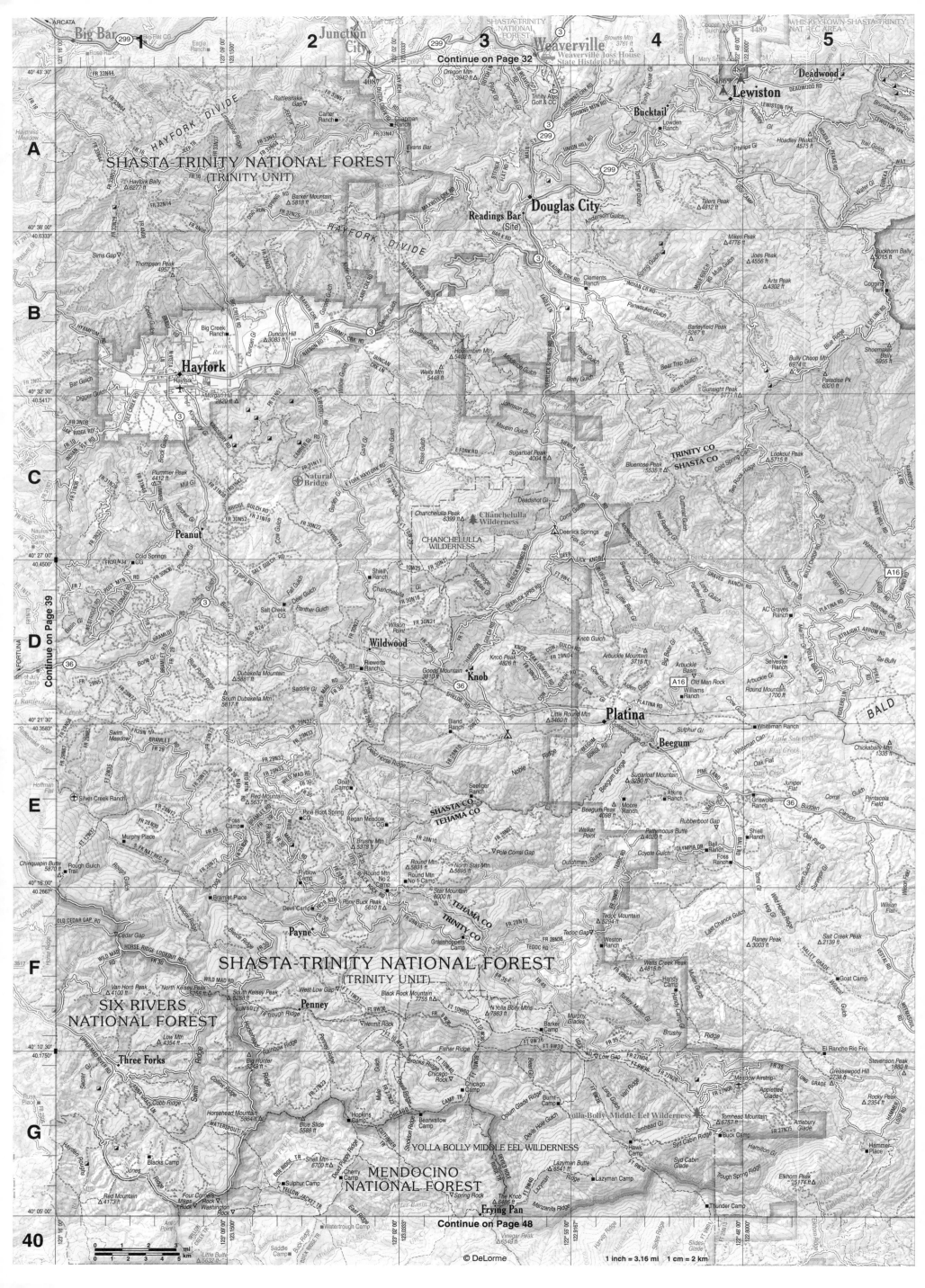

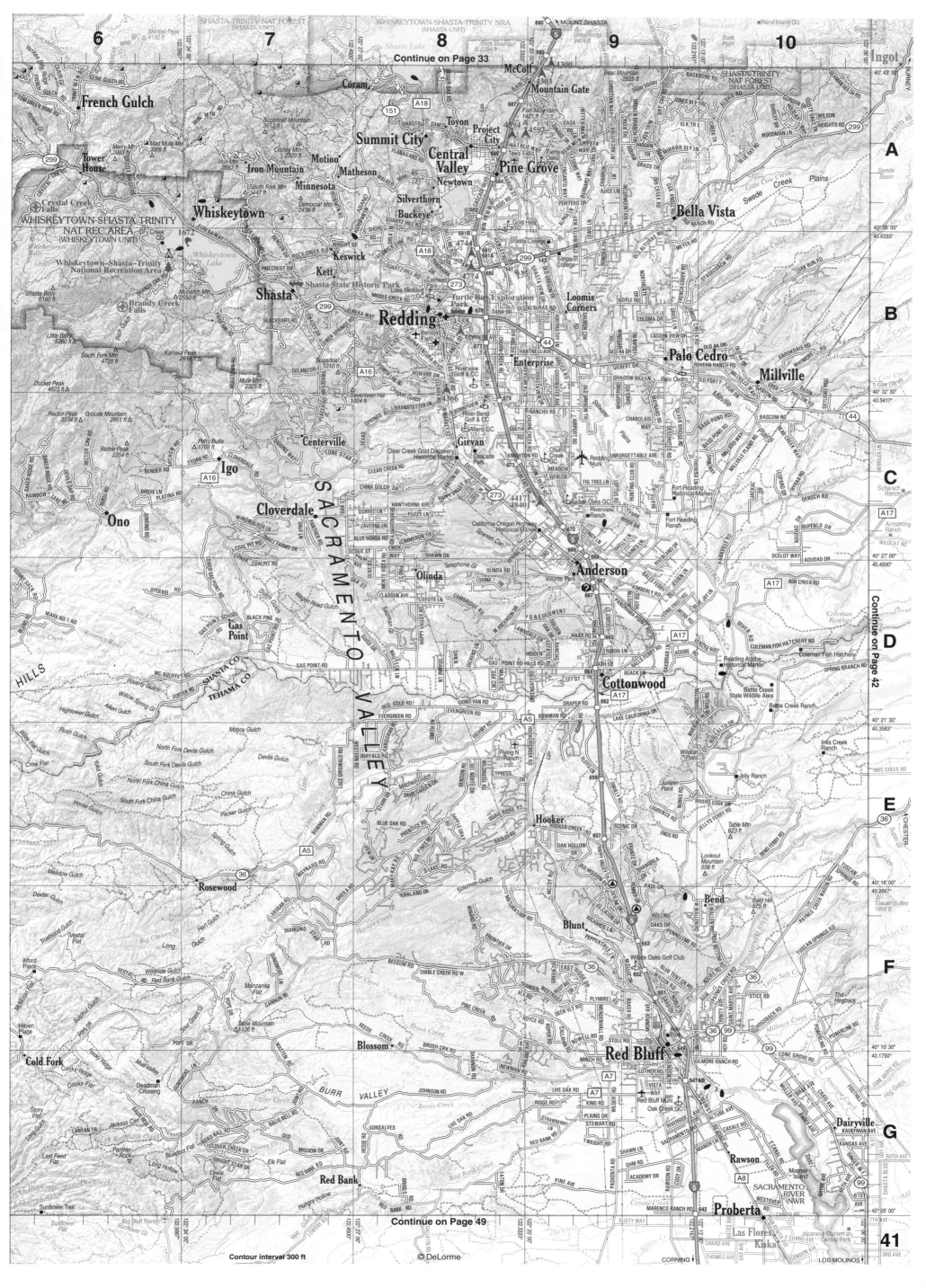

Continue on Page 33

SHASTA-TRINITY NAT FOREST
(SHASTA UNIT)

WHISKEYTOWN-SHASTA-TRINITY NRA
(SHASTA UNIT)

MOUNT SHASTA

Reed Island CG

Ingot

McColl

Mountain Gate

French Gulch

Coram

SHASTA-TRINITY
NAT FOREST
(SHASTA UNIT)

Tower
House

Summit City

Toyon

Project City

Central Valley

Pine Grove

Bella Vista

Motion

Whiskeytown

Matheson

Newtown

Iron Mountain

Minnesota

Silverthorn

Buckeye

WHISKEYTOWN-SHASTA-TRINITY
NAT REC AREA
(WHISKEYTOWN UNIT)

Whiskeytown-Shasta-Trinity
National Recreation Area

Keswick

Kett

Loomis
Corners

Shasta

Shasta State Historic Park

Redding

Enterprise

Palo Cedro

Millville

Benton

Centerville

Girvan

Igo

Cloverdale

SACRAMENTO VALLEY

Ono

Olinda

Anderson

Gas
Point

HILLS

SHASTA CO

TEHAMA CO

Cottonwood

Continue on Page 42

Rosewood

Hooker

Bend

Blunt

Blossom

Red Bluff

Cold Fork

BURR VALLEY

Dairyville

Rawson

Red Bank

SACRAMENTO
RIVER
NWR

Proberta

Continue on Page 49

Las Flores
Kiska

Contour interval 300 ft

© DeLorme

A

B

C

D

E

F

G

41

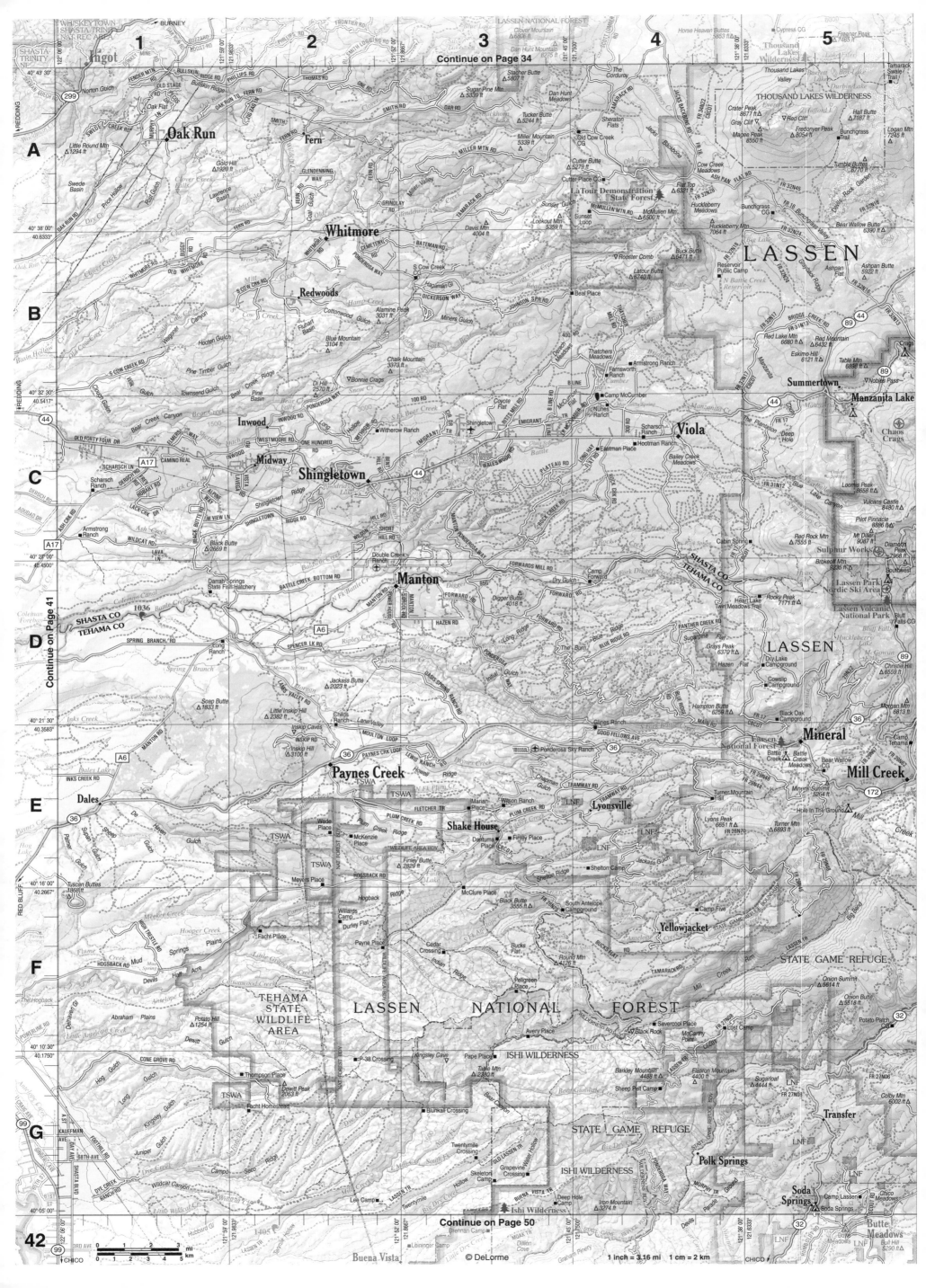

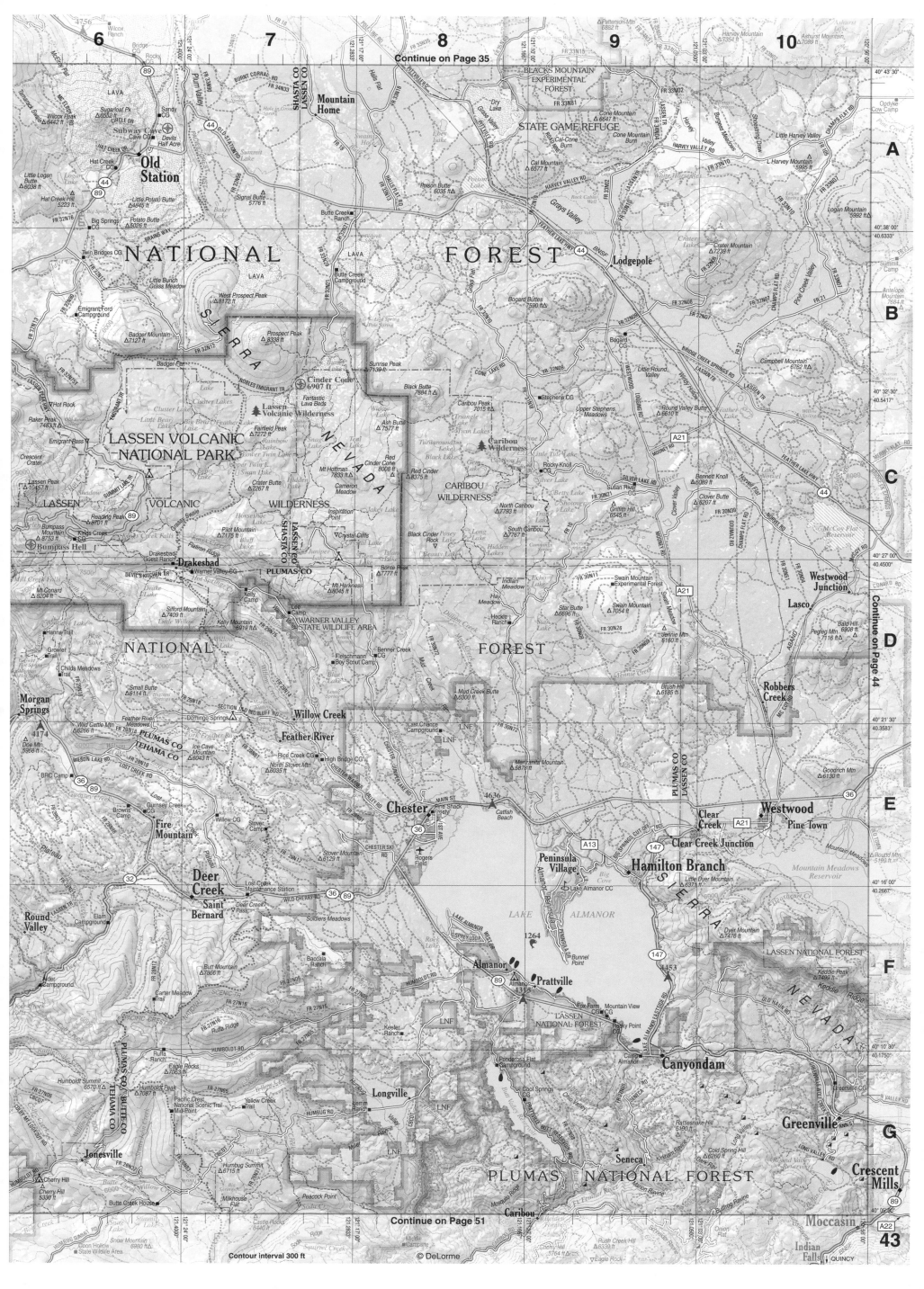

Continue on Page 35

Continue on Page 44

Continue on Page 51

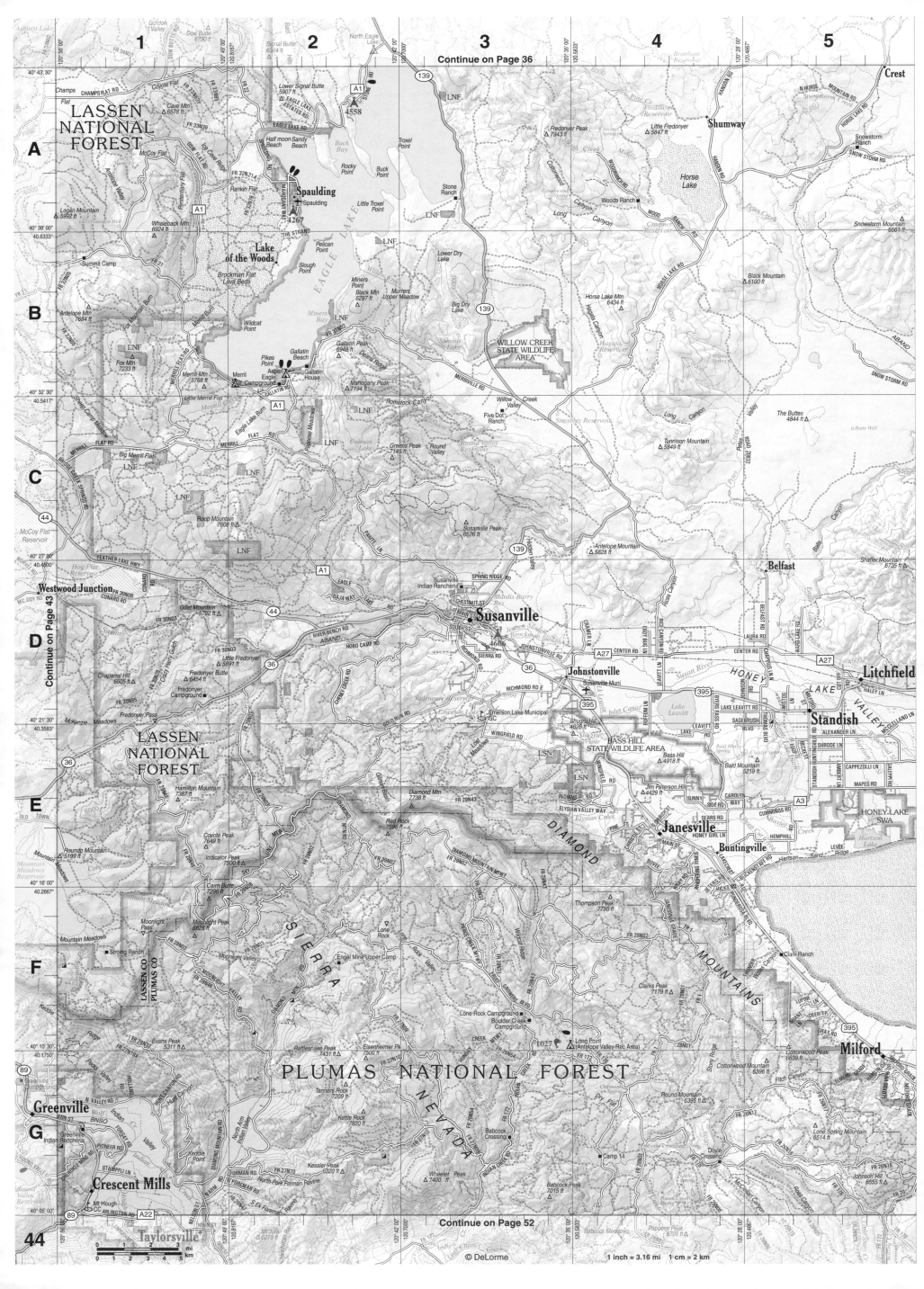

Continue on Page 36

Continue on Page 43

Continue on Page 52

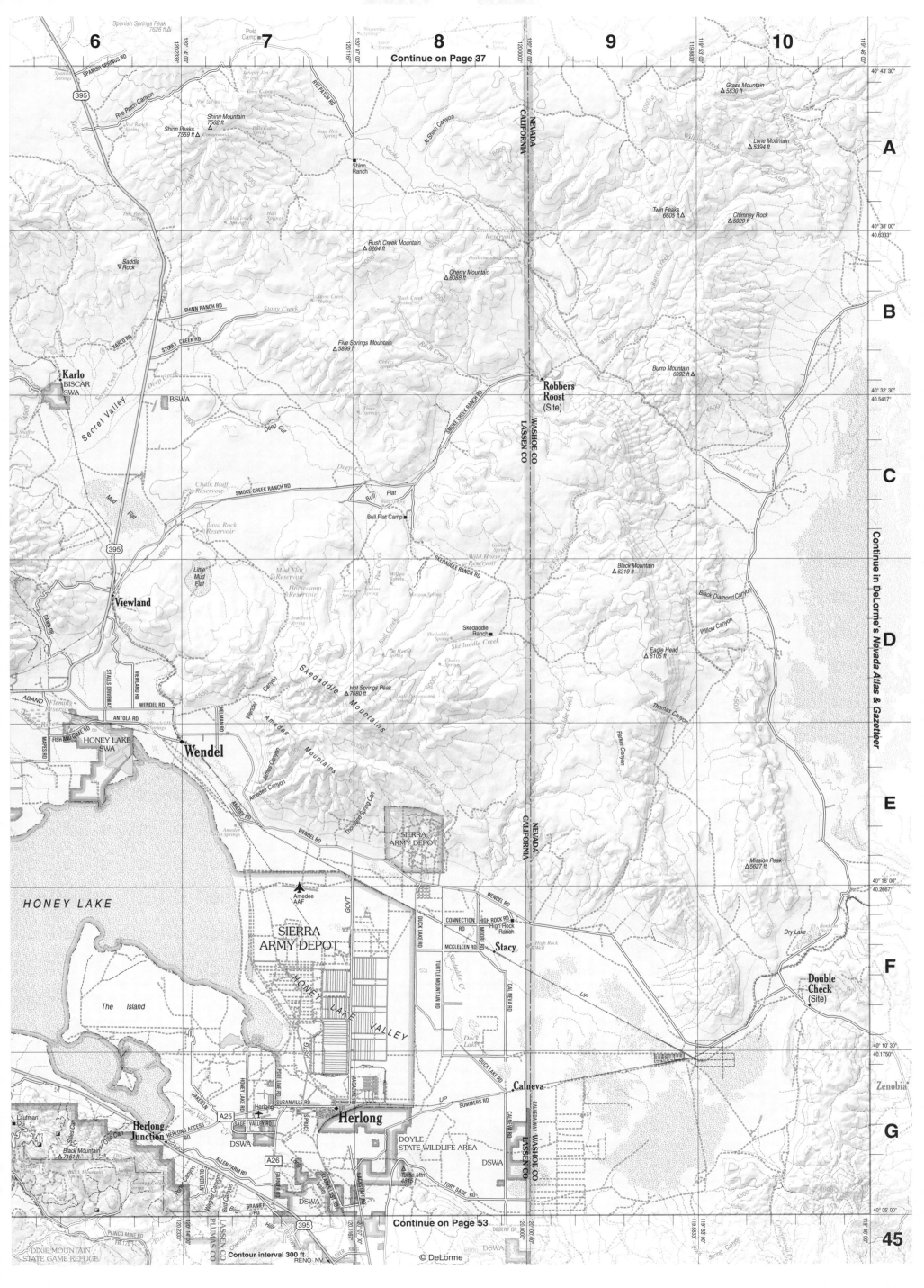

Continue on Page 37

Continue in DeLorme's Nevada Atlas & Gazetteer

6   7   8   9   10

A   B   C   D   E   F   G

Spanish Springs Peak
7626 ft △

Rye Patch Canyon

Shinn Mountain
7562 ft △

Shinn Peaks
7559 ft △

Shinn Ranch

Grass Mountain
△ 5830 ft

Lone Mountain
△ 5394 ft

Twin Peaks
6605 ft △

Chimney Rock
△ 5929 ft

Rush Creek Mountain
△ 6264 ft

Cherry Mountain
△ 8088 ft

Burro Mountain
△ 6092 ft △

Five Springs Mountain
△ 5899 ft

SHINN RANCH RD

Stony Creek

Saddle
▽ Rock

Karlo
BISCAR
SWA

BSWA

Robbers
Roost
(Site)

SMOKE CREEK RANCH RD

Secret Valley

Mud Flat

Smoke Creek

Chalk Bluff
Reservoir

SMOKE CREEK RANCH RD

Bull   Flat

Bull Flat Camp ■

Black Mountain
△ 6219 ft

Black Diamond Canyon

Willow Canyon

Lava Rock
Reservoir

Little
Mud
Flat

Mud Flat
Reservoir

Horsecamp
Reservoir

SKEDADDLE RANCH RD

Wild Horse
Reservoir

Skedaddle
Ranch ■

Eagle Head
△ 6105 ft

Viewland

Skedaddle Creek

Thomas Canyon

DAWN DR

Skedaddle   Mountains

Hot Springs Peak
△ 7680 ft

WENDEL RD

ANTOLA RD

FISH AND GAME RD

HONEY LAKE
SWA

Wendel

Amedee   Mountains

Mission Peak
△ 5627 ft

Parker Canyon

MAPES RD

Amedee Canyon

AMEDEE RD

WENDEL RD

WENDEL RD

CONNECTION
RD

HIGH ROCK RD

High Rock
Ranch ■

Dry Lake

HONEY LAKE

Amedee
AAF

SIERRA
ARMY DEPOT

GOVT

MCCLELLEN RD

MOORE RD

Stacy

DUCK LAKE RD

CAL NEVA RD

High Rock Slough

Up

Double
Check
(Site)

The   Island

SIERRA
ARMY DEPOT

HONEY LAKE VALLEY

TURTLE MOUNTAIN RD

Duck
Lake

Zenobia

Lautman
CG

Black Mountain
△ 7161 ft

Herlong
Junction

JACKS LN

HONEY LAKE RD

SUSANVILLE RD

MAGAZINE RD

Herlong

Calneva

SUMMERS RD

UP

DUCK LAKE RD

CALNEVA WY

A25

SAGE VALLEY RD

SPRUCE

DSWA

DOYLE
STATE WILDLIFE AREA

DSWA

DIXIE MOUNTAIN
STATE GAME REFUGE

ALLEN FARM RD

A26

DSWA

Turtle Mtn
△ 4815 ft

FORT SAGE RD

DSWA

395

RENO NV

WASHOE CO
LASSEN CO

NEVADA
CALIFORNIA

Continue on Page 53

Contour interval 300 ft

© DeLorme

45

40° 43' 30"
40° 38' 00"   40.6333°
40° 32' 30"   40.5417°
40° 16' 00"   40.2667°
40° 10' 30"   40.1750°
40° 05' 00"

120° 14' 00"   120° 07' 00"   120° 00' 00"   119° 53' 00"   119° 46' 00"

120.2333°   120.1167°   120.0000°   119.8833°   119.7667°

Continue on Page 38

King Range
National
Conservation Area

Horse Mtn
920 ft

Horse Mountain
Campground

Tolkan
CG

Queen Peak
2840 ft

Thorn
Junction

Shelter Cove
Golf Links

Shelter
Cove

Point
Delgada

Nadelos CG
Chamisal Mtn
2598 ft

Wailaki
Campground

SHELTER

Whitethorn

HUNGRY

GULCH

SHELTER COVE RD

SWSP

King Range
National
Rec Area

HUMBOLDT CO
MENDOCINO CO

SWSP

Point No
Pass

**Four
Corners**

Sinkyone Wilderness
State Park

High Tid
372 ft

Bear Harbor
Ranch

Bear
Harbor

**Kenny
(Site)**

SINKYONE WILDERNESS
STATE PARK

Jackson
Pinnacle

**Wheeler
(Site)**

Chimney Rock
404 ft

Anderson
Cliff

Mistake
Point

TIMBER

Timber
Point

Rose Peak
2026 ft

JEEP Tr

MOODY RD

PACIFIC   OCEAN

0 1 2 3   mi
0 1 2 3 4 5 km

© DeLorme

1 inch = 3.16 mi   1 cm = 2 km

124° 26' 00"
124° 19' 00"
124.3167°
124° 12' 00"
124.2000°
124° 05' 00"
124.0833°
123° 58' 00"
123.9667°

40° 05' 00"
39° 59' 30"
39.9917°
39° 54' 00"
39.9000°
39° 48' 30"
39.8083°
39° 43' 00"
39.7167°
39° 37' 30"
39.6250°
39° 32' 00"
39.5333°
39° 26' 30"

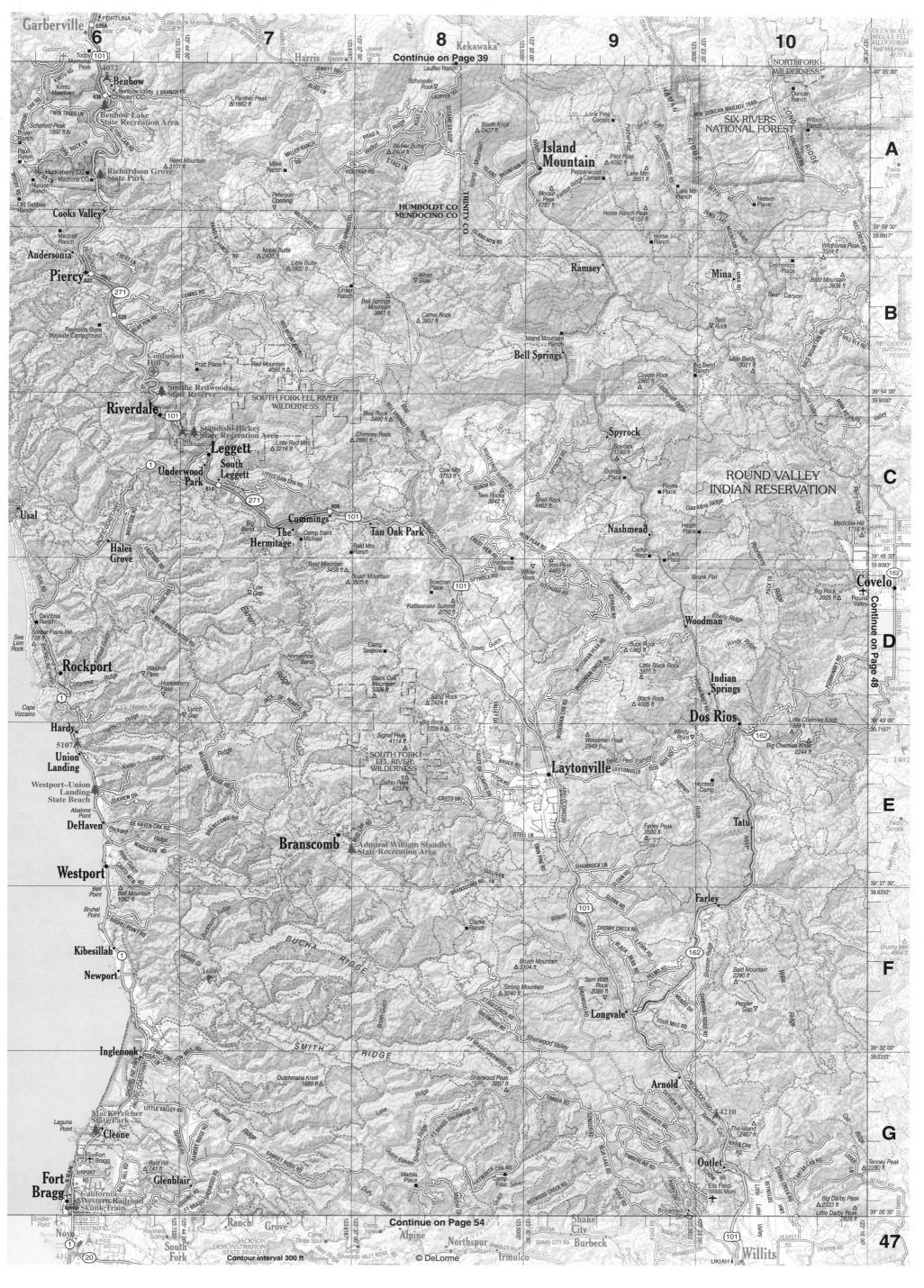

Continue on Page 39

Continue on Page 48

Continue on Page 54

Contour interval 300 ft

© DeLorme

47

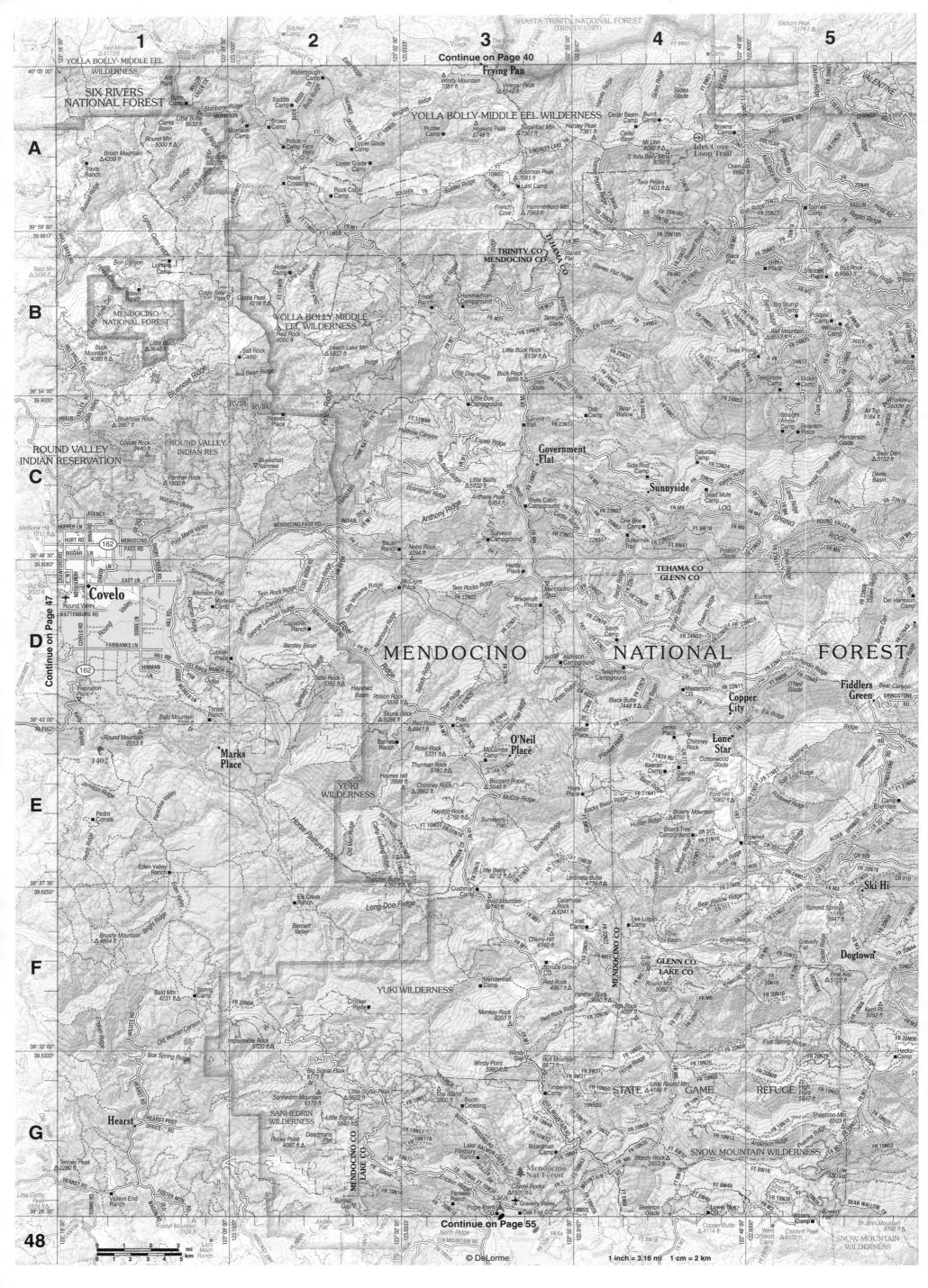

Continue on Page 40

Continue on Page 47

Continue on Page 55

MENDOCINO NATIONAL FOREST

© DeLorme

1 inch = 3.16 mi   1 cm = 2 km

48

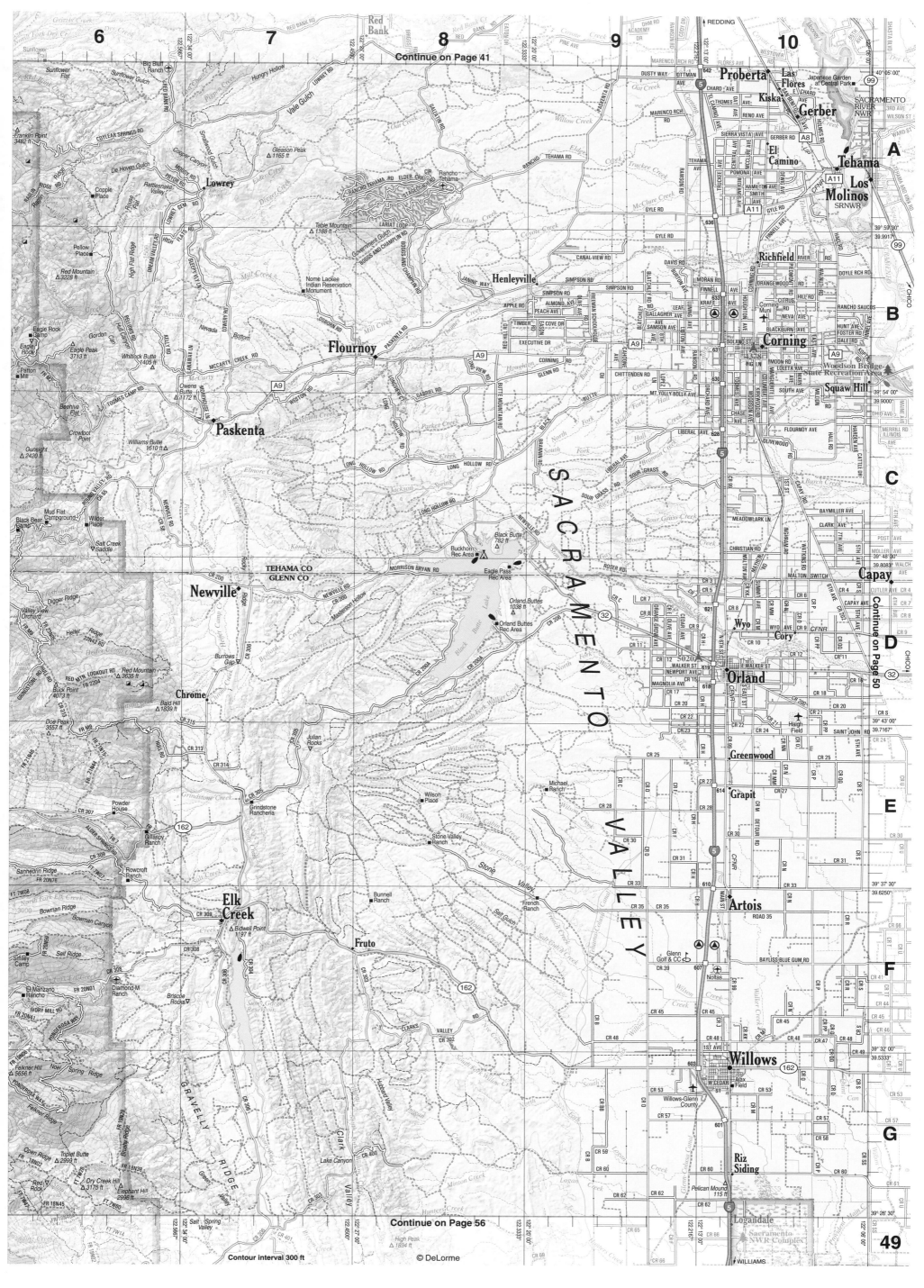

Continue on Page 41

Continue on Page 50

Continue on Page 56

Contour interval 300 ft

© DeLorme

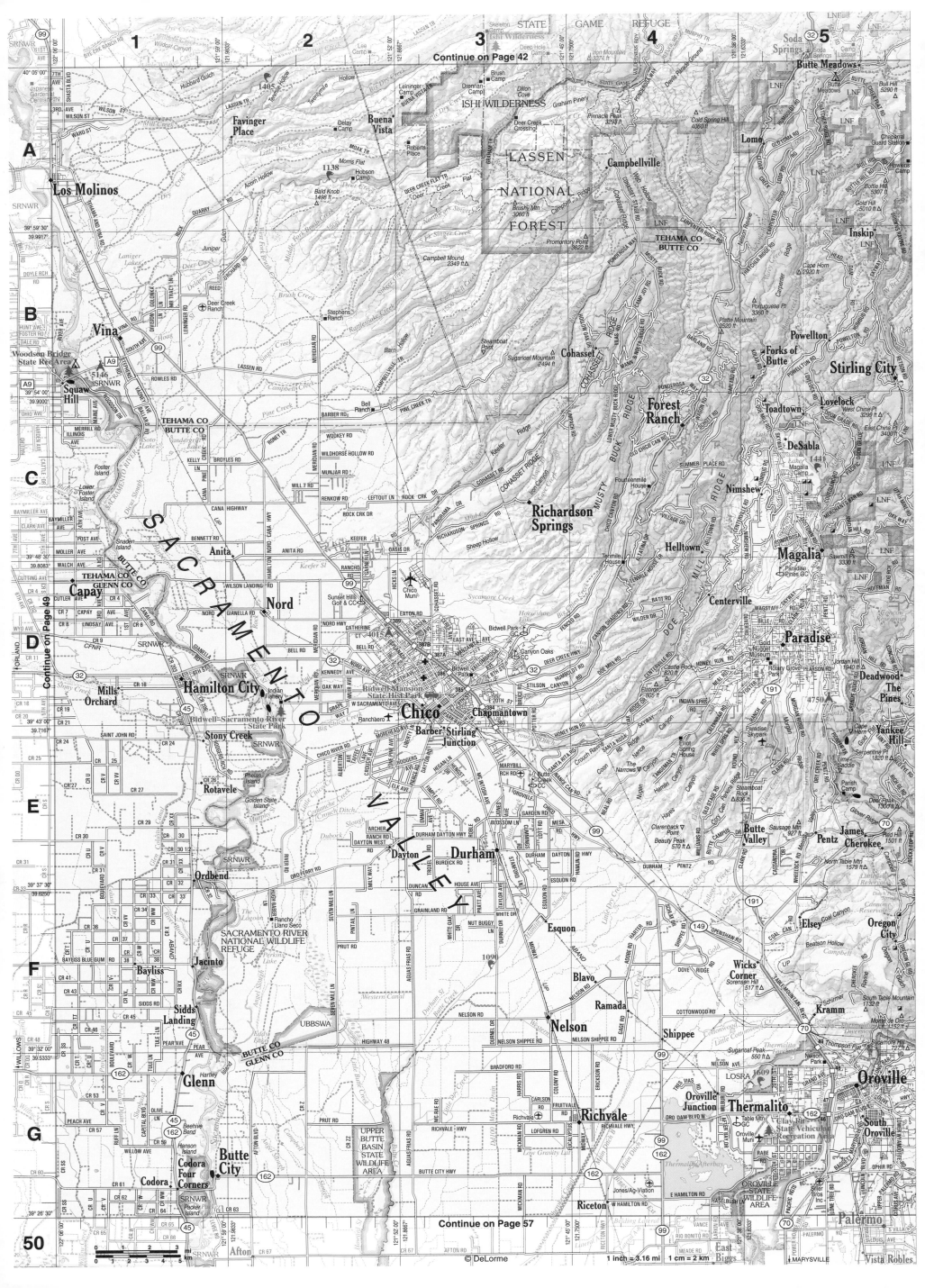

Continue on Page 42

Continue on Page 49

Continue on Page 57

50

1 inch = 3.16 mi   1 cm = 2 km

© DeLorme

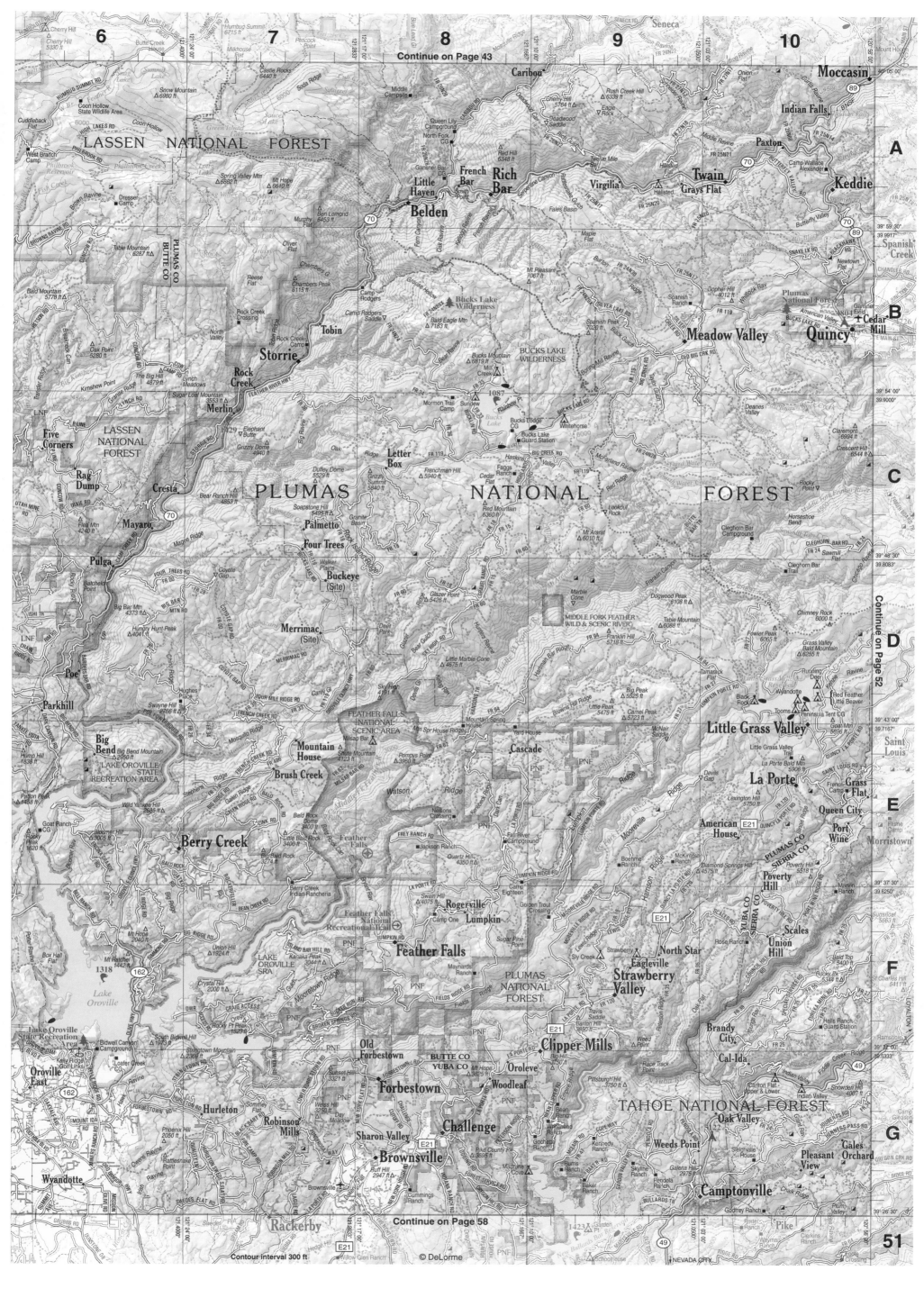

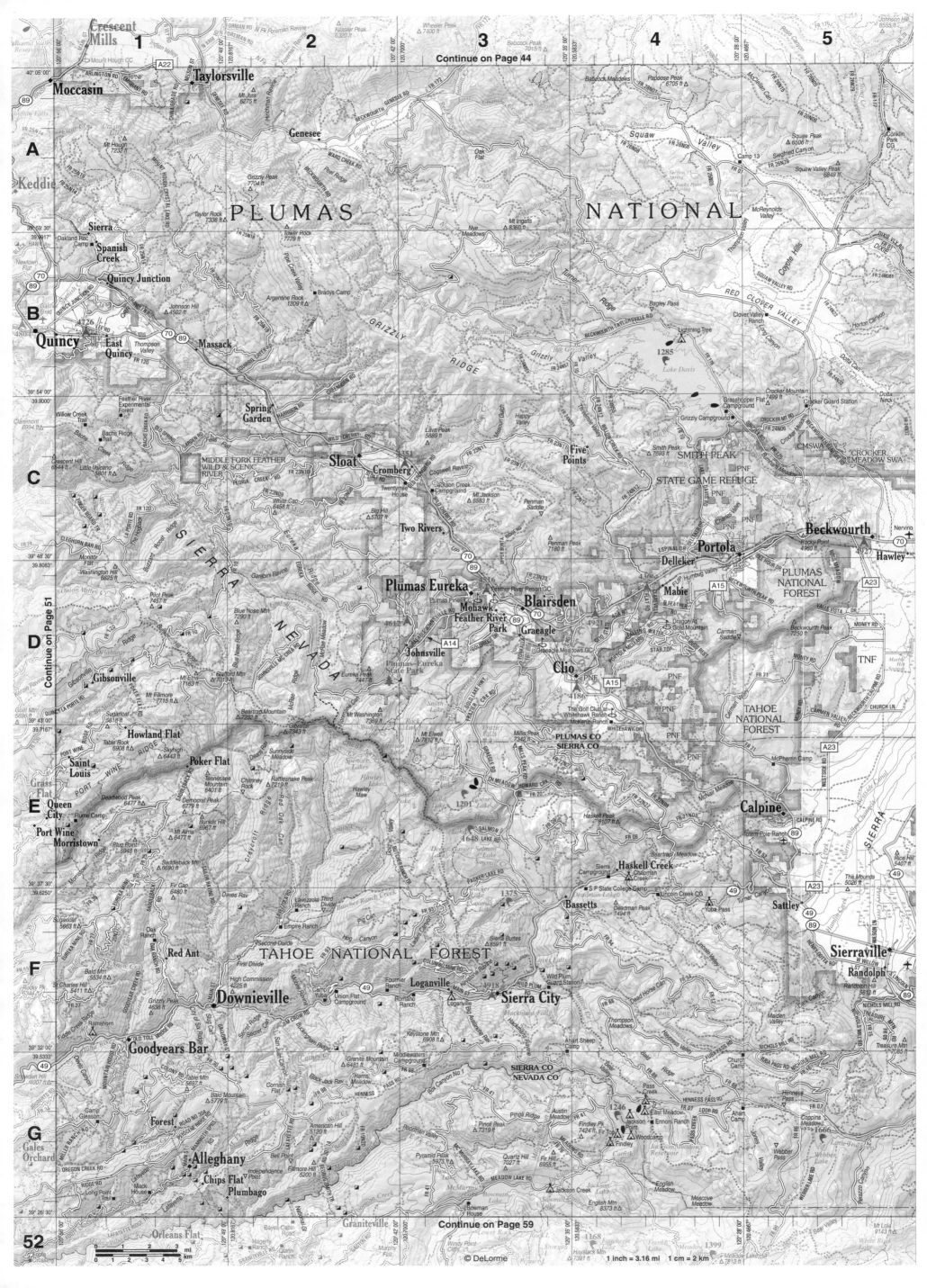

Continue on Page 59

Continue on Page 51

1 inch = 3.16 mi   1 cm = 2 km

© DeLorme

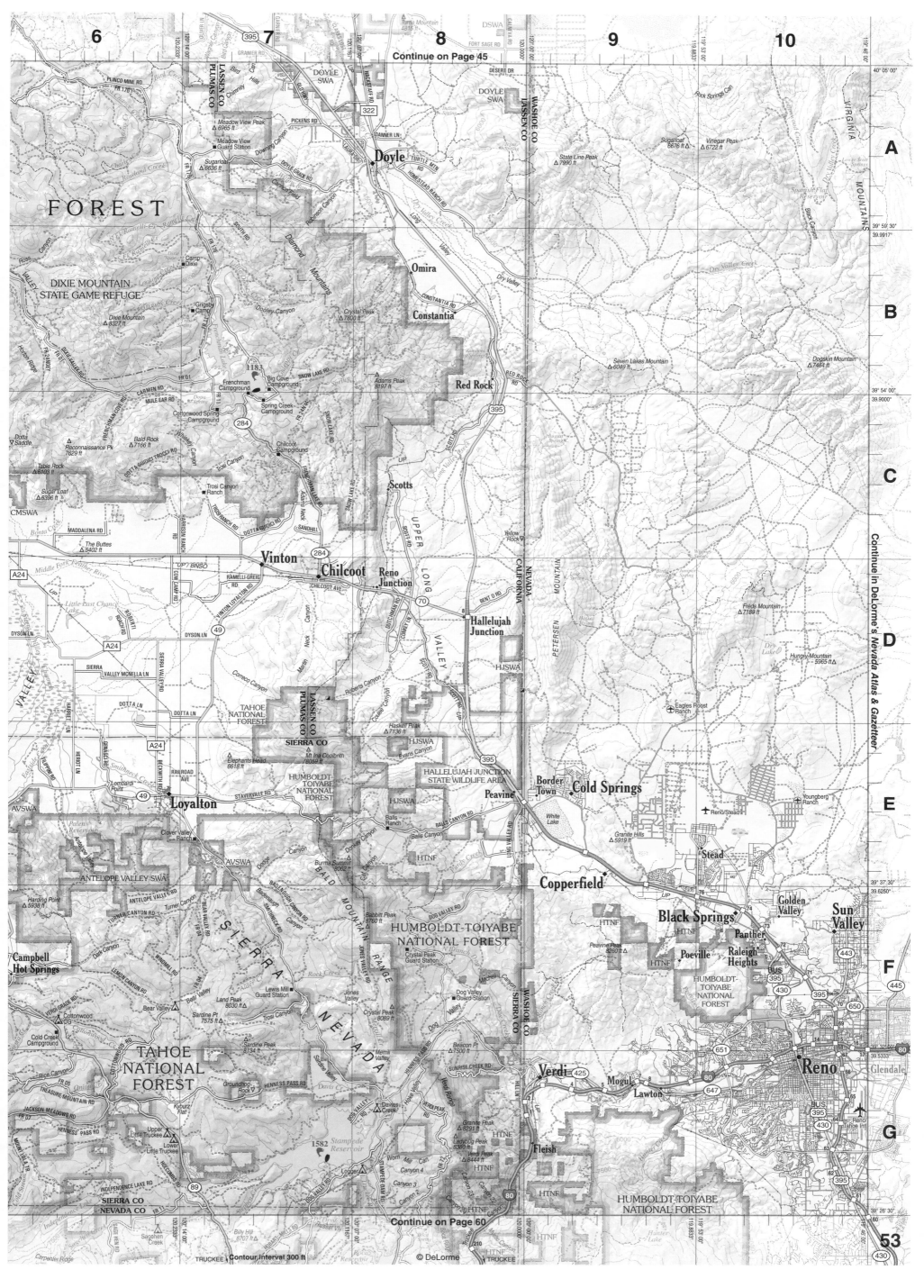

Continue on Page 45

FOREST

DIXIE MOUNTAIN
STATE GAME REFUGE

Doyle

Omira

Constantia

Red Rock

Scotts

Vinton   Chilcoot   Reno Junction

Hallelujah Junction

TAHOE NATIONAL FOREST

LASSEN CO / PLUMAS CO

SIERRA CO

HUMBOLDT-TOIYABE NATIONAL FOREST

HALLELUJAH JUNCTION STATE WILDLIFE AREA

Peavine

Border Town

Cold Springs

Loyalton

Copperfield

ANTELOPE VALLEY SWA

Black Springs

Golden Valley

Sun Valley

Stead

Panther

Poeville   Raleigh Heights

HUMBOLDT-TOIYABE NATIONAL FOREST

Campbell Hot Springs

SIERRA
NEVADA

BALD MOUNTAIN RANGE

HUMBOLDT-TOIYABE NATIONAL FOREST

Verdi   Mogul   Lawton

Reno

Glendale

Fleish

TAHOE NATIONAL FOREST

SIERRA CO / NEVADA CO

HUMBOLDT-TOIYABE NATIONAL FOREST

Continue on Page 60

TRUCKEE • Contour interval 300 ft

© DeLorme

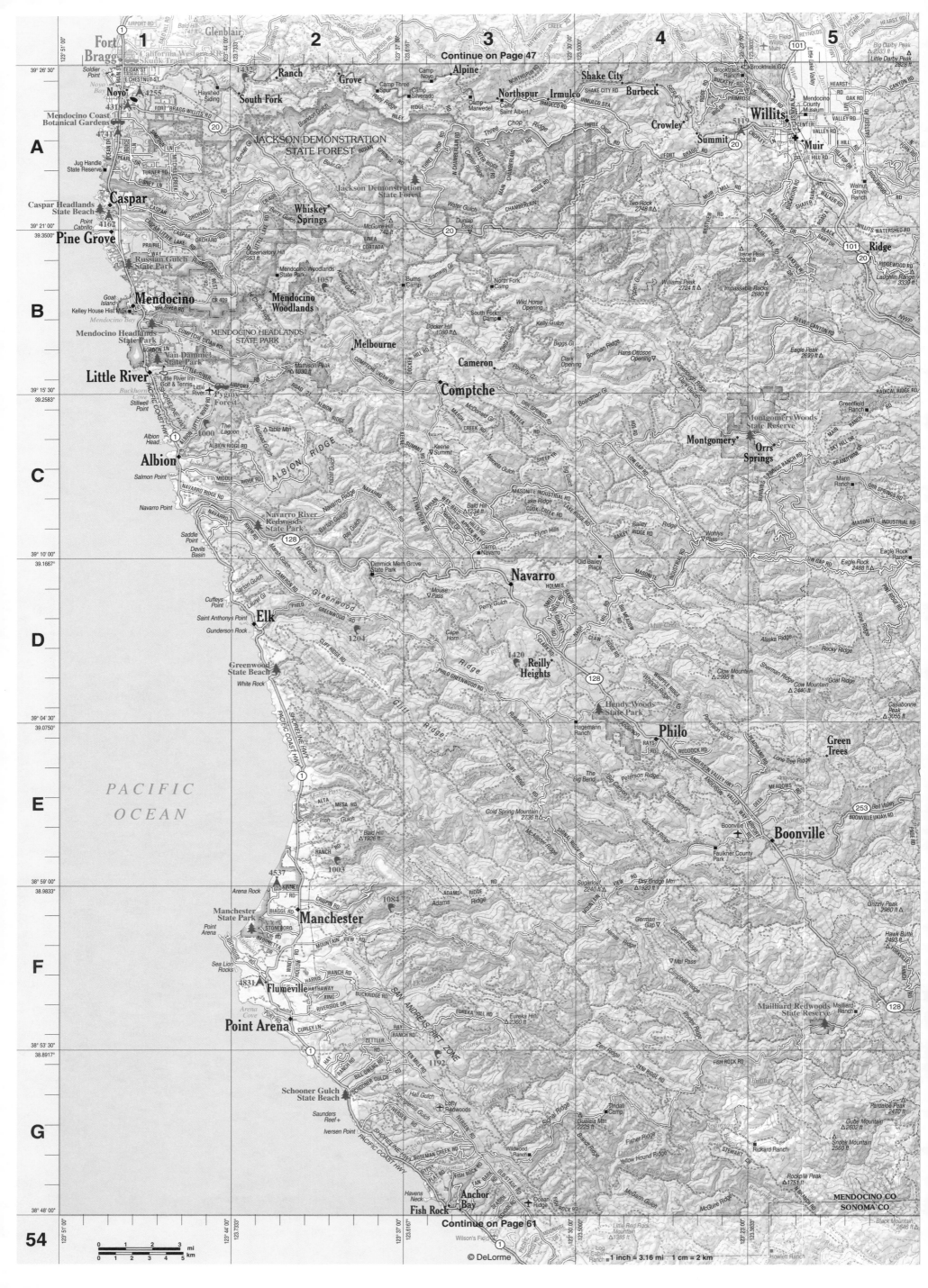

PACIFIC OCEAN

Fort Bragg

Willits

Mendocino

Boonville

Point Arena

© DeLorme

1 inch = 3.16 mi   1 cm = 2 km

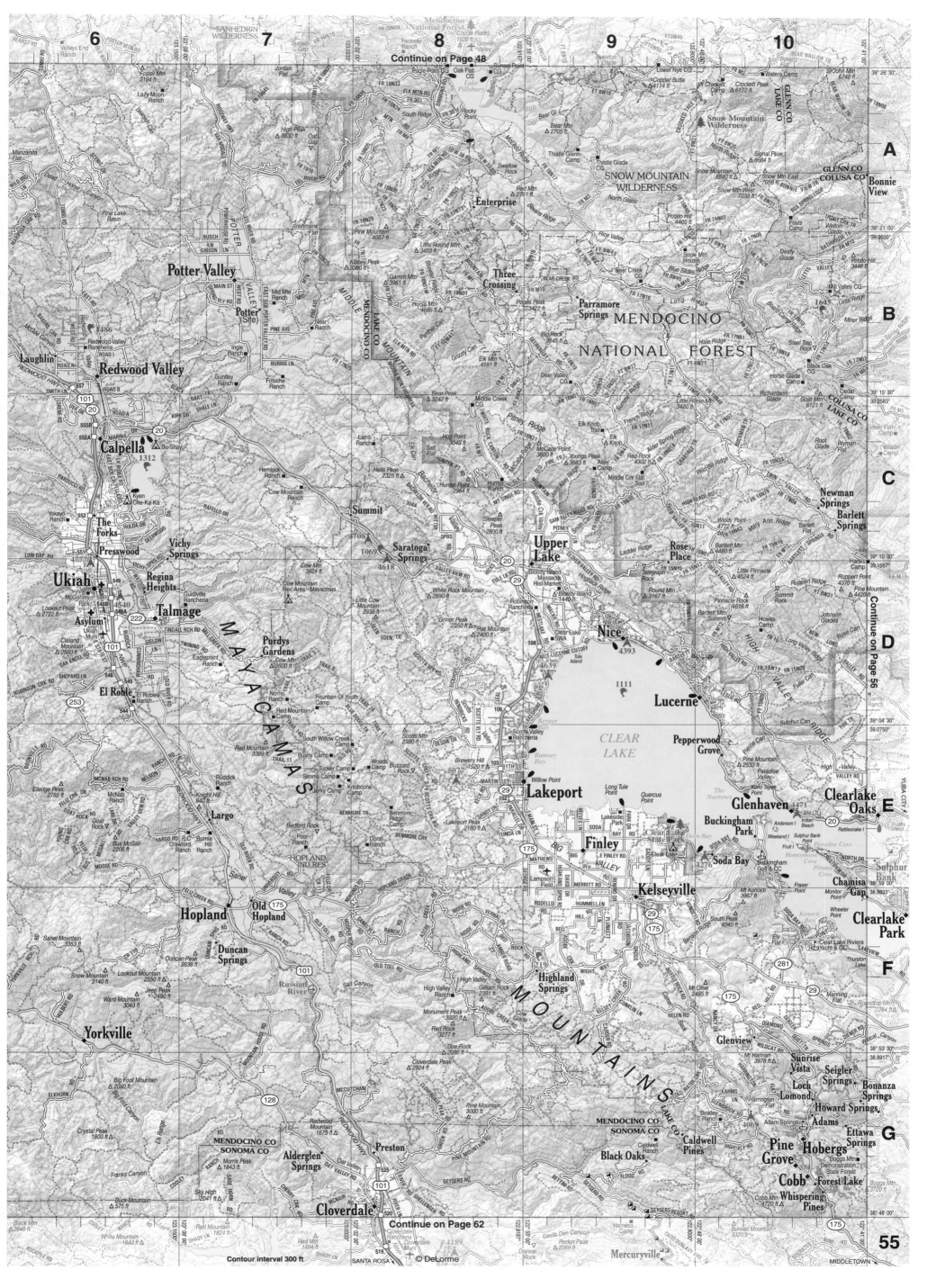

Continue on Page 48

Continue on Page 56

Continue on Page 62

Contour interval 300 ft

© DeLorme

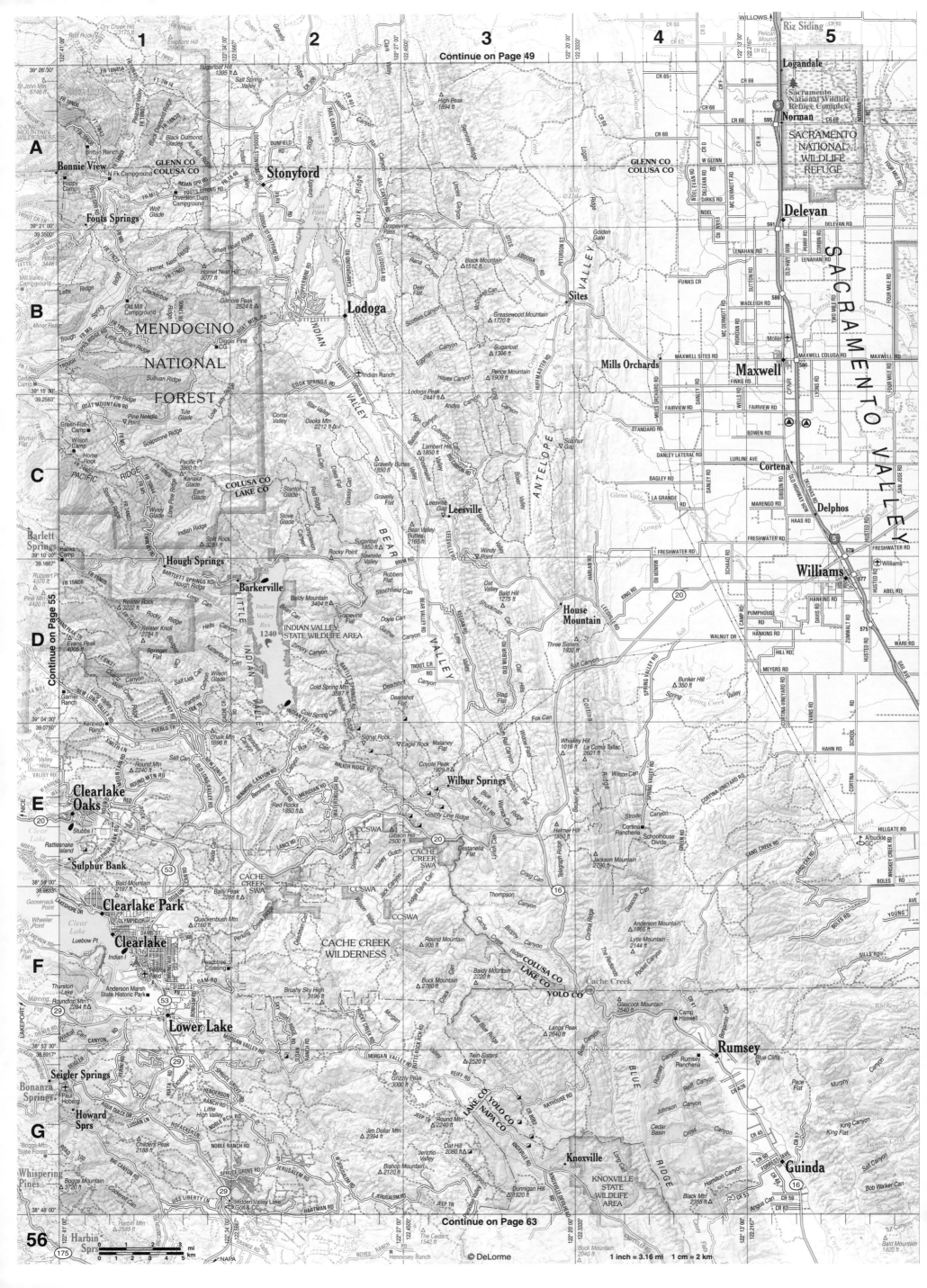

Continue on Page 49

Continue on Page 55

Continue on Page 63

56

1 inch = 3.16 mi   1 cm = 2 km

© DeLorme

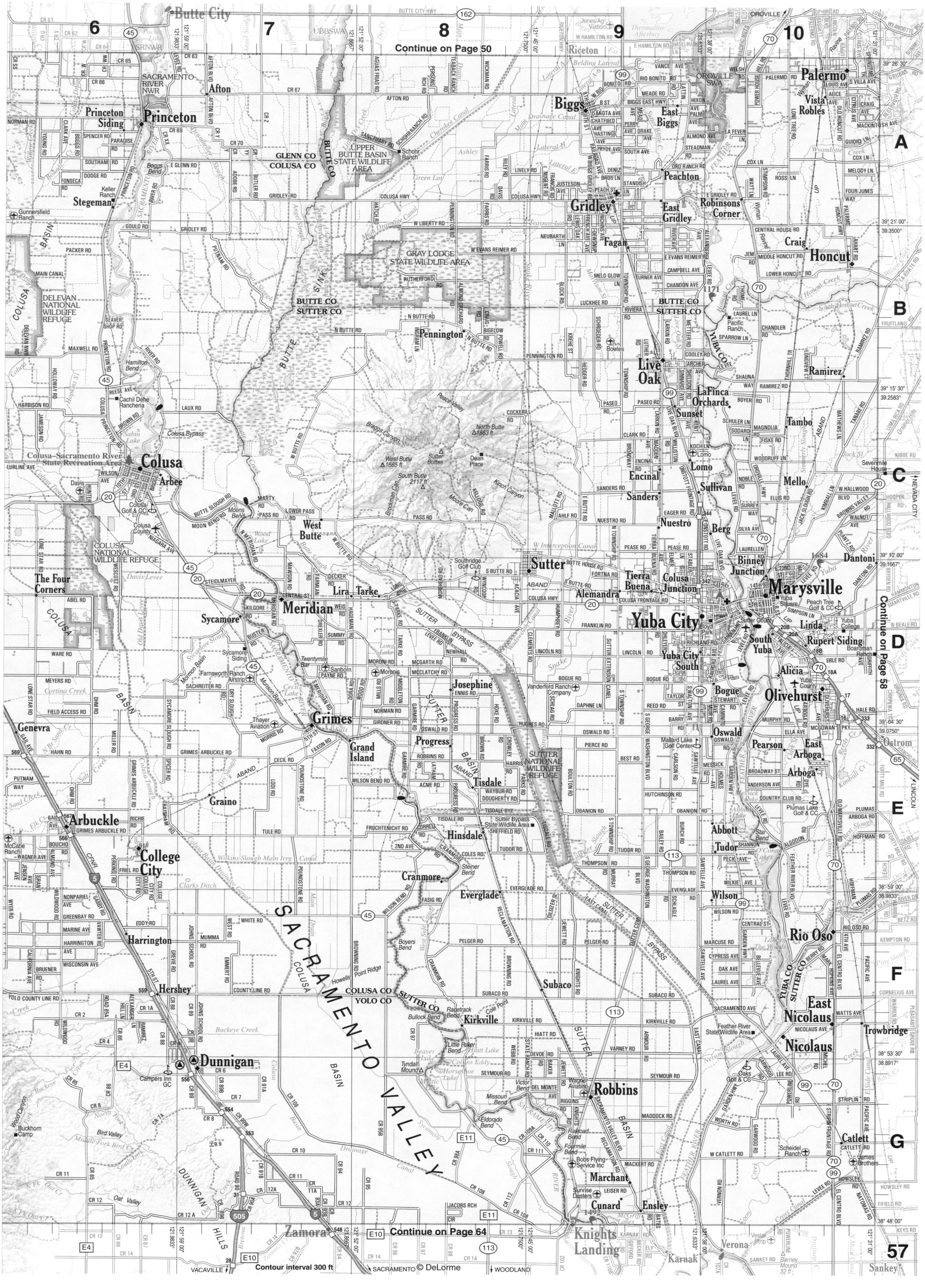
Continue on Page 50
Continue on Page 58
Continue on Page 64
Contour interval 300 ft
© DeLorme
Butte City
Princeton
Princeton Siding
Afton
Stegeman
Sacramento River NWR
Upper Butte Basin State Wildlife Area
Glenn Co
Colusa Co
Butte Co
Sutter Co
Yuba Co
Yolo Co
Biggs
East Biggs
Richvale
Peachton
Gridley
East Gridley
Robinsons Corner
Palermo
Vista Robles
Honcut
Craig
Fagan
Gray Lodge State Wildlife Area
Delevan National Wildlife Refuge
Colusa National Wildlife Refuge
Pennington
Live Oak
LaFinca Orchards
Sunset
Ramirez
Tambo
Colusa
Arbee
Colusa-Sacramento River State Recreation Area
West Butte
Sutter Buttes
South Butte 2117 ft
North Butte 1863 ft
West Butte 1685 ft
Encinal
Lomo
Sullivan
Sanders
Nuestro
Berg
Mello
Sutter
Tierra Buena
Colusa Junction
Binney Junction
Marysville
Dantoni
Alemandra
Yuba City
South Yuba
Linda
Rupert Siding
Yuba City South
Alicia
Olivehurst
Meridian
Lira
Tarke
Sycamore
The Four Corners
Josephine
Grimes
Grand Island
Progress
Tisdale
Sutter National Wildlife Refuge
Oswald
Pearson
East Arboga
Arboga
Graino
Genevra
Arbuckle
Abbott
Tudor
Hinsdale
College City
Cranmore
Everglade
Wilson
Rio Oso
Harrington
Hershey
Subaco
Kirkville
East Nicolaus
Nicolaus
Trowbridge
Dunnigan
Robbins
Catlett
Marchant
Cunard
Ensley
Knights Landing
Zamora
Verona
Karnak
Sankey
Sacramento Valley
Sacramento River
Feather River
Dunnigan Hills

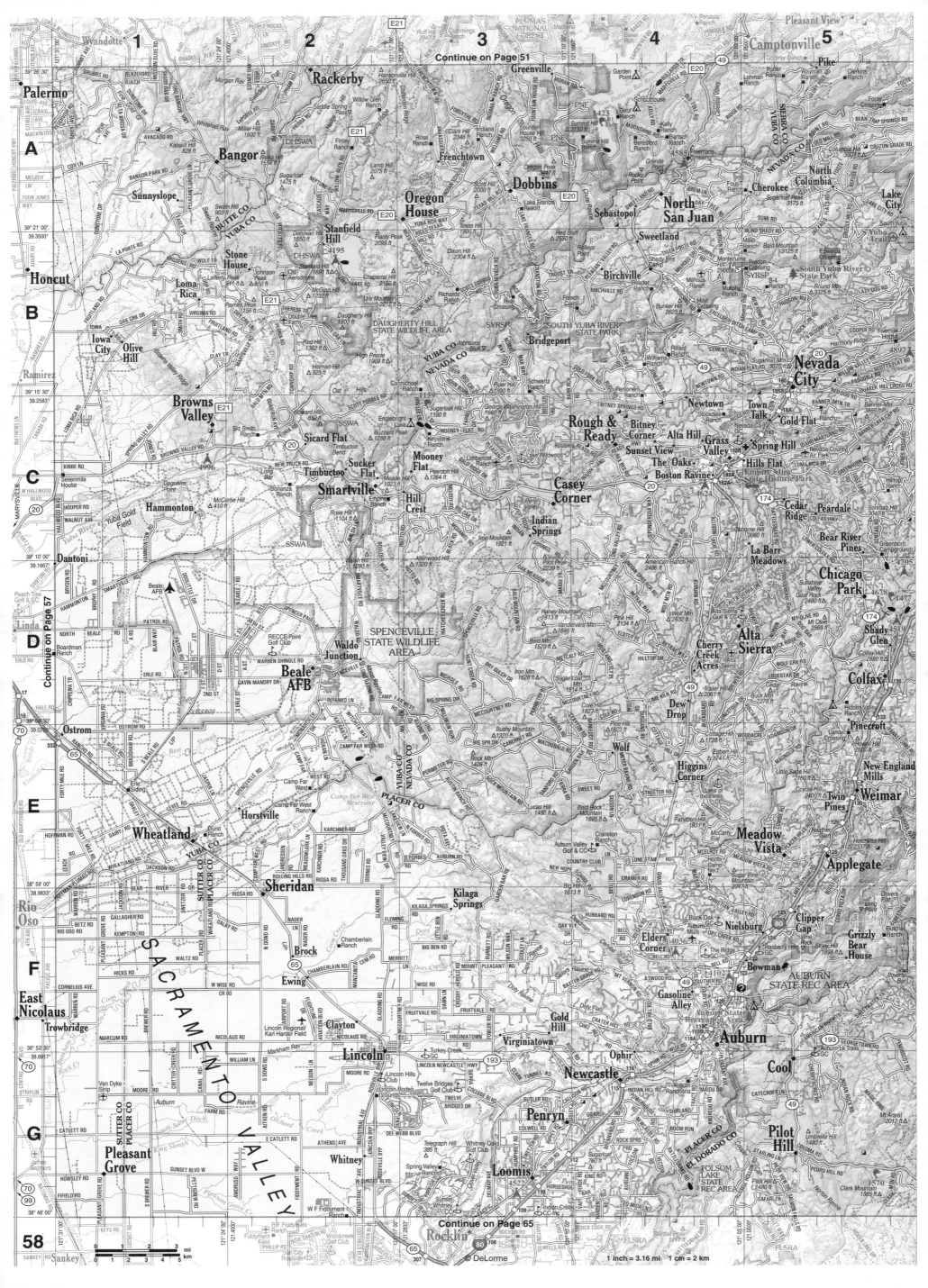

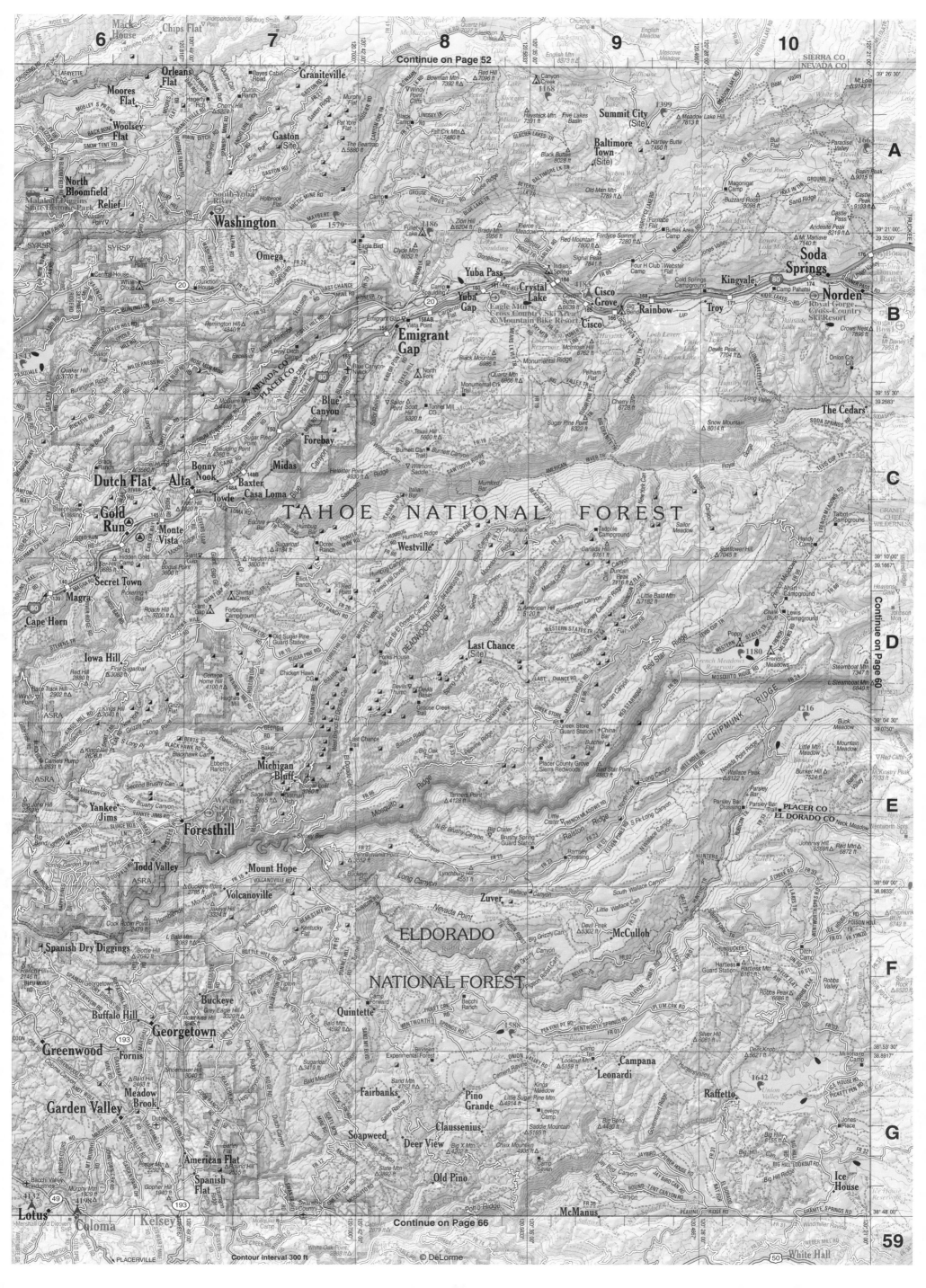

Continue on Page 52

Continue on Page 60

Continue on Page 66

Contour interval 300 ft   © DeLorme

59

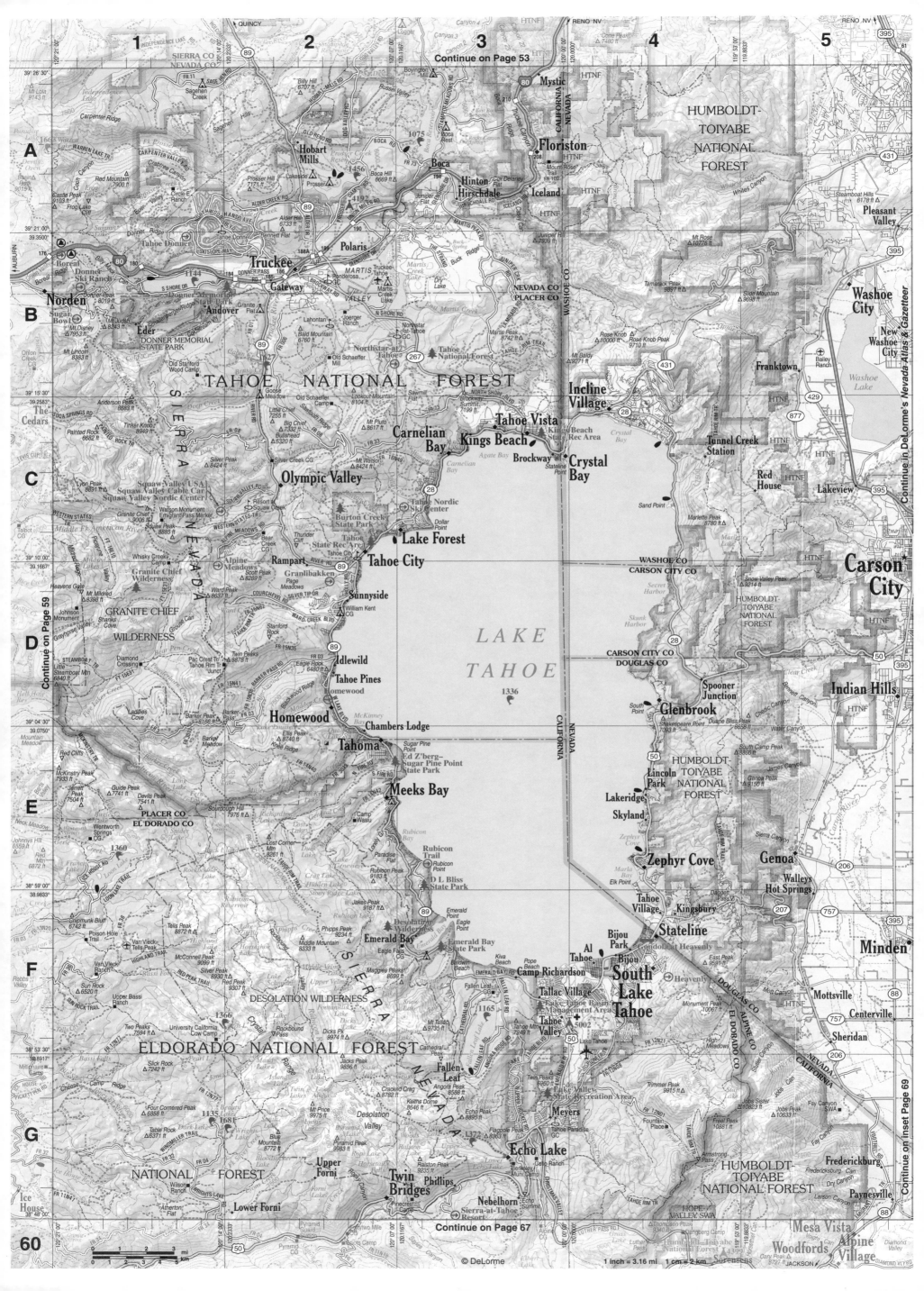

HUMBOLDT-
TOIYABE
NATIONAL
FOREST

TAHOE NATIONAL FOREST

SIERRA

NEVADA

GRANITE CHIEF
WILDERNESS

LAKE
TAHOE

1336

DESOLATION WILDERNESS

ELDORADO NATIONAL FOREST

NATIONAL FOREST

HUMBOLDT-
TOIYABE
NATIONAL FOREST

HUMBOLDT-
TOIYABE
NATIONAL FOREST

Carson City

60

Continue on Page 59

Continue on Page 67

Continue on inset Page 69

© DeLorme   1 inch = 3.16 mi   1 cm = 2 km

0 1 2 3 mi
0 1 2 3 4 5 km

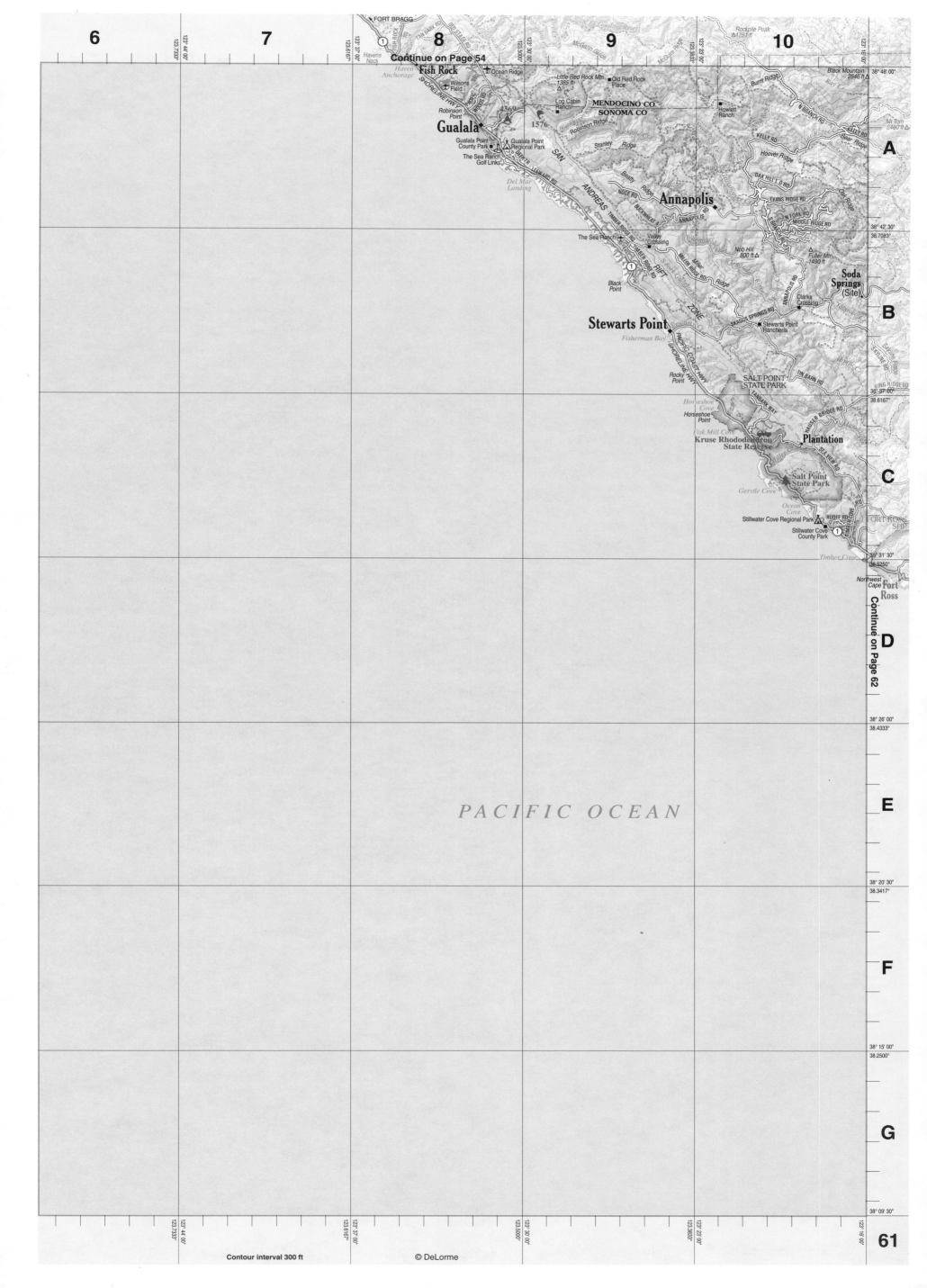

Continue on Page 54

6 **7** **8** **9** **10**

FORT BRAGG

Fish Rock

Haven Anchorage

Robinson Point

Wilsons Field

Gualala

Gualala Point County Park

Gualala Point Regional Park

The Sea Ranch Golf Links

Del Mar Landing

Ocean Ridge

Little Red Rock Mtn 1385 ft

Old Red Rock Place

Log Cabin Ranch

MENDOCINO CO
SONOMA CO

Robinson Ridge

Stanley Ridge

Beatty Ridge

Noce Rd

Buckwheat Rd

Rockpile Peak 1751 ft

Black Mountain 2646 ft

Burn Ridge

N BRANCH RD

Howlett Ranch

Mt Tom 2480 ft

KELLY RD

Hoover Ridge

OAK HILL L O RD

Oak Ridge

Annapolis

Annapolis

Evans Ridge Rd

N FORK RD

MIDDLE RIDGE RD

Nob Hill 800 ft

Fuller Mtn 1490 ft

Soda Springs (Site)

Clarks Crossing

The Sea Ranch

Valley Crossing

Black Point

SAN ANDREAS RIFT ZONE

MILLER RIDGE RD

ANNAPOLIS RD

SKAGGS SPRINGS RD

Stewarts Point Rancheria

King Ridge Rd

Stewarts Point

Fisherman Bay

Rocky Point

PACIFIC COASTHWY

SHORELINE HWY

TIN BARN RD

SALT POINT STATE PARK

Horseshoe Cove

Horseshoe Point

Fisk Mill Cove

TANBARK WAY

HAUSER BRIDGE RD

SEA VIEW RD

Plantation

Kruse Rhododendron State Reserve

Gerstle Cove

Salt Point State Park

Ocean Cove

Stillwater Cove Regional Park

Stillwater Cove County Park

RUOFF RD

FORT ROSS SHP

Timber Cove

Northwest Cape

Fort Ross

Continue on Page 62

PACIFIC OCEAN

123° 44' 00"
123.7333°

123° 37' 00"
123.6167°

123° 30' 00"
123.5000°

123° 23' 00"
123.3833°

123° 16' 00"

38° 48' 00"

38° 42' 30"
38.7083°

38° 37' 00"
38.6167°

38° 31' 30"
38.5250°

38° 26' 00"
38.4333°

38° 20' 30"
38.3417°

38° 15' 00"
38.2500°

38° 09' 30"

A
B
C
D
E
F
G

61

Contour interval 300 ft

© DeLorme

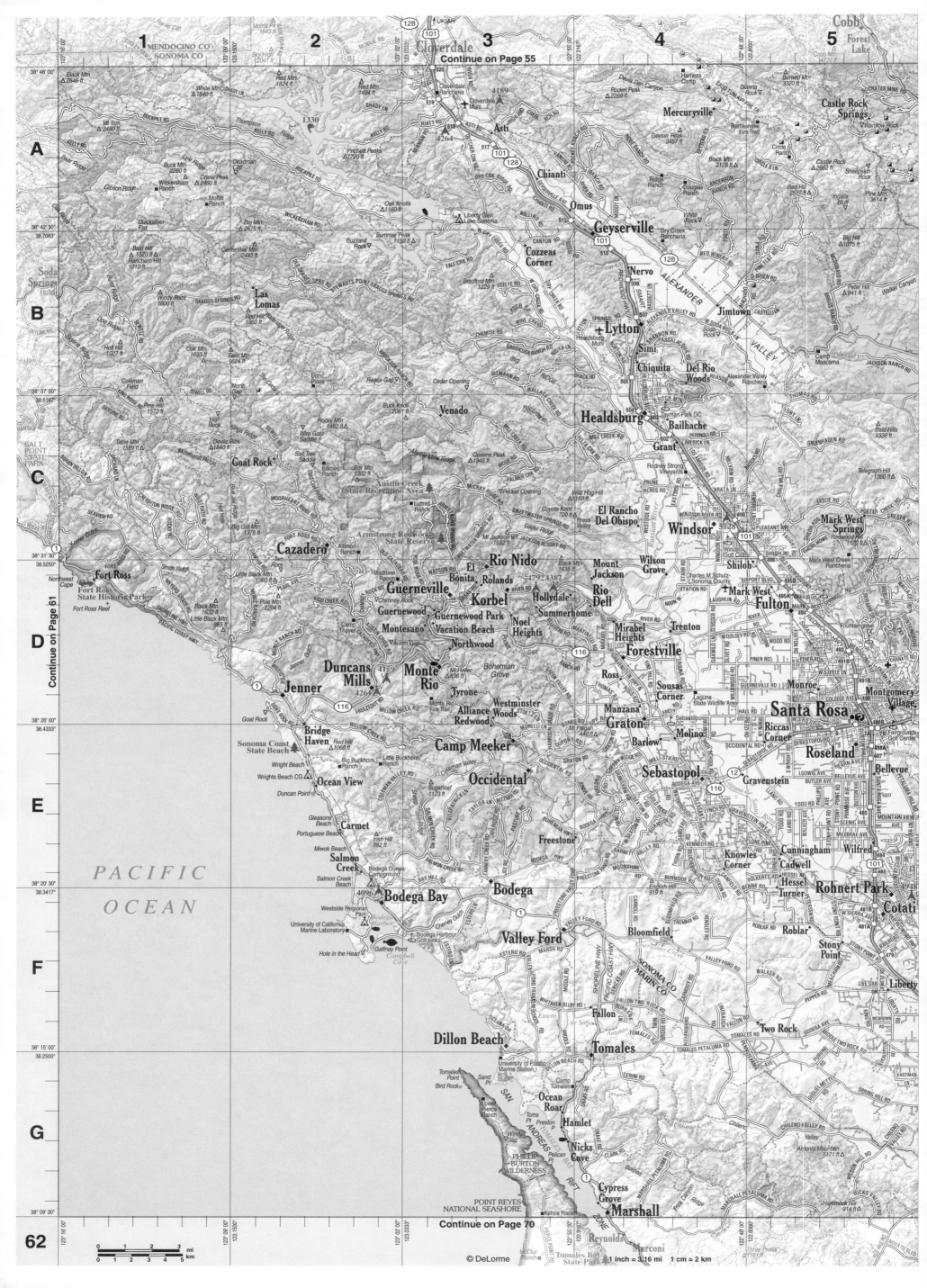

Continue on Page 55

Continue on Page 61

PACIFIC

OCEAN

Continue on Page 70

62

© DeLorme

1 inch = 3.16 mi   1 cm = 2 km

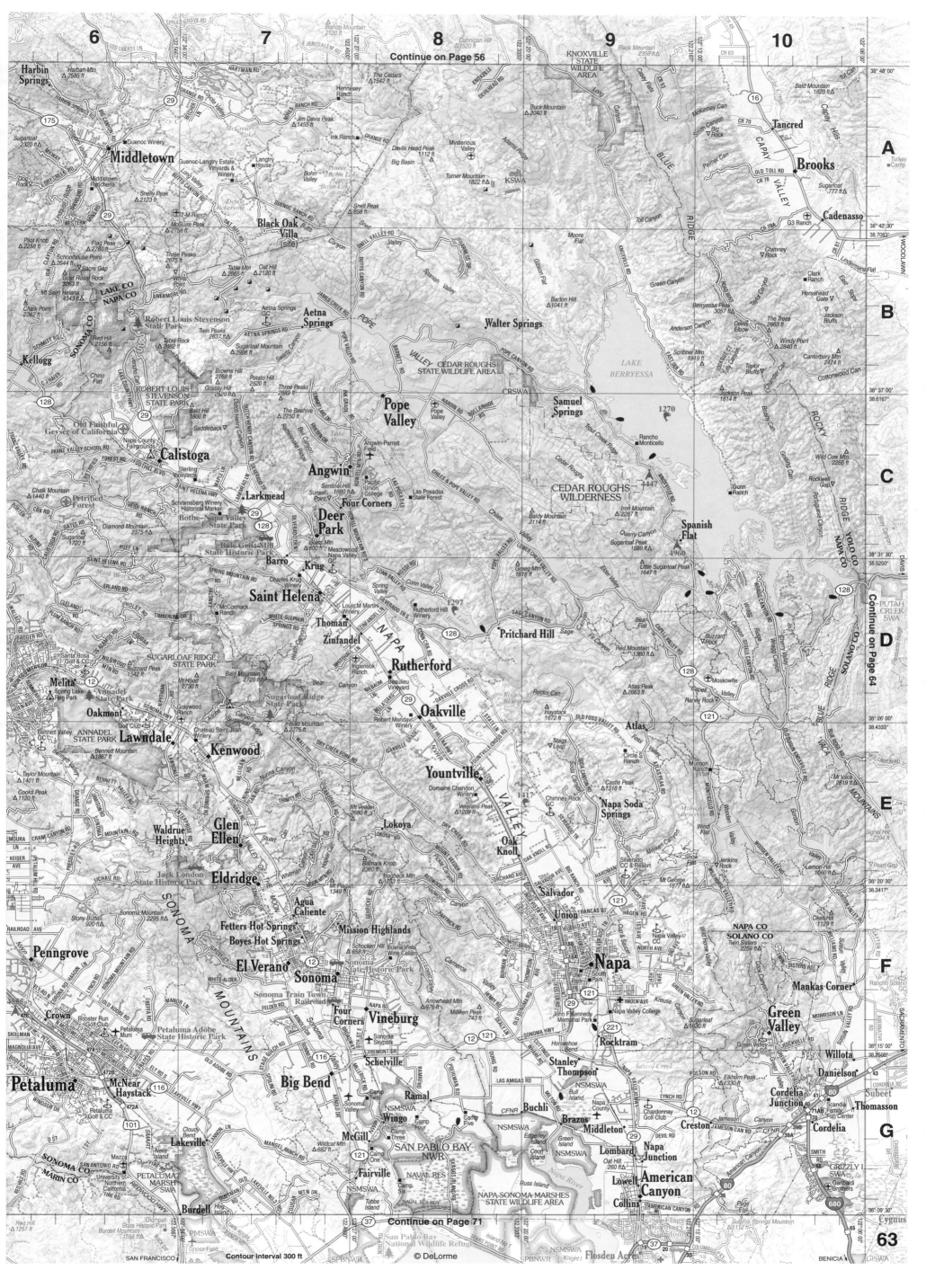

Continue on Page 56

Continue on Page 64

Continue on Page 71

Contour interval 300 ft

© DeLorme

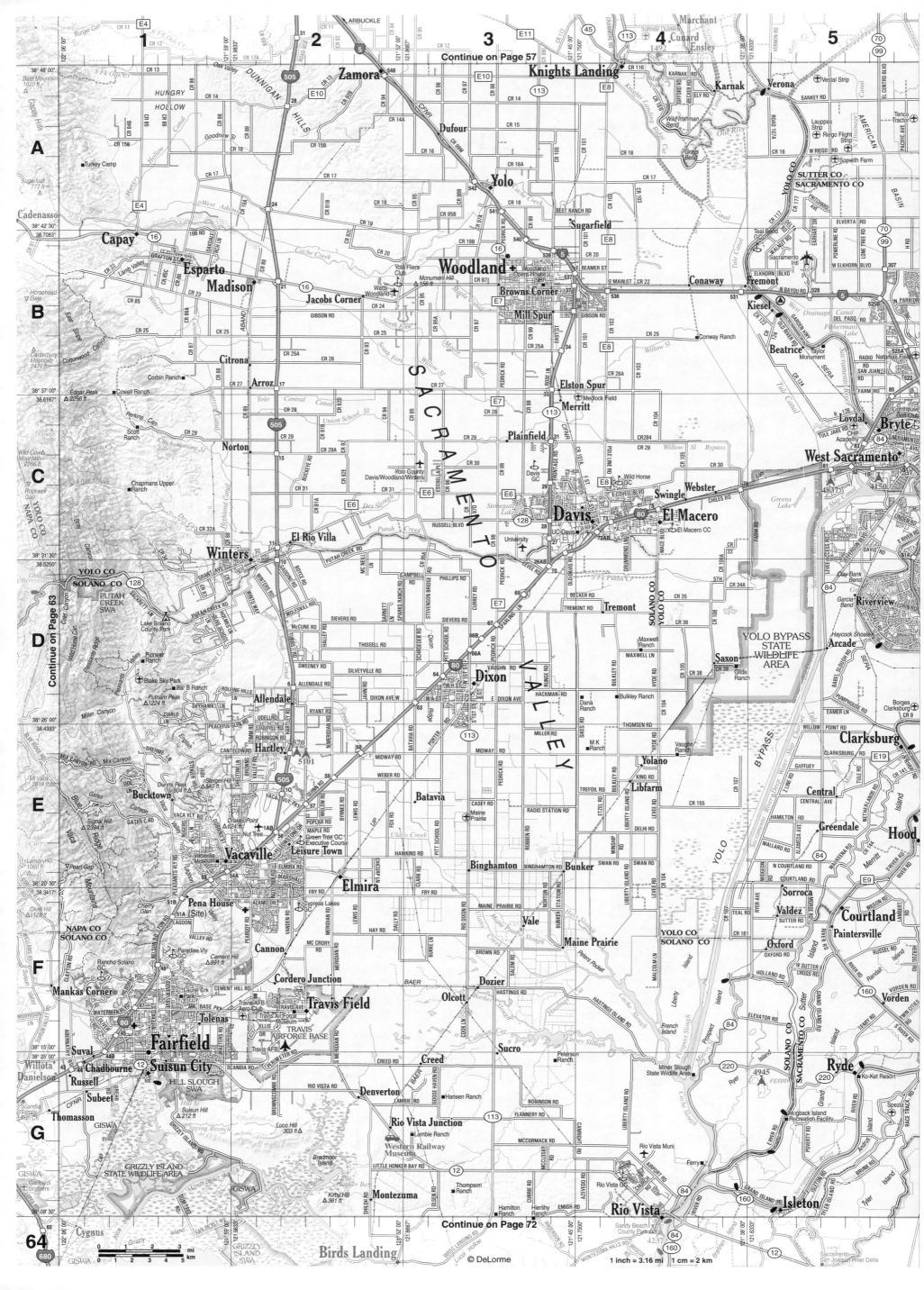

Continue on Page 63

1 inch = 3.16 mi   1 cm = 2 km

© DeLorme

Birds Landing

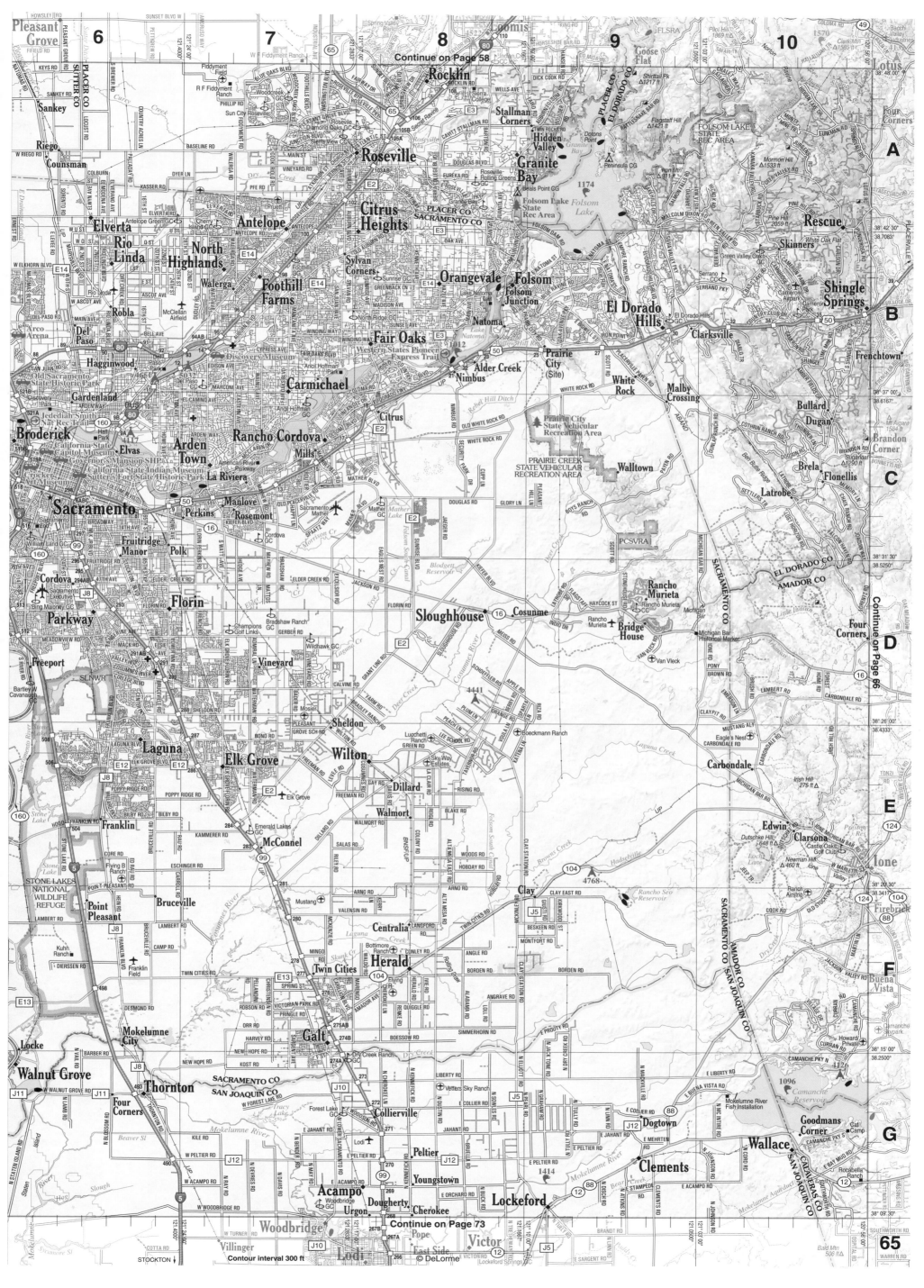

Continue on Page 58

Continue on Page 66

Continue on Page 73

Contour interval 300 ft   © DeLorme

1 **2** **3** **4** **5**

A

Coloma Kelsey
Four Corners
Gold Hill
Cold Springs
Smithflat
Motor City
Camino
Five Mile Terrace
Placerville
Apex

Pollock Pines
Fresh Pond Pacific
Riverton
White Hall

B

Missouri Flat
Shaw Mine Mill
Perks Corner
Diamond Springs
El Dorado Kingsville
Shingle Springs
Old Fort Jim
Avinsino Corner
Newtown
Tiger Lily Hanks Exchange
Pleasant Valley

Happy Valley
Sweeneys Crossing
Grizzly Flat
Gilberts

ELDORADO
Bryants
Darlington
Griminger
Bonetti
Voss
Capps Crossing

Frenchtown
Somerset

C

Brandon Corner
Nashville
Enterprise
River Pines
Mount Aukum
Melsons Corner
Outingdale
Fair Play
Coyoteville
Tylers Corner
Omo Ranch
Caldor
Croft
Five Corners

D

Plymouth
Four Corners
Drytown
Fiddletown

Volcano
Pioneer
Barton

E

New Chicago
Bunker Hill
Amador City
Sutter Creek
Sutter Hill
Martell
Jackson Gate
Pine Grove
Clinton
West Point
Bummerville
Sandy Gulch
Wilseyville
Independence

F

Ione
Lanes
Firebrick
Jackson
Scottsville
Bonnefoy
Big Bar
Mokelumne Hill
Electra
Rich Gulch
Glencoe
Rail Road Flat

Buena Vista
Jesus Maria
Paloma

G

Burson
Valley Springs
Campo Seco
Toyon
San Andreas
Kentucky House
Calaveritas
Mountain Ranch
Sheep Ranch
Fisher Place
Avery
Hathaway Pines
Arnold
Red Apple
Forest Meadows

Continue on Page 65

Continue on Page 74

66

1 inch = 3.16 mi 1 cm = 2 km

© DeLorme

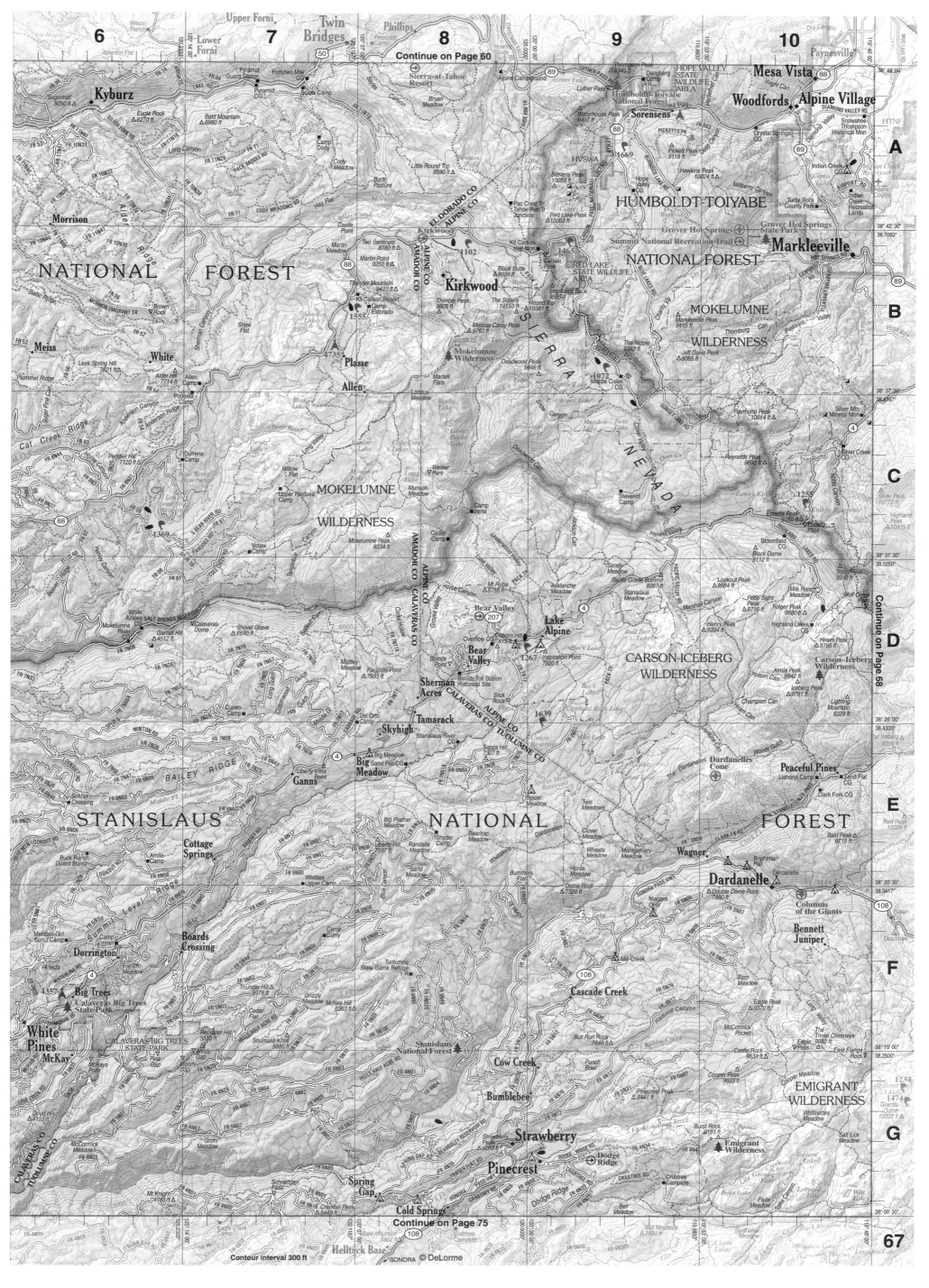

Continue on Page 60

Continue on Page 68

Continue on Page 75

Contour interval 300 ft

© DeLorme

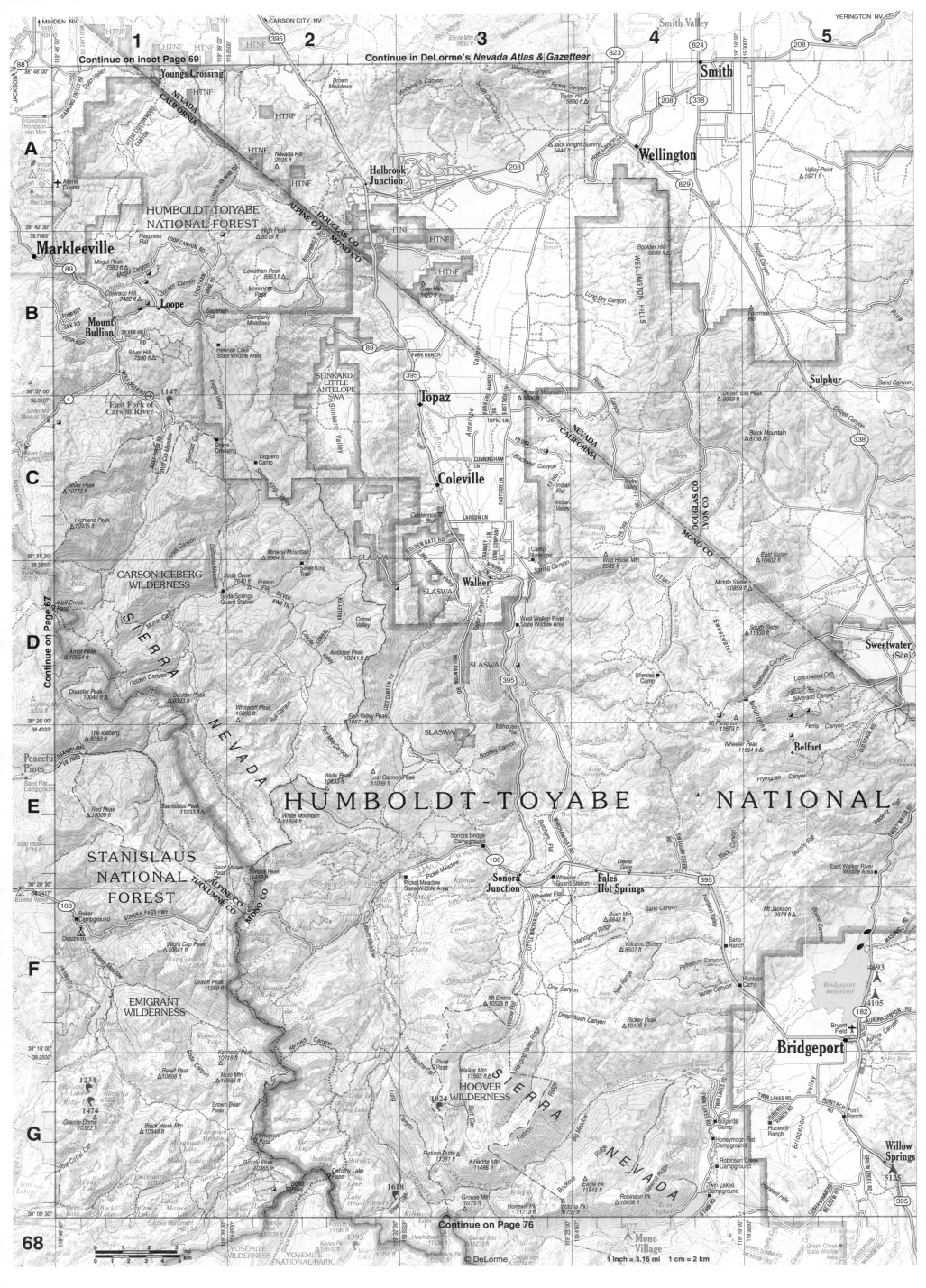

Continue on inset Page 69
Continue in DeLorme's *Nevada Atlas & Gazetteer*
Continue on Page 67
Continue on Page 76

Map labels (selected):

MINDEN NV, CARSON CITY NV, YERINGTON NV, Smith Valley, JACKSON

Youngs Crossing, NEVADA, CALIFORNIA, Smith

HUMBOLDT-TOIYABE NATIONAL FOREST, Holbrook Junction, Wellington

Markleeville, Haypress Flat, DOUGLAS CO, MONO CO

Mogul Peak 7583 ft, Loope, Mount Bullion, Silver Hill 7500 ft, Leviathan Peak 8963 ft, Monitor Pass, Gray Hills 5420 ft, Boulder Hill 6688 ft, WELLINGTON HILLS, Fourmile Hill

East Fork of Carson River, SLINKARD/LITTLE ANTELOPE SWA, Topaz, Sulphur, Desert Crk Peak 8969 ft

Silver Peak 10772 ft, Highland Peak 10935 ft, Grays Crossing, Vaquero Camp, Coleville, Cunningham, Black Mountain 8158 ft

CARSON-ICEBERG WILDERNESS, Mineral Mountain 8964 ft, Soda Cone 7640 ft, SLASWA, Walker, East Sister 10402 ft

SIERRA, NEVADA, Arnot Peak 10054 ft, Disaster Peak 10046 ft, Boulder Peak 9393 ft, Whitecliff Peak 10800 ft, Antelope Peak 10241 ft, Middle Sister 10859 ft, South Sister 11339 ft, Sweetwater, Mt Patterson 11679 ft

Peaceful Pines, The Iceberg 8350 ft, Fish Valley Peak 10571 ft, Wheeler Peak 11664 ft, Belfort

Red Peak 10009 ft, Stanislaus Peak 11233 ft, White Mountain 11398 ft, Wells Peak 10633 ft, Lost Cannon Peak 11099 ft, HUMBOLDT-TOYABE NATIONAL

STANISLAUS NATIONAL FOREST, Sonora Peak 11459 ft, Sonora Bridge Campground, Sonora Junction, Fales Hot Springs

Baker Campground, Deadman, Night Cap Peak 10641 ft, Leavitt Peak 11569 ft, Mt Jackson 9378 ft

EMIGRANT WILDERNESS, Kennedy Peak 10718 ft, Relief Peak 10808 ft, Molo Mtn 10885 ft, Walker Mtn 11563 ft, Bridgeport

Granite Dome 10322 ft, Black Hawk Mtn 10348 ft, Emigrant Pass, HOOVER WILDERNESS, Grouse Mtn 10775 ft, Eagle Pk 11845 ft, Robinson Pk 10806 ft, Willow Springs

YOSEMITE WILDERNESS, YOSEMITE NATIONAL PARK, Mono Village

1 inch = 3.16 mi   1 cm = 2 km

© DeLorme

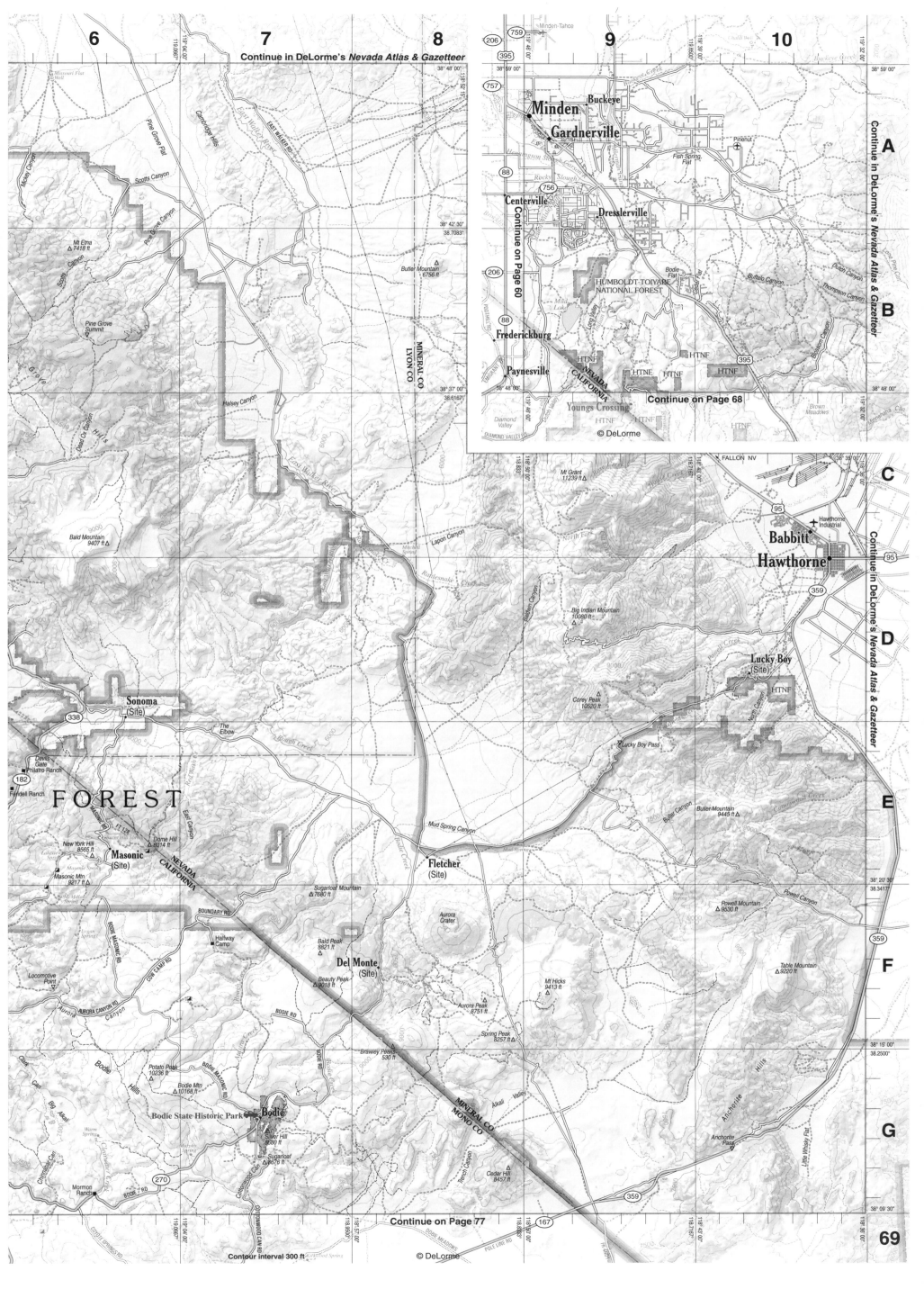

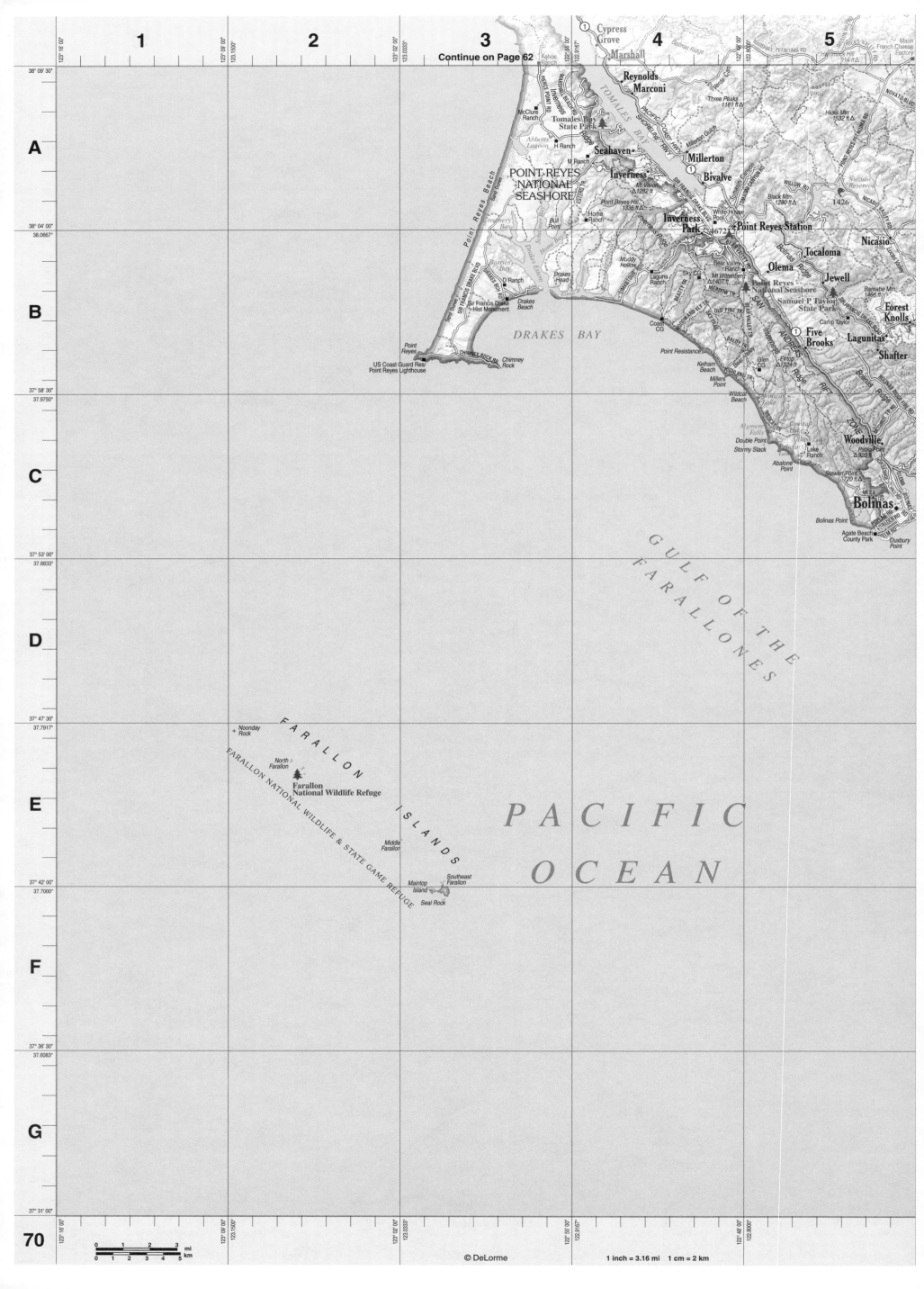

Continue on Page 62

Cypress Grove
Marshall
Reynolds
Marconi
McClure Ranch
Tomales Bay State Park
Abbotts Lagoon
H Ranch
Seahaven
POINT REYES NATIONAL SEASHORE
Inverness
Millerton
Bivalve
Mt Vision 1282 ft
Point Reyes Hill 1336 ft
Black Mtn 1280 ft
1426
Bull Point
Home Ranch
White House Pool
Inverness Park
1672
Point Reyes Station
Tocaloma
Nicasio
Olema
Jewell
Drakes Head
Muddy Hollow
Laguna Ranch
Bear Valley Ranch
Mt Wittenberg 1407 ft
Point Reyes National Seashore
Samuel P Taylor State Park
Barnabe Mtn 1466 ft
Forest Knolls
Sir Francis Drake Hist Monument
Drakes Beach
Coast CG
Sky CG
Old Pine Tr
Camp Taylor
Five Brooks
Lagunitas
Shafter
DRAKES BAY
Point Reyes
Point Resistance
Glen CG
Firtop 1324 ft
US Coast Guard Res/
Point Reyes Lighthouse
Chimney Rock Rd
Chimney Rock
Kelham Beach
Millers Point
Woodville
Pablo Point 920 ft
Wildcat Beach
Alamere Falls
Double Point
Stormy Stack
Lake Ranch
Stewart Point 720 ft
Abalone Point
Bolinas
Bolinas Point
Agate Beach County Park
Duxbury Point

G U L F O F T H E
F A R A L L O N E S

Noonday Rock
North Farallon
Farallon National Wildlife Refuge
FARALLON NATIONAL WILDLIFE & STATE GAME REFUGE
F A R A L L O N
I S L A N D S
Middle Farallon
Maintop Island
Southeast Farallon
Seal Rock

P A C I F I C
O C E A N

0 1 2 3 mi
0 1 2 3 4 5 km

© DeLorme   1 inch = 3.16 mi   1 cm = 2 km

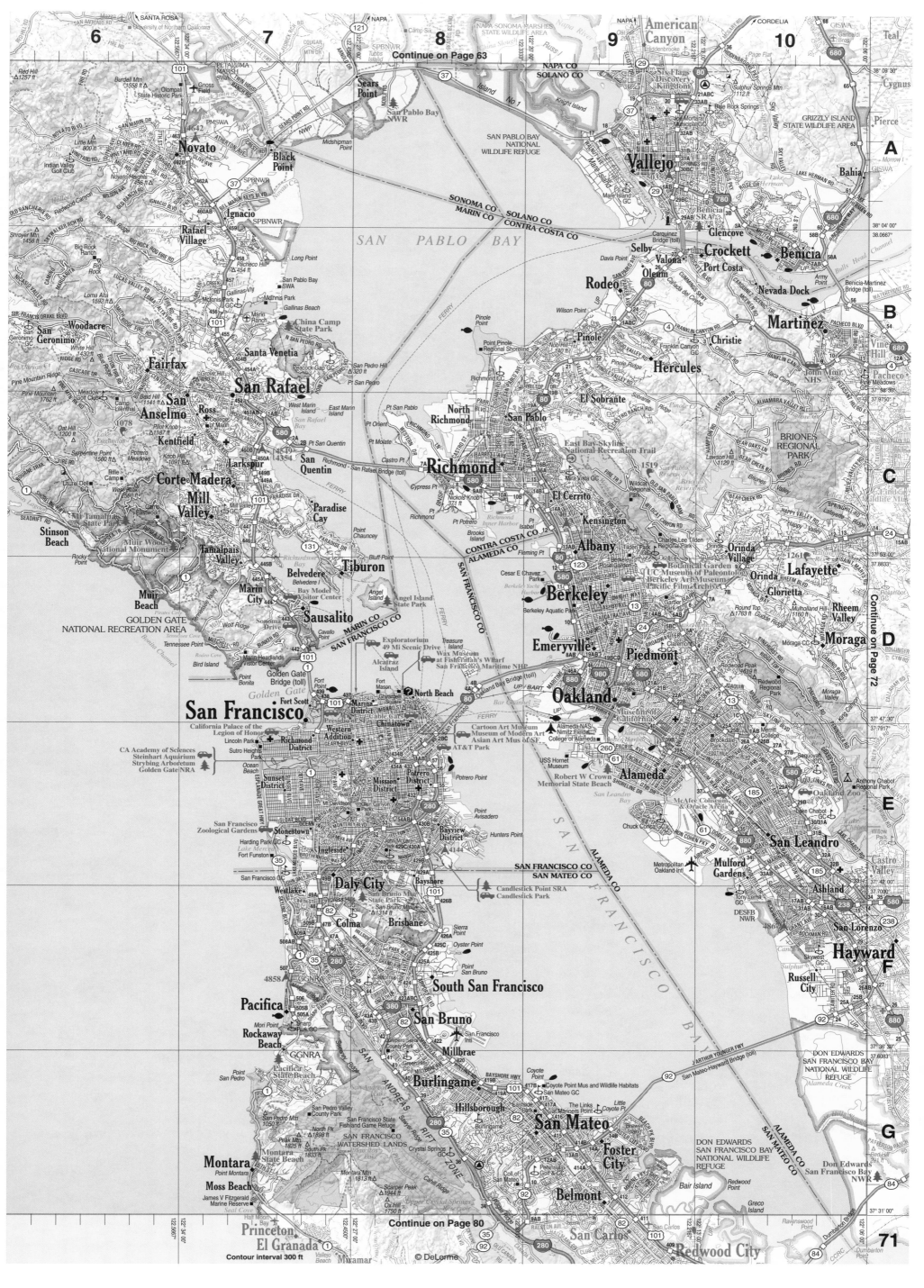

Continue on Page 63

Continue on Page 72

Continue on Page 80

SAN PABLO BAY

SAN PABLO BAY
NATIONAL
WILDLIFE REFUGE

GOLDEN GATE
NATIONAL RECREATION AREA

San Francisco

Oakland

Berkeley

Richmond

San Rafael

Novato

Vallejo

Benicia

Martinez

Hayward

San Leandro

San Mateo

Daly City

South San Francisco

San Bruno

Burlingame

Pacifica

Contour interval 300 ft

© DeLorme

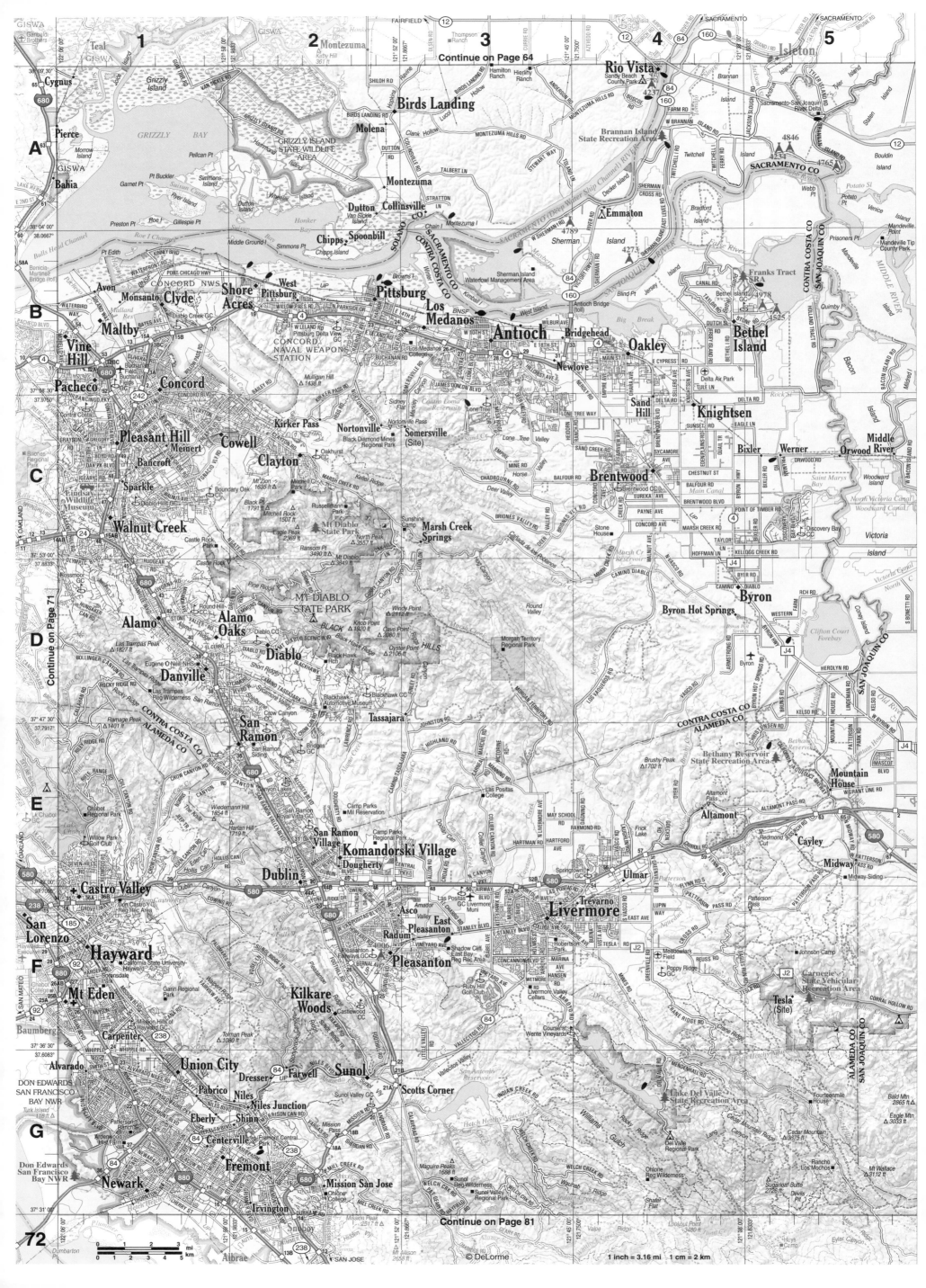

Continue on Page 64

Continue on Page 71

Continue on Page 81

© DeLorme

1 inch = 3.16 mi   1 cm = 2 km

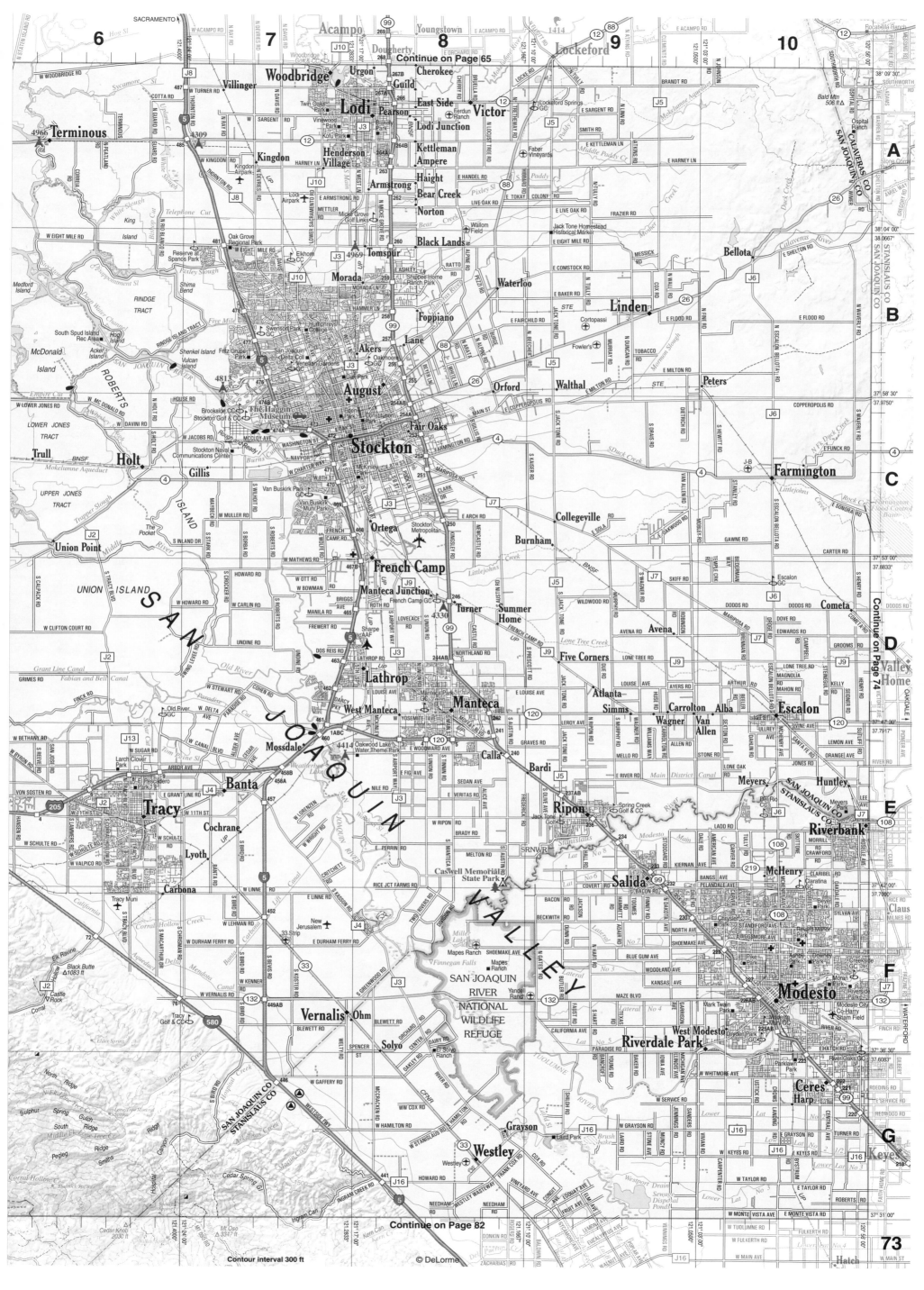

Continue on Page 65

Continue on Page 74

Continue on Page 82

Contour interval 300 ft

© DeLorme

73

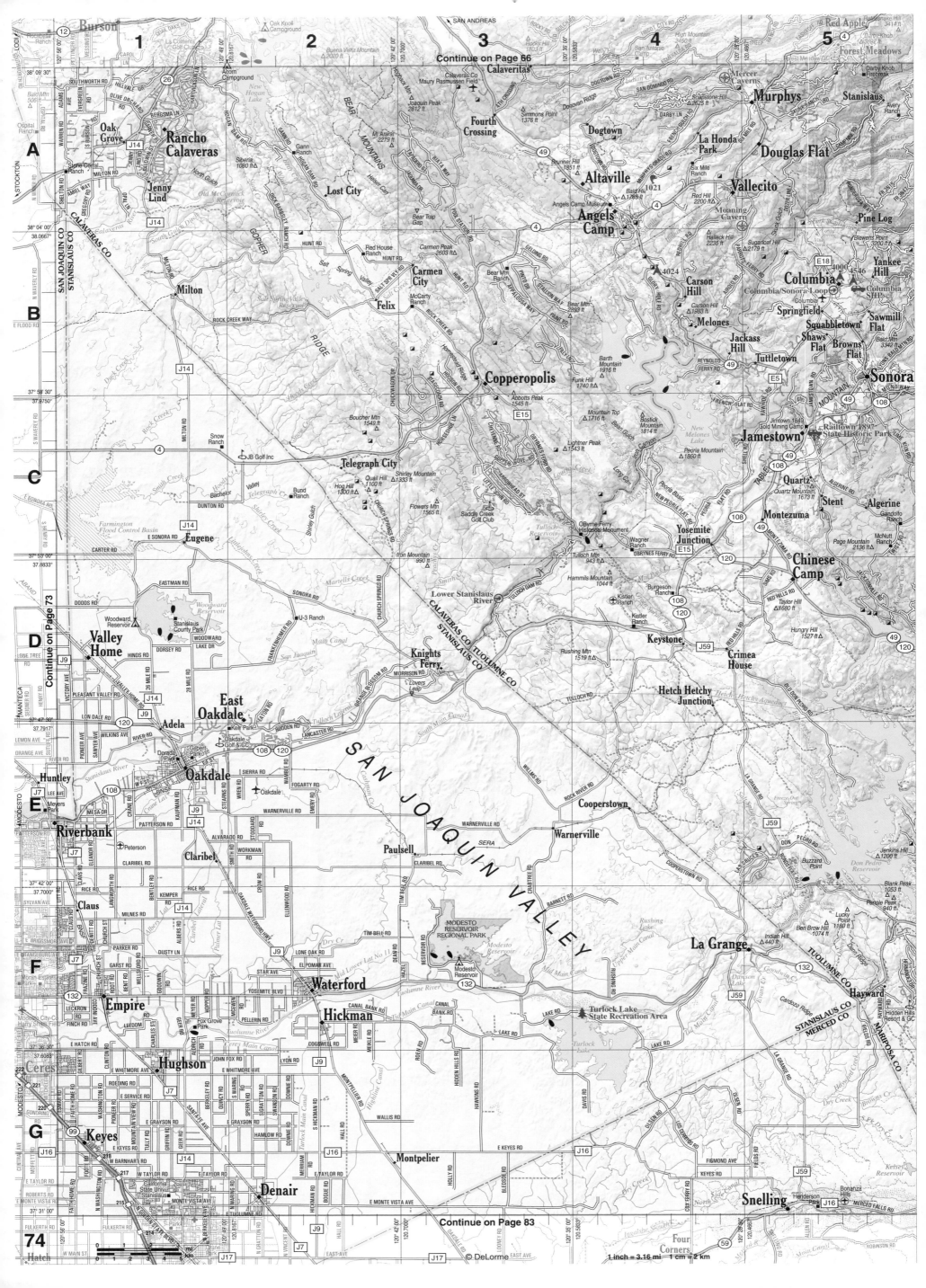

Continue on Page 66

Continue on Page 73

Continue on Page 83

SAN JOAQUIN VALLEY

1 inch = 3.16 mi   1 cm = 2 km

© DeLorme

74

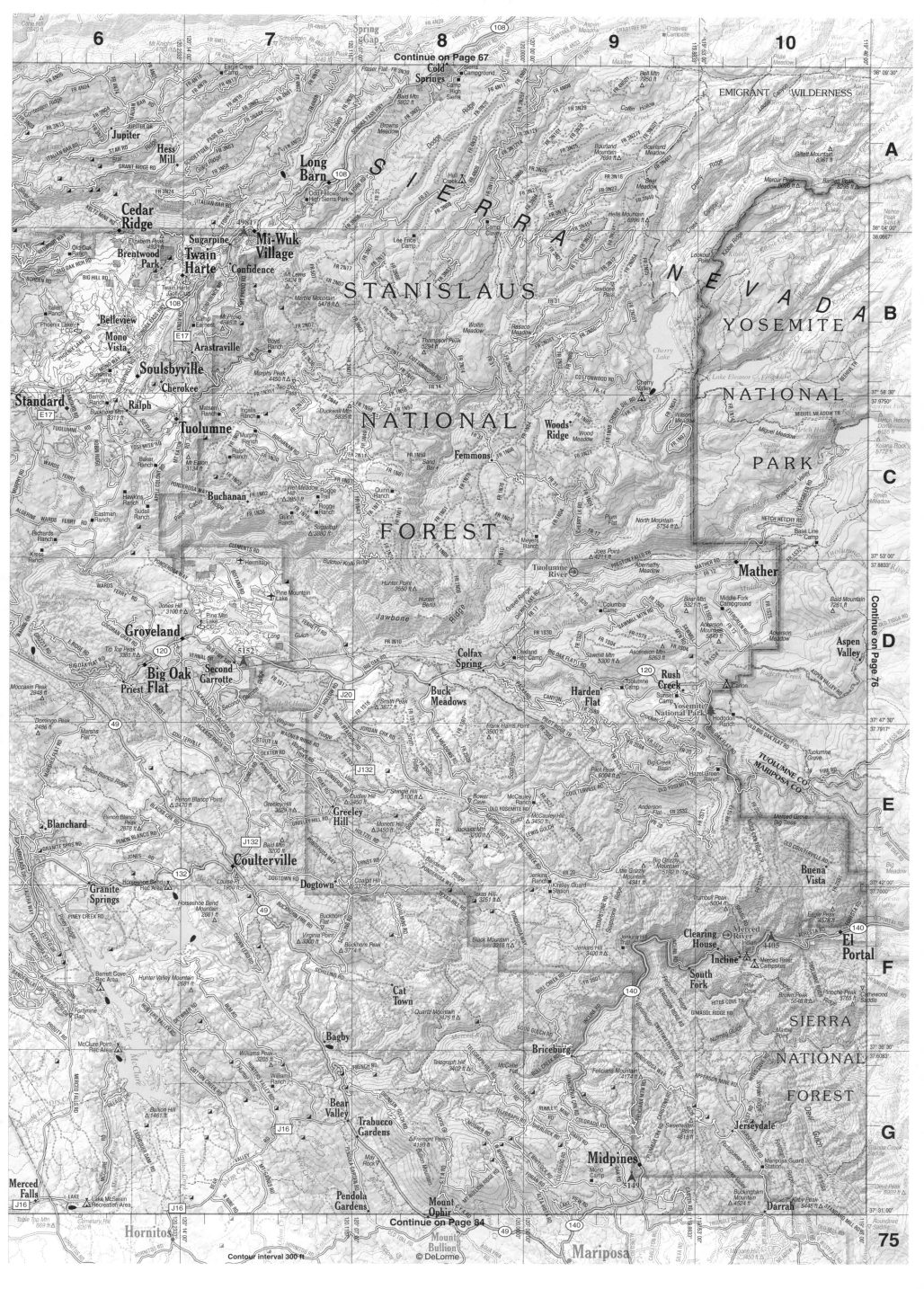

Continue on Page 67

Continue on Page 76

Continue on Page 84

Contour interval 300 ft

© DeLorme

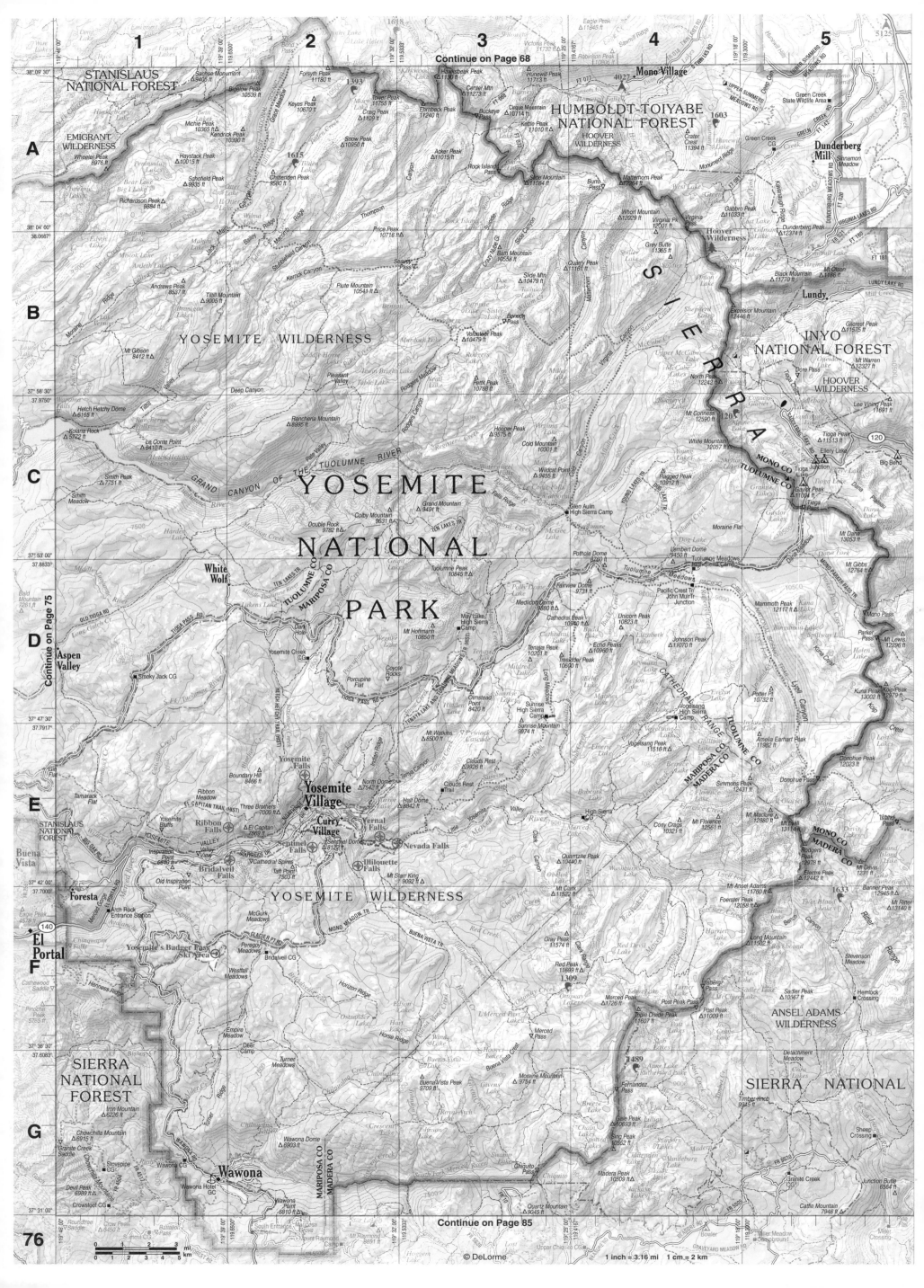

Continue on Page 68

Continue on Page 85

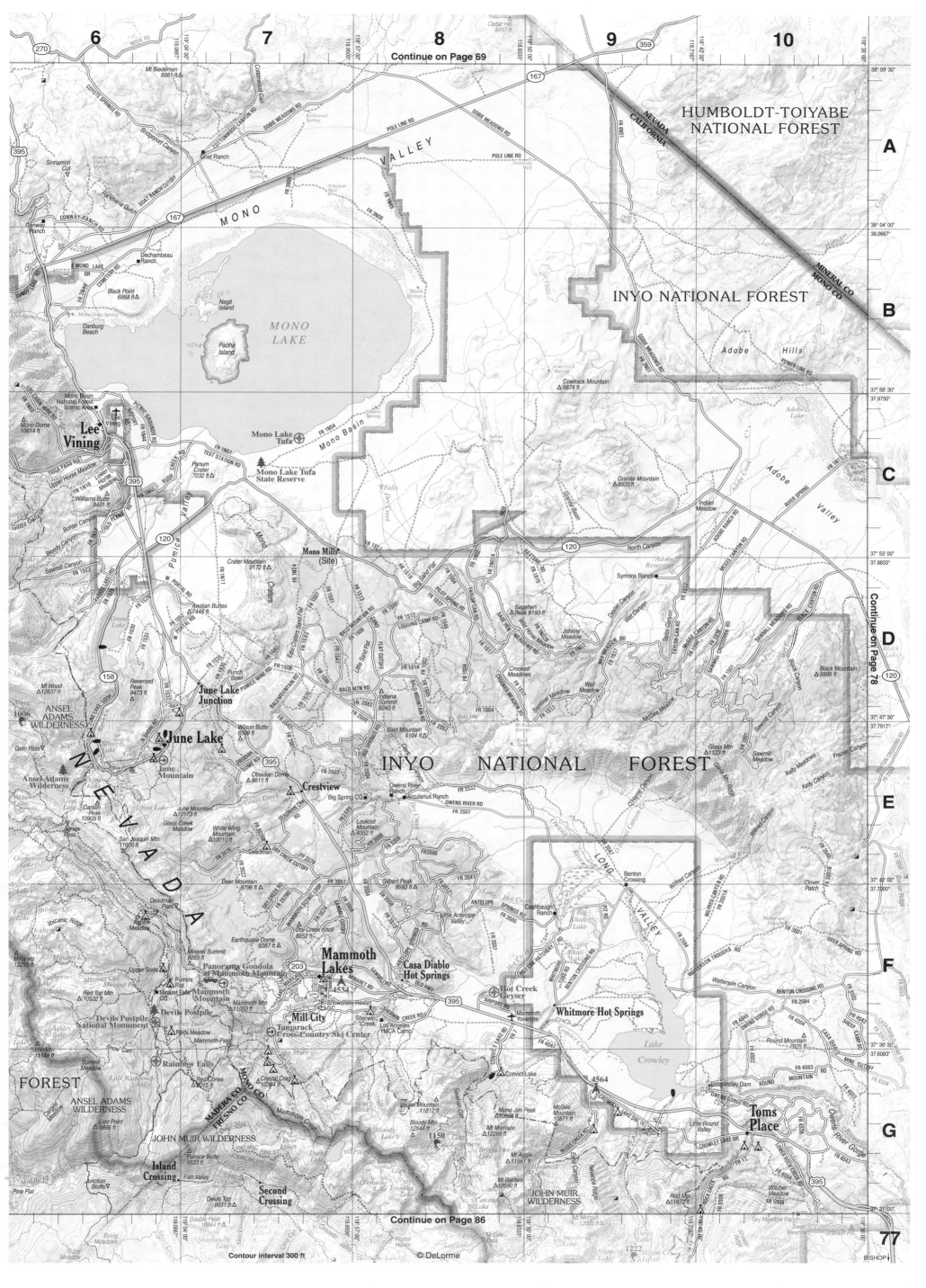

Continue on Page 69

HUMBOLDT-TOIYABE
NATIONAL FOREST

INYO NATIONAL FOREST

MONO LAKE

Lee Vining

INYO NATIONAL FOREST

June Lake

NEVADA

Mammoth Lakes

ANSEL ADAMS WILDERNESS

JOHN MUIR WILDERNESS

Toms Place

Continue on Page 78

Continue on Page 86

Contour interval 300 ft

© DeLorme

1   **2**   **3**   **4**   **5**

A

B

C

D

E

F

G

HUMBOLDT-TOIYABE
NATIONAL FOREST

Dry Lake

Government Well

Huntoon

Jack Spring Canyon

Columbus
(Site)

MINERAL CO
ESMERALDA CO

Candelaria Hills

Miller Mountain
8729 ft △

360

NEVADA
CALIFORNIA

Pizona
(Site)

McBride Flat

Truman Meadows

Truman
Springs

Basalt
(Site)

**Mount
Montgomery**

Montgomery
Pass

6

Volcanic Hills

INYO   NATIONAL   FOREST

264

773

FR 1N13

Pizona

Sugarloaf
9182 ft △

Gold Hit
(Site)

Saghen
Flat

Cedar
Springs

Sand Spring Canyon

Antelope
Mountain
Lake

Antelope Mountain
△ 7617 ft

Bramlette
Ranch

RANCHARD EXTENDED RD

TRUMAN MEADOWS RD

Mustang Point
9869 ft △

Kennedy
Flats

Mustang Can

Queen

Pinto Hill
6046 ft
△

River
Spring
Lakes

MINERAL CO
ESMERALDA CO

Buffalo Point
△ 9643 ft

Kennedy Point
△ 10410 ft

Wildhorse
Flat

North
Valley

Queen Valley

Can

120

ADOBE VALLEY

Trafton Mountain
7825 ft △

Benton

FOOTHILL RD

Pedro
Ranch

Morris Creek

PEDRO RCH RD

Trail Canyon
Saddle

Trail Canyon

Black
Lake

SIPES RANCH RD

Montgomery City

Montgomery Peak
13441 ft △

Black Mountain
9704 ft △

Chiatovich Creek

264

Benton

120

S I E R R A

Davis Mountain
9369 ft

Benton Hot
Springs

Dutch Pete's
Ranch

CATTLE DRIVE RD

Modoc
Peak
6880 ft △

Blind Spring Hill

BENTON RANGE

Anderson Peak
6920 ft △

Diana Peak
7080 ft

Marble Creek

The Jumpoff
13484 ft △

Mt Dubois
13559 ft △

Queen Dicks Canyon

NEVADA
CALIFORNIA

Post
Meadow

Marble Creek

Circle L
Ranch

Leidy Creek

Fish
Lake

Frazier Canyon

Kelty
Canyon

Watterson
Meadow

POLE RD

POLE RD

JACKET RD

Yellowjacket Canyon

**Queen
Dicks**

Falls

Canyon

Pellisier
Flats

W H I T E

Mt Hogue
12751 ft △

INYO

BENTON CROSSING RD

FR 3S06

Banner Ridge

FR 3S09

FR 3S09

6

FALLS CRK
RD

Middle

Canyon

M O U N T A I N S

Pinyon Mountain
8773 ft △

Dyer

ESMERALDA CO
MONO CO

264

NATIONAL

BLACK ROCK MINE RD

Hammil Valley

Harris Bros
Ranch

Indian Peak
11297 ft △

Headley Peak
12678 ft △

N E V A D A

Juniper Mountain
7662 ft △

FR 3S01

CHIDAGO CANYON RD

Red Rock Canyon

DAWSON RCH RD

Hammil

Devinlos
Ranch

Cottonwood

Canyon

INYO

FOREST

POLE RD

Red Canyon
Petroglyphs

Symons
Ranch

Cashbaugh
Ranch

Hill
Ranch

White Mountain Peak
14246 ft △

Red Mountain
△ 7988 ft

NATIONAL

Chidago
Flat

CHIDAGO LOOP

Casa Diablo Mtn
△ 7912 ft

FR 4S41

Chidago

FISH SLOUGH RD

Jeffrey
Mine

Sabies

Canyon

Mt Barcroft
13040 ft △

McAfee Meadow

Tres Plumas
Meadow

F O R E S T

CASA DIABLO MINE CUTOFF

FR 4S04

FR 4S02

FR 4S03

FR 4S04

CHALFANT

Straight

Canyon

Sacramento

Can

Canyon

Lamb
Camp

Piute Mtn
12564 ft △

WHT MTN RD

FR 4S01

Sheep Mountain
12497 ft △

Tres Plumas
Flat

Basin

McCloud
Camp

Standel Peak

395

Mesa
Camp

VOLCANIC
TABLELAND

SLIM PRINCESS RD

Chalfant

6

Piute Creek

Campito
Meadow

Campito Mountain
11543 ft △

BISHOP

Continue on Page 77

Continue on Page 87

MAMMOTH LAKES

Owens River

BISHOP

78

1 inch = 3.16 mi   1 cm = 2 km

© DeLorme

0 1 2 3 mi
0 1 2 3 4 5 km

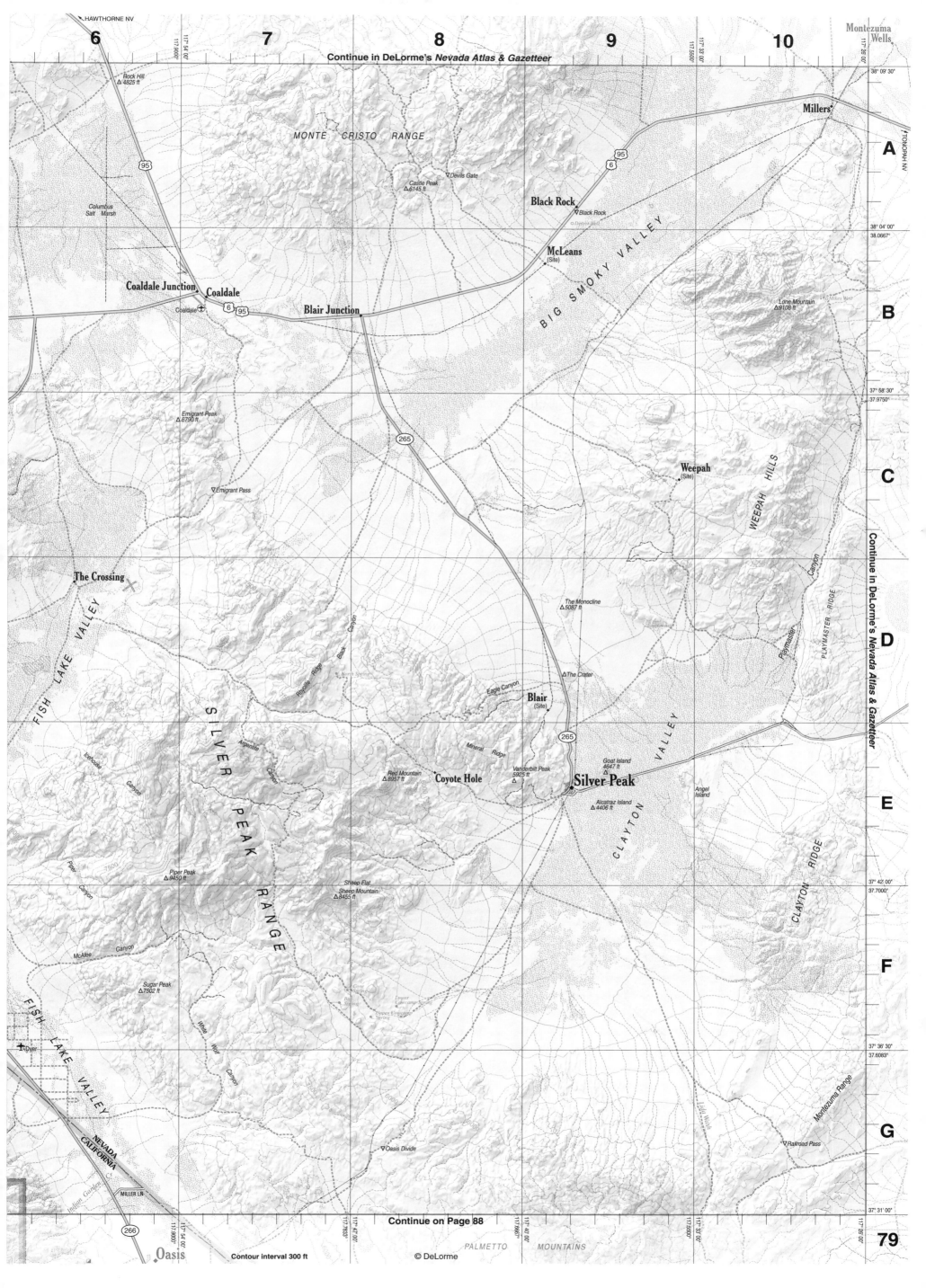

Rock Hill
△4825 ft

MONTE CRISTO RANGE

Millers

Columbus Salt Marsh

Castle Peak
△6145 ft

▽Devils Gate

A

95

Black Rock
▽Black Rock
○Devils Well

McLeans
(Site)

BIG SMOKY VALLEY

Lone Mountain
△9108 ft

Millers Well

B

Coaldale Junction ⊕ Coaldale
Coaldale ⊕

Blair Junction

6 95

95

Emigrant Peak
△6790 ft

265

Weepah
(Site)

WEEPAH HILLS

C

▽Emigrant Pass

The Crossing ✕

FISH LAKE VALLEY

Black Canyon

The Monocline
△5087 ft

PLAYMASTER RIDGE

PLAYMASTER RIDGE

Canyon

D

Rhyolite Ridge

North Spring

Eagle Canyon

Blair
(Site)

△The Crater

265

SILVER PEAK RANGE

Argentite Canyon

Mineral Ridge

Red Mountain
△8957 ft

Coyote Hole

Vanderbilt Peak
5925 ft
△

Goat Island
4647 ft

Silver Peak

Alcatraz Island
△4406 ft

Angel Island

CLAYTON VALLEY

CLAYTON RIDGE

E

Icehouse Canyon

Piper Canyon

Piper Peak
△9450 ft

Sheep Flat
Sheep Mountain
△8455 ft

6000

F

McAfee Canyon

Sugar Peak
△7502 ft

White Wolf Canyon

Cave Spring

Lower Encampment Spring

Dyer Vineyard Spring

Lida Wash

G

FISH LAKE VALLEY

Dyer ⊕

NEVADA
CALIFORNIA

▽Oasis Divide

Montezuma Range

▽Railroad Pass

MILLER LN.

266

○Oasis

Continue on Page 88

PALMETTO MOUNTAINS

Contour interval 300 ft

© DeLorme

79

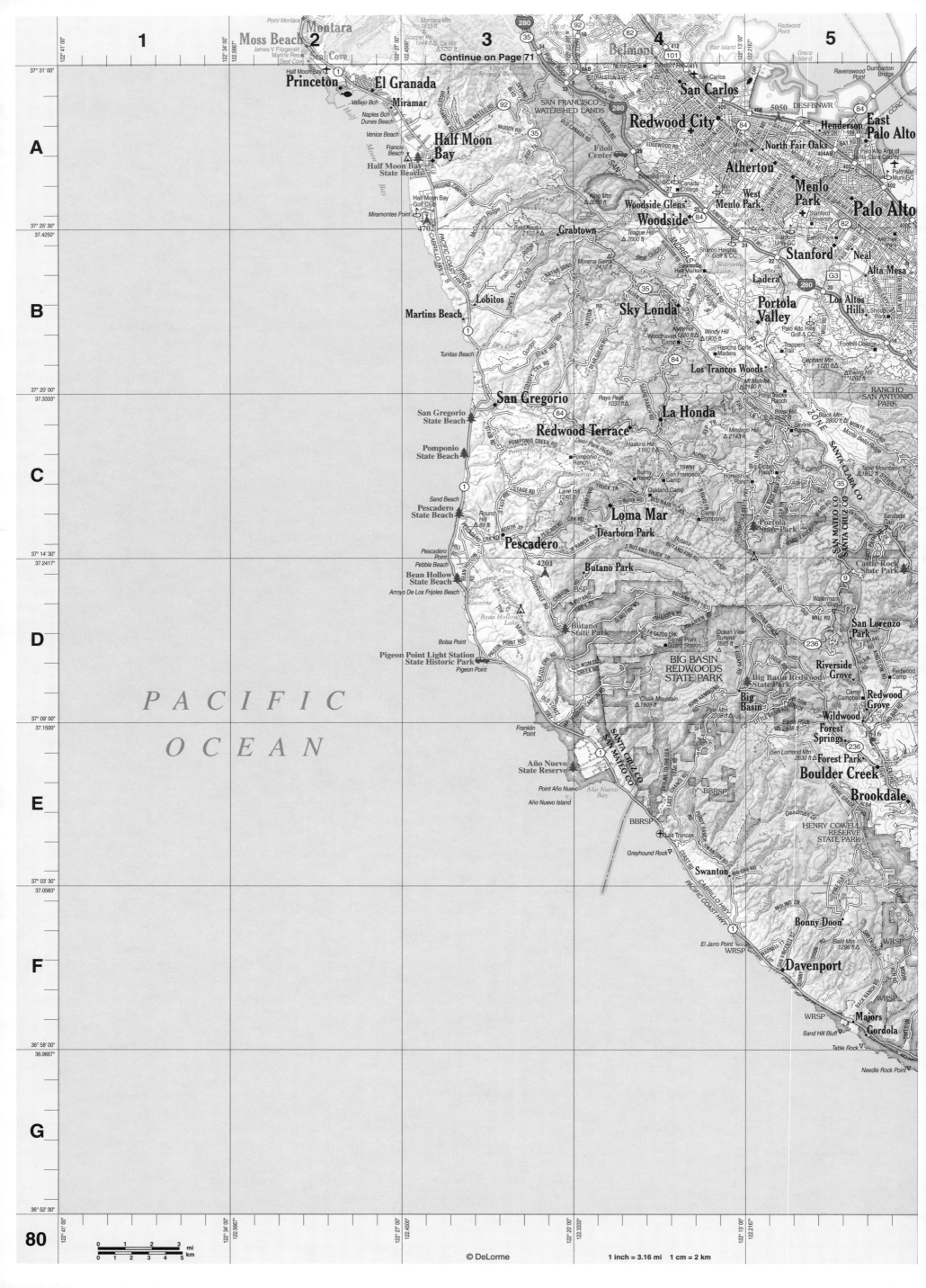

Continue on Page 71

PACIFIC

OCEAN

80

© DeLorme

1 inch = 3.16 mi   1 cm = 2 km

Continue on Page 72

Continue on Page 82

Continue on Page 90

Contour interval 300 ft

© DeLorme

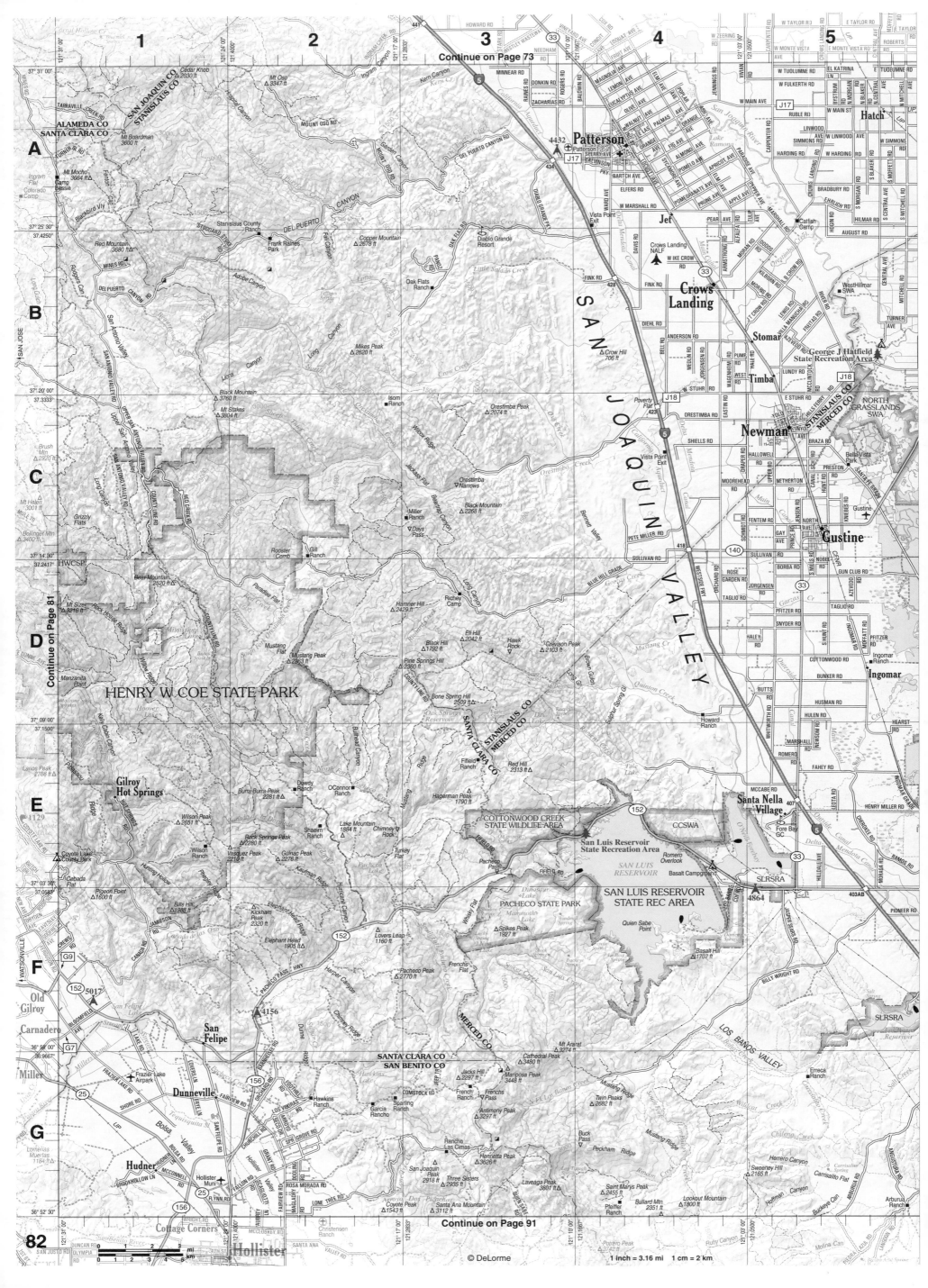

Continue on Page 73

A

B

C

D

E

F

G

Continue on Page 81

HENRY W COE STATE PARK

Gilroy
Hot Springs

COTTONWOOD CREEK
STATE WILDLIFE AREA

San Luis Reservoir
State Recreation Area

SAN LUIS RESERVOIR
STATE REC AREA

PACHECO STATE PARK

SAN JOAQUIN VALLEY

Patterson

Jet

Crows
Landing

Stomar

Timba

Newman

Gustine

Santa Nella
Village

Ingomar

Hatch

Old
Gilroy

Carnadero

Miller

San Felipe

Dunneville

Hudner

Hollister

Continue on Page 91

© DeLorme

1 inch = 3.16 mi   1 cm = 2 km

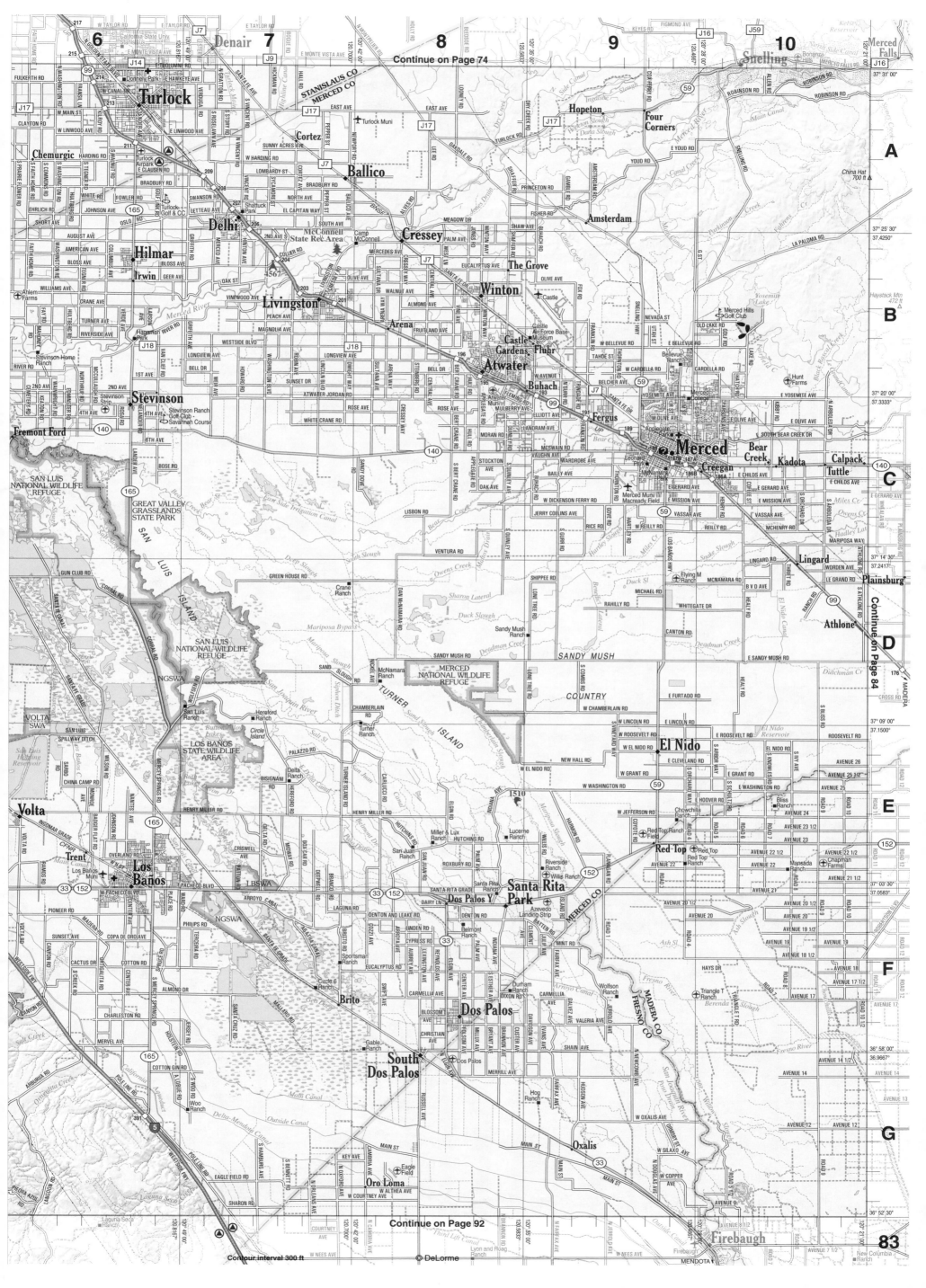

Continue on Page 74

Continue on Page 84

Continue on Page 92

Contour interval 300 ft

© DeLorme

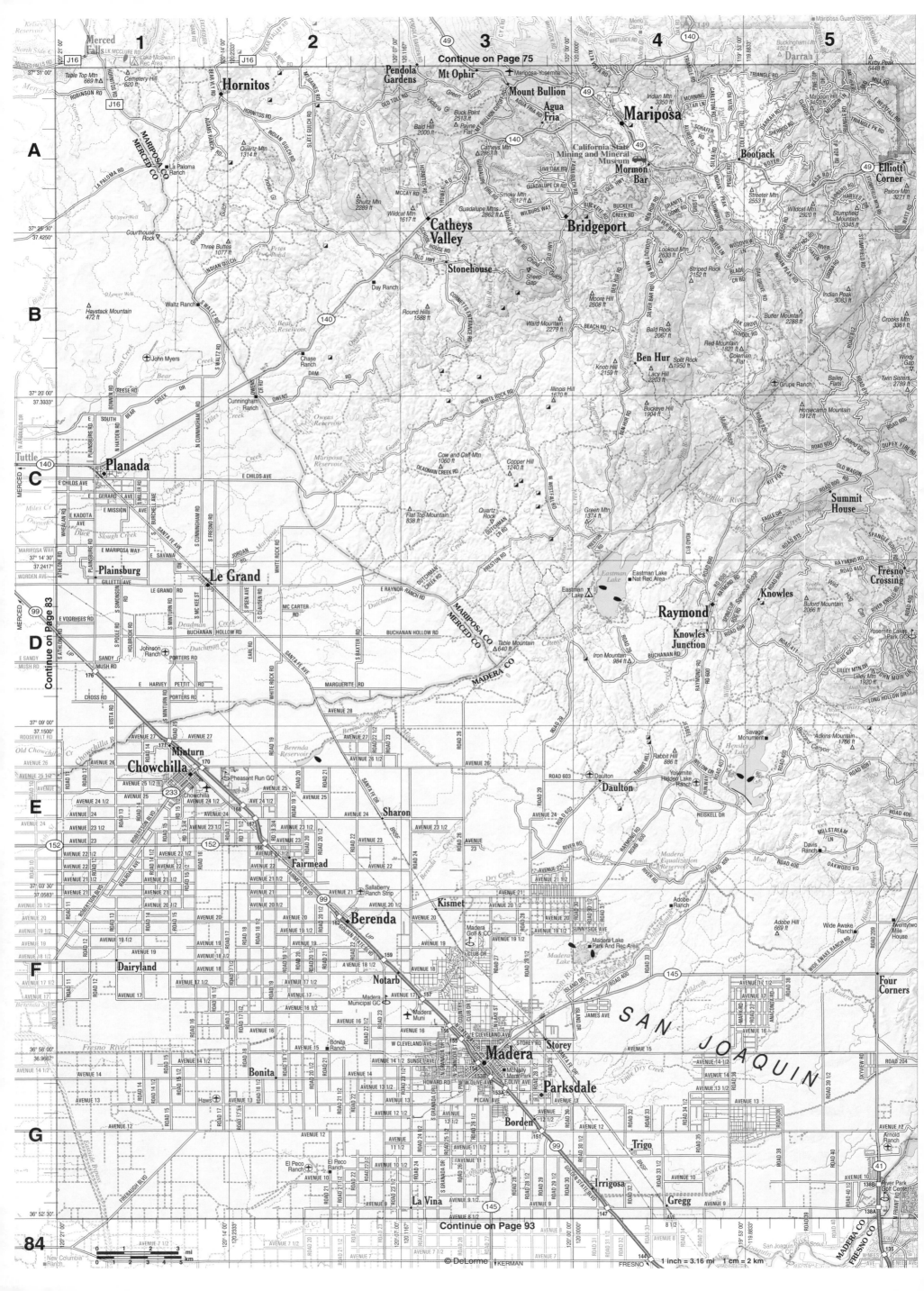

Continue on Page 75

Continue on Page 83

Continue on Page 93

84

1 inch = 3.16 mi   1 cm = 2 km

© DeLorme

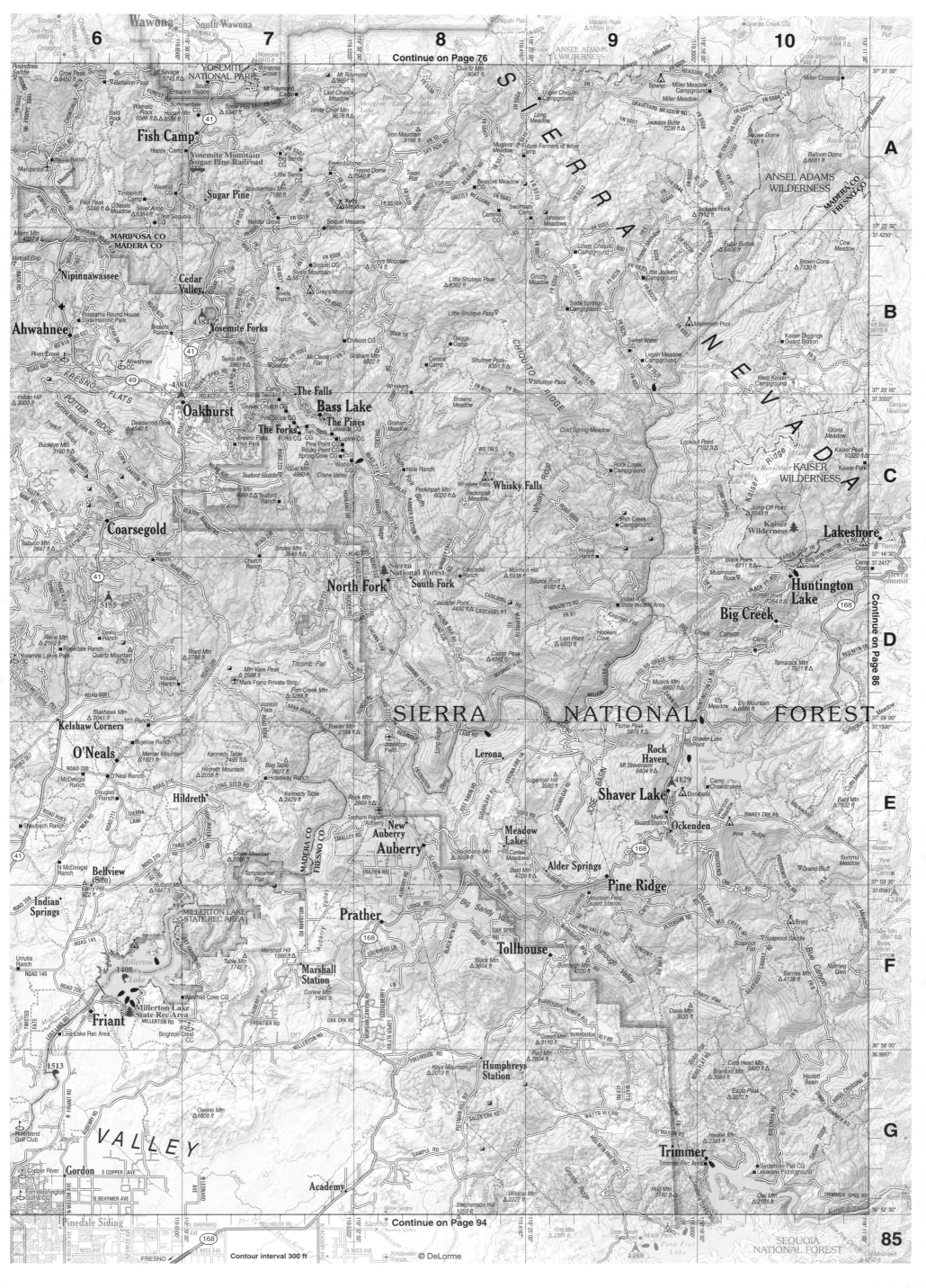

Continue on Page 76

Wawona
South Wawona

YOSEMITE NATIONAL PARK

Fish Camp
Yosemite Mountain Sugar Pine Railroad

Sugar Pine

MARIPOSA CO
MADERA CO

Nipinnawassee
Cedar Valley

Ahwahnee
Yosemite Forks

Oakhurst
The Falls
Bass Lake
The Pines
The Forks

Coarsegold

Whisky Falls

North Fork
South Fork

Huntington Lake
Big Creek

Lakeshore

KAISER WILDERNESS

Kaiser Wilderness

SIERRA NATIONAL FOREST

Kelshaw Corners
O'Neals
Hildreth

Rock Haven
Shaver Lake
Ockenden

New Auberry
Auberry

Lerona
Meadow Lakes

Alder Springs

Pine Ridge

Bellview (Site)

Indian Springs

Prather

Tollhouse

Marshall Station

Millerton Lake State Rec Area

Friant
Millerton Lake State Rec Area

Humphreys Station

VALLEY
Gordon

Academy

Trimmer

Continue on Page 94

Contour interval 300 ft
© DeLorme

SEQUOIA NATIONAL FOREST

A
B
C
D
E
F
G

Continue on Page 86

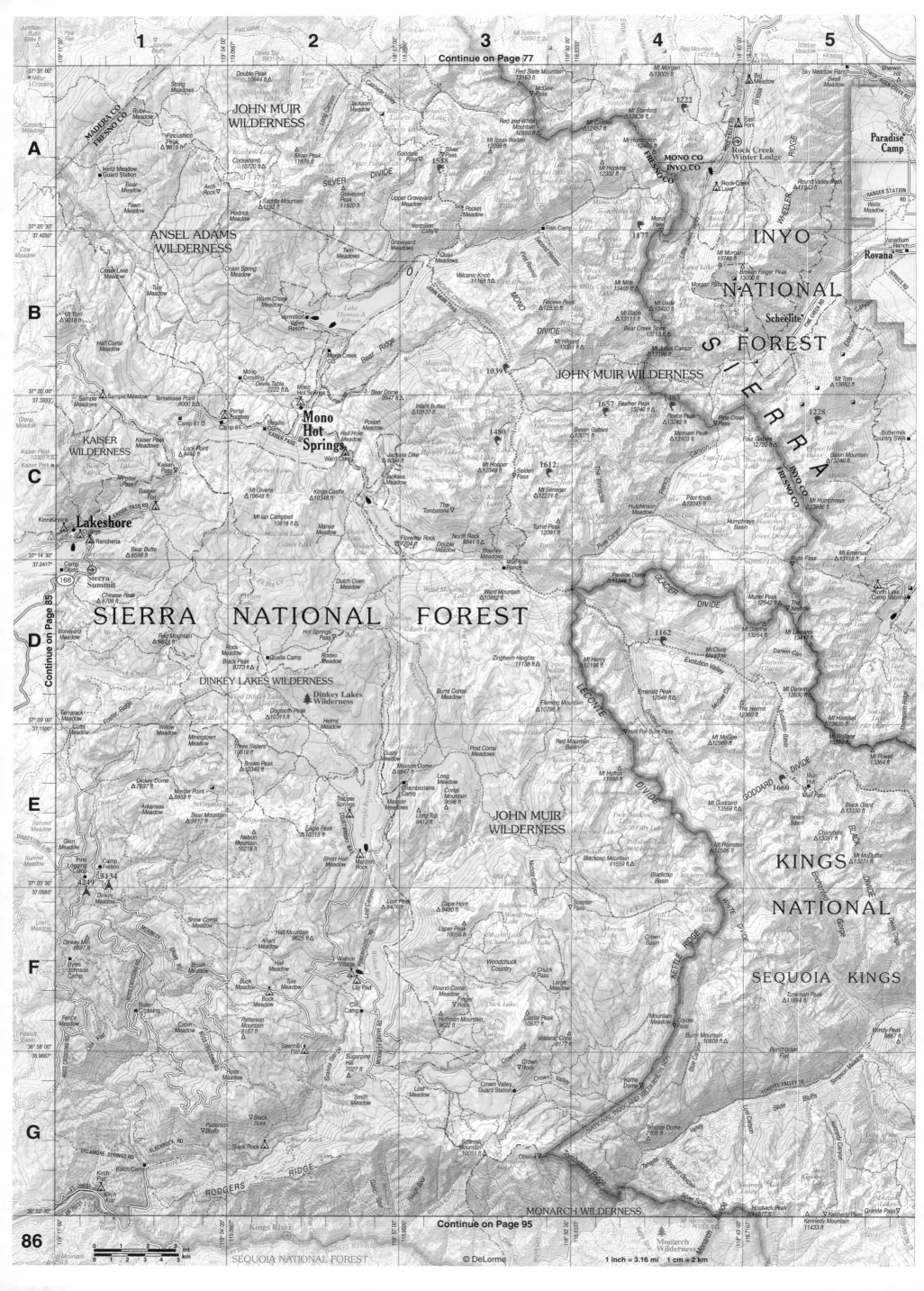

Continue on Page 77

Continue on Page 85

Continue on Page 95

© DeLorme

1 inch = 3.16 mi 1 cm = 2 km

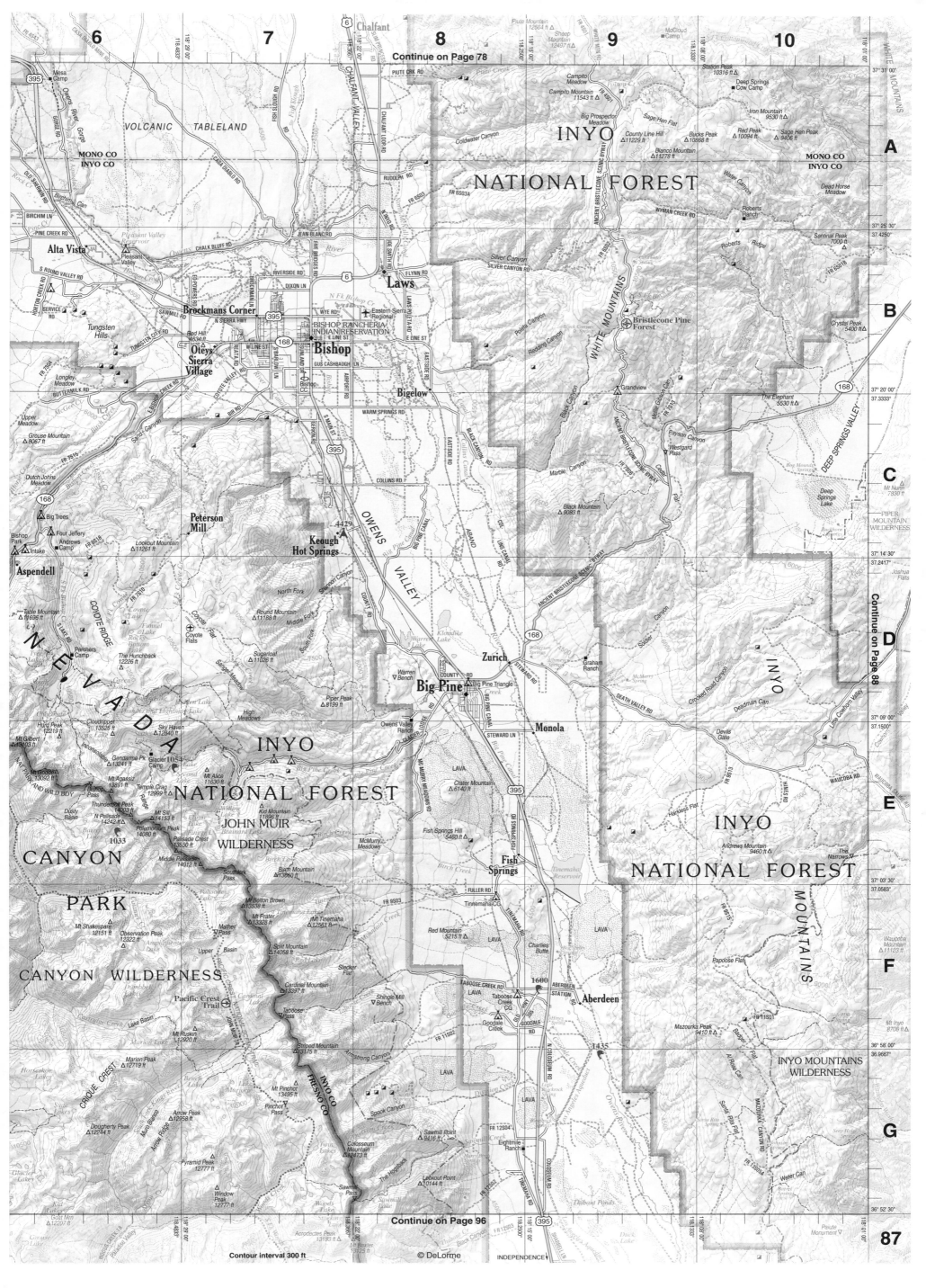

Continue on Page 78

Chalfant

VOLCANIC TABLELAND

MONO CO
INYO CO

INYO

NATIONAL FOREST

WHITE MOUNTAINS

Alta Vista
Pleasant Valley
Reservoir

Tungsten Hills

Laws

Brockmans Corner

Oteys
Sierra Village
Bishop
Bishop Rancheria
Indian Reservation

Bigelow

Bristlecone Pine Forest

Grandview

The Elephant
5530 ft

DEEP SPRINGS VALLEY

Peterson Mill

Keough Hot Springs

OWENS VALLEY

Aspendell

Bishop Park

NEVADA

COYOTE RIDGE

Big Trees
Four Jeffery
Andrews Camp
Intake

Lookout Mountain
11261 ft

North Fork

Round Mountain
11188 ft

Sugarloaf
11026 ft

Deep Springs Lake

PIPER MOUNTAIN WILDERNESS

Zurich

Big Pine

Monola

INYO

NATIONAL FOREST

CANYON

PARK

CANYON WILDERNESS

JOHN MUIR

WILDERNESS

Fish Springs

INYO

NATIONAL FOREST

MOUNTAINS

Aberdeen

INYO MOUNTAINS WILDERNESS

Pacific Crest Trail

Continue on Page 88

Continue on Page 96

Contour interval 300 ft   © DeLorme   INDEPENDENCE

A
B
C
D
E
F
G

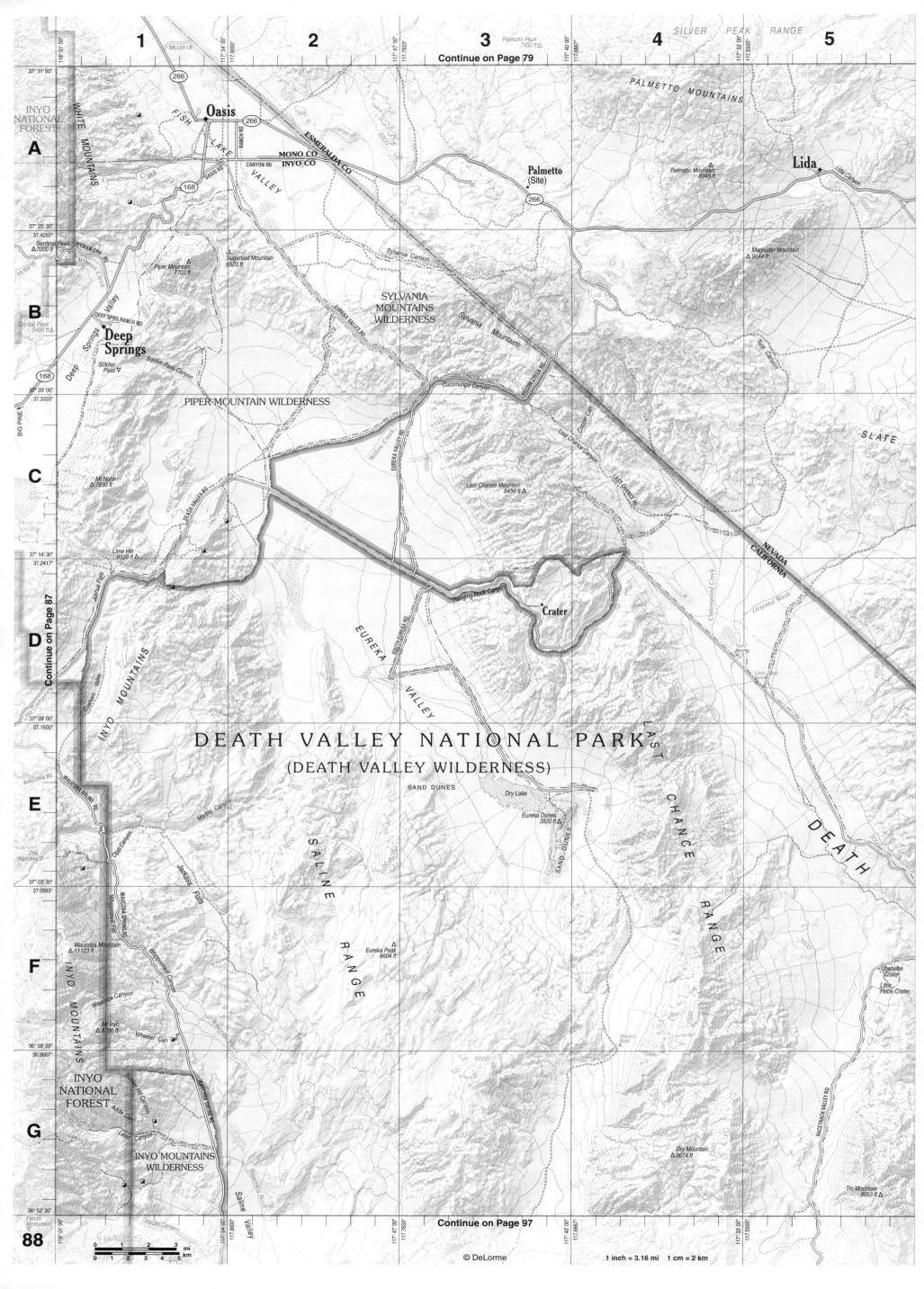

1 2 3 4 5

SILVER   PEAK   RANGE

Palmetto Peak
7450 ft △

PALMETTO   MOUNTAINS

INYO
NATIONAL
FOREST

WHITE

Oasis

FISH   LAKE

VALLEY

Palmetto
(Site)

Palmetto Mountain
8945 ft △

Lida

Lida Canyon

A

MOUNTAINS

Cottonwood Creek

ESMERALDA CO

MONO CO
INYO CO

CANYON RD

OASIS RD

ESMERALDA CO

B

Sentinel Peak
△ 7000 ft

WYMAN CRK

Piper Mountain
7703 ft △

Sugarloaf Mountain
6520 ft

Sylvania Canyon

Magruder Mountain
△ 9044 ft

Crystal Peak
5400 ft △

Wyman Creek

Deep
Springs

SYLVANIA
MOUNTAINS
WILDERNESS

Sylvania   Mountains

Tule Canyon

Deep Springs Valley

DEEP SPRS RANCH RD

EUREKA VALLEY RD

Cucomungo Canyon

Copper Can

SLATE

PIPER MOUNTAIN WILDERNESS

Soldier
Pass ▽

Soldier Pass Canyon

Wilson Creek

Last Chance Canyon

LAST CHANCE RD

Roosevelt
Well

C

Mt Nunn
△ 7830 ft

JUDATH VALLEY RD

EUREKA VALLEY RD

Last Chance Mountain
8456 ft △

NEVADA
CALIFORNIA

Lime Hill
6520 ft △

Joshua Falls

INYO

Hanging Rock Canyon

•Crater

D

Continue on Page 87

MOUNTAINS

Cowhorn Valley

EUREKA

SOUTH EUREKA RD

VALLEY

Oriental Wash

LAST

Little Sand Narrows

WAUCOBA RD

WAUCOBA SALINE RD

E

The Narrows ▽

Marble Canyon

Opal Canyon

Jackass Fields

DEATH VALLEY NATIONAL PARK
(DEATH VALLEY WILDERNESS)

SAND DUNES

Dry Lake

Eureka Dunes
3520 ft △

SAND DUNES

CHANCE

DEATH

SALINE

Waucoba Mountain
△ 11123 ft

WAUCOBA SPRING RD

Whippoorwill Flat

Waucoba Spring

Waucoba Canyon

Whippoorwill Canyon

F

RANGE

Eureka Peak
6604 ft △

RANGE

Ubehebe
Crater

Little
Hebe Crater

Mt Inyo
△ 8706 ft

Wheeler Can

Marble Bath

INYO

MOUNTAINS

Saline Valley

WAUCOBA SALINE RD

G

INYO
NATIONAL
FOREST

Beveridge Canyon

Addie Can

Lead Canyon

INYO MOUNTAINS
WILDERNESS

Saline

Valley

Dry Mountain
△ 8674 ft

RACETRACK VALLEY RD

Tin Mountain
8953 ft △

88

mi
0 1 2 3
km
0 1 2 3 4 5

© DeLorme

1 inch = 3.16 mi   1 cm = 2 km

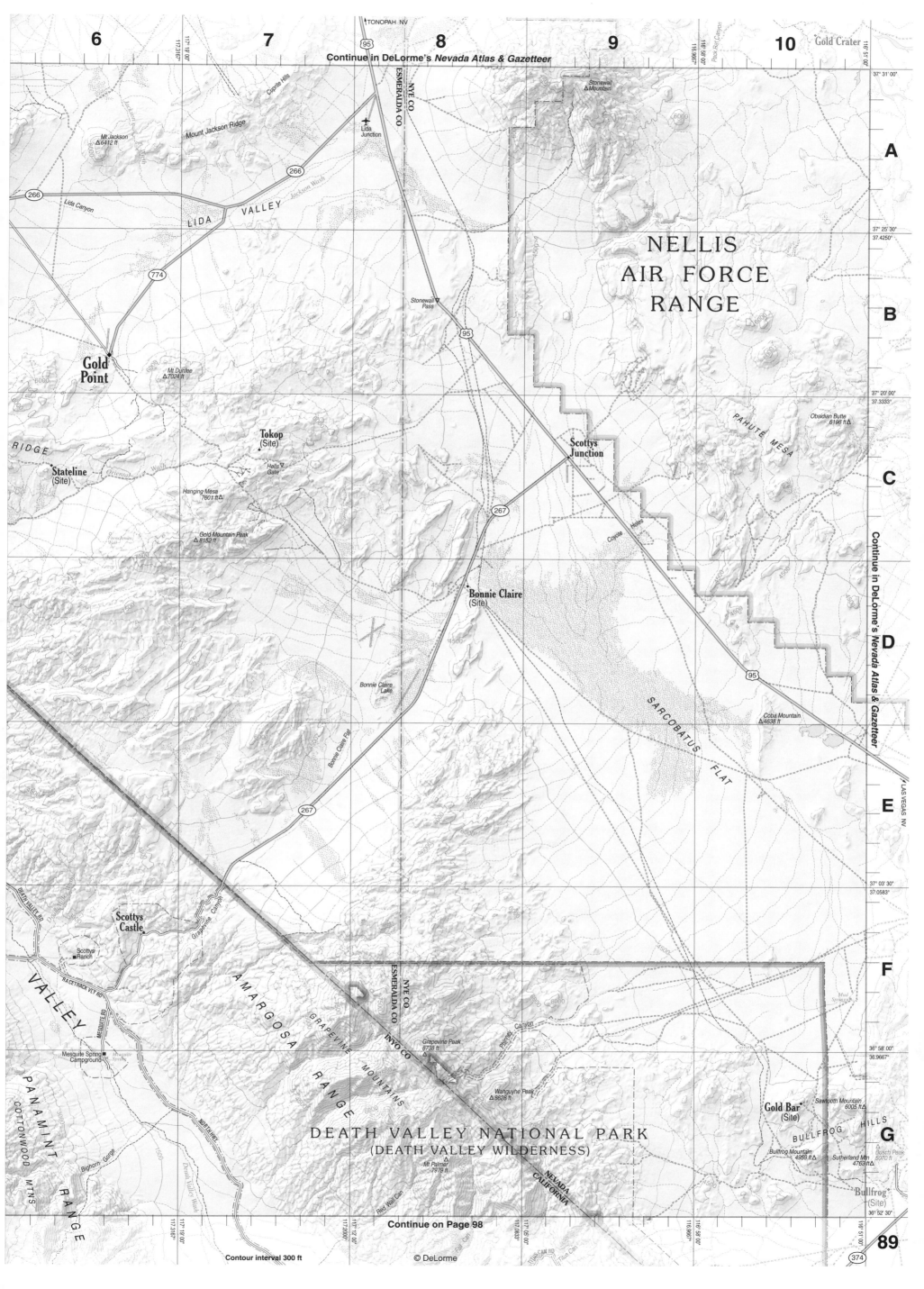

TONOPAH NV

Gold Crater

95

Continue in DeLorme's *Nevada Atlas & Gazetteer*

A

NYE CO
ESMERALDA CO

Cuprite Hills

Mt Jackson
△6412 ft

Mount Jackson Ridge

Lida
Junction

Stonewall
△Mountain

266

NELLIS
AIR FORCE
RANGE

LIDA VALLEY

Jackson Wash

266

B

774

Stonewall ▽
Pass

95

Gold
Point

Mt Dunfee
△7024 ft

PAHUTE MESA

Obsidian Butte
6198 ft△

RIDGE

Tokop
(Site)

Anderson Well

Hells ▽
Gate

Scottys
Junction

C

Stateline
(Site)

Oriental Wash

Hanging Mesa
7601 ft△

267

Coyote Holes

Gold Mountain Peak
△8152 ft

Frenchman Well

Continue in DeLorme's *Nevada Atlas & Gazetteer*

Bonnie Claire
(Site)

D

4500

Bonnie Claire
Lake

95

Coba Mountain
△4638 ft

SARCOBATUS FLAT

Bonnie Clare Flat

6000

4500

E

267

LAS VEGAS NV

DEATH VALLEY RD

Scottys
Castle

Grapevine Canyon

F

Scottys
Ranch

RACETRACK VLY RD

NYE CO
ESMERALDA CO

AMARGOSA RANGE

GRAPEVINE MOUNTAINS

Grapevine Peak
△8738 ft

Phinney Canyon

Mud
Springs

NORTH HWY

MESQUITE RD

Mesquite Spring
Campground

Mesquite
Spring

Wahguyhe Peak
△8628 ft

Gold Bar
(Site)

Sawtooth Mountain
6005 ft△

G

PANAMINT RANGE

COTTONWOOD MTNS

Bighorn Gorge

VALLEY

DEATH VALLEY NATIONAL PARK
(DEATH VALLEY WILDERNESS)

Mt Palmer
△7979 ft

Red Wall Can

BULLFROG HILLS

Busch Peak
5070 ft

Bullfrog Mountain
4959 ft△

Sutherland Mtn
4763 ft△

Bullfrog
(Site)

INYO CO

DEATH VALLEY WASH

Silk Can

NEVADA
CALIFORNIA

Continue on Page 98

TITUS CAN RD

Titus Can

374

89

Contour interval 300 ft

© DeLorme

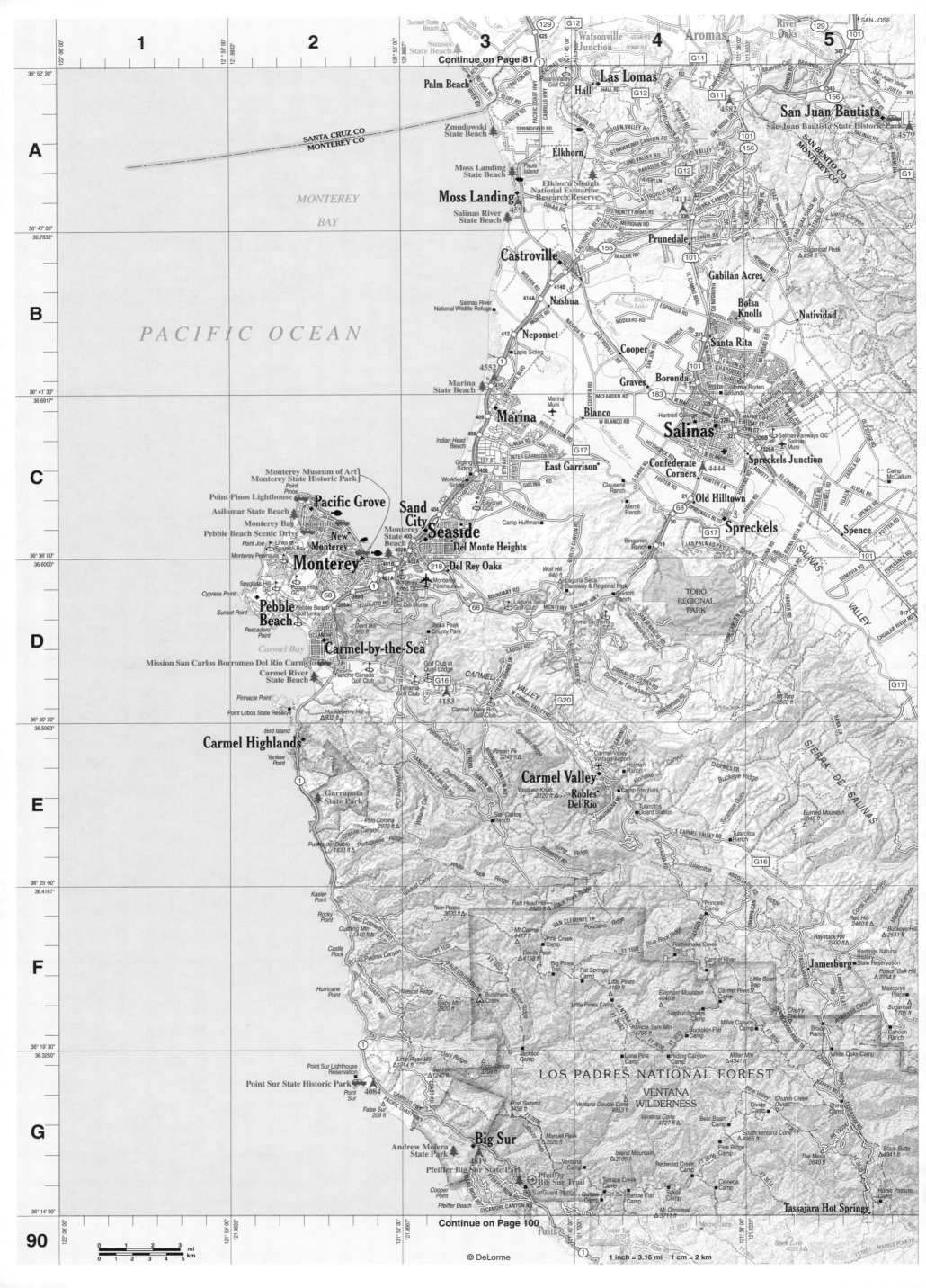

Continue on Page 81

Continue on Page 100

90

1 inch = 3.16 mi   1 cm = 2 km

© DeLorme

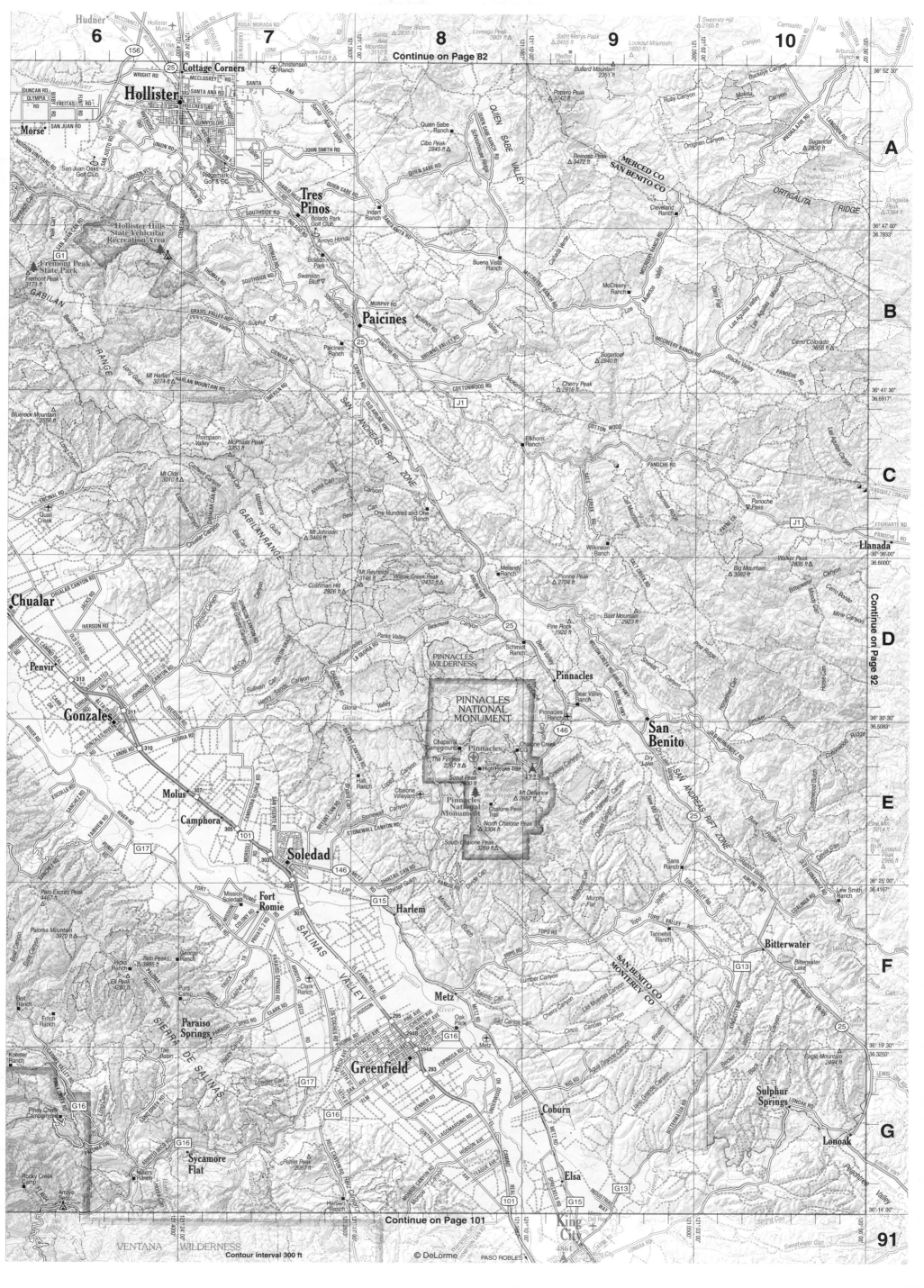

Continue on Page 82

Continue on Page 92

Continue on Page 101

Contour interval 300 ft

© DeLorme

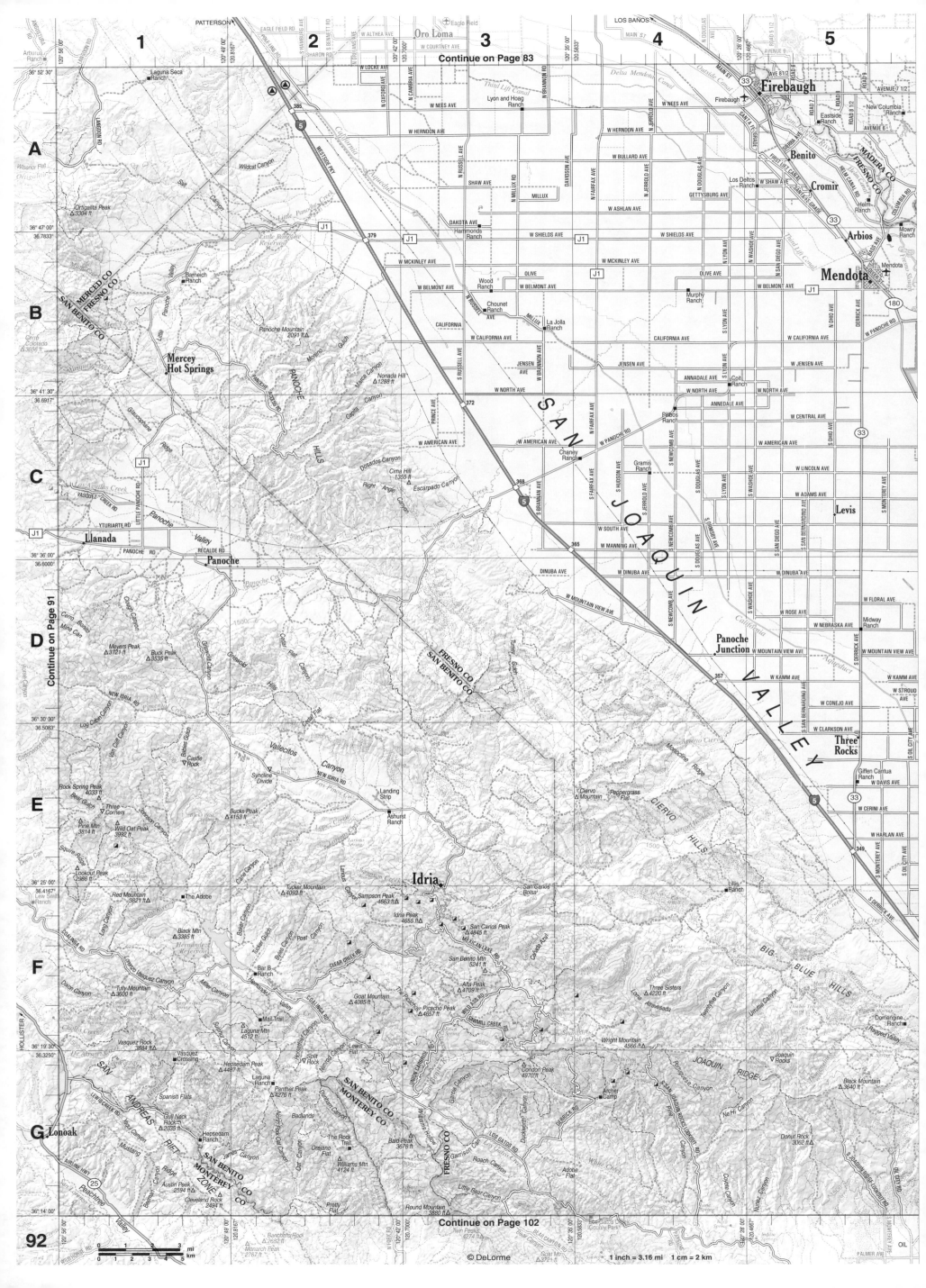

Continue on Page 91

Continue on Page 102

© DeLorme

1 inch = 3.16 mi   1 cm = 2 km

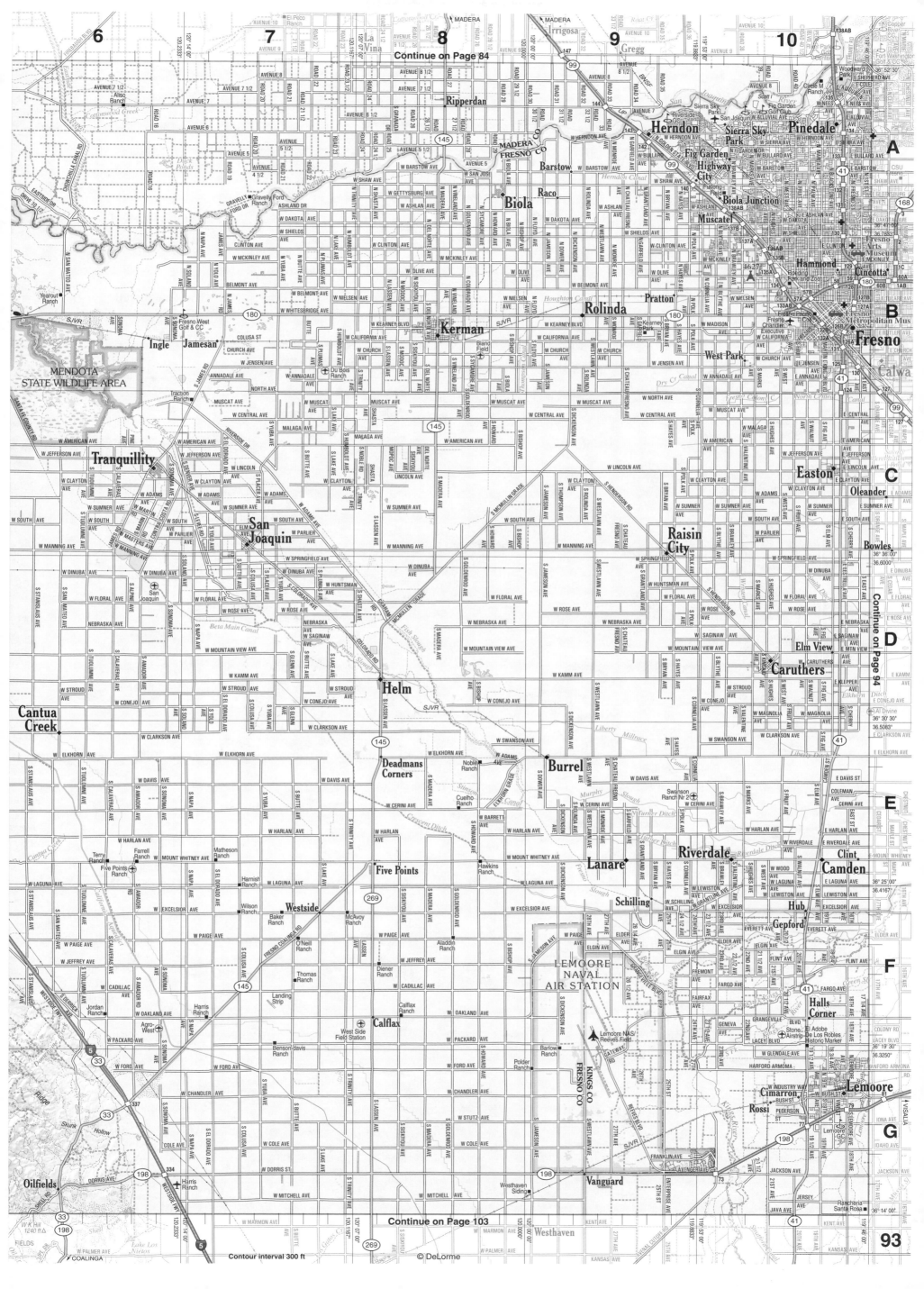

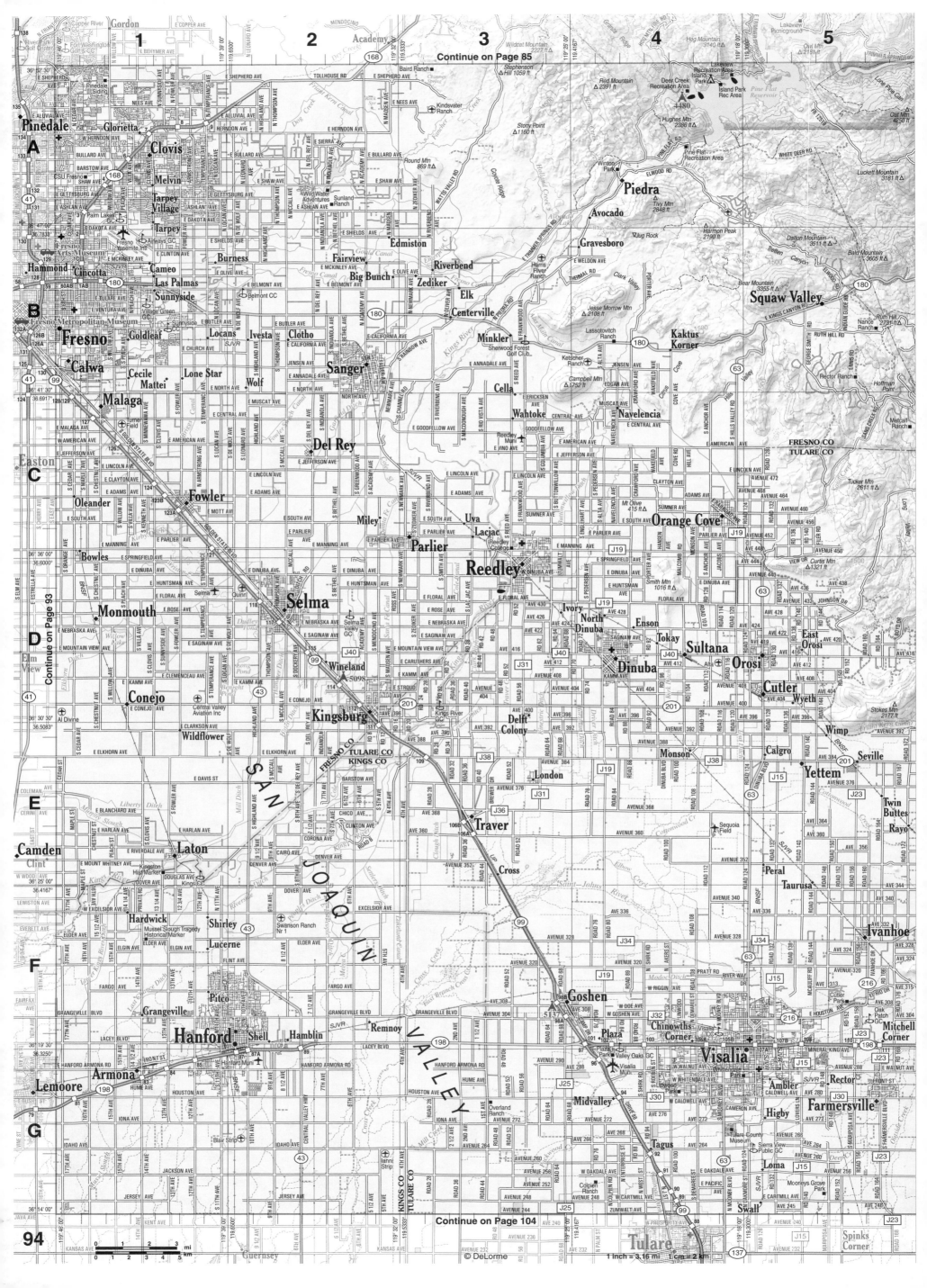

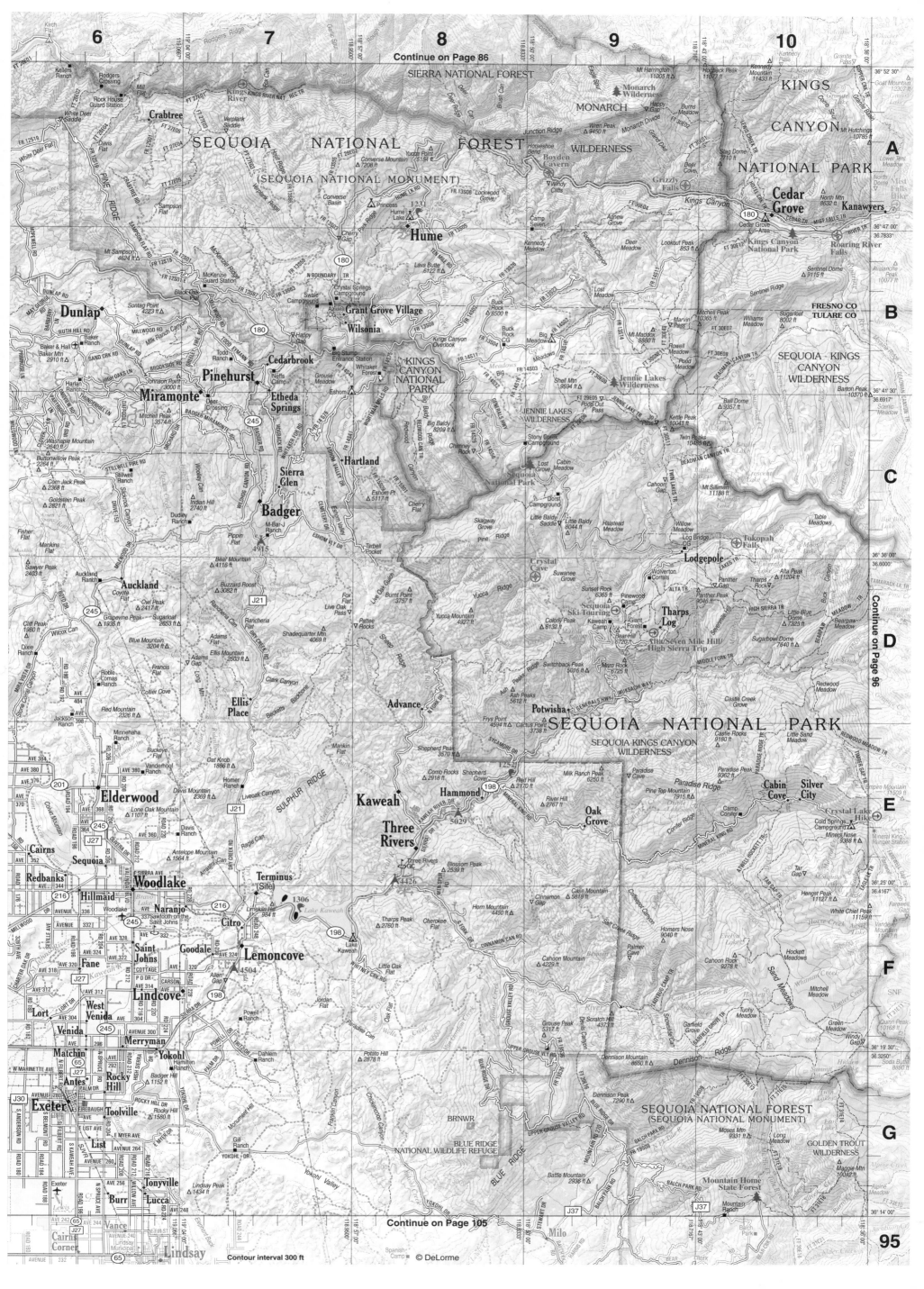

Continue on Page 86

SIERRA NATIONAL FOREST

KINGS

MONARCH

CANYON

SEQUOIA   NATIONAL   FOREST

WILDERNESS

NATIONAL PARK

(SEQUOIA NATIONAL MONUMENT)

Cedar
Grove   Kanawyers

A

Hume

FRESNO CO
TULARE CO

B

Dunlap

Grant Grove Village

Wilsonia

Pinehurst

Cedarbrook

Miramonte

Etheda
Springs

SEQUOIA - KINGS
CANYON
WILDERNESS

KINGS
CANYON
NATIONAL PARK

Jennie Lakes
Wilderness

JENNIE LAKES
WILDERNESS

C

Sierra
Glen

Hartland

Badger

Sequoia
National Park

Lodgepole

D

Auckland

SEQUOIA NATIONAL PARK

Tharps
Log

Ellis
Place

Advance

Potwisha

SEQUOIA - KINGS CANYON
WILDERNESS

E

Elderwood

Kaweah

Hammond

Oak
Grove

Cabin
Cove

Silver
City

Three
Rivers

Crystal Lake
Hike

Cairns

Sequoia

Redbanks

Woodlake

Terminus
(Site)

Hillmaid

Naranjo

Citro

Saint
Johns

Goodale

Lemoncove

Fane

F

West
Venida

Lindcove

Venida

Merryman

Yokohl

Matchin

Rocky
Hill

Antes

Exeter

Toolville

SEQUOIA NATIONAL FOREST
(SEQUOIA NATIONAL MONUMENT)

GOLDEN TROUT
WILDERNESS

G

List

BRNWR

BLUE RIDGE
NATIONAL WILDLIFE REFUGE

Burr

Lucca

Tonyville

Mountain Home
State Forest

Cairns
Corner

Lindsay

Contour interval 300 ft   © DeLorme

Continue on Page 96

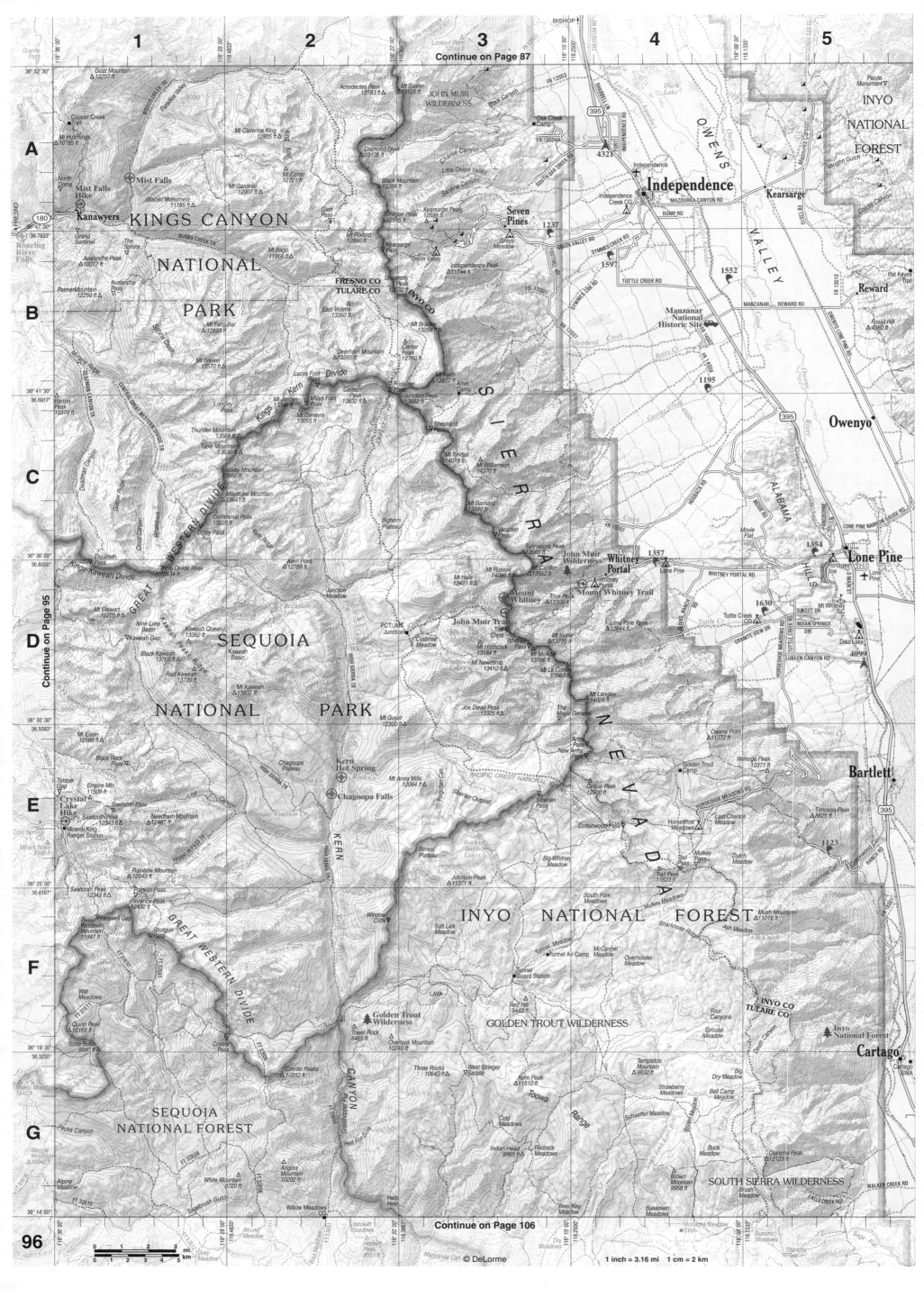

Continue on Page 95

1 inch = 3.16 mi   1 cm = 2 km

© DeLorme

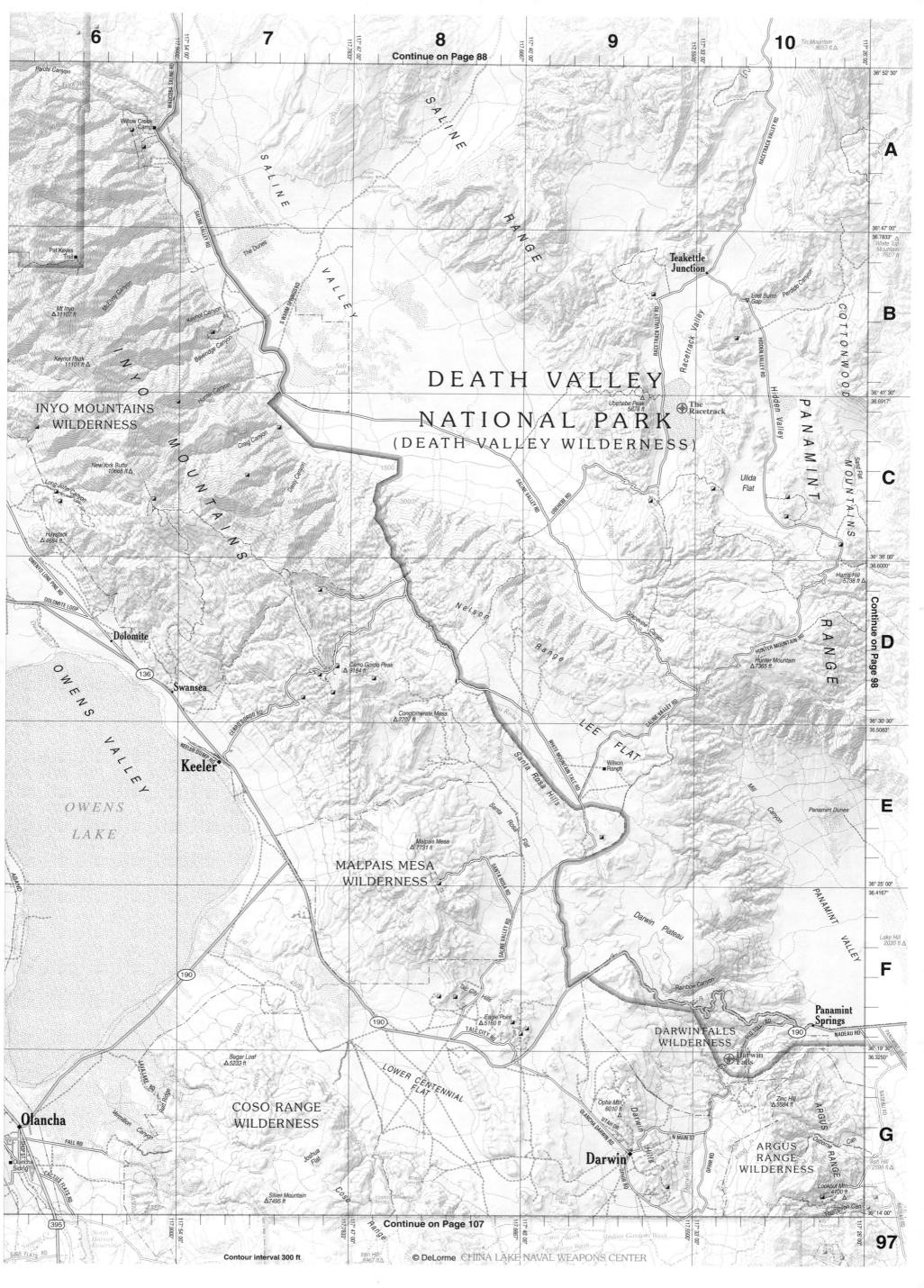

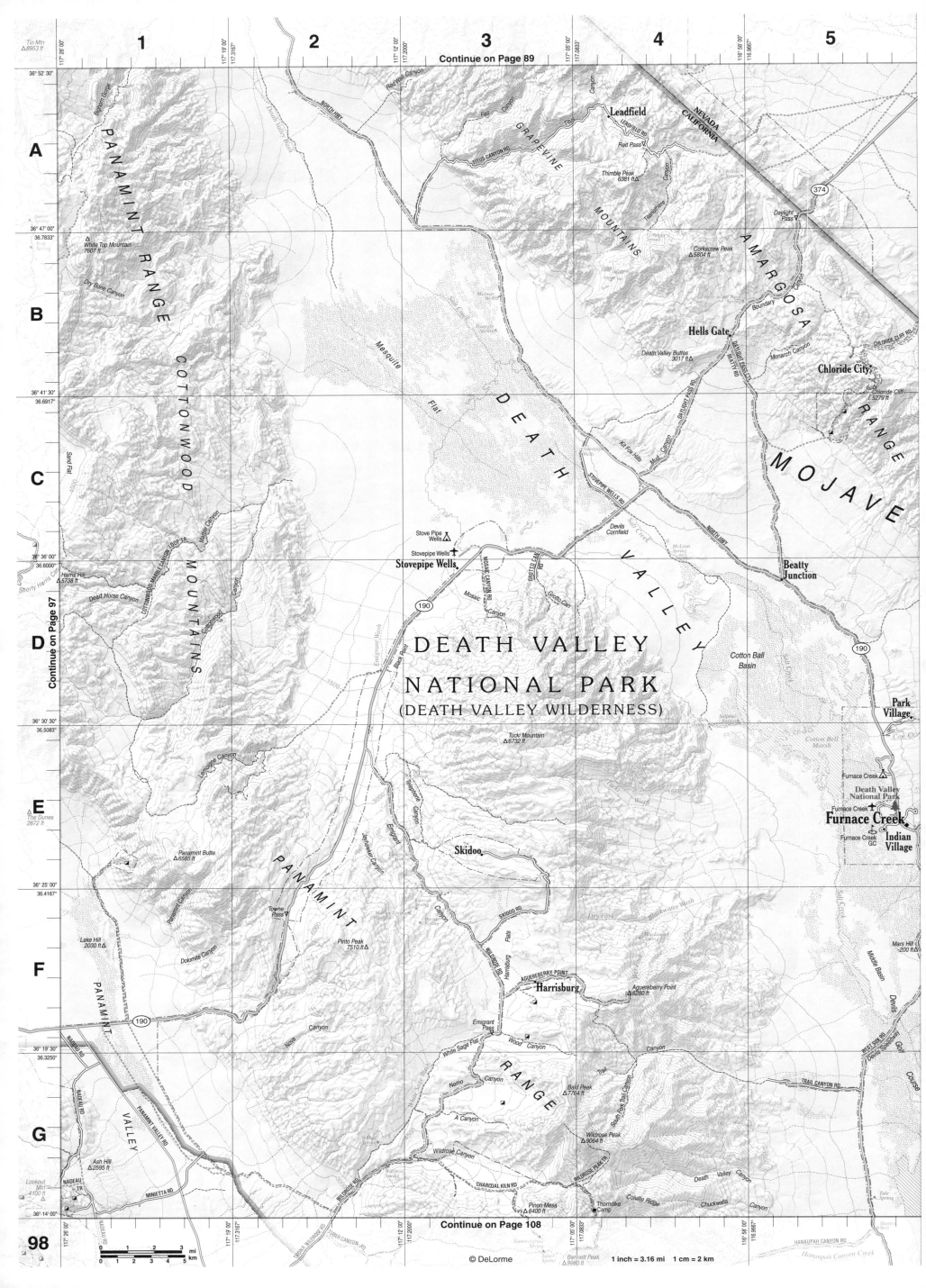

Continue on Page 89

A

B

C

D

E

F

G

Continue on Page 97

PANAMINT RANGE

COTTONWOOD MOUNTAINS

Tin Mtn
△8953 ft

Bighorn Gorge

△ White Top Mountain
7607 ft

Dry Bone Canyon

6000

Sand Flat

Harris Hill
△5738 ft

Shorty Harris Cn

Dead Horse Canyon

Marble Canyon

Cottonwood Canyon

COTTONWOOD MARBLE CANYON LOOP TR

△ The Dunes
2672 ft

Lake Hill
2030 ft△

Panamint Butte
△6585 ft

Panamint Canyon

Dolomite Canyon

PANAMINT

Nova Canyon

VALLEY

Ash Hill
△2595 ft

Lookout Mtn
4100 ft △

NADEAU TR

NADEAU RD

PANAMINT VALLEY RD

MINIETTA RD

WILDROSE RD

Red Wall Canyon

Fall Canyon

NORTH HWY

Death Valley Wash

Titus Canyon

TITUS CANYON RD

GRAPEVINE MOUNTAINS

Leadfield
Leadfield Rd
Red Pass

NEVADA
CALIFORNIA

Thimble Peak
6381 ft△

AMARGOSA

Corkscrew Peak
△5804 ft

Daylight Pass

374

Hells Gate

Death Valley Buttes
3017 ft△

Boundary

DAYLIGHT PASS RD

BEATTY RD

Monarch Canyon

CHLORIDE CLIFF RD

Chloride City

Chloride Cliff
5279 ft

MOJAVE

RANGE

Mesquite Flat

Salt Creek

D E A T H

Kit Fox Hills

Mud Canyon

STOVEPIPE WELLS RD

Devils Cornfield

McLean Spring

Stove Pipe Wells △

Stovepipe Wells

Stovepipe Wells

Mosaic Canyon

MOSAIC CANYON RD

GROTTO CAN RD

Grotto Can

NORTH HWY

V A L L E Y

Beatty Junction

190

Black Pnt

Emigrant Wash

1500

Cotton Ball Basin

Sulphur

190

Park Village

DEATH VALLEY

NATIONAL PARK

(DEATH VALLEY WILDERNESS)

Tucki Mountain
△6732 ft

Cotton Ball Marsh

Furnace Creek △

Death Valley National Park

Lemoigne Canyon

Telescope Canyon

Tucki Wash

Furnace Creek

Furnace Creek

Furnace Creek
GC

Indian Village

PANAMINT

Jayhawker Canyon

Emigrant

Skidoo

Towne Pass

Pinto Peak
7510 ft△

SKIDOO RD

Emigrant Flats

WILDROSE RD

Dry Lake

Buckwheat Wash

Mars Hill
-200 ft△

Harrisburg

AGUEREBERRY POINT

Aguereberry Point
△6280 ft

1500

RANGE

Emigrant Pass

White Sage Flat

Wood Canyon

Nemo Canyon

A Canyon

Bald Peak
△7764 ft

Wildrose Peak
△9064 ft

South Fork Trail Canyon

TRAIL CANYON RD

Devils

WEST SIDE RD

190

PANAMINT

Wildrose Canyon

CHARCOAL KILN RD

WILDROSE PEAK TR

Pinon Mesa
△6400 ft

Thorndike Camp

Colville Ridge

Death Valley Canyon

Chuckwalla Canyon

Devils

Tule Spring

Hanaupah Canyon Creek

HANAUPAH CANYON RD

© DeLorme

Continue on Page 108

0 1 2 3 mi
0 1 2 3 4 5 km

1 inch = 3.16 mi   1 cm = 2 km

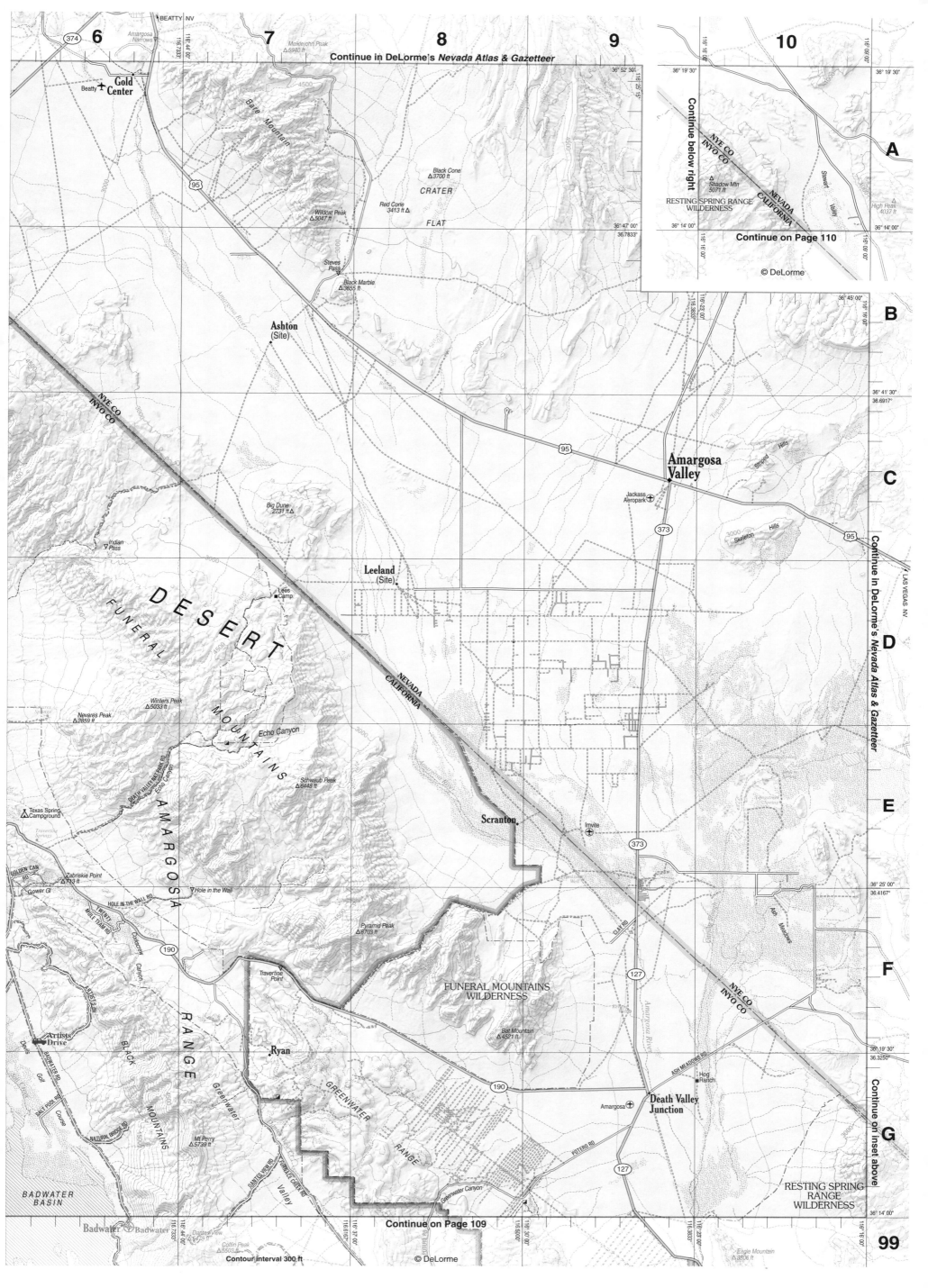

BEATTY NV

374

Gold Center

Beatty

Amargosa Narrows

116.7333°

Meiklejohn Peak
△5940 ft

Continue in DeLorme's *Nevada Atlas & Gazetteer*

Bare Mountain

95

4500

Black Cone
3700 ft △

Red Cone
3413 ft △

CRATER

Wildcat Peak
△5047 ft

FLAT

116.25° 15'

36° 52' 30'

36° 47' 00'
36.7833°

Steves Pass

Black Marble
△3655 ft.

116° 16' 00'

Continue below right

NYE CO
INYO CO

△ Shadow Mtn
5071 ft

**RESTING SPRING RANGE
WILDERNESS**

NEVADA
CALIFORNIA

Stewart Valley

High Peak
4037 ft

36° 19' 30'

A

Continue on Page 110

© DeLorme

36° 14' 00'
116° 16' 00'

Ashton
(Site)

NYE CO
INYO CO

95

Amargosa Valley

Jackass Aeropark

373

Striped Hills

Skeleton Hills

3000

95

36° 45' 00'
116° 16' 00'

B

36° 41' 30'
36.6917°

C

Big Dune
2731 ft △

Indian Pass

Leeland
(Site)

Lees Camp

D E S E R T

F U N E R A L

Winters Peak
△5033 ft

Nevares Peak
△2859 ft

Echo Canyon

DEATH VALLEY NAT'L PARK RD

M O U N T A I N S

A M A R G O S A

Schwaub Peak
△6448 ft

Echo Canyon

3000

3000

NEVADA
CALIFORNIA

Continue in DeLorme's *Nevada Atlas & Gazetteer*

LAS VEGAS NV

D

Scranton

Imvite

373

E

Texas Spring Campground

Travertine Springs

GOLDEN CAN RD

Zabriskie Point
△713 ft

Gower Gl

Hole in the Wall

TWENTY MILE TEAM RD

Coffeeberry Creek

Pyramid Peak
△6703 ft

36° 25' 00'
36.4167°

R A N G E

190

F

Travertine Point

Artists Drive

BARNWATER RD

Devils Golf Course

SALT POOL RD

B L A C K

Ryan

NATURAL BRIDGE RD

Mt Perry
△5739 ft

Greenwater

DANTES VIEW RD

FURNACE CREEK RD

M O U N T A I N S

G R E E N W A T E R

**FUNERAL MOUNTAINS
WILDERNESS**

Bat Mountain
△4521 ft

CLAY RD

127

NYE CO
INYO CO

Amargosa River

36° 19' 30'
36.3250°

ASH MEADOWS RD

Hog Ranch

Ash Meadows

G

Continue on inset above

BADWATER BASIN

Badwater

Badwater

Dantes View

Coffin Peak
△5503 ft

Greenwater Canyon

V a l l e y

Greenwater Canyon

190

Amargosa

Death Valley Junction

POTERO RD

127

**RESTING SPRING RANGE
WILDERNESS**

Eagle Mountain
△3806 ft

36° 14' 00'
116° 16' 00'

116.7333°
116° 44' 00'

116.6167°
116° 37' 00'

116.6°
116° 30' 00'

116.3833°
116° 23' 00'

Continue on Page 109

Contour interval 300 ft

© DeLorme

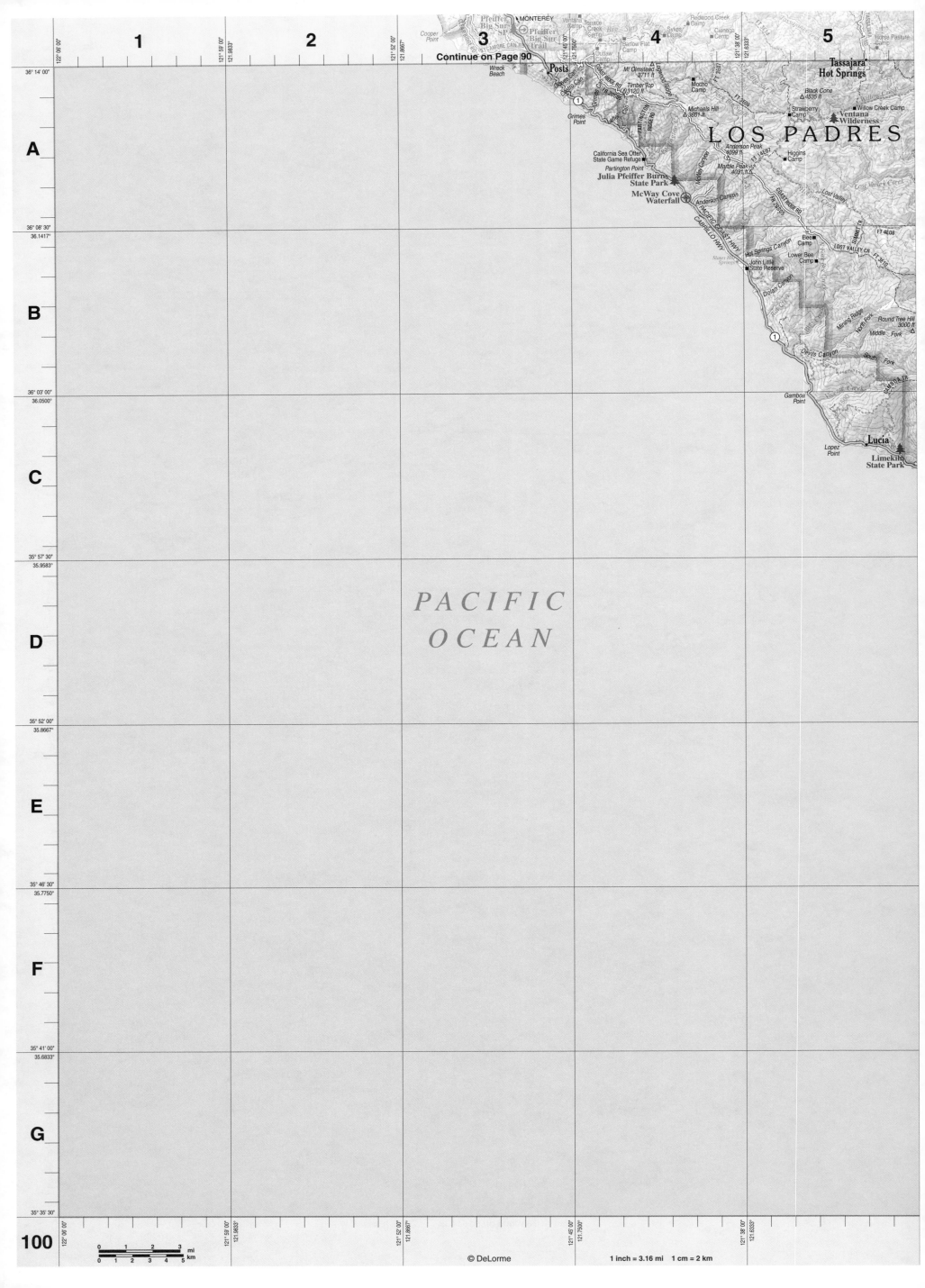

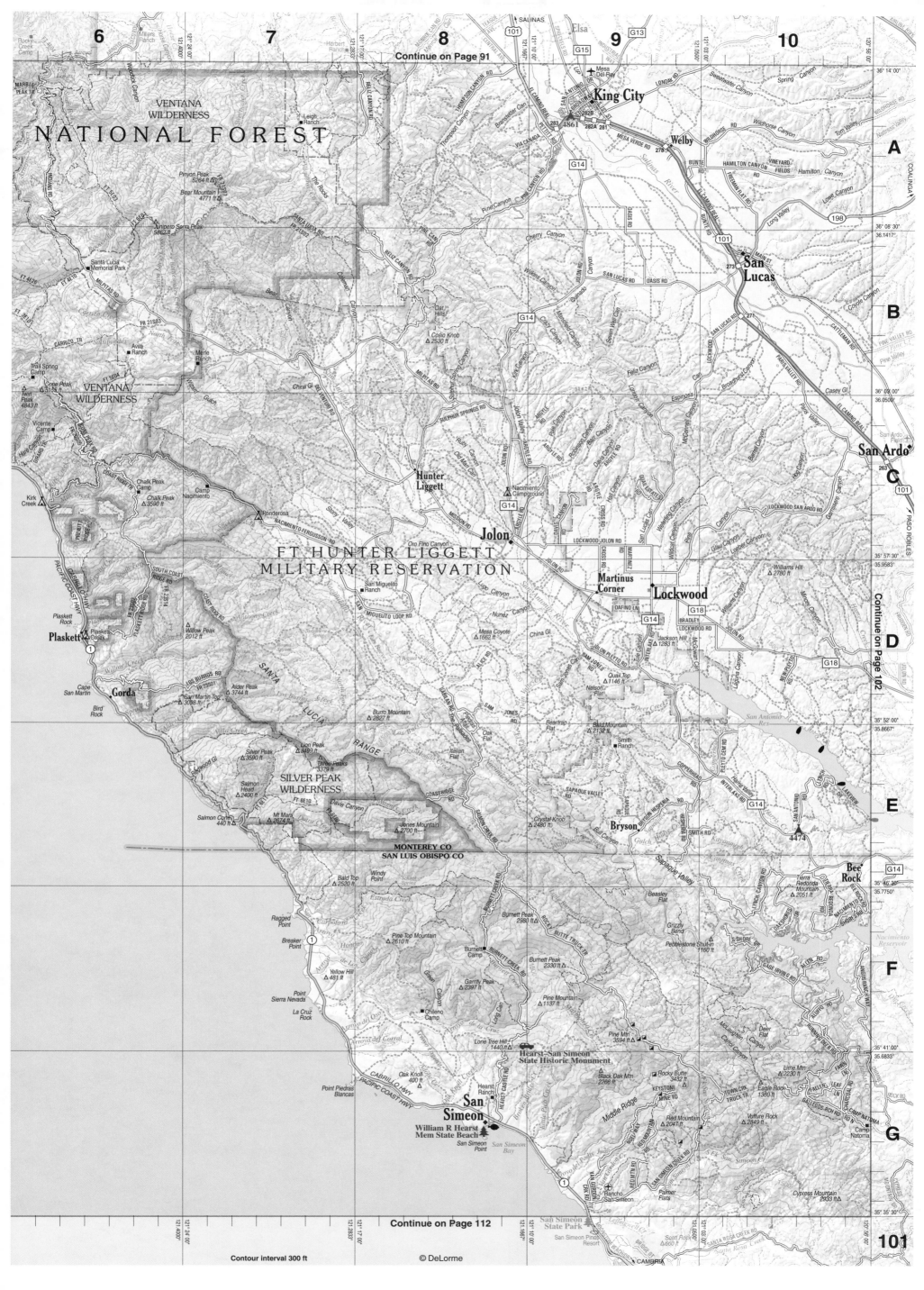

Continue on Page 91

VENTANA
WILDERNESS

NATIONAL FOREST

King City

Welby

San Lucas

VENTANA
WILDERNESS

San Ardo

Hunter
Liggett

Jolon

FT. HUNTER LIGGETT
MILITARY RESERVATION

Martinus
Corner   Lockwood

Continue on Page 102

Plaskett

Gorda

SANTA

LUCIA

SILVER PEAK
WILDERNESS

RANGE

Bryson

Bee
Rock

MONTEREY CO
SAN LUIS OBISPO CO

Ragged
Point

Breaker
Point

Point
Sierra Nevada

La Cruz
Rock

Hearst-San Simeon
State Historic Monument

Point Piedras
Blancas

San
Simeon

William R Hearst
Mem State Beach

Continue on Page 112

A

B

C

D

E

F

G

101

Contour interval 300 ft   © DeLorme

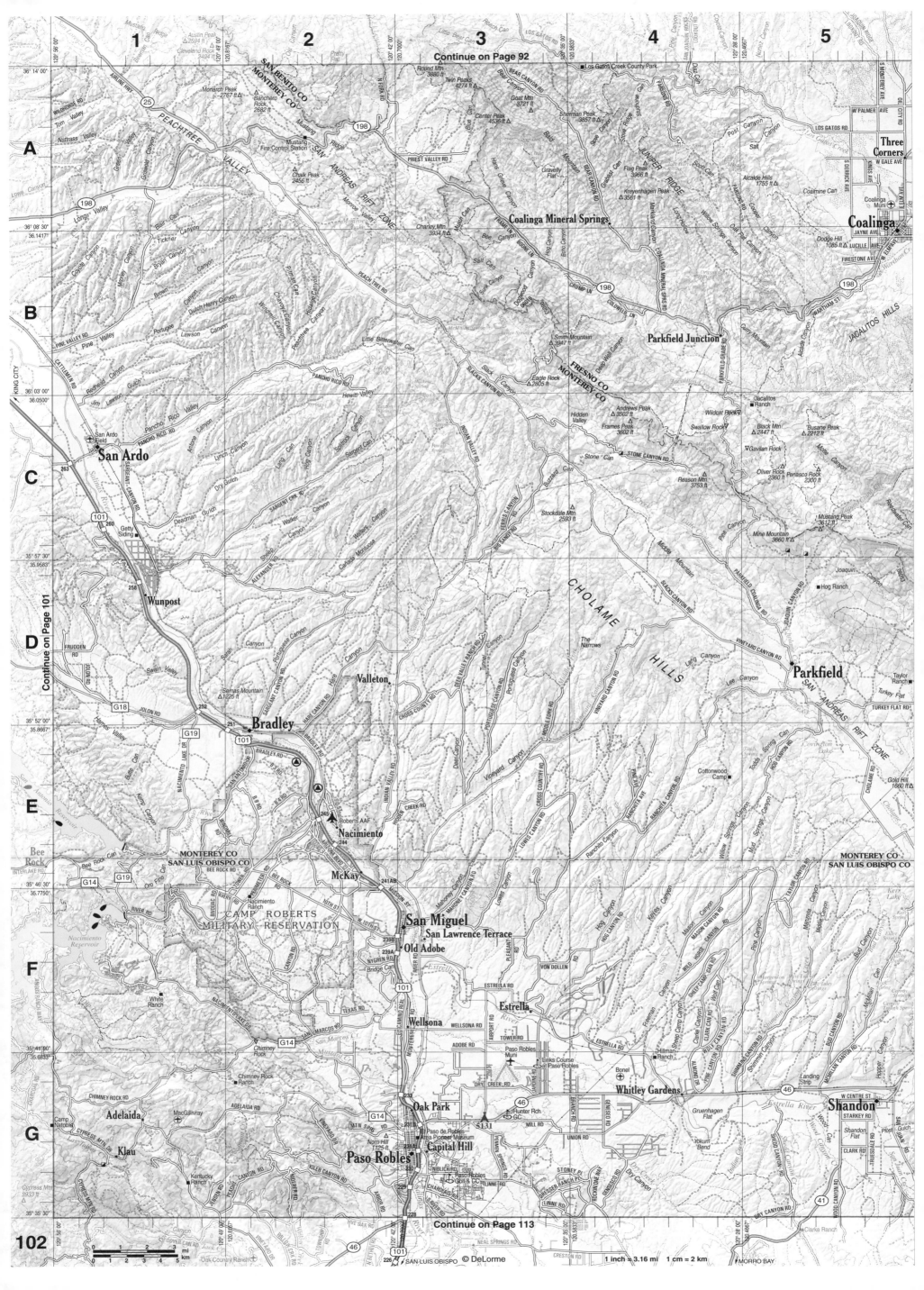

Continue on Page 92

Continue on Page 101

Continue on Page 113

102

1 inch = 3.16 mi   1 cm = 2 km

© DeLorme

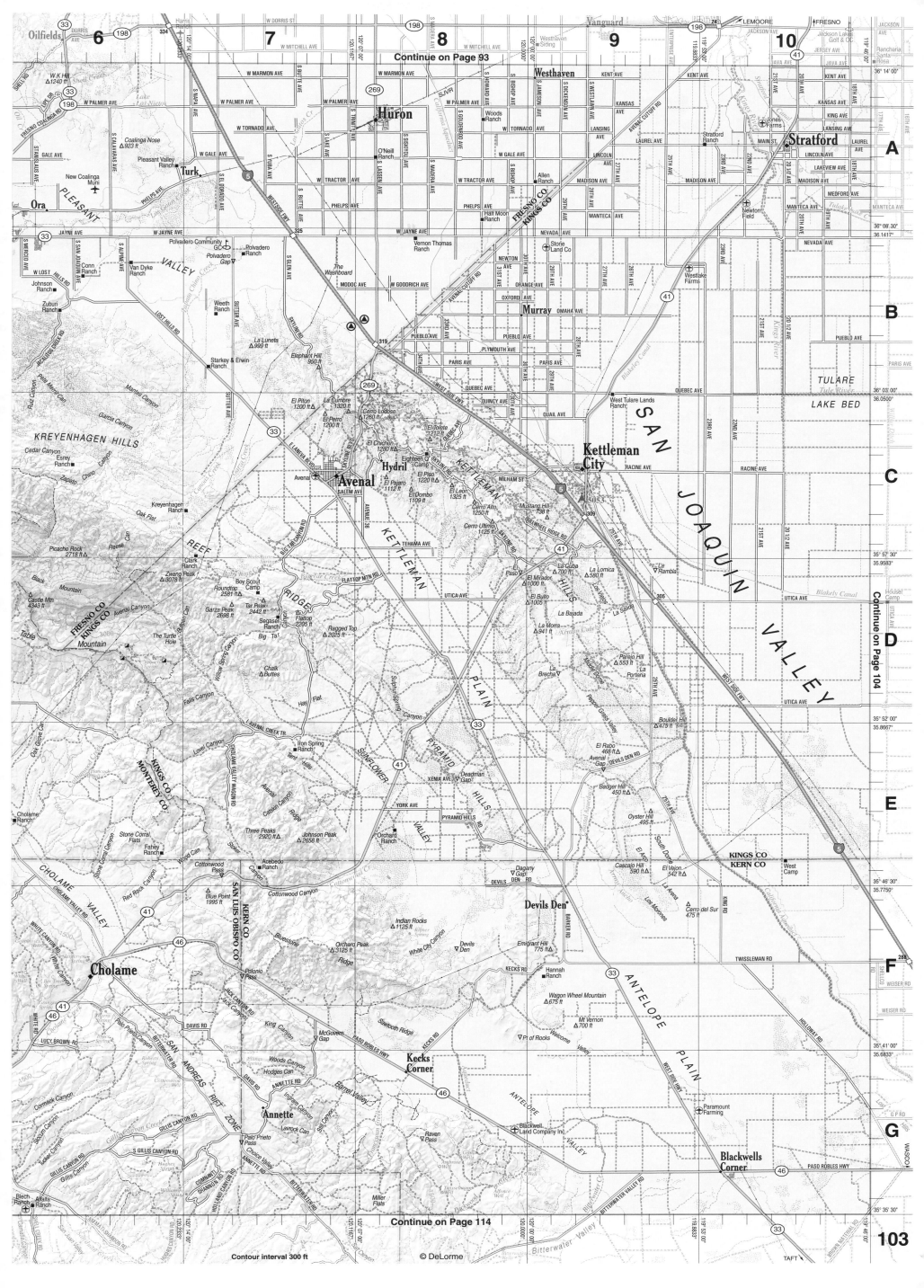

Continue on Page 93

Continue on Page 104

Continue on Page 114

Oilfields

Huron

Westhaven

Stratford

Turk

Ora

PLEASANT

VALLEY

Murray

TULARE

LAKE BED

KREYENHAGEN HILLS

Kettleman City

SAN

JOAQUIN

Hydril

Avenal

REEF

RIDGE

KETTLEMAN

PLAIN

HILLS

VALLEY

SUNFLOWER

PYRAMID

HILLS

KINGS CO

MONTEREY CO

KINGS CO

KERN CO

West Camp

Devils Den

ANTELOPE

CHOLAME

VALLEY

Cholame

SAN LUIS OBISPO CO

KERN CO

SAN ANDREAS RIFT ZONE

Kecks Corner

PLAIN

Annette

Blackwells Corner

© DeLorme

Contour interval 300 ft

103

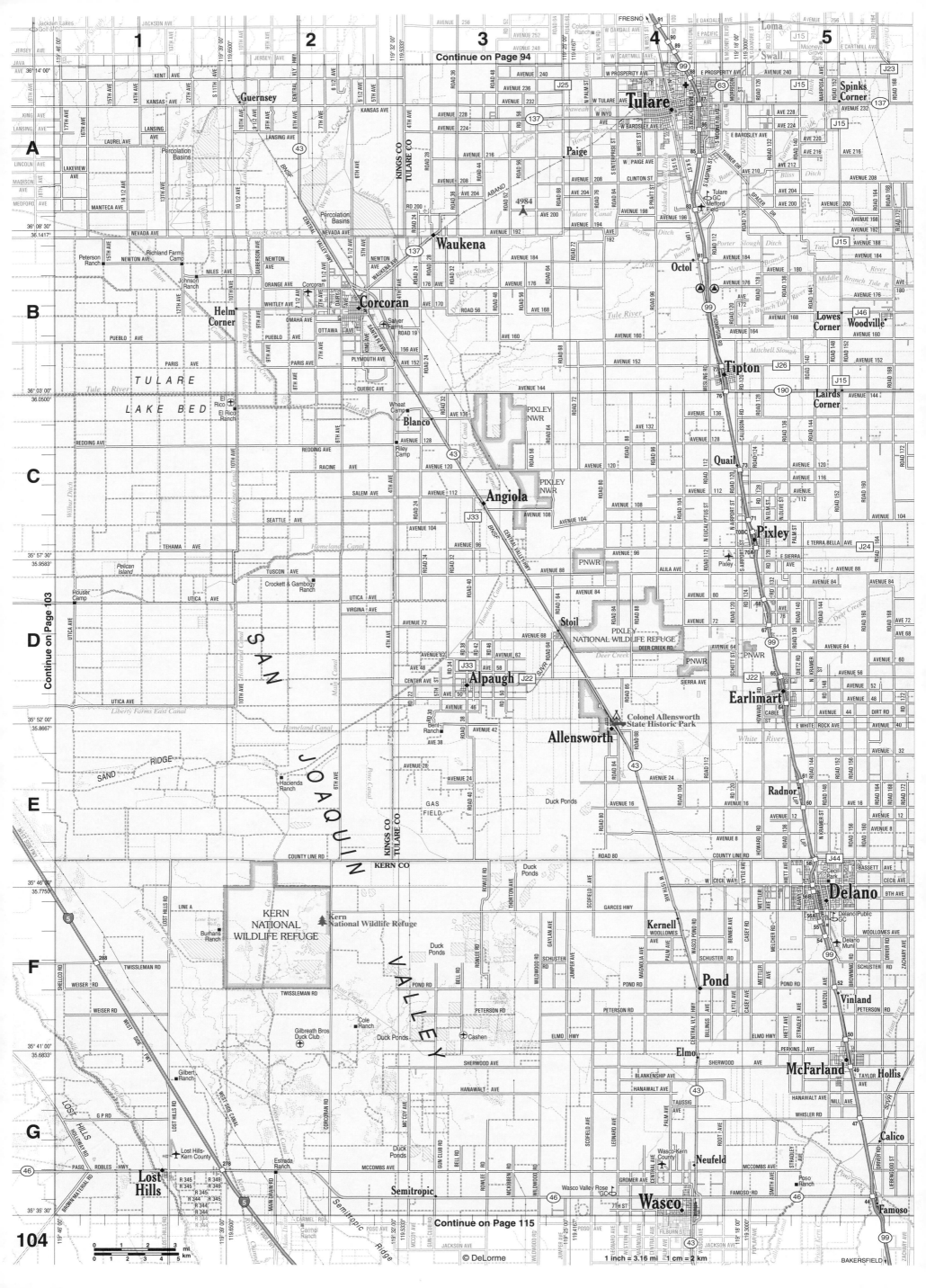

Continue on Page 94

Continue on Page 103

Continue on Page 115

104

© DeLorme

1 inch = 3.16 mi   1 cm = 2 km

BAKERSFIELD

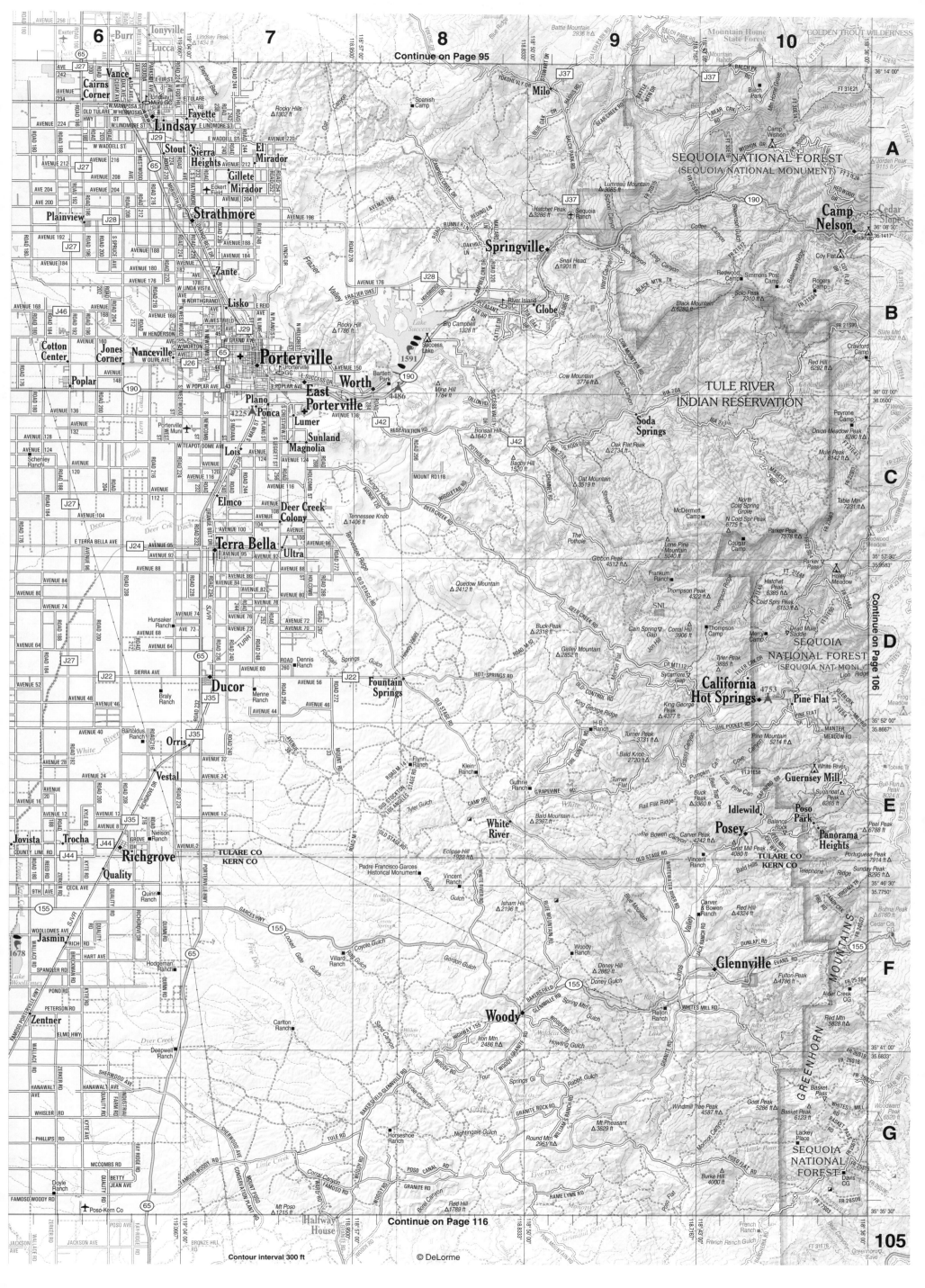

Continue on Page 95

GOLDEN TROUT WILDERNESS

SEQUOIA NATIONAL FOREST
(SEQUOIA NATIONAL MONUMENT)

Milo

Springville

Globe

Camp Nelson

Lindsay

Fayette

Stout

Sierra Heights

El Mirador

Gillete Mirador

Strathmore

Plainview

Zante

Lisko

Cotton Center

Jones Corner

Nanceville

Poplar

Porterville

Worth

East Porterville

Plano Ponca

Lumer

Sunland

Magnolia

Lois

Elmco

Deer Creek Colony

Terra Bella

Ultra

TULE RIVER
INDIAN RESERVATION

Soda Springs

SEQUOIA
NATIONAL FOREST
(SEQUOIA NAT-MON)

California
Hot Springs

Pine Flat

Ducor

Fountain Springs

Orris

Vestal

Jovista

Trocha

Richgrove

Quality

White River

Posey

Guernsey Mill

Idlewild

Poso Park

Panorama Heights

TULARE CO
KERN CO

Jasmin

Zentner

Glennville

Woody

GREENHORN

MOUNTAINS

SEQUOIA
NATIONAL
FOREST

Contour interval 300 ft

© DeLorme

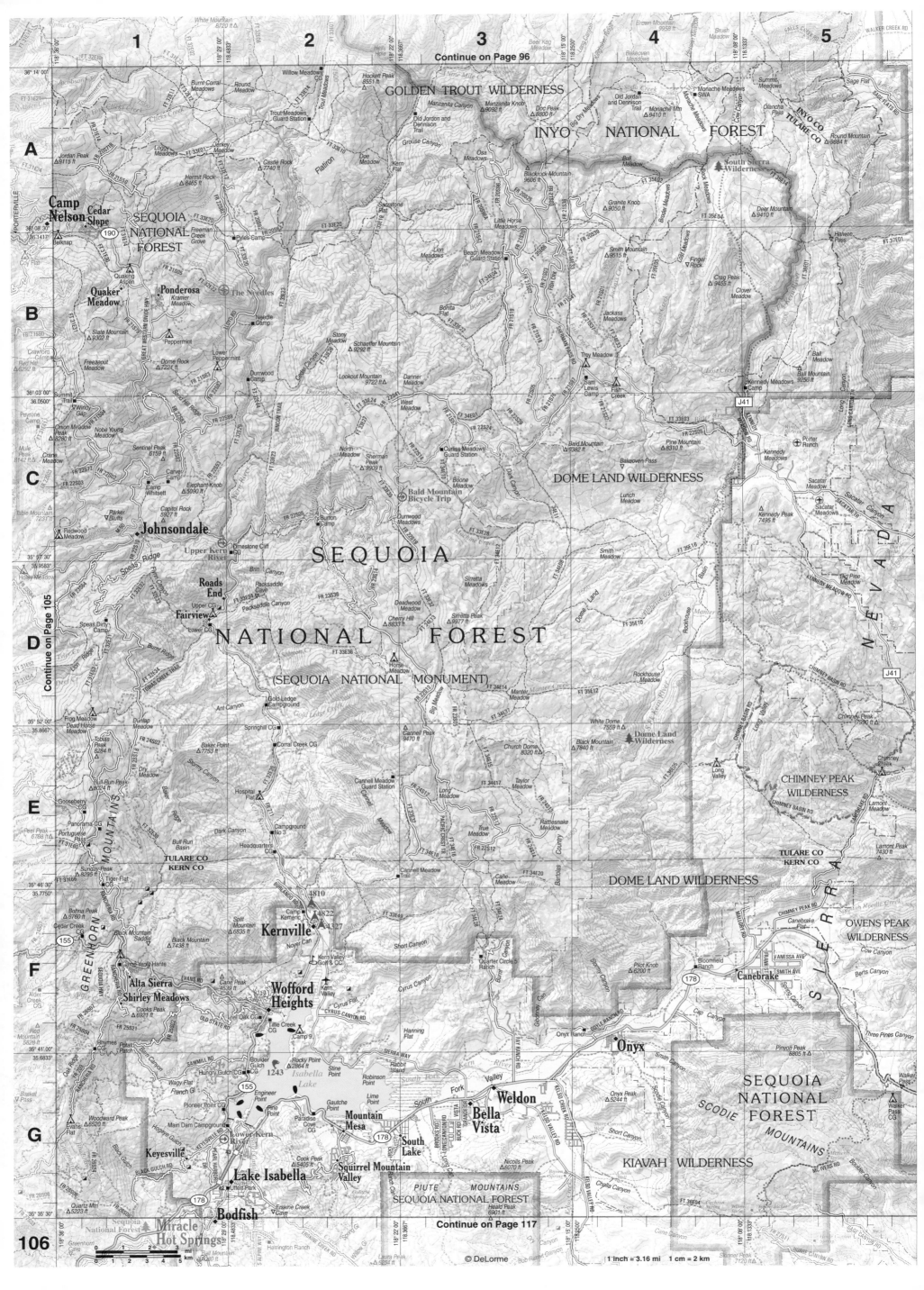

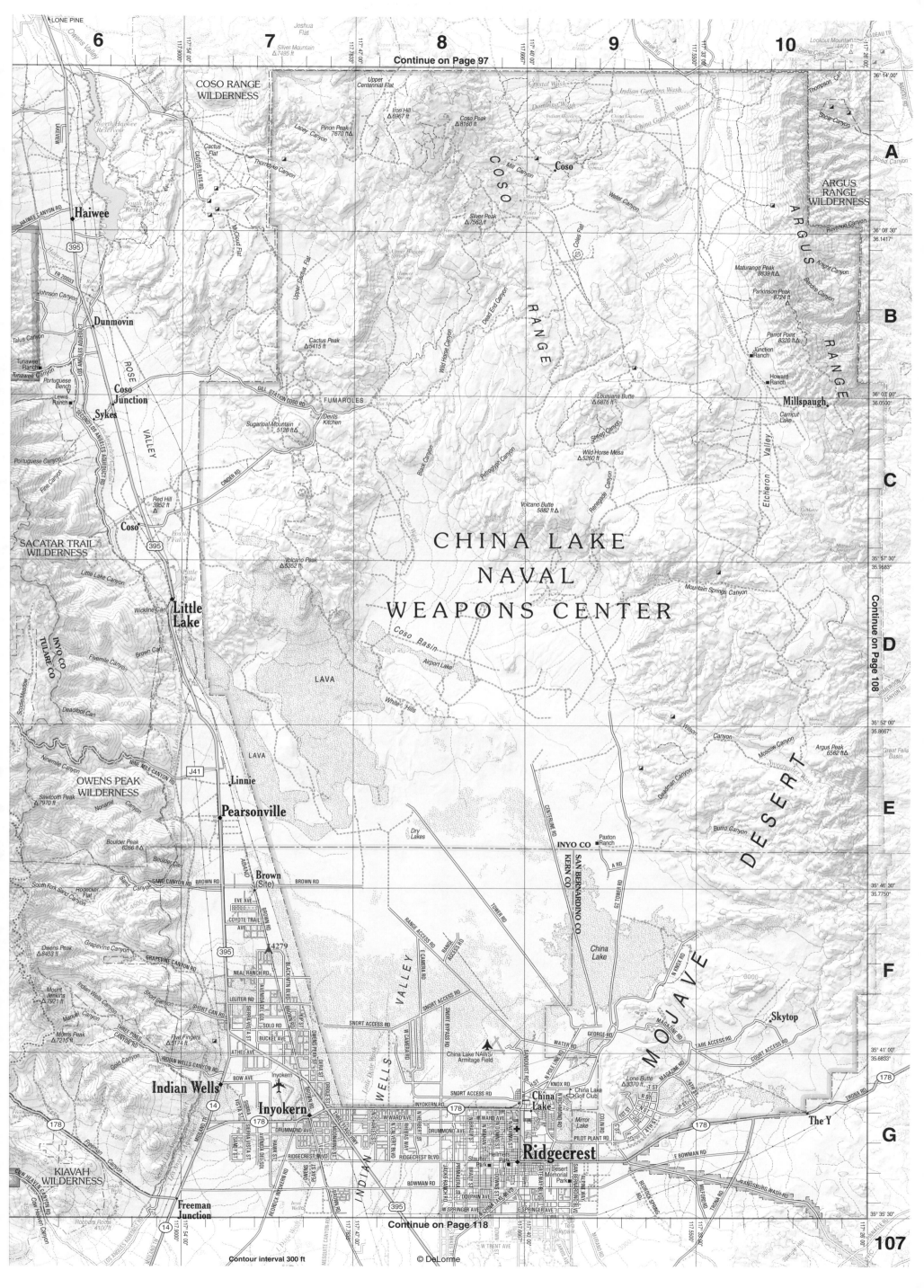

6   **7**   **8**   **9**   **10**

LONE PINE

Owens Valley

Joshua Flat

Lookout Mountain 4400 ft

Spear Canyon

Wood Canyon

COSO RANGE WILDERNESS

North Haiwee Reservoir

Upper Centennial Flat

Crystal Wash

Indian Gardens Wash

A

Silver Mountain 7495 ft

Iron Hill 6967 ft

Coso Peak 8160 ft

China Gardens Wash

ARGUS RANGE WILDERNESS

HAIWEE CANYON RD

Cactus Flat

Lacey Canyon

Pinon Peak 7670 ft

China Gardens Spring

Cactus Flats Rd

Thorndike Canyon

McCloud Flat

Coso Springs

Coso

Water Canyon

Revenue Canyon

Knight Canyon

Haiwee

South Haiwee Reservoir

Upper Cactus Flat

C O S O

Silver Peak 7562 ft

Darwin Wash

Maturango Peak 8839 ft

Parkinson Peak 8724 ft

Banana Canyon

B

Talus Canyon

Johnson Canyon

Dunmovin

Upper Haiwee Springs

Haiwee Springs

Wild Horse Spring

R A N G E

Parrot Point 8320 ft

Junction Ranch

Tunawee Canyon

Tunawee Canyon

Portuguese Bench

Lewis Ranch

Coso Junction

GILL STATION COSO RD

FUMAROLES

Iron Hot Springs

Dead End Canyon

Wild Horse Canyon

Louisiana Butte 6876 ft

Howard Ranch

36° 03' 00"
36.0500°

Millspaugh

Carricut Lake

Portuguese Canyon

Sykes

Sugarloaf Mountain 5128 ft

Devils Kitchen

Black Canyon

Sheep Canyon

Renegade Canyon

Etcheron Valley

A R G U S   R A N G E

C

Pine Canyon

ROSE VALLEY

CINDER RD

Petroglyph Canyon

Wild Horse Mesa 5260 ft

SACATAR TRAIL WILDERNESS

Red Hill 3952 ft

Coso

395

Volcano Butte 5882 ft

CHINA LAKE

35° 57' 30"
35.9583°

Little Lake Canyon

Volcano Peak 5352 ft

NAVAL

D

Mountain Springs Canyon

Little Lake

Wickline Can

WEAPONS CENTER

Coso Basin

Continue on Page 108

INYO CO TULARE CO

Fivemile Canyon

Brown Can

Airport Lake

White Hills

LAVA

Deadfoot Can

Ninemile Canyon

LAVA

Argus Peak 6562 ft

35° 52' 00"
35.8667°

OWENS PEAK WILDERNESS

Moscow Canyon

Great Falls Basin

Sawtooth Peak 7970 ft

J41

Linnie

Noname Canyon

Deadman Canyon

Burro Canyon

Sweetwater

E

NINE MILE CANYON RD

Pearsonville

Dry Lakes

CENTERLINE RD

Paxton Ranch

Boulder Peak 6266 ft

Boulder Can

INYO CO
KERN CO

A RD

San Bernardino Co

35° 46' 30"
35.7750°

South Fork Sand Canyon

Sand Canyon

SAND CANYON RD

BROWN RD

Brown (Site)

BROWN RD

D2 TOWER RD

Rodecker Flat

ABAND

EVE AVE

F

Owens Peak 8453 ft

Grapevine Canyon

395

COYOTE TRAIL AVE

RANGE ACCESS RD

TOWER RD

China Lake

Mount Jenkins 7921 ft

GRAPEVINE CANYON RD

4279

NEAL RANCH RD

E CAMERA RD

RANGE ACCESS RD

INYOKERN RD

George Rd

Skytop

Manzar RD

Morris Peak 7215 ft

THREE PINS CANYON RD

LELITER RD

BLACK MTN BLVD

SNORT ACCESS RD

SNORT BYPASS RD

WATER RD

TARE ACCESS RD

COURT ACCESS RD

35° 41' 00"
35.6833°

Five Fingers 5174 ft

Five Fingers

SOLO RD

BUCKEL AVE

SNORT ACCESS RD

China Lake NAWS/ Armitage Field

M O J A V E

Lone Butte 3370 ft

Mirror Lake

SHORT CAN RD

ATHEL AVE

I N D I A N   W E L L S   V A L L E Y

GEORGE RD

KNOX RD

China Lake Golf Club

Indian Wells

14

BOW AVE

Inyokern

W WARD AVE

China Lake

178

The Y

Manuel Canyon

Inyokern

178

DRUMMOND AVE

DRUMMOND AVE

PILOT PLANT RD

G

KIAVAH WILDERNESS

178

RIDGECREST BLVD

RIDGECREST BLVD

Stauter Park

Ridgecrest

Desert Memorial Park

BOWMAN RD

BOWMAN RD

Freeman Junction

14

395

INDIAN WELLS

Inyo Wells

178

178

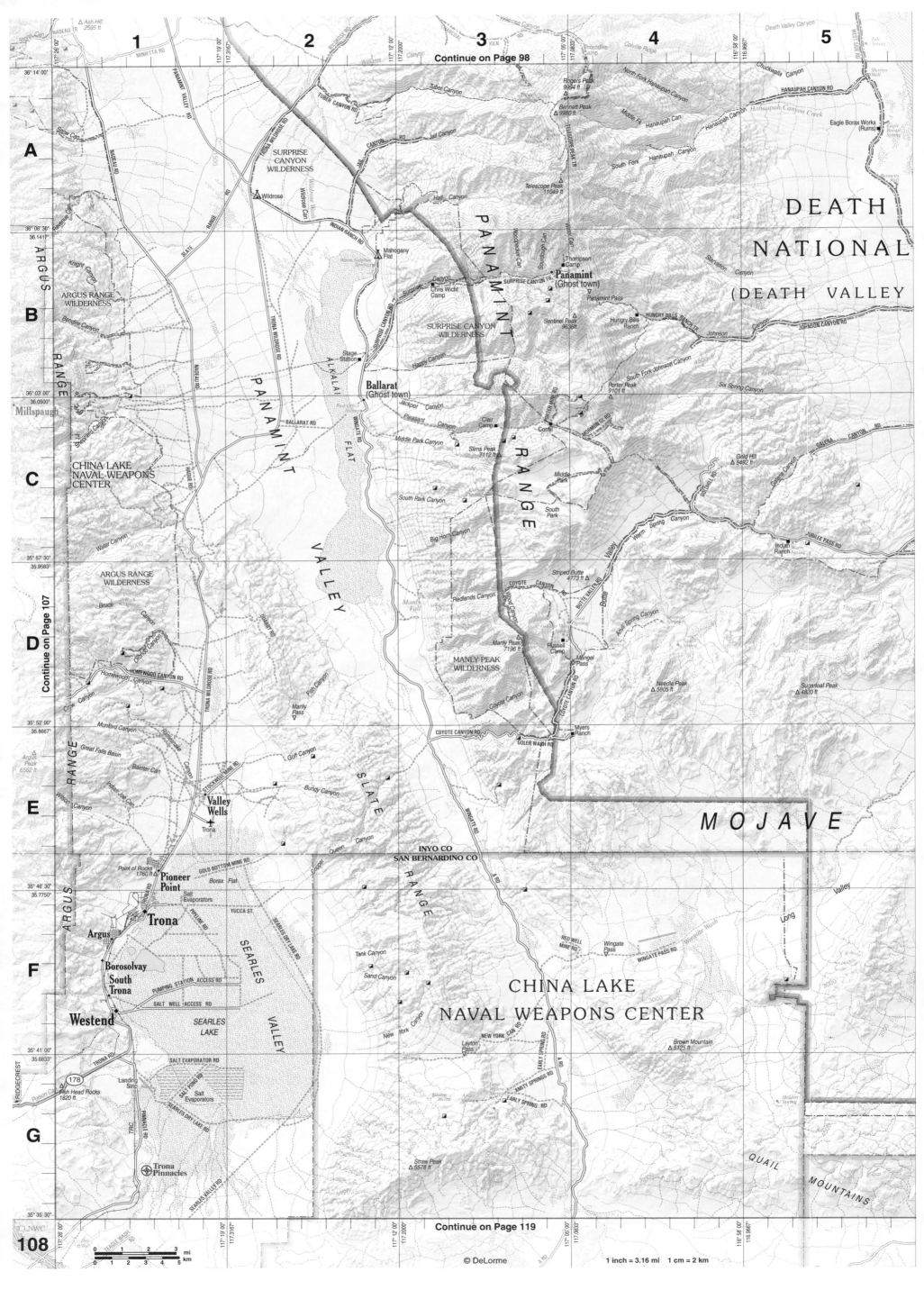

DEATH

NATIONAL

(DEATH VALLEY

MOJAVE

CHINA LAKE
NAVAL WEAPONS CENTER

Continue on Page 119

Continue on Page 107

© DeLorme   1 inch = 3.16 mi   1 cm = 2 km

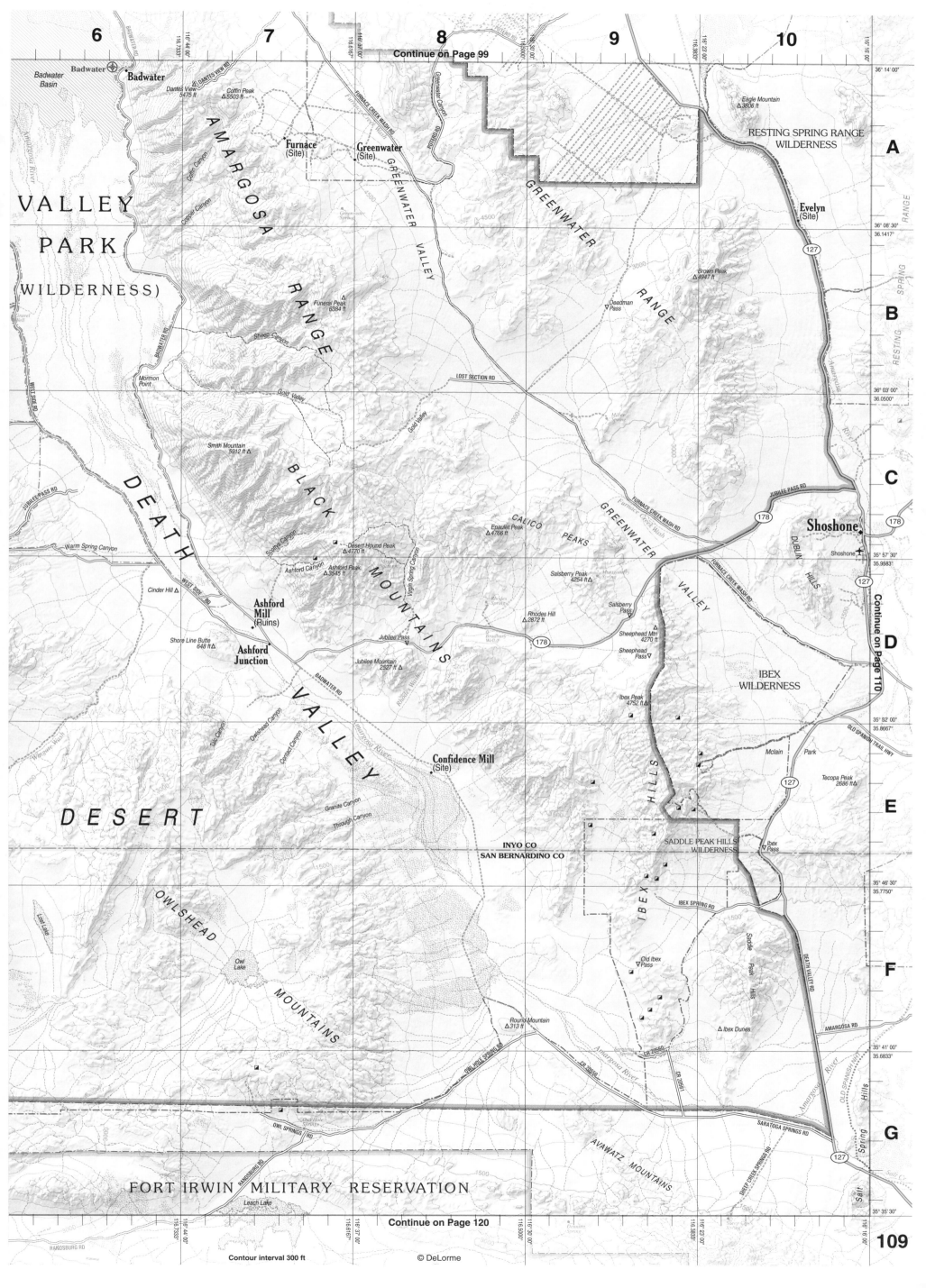

Continue on Page 99

116° 44' 00"
116° 37.333"
116° 37' 00"
116° 30' 30"
116° 30' 00"
116° 23' 00"
116° 16' 00"

36° 14' 00"

Badwater Basin
Badwater •Badwater

Dantes View 5475 ft △
Coffin Peak △5503 ft

RESTING SPRING RANGE WILDERNESS

A

Eagle Mountain △3806 ft

Furnace (Site)
Greenwater (Site)

Evelyn (Site)

36° 08' 30"
36.1417°

127

VALLEY

A M A R G O S A   R A N G E

G R E E N W A T E R   V A L L E Y

G R E E N W A T E R   R A N G E

Brown Peak △4947 ft

PARK

(WILDERNESS)

Funeral Peak 6384 ft △

Deadman Pass ▽

B

Sheep Canyon

Mormon Point

LOST SECTION RD

36° 03' 00"
36.0500°

Gold Valley

Smith Mountain 5912 ft △

Gold Valley

Miller Spring

JUBILEE PASS RD

C

Jubilee Pass Rd

CALICO PEAKS

G R E E N W A T E R

Furnace Creek Wash

FURNACE CREEK WASH RD

Shoshone

178

Epaulet Peak △4766 ft

Salsberry Peak 4254 ft △

Salsberry Pass

FURNACE CREEK WASH RD

DUBLIN HILLS

Shoshone ✚

35° 57' 30"
35.9583°

127

W A R M   S P R I N G   C A N Y O N

B L A C K

Desert Hound Peak △4770 ft

Virgin Spring Canyon

Rhodes Spring

Rhodes Hill △2872 ft

Sheephead Mtn 4270 ft ▽

V A L L E Y

Continue on Page 110

D

Cinder Hill △

Ashford Canyon
Ashford Peak △3545 ft

Scotty's Canyon

Bradbury Well

178

Sheephead Pass ▽

IBEX WILDERNESS

Ashford Mill (Ruins)

Jubilee Pass ▽

M O U N T A I N S

Ibex Peak 4752 ft △

35° 52' 00"
35.8667°

Shore Line Butte 648 ft △

Ashford Junction

Jubilee Mountain 2527 ft △

Mclain   Park

OLD SPANISH TRAIL HWY

BADWATER RD

Tecopa Peak 2686 ft △

127

D E A T H

Tule Canyon
Owlshead Canyon
Contact Canyon

Confidence Mill (Site)

Rhodes Wash

Amargosa River

I B E X
H I L L S

E

D E S E R T

Granite Canyon
Through Canyon

Ibex Pass ▽

35° 46' 30"
35.7750°

INYO CO
SAN BERNARDINO CO

SADDLE PEAK HILLS WILDERNESS

O W L S H E A D

I B E X

IBEX SPRING RD

Saddle Peak Hills

DEATH VALLEY RD

F

Lost Lake

Owl Lake

Old Ibex Pass ▽

△ Ibex Dunes

AMARGOSA RD

M O U N T A I N S

Round Mountain △313 ft

CR 20580

35° 41' 00"
35.6833°

OWL HOLE SPRINGS RD

Amargosa River

CR 20560

CR 20561

SARATOGA SPRINGS RD

Salt Spring Hills

G

RANDSBURG RD

OWL SPRINGS RD

Owl Hole Springs

A V A W A T Z   M O U N T A I N S

SHEEP CREEK SPRINGS RD

127

35° 35' 30"

F O R T   I R W I N   M I L I T A R Y   R E S E R V A T I O N

116° 44' 00"
116° 37.333"
116° 37' 00"
116° 30' 30"
116° 30' 00"
116° 23' 00"
116° 16' 00"

Continue on Page 120

Contour interval 300 ft   © DeLorme

109

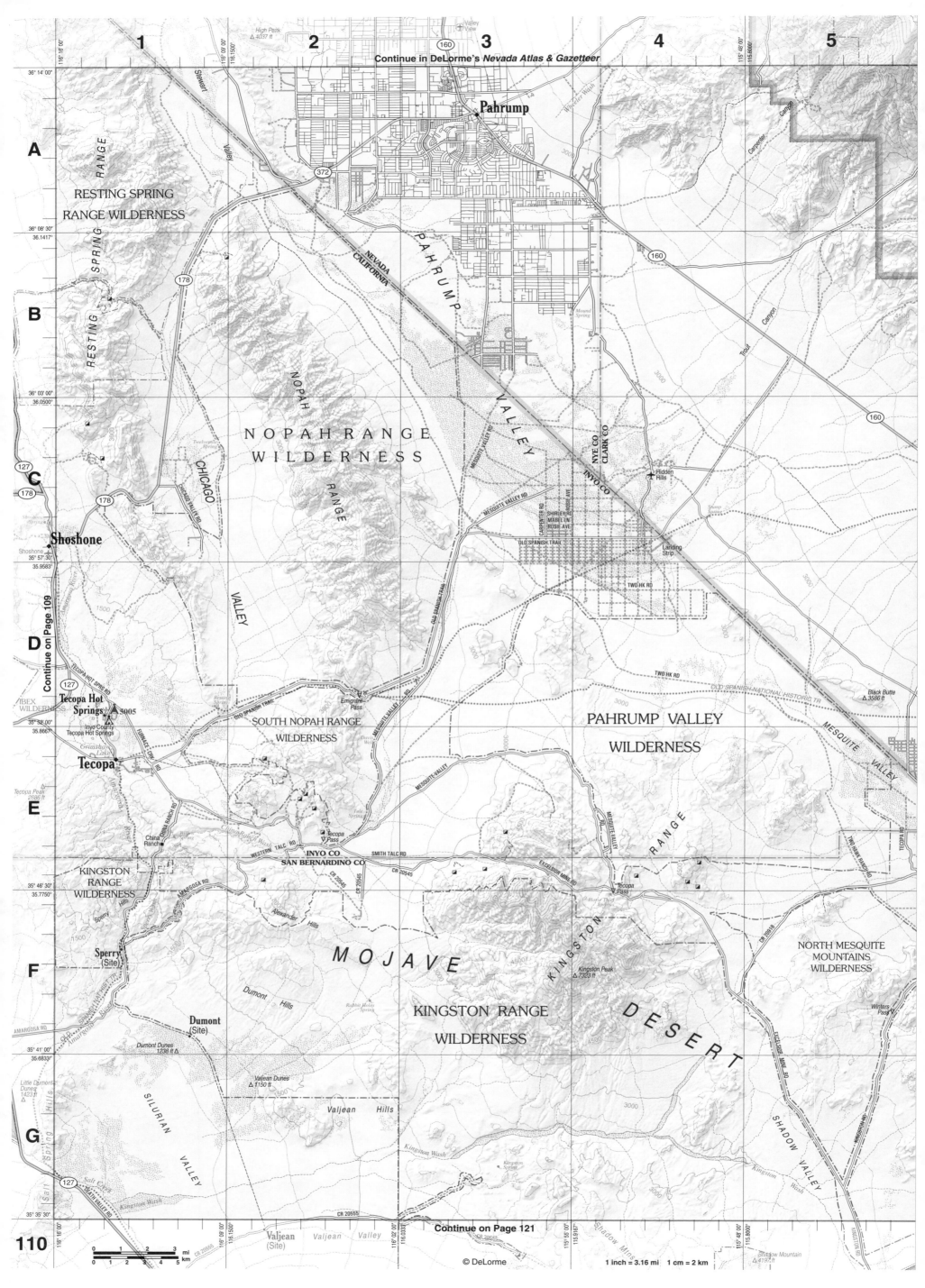

Pahrump

A

RESTING SPRING
RANGE WILDERNESS

B

NOPAH RANGE
WILDERNESS

PAHRUMP VALLEY

RESTING SPRING RANGE

CHICAGO

C

Shoshone

NOPAH RANGE

NYE CO
CLARK CO
INYO CO

Hidden
Hills

OLD SPANISH TRAIL

D

VALLEY

Tecopa Hot
Springs

Emigrant
Pass

SOUTH NOPAH RANGE
WILDERNESS

PAHRUMP VALLEY

WILDERNESS

Black Butte
△3586 ft

E

Tecopa

China
Ranch

Tecopa
Pass

INYO CO
SAN BERNARDINO CO

MESQUITE RANGE

KINGSTON
RANGE
WILDERNESS

Sperry

Tecopa
Pass

NORTH MESQUITE
MOUNTAINS
WILDERNESS

F

Sperry
(Site)

M O J A V E

Dumont
Hills

Rabbit Holes
Spring

KINGSTON RANGE

WILDERNESS

Kingston Peak
△7323 ft

D E S E R T

Winters
Pass

Dumont
(Site)

Dumont Dunes
1238 ft △

G

Little Dumont
Dunes
1423 ft △

SILURIAN

VALLEY

Valjean Dunes
△1150 ft

Valjean Hills

Kingston Wash

SHADOW VALLEY

Continue on Page 109

Valjean
(Site)

© DeLorme

0 1 2 3 mi
0 1 2 3 4 5 km

1 inch = 3.16 mi   1 cm = 2 km

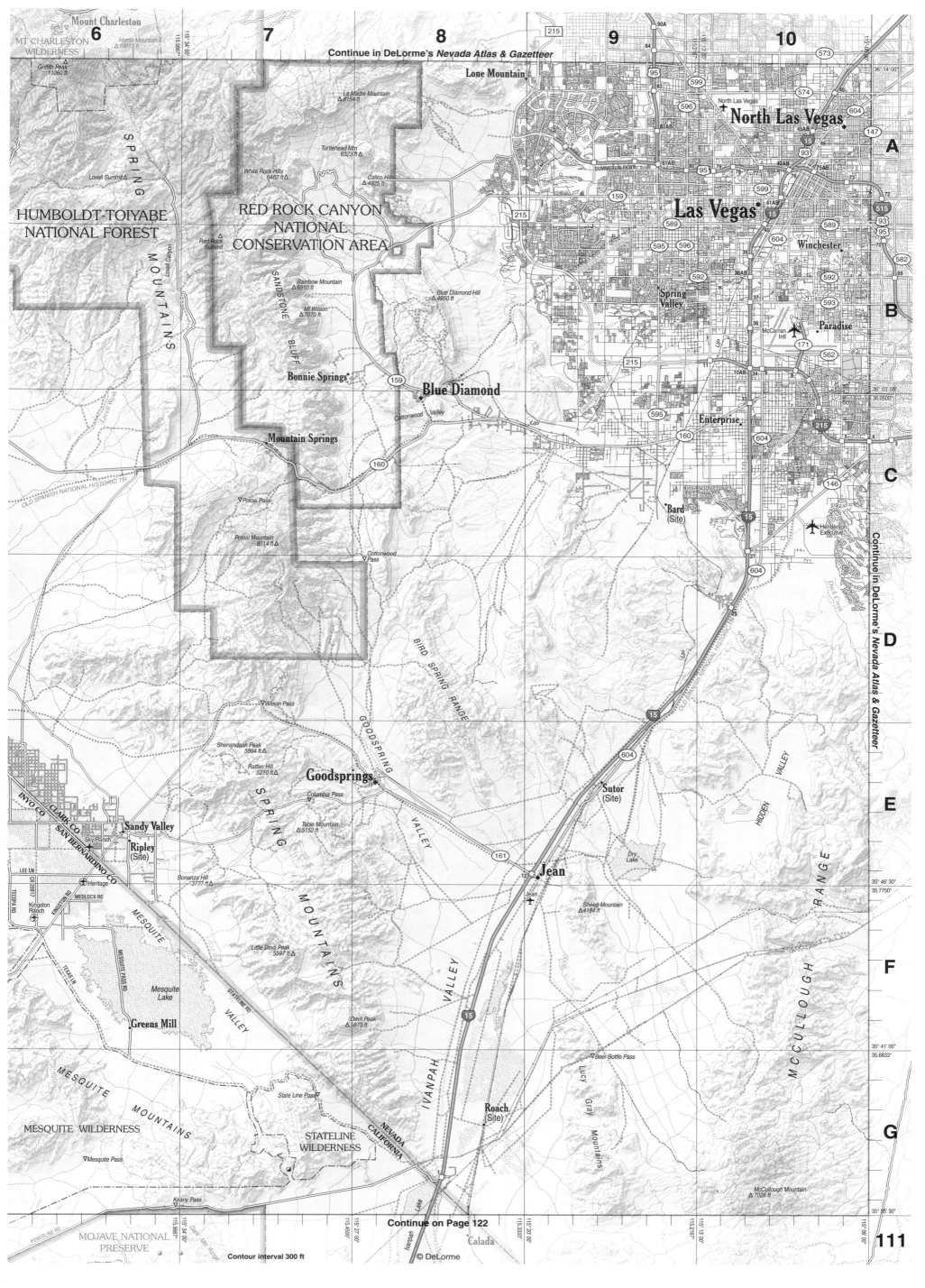

Mount Charleston

MT CHARLESTON
WILDERNESS

Echo
Cliff

Griffith Peak
△11060 ft

Harris Mountain
△10013 ft

Continue in DeLorme's *Nevada Atlas & Gazetteer*

Lone Mountain

215

90A

84

95

573

599

North Las Vegas

574

604

147

La Madre Mountain
△8154 ft

596

82AB

81AB

80

95

78

77

42AB

45AB

5AB

North Las Vegas

15

93

A

Lovell Summit

SPRING

Turtlehead Mtn
6323 ft △

White Rock Hills
6462 ft △

Calico Hills
△4925 ft

159

215

599

Las Vegas

15

93

95

70

515

**HUMBOLDT-TOIYABE
NATIONAL FOREST**

RED ROCK CANYON
NATIONAL
CONSERVATION
AREA

Red Rock
Summit

589

740

604

Winchester

582

69

M
O
U
N
T
A
I
N
S

SANDSTONE BLUFF

Rainbow Mountain
△6810 ft

Mt Wilson
△7070 ft

Blue Diamond Hill
△4950 ft

595

596

592

38AB

37

39

**Spring
Valley**

36

McCarran
Intl

171

Paradise

592

593

562

B

Bonnie Springs

159

Blue Diamond

215

11

10AB

34

35

8

Enterprise

S

Mountain Springs

Cottonwood   Valley

160

UP

595

160

33

604

215

C

146

▽Potosi Pass

Bard
(Site)

15

Potosi Mountain
8514 ft △

▽Cottonwood
Pass

27

604

D

▽Wilson Pass

BIRD SPRING RANGE

15

Shenandaah Peak
5864 ft △

Rattler Hill
5210 ft △

GOODSPRING

604

HIDDEN   VALLEY

Continue in DeLorme's *Nevada Atlas & Gazetteer*

INYO CO
CLARK CO

SAN BERNARDINO CO

Goodsprings

Columbia Pass

Sutor
(Site)

E

Sandy Valley

Sky Ranch

Table Mountain
△5152 ft

SPRING

161

VALLEY

Dry
Lake

MCCULLOUGH   RANGE

Ripley
(Site)

LEE LN

Bonanza Hill
3777 ft △

12

Jean

35° 46' 30"
35.7750°

CR 20917

TECOPA RD

Kingston
Ranch

MEDLOCK RD

Heritage

Club Well

Jean

Sheep Mountain
△4184 ft

Lucy Gray Mountains

F

KINGSTON RD

MESQUITE

Little Devil Peak
5597 ft △

M
O
U
N
T
A
I
N
S

15

TEXAS LN

STATELINE RD

Mesquite Lake

Government

Devil Peak
△5873 ft

35° 41' 00"
35.6833°

Greens Mill

VALLEY

MOUNTAINS

IVANPAH   VALLEY

NEVADA
CALIFORNIA

▽Beer Bottle Pass

G

Roach
(Site)

McCullough Mountain
△7026 ft

MESQUITE WILDERNESS

State Line Pass▽

STATELINE
WILDERNESS

15

▽Mesquite Pass

Keany Pass▽

POWERLINE RD

**MOJAVE NATIONAL
PRESERVE**

Ivanpah
Lake

Calada

35° 35' 00"

Contour interval 300 ft

© DeLorme

115° 34' 00"
115.5667°

115° 34' 00"
115.5667°

115° 27' 00"
115.4500°

115° 20' 00"
115.3333°

115° 13' 00"
115.2167°

115° 06' 00"

36° 14' 00"

36° 03' 00"
36.0500°

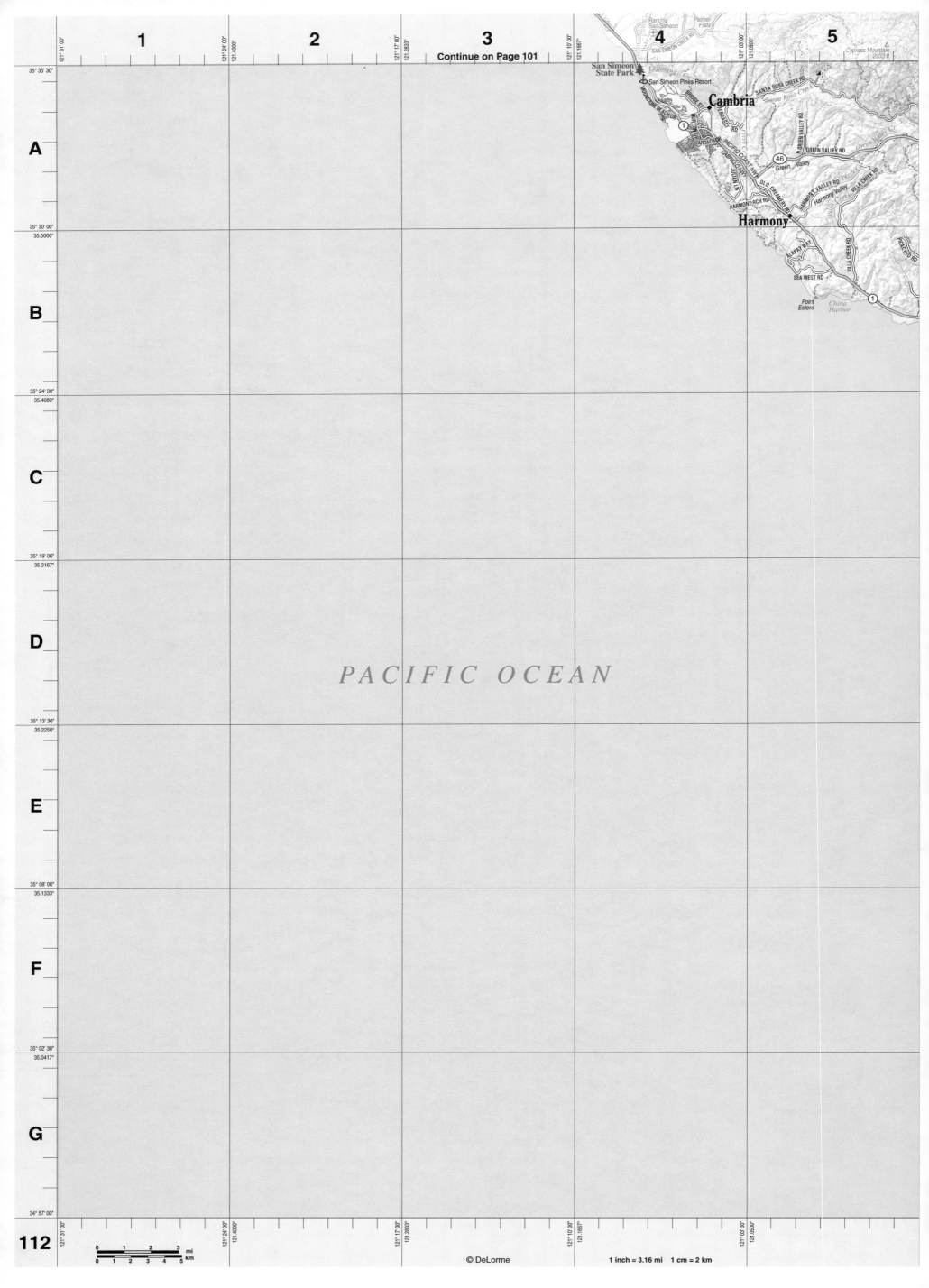

Continue on Page 101

PACIFIC OCEAN

1 inch = 3.16 mi   1 cm = 2 km

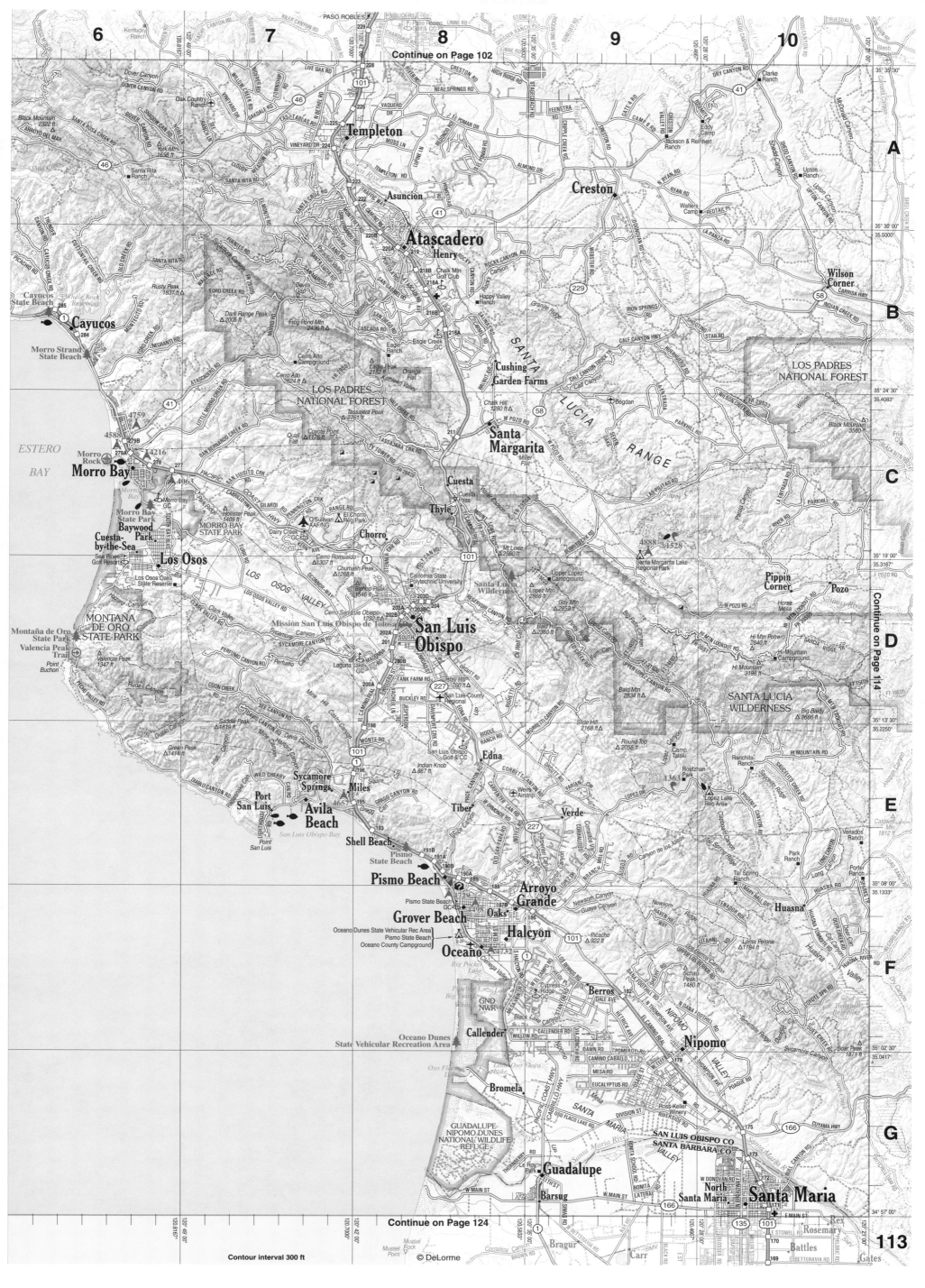

Continue on Page 102

Continue on Page 114

Contour interval 300 ft

© DeLorme

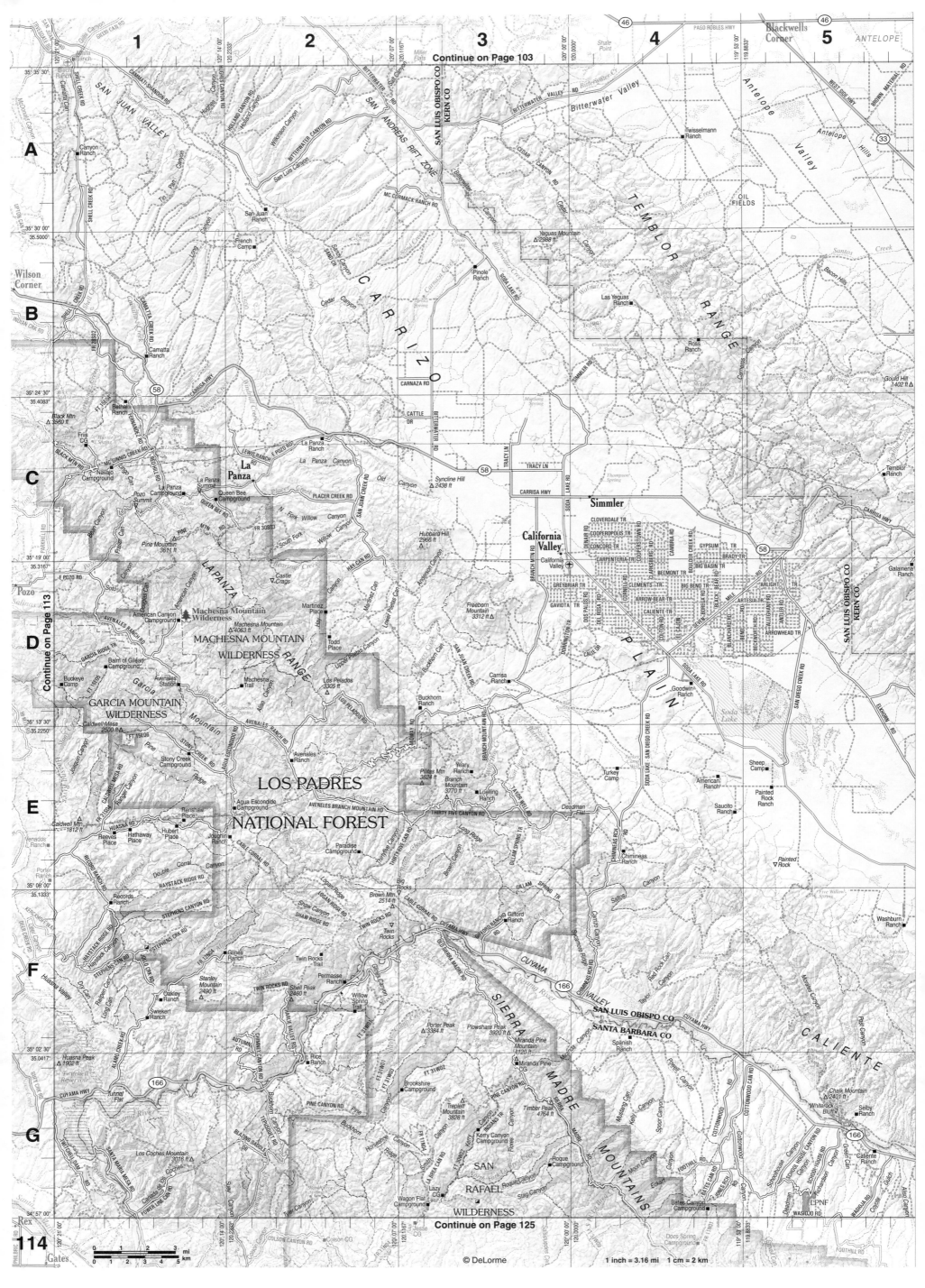

A
B
C
D
E
F
G

LOS PADRES

NATIONAL FOREST

MACHESNA MOUNTAIN

WILDERNESS RANGE

GARCIA MOUNTAIN
WILDERNESS

SAN JUAN VALLEY

CARRIZO

TEMBLOR RANGE

PLAIN

California Valley

Simmler

LA PANZA RANGE

SIERRA

MADRE

MOUNTAINS

SAN

RAFAEL

WILDERNESS

CALIENTE

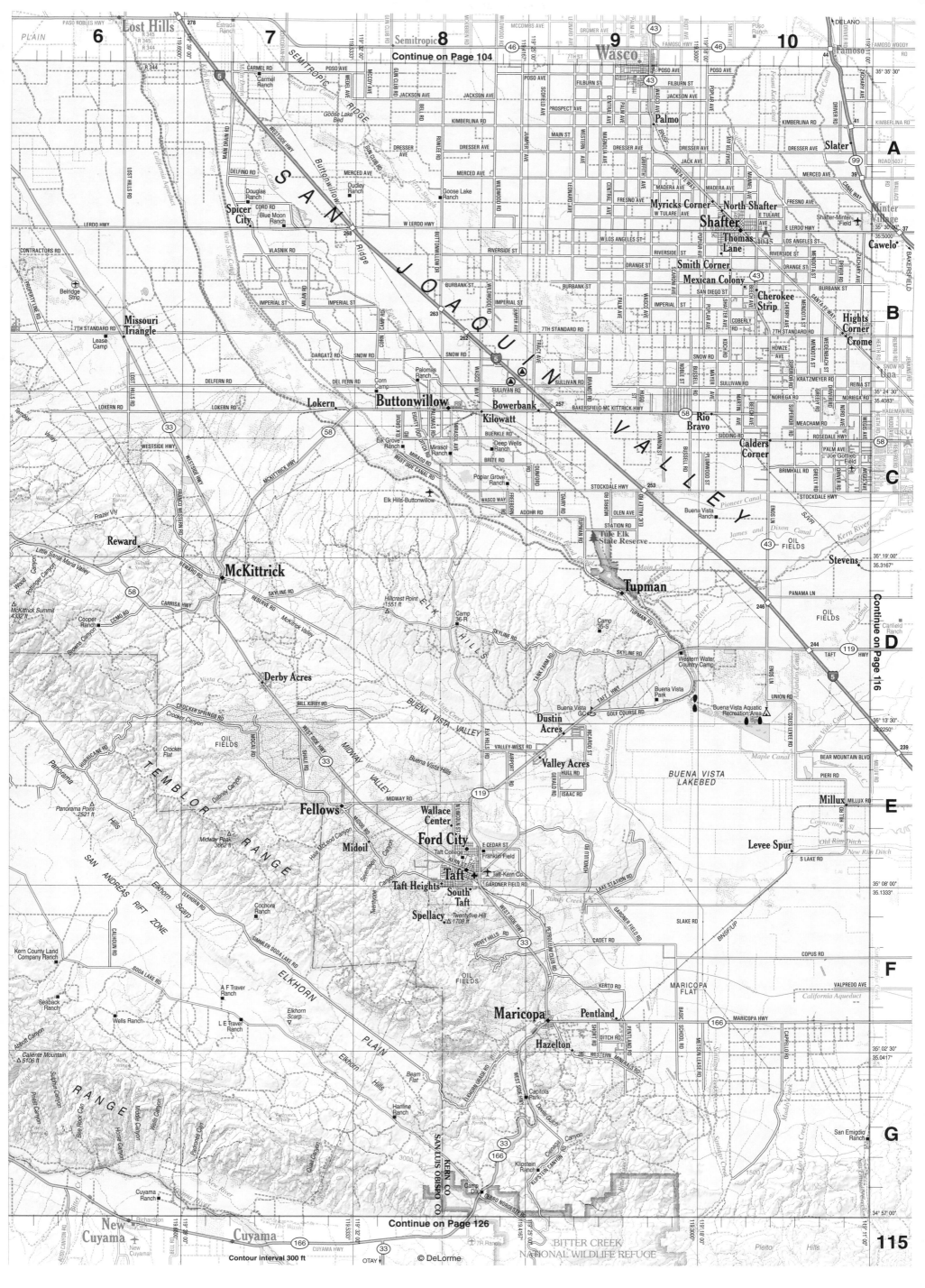

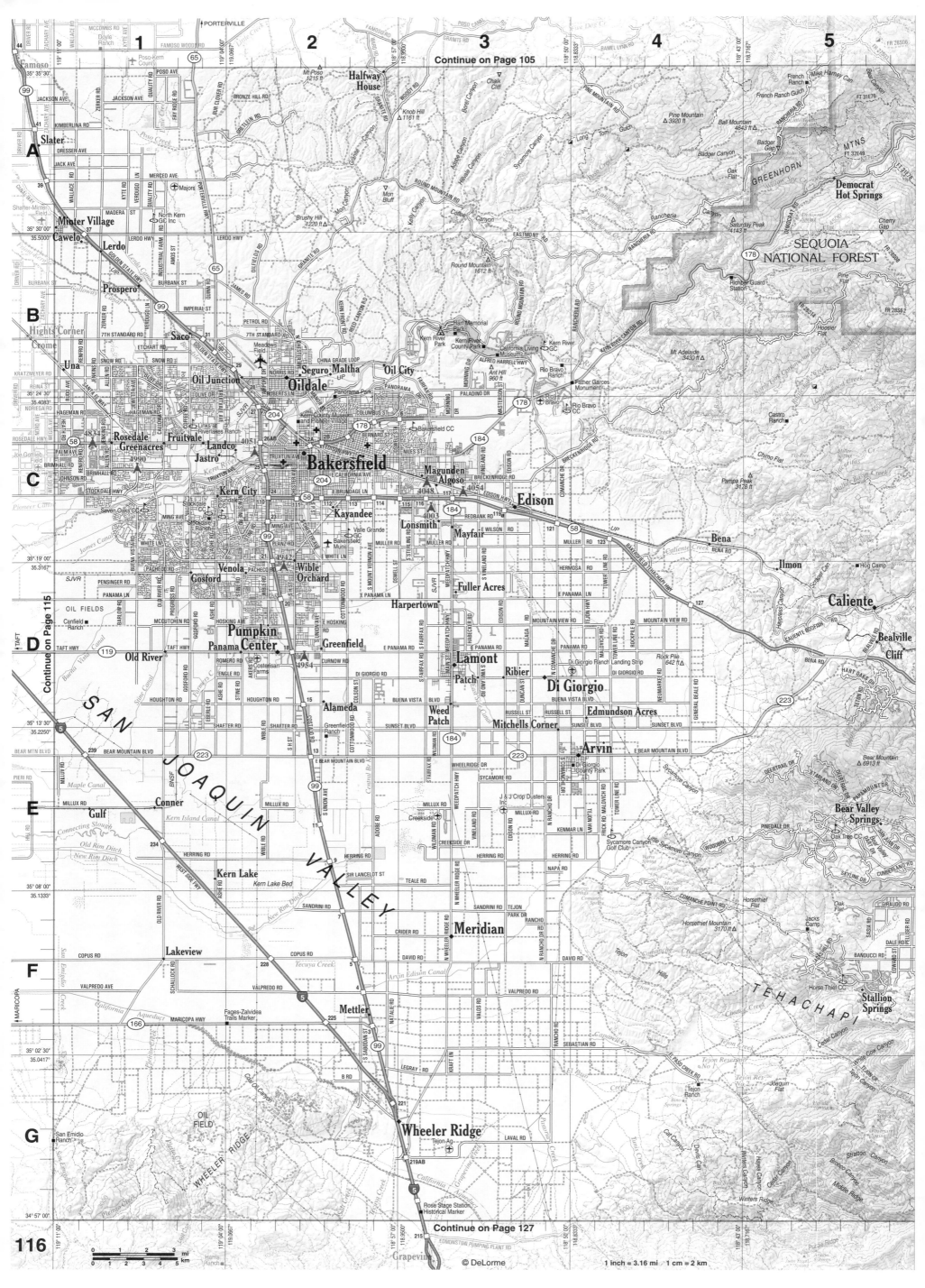

Continue on Page 105

Continue on Page 115

Continue on Page 127

© DeLorme

1 inch = 3.16 mi   1 cm = 2 km

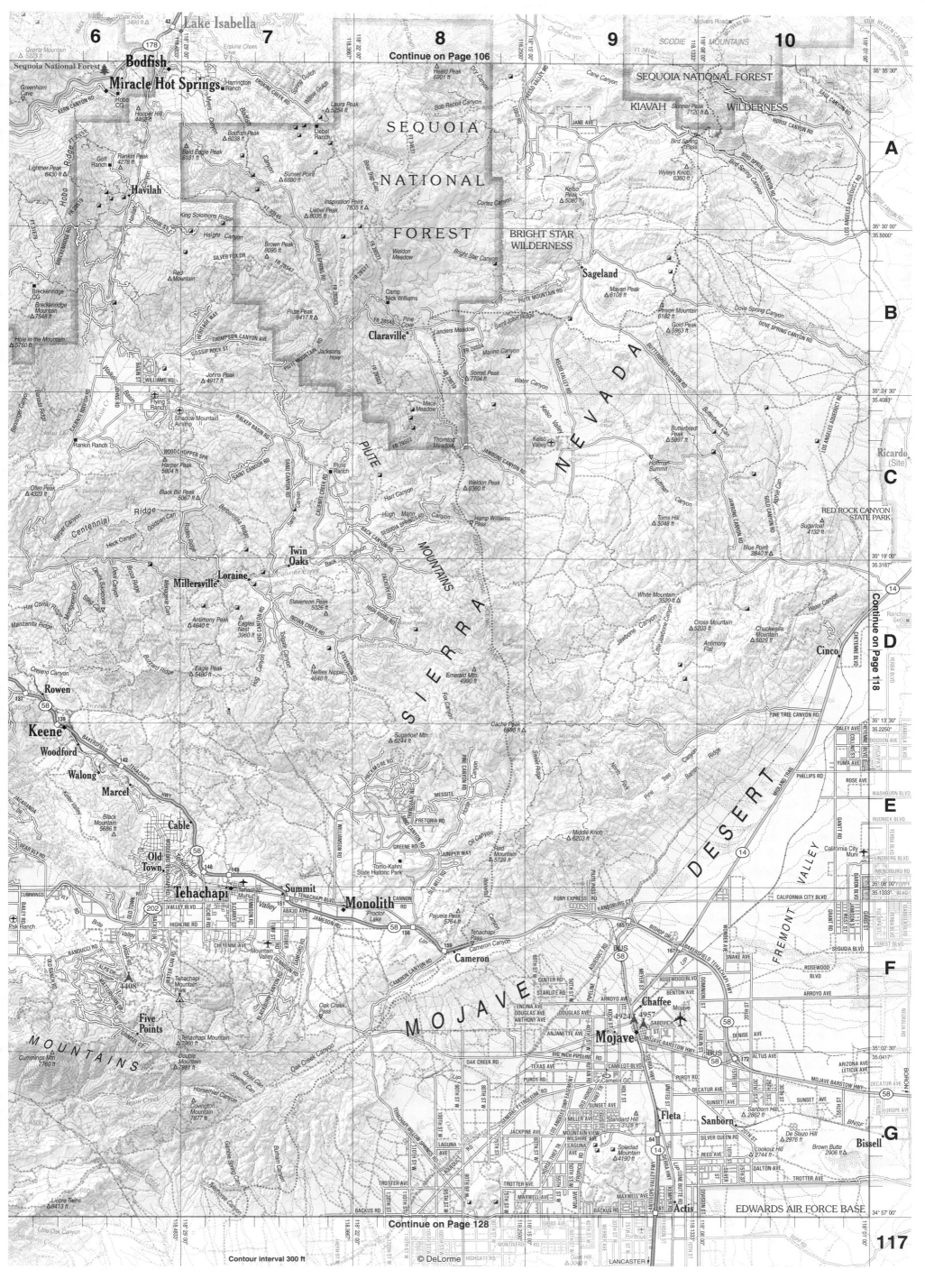

Continue on Page 106

A

B

C

Continue on Page 118

D

E

F

G

Continue on Page 128

Contour interval 300 ft

© DeLorme

Continue on Page 107

SEQUOIA NAT FOR

KIAVAH WILDERNESS

OWENS PEAK WILDERNESS

LONE PINE

Freeman Junction

Robbers Roost 4100 ft

INDIAN WELLS VALLEY

Armistead

EL PASO MOUNTAINS WILDERNESS

Harts Place

Black Hills   Black Mountain △5244 ft

El Paso Peaks 4578 ft△   Laurel Mountain △4460 ft

Searles

SUMMIT   RANGE

MOJAVE

RED ROCK CANYON STATE PARK

Holland Camp

Colorado Camp

Owens Camp   Gerbracht Camp

Bickel Camp

Red Buttes △3708 ft

Cudahy Camp

Schmidt Camp

The Narrows

Mormon Flat

Goler Heights   Landing Strip

Rand   R122

Dome Mountain △4974 ft

Klinker Mtn 4562 ft△

LAVA   MOUNTAINS

Ricardo (Site)

Red Rock Canyon

Red Rock Canyon State Park

Garlock Hist Marker

Garlock

GOLDEN VALLEY WILDERNESS

Almond Mountain 4155 ft△

Saltdale

Ceneda

Johannesburg

Randsburg   Red Mountain

Browns Ranch

Almond Cove

Gypsite

Koehn Lake

Government Peak 4741 ft△

Red Mountain △5261 ft

Cantil

LAKE RD

Sidney Peak 4372 ft△

Atolia

Cuddeback Lake

Rancho Seco

Quartz Hill

FREMONT

VALLEY

Notre Dame Rd   Gonzaga

Colgate Rd

COLUMBIA RD

KINGSTON AVE

CUDDEBACK RD

HOFFMAN RD

BUCKNELL RD

Galileo Park   Galileo Hill △3310 ft

Fremont (Site)

Fremont Peak 4584 ft△

California City

Tierra Del Sol   California City Golf Club   California City Municipal GC

Castle Butte 3124 ft△

Aerial Acres

Desert Butte 2849 ft△

Twin Buttes

Saddleback Mountain 3087 ft△

Landing Strip

North Edwards

Thundering Herd Ranch

Desert Lake

Boron Airstrip

Arabian Trailer Oasis

Kramer Junction

Bissell

Edwards Siding

Edwards AF Aux North Base

Silt

Desert Lake

Kern County Park   Boron

Brown Butte 2906 ft△

Rogers Lake

EDWARDS AIR FORCE BASE

Rich

Jimgrey

KERN CO   SAN BERNARDINO CO

Continue on Page 129

Continue on Page 117

Edwards

SALINAS RD

ADELANTO

118

© DeLorme

1 inch = 3.16 mi   1 cm = 2 km

Salton

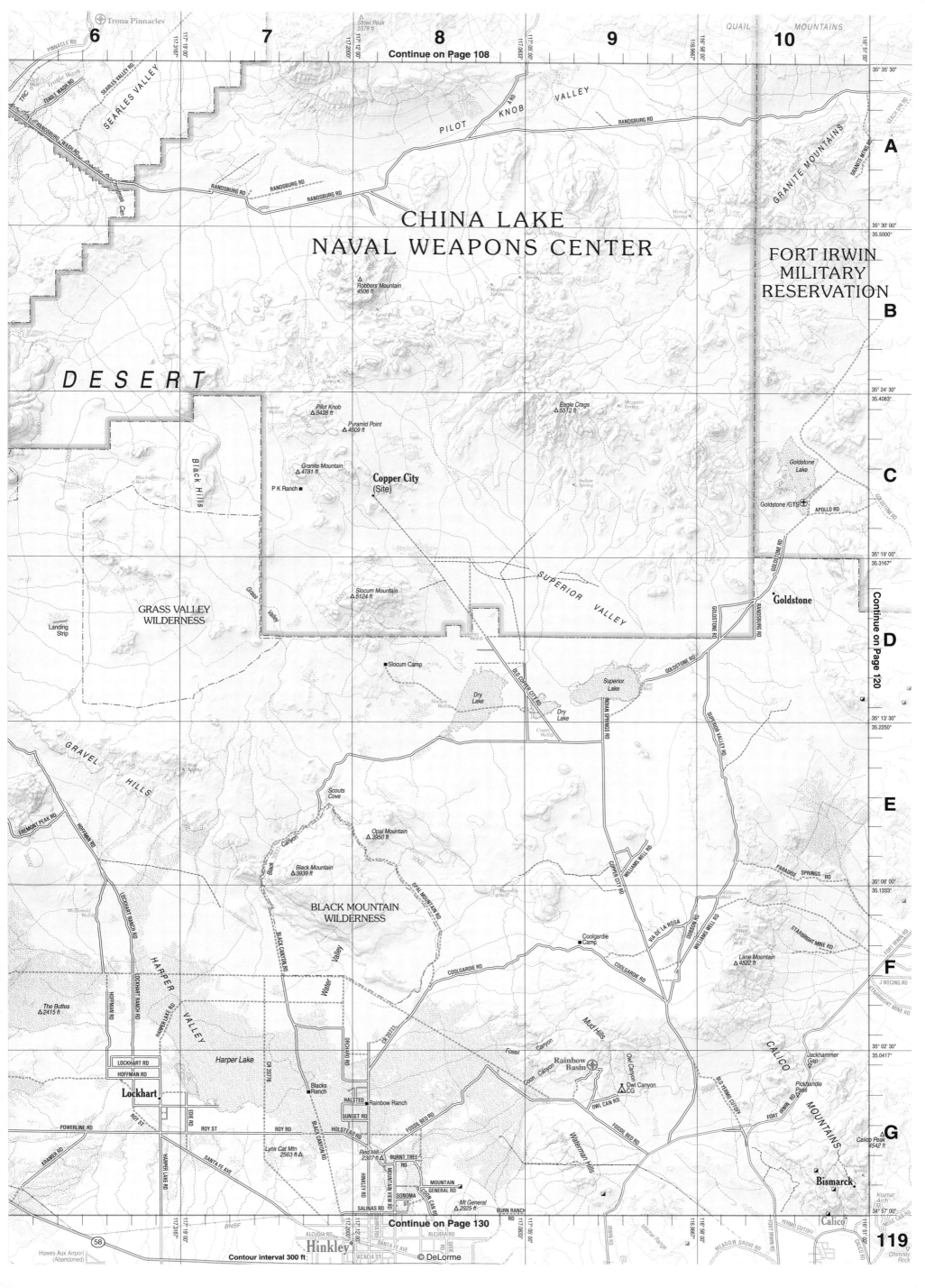

Continue on Page 108

Continue on Page 120

Continue on Page 130

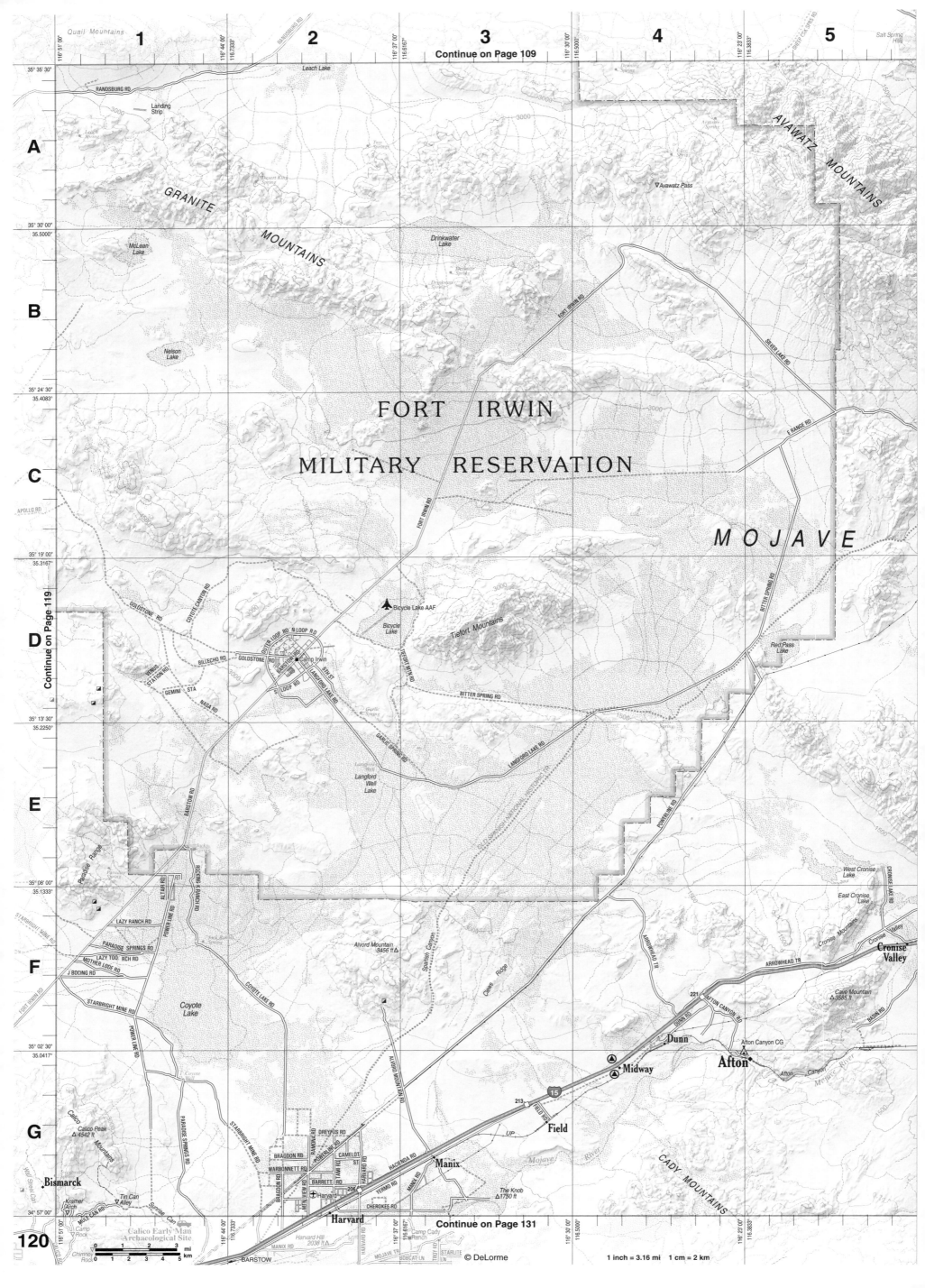

Continue on Page 109

Quail Mountains

Salt Spring Hills

RANDSBURG RD

Leach Lake

Landing Strip

AVAWATZ MOUNTAINS

GRANITE

McLean Lake

MOUNTAINS

Drinkwater Lake

Avawatz Pass

FORT IRWIN RD

Nelson Lake

SILVER LAKE RD

FORT IRWIN

E RANGE RD

MILITARY RESERVATION

MOJAVE

Continue on Page 119

Bicycle Lake AAF

BITTER SPRING RD

GOLDSTONE RD

COYOTE CANYON RD

Bicycle Lake

Tiefort Mountains

Red Pass Lake

BILLECHO RD

GOLDSTONE RD

OUTER LOOP RD N LOOP RD

Camp Irwin

VENUS STATION RD

BARSTOW RD

5TH ST

GEMINI STA

S LOOP RD

LANGFORD LAKE RD

NASA RD

TIEFORT MTN RD

Garlic Spring

BITTER SPRING RD

GARLIC SPRING RD

LANGFORD LAKE RD

Langford Well Lake

OLD SPANISH NATIONAL HISTORIC TR

POWERLINE RD

Paradise Range

BARSTOW RD

West Cronise Lake

East Cronise Lake

ALTAIR RD

BICENO RANCH RD

POWER LINE RD

Alvord Mountain 3456 ft △

Spanish Canyon

Clews Ridge

ARROWHEAD TR

Cronise Mountains

Cronise Valley

LAZY RANCH RD

ARROWHEAD TR

Cronise Valley

PARADISE SPRINGS RD

LAZY TOO RCH RD

221

Cave Mountain △3585 ft

AFTON CANYON RD

MOTHER LODE RD

J BOCING RD

FORT IRWIN RD

STARBRIGHT MINE RD

Coyote Lake

COYOTE LAKE RD

DUNN RD

Dunn

Afton Canyon CG

Afton

Afton Canyon

Mojave River

Midway

PARADISE SPRINGS RD

Calico Peak △4542 ft

Calico Mountains

Mojave River

213

FIELD RD

15

Field

UP

CADY MOUNTAINS

Bismarck

Kramer Arch

Tin Can Alley

MULE CAN RD

STARBRIGHT MINE RD

Camp Rock

BRAGDON RD

DREYFUS RD

RAMONA RD

CAMELOT

BORDERLINE RD

HACIENDA RD

Manix

WARBONNETT RD

TAMI RD

HARVARD ST

BRAGDON RD

MTN VIEW RD

BARRETT

Harvard

206

MANIX RD

The Knob △1750 ft

YERMO RD

Wall Street Cyn

CHEROKEE RD

Camp Cady Ranch

Continue on Page 131

Harvard

Harvard Hill 2038 ft △

Calico Early Man Archaeological Site

Chimney Rock

MOJAVE TR

MANIX RD

HARVARD RD

BOBCAT LN

TROY RD

STARLITE LN

BARSTOW

© DeLorme

120

0 1 2 3 4 5 mi
0 1 2 3 4 5 km

1 inch = 3.16 mi   1 cm = 2 km

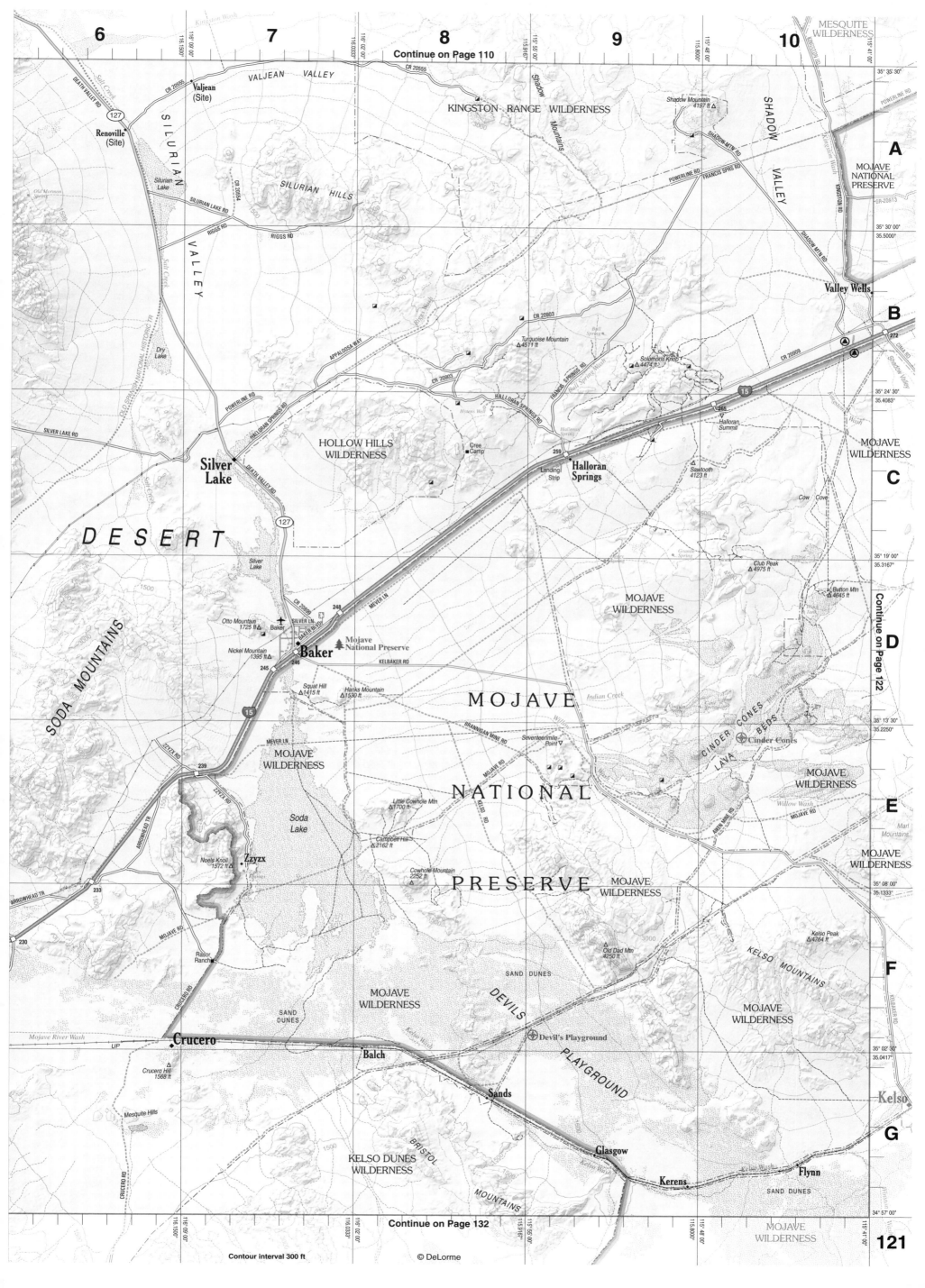

MESQUITE WILDERNESS

VALJEAN VALLEY

Valjean (Site)

Renoville (Site)

CR 20555

KINGSTON RANGE WILDERNESS

Shadow Mountains

Shadow Mountain 4197 ft △

SHADOW VALLEY

MOJAVE NATIONAL PRESERVE

A

SILURIAN VALLEY

Silurian Lake

SILURIAN HILLS

Old Mormon Spring

Dry Lake

DEATH VALLEY RD

127

POWERLINE RD

FRANCIS SPRGS RD

Valley Wells

272

B

Turquoise Mountain △4511 ft

Solomons Knob △4474 ft

CR 20903

15

265

MOJAVE WILDERNESS

SILVER LAKE RD

POWERLINE RD

HALLORAN SPRINGS RD

HOLLOW HILLS WILDERNESS

Cree Camp

Hyten Well

Halloran Spring

Landing Strip

259

Halloran Springs

Halloran Summit

Sawtooth 4123 ft

Cow Cove

C

Silver Lake

DEATH VALLEY RD

127

Silver Lake

DESERT

3000

MOJAVE WILDERNESS

Club Peak △4975 ft

Button Mtn △4645 ft

D

SODA MOUNTAINS

Otto Mountain 1725 ft △

SILVER LN

Baker

248

MCVER LN

Nickel Mountain 1395 ft △

Baker

245

246

KELBAKER RD

Squat Hill △1415 ft

Hanks Mountain △1530 ft

M O J A V E

Indian Creek

Continue on Page 122

15

ZZYZX RD

MCVER LN

MOJAVE WILDERNESS

BRANNIGAN MINE RD

Seventeenmile Point ▽

N A T I O N A L

MOJAVE RD

KELSO RD

AMON MINE RD

CINDER CONES LAVA BEDS

Cinder Cones

MOJAVE WILDERNESS

E

239

Soda Lake

Little Cowhole Mtn △1700 ft

Willow Wash

MOJAVE RD

Marl Mountains

ARROWHEAD TR

Noels Knoll 1572 ft △

Zzyzx

Campbell Hill △2162 ft

Cowhole Mountain 2252 ft

P R E S E R V E

MOJAVE WILDERNESS

MOJAVE WILDERNESS

233

230

MOJAVE RD

Razor Ranch

Old Dad Mtn 4250 ft

Kelso Peak △4764 ft

KELSO MOUNTAINS

F

SAND DUNES

MOJAVE WILDERNESS

DEVILS

MOJAVE WILDERNESS

KELBAKER RD

CRUCERO RD

Mojave River Wash

UP

Crucero

Balch

Kelso Wash

Devil's Playground

P L A Y G R O U N D

Kelso

G

Crucero Hill △1568 ft

Sands

ARROWHEAD TR

Mesquite Hills

KELSO DUNES WILDERNESS

BRISTOL

MOUNTAINS

Glasgow

Kerens

Flynn

SAND DUNES

MOJAVE WILDERNESS

Continue on Page 132

Contour interval 300 ft

© DeLorme

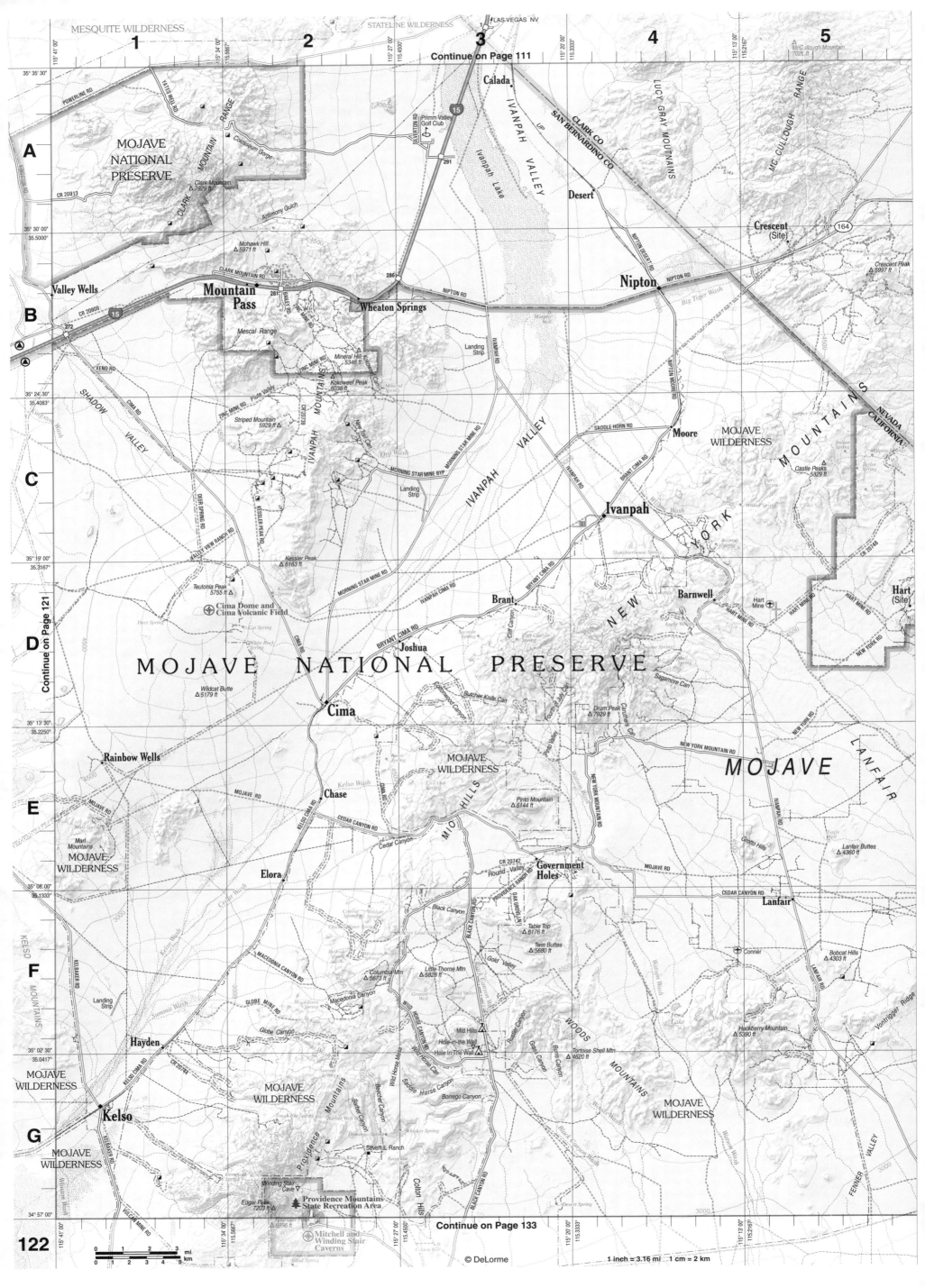

MESQUITE WILDERNESS   STATELINE WILDERNESS   LAS VEGAS NV

Continue on Page 111

Calada

MOJAVE
NATIONAL
PRESERVE

Clark Mountain
△ 7923 ft

LUCY GRAY MOUNTAINS

MC CULLOUGH RANGE

McCullough Mountain
△ 7026 ft

Primm Valley
Golf Club

CLARK CO
SAN BERNARDINO CO

Desert

Crescent
(Site)

Crescent Peak
△ 5997 ft

Antimony Gulch

Mohawk Hill
△ 5971 ft

Valley Wells

**Mountain
Pass**

CLARK MOUNTAIN RD

Wheaton Springs

NIPTON RD

Nipton

NIPTON RD

Big Tiger Wash

Mescal Range

Mineral Hill
△ 5346 ft

Kokoweef Peak
△ 6038 ft

Landing
Strip

MOJAVE
WILDERNESS

Xeno Rd

SHADOW

VALLEY

Striped Mountain
5929 ft △

SADDLE HORN RD

Moore

NEW

Castle Peaks
△ 5329 ft

DEER SPRING RD

MORNING STAR MINE BYP

Landing
Strip

IVANPAH

VALLEY

Ivanpah

YORK

Kessler Peak
△ 6163 ft

Teutonia Peak
5755 ft △

**Cima Dome and
Cima Volcanic Field**

Wildcat Butte
△ 5179 ft

BRYANT CIMA RD

Brant

Barnwell

Hart
Mine

Hart
(Site)

Joshua

M O J A V E   N A T I O N A L   P R E S E R V E

CIMA RD

Cima

Drum Peak
△ 7929 ft

Sagamore Can

Rainbow Wells

MOJAVE
WILDERNESS

NEW YORK MOUNTAIN RD

M O J A V E

L A N F A I R

Kelso Wash

Chase

CEDAR CANYON RD

M
I
O

Pinto Mountain
△ 6144 ft

Cedar Canyon

HILLS

Lanfair Buttes
△ 4360 ft

MOJAVE
WILDERNESS

Marl
Mountains

MOJAVE
ROD

Cedar Canyon

Elora

CR 20742
Round Valley

**Government
Holes**

MOJAVE RD

Lanfair

CEDAR CANYON RD

Table Top
△ 6176 ft

Twin Buttes
△ 5680 ft

Conner

Bobcat Hills
△ 4303 ft

KELBAKER RD

MACEDONIA CANYON RD

Black Canyon

Columbia Mtn
△ 5673 ft

Little Thorne Mtn
△ 5828 ft

Gold Valley

Hackberry Mountain
△ 5390 ft

Landing
Strip

GLOBE MINE RD

Macedonia Canyon

Globe Canyon

W O O D S

MOUNTAINS

Tortoise Shell Mtn
△ 4620 ft

Hayden

KELSO CIMA RD

Mid Hills
Hole-in-the-Wall
Hole In The Wall

MOJAVE
WILDERNESS

MOJAVE
WILDERNESS

CR 20744

MOJAVE
WILDERNESS

Kelso

MOJAVE
WILDERNESS

Providence
Mountains

BLACK CANYON RD

Colton
Hills

Winding Stair
Cave

Edgar Peak
7203 ft △

**Providence Mountains
State Recreation Area**

**Mitchell and
Winding Stair
Caverns**

Continue on Page 121

Continue on Page 133

122

0 1 2 3   mi
0 1 2 3 4   km

© DeLorme

1 inch = 3.16 mi   1 cm = 2 km

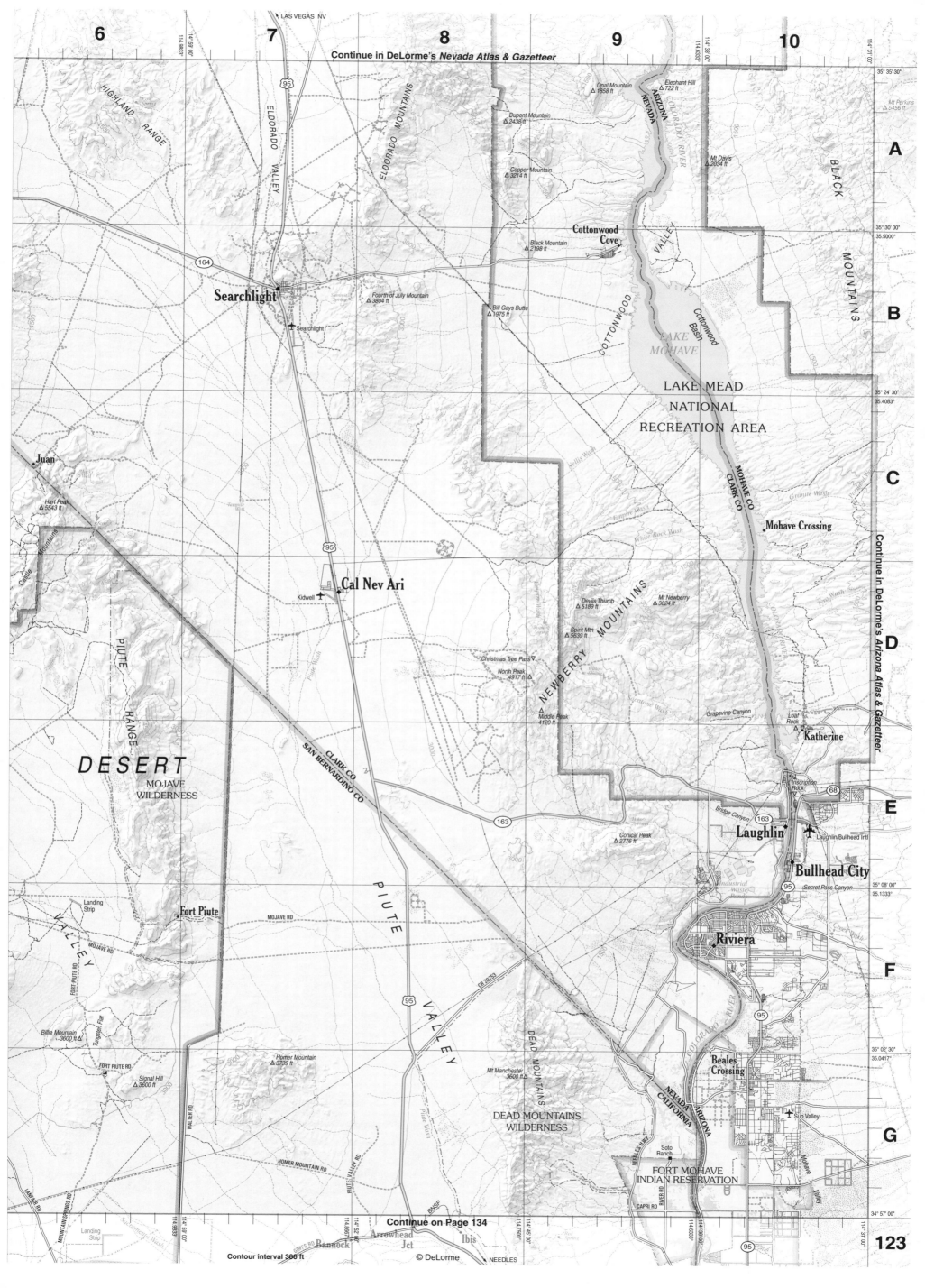

LAS VEGAS NV

Continue in DeLorme's *Nevada Atlas & Gazetteer*

35° 35' 30"

Mt Perkins △ 5456 ft

HIGHLAND RANGE

ELDORADO VALLEY

ELDORADO MOUNTAINS

Opal Mountain △ 1858 ft

Elephant Hill △ 722 ft

ARIZONA
NEVADA

COLORADO RIVER

Dupont Mountain △ 2438 ft

A

Mt Davis △ 2034 ft

BLACK MOUNTAINS

Copper Mountain △ 3214 ft

95

164

Cottonwood Cove

35° 30' 00"
35.5000°

COTTONWOOD VALLEY

Cottonwood Basin

Black Mountain △ 2198 ft

Searchlight

Summit Spring

Fourth of July Mountain △ 3804 ft

Boat Ramp

Searchlight

B

Bill Gays Butte △ 1975 ft

Lake Mohave

Top Joe

LAKE MEAD

NATIONAL

RECREATION AREA

35° 24' 30"
35.4083°

Juan

Hart Peak △ 5543 ft

Castle Mountains

C

Temple Well

Temple Wash

Nellis Wash

MOHAVE CO
CLARK CO

Granite Wash

Empire Wash

Mohave Crossing

White Rock Wash

95

Cal Nev Ari

Kidwell

NEWBERRY MOUNTAINS

Devils Thumb △ 5189 ft

Mt Newberry △ 3624 ft

Continue in DeLorme's *Arizona Atlas & Gazetteer*

D

Spirit Mtn △ 5639 ft

Christmas Tree Pass

North Peak △ 4917 ft

Grapevine Canyon

Loaf Rock

Katherine

PIUTE RANGE

Middle Peak △ 4120 ft

DESERT

MOJAVE WILDERNESS

SAN BERNARDINO CO
CLARK CO

163

Inscription Rock

68

Bridge Canyon

E

163

Laughlin

Laughlin/Bullhead Intl

Conical Peak △ 2776 ft

PIUTE VALLEY

Fort Piute

Landing Strip

VALLEY

MOJAVE RD

MOJAVE RD

Bullhead City

95

Secret Pass Canyon

35° 08' 00"
35.1333°

Industrial Wash

Riviera

F

FORT PIUTE RD

CR 20755

Billie Mountain △ 3600 ft

Tungsten Flat

FORT PIUTE RD

Signal Hill △ 3600 ft

95

Homer Mountain △ 3739 ft

DEAD MOUNTAINS

Mt Manchester 3600 ft △

Beales Crossing

35° 02' 30"
35.0417°

MOUNTAIN SPRINGS RD

LANFAIR RD

Landing Strip

HOMER MOUNTAIN RD

PIUTE VALLEY RD

DEAD MOUNTAINS WILDERNESS

NEVADA
CALIFORNIA

NEEDLES HWY

Sun Valley

G

Soto Ranch

RIVER RD

FORT MOHAVE INDIAN RESERVATION

CAPRI RD

34° 57' 00"

Sacramento Wash

LOST RD

Continue on Page 134

Bannock

Arrowhead Jct

Ibis

114° 46' 00"

114° 45' 00"

114° 38' 00"

95

123

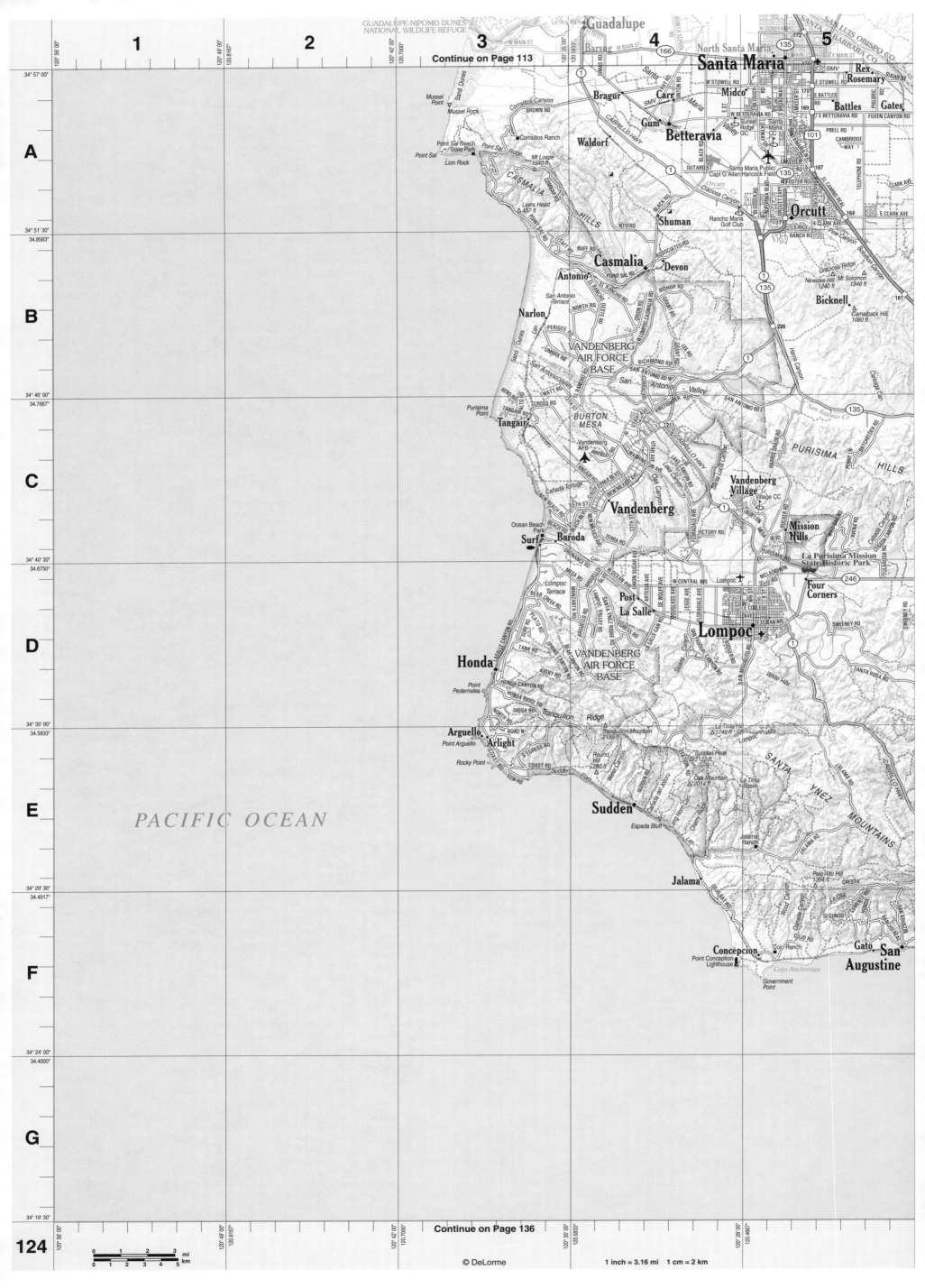

1 **2** **3** **4** **5**

Continue on Page 113

Guadalupe

Santa Maria

North Santa Maria

Rex
Rosemary

Barsug

W MAIN ST

Bragur
Carr
Midco

SMV

Battles
Gates

Gum

Betteravia

Waldorf

Shuman

Casmalia

Devon
Antonio

Bicknell

Narlon

Camelback Hill
1080 ft

VANDENBERG
AIR FORCE
BASE

PURISIMA
HILLS

Purisima
Point

Tangair

BURTON
MESA

Vandenberg
AFB

Vandenberg
Village

A

B

C

D

E

F

G

Vandenberg

Mission
Hills

Surf
Baroda

La Purisima Mission
State Historic Park

Four
Corners

Post
La Salle

Lompoc

Honda

VANDENBERG
AIR FORCE
BASE

Point
Pedernales

Tranquillon Ridge

Arguello
Point Arguello
Arlight

Rocky Point

Sudden

SANTA
YNEZ

MOUNTAINS

Jalama

Concepcion
Point Conception
Lighthouse

Gato
Augustine

San

Government
Point

PACIFIC OCEAN

124

Continue on Page 136

© DeLorme

1 inch = 3.16 mi   1 cm = 2 km

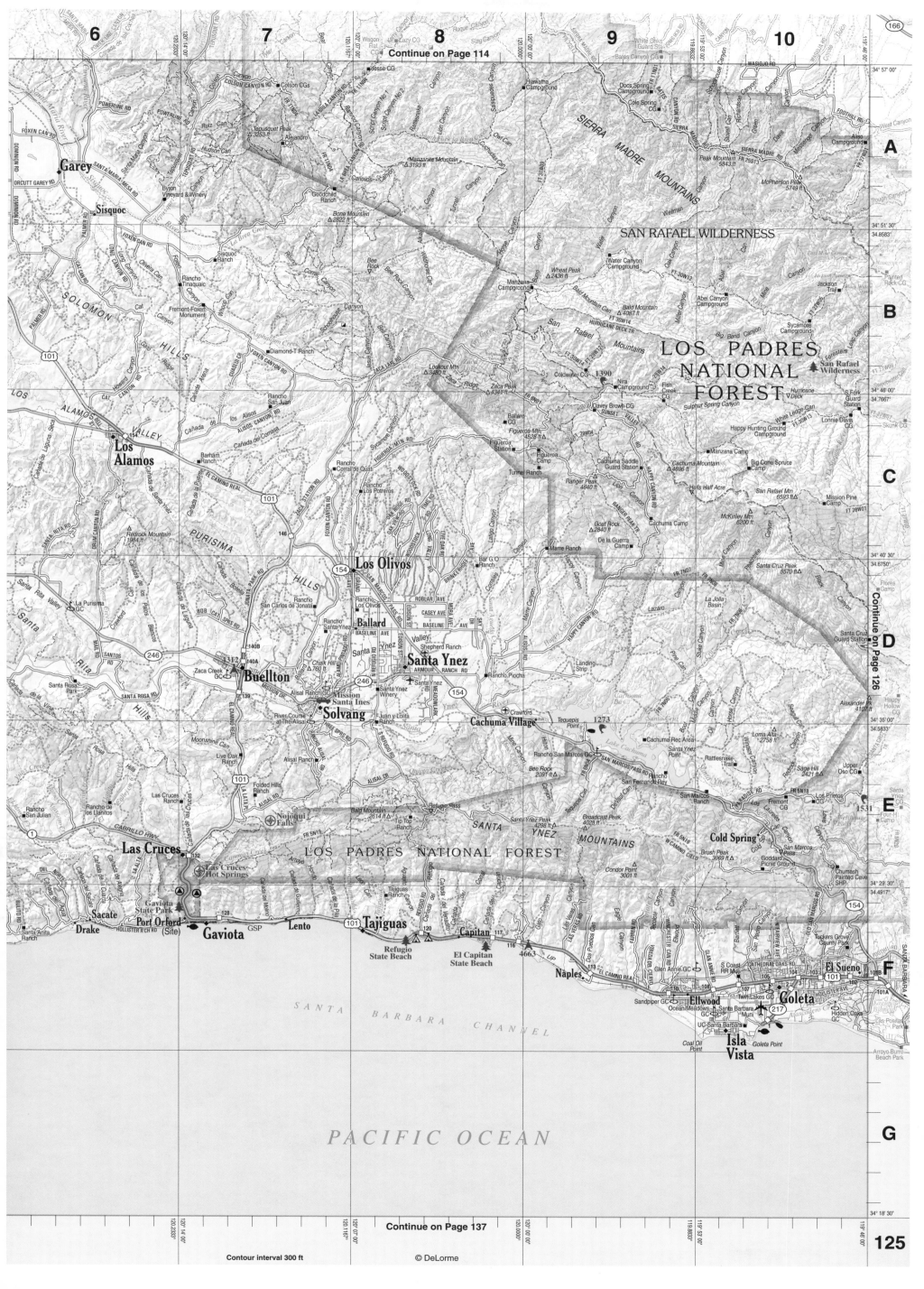

Continue on Page 114

Continue on Page 126

SIERRA MADRE MOUNTAINS

SAN RAFAEL WILDERNESS

LOS PADRES NATIONAL FOREST

San Rafael Wilderness

PURISIMA HILLS

SOLOMON HILLS

LOS ALAMOS VALLEY

SANTA RITA HILLS

SANTA ROSA HILLS

Garey

Sisquoc

Los Alamos

Buellton

Solvang

Los Olivos

Ballard

Santa Ynez

Cachuma Village

SANTA YNEZ MOUNTAINS

Cold Spring

Las Cruces

Sacate
Drake

Gaviota

Port Orford (Site)

Lento

Tajiguas

Capitan

Naples

Ellwood

Goleta

El Sueno

Isla Vista

Refugio State Beach

El Capitan State Beach

LOS PADRES NATIONAL FOREST

PACIFIC OCEAN

SANTA BARBARA CHANNEL

Continue on Page 137

Contour interval 300 ft

© DeLorme

125

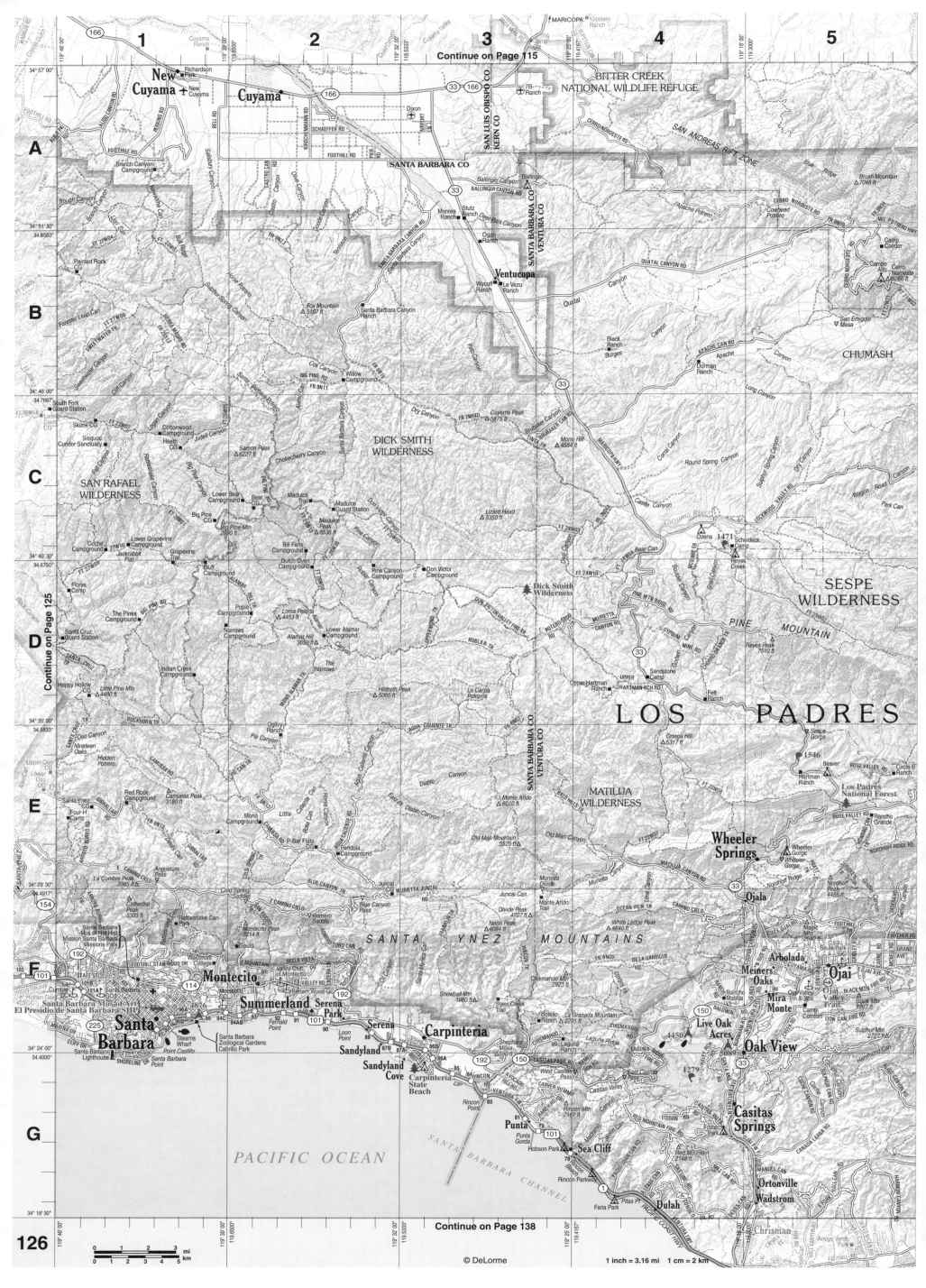

Continue on Page 115

1 **2** **3** **4** **5**

A

B

C

D

E

F

G

BITTER CREEK NATIONAL WILDLIFE REFUGE

New Cuyama

Cuyama

Ventucopa

CHUMASH

SAN RAFAEL WILDERNESS

DICK SMITH WILDERNESS

SESPE WILDERNESS

Dick Smith Wilderness

PINE MOUNTAIN

LOS PADRES

MATILIJA WILDERNESS

Los Padres National Forest

Wheeler Springs

Ojala

SANTA YNEZ MOUNTAINS

Arbolada

Meiners Oaks

Ojai

Mira Monte

Live Oak Acres

Oak View

Montecito

Summerland

Serena Park

Serena

Carpinteria

Sandyland

Sandyland Cove

Carpinteria State Beach

Santa Barbara

El Presidio de Santa Barbara SHP

Casitas Springs

Punta

Sea Cliff

Dulah

Ortonville

Wadstrom

PACIFIC OCEAN

SANTA BARBARA CHANNEL

Continue on Page 138

Continue on Page 125

© DeLorme

1 inch = 3.16 mi   1 cm = 2 km

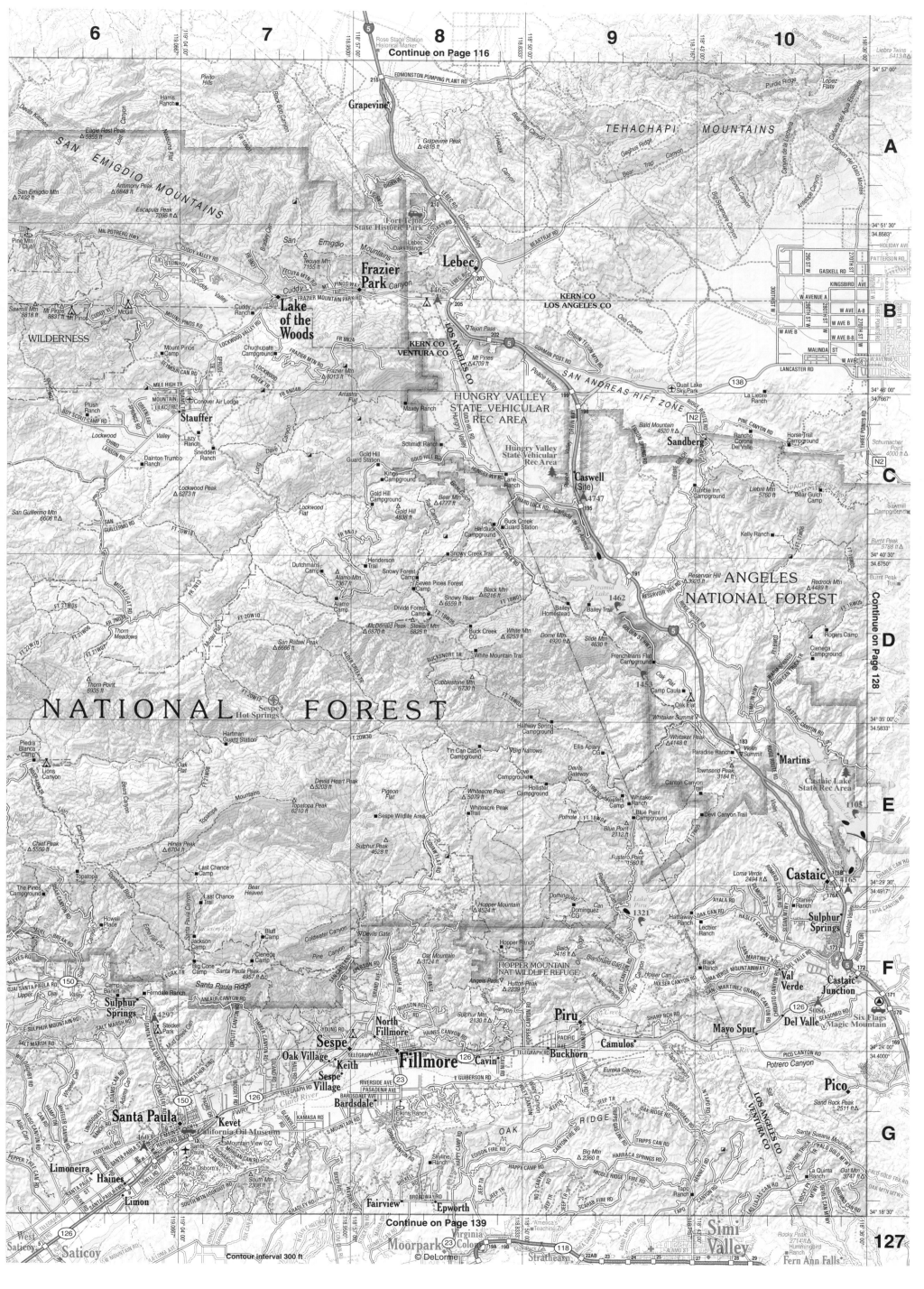

Continue on Page 116

A

B

Continue on Page 128

C

D

E

F

G

SAN EMIGDIO MOUNTAINS

TEHACHAPI MOUNTAINS

WILDERNESS

Grapevine

Frazier Park

Lebec

Lake of the Woods

KERN CO
LOS ANGELES CO

KERN CO
VENTURA CO

HUNGRY VALLEY
STATE VEHICULAR
REC AREA

SAN ANDREAS RIFT ZONE

Stauffer

Sandberg

Hungry Valley
State Vehicular
Rec Area

Caswell
(Site)
4747

ANGELES
NATIONAL FOREST

NATIONAL FOREST

Sespe
Hot Springs

Martins

Castaic Lake
State Rec Area

Castaic

Sulphur Springs

Sulphur
Springs

HOPPER MOUNTAIN
NAT WILDLIFE REFUGE

Piru

Val Verde

Castaic
Junction

Del Valle

Six Flags
Magic Mountain

Mayo Spur

Camulos

Buckhorn

North
Fillmore

Sespe

Oak Village

Keith

Sespe
Village

Fillmore

Cavin

Pico

Santa Paula

Bardsdale

Kevet

California Oil Museum

Limoneira

Haines

Limon

Fairview

Epworth

Continue on Page 139

Moorpark

Saticoy

West
Saticoy

Virginia
Colony

Simi
Valley

Stratheam

Fern Ann Falls

Contour interval 300 ft

© DeLorme

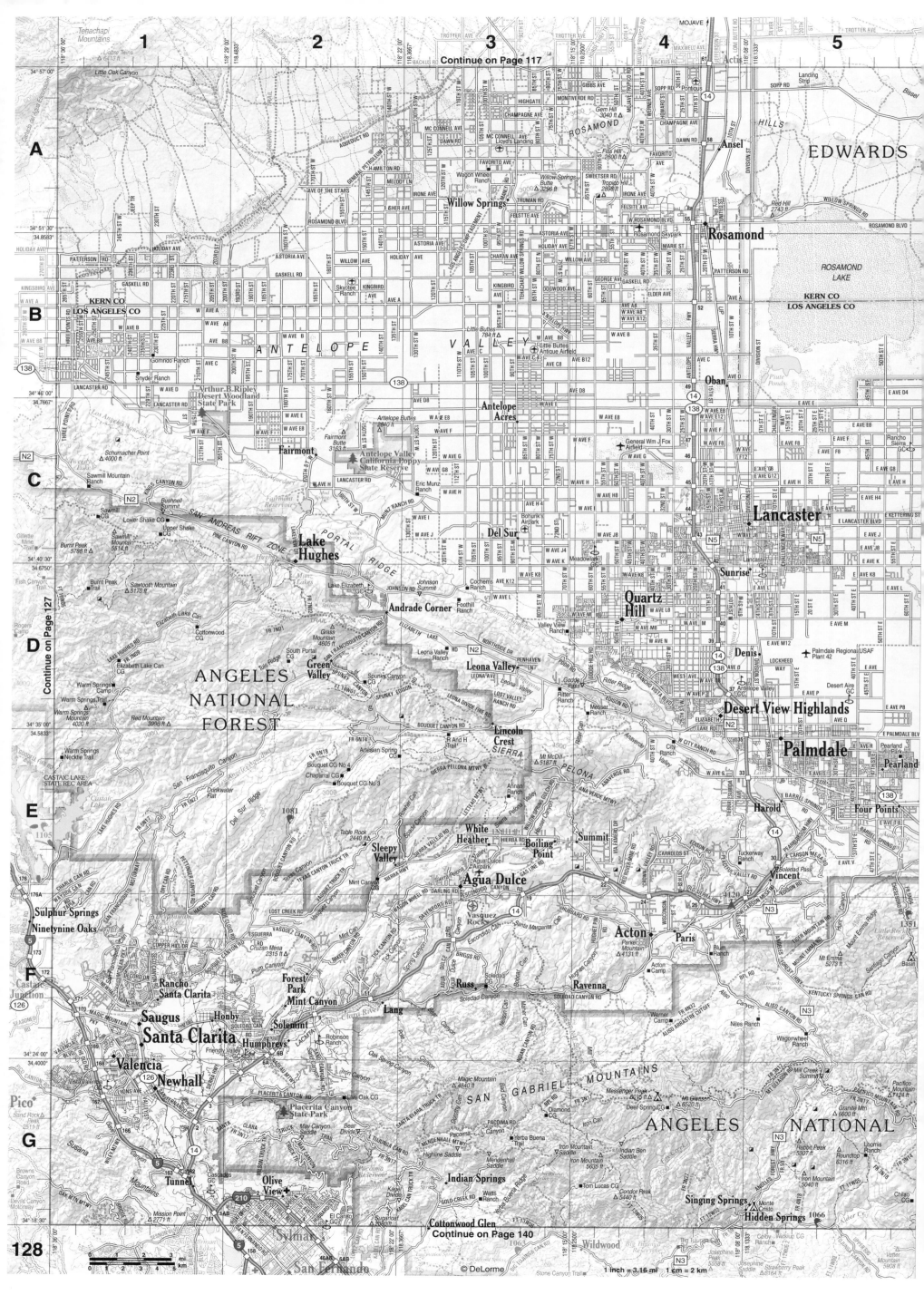

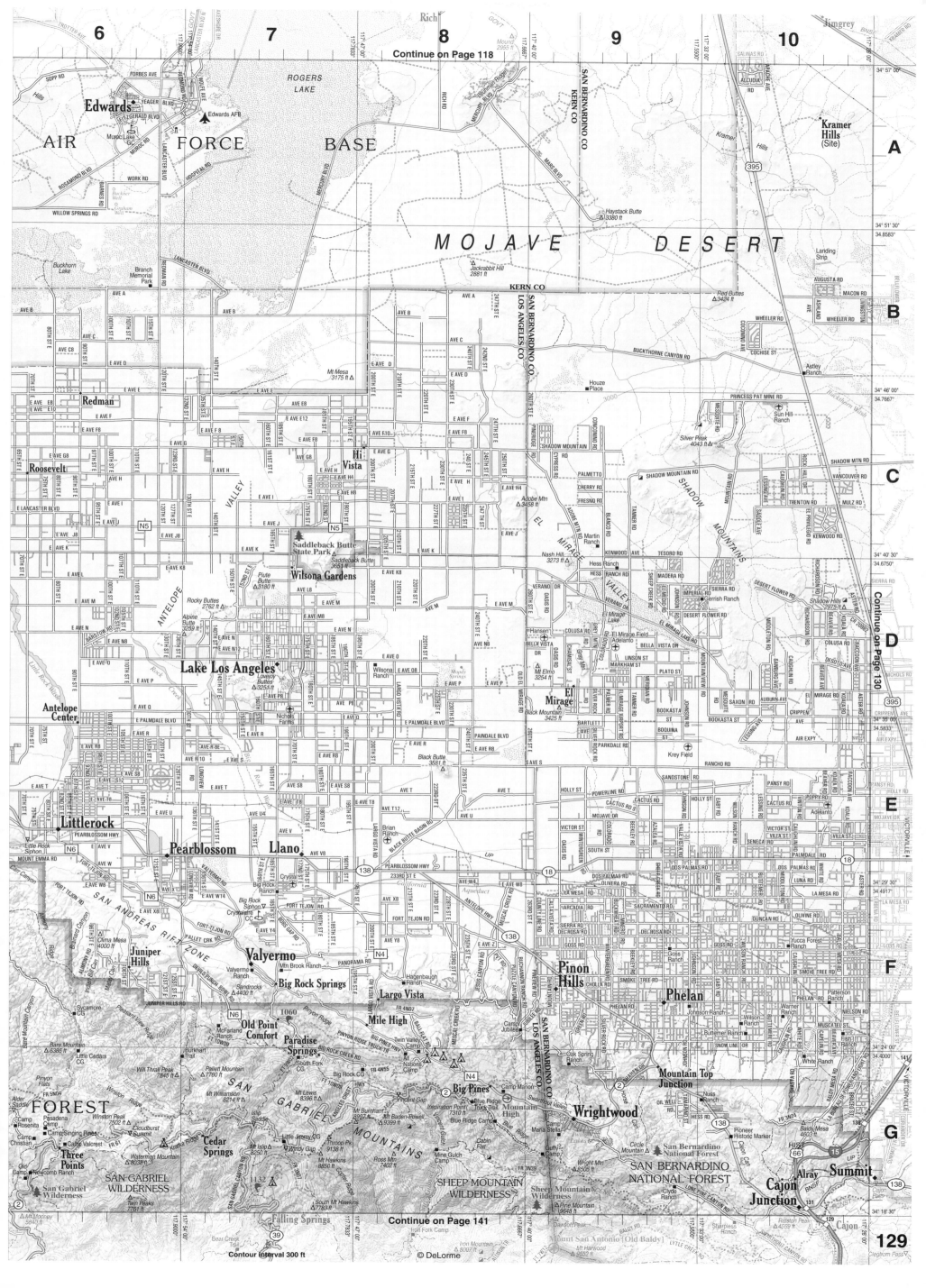

Continue on Page 118

MOJAVE   DESERT

Continue on Page 130

Continue on Page 141

Contour interval 300 ft

© DeLorme

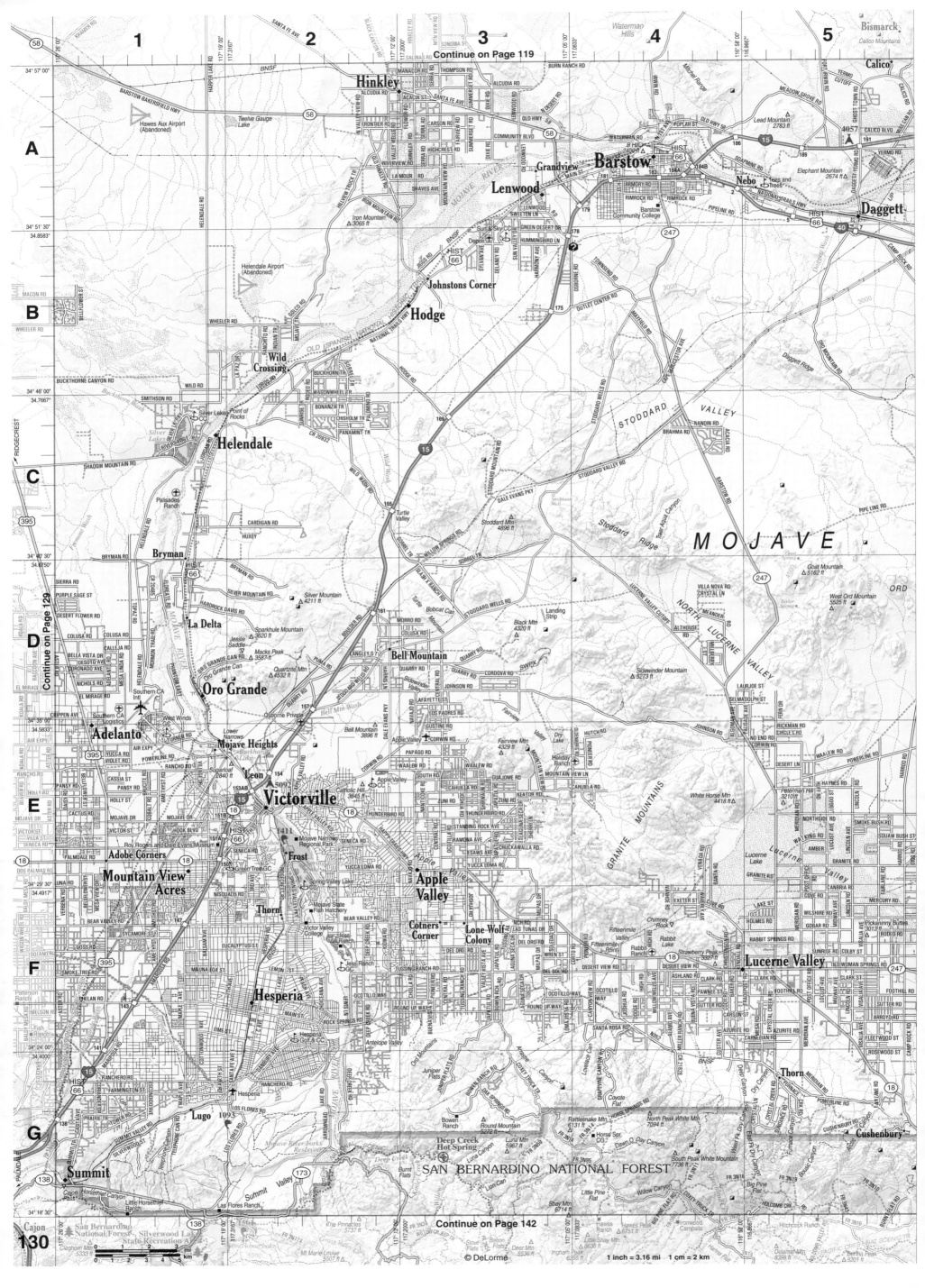

Continue on Page 119

Continue on Page 142

Continue on Page 129

130

SAN BERNARDINO NATIONAL FOREST

MOJAVE

1 inch = 3.16 mi   1 cm = 2 km

© DeLorme

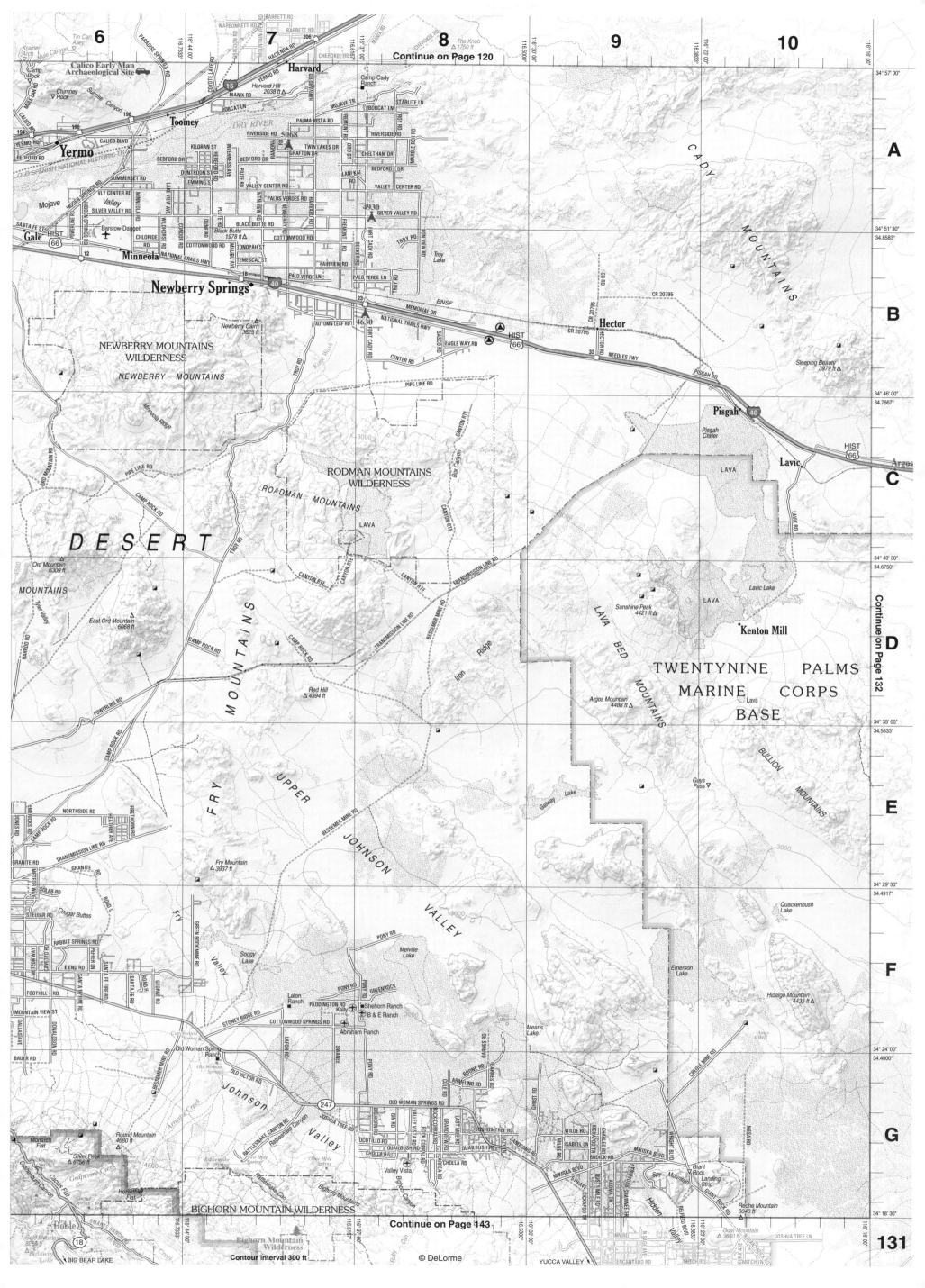

Continue on Page 120

Continue on Page 132

Continue on Page 143

© DeLorme

Contour interval 300 ft

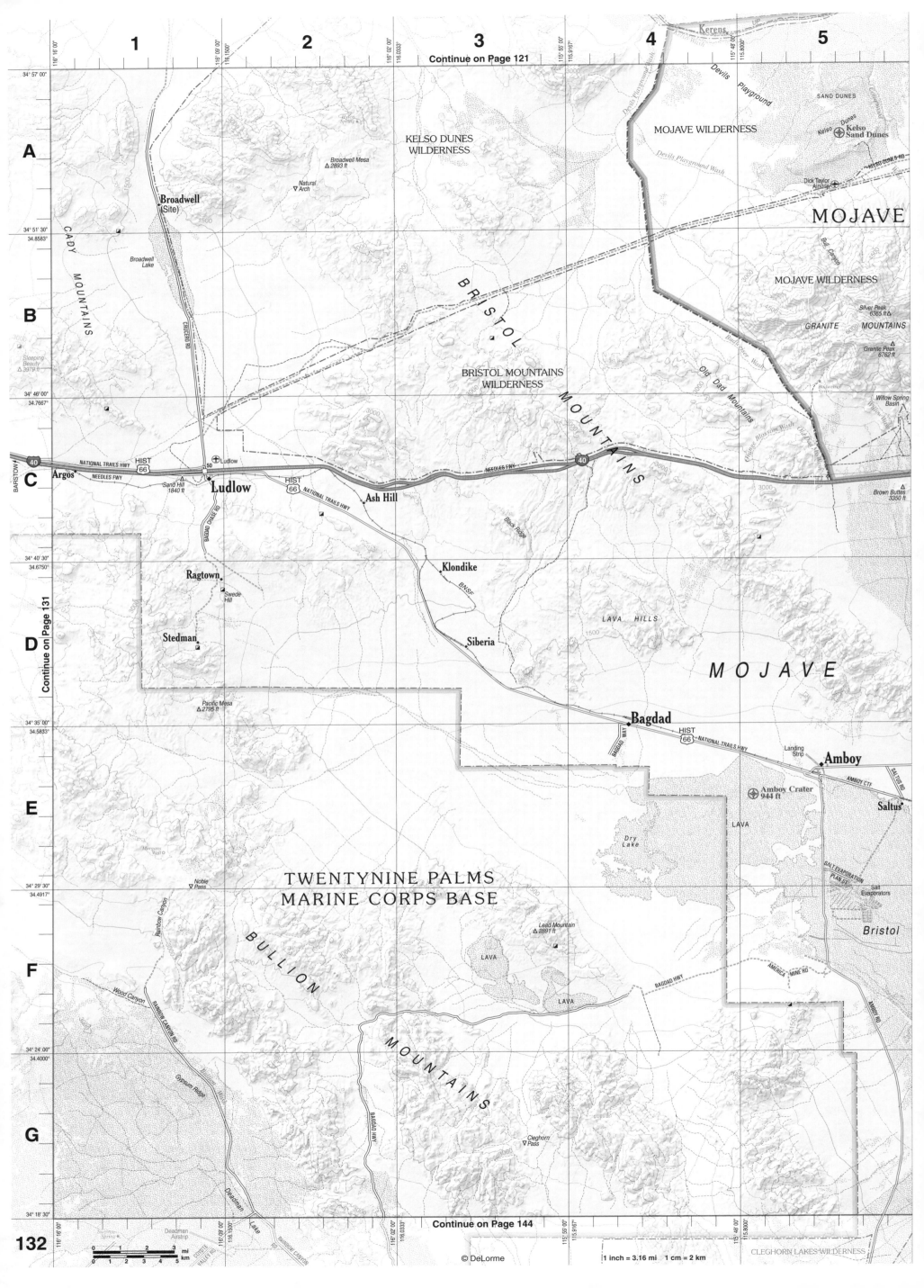

Continue on Page 121

1 **2** **3** **4** **5**

34° 57' 00"

A

MOJAVE

KELSO DUNES
WILDERNESS

MOJAVE WILDERNESS

SAND DUNES

Devils Playground

Kelso Dunes

Kelso
Sand Dunes

KELSO DUNES RD

Broadwell Mesa
△ 2893 ft

Natural
▽ Arch

Hidden
Spring

Devils Playground Wash

Dick Taylor
Airstrip

Broadwell
(Site)

34° 51' 30"
34.8583°

B

CADY
MOUNTAINS

Broadwell Lake

CRUCERO RD

MOJAVE WILDERNESS

Bull Canyon

Silver Peak
6365 ft △

GRANITE MOUNTAINS

Sleeping Beauty
△ 3979 ft

BRISTOL   MOUNTAINS

Budweiser Wash

Granite Peak
6762 ft

34° 46' 00"
34.7667°

BRISTOL MOUNTAINS
WILDERNESS

Old Dad Mountains

Budweiser
Spring

Willow Spring
Basin

BARSTOW

C

40

NATIONAL TRAILS HWY

HIST
66

50

⊕ Ludlow

Needles Hwy

Needles Fwy

40

3000

Brown Buttes
3350 ft

Argos

NEEDLES FWY

Sand Hill
1840 ft

Ludlow

HIST
66

NATIONAL TRAILS HWY

Ash Hill

Black Ridge

34° 40' 30"
34.6750°

Continue on Page 131

D

BAGDAD CHASE RD

Ragtown

Swede
Hill

Klondike

BNSF

LAVA   HILLS

M O J A V E

Stedman

Siberia

1500

34° 35' 00"
34.5833°

E

Pacific Mesa
△ 2795 ft

Bagdad

BAGDAD WAY

HIST
66

NATIONAL TRAILS HWY

Landing
Strip

Amboy

AMBOY CTF

Saltus

Amboy Crater
944 ft

LAVA

Dry
Lake

SALTUS RD

34° 29' 30"
34.4917°

F

**TWENTYNINE PALMS
MARINE CORPS BASE**

Mercuria
Well ▽

Noble
▽ Pass

SALT EVAPORATION
PLANT

Salt
Evaporators

Bristol

Rainbow Canyon

B U L L I O N

Lead Mountain
△ 2891 ft

LAVA

LAVA

Bagdad Hwy

AMERICA MINE RD

AMBY RD

Wood Canyon

RAINBOW CANYON RD

34° 24' 00"
34.4000°

G

Gypsum Ridge

M O U N T A I N S

BAGDAD HWY

Cleghorn
▽ Pass

Sleeping
Spring

Deadman
Airstrip

Deadman
Lake

CORTEZ
VALLEY RD

RAINBOW CANYON RD

CLEGHORN LAKES WILDERNESS

34° 18' 30"

132

Continue on Page 144

116° 16' 00"
116° 16' 00"

116° 09' 00"
116° 1500"

116° 02' 00"
116° 02' 00"
116.0333"

115° 55' 00"
115.9167°

115° 48' 00"
115.8000°

0 1 2 3 mi
0 1 2 3 4 5 km

© DeLorme

1 inch = 3.16 mi   1 cm = 2 km

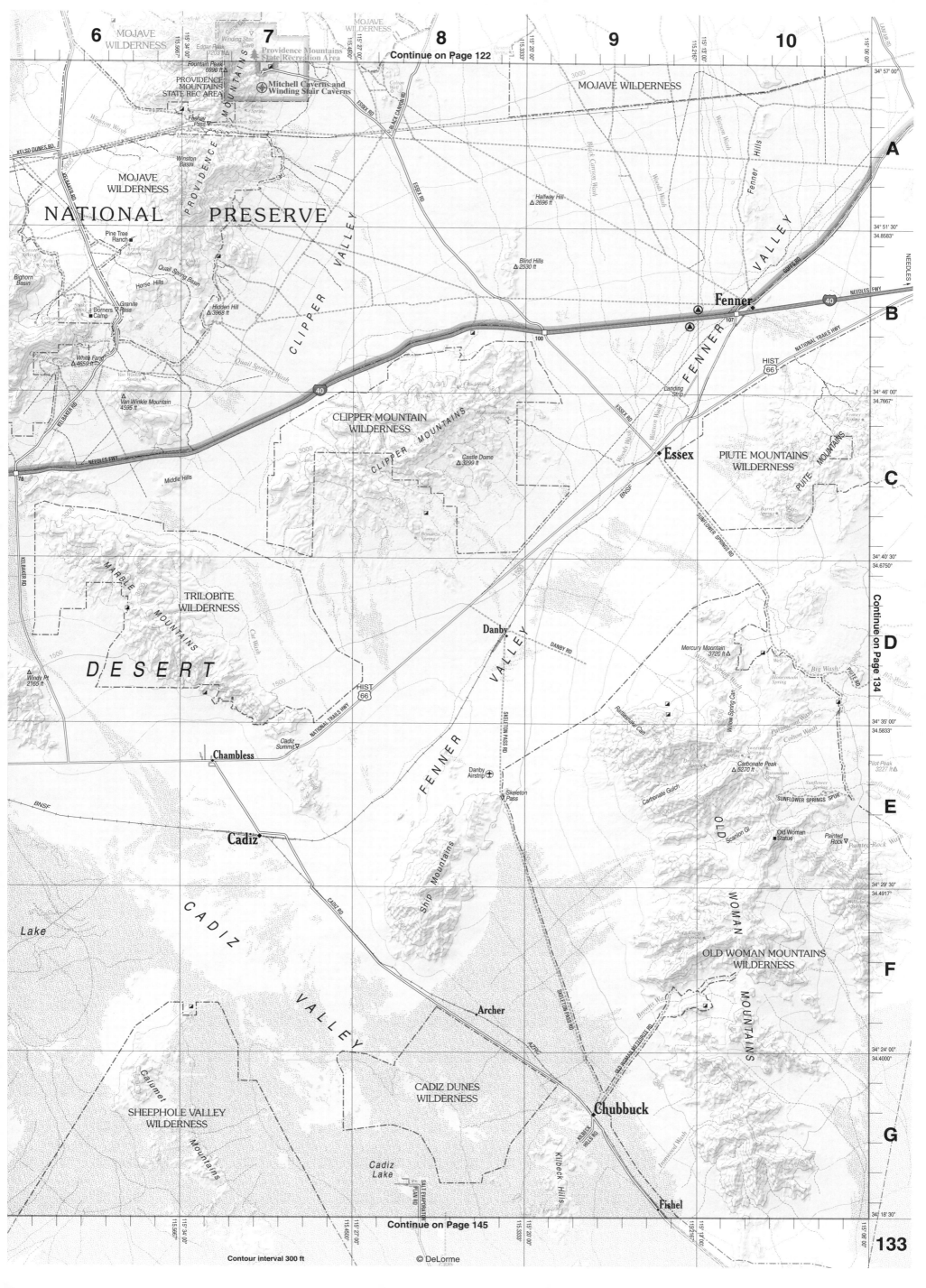

MOJAVE
WILDERNESS

MOJAVE
WILDERNESS

Continue on Page 122

Providence Mountains
State Recreation Area

MOJAVE WILDERNESS

Mitchell Caverns and
Winding Stair Caverns

Fountain Peak
6996 ft

PROVIDENCE
MOUNTAINS
STATE REC AREA

Foshay
Pass

Winston Basin

MOJAVE
WILDERNESS

NATIONAL   PRESERVE

Pine Tree
Ranch

Horse Hills

Hidden Hill
3968 ft

Bighorn
Basin

Dorners
Camp

Granite
Pass

CLIPPER   VALLEY

Fenner

40   Needles Fwy

NEEDLES FWY

34° 57' 00"

34° 51' 30"
34.8583°

A

White Fang
4650 ft

Quail Spring Wash

Van Winkle Mountain
4595 ft

100

Halfway Hill
2696 ft

Blind Hills
2530 ft

FENNER   VALLEY

B

107

HIST
66   NATIONAL TRAILS HWY

Landing
Strip

34° 46' 00"
34.7667°

NEEDLES FWY

78

40

Middle Hills

CLIPPER MOUNTAIN
WILDERNESS

CLIPPER   MOUNTAINS

Castle Dome
3299 ft

Bonanza
Spring

Essex

BNSF

PIUTE MOUNTAINS
WILDERNESS

PIUTE   MOUNTAINS

Barrel
Spring

C

MARBLE

TRILOBITE
WILDERNESS

Cut Wash

DESERT

Windy Pt
2165 ft

1500

1500

MOUNTAINS

Cadiz
Summit

HIST
66

NATIONAL TRAILS HWY

Danby

DANBY RD

FENNER   VALLEY

SKELETON PASS RD

Mercury Mountain
3720 ft

Willow Spring Wash

Well

Hidden Smoke
Spring

Colton Wash

34° 40' 30"
34.6750°

Parahana Wash

34° 35' 00"
34.5833°

Pilot Peak
3227 ft

D

Continue on Page 134

Chambless

KELBAKER RD

Rattlesnake Can

Carbonate Peak
5270 ft

Carbonate Gulch

Defiance
Spring

Scanlon Gl

SUNFLOWER SPRINGS SPUR

OLD

Old Woman
Statue

Painted
Rock

E

Cadiz

Danby
Airstrip

Skeleton
Pass

Ship Mountains

CADIZ

Lake

CADIZ   VALLEY

CADIZ RD

WOMAN

OLD WOMAN MOUNTAINS
WILDERNESS

MOUNTAINS

34° 29' 30"
34.4917°

F

Archer

SKELETON PASS RD

Brown's Wash

34° 24' 00"
34.4000°

G

Calumet

SHEEPHOLE VALLEY
WILDERNESS

Mountains

CADIZ DUNES
WILDERNESS

AZTEC

Chubbuck

Kilbeck Hills

KILBECK HILLS RD

Cadiz
Lake

SALT EVAPORATORS
BRINE RD

Fishel

Continue on Page 145

Contour interval 300 ft

© DeLorme

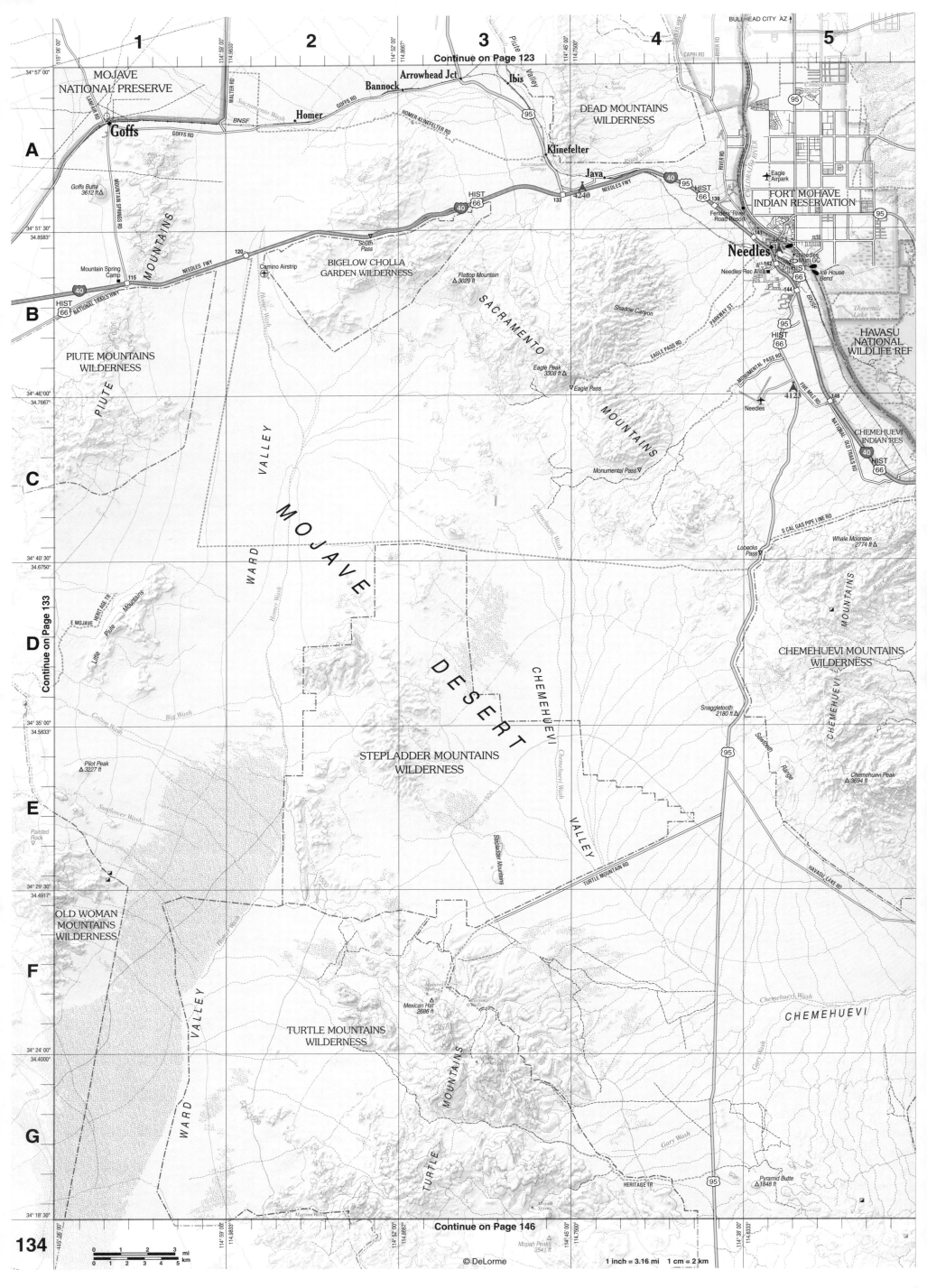

MOJAVE
NATIONAL PRESERVE

Goffs

Continue on Page 123

Arrowhead Jct

Bannock

Homer

Ibis

DEAD MOUNTAINS
WILDERNESS

Klinefelter

Java

BULLHEAD CITY AZ

FORT MOHAVE
INDIAN RESERVATION

Eagle Airpark

Needles

Goffs Butte
3612 ft

MOUNTAIN SPRINGS RD

Mountain Spring
Camp

NATIONAL TRAILS HWY

BIGELOW CHOLLA
GARDEN WILDERNESS

Camino Airstrip

Flattop Mountain
3029 ft

SACRAMENTO

Shadow Canyon

HAVASU
NATIONAL
WILDLIFE REF

PIUTE MOUNTAINS
WILDERNESS

PIUTE

Eagle Peak
3308 ft

Eagle Pass

MOUNTAINS

Needles
4123

CHEMEHUEVI
INDIAN RES

MOJAVE

WARD

VALLEY

Monumental Pass

Whale Mountain
2774 ft

Lobecks
Pass

E MOJAVE
HERT HSE TR.

Piute

Little

Mountains

Big Wash

DESERT

CHEMEHUEVI

CHEMEHUEVI MOUNTAINS
WILDERNESS

Cotton Wash

Pilot Peak
3227 ft

Sunflower Wash

STEPLADDER MOUNTAINS
WILDERNESS

Stepladder Mountains

Snaggletooth
2180 ft

MOUNTAINS

Chemehuevi Peak
3694 ft

VALLEY

Sawtooth
Range

Painted
Rock

Continue on Page 133

OLD WOMAN
MOUNTAINS
WILDERNESS

WARD

VALLEY

Turtle Mountain Rd

HAVASU LAKE RD

TURTLE MOUNTAINS
WILDERNESS

Mexican Hat
2686 ft

TURTLE

MOUNTAINS

CHEMEHUEVI

Chemehuevi Wash

Gary Wash

Pyramid Butte
1848 ft

HERITAGE TR

Mopah Peaks
3541 ft

© DeLorme

1 inch = 3.16 mi   1 cm = 2 km

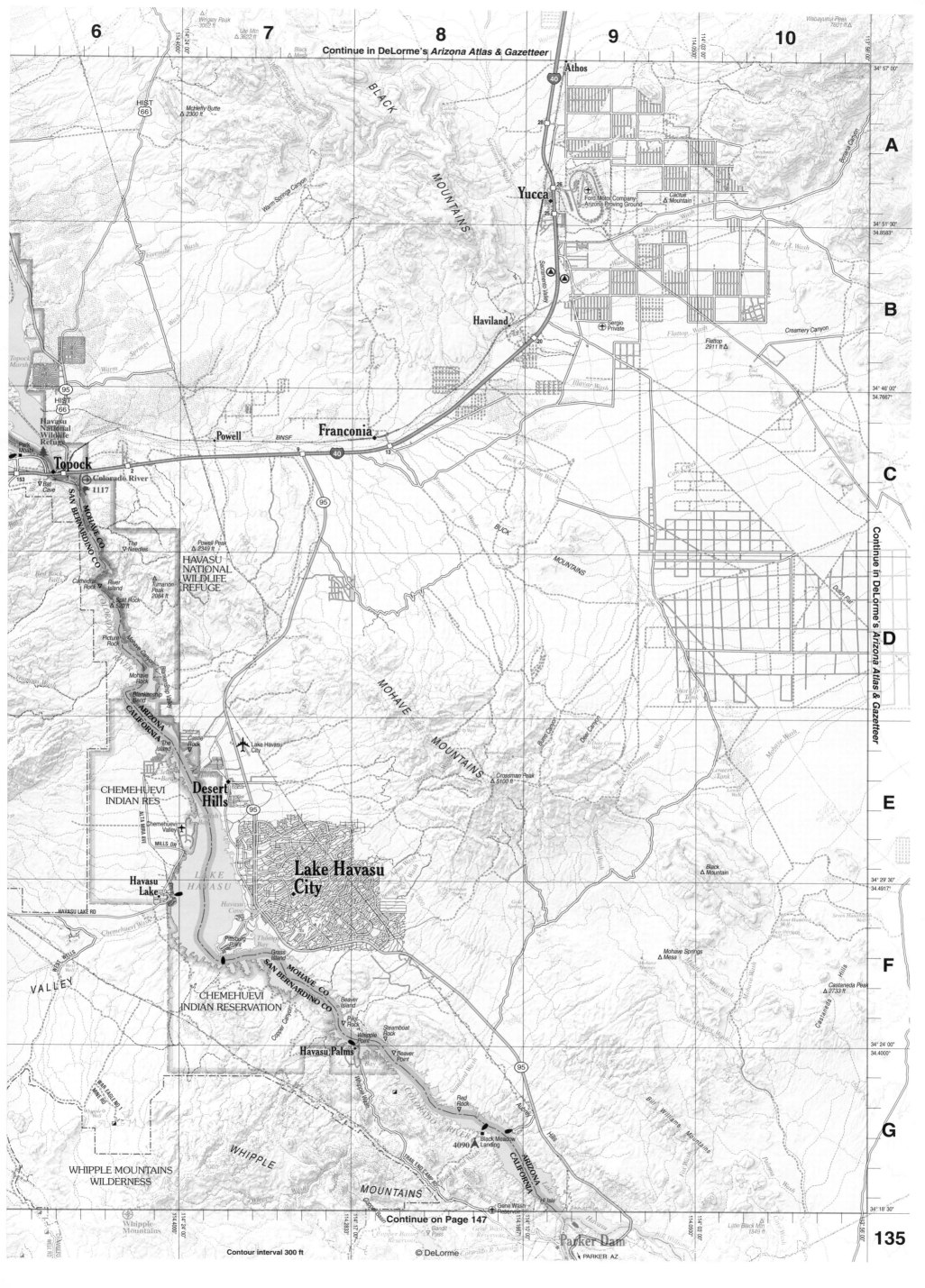

Continue in DeLorme's *Arizona Atlas & Gazetteer*

Athos

Yucca

Ford Motor Company
Arizona Proving Ground

Haviland

Powell   BNSF   Franconia

Topock

Colorado River

HAVASU
NATIONAL
WILDLIFE
REFUGE

Lake Havasu
City

CHEMEHUEVI
INDIAN RES

Desert
Hills

Havasu Lake

**Lake Havasu
City**

CHEMEHUEVI
INDIAN RESERVATION

Havasu Palms

WHIPPLE MOUNTAINS
WILDERNESS

WHIPPLE

MOUNTAINS

Continue on Page 147

Contour interval 300 ft   © DeLorme

Parker Dam
PARKER AZ

A

B

C

D

E

F

G

Continue in DeLorme's *Arizona Atlas & Gazetteer*

135

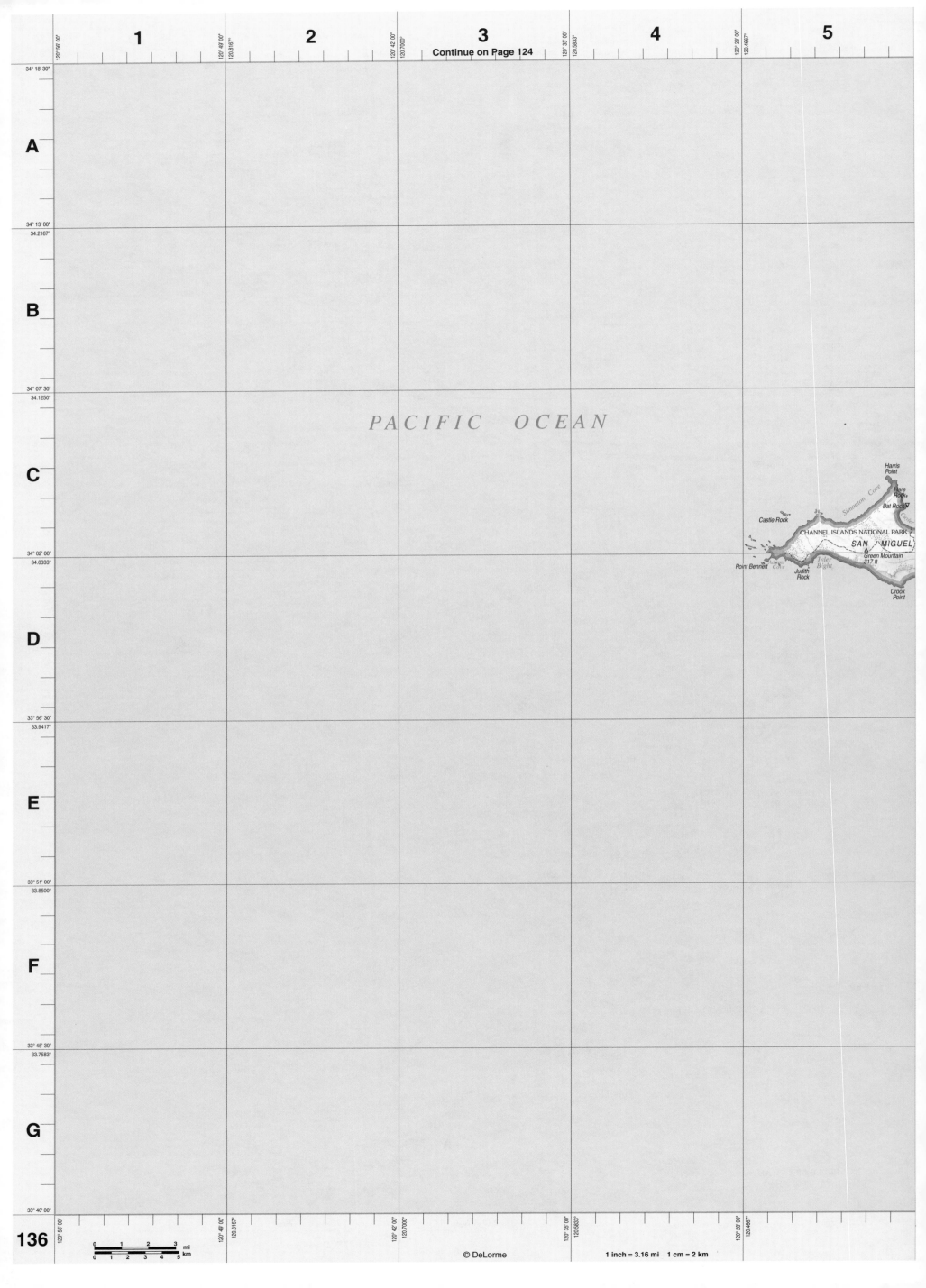

120° 56' 00"
120° 49' 00"
120.8167°
120° 42' 00"
120.7000°
120° 35' 00"
120.5833°
120° 28' 00"
120.4667°

Continue on Page 124

34° 18' 30"
34° 13' 00"
34.2167°
34° 07' 30"
34.1250°
34° 02' 00"
34.0333°
33° 56' 30"
33.9417°
33° 51' 00"
33.8500°
33° 45' 30"
33.7583°
33° 40' 00"

A
B
C
D
E
F
G

PACIFIC OCEAN

Harris
Point
Hare
Rock
Bat Rock
Simonton Cove
Castle Rock
CHANNEL ISLANDS NATIONAL PARK
SAN MIGUEL
Green Mountain
317 ft
Point Bennett
Judith
Rock
Crook
Point

0 1 2 3 mi
0 1 2 3 4 5 km

© DeLorme

1 inch = 3.16 mi   1 cm = 2 km

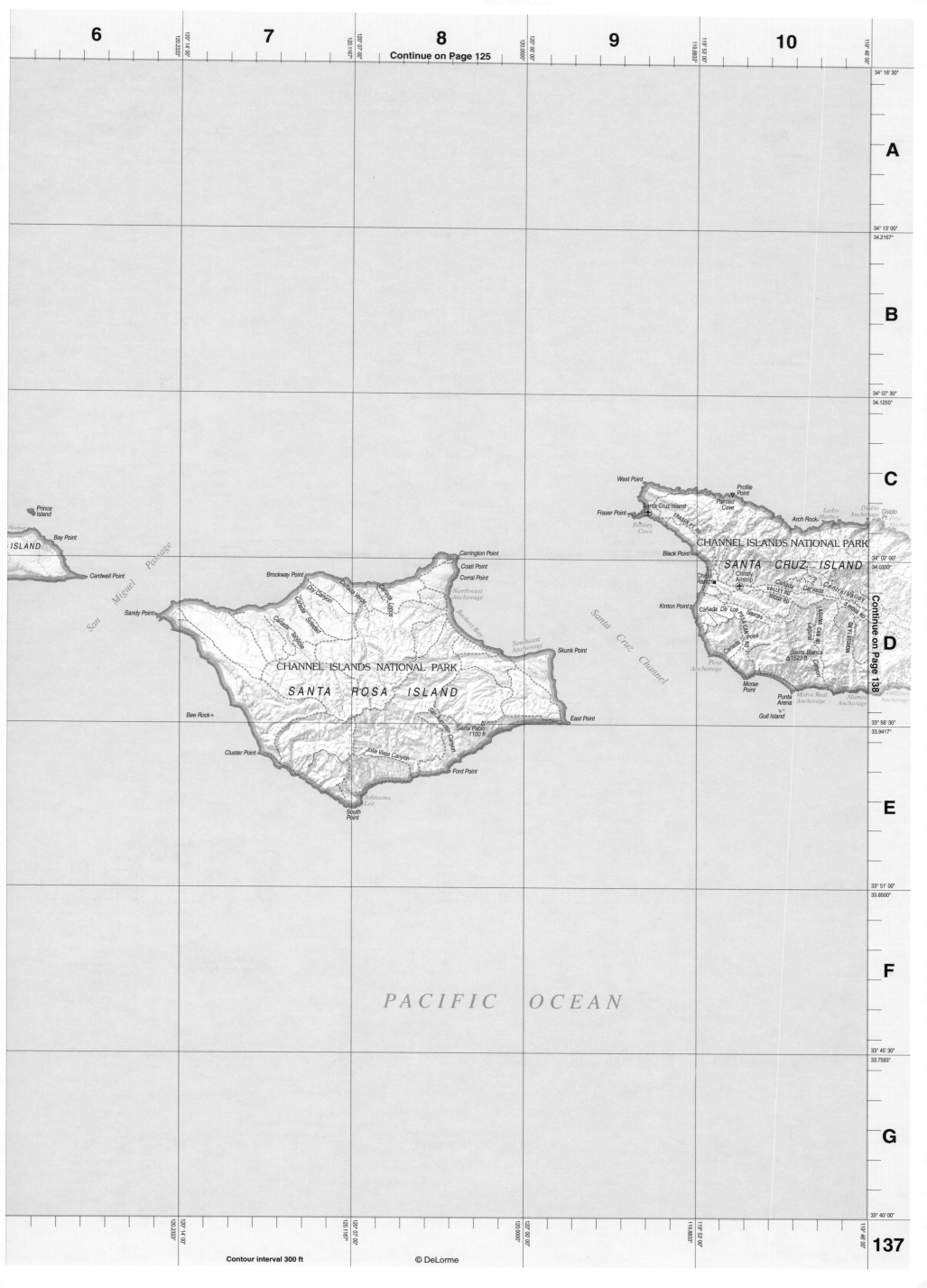

Continue on Page 125

Continue on Page 138

Contour interval 300 ft   © DeLorme

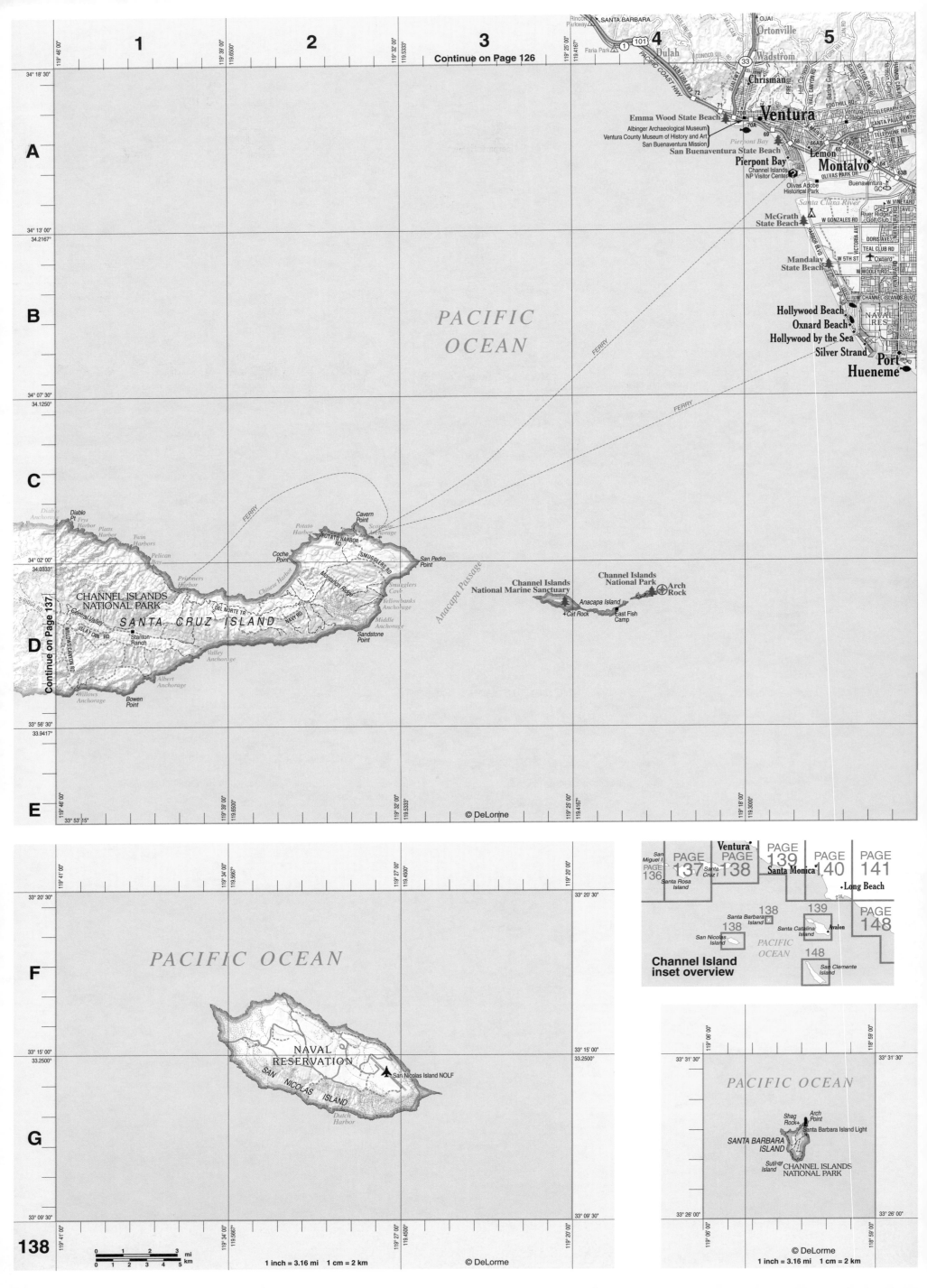

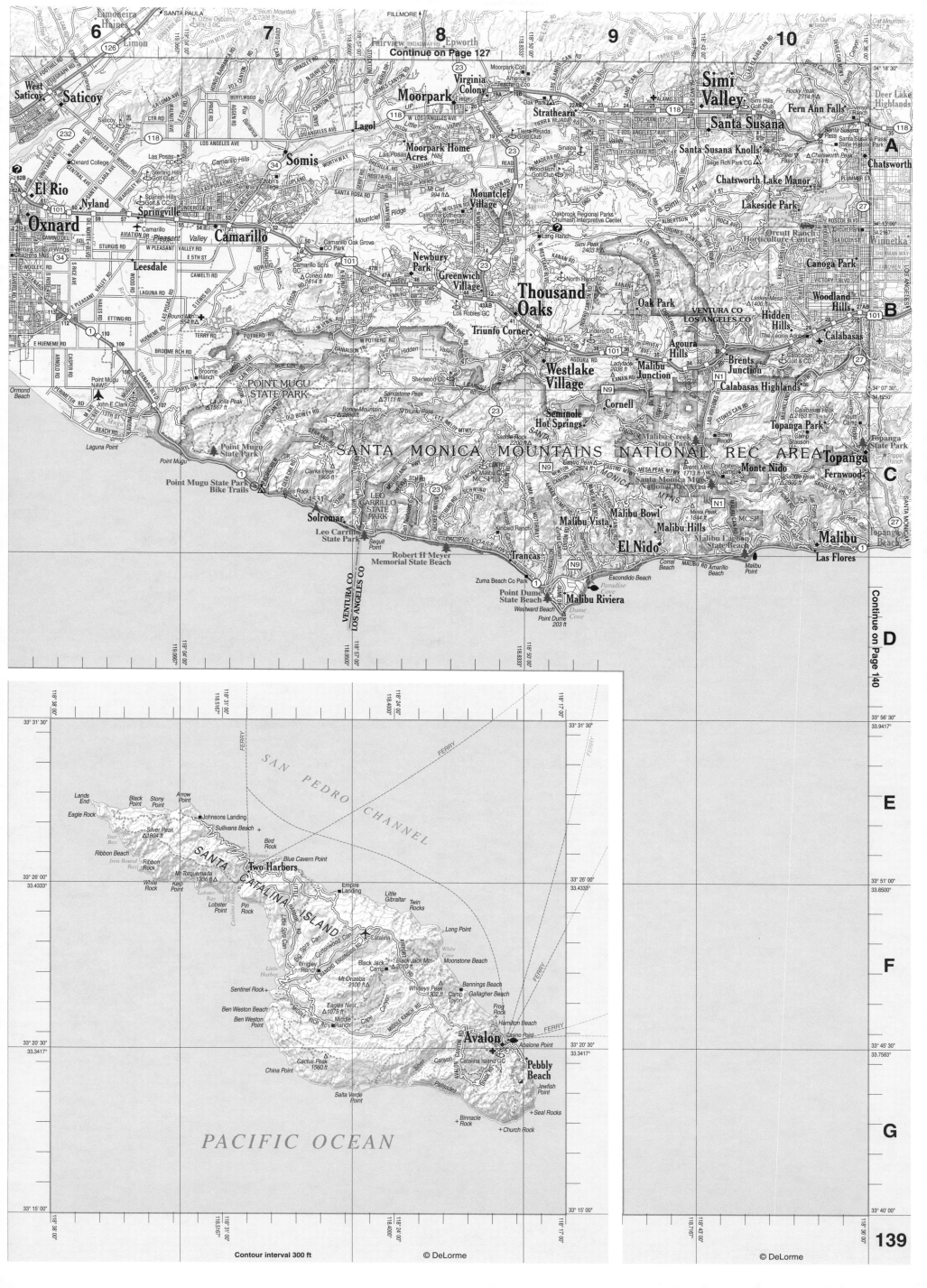

Continue on Page 127

Continue on Page 140

6   **7**   **8**   **9**   **10**

A
B
C
D
E
F
G

Emoneira Haines
SANTA PAULA
FILLMORE
West Saticoy
Saticoy
El Rio
Nyland
Oxnard
Springville
Leesdale
Camarillo
Somis
Ormond Beach
Point Mugu NAWS
Laguna Point
Point Mugu State Park
Point Mugu State Park Bike Trails
Solromar
Leo Carrillo State Park
Seguit Point
Robert H Meyer Memorial State Beach

Fairview Broadway Rd Epworth
Moorpark
Virginia Colony
Lagol
Moorpark Home Acres
Newbury Park
Greenwich Village
Thousand Oaks
Triunfo Corner
Westlake Village
POINT MUGU STATE PARK
Sandstone Peak 3111 ft
Boney Mountain 2886 ft
Triunfo Pass
Seminole Hot Springs
SANTA MONICA MOUNTAINS NATIONAL REC AREA
Trancas
Zuma Beach Co Park
Point Dume State Beach
Westward Beach
Point Dume 203 ft
Malibu Riviera
Dume Cove
Paradise Cove
Escondido Beach

Simi Valley
Fern Ann Falls
Santa Susana
Santa Susana Knolls
Chatsworth
Deer Lake Highlands
Chatsworth Lake Manor
Lakeside Park
Canoga Park
Woodland Hills
Winnetka
Calabasas
Hidden Hills
Agoura Hills
Oak Park
Brents Junction
Calabasas Highlands
Malibu Junction
Cornell
Topanga Park
Topanga State Park
Monte Nido
Topanga
Fernwood
Malibu Vista
Malibu Bowl
Malibu Hills
El Nido
Malibu
Las Flores
Malibu Point
Corral Beach
Malibu Lagoon State Beach

VENTURA CO / LOS ANGELES CO

Contour interval 300 ft   © DeLorme   © DeLorme

SAN PEDRO CHANNEL
FERRY
Lands End
Eagle Rock
Black Point
Stony Point
Arrow Point
Johnsons Landing
Sullivans Beach
Bird Rock
Silver Peak 1804 ft
Blue Cavern Point
Ribbon Beach
Star Bay
Ribbon Rock
Iron Bound Bay
SANTA CATALINA ISLAND
Two Harbors
White Rock
Kelp Point
Lobster Bay
Lobster Point
Pin Rock
Mt Torquemada 1336 ft
Empire Landing
Little Gibralter
Twin Rocks
Long Point
Catalina
Black Jack Mtn 2010 ft
Black Jack Camp
Moonstone Beach
Wrigley Ranch
Mt Orizaba 2100 ft
Whitleys Peak 302 ft
Bannings Beach
Gallagher Beach
Camp Toyon
Sentinel Rock
Eagles Nest 1075 ft
Middle Ranch
Frog Rock
Hamilton Beach
Ben Weston Beach
Ben Weston Point
Cape Canyon
Avalon
Casino Point
Abalone Point
Pebbly Beach
Cactus Peak 1560 ft
Catalina Island GC
Jewish Point
China Point
Palisades
Salta Verde Point
Binnacle Rock
Seal Rocks
Church Rock

PACIFIC OCEAN

139

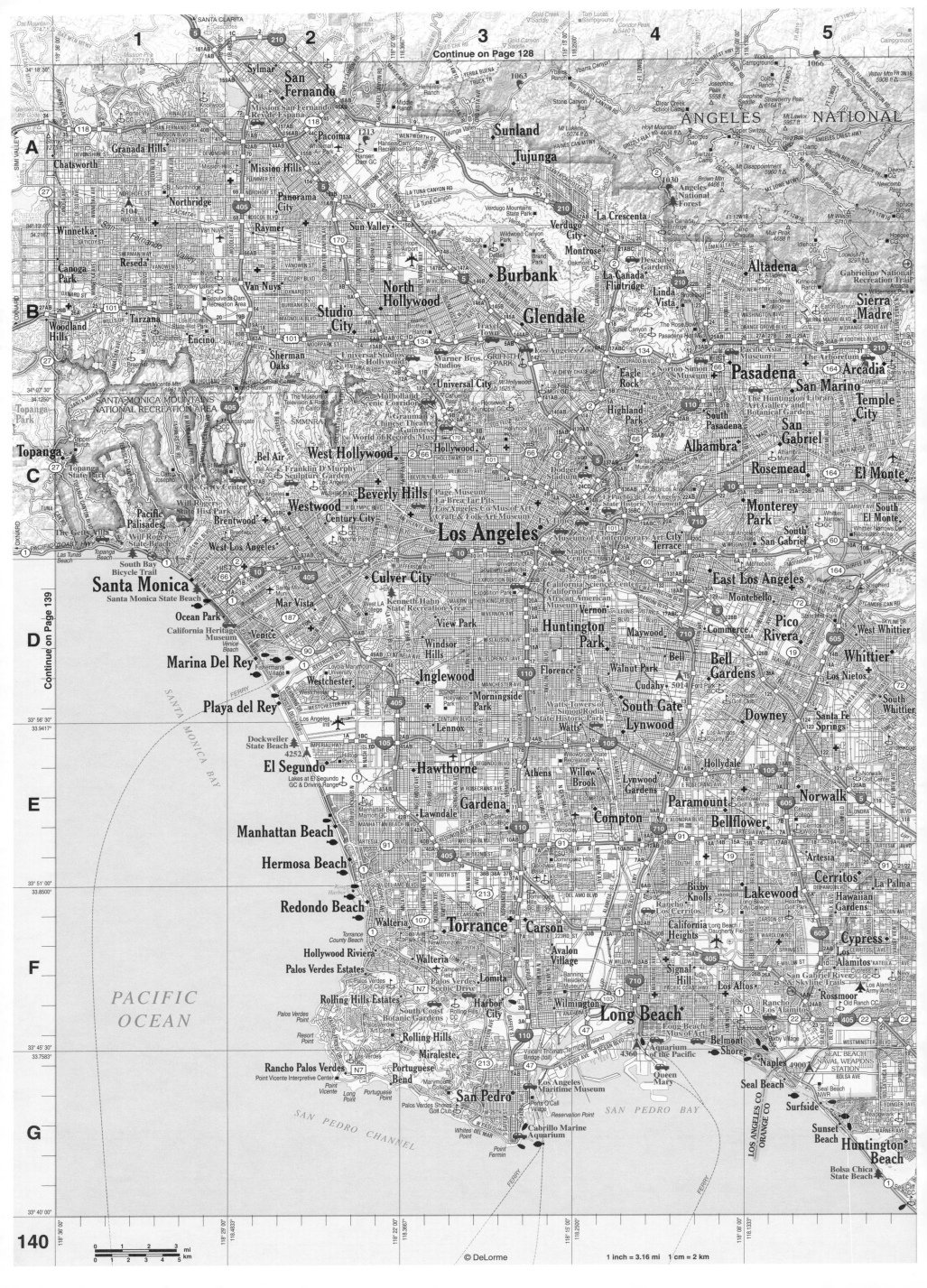

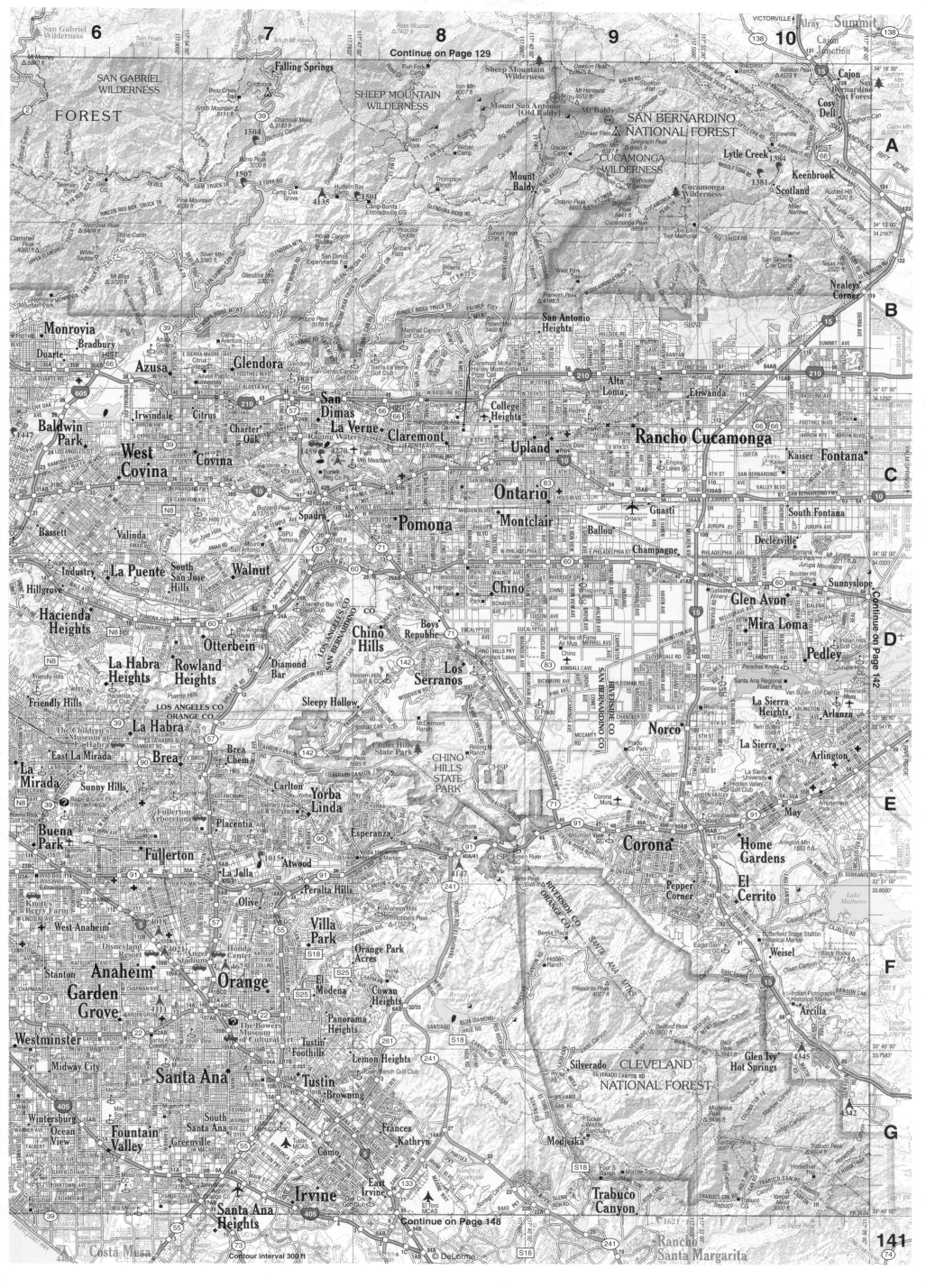

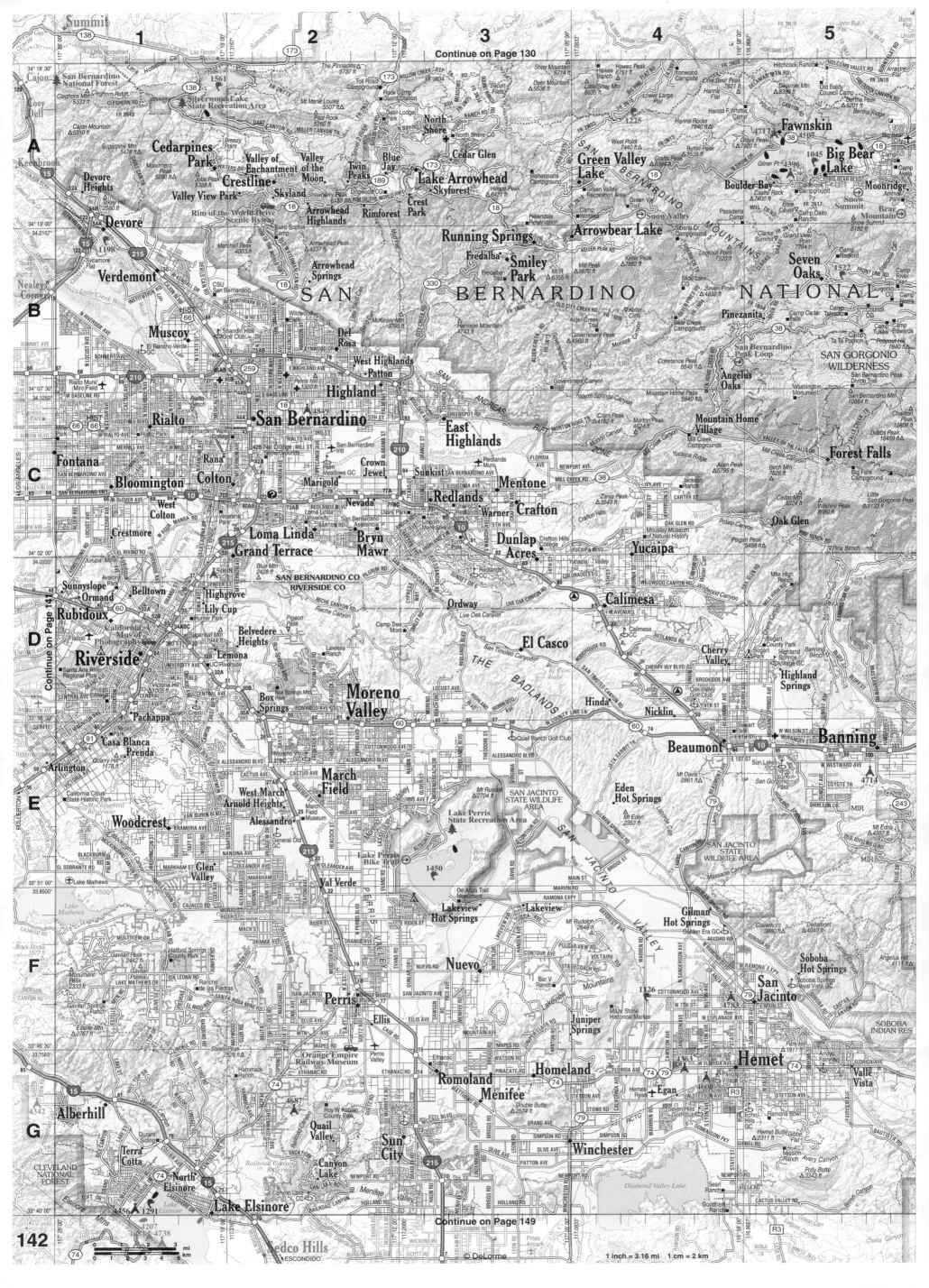

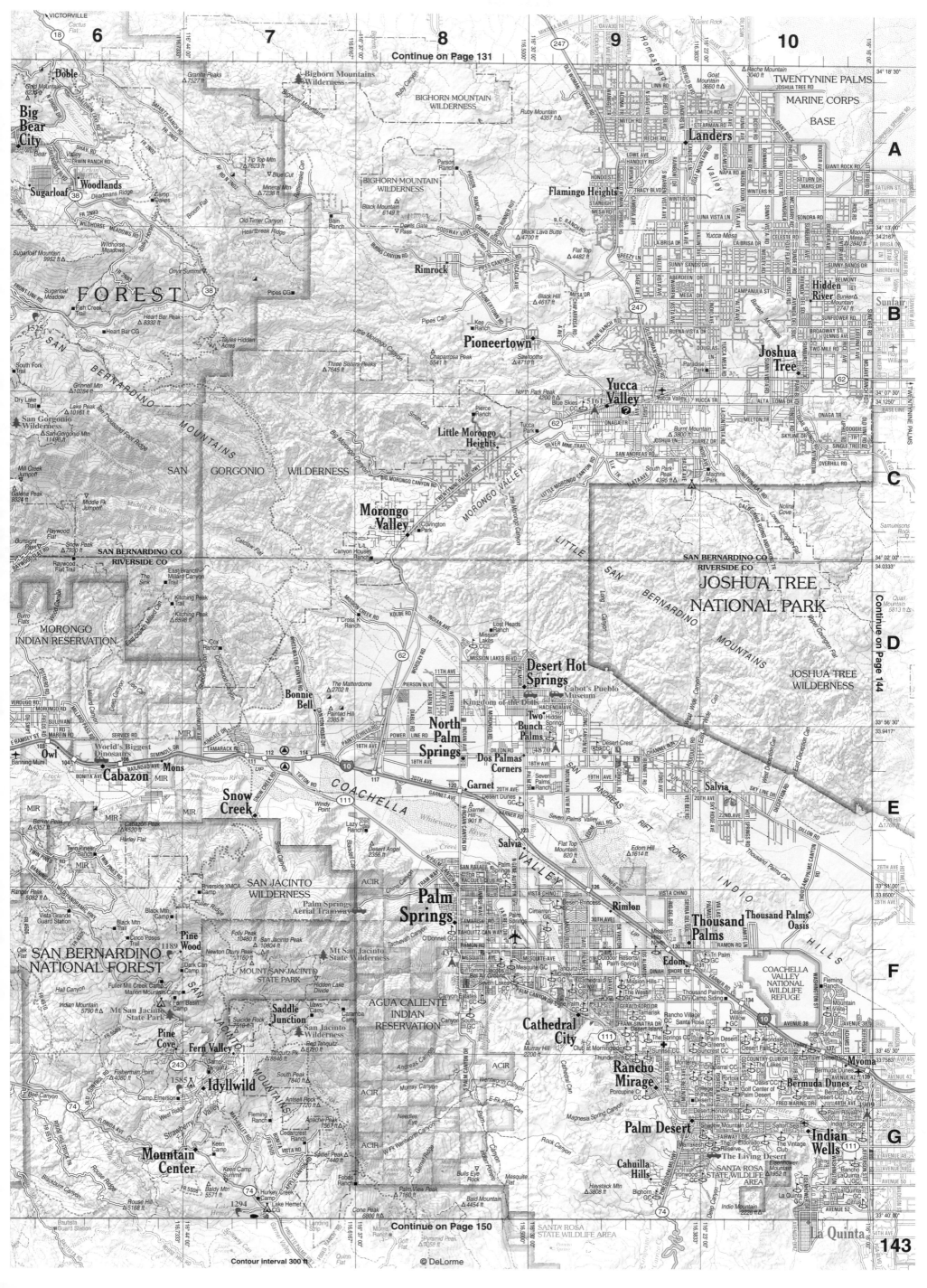

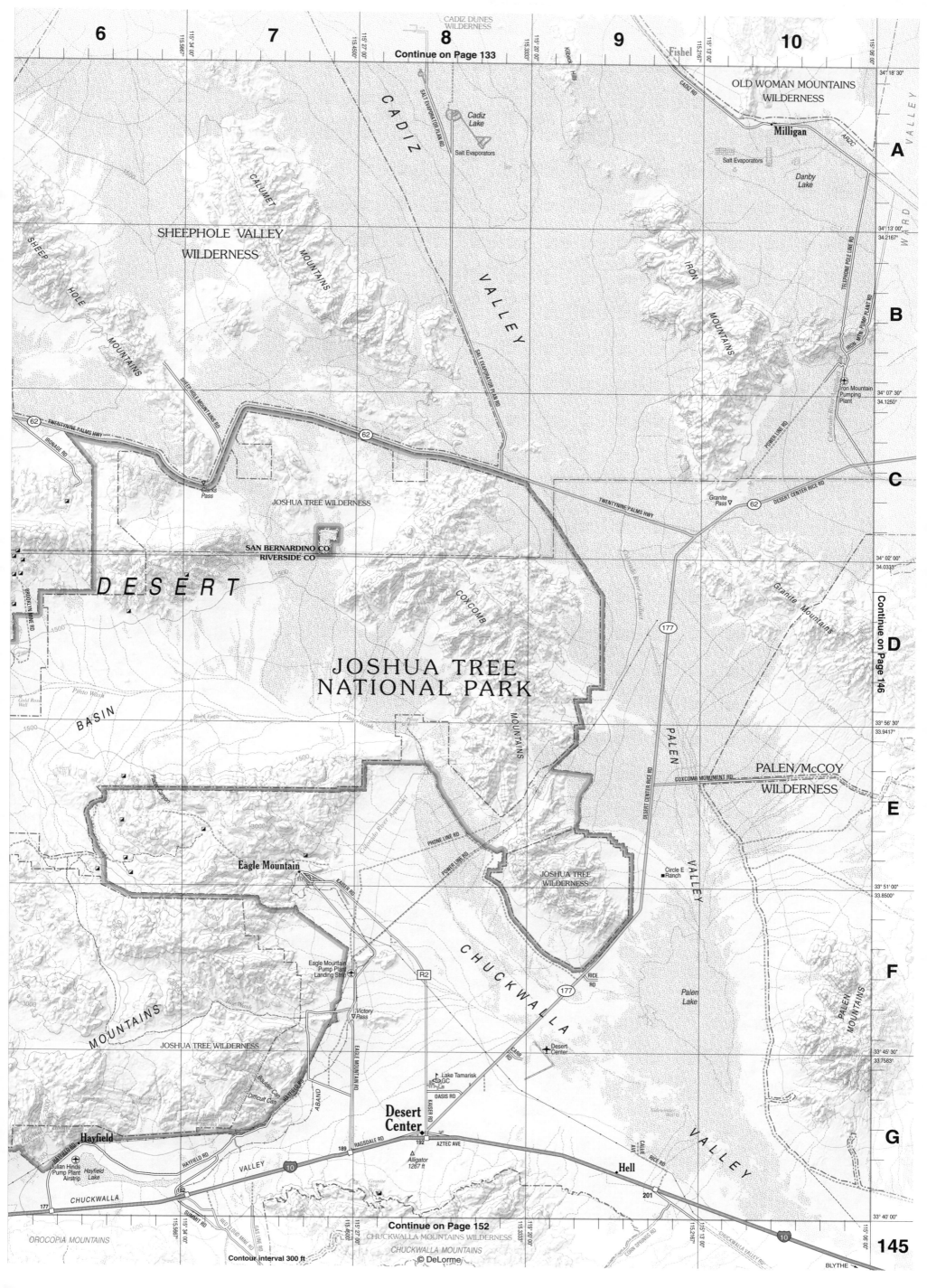

Continue on Page 133

CADIZ DUNES WILDERNESS

115° 34' 00"
115.5667°

115° 27' 00"
115.4500°

115° 33.33"

115° 20' 00"
115.3333°

115° 13' 00"
115.2167°

115° 06' 00"

WARD VALLEY

OLD WOMAN MOUNTAINS WILDERNESS

34° 18' 30"

Milligan

Salt Evaporators

Danby Lake

34° 13' 00"
34.2167°

A

CADIZ

Cadiz Lake

Salt Evaporators

VALLEY

CALUMET

SHEEPHOLE VALLEY WILDERNESS

MOUNTAINS

IRON

MOUNTAINS

Kilbeck Hills

34° 07' 30"
34.1250°

B

Iron Mountain Tunnel

Iron Mountain Pumping Plant

TELEPHONE POLE LINE RD

CADIZ RD

AR2C

Fishel

SHEEP HOLE MOUNTAINS RD

SHEEP HOLE MOUNTAINS

62 Twentynine Palms Hwy

IRONAGE RD

Clarks Pass

62

Twentynine Palms Hwy

62

Granite Pass

Desert Center Rice Rd

POWER LINE RD

Colorado River Aqueduct

34° 07' 30"

C

JOSHUA TREE WILDERNESS

SAN BERNARDINO CO
RIVERSIDE CO

DESERT

BROOKLYN MINE RD

1500

Gold Road Well

Pinto Wash

BASIN

1500

Black Eagle Pinto Wash

COXCOMB

JOSHUA TREE
NATIONAL PARK

MOUNTAINS

Granite Mountains

34° 02' 00"
34.0333°

177

PALEN

Continue on Page 146

D

33° 56' 30"
33.9417°

Pinto Wash

1500

3000

PLACER CANYON

Colorado River Aqueduct

PHONE LINE RD

POWER LINE RD

Coxcomb Tunnel

Coxcomb Monument Rd

PALEN/McCOY
WILDERNESS

33° 51' 00"
33.8500°

E

Circle E Ranch

VALLEY

Eagle Mountain

KAISER RD

3000

JOSHUA TREE
WILDERNESS

3000

RICE RD

PALEN

MOUNTAINS

F

Eagle Mountain Pump Plant Landing Strip

EAGLE MOUNTAIN RD

R2

177

Palen Lake

MOUNTAINS

Victory Pass

ABAND

Desert Center

33° 45' 30"
33.7583°

JOSHUA TREE WILDERNESS

Boulder Can

Difficult Can

3000

Lake Tamarisk
GC

CADIZ RD

CHUCKWALLA

VALLEY

Hayfield

HAYFIELD RD

Julian Hinds Pump Plant Airstrip

Hayfield Lake

VALLEY

OASIS RD

Desert
Center

192 AZTEC AVE

Hell

CALLE AVE

RICE RD

G

Alligator 1267 ft

201

10

33° 40' 00"

189 RAGSDALE RD

10

182

177

OROCOPIA MOUNTAINS

SUMMIT RD

RED CLOUD MINE RD

GAS LINE RD

115° 34' 00"

115° 27' 00"
115.4500°

CHUCKWALLA

Continue on Page 152

CHUCKWALLA MOUNTAINS WILDERNESS

CHUCKWALLA MOUNTAINS

115° 20' 00"
115.3333°

CORN SPRINGS RD

CHUCKWALLA VALLEY RD

115° 13' 00"
115.2167°

115° 06' 00"

Contour interval 300 ft

© DeLorme

BLYTHE

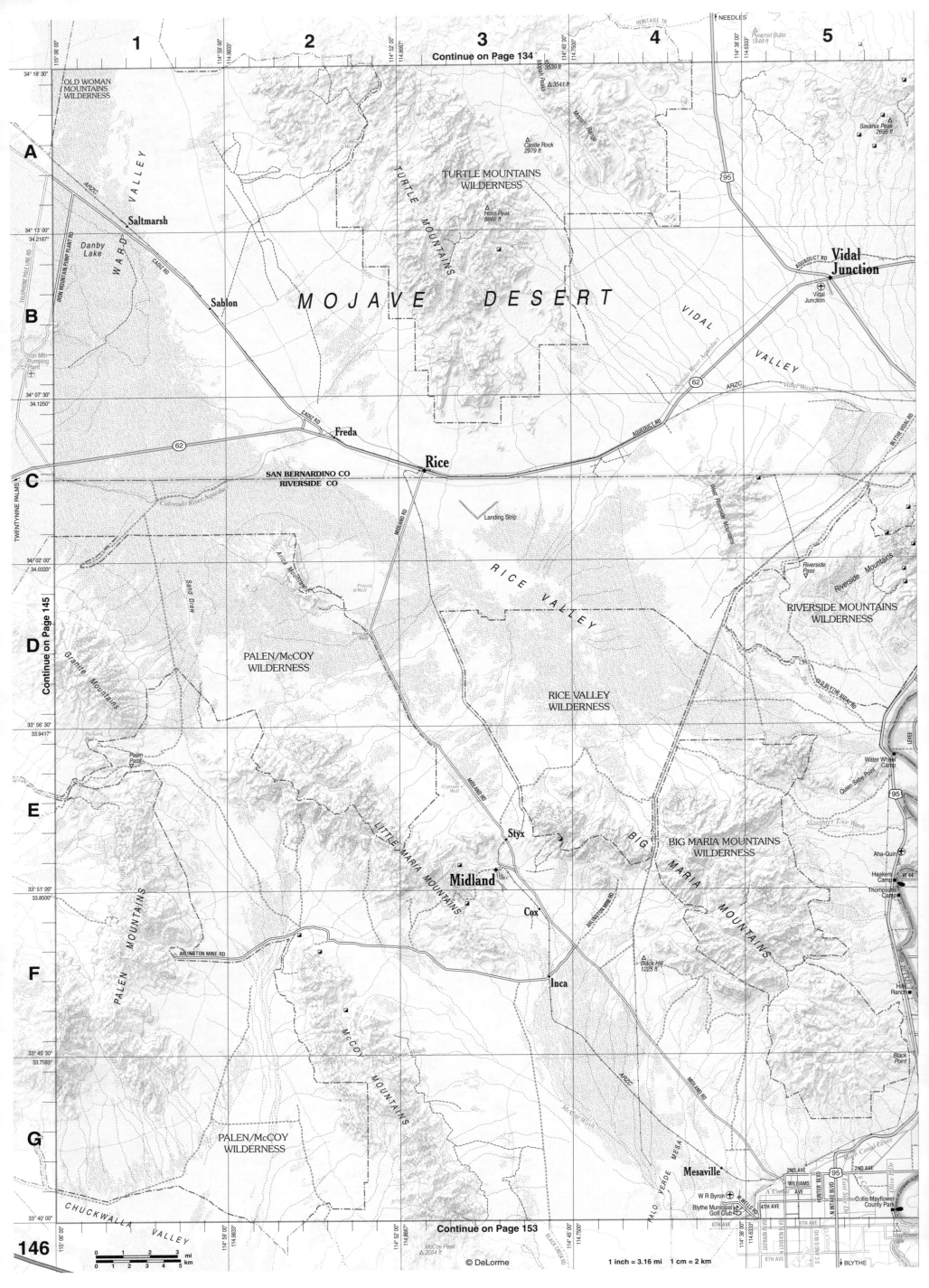

Continue on Page 134

A

OLD WOMAN
MOUNTAINS
WILDERNESS

Pyramid Butte
1848 ft

NEEDLES

HERITAGE TR

Mopah Peaks
3539 ft
3541 ft

Savahia Peak
2695 ft

Castle Rock
2979 ft

TURTLE MOUNTAINS
WILDERNESS

Saltmarsh

Danby
Lake

B

Horn Peak
8866 ft

Horn
Spring

Vidal
Junction

**Vidal
Junction**

Sablon

M O J A V E   D E S E R T

Colorado River Aqueduct

VIDAL

VALLEY

Vidal Wash

ARZC

62

Continue on Page 145

C

Freda

62

Rice

SAN BERNARDINO CO
RIVERSIDE CO

West Riverside Mountains

Landing Strip

Riverside
Pass

Riverside Mountains

R I C E   V A L L E Y

RIVERSIDE MOUNTAINS
WILDERNESS

Colorado River Aqueduct

Priests
Well

D

Granite Mountains

Sand Draw

PALEN/McCOY
WILDERNESS

Browns
Well

RICE VALLEY
WILDERNESS

Old Blythe Vidal Rd

Water Wheel
Camp

Quien Sabe Point

E

Palen
Pass

Gypsum
Well

B I G

Slaughter Tree Wash

LEVEE

95

Styx

M A R I A

BIG MARIA MOUNTAINS
WILDERNESS

Aha-Quin

L I T T L E   M A R I A   M O U N T A I N S

Midland

Cox

Haskers
Camp

Thompsons
Camp

IR 44

F

PALEN MOUNTAINS

ARLINGTON MINE RD

Inca

Black Hill
1225 ft

M O U N T A I N S

Black Point

Hitt
Ranch

McCOY   MOUNTAINS

McCoy Wash

PALO VERDE MESA

ARZC

G

PALEN/McCOY
WILDERNESS

Mesaville

W R Byron

Blythe Municipal
Golf Club

2ND. AVE

2ND. AVE

WILLIAMS   AVE

95

Collis Mayflower
County Park

Mayflower

CHUCKWALLA   VALLEY

McCoy Peak
2054 ft

Continue on Page 153

4TH. AVE

6TH AVE

BLYTHE

© DeLorme

1 inch = 3.16 mi   1 cm = 2 km

0 1 2 3 mi
0 1 2 3 4 5 km

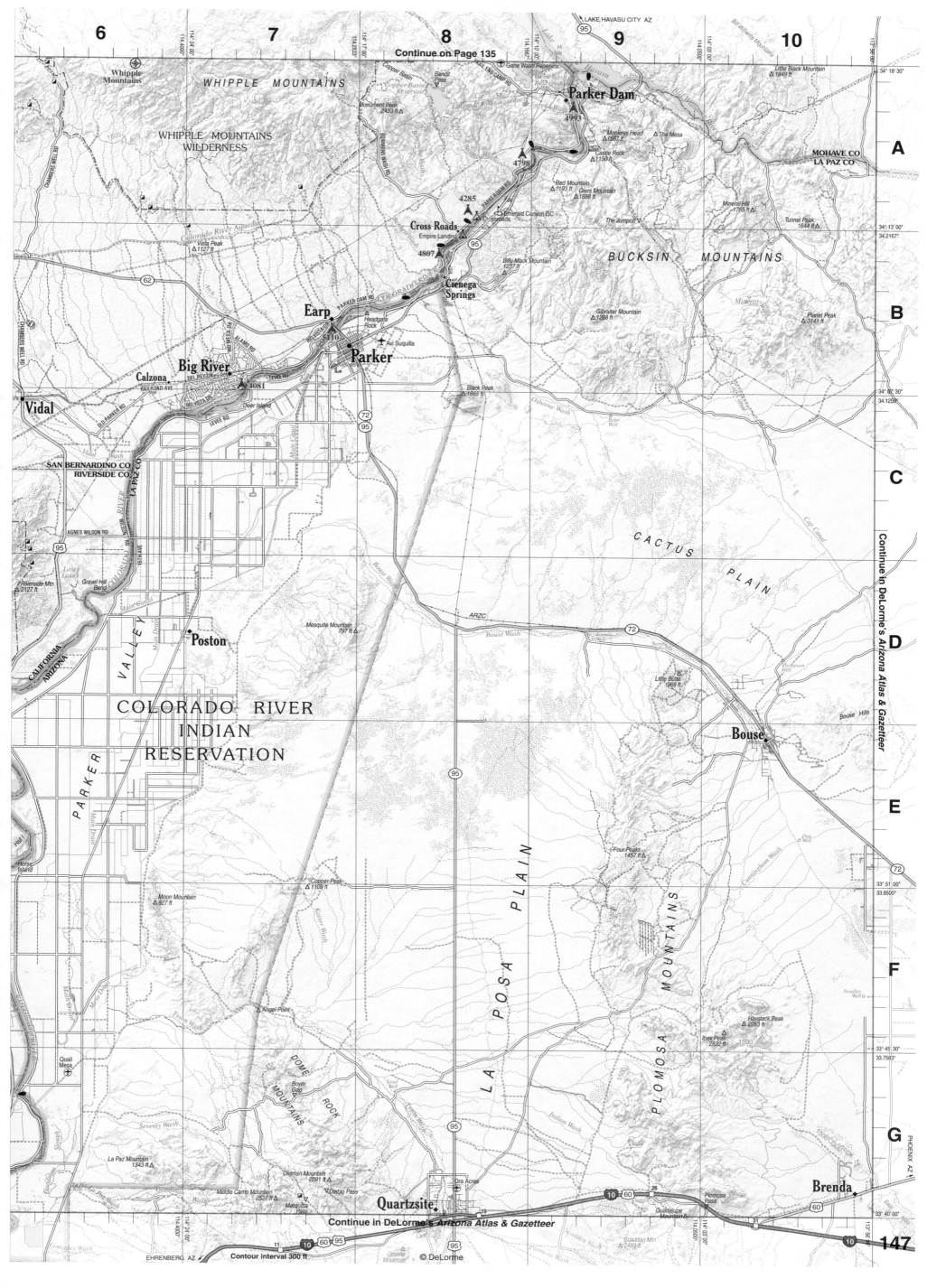

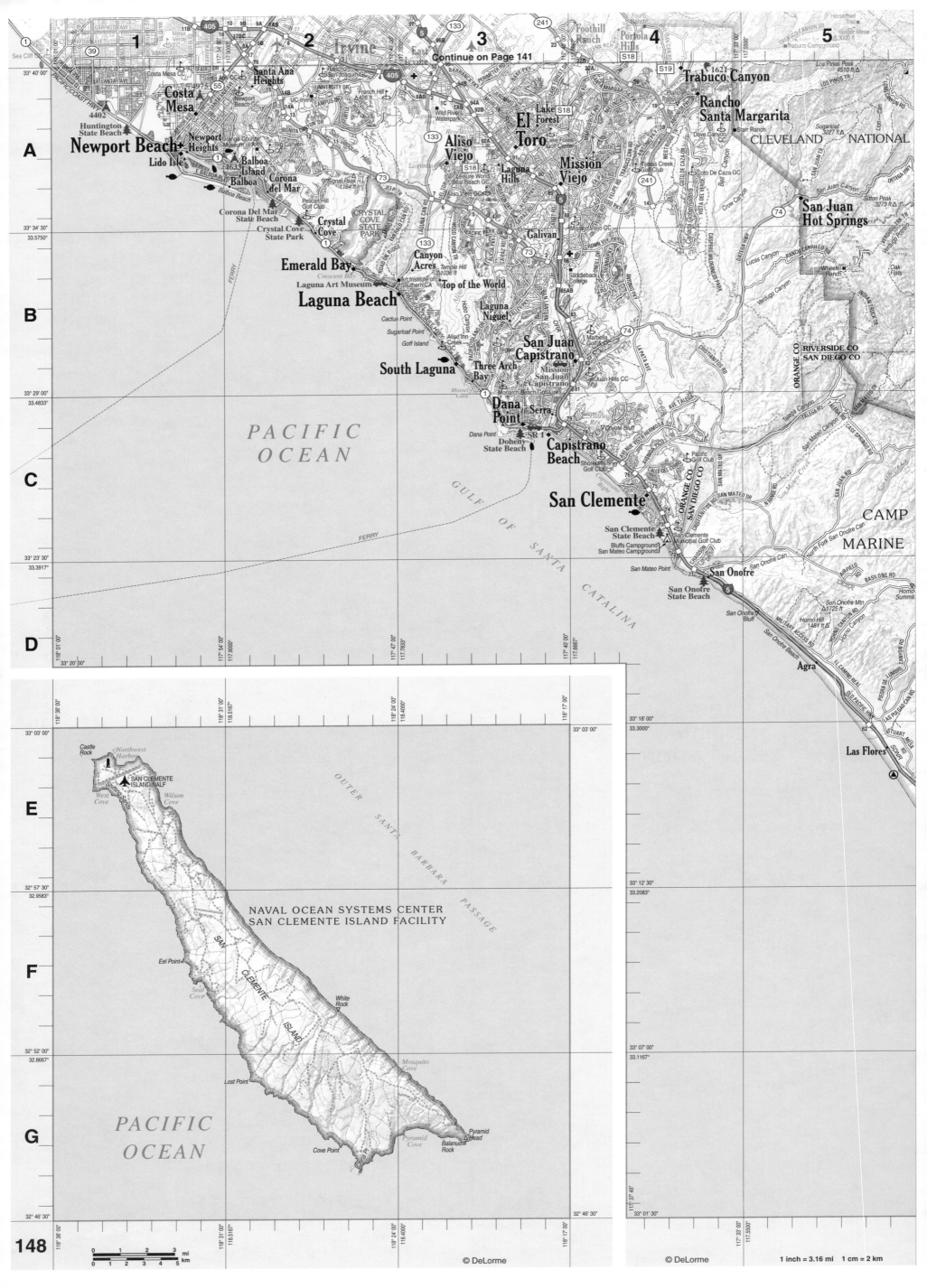

Continue on Page 141

PACIFIC OCEAN

GULF OF SANTA CATALINA

CLEVELAND NATIONAL

Newport Beach
Costa Mesa
Huntington State Beach
Santa Ana Heights
Irvine
Lido Isle
Balboa Island
Balboa
Corona del Mar
Newport Heights
Corona Del Mar State Beach
Crystal Cove State Beach
Crystal Cove
CRYSTAL COVE STATE PARK

El Toro
Lake Forest
Aliso Viejo
Mission Viejo
Laguna Hills
Emerald Bay
Laguna Art Museum
Laguna Beach
Canyon Acres
Top of the World
Laguna Niguel
South Laguna
Three Arch Bay
San Juan Capistrano
Mission San Juan Capistrano
Dana Point
Serra
Doheny State Beach
Capistrano Beach
San Clemente
San Clemente State Beach
Bluffs Campground
San Mateo Campground
San Mateo Point
San Onofre State Beach
San Onofre

Trabuco Canyon
Rancho Santa Margarita
San Juan Hot Springs

RIVERSIDE CO
SAN DIEGO CO

ORANGE CO
SAN DIEGO CO

CAMP MARINE

Agra
Las Flores

PACIFIC OCEAN

NAVAL OCEAN SYSTEMS CENTER
SAN CLEMENTE ISLAND FACILITY

Castle Rock
Northwest Harbor
SAN CLEMENTE ISLAND NALF
West Cove
Wilson Cove
SAN CLEMENTE ISLAND
Eel Point
Seal Cove
White Rock
Mosquito Cove
Lost Point
Pyramid Head
Cove Point
Pyramid Cove
Balanada Rock

OUTER SANTA BARBARA PASSAGE

© DeLorme

© DeLorme

1 inch = 3.16 mi   1 cm = 2 km

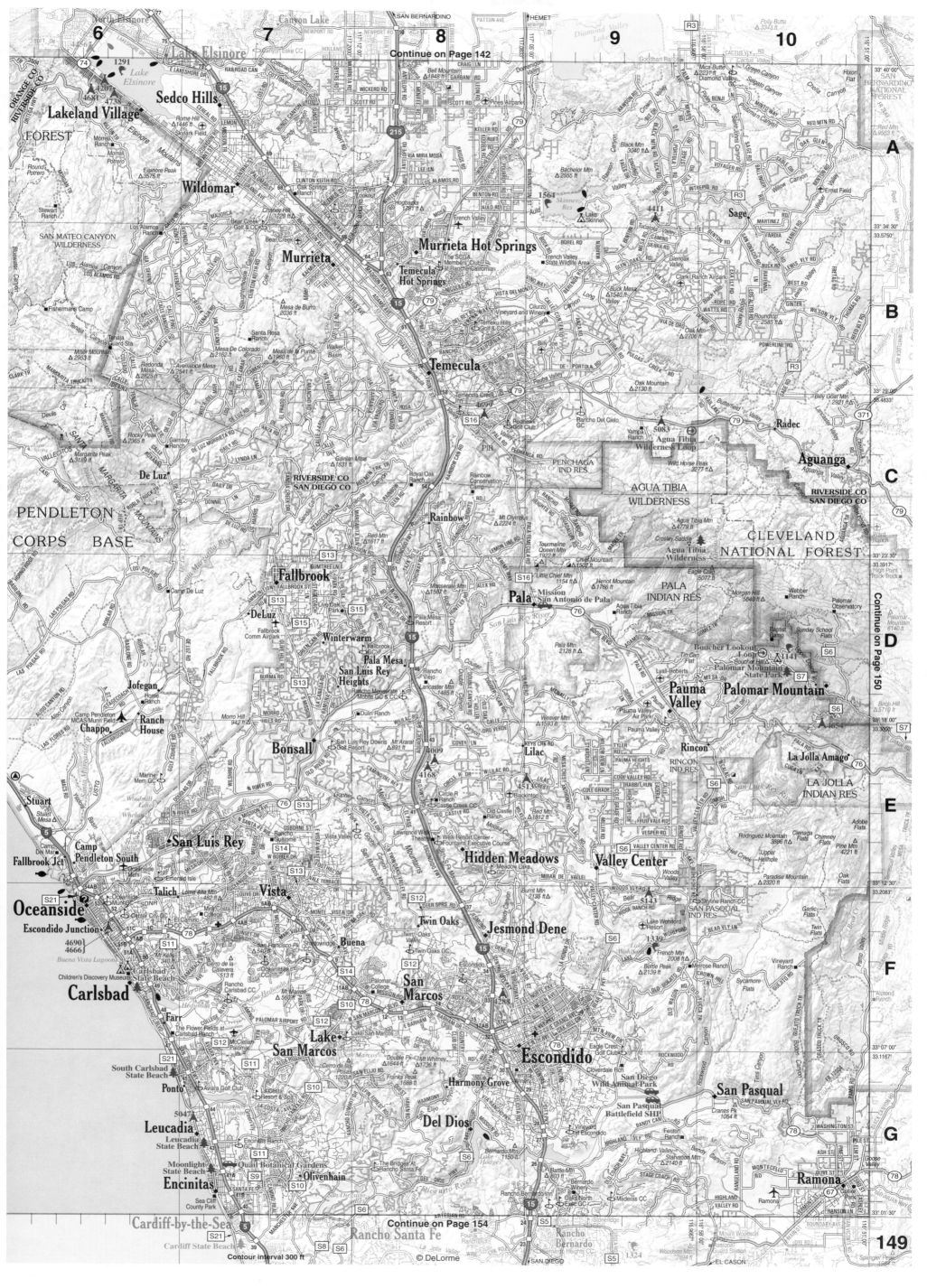

Continue on Page 142

Continue on Page 150

Continue on Page 154

Contour interval 300 ft

© DeLorme

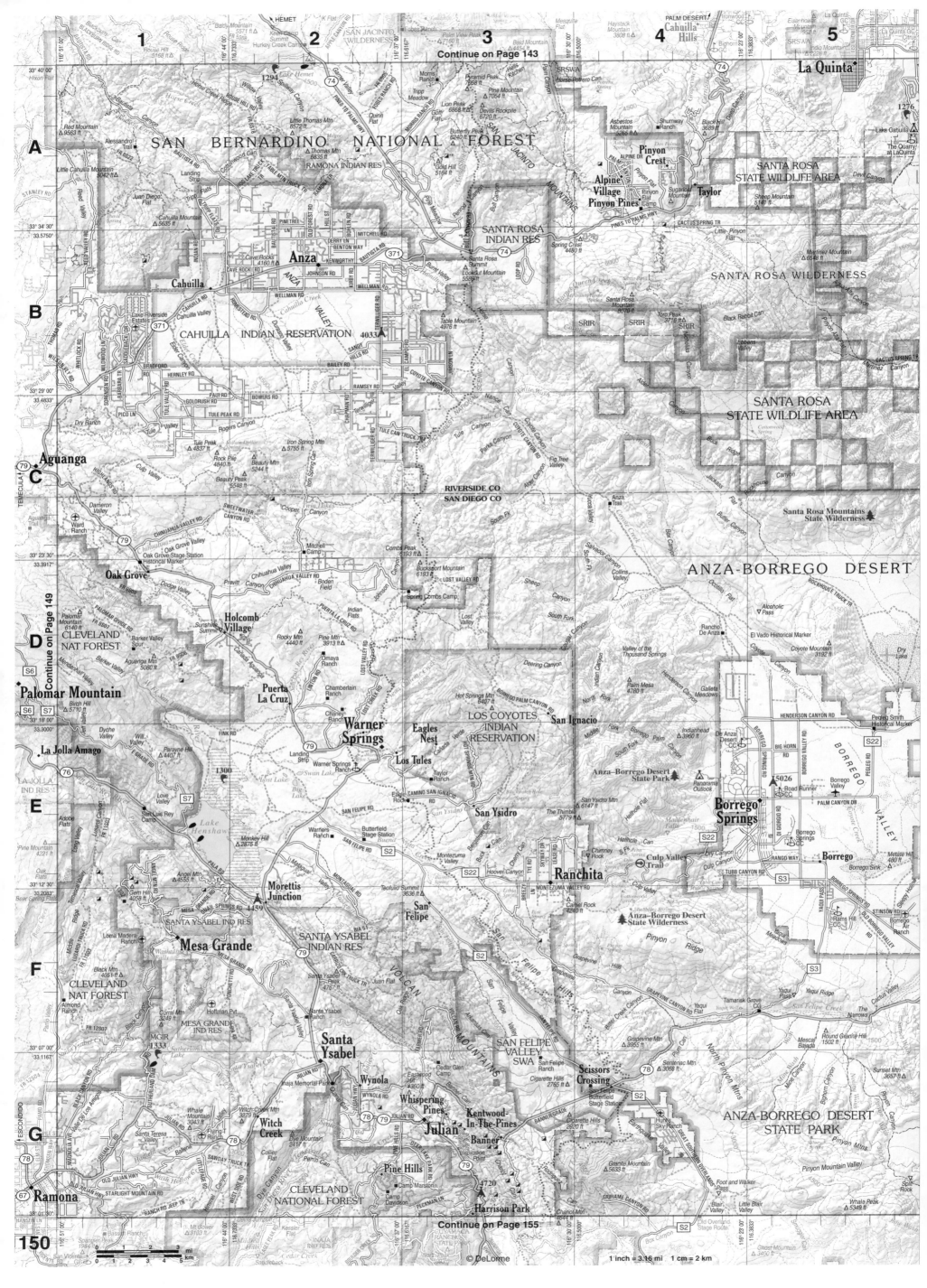

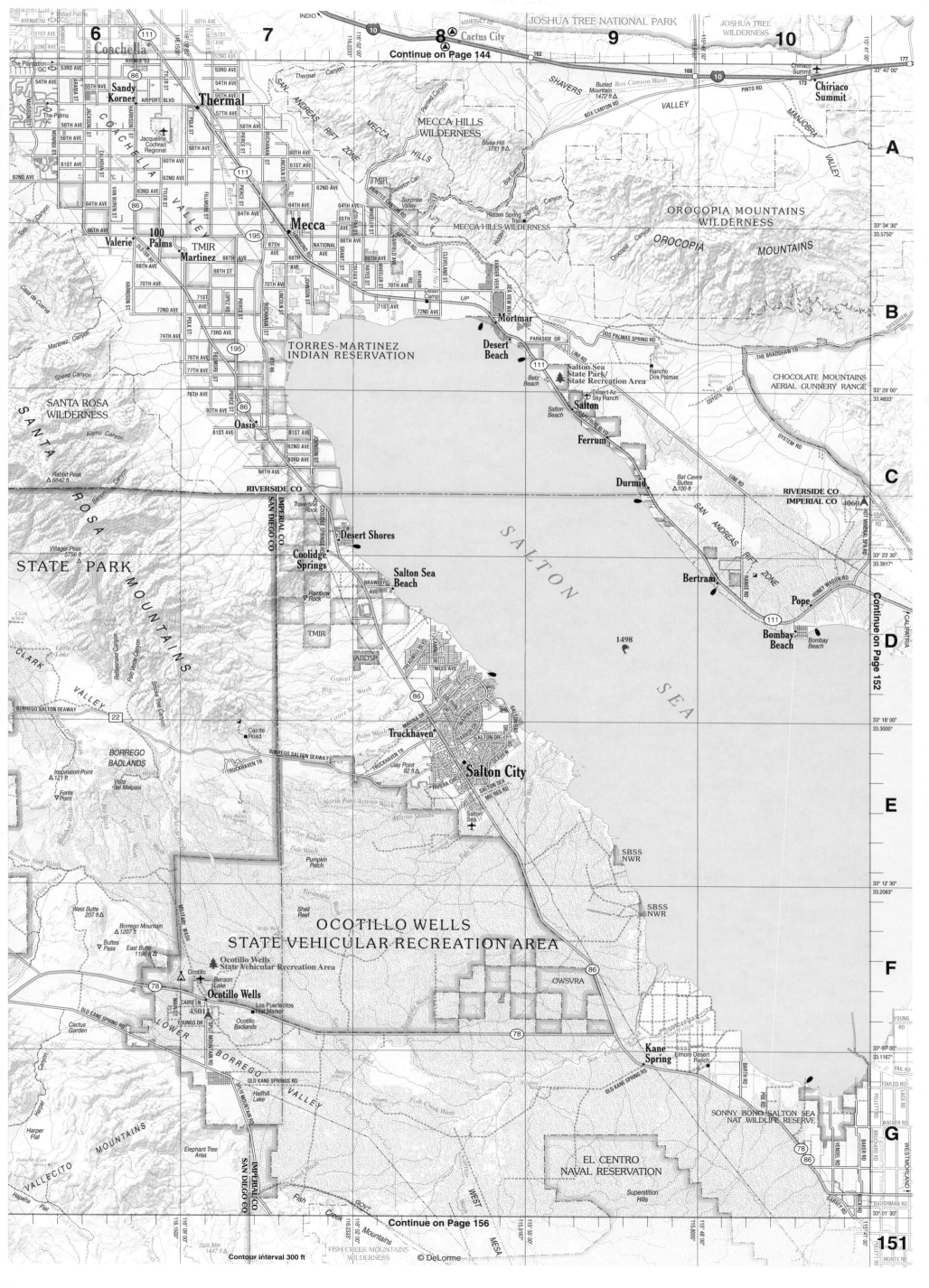

Continue on Page 144

Continue on Page 152

Continue on Page 156

A

B

C

D

E

F

G

Contour interval 300 ft

© DeLorme

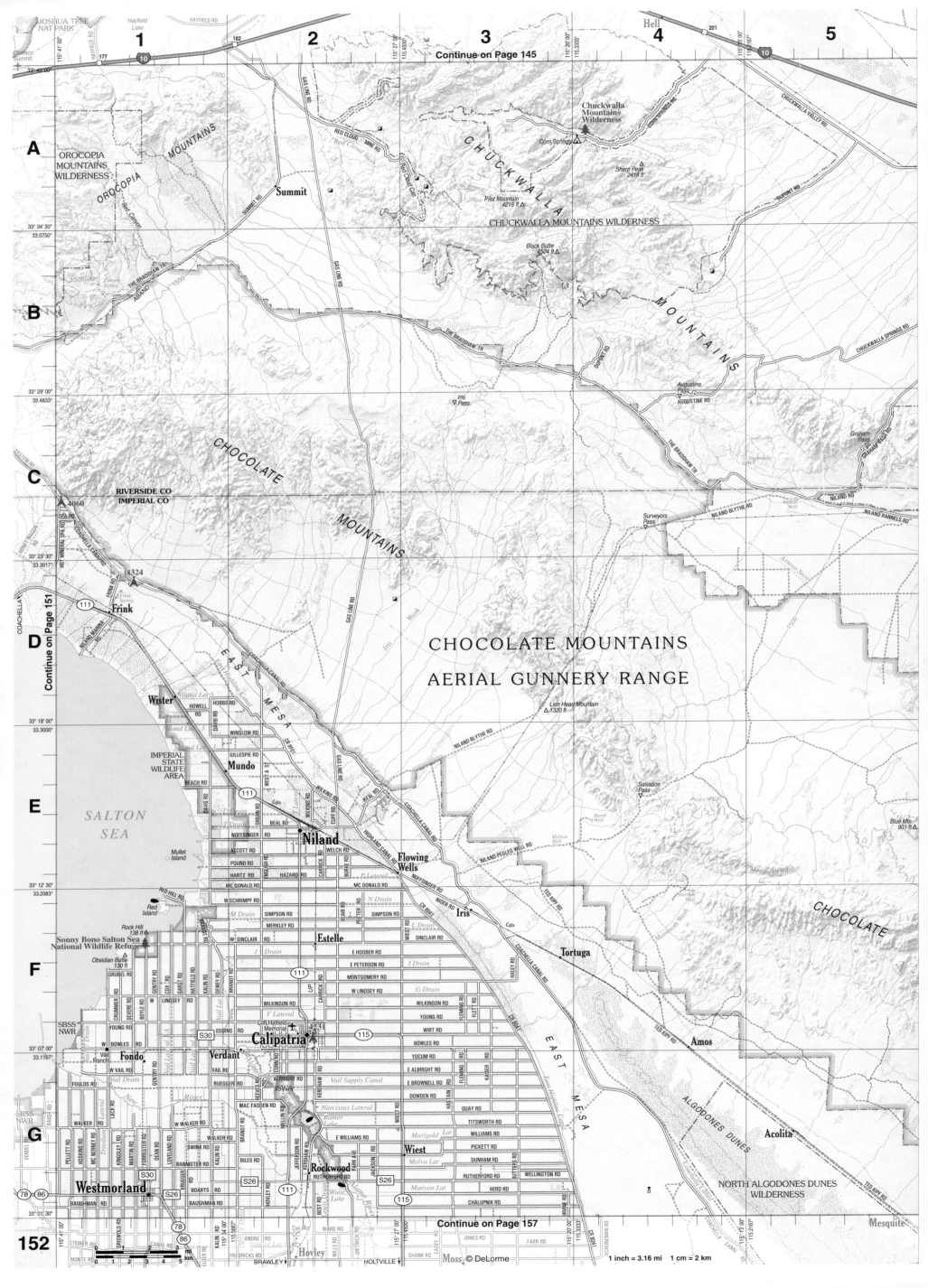

1 **2** **3** **4** **5**

JOSHUA TREE NAT PARK

Hayfield Lake

HAYFIELD RD

Chiriaco Summit

Hell

201

Orocopia Mountains Wilderness

OROCOPIA MOUNTAINS WILDERNESS

OROCOPIA   MOUNTAINS

Summit

CHUCKWALLA

Chuckwalla Mountains Wilderness

Corn Springs

Sharp Peak 2418 ft

Pilot Mountain 4216 ft

CHUCKWALLA MOUNTAINS WILDERNESS

MOUNTAINS

Black Butte 1504 ft

DUPONT RD

CHUCKWALLA SPRINGS RD

THE BRADSHAW TR

Iris Pass

Augustine Pass
AUGUSTINE RD

CHOCOLATE

Arroyo Seco

THE BRADSHAW TR

Graham Pass
GRAHAM PASS RD

MOUNTAINS

RIVERSIDE CO
IMPERIAL CO

Surveyors Pass

NILAND RD

NILAND-BLYTHE RD
NILAND RANNELS RD

4324

Frink Spring

111 Frink

CHOCOLATE MOUNTAINS

AERIAL GUNNERY RANGE

EAST

MESA

Lion Head Mountain 1320 ft

Salvation Pass

Continue on Page 151

Wister

HOWELL RD

HOBBS RD

DAVIS RD

WINSLOW RD

IMPERIAL STATE WILDLIFE AREA

GILLESPIE RD

Mundo

BEACH RD

111

WEST ST

DAVIS RD

NOFFSINGER RD

BEAL RD

ALCOTT RD

POUND RD

HARTZ RD

HAZARD RD

MC DONALD RD

W SCHRIMPF RD

WILKINS RD

CLIFF RD

WELCH RD

CARRICK RD

BURKE RD

Niland

HIGHLAND CANAL RD

COACHELLA CANAL RD

REAL RD

GAS LINE RD

Flowing Wells

NOFFSINGER RD

NILAND PEGLEG WELL RD

Barth Well

Melson Well

Blue Mtn 901 ft

SALTON SEA

Mullet Island

Red Island

Rock Hill 138 ft

Sonny Bono Salton Sea National Wildlife Refuge

Obsidian Butte 130 ft

SBSS NWR

M Drain

SIMPSON RD

MERKLEY RD

Estelle

SINCLAIR RD

W SINCLAIR RD

E HOOBER RD

E PETERSON RD

MONTGOMERY RD

Iris

TED KIPF RD

CHOCOLATE

McDONALD RD

N Drain

SIMPSON RD

I Drain

Tortuga

WIEST RD

CR 804

UP

MC DONALD RD

GRUBEL RD

CRUMMER RD

YOUNG RD

BOWLES RD

Fondo

Vail Ranch

W VAIL RD

VAIL RD

Verdant

Calipatria

Cliff Hatfield Memorial

ISWA

ALBRIGHT RD

RUEGGER RD

MAC FADDEN RD

W WALKER RD

WALKER RD

BAKER RD

VENDEL RD

SBSS NWR

WALKER RD

PELLETT RD

HOSKINS RD

MC NERNEY RD

KINGSLEY RD

MARTIN RD

FORRESTER RD

LOVELAND RD

SWINK RD

KALIN RD

BANNISTER RD

Westmorland

78 86

S30

S26

BAUGHMAN RD

Rockwood

RUTHERFORD RD

Wiest

PICKETT RD

DUNHAM RD

RUTHERFORD RD

WELLINGTON RD

HERD RD

CHALUPNIK RD

NORTH ALGODONES DUNES WILDERNESS

ALGODONES DUNES

EAST MESA

Amos

Acolita

Mesquite

1 inch = 3.16 mi   1 cm = 2 km

Moss. © DeLorme

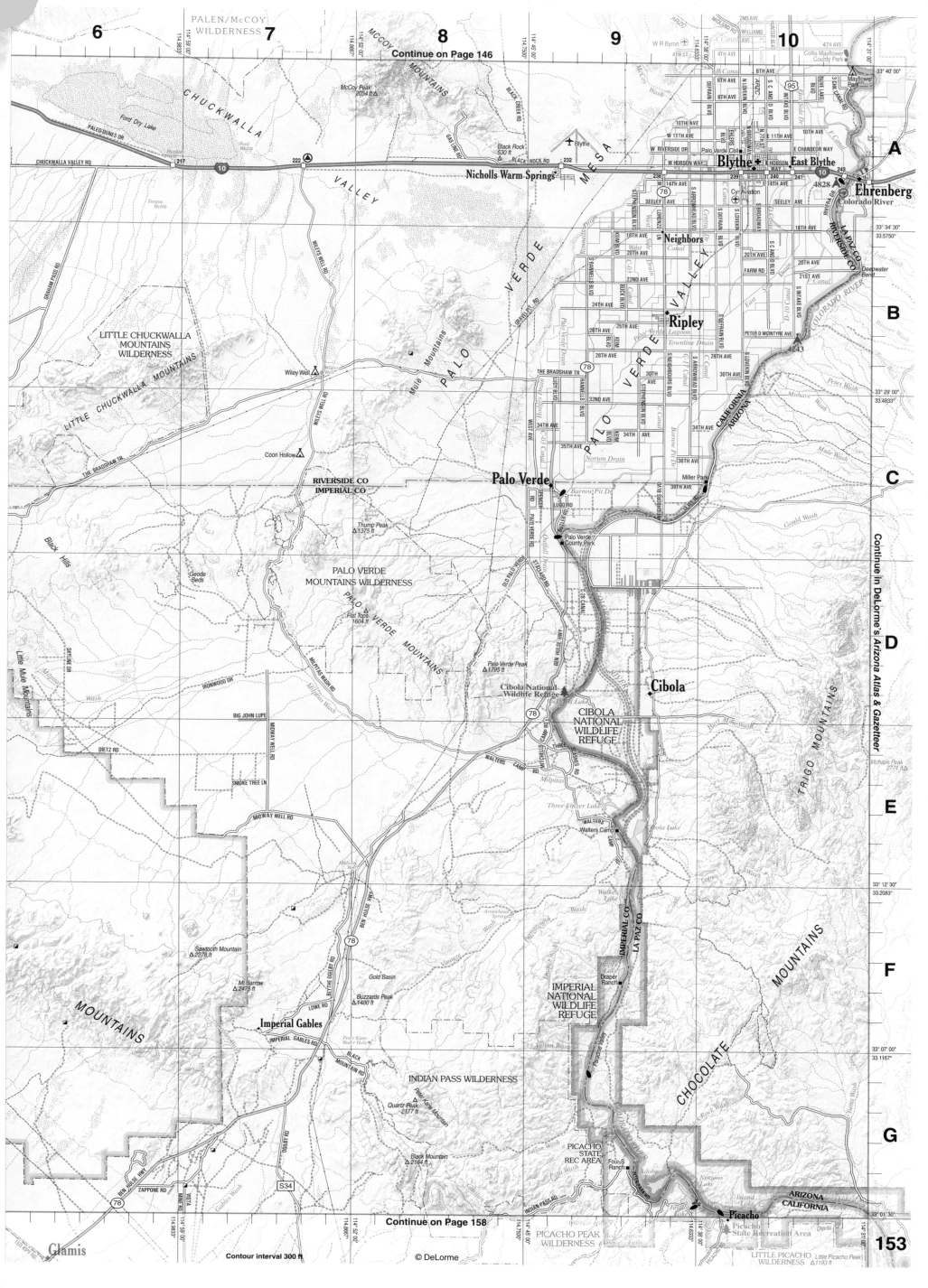

PALEN/McCOY
WILDERNESS

Continue on Page 146

McCOY MOUNTAINS

McCoy Peak
2054 ft

CHUCKWALLA

Ford Dry Lake

PALEO DUNES DR

Ford Wells

Teague Wells

CHUCKWALLA VALLEY RD

W HOBSON WAY

Black Rock
530 ft

Blythe

Black Rock Rd

GAS LINE RD

BLACK CREEK RD

GRAHAM PASS RD

217   222   10   232

Nicholls Warm Springs

VALLEY

MESA

PALO VERDE

A

Collis Mayflower
County Park

Mayflower
Park

95

Blythe ✛

East Blythe

Ehrenberg
Colorado River

33° 40' 00"

4828

243

33° 34' 30"
33.5750°

Neighbors

PALO VERDE VALLEY

B

Deepwater
Bend

Ripley

243

33° 29' 00"
33.4833°

LITTLE CHUCKWALLA
MOUNTAINS
WILDERNESS

Wiley Well

LITTLE CHUCKWALLA MOUNTAINS

WILEYS WELL RD

Mule Mountains

THE BRADSHAW TR

78

Coon Hollow

RIVERSIDE CO
IMPERIAL CO

Pete's Wash

Mohave
Wash

CALIFORNIA
ARIZONA

33° 29' 00"
33.4833°

C

Palo Verde

Miller Park

Gould Wash

Black Hills

Geode Beds

Thump Peak
1375 ft

PALO VERDE
MOUNTAINS WILDERNESS

Flat Tops
1604 ft

PALO VERDE MOUNTAINS

SKYLINE DR

IRONWOOD DR

MILPITAS WASH RD

BIG JOHN LUPE

Palo Verde
County Park

C-28 CANAL

D

Little Mule
Mountains

Wash

DIETZ RD

MIDWAY WELL RD

SMOKE TREE LN

MIDWAY WELL RD

Palo Verde Peak
1795 ft

Cibola National
Wildlife Refuge

78

Cibola

CIBOLA
NATIONAL
WILDLIFE
REFUGE

TRIGO MOUNTAINS

Continue in DeLorme's Arizona Atlas & Gazetteer

Mohave Peak
2771 ft

E

WALTERS CAMP RD

Three Fingers
Lakes

WALTERS CAMP RD

Walters Camp

Cibola Lake

33° 12' 30"
33.2083°

F

MOUNTAINS

BLYTHE OGILBY RD

78

LOWE RD

Sawtooth Mountain
2278 ft

Mt Barrow
2475 ft

Gold Basin

Buzzards Peak
1400 ft

Imperial Gables

IMPERIAL GABLES RD

BEN HULSE HWY

Peter Kane
Water Hole

IMPERIAL
NATIONAL
WILDLIFE
REFUGE

Draper
Ranch

IMPERIAL CO
LA PAZ CO

CHOCOLATE

33° 07' 00"
33.1167°

G

BLACK MOUNTAIN RD

INDIAN PASS WILDERNESS

Quartz Peak
2177 ft

Peter Kane Mountain

Black Mountain
2164 ft

PICACHO
STATE
REC AREA

Four-S
Ranch

MOUNTAINS

78

S34

ZAPPONE RD

VISTA RD

INDIAN PASS RD

ARIZONA
CALIFORNIA

Picacho

Picacho
State Recreation Area

153

Continue on Page 158

Glamis

Contour interval 300 ft

© DeLorme

PICACHO PEAK
WILDERNESS

LITTLE PICACHO
WILDERNESS   Little Picacho Peak
1193 ft

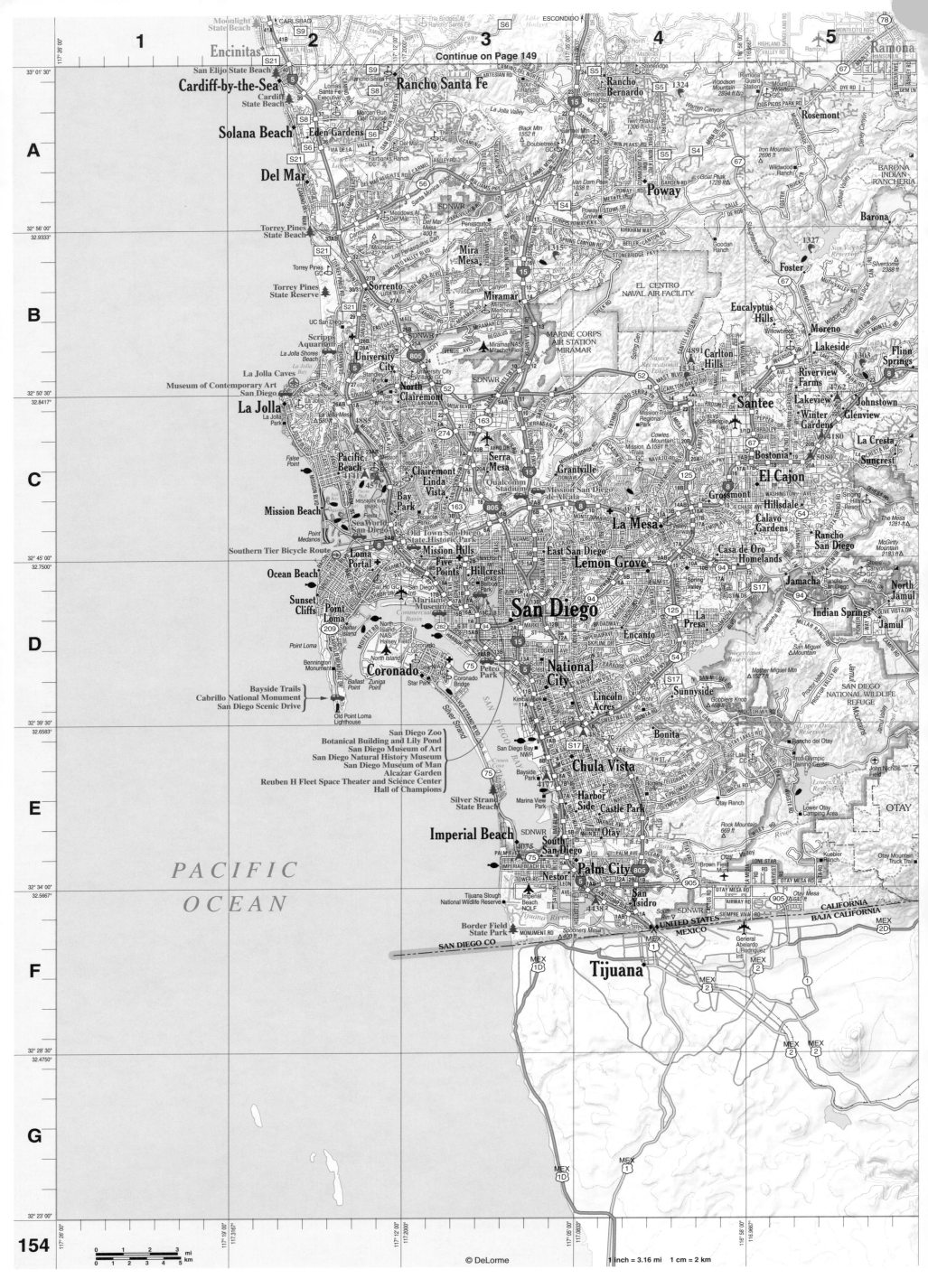

PACIFIC OCEAN

Tijuana

San Diego

Coronado

Chula Vista

Imperial Beach

El Cajon

La Mesa

National City

Poway

Santee

Ramona

© DeLorme

1 inch = 3.16 mi   1 cm = 2 km

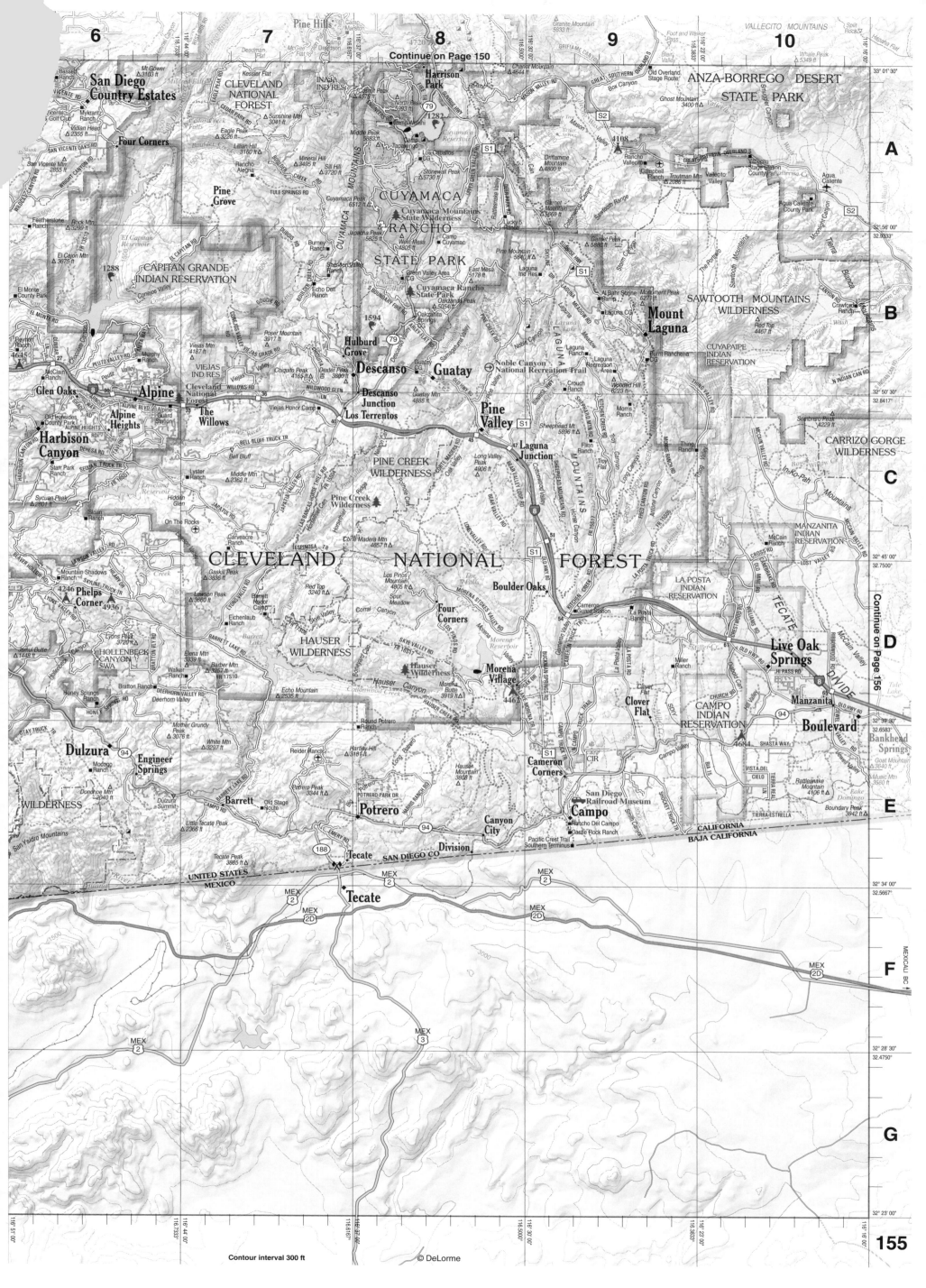

Continue on Page 156

Contour interval 300 ft

© DeLorme

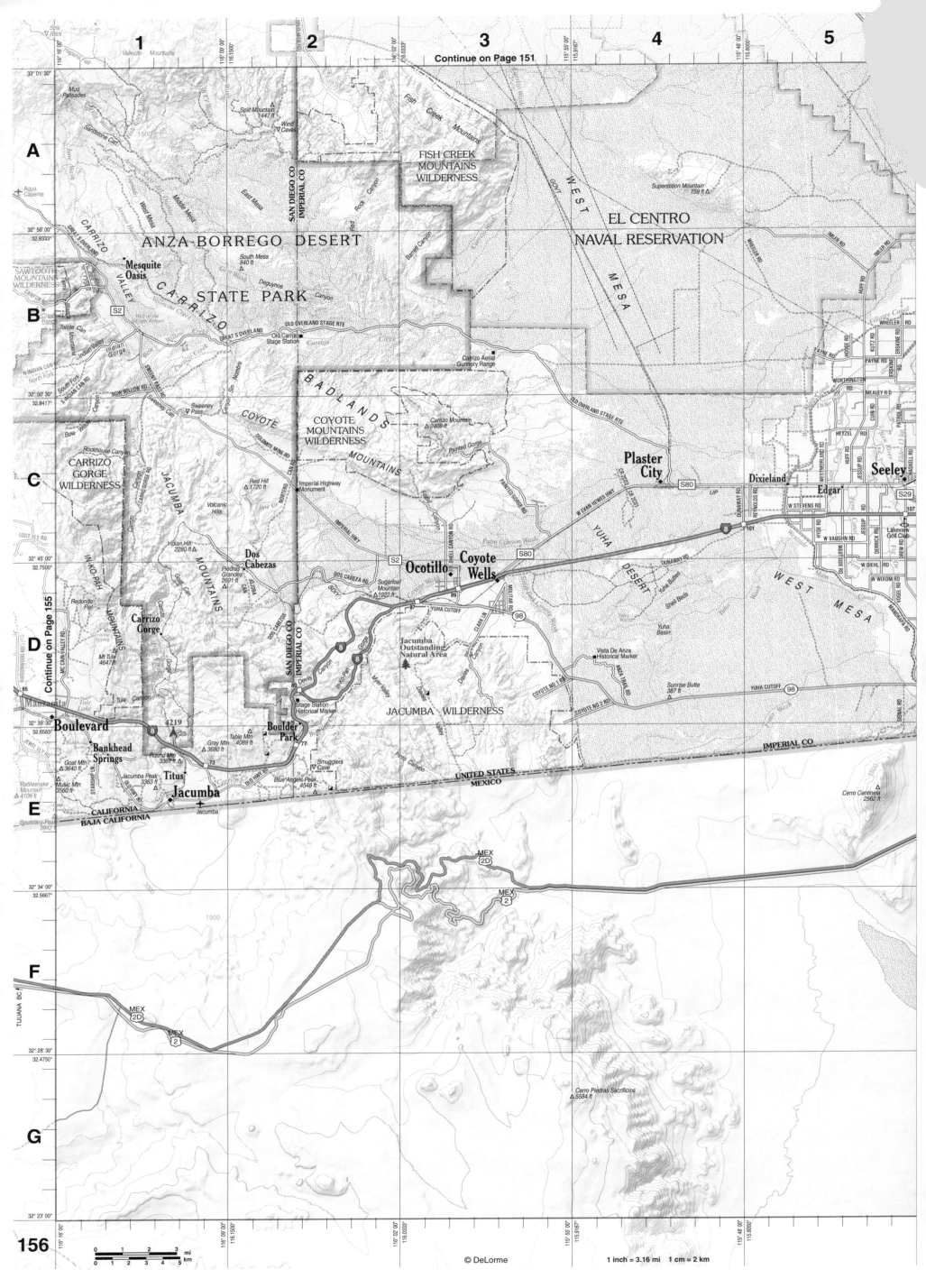

Continue on Page 151

33° 01' 30"

A

116° 16' 00"
116° 09' 00"

Split
Rock

Mud
Palisades

Vallecito Mountains

Fish Creek Mountains

Split Mountain
1447 ft

Wind
Caves

FISH CREEK
MOUNTAINS
WILDERNESS

116° 02' 00"
116.0333°

115° 55' 00"
115.9167°

115° 48' 00"
115.800°

Superstition Mountain
759 ft

WEST
MESA

32° 56' 00"
32.9333°

Agua
Caliente

SAWTOOTH
MOUNTAINS
WILDERNESS

CARRIZO

ANZA-BORREGO DESERT

Sandstone Canyon

West Mesa

Middle Mesa

East Mesa

Red Rock Canyon

SAN DIEGO CO
IMPERIAL CO

South Mesa
840 ft

Deguynos Canyon

EL CENTRO
NAVAL RESERVATION

Barrett Canyon

B

Mesquite
Oasis

STATE PARK

VALLEY

S2

Carrizo

Torote Can

Indian
Gorge

Indian Valley

Great S Overland

Old Overland Stage Rte

Old Carrizo
Stage Station

Carrizo

Carrizo Aerial
Gunnery Range

GOVT RD

OLD OVERLAND STAGE RTE

WHEELER RD

Village Canal

Wheeler RD

32° 50' 30"
32.8417°

S INDIAN CAN RD
North Fork

Bow Willow RD

Sweeney Pass RD

Sweeney
Pass

Bow Willow

Canyon Sin Nombre

BADLANDS

COYOTE

MOUNTAINS

PAYNE RD

MOOSE RD

KUTT RD

ERSKINE RD

MEALEY RD

C

CARRIZO
GORGE
WILDERNESS

Rockhouse Canyon

JACUMBA

MOUNTAINS

Red Hill
1720 ft

Volcanic
Hills

Dolomite Mine RD

Coyote Canyon RD

COYOTE
MOUNTAINS
WILDERNESS

Carrizo Mountain
2408 ft

Painted Gorge

Imperial Highway
Monument

PAINTED GORGE RD

Fossil Canyon

Plaster
City

S80

Dixieland

Edgar

Seeley

CR 201

HETZEL

WORTHINGTON
RD

DIXIE RD

HUFF RD

WESTSIDE RD

S29

107

32° 45' 00"
32.7500°

LOST VLY RD

Indian Hill
2280 ft

Dos
Cabezas

Piedras
Grandes
2601 ft

DOS CABEZA RD

IMPERIAL HWY

Dos Cabeza Canyon

Sugarloaf
Mountain
1022 ft

S2

Ocotillo

Coyote
Wells

W EVAN HEWES HWY

YUHA

DESERT

UP

8

101

W STEVENS RD

W VAUGHN RD

W DIEHL RD

W WIXOM RD

Lakeview
Golf Club

IN-KO-PAH

Redondo
Flat

MOUNTAINS

Gear Can

Palmo Can Wash

87

89

8

Yuha Cutoff

98

Dunawin RD

Yuha Buttes

Shell Beds

Yuha
Basin

WEST

MESA

D

Continue on Page 155

65

Manzanita

Mt Tule
4647 ft

Tule Can

Carrizo Gorge

SAN DIEGO CO
IMPERIAL CO

8

Devils Canyon

In-Ko-Pah Gorge

Jacumba
Outstanding
Natural Area

Myers Valley

Stage Station
Historical Marker

Davies Canyon

Vista De Anza
Historical Marker

COYOTE NO 1 RD

Sunrise Butte
387 ft

Yuha Cutoff

98

32° 39' 30"
32.6583°

Boulevard

Bankhead
Springs

8

4219

Round Mtn
3367 ft

Gray Mtn
3680 ft

Table Mtn

77

JACUMBA WILDERNESS

Pinto Canyon

COYOTE NO 2 RD

IMPERIAL CO

E

Goat Mtn
3640 ft

Rattlesnake
Mountain
4106 ft

STARSHIP LN

Jacumba Peak
3363 ft

73

Titus

Jacumba

Music Mtn
3560 ft

OLD HWY 80

Blue Angels Peak
4548 ft

Smugglers
Cave

UNITED STATES
MEXICO

Cerro Centinela
2562 ft

CALIFORNIA
BAJA CALIFORNIA

Boundary Peak
3942 ft

Jacumba

MEX
2D

1500

MEX
2

32° 34' 00"
32.5667°

1500

F

TIJUANA BC

MEX
2D

MEX
2

Cerro Piedras Sacrificios
5584 ft

32° 28' 30"
32.4750°

G

32° 23' 00"

0   1   2   3 mi
0 1 2 3 4 5 km

1 inch = 3.16 mi   1 cm = 2 km

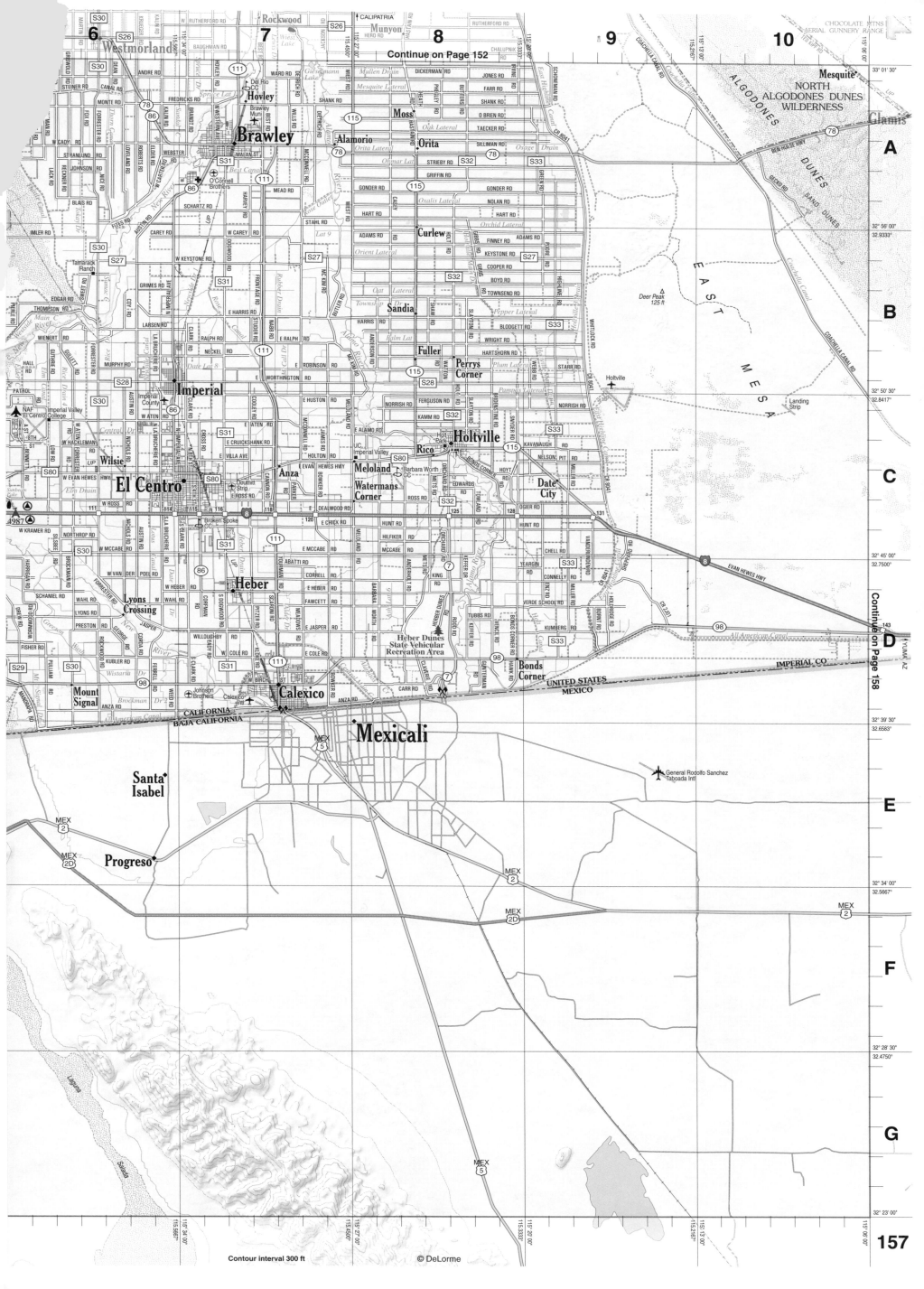

Continue on Page 158

Brawley

Imperial

El Centro

Heber

Calexico

Mexicali

Holtville

Westmorland

Rockwood

Hovley

Moss

Alamorio

Orita

Curlew

Sandia

Fuller

Perrys Corner

Rico

Meloland

Watermans Corner

Date City

Bonds Corner

Mount Signal

Wilsie

Lyons Crossing

Anza

Santa Isabel

Progreso

CALIPATRIA

Munyon

Mesquite

NORTH ALGODONES DUNES WILDERNESS

Glamis

CHOCOLATE MTNS AERIAL GUNNERY RANGE

EAST MESA

Deer Peak 125 ft

Holtville

Landing Strip

Heber Dunes State Vehicular Recreation Area

Barbara Worth CC

Imperial Valley College

NAF El Centro

Broken Spoke CC

Del Rio CC

Brawley Muni

Imperial County

UC Imperial Valley

O'Connell Brothers

Johnson Brothers

Calexico Intl

General Rodolfo Sanchez Taboada Intl

UNITED STATES
MEXICO

IMPERIAL CO.

CALIFORNIA
BAJA CALIFORNIA

YUMA, AZ

All American Canal

Coachella Canal

New River

Alamo River

157

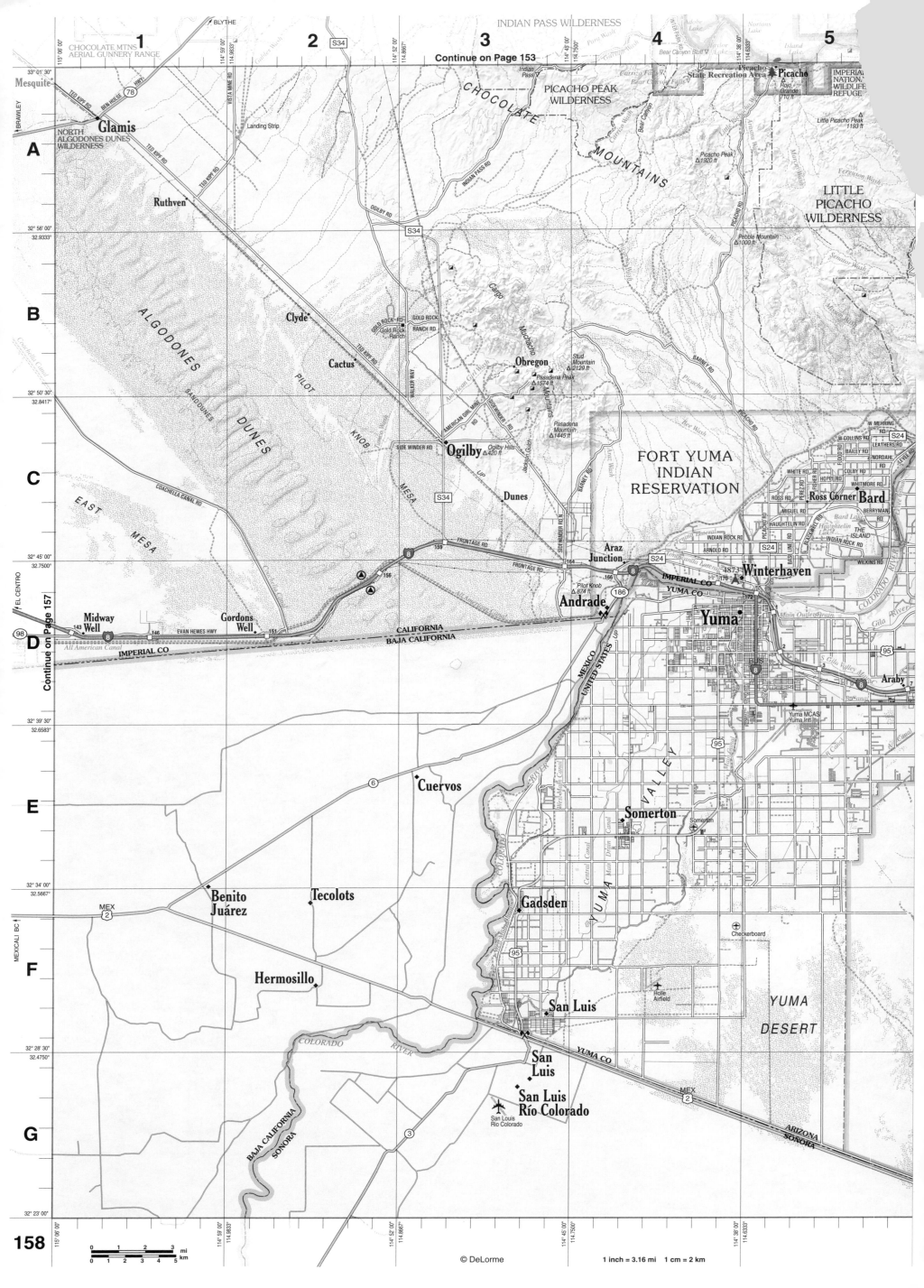

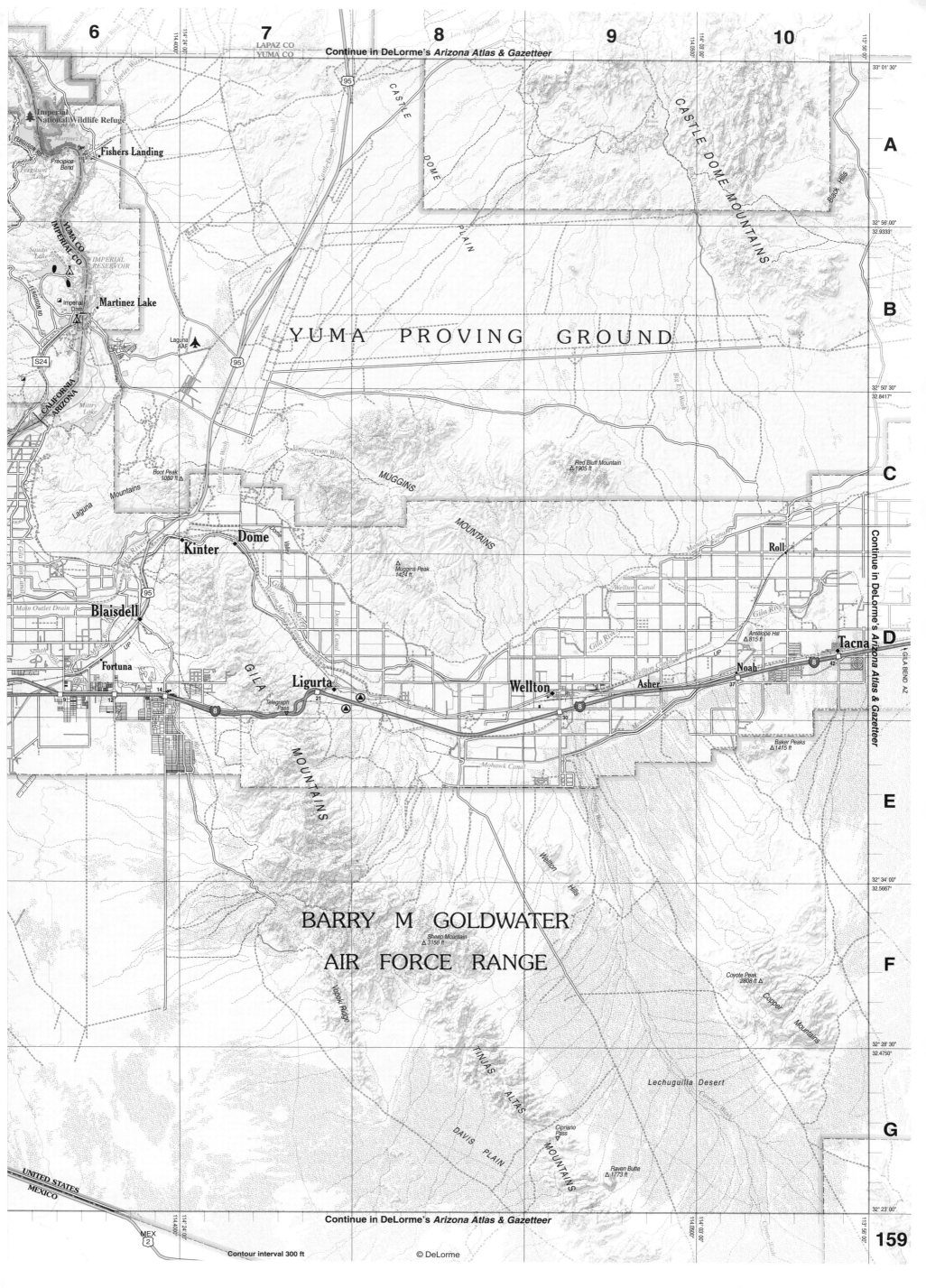

LAPAZ CO
YUMA CO

Continue in DeLorme's *Arizona Atlas & Gazetteer*

33° 01' 30"

A

32° 56' 00"
32.9333°

B

32° 50' 30"
32.8417°

Imperial
National Wildlife Refuge

Fishers Landing

Precipice
Bend

Ferguson
Lake

YUMA CO
IMPERIAL CO

Squaw
Lake

IMPERIAL
RESERVOIR

Martinez L.

Imperial
Dam

Martinez Lake

Laguna AAF

CALIFORNIA
ARIZONA

Mittry
Lake

YUMA   PROVING   GROUND

CASTLE DOME MOUNTAINS

Black Hills

Castle Dome

CASTLE

DOME

PLAIN

Dixon Springs

Big Eye Wash

Red Bluff Mountain
△1905 ft

C

Boot Peak
1080 ft △

Mountains

Laguna

Vinegarroon Wash

MUGGINS

MOUNTAINS

Muggins Peak
1424 ft

Mohawk Canal

Roll

Wellton Canal

D

32° 50' 30"
32.8417"

Kinter   **Dome**

Dome
Valley

Gila River

Gila River

Antelope Hill
△815 ft

Tacna

Blaisdell

Fortuna

GILA

Dome Canal

Telegraph Pass

Ligurta

21

14

8

Wellton

Asher

Noah

8   42

37

30

Baker Peaks
△1415 ft

GILA BEND AZ

Continue in DeLorme's *Arizona Atlas & Gazetteer*

E

32° 34' 00"
32.5667°

MOUNTAINS

Wellton
Hills

BARRY   M   GOLDWATER

Sheep Mountain
△3156 ft

Coyote Peak
2808 ft △

F

AIR   FORCE   RANGE

Yopoki Ridge

Copper

Mountains

32° 28' 30"
32.4750°

TINAJAS

ALTAS

DAVIS

PLAIN

MOUNTAINS

Lechuguilla Desert

Cipriano
Pass

Raven Butte
△1773 ft

G

32° 23' 00"

UNITED STATES

MEXICO

MEX
2

Contour interval 300 ft

© DeLorme

NUMBER, NAME	PAGE & GRID	BASS	CATFISH	TROUT	SALMON	BLUEGILL	CRAPPIE
1000 Albion River	54 C1			●	●		
1003 Alder Creek	54 E2			●			
1006 Alger Lakes	77 E6			●			
1009 Amador Lake	66 F1			●			
1012 American River	65 B8	●		●	●		
1015 Anaheim Lake	141 E7			●			
1018 Anderson Lake	81 D10	●	●				●
1021 Angels Creek	74 A4			●			
1024 Anna Lake	68 G3			●			
1027 Antelope Lake	44 F3			●			
1030 Arroyo Sec Creek	140 A4			●			
1033 Barrett Lakes	87 E6			●			
1036 Battle Creek	42 D1			●			
1039 Bear Creek	86 B3			●			
1042 Bear River	38 C1			●	●		
1045 Big Bear Lake	142 A5	●	●	●	●	●	●
1048 Big Bear Lake	32 B5			●			
1051 Big Duck Lake	32 A3			●			
1054 Big Pine Lakes	87 E6			●			
1057 Big River	54 B2			●	●		
1060 Big Rock Creek	129 F7			●			
1063 Big Tujunga Creek	140 A3			●			
1066 Big Tujunga Creek	128 G5			●			
1069 Blue Lakes	55 C8	●	●	●			●
1072 Blue Lakes	67 B9			●			
1075 Boca Reservoir	60 A3			●	●		
1078 Bon Tempe Lake	71 C6			●			
1081 Bouquet Canyon Creek	128 E2			●			
1084 Brush Creek	54 F2			●			
1087 Bucks Lake	51 C8			●			
1090 Butte Creek	50 F3			●			
1093 California Aqueduct	130 G2	●	●			●	●
1096 Camanche Reservoir	65 G10			●	●		
1099 Campbell Lake	24 F2			●			
1102 Caples Lake	67 B8			●			
1105 Castaic Lake	127 E10	●	●	●			
1108 Clair Engle Lake	33 E6			●	●		
1111 Clear Lake	55 E9	●	●				●
1114 Cliff Lake	24 F2			●			
1117 Colorado River	135 C6	●	●			●	
1120 Conness Lakes	76 C4			●			
1123 Cottonwood Creek	96 E5			●			
1126 Cottonwood Lake	142 F4	●	●	●			
1129 Coyote Lake	81 E10			●			
1132 Crystal Lake	129 G7	●	●	●			●
1135 Dark Lake	60 G1			●			
1138 Deer Creek	50 A2			●			
1141 Doane Pond	149 D10	●	●	●			
1144 Donner Lake	60 B1			●			
1147 East Fork of Carson River	68 C1			●			
1150 Edith Lake	77 G8			●			
1153 Eel River	39 F7			●	●		
1156 Elk River	30 G3			●	●		
1159 Englebright Lake	58 C3			●			
1162 Evolution Creek	86 D4			●			
1165 Fallen Leaf Lake	60 F3				●		
1168 Faucherie Lake	59 A9			●			
1171 Feather River	57 B10	●		●	●		
1174 Folsom Lake	65 A9			●	●		
1177 Fourth Recess Creek	86 B4			●			
1180 French Meadows Reservoir	59 D10			●			
1183 Frenchman Lake	53 B7			●			
1186 Fuller Lake	59 B8			●			
1189 Fuller Mill Creek	143 F6			●			
1192 Garcia River	54 G3			●	●		
1195 George Creek	96 B4			●			
1198 Glen Helen Park	142 B1	●	●	●			
1201 Gold Lake	52 E3			●			
1204 Greenwood Creek	54 D2			●			
1207 Grizzly Lake	32 D2			●			
1210 Hancock Lake	24 G1			●			
1213 Hansen Dam	140 A2	●	●	●		●	
1216 Hell Hole Reservoir	59 D10			●			
1219 Highland Springs Reservoir	55 F9	●	●				●
1222 Hilton Creek Lakes	86 A4			●			
1225 Holcomb Creek	142 A4			●			
1228 Horton Lake	86 C5			●			
1231 Hume Lake	95 A8			●			
1234 Iceland Lake	68 G1			●			
1237 Independence Creek	96 B3			●			
1240 Indian Valley Reservoir	56 D2	●	●	●			●
1243 Isabella Lake	106 G2	●	●	●		●	●
1246 Jackson Meadow Reservoir	52 G4			●			
1249 Jenkinson Lake	66 A4			●			
1252 Kaweah River	95 E8			●			
1255 Kinney Reservoir	67 C10			●			
1258 Klamath River	24 B1			●	●		
1261 Lafayette Reservoir	71 D10	●	●	●		●	
1264 Lake Almanor	43 F9			●			
1267 Lake Alpine	67 D9			●			
1270 Lake Berryessa	63 C9			●			
1273 Lake Cachuma	125 E9	●	●	●		●	●
1276 Lake Cahuilla	150 A5	●	●	●			
1279 Lake Casitas	126 G4	●	●	●		●	●
1282 Lake Cuyamaca	155 A8			●			
1285 Lake Davis	52 B4			●			
1288 Lake El Capitan	155 B6	●	●				●
1291 Lake Elsinore	149 A6	●	●				●
1294 Lake Hemet	150 A2	●	●	●		●	
1297 Lake Hennessey	63 D8	●	●	●		●	
1300 Lake Henshaw	150 E1	●	●			●	
1303 Lake Jennings	154 B5	●	●	●			
1306 Lake Kaweah	95 F7	●	●			●	
1309 Lake Lower Otay	76 F3	●	●			●	
1312 Lake Mendocino	55 C6	●	●	●			
1315 Lake Miramar	154 B3	●	●	●			●
1318 Lake Oroville	51 F6			●	●		
1321 Lake Piru	127 F9	●	●				●
1324 Lake Poway	154 A4	●	●	●			
1327 Lake San Vincente	154 B5	●	●				●
1330 Lake Sonoma	62 A2	●	●				●
1333 Lake Sutherland	150 G1	●	●				●
1336 Lake Tahoe	60 D3			●	●		
1339 Lake Wohlford	149 F9	●	●	●			●
1342 Lewiston Lake	32 G4			●	●		
1345 Lexington Reservoir	81 D6	●	●				●
1348 Little River	30 D4			●	●		
1351 Little Rock Reservoir	128 F5	●	●	●			
1354 Lone Pine Creek, Lower	96 C5			●			
1357 Lone Pine Creek, Upper	96 D4			●			
1360 Loon Lake	60 E1			●			
1363 Lopez Lake	113 E9	●	●	●		●	●
1366 Lost Lake	60 F1			●			
1369 Lower Bear River Reservoir	67 C6			●			
1372 Lower Echo Lake	60 G3			●			
1375 Lower Sardine Lake	52 F3			●			
1378 Lower Wright Lake	24 E2			●			
1381 Lytle Creek, Middle Fork	141 A10			●			
1384 Lytle Creek, North Fork	141 A10			●			
1387 Mad River	39 A6			●	●		
1390 Manzana Creek	125 B9			●			
1393 Mary Lake	76 A2			●			
1396 Mattole River	38 E2			●	●		
1399 Meadow Lake	59 A9			●			
1402 Middle Fork of Eel River	48 E1			●	●		
1405 Mill Creek	50 A2			●			
1408 Millerton Lake	85 F6	●	●				
1411 Mojave Narrows Park	130 E2	●	●	●			
1414 Mokelumne River	65 G9				●		
1417 Napa River	63 E9					●	
1420 Navarro River	54 D3			●	●		
1423 New Bullards Bar Reservoir	58 A4					●	
1426 Nicasio Reservoir	70 A5	●	●				●
1429 North Fork of Feather River	51 C7			●			
1432 Noyo River	54 A2			●	●		
1435 Owens River	87 G9			●			
1438 Papoose Lake	32 E2			●			
1441 Paradise Lake	50 C5			●			
1444 Pardee Reservoir	66 F1			●	●		●
1447 Peck Road Water Conservation Park	141 C6	●	●			●	●
1450 Perris Reservoir	142 E3	●	●	●		●	●
1453 Piru Creek	127 D9			●			
1456 Prosser Creek Reservoir	60 A2			●	●		
1459 Puddingstone Lake	141 C7	●	●	●		●	●
1462 Pyramid Lake	127 D9	●	●	●		●	●
1465 Red Lake	67 B9			●			
1468 Redwood Creek	31 F6			●	●		
1471 Reyes Creek	126 C4			●			
1474 Ridge Lake	68 G1			●			
1477 Rollins Lake	58 D5			●			
1480 Rose Lake	86 C3			●			
1483 Royce Lakes	86 C4			●			
1486 Russian River	55 B6			●	●		
1489 Rutherford Lake	76 G4			●			
1492 Sacramento River	57 G9		●	●	●		
1495 Salmon River	31 A10			●	●		
1498 Salton Sea	151 D9						
1501 San Gabriel River, East Fork	141 A7			●			
1504 San Gabriel River, North Fork	141 A7			●			
1507 San Gabriel River, West Fork	141 A7			●			
1510 San Joaquin River	83 E8			●			
1513 San Joaquin River	85 G6	●	●	●			
1516 San Lorenzo River	80 E5			●	●		
1519 San Pablo Reservoir	71 C9	●	●	●		●	
1522 Santa Ana River	142 B5	●	●	●		●	
1525 Santa Ana River, South Fork	143 B6			●			
1528 Santa Margarita Lake	113 C9	●	●	●		●	●
1531 Santa Ynez River	125 E10			●			
1534 Santee Lakes	154 B4	●	●				●
1537 Schaads Reservoir	66 E5			●			
1540 Scott River	24 G4			●	●		
1543 Scotts Flat Reservoir	59 B6			●			
1546 Sespe Creek, Upper Section	126 E5			●			
1549 Shasta Lake	33 G8	●	●	●			●
1552 Shepherd's Creek	96 B4			●			
1555 Silver Lake	67 B8			●			
1558 Silver Pass Lake	86 A3			●			
1561 Silverwood Lake	142 A1	●	●	●		●	●
1564 Skinner Reservoir	149 A9	●	●	●			●
1567 Smith River	22 B3			●	●		
1570 South Fork of American River	58 G5			●	●		
1573 South Fork of Eel River	38 E5			●	●		
1576 South Fork of Gualala River	61 A9			●	●		
1579 South Yuba River	59 A7			●			
1582 Stampede Reservoir	53 G7			●	●		
1585 Strawberry Creek	143 G6			●			
1588 Stumpy Meadows Lake	59 F8			●			
1591 Success Lake	105 B8	●	●	●		●	●
1594 Sweetwater River	155 B8			●			
1597 Symmes Creek	96 B4			●			
1600 Taboose Creek	87 F9			●			
1603 Tamarack Lake	76 A4			●			
1606 Ten Mile River	47 F7			●	●		
1609 Thermalito Forebay	50 G5			●			
1612 Three Island Lake	86 C3			●			
1615 Tilden Lake	76 A2			●			
1618 Tower Canyon Creek	68 G2			●			
1621 Trabuco Creek	148 A4			●			
1624 Trinity River	31 G10			●	●		
1627 Truckee River	60 B2			●			
1630 Tuttle Creek	96 D5			●			
1633 Twin Island Lakes	76 F5			●			
1636 Ukonom Lake	23 E10			●			
1639 Union Reservoir	67 E9			●			
1642 Union Valley Reservoir	59 G10			●			
1645 Upper Letts Lake	55 B10			●			
1648 Upper Salmon Lake	52 E3			●			
1651 Uvas Reservoir	81 E9	●	●				●
1654 Van Duzen River	38 C4			●	●		
1657 Vee Lake	86 C4			●			
1660 Wanda Lake	86 E5			●			
1663 Warren Lake	59 A10			●			
1666 Webber Lake	52 G5			●			
1669 West Fork of Carson River	67 A9			●			
1672 Whiskeytown Lake	41 B7	●	●	●		●	●
1675 Wooley Creek	23 G10			●			
1678 Woollomes Lake	105 F6	●	●			●	
1681 Wrights Lake	60 G2			●			
1684 Yuba River	57 D10			●	●		